THE PAPERS OF

WOODROW WILSON

VOLUME 56

MARCH 17-APRIL 4, 1919

SPONSORED BY THE WOODROW WILSON
FOUNDATION
AND PRINCETON UNIVERSITY

THE PAPERS OF

WOODROW WILSON

ARTHUR S. LINK, *EDITOR*

DAVID W. HIRST, *SENIOR ASSOCIATE EDITOR*

JOHN E. LITTLE, *ASSOCIATE EDITOR*

FREDRICK AANDAHL, *ASSOCIATE EDITOR*

MANFRED F. BOEMEKE, *ASSOCIATE EDITOR*

DENISE THOMPSON, *ASSISTANT EDITOR*

PHYLLIS MARCHAND AND MARGARET D. LINK,
EDITORIAL ASSISTANTS

Volume 56
March 17-April 4, 1919

PRINCETON, NEW JERSEY

PRINCETON UNIVERSITY PRESS

1987

INTRODUCTION

AS this volume opens, the Supreme War Council meets in a long session which, except for a few details, results in agreement by Wilson and the Allied Prime Ministers and their advisers on the military, naval, and aerial terms to be imposed upon Germany. The general harmony of this meeting is in stark contrast to the discord and bitter argument that characterizes the meetings of the four heads of government recorded in the balance of this volume.

Controversy erupts when Marshal Foch demands annexation by France of German territory on the left bank of the Rhine in order to assure the perpetual security of his country against future German aggression. Backing away somewhat from this extreme proposal, Clemenceau and his advisers insist, as an alternative, upon the creation of a Rhenish Republic under French control. Wilson, with strong support from Lloyd George, resists both initiatives on the ground that they would constitute a gross violation of the principle of self-determination. The dispute is settled only after the American President and the British Prime Minister agree to submit to their respective parliamentary bodies treaties pledging the United States and Great Britain to come to the immediate aid of France in the event of unprovoked German aggression against her. In addition, Wilson and Lloyd George agree that the Allied and Associated Governments, but principally France, would occupy the Rhineland and the great river's bridgeheads for a period of at least fifteen years, or until Germany has completely fulfilled her obligations under the peace treaty. Even so, the leaders in Paris still have not agreed on the specific arrangements for this occupation when this volume ends.

An even more bitter struggle ensues when Clemenceau calls for the outright annexation by France of the Saar Basin, one of the great sources of coal for Germany, to compensate for the wanton German destruction of French mines in the Nord. Wilson singlehandedly, without support from Lloyd George and contrary to the advice of his own experts, opposes Clemenceau's demand. For a moment, it seems as if the conference is on the verge of disruption over this issue, so bitter are the exchanges between Clemenceau and Wilson. But tempers cool, and Clemenceau gives evidence of his willingness to accept a compromise solution.

The fight over reparation by Germany reaches a crescendo during the weeks covered in this volume. Lloyd George and Clemenceau, cowed by their respective public opinions, continue to demand astronomical payments by Germany, with no definite sum or time limit laid down. Wilson and his economic advisers persist in arguing patiently but forcefully for a reparation bill based upon Germany's capacity to pay, and one limited both in amount and the duration of payments. The American, British, and French economic advisers strive hard to reach a mutually acceptable compromise, but this compromise is not in sight as this volume ends.

The so-called Big Four—Wilson, Lloyd George, Clemenceau, and Orlando—agree, on March 23 and 24, to meet secretly and privately to settle their differences apart from the distractions of the noisy and overly large Council of Ten. However, the Big Four are at another impasse by early April, and discussions grind to a halt when Wilson suffers a viral infection that puts him out of commission for four or five days.

Meanwhile, Wilson finds time to reconvene the Commission on the League of Nations in order to obtain amendments to the Covenant which former President Taft and others have warned him are necessary for the Senate's approval of a treaty which includes the Covenant.

To make bad matters worse, the statesmen in Paris have to struggle with a host of other problems, for example, the fighting between Poles and Ukrainians around Lemberg, obtaining German consent to send a Polish army from France by way of Danzig to defend its homeland, and continued Rumanian aggression against a prostrate Hungary. The seemingly most urgent of the new problems is the takeover of the Hungarian government by the Communist, Béla Kun, and the establishment of a Soviet Republic on March 22. In panic, Marshal Foch urges the dispatch of an inter-Allied army to Vienna, from which point it would establish contact with Rumanian and Polish forces in order to create a *cordon sanitaire* against the spread of Bolshevism into Central Europe. Wilson and Lloyd George absolutely veto this proposal on the grounds that Hungary was ripe for revolution and that the Kun government poses no serious threat to anyone.

The specter of Soviet Russia still haunts the statesmen in Paris. At the initiative of Colonel House, William C. Bullitt of the Russian Section of the A.C.N.P. goes to Petrograd and Moscow and returns with proposals from Lenin and his colleagues which seem to offer some grounds for accommodation between Soviet Russia and the western powers. Wilson has been leaning toward a *de facto* recognition of the Soviet regime, but the political explosion in the United States, Great Britain, and France which follows the leak of the news of Bullitt's mission forces him to attempt to find another route to Moscow. As this volume closes, plans are already under way for the creation of a commission, headed by the Norwegian explorer and humanitarian, Fridtjof Nansen, to supply Russia with desperately needed food and raw materials in cooperation with the Soviet authorities.

As the reader will quickly see, Wilson, during the protracted and often acrimonious discussions from the middle to the end of March, usually succeeds in standing firmly behind his principles, but without rancor and in a dignified and conciliatory manner. However, it is evident that his suppressed frustration, anger, and despair are mounting daily and might soon lead to some kind of drastic action on his part. The first dire crisis of the conference is actually at hand.

During all this time, of course, Wilson has to deal daily with matters at home. The most important of these is a bitter controversy between Secretary Redfield's newly created Industrial Board and the Director General of Railroads, Walker D. Hines, over the price that the Railroad Administration should pay for steel rails and other such materials. By the time that this volume ends, it is obvious that Wilson will support the Railroad Administration in its opposition to the Industrial Board's plan for noncompetitive prices for steel rails, and that this spells the doom of the Industrial Board.

"VERBATIM ET LITERATIM"

In earlier volumes of this series, we have said the following: "All documents are reproduced *verbatim et literatim*, with typographical and spelling errors corrected in square brackets only when necessary for clarity and ease of reading." The following essay explains our textual methods and review procedures.

We have never printed and do not intend to print critical, or corrected, versions of documents. We print them exactly as they are, with a few exceptions which we always note. We never use the word *sic* except to denote the repetition of words in a document; in fact, we think that a succession of *sics* defaces a page.

We usually repair words in square brackets when letters are missing. As we have said, we also repair words in square brackets for clarity and ease of reading. Our general rule is to do this when we, ourselves, cannot read the word without having to stop to puzzle out its meaning. Jumbled words and names misspelled beyond recognition of course have to be repaired. We correct the misspelling of names in documents in the footnotes identifying those persons.

However, when an old man writes to Wilson saying that he is glad to hear that Wilson is "comming" to Newark, or a semiliterate farmer from Texas writes phonetically, we see no reason to correct spellings in square brackets when the words are perfectly understandable. We do not correct Wilson's misspellings unless they are unreadable, except to supply in square brackets letters missing in words. For example, he consistently spelled "belligerent" as "belligerant." Nothing would be gained by correcting "belligerant" in square brackets.

We think that it is very important for several reasons to follow the rule of *verbatim et literatim*. Most important, a document has its own integrity and power, particularly when it is not written in perfect literary form. There is something very moving in seeing a Texas dirt farmer struggling to express his feelings in words, or a semiliterate former slave doing the same thing. Second, in Wilson's case it is essential to reproduce his errors in letters which he typed himself, since he usually typed badly when he was in an agitated state. Third, since style is the essence of the person, we would never correct grammar or make tenses consistent, as one correspondent has urged us to do. Fourth, we think that it is very important that we print exact transcripts of Charles L. Swem's copies of Wilson's letters. Swem made many mistakes (we correct them in footnotes from a reading of his shorthand books), and Wilson let them pass. We thus have to assume that Wilson often did not read his letters before signing them, and this, we think, is a significant fact.

We think that our series would be worthless if we produced unreliable texts, and we go to considerable effort to make certain that the texts are authentic.

Our typists are highly skilled and proofread their transcripts carefully as soon as they have typed them. The Editor sight proofreads documents once he has assembled a volume and is setting its annotation. The Editors who write the notes read through documents several times and are careful to check any anomalies. Then, once the manuscript volume has been completed and all notes checked, the Editor and Senior Associate Editor orally proofread the documents against the copy. They read every comma, dash, and character. They note every absence of punctuation. They study every nearly illegible word in written documents.

Once this process of "establishing the text" is completed, the manuscript volume goes to our editor at Princeton University Press, who checks the volume carefully and sends it to the printing plant. The galley proofs are read against copy in the proofroom at the Press. And we must say that the proofreaders there are extraordinarily skilled. Some years ago, before we found a way to ease their burden, they queried every misspelled word, inconsistencies in punctuation and capitalization, absence of punctuation, or other such anomalies. Now we write "O.K." above such words or spaces on the copy.

We read the galley proofs at least four times. Our copyeditor gives them a sight reading against the manuscript copy to look for remaining typographical errors and to make sure that no line has been dropped. The Editor, Senior Associate Editor, and Associate Editor Boemeke sight read them against documents and copy. We then get the page proofs, which have been corrected at the Press. We check all the changes three times. In addition, we get *revised* pages and check them twice.

This is not the end. The Editor, Senior Associate Editor, and Dr. Boemeke give a final reading to headings, description-location lines, and notes. Finally, our indexer of course reads the pages word by word. Before we return the pages to the Press, she brings in a list of queries, all of which are answered by reference to the documents.

Our rule in the Wilson Papers is that our tolerance of error is zero. No system and no person can be perfect. There may be errors in our volumes. However, we believe that we have done everything humanly possible to avoid error; the chance is remote that what looks at first glance like a typographical error is indeed an error.

With this volume, we begin to print translations of Professor Paul Mantoux's notes of the deliberations of the Council of Four, which we described in the Introduction to Volume 53. These are our own translations, and they are not compacted or abridged in any way. Although it is impossible to translate a foreign-language text into English literally, we have tried to present translations that are faithful to Professor Mantoux's prose. Our task was facilitated by the fact that his French prose is straightforward and not convoluted or contrived. It is also vivid, rich, and beautiful in language.

We are deeply indebted to the late Mme. Paul Mantoux and to her sons, Philippe-Roger and Jacques Mantoux, for their generous approval of our use of materials from *Les Délibérations du Conseil des Quatres* and for their keen interest in *The Papers*. We are particularly indebted to Philippe-Roger Mantoux, a professional translator and (like the other members of his family) bilingual in French and English. He reviewed our translations of his father's notes and made many suggestions that improved our versions notably.

We are also indebted to members of the Mantoux family for giving us the exclusive right to produce a separate, complete, and appropriately annotated English-language edition of *Les Délibérations*, one that will do full justice to Professor Mantoux's monumentally important work.

We here take note of the death of our colleague, John Wells Davidson, on June 14, 1986, at the age of eighty-three. Dr. Davidson joined the Editor as the first Associate Editor of *The Papers* in 1958.

From that date until November 1963, he was largely responsible for the gathering and organization of the bulk of our collection. In addition, he mastered the Graham system of shorthand, which Wilson used, and supervised the transcription of Wilson's shorthand manuscripts, marginalia, etc. He retired on June 30, 1971, but his interest in and concern for *The Papers* continued unabated until his last days. We here record our gratitude to him for all his contributions to *The Papers*, our respect for his scholarly integrity, and our admiration for his dedication to the cause of Wilsonian historiography. Farewell, old friend!

We continue to be indebted to our faithful reviewers and critics among the Editorial Advisory Committee—John Milton Cooper, Jr., William H. Harbaugh, Richard W. Leopold, and Betty Miller Unterberger—and to Alice Calaprice, our editor at Princeton University Press. We thank Jacques Mantoux for supplying us with the handsome portrait of his father, which appears in the illustration section of this volume. We are indebted to Drs. A. Stanley Link, Jr., Richard S. Marx, and Samuel Pegram for their fine commentaries on Wilson's illness in early April 1919. Finally, we thank Virginia Reinburg and Alice L. Conklin for preparing a draft translation of *Les Délibérations*.

Readers will note that the title of Dr. Bert E. Park's book on the impact of illness on Wilson and other political leaders, mentioned in the "Special Note" in the Introduction to Volume 54, has been changed from *Fit to Lead? The Impact of Illness on World Leaders* to *The Impact of Illness on World Leaders*. It will be published by the University of Pennsylvania Press in November 1986. In this "Special Note," we omitted the work of a pioneer in the field of lacunar infarctions, or infarcts: Walter C. Alvarez, M.D., *Little Strokes* (Philadelphia and Toronto, 1966). We thank Dr. James F. Toole for calling this work to our attention.

THE EDITORS

Princeton, New Jersey
September 5, 1986

CONTENTS

General Diplomatic and Military Affairs

Domestic Affairs

Personal Affairs

ILLUSTRATIONS

Following page 360

ABBREVIATIONS

A.C.N.P.	American Commission to Negotiate Peace
ALS	autograph letter signed
ASB	Albert Sidney Burleson
CC	carbon copy
CCL	carbon copy of letter
CLSsh	Charles Lee Swem shorthand
EMH	Edward Mandell House
ENH	Edward Nash Hurley
FKL	Franklin Knight Lane
FLP	Frank Lyon Polk
FR	*Papers Relating to the Foreign Relations of the United States*
FR Russia, *1919*	*Papers Relating to the Foreign Relations of the United States, 1919, Russia*
HCH	Herbert Clark Hoover
Hw, hw	handwriting, handwritten
HwLS	handwritten letter signed
JPT	Joseph Patrick Tumulty
MS, MSS	manuscript, manuscripts
NDB	Newton Diehl Baker
PPC	*Papers Relating to the Foreign Relations of the United States, The Paris Peace Conference, 1919*
RG	record group
RL	Robert Lansing
T	typed
TC	typed copy
TCL	typed copy of letter
TI	typed initialed
TL	typed letter
TLI	typed letter initialed
TLS	typed letter signed
TS	typed signed
WBW	William Bauchop Wilson
WCR	William Cox Redfield
WW	Woodrow Wilson
WWhw	Woodrow Wilson handwriting, handwritten
WWsh	Woodrow Wilson shorthand
WWT	Woodrow Wilson typed

ABBREVIATIONS FOR COLLECTIONS AND REPOSITORIES

Following the National Union Catalog of the Library of Congress

CSt-H	Hoover Institution on War, Revolution and Peace
CtY	Yale University
DARC	American National Red Cross
DLC	Library of Congress
DNA	National Archives

FO	British Foreign Office
MH-BA	Harvard University Graduate School of Business Administration
NjP	Princeton University
NNC	Columbia University
PRO	Public Record Office
RSB Coll., DLC	Ray Stannard Baker Collection of Wilsoniana, Library of Congress
SDR	State Department Records
WC, NjP	Woodrow Wilson Collection, Princeton University
WP, DLC	Woodrow Wilson Papers, Library of Congress

SYMBOLS

[March 22, 1919]	publication date of published writing; also date of document when date is not part of text
[March 19, 1919]	composition date when publication date differs
[[April 2, 1919]]	delivery date of speech if publication date differs
**** ***	text deleted by author of document

THE PAPERS OF
WOODROW WILSON
VOLUME 56
MARCH 17-APRIL 4, 1919

THE PAPERS OF
WOODROW WILSON

From the Diary of Dr. Grayson

Monday, March 17, 1919.

A decided sensation had been created overnight as the result of the weekly conference between Pichon and the American newspapermen. At this conference Pichon declared emphatically that the French would not care to have the League of Nations being made a part of the preliminary peace conference. Pichon told the newspapermen that France intended forcing her original plans and having a treaty signed within the next ten days which would include the military and naval and economic conditions, and that there would be plenty of time after that to go ahead with the League of Nations program.[1] As a matter of fact what Pichon and the other French representatives wanted, it subsequently developed, was an opportunity to work their will in connection with the peace terms and later on to talk the League of Nations to death. At no time have the French delegates been sincere in their endorsement of the League of Nations. Their leading advocate, Bourgeois, who had represented France on the League of Nations committee, had in reserve a plan whereby the League of Nations would really become a police body and would have at its disposal a big international army. This plan had been turned down and the result was that the French were entirely opposed to the League. When Pichon's address was called to the attention of the President he immediately cabled to Tumulty at Washington, as follows: [blank][2]

Afterwards the President called attention to the fact that the Plenary Conference was on record and a formal statement was issued dealing with that phase: [blank][3]

In the afternoon the President attended the session of the Supreme War Council at the Quai D'Orsay. All of the military, naval and economic proposals dealing with Germany were discussed at length and the majority were approved. However, the disposition of the Kiel Canal and the question of the Helgoland fortification was deferred to be decided later on by the President and Premiers Lloyd-George and Clemenceau.

In order to get some badly needed exercise the President, Mrs. Wilson and myself walked from the new White House to the Foreign Office. The President asked Mrs. Wilson especially to buy him a map so that he could study out the streets and routes himself—which was done. We followed a course picked out by him this afternoon.

T MS (received from James Gordon Grayson and Cary T. Grayson, Jr.). About this diary, see n. 1 to the entry from the Grayson Diary printed at Dec. 3, 1918, Vol. 53.

[1] Pichon spoke to press representatives from several nations at his news conference on March 16. According to one report of the event, he had expressed the opinion that "one cannot think of inserting the project of the League in the Preliminaries of Peace." The principle of the League, he said, might be stated in the preliminary agreement, but even this, he thought, "was not necessary," since "all of the delegates to the Peace Conference are in full accord on the principle." The French government, responding to American protests, attempted to suppress Pichon's remarks on the League. Most of the Paris press did omit them, with the exceptions of *L'Oeuvre*, *La Libre Parole*, and the Paris edition of the *New York Herald*. Many French provincial newspapers, however, carried the entire interview. See George Bernard Noble, *Policies and Opinions at Paris, 1919: Wilsonian Diplomacy, the Versailles Peace, and French Public Opinion* (New York, 1935), pp. 128-29. Varying versions of Pichon's remarks on the League appeared in the New York *Sun*, the *New York Tribune*, and the New York *World*, all on March 17, 1919, and in the *New York Times*, March 18, 1919. The quotations above, from Noble's book, appeared in the Paris edition of the *New York Herald*.

[2] Grayson's chronology is a bit confused. He certainly refers here to WW to JPT, March 15, 1919, Vol. 55.

[3] Again, the chronology is confused or misleading. Grayson refers to Ray Stannard Baker's statement or press release of March 15, 1919, about which see the extract from Baker's diary printed at that date and n. 1 thereto, Vol. 55.

From the Diary of Colonel House

March 17, 1919.

I began early this morning with Ray Stannard Baker, Commander Carter[1] and Wiseman. Carter came to give me Benson's report on the Naval Terms which I ask[ed] for last night. I asked General Bliss for a similar statement. Benson's came in ten lines and was terse and explicit. Bliss' covered eight or ten pages. The President merely wanted to know what we had accepted in the Naval and Military terms so as to be prepared for the meeting this afternoon.

When I took them up this morning, he read Benson's with delight and groaned when he saw Bliss'. Bliss is too prolix and is getting more so rather than less. The President and I got through with our business in short order. We started at twelve and at twenty minutes after had completely finished. I had to go to the meeting of the Economic Committee which is always held in my rooms at noon on Monday. I suggested to the President that he go down to the Crillon and attend it. It always pleases them to have the President come to the meetings.

I found Wiseman waiting for me. He came to tell me that, acting upon my suggestion earlier in the morning, he had seen Lloyd George and explained the necessity of his remaining in Paris all of this week and next. I asked him to say to George that there were no political matters in England that could not better be attended to in Paris. It was here that the eyes of the world were focussed and if we did our work well or badly, quickly or slowly, we would be judged by results. George replied that if I would get the President to write him a letter requesting him to remain, and would get Clemenceau and Orlando also to sign it, he thought he could put off going to London for two weeks.[2]

When I told the President this I handed him a pad and asked if he would not write the letter. He wrote it largely at the dicatation [dictation] of Wiseman and myself. I had it typed while he was talking to the Economic Council, and when he had finished, I got him to sign it. I then sent Frazier to the Ministry of War to get Clemenceau's signature and to the Hotel Eduard 7th for Orlando's. I told Frazier to ask them both to sign it at my earnest request. The letter was back here by 2.30 and I immediately sent it to the Quai d'Orsay to be handed Lloyd George just before the meeting. It was quick work and I feel happy at having been able to hold George here. His going would have meant delaying of peace for just so long as he remained away.

Wiseman came again after lunch and said George was worried about the question of reparation, both as to amount and as to how he was to satisfy the British public. I wrote out a plan which I told Wiseman to submit to him and which I thought might cover the case.[3] The feature of my suggestion was that the sum of thirty billion dollars could be set as a maximum figure, and that a commission should meet once a year to determine how much Germany could pay the following year and also determine whether the amount of thirty billions was excessive for reparation demands. In this way, the French and English could let Germany evade an impossible payment.

I also suggested a plan for the settlement of the left bank of the Rhine question which I thought might meet the President's, Lloyd George's and Clemenceau's views. This suggestion was that a buffer state should be created for a period of five years and then the League of Nations should decide whether the buffer state should exercise self determination or should continue for another five year period.

In talking with the President this morning, he insisted that peace should be made simultaneously with Germany, Austria-Hungary, Bulgaria and Turkey. His thought was that Germany should be tied up with the settlements made with these countries. Since both Austria-Hungary and Turkey are being dismembered, I insisted this would delay peace for an interminable time and I thought another way out could be found. A clause could be put in the treaty with Germany binding her to accept the treaties which were subsequently to be made with the other states.

T MS (E. M. House Papers, CtY).
    [1] Comdr. Andrew Francis Carter, U.S.N., aide to the Chief of Naval Operations and a technical adviser on naval questions at the peace conference.
    [2] Wilson's draft is printed below, following the minutes of the Supreme War Council.
    [3] Not found.

A Memorandum by Tasker Howard Bliss

Paris, March 17, 1919.

MEMORANDUM FOR THE PRESIDENT.

Subject: *The Proposed Military Terms of Peace with Germany.*

1. The OBJECT of the proposed Military Terms is to effect a reduction in the military power of Germany.

It is proposed to effect this reduction in the following ways:

A. A reduction in personnel and matériel of war. This is to be accomplished within a time not to exceed three months from the date of signature.

B. By a series of injunctions and prohibitions which extend over an unlimited time and which, for the most part, it is proposed shall be embodied in the German Military Law.

2. The reduction in the personnel of the German Army is effected by the Articles of Chap. I, in five Articles. I recommend that these Articles be accepted.

When the proposed terms are finally considered by the Supreme Council, it is understood that the French will propose the following as Art. 6:

"*Art.* 6. The number of the employees or functionaries of the German States, such as Customs House Employees, Forest Guards, Coast Guards, shall not exceed the number of employees or functionaries exercising these functions in 1913.

"The number of gendarmes or of employees or functionaries of local or municipal police forces can be increased only in proportion to the increase in the population since 1913 in the localities or municipalities which employ them.

"These employees or functionaries shall never be assembled for participation in any military exercise."

This proposed Art. 6 would take the place of Art. 8 of Chap. III. of the *original* draft which reads as follows:

"Art. 8 Public servants such as Gendarmes, Customs House Officials, Forest and Coast Guards, and local and municipal Police

Officials shall never be assembled to take part in any military training."

It will be observed, on comparing the old Art. 8 of Chap. III. with the proposed Art. 6 of Chap. I, that the change effected by the latter consists in an attempt to fix the number of State employees. Customs House officials, forest guards and coast guards shall *never* exceed the number employed in 1913. The number of gendarmes and of local and municipal police can be increased *only* in proportion to an increase in the population. Attempts to enforce these provisions will doubtless lead to endless friction. To do so will require perpetual control of Germany. But this is no more true of this Article than of a number of others. The other Powers are agreed upon these provisions and thus far have insisted upon them. If the other Powers insist, I recommend acceptance of proposed Art. 6.

3. The reduction in armament, munitions and matériel is effected by Chap. II., Arts. 7-13. I recommend that these Articles be accepted.

4. Chap. III., Arts. 14-19, covers the subjects of the method of raising the army and of military instruction. I recommend that these Articles be accepted.

5. Chap. IV. (Art. 20) relates to the disarmament and dismantling of all German fortifications between the right bank of the Rhine and a line drawn fifty kilometers east of the Rhine. It prohibits the construction of any new fortifications within this zone. It provides that fortifications on the southern and eastern frontiers of Germany shall remain in their present condition. I recommend that this Article be accepted.

6. Arts. 21-45, inclusive, relate to the Naval and Air Terms of Peace. I have not touched upon them in this memorandum because the request received by me from Mr. House (through Admiral Benson) was that I should prepare a memorandum on the subject of the Military Terms alone.

7. The general Arts. 46-47 relate to the Military Terms, because they provide that within three months after signature German legislation must be modified and thereafter must be maintained in conformity with the requirements of these terms.

Art. 47 provides that the terms of the Armistice of November 11, 1918, and the subsequent Armistice Conventions, shall remain in force insofar as they are not in conflict with these terms. I think that there will be a chance of great confusion and dispute if we attempt to carry over the terms of the Armistice into the terms of peace. I think that it will be much safer and wiser to demand that all terms of the Armistice and subsequent Armistice Conventions, which are to be continued after the signature of peace, shall be specifically embodied in the terms of peace or in an Annex thereto.

With the exception just noted, I recommend that these Articles be accepted.

8. Sec. 5 relates to the subject of Inter-Allied Commissions of Control in Germany and comprises Arts. 48-54. A footnote to Article 48 reads as follows:

"It belongs to the Allied and Associated Governments to agree among themselves and to establish in an agreement the conditions for the appointment, the functioning, and the duration of the Commissions of Control.

"The Delegates of the United States desire to present an absolute reserve in regard to the participation of the United States in a Commission of Control of indefinite duration."

I regard the Military, Naval and Air Terms as fraught with very great danger, although I do not see how this danger can be avoided. This danger will grow out of the fact that these terms must be enforced by very large Commissions of military and Naval officers. The spirit in which officers of the European Allies have heretofore conducted negotiations with the enemy suggests the possibility, if not probability, of great friction with the Germans. The spirit of irritation which will undoubtedly be aroused in the latter will result in constant petty delays and disputes. It can only be hoped that the Germans will quickly do the things required of them in order to get rid of these Commissions as quickly as possible. But it must be remembered that the latter will not be dealing with one or two principal officials of the German Government, but will be dealing with all sorts of people in every city and town in Germany, and the radical element now opposing the German Government will have every temptation to make trouble.

Moreover, how can a Commission of Control oblige a German legislature to agree upon and enact a very complicated system of military law within the time-limit of three months imposed?

The footnote quoted above, as I understand it, means that the Allied and Associated Governments must agree upon the duration of the Commission of Control. When the original draft of the Military Terms was prepared, it was proposed by all of the Powers except the United States that the duration of the control of the Inter-Allied Military Commissions in Germany should be unlimited. I declined to accept this and it was finally agreed that they should be limited to the maximum time-limit necessary for the execution of those terms which could be executed within a definite fixed time, i.e., three months. At the end of that time, if any of the imposed conditions were not executed, the Delegates of each nation in the

Commissions of Control were to report to their respective governments for further instructions. This would give each government an opportunity to decide for itself whether it was necessary or desirable for it to participate longer in the control. This provision has been again changed by the Drafting Committee, so as to provide that the control shall last as long as the Allied and Associated Governments may choose to require it.

If the United States participates in a system of control the time-limit of which is not definitely fixed at the outset, it will find great difficulty in withdrawing at any subsequent time. I, therefore, suggest the following for the consideration of the President:

(a) That the time-limit originally agreed upon for the reduction in the military personnel, the reduction in armament, and the disarmament and dismantling of the fortifications east of the Rhine, 3 months, be fixed as the time-limit of this control, leaving to each nation thereafter full liberty of action as to its withdrawal or its continued participation in the control. I assume, of course, that if at the end of that time it appears that Germany is defiantly refusing or failing to execute the terms which can be executed in three months, the United States will agree with the European Allies in taking whatever steps may be absolutely necessary to enforce compliance.

(b) That if these terms be reasonably well executed within the time-limit prescribed, the Commissions of Control shall be withdrawn even though the required German military legislation be not yet enacted. I recommend this for the reason that these Commissions of Control can exercise no power whatever in forcing a German legislature to take action. The Allied Governments will know quite as well as the Commissions whether the required legislation has been enacted or not and it will be in the power of these governments to take whatever action the circumstances of the case require.   Tasker H. Bliss.

TS MS (WP, DLC).

A Translation of a Letter from Georges Clemenceau, with Enclosure

My dear President,   Paris, March 17, 1919

Following through on our conversation of Saturday,[1] I send you enclosed a note which I believe will make precise the ideas exchanged in order to facilitate the solution.

Believe me, my dear President,

Very cordially yours,   G Clemenceau

T translation of TLS (WP, DLC).
    ¹ March 15, 1919, about which see the extract from the Grayson Diary printed at that date in Vol. 55.

E N C L O S U R E

TRANSLATION   March 17, 1919.

NOTE ON THE SUGGESTION PRESENTED MARCH 14.

I

RESUMÉ ON THE FRENCH PROPOSITION.

1) The military occupation of the Rhine by an interallied force (with the immediate and durable consequence of a rupture of the left bank with the *empire* and the *German customs Union*) is, in the present state of international relations, of vital necessity for France and of common interest to the Allies. A detailed memorandum justifies this assertion.

It is a question of preventing the recurrence of what we have undergone twice in fifty years, and, to this end, to deprive Germany of her essential means (the left bank, the railways and the bridges on the Rhine).

As a guarantee of this clause, the military occupation of the line of the Rhine is indispensable to France, which has but half of the population of Germany, is deprived of the Russian alliance and has no good natural frontier.

On the other hand, the democracies across the seas cannot fight in Europe, if the French ports and railways are not solidly covered. The last war has demonstrated to them the gravity of this danger which might shut them off from any European battlefield.

2) The limitation of German military forces is not a sufficient guarantee against this peril as long as experience shall not have enlightened us upon its efficacity; above all, as long as Germany can dispose of more than three million men trained in war, by means of having participated in it. The total suppression of the German fleet has not been a sufficient reason for the maritime countries to disarm their fleets. On land, France has need also of a physical guarantee.

The League of Nations is not a sufficient guarantee either. In its present state, it makes a final victory almost a certainty, but the machinery is too slow to prevent the invasion of territory at the commencement of a war. Therefore, here again, a physical guarantee is necessary.

This physical guarantee is the Rhine militarily occupied and the control of the traffic of its bridges.

3) The Objections which have been presented do not modify this conclusion.

A movement for the union of the left bank with Germany is feared. France has information to the contrary. The left bank is different from the rest of Germany. It dreads Bolshevism and war taxes. It is conscious of its economic peculiarities. It does not like the Prussian functionaries imposed upon it by the Empire. Separatist tendencies have already manifested themselves in spite of our entire discretion.

Nationalist irritation in Germany is anticipated. This sentiment is the result of their defeat. The whole question is one of protection against its possible consequences.

It is thought that the proposed solution might be suspected of imperialism. But this is not a question of annexation, it is a question of constituting an independent state under the protection of the League of Nations in conformity with the interests of the inhabitants and the aspirations of a large majority of them. This is not Bismarkian solution.

People are apprehensive of the effect which might be produced upon British and American opinion. But the last war has taught us that the Rhine is the military frontier necessary not only for France and Belgium but also for the democracies beyond the seas. It is the "frontier of liberty," to quote the expression of President Wilson. These democracies will understand it as they have understood the necessity of conscription during the war; and as the English democracy to-day understands the tunnel under the Channel.

The danger of an indefinite occupation is pointed out. But as any organization on the left bank would be in the hands of the League of Nations, the latter would always have the right to modify it.

Therefore, the physical guarantee, which would prevent a recurrence of the situation of 1914, remains a vital necessity for France, in the present state of the relations between peoples.

II

EXAMINATION OF THE SUGGESTION PRESENTED.

I

The suggestion presented on March 14th, by the terms of which Great Britain and the United States would bind themselves to bring to France without delay in case of a German aggression,[1] the help of their military forces recognizes that France is in need of a special guarantee: but, in place of the physical guarantee, asked for by France, it substitutes a political guarantee, of a kind which by a positive engagement, will shorten the time which would elapse between the menace of war and the pooling of the Allied forces.

The French Government fully appreciates the great value of such a guarantee, which would produce an important modification of the international situation, and is quite disposed to welcome it. But it points out that the guarantee must be completed and defined in order to be efficacious.

2) In the first place, in view of the distance, there will always be a period during which France, in case of an attack, would have to defend herself alone without her allies beyond the seas: it is necessary that she should be able to do so under better conditions than in the past.

On the other hand, it is necessary that there should be no doubt as to the substance and extent of the engagement, that is to say as to the obligations imposed upon Germany, the means of control to be applied there, the definition of acts which would constitute a threat of war, the right of defence which would thereby accrue to France, the military aid of which would be forthcoming from Great Britain and the Uni[t]ed States.

3) In other words, in order that we may be able to envisage the

---

[1] The reader will recall that Wilson had met with Lloyd George at noon on March 14 and with both Lloyd George and Clemenceau later that afternoon. See the extract from the Diary of Col. House printed at the date, Vol. 55. The only comments on what took place at those meetings are in the reminiscences of the peace conference by Lloyd George and André Tardieu. Lloyd George remembered that, shortly before these meetings, Clemenceau had asked him if he had any counterproposals to make to the French project of the occupation of the left bank of the Rhine. "I then conceived," Lloyd George wrote, "the idea of a joint military guarantee by America and Britain to France against any aggression by Germany in the future. President Wilson agreed to this proposal. On the 14th of March, 1919, President Wilson and I informed M. Clemenceau that we could not consent to any occupation of the left bank of the Rhine, except a short occupation as provisional guarantee for payment of the German debt. On the other hand, we formally offered our immediate military guarantee against any unprovoked aggression on the part of Germany against France." See David Lloyd George, *The Truth About the Peace Treaties* (2 vols., London, 1938), I, 403, or the American edition of the same book, *Memoirs of the Peace Conference* (2 vols., New Haven, Conn., 1939), I, 265-66. Tardieu recalled that Wilson and Lloyd George had offered France "a formal pledge of alliance:—their immediate military guarantee against any unprovoked aggression on the part of Germany." He added that Clemenceau had immediately said that he attached great value to this offer but had requested time to reflect and take counsel upon it. André Tardieu, *The Truth about the Treaty* (London, 1921), pp. 176-77. For discussions of the background of the Anglo-American proposal of March 14, see Louis A. R. Yates, *United States and French Security, 1917-1921* (New York, 1957), pp. 44-50; Harold I. Nelson, *Land and Power: British and Allied Policy on Germany's Frontiers, 1916-19* (London and Toronto, 1963), pp. 212-21; and Keith L. Nelson, *Victors Divided: America and the Allies in Germany, 1918-1923* (Berkeley, Los Angeles, and London, 1975), pp. 76-80.

relinquishment of the first guarantee (of a material order and based upon distance), it is necessary that a second guarantee (based upon time, that is to say, upon the rapid help of our Allies) be liable to no incertainty and that it be supplemented by other assurances borrowed from the first system.

It is therefore not possible in such case, for France, to renounce positive security for a condition resting on hope.

III

CLAUSES OPEN TO AGREEMENT

Desirous of responding to the suggestion which had been made to it, the French Government believes it is necessary to find a general basis upon which an agreement could be reached: this basis representing for France a minimum of guarantees considered indispensable.

In the first place, it should be agreed that:

In case Germany, in violation of the conditions of Peace imposed upon her by the Allied and Associated Governments, should commit an act [of] aggression against France,—Great Britain, and the United States would, without delay, give France the aid of their military forces.

In consequence:

1) The date and the conditions of evacuation of the bridge-heads of the right bank and the territories on the left bank of the Rhine should be fixed by the treaty of Peace (*in connection with the guarantees to be taken for at least the partial execution of the financial clauses*).

2) Germany should not maintain on the left bank of the Rhine or in a zone of 50 kilometers East of the river either military forces or military organizations. The German army should not execute manoeuvres there. German recruiting should be forbidden, even by appeal to volunteers. Fortifications should be destroyed. No new fortification should be constructed there. No materiel of war should be manufactured there. (*Certain of these clauses appear in the project of the Preliminaries of Peace: but, it is necessary in the present hypothesis to reinforce them.*)

3) In the above mentioned zone, Great-Britain, the United and France [States] and France, should have the right to assure the execution of the engagements imposed upon Germany by means of a permanent Commission of Inspection (*for, without this right the preceeding clause would be valueless*)

4) Great-Britain, the United States and France should agree to consider as an act of aggression any entry or attempt at entry of all or part of the German army into the zone delimited by paragraph 2.

5) Moreover, Great-Britain and the United States should acknowledge that France would have the right to occupy the line of the Rhine with five bridge-heads, of a radius of 20 kilometers, in case Germany in the opinion of the Commission of Inspection should fail to execute the engagements under Paragraph 2, or any of the military, aerial and naval clauses of the Preliminaries of Peace. (*Therefore, if France renounces a permanent occupation, in case of any danger of war resulting from Germany breaking her engagements, she should at least be able to advance her troops to the only good defensive position, that is to say to the Rhine.*)

6) Great-Britain and the United States should agree to allow France to have the frontier of 1814 with the right of occupation, without annexation, of that portion of the mining basin of the Sarre not included in the frontier, on the ground of reparation.

It goes without saying that the French Government understands by act of aggression against France, any aggression against Belgium.

T MS (WP, DLC).

Hankey's Notes of a Meeting of the Supreme War Council[1]

Quai d'Orsay, March 17, 1919, 3 p.m.

BC-52, SWC-18

1. M. CLEMENCEAU said that the first question on the Agenda related to the Military, Naval and Aerial Terms of Peace, and he would call upon M. Mantoux to read the document which had been circulated, Article by Article. He understood there were certain parts which had been reserved; and he enquired whether the Commission had prepared any special reports in regard to those paragraphs, or whether Marshal Foch or General Weygand would be in a position to give the necessary explanations.

GENERAL WEYGAND explained that the sub-Committees which had dealt with subjects such as the Kiel Canal, and Cables, had submitted special reports, which had been duly considered by the Allied Military, Naval and Aerial Commission. When the time came, he would if so desired, give the summary of those reports.

[1] The full text of these minutes is printed in *PPC*, IV, 355-403.

(M. Mantoux then read the draft Military, Naval and Aerial Terms of Peace, Article by Article. For full text, see Annexure "A.")[2]

Annexure "A"

Naval, Military and Air Conditions of Peace

SECTION I. *Military Clauses*

Chapter I. Effectives and Cadres of the German Army

Article 1.

Within two months of the signature of the present stipulations the German military forces shall be demobilised to the extent prescribed hereinafter.

(Read and approved.)

Article 2.

The German Army must not comprise more than seven divisions of infantry and three divisions of cavalry.

In no case must the total number of effectives in the army of the States constituting Germany ever exceed 100,000 men, including officers and establishment of depots. The army shall be devoted exclusively to the maintenance of order within the territory and to the control of the frontiers.

The total effective strength of officers, including the personnel of staffs, whatever their composition, must not exceed 4,000.

PRESIDENT WILSON asked to be assured that the exterior dangers from the Bolsheviks and so forth, which the Germans might have to meet on their eastern frontiers had been considered by the military experts in fixing the total number of effectives to be allowed to Germany.

MARSHAL FOCH replied that the Commission considered that the 100,000 men allowed, in addition to the gendarmerie, would be quite sufficient for the maintenance of order within the territory of Germany and for the defence of her frontiers.

MR. LLOYD GEORGE enquired, following up President Wilson's point, how many German troops had been engaged in suppressing the various Spartacist insurrections through Germany, including Bavaria.

MARSHAL FOCH replied that he had no exact idea; only vague estimates were available.

MR. LLOYD GEORGE enquired whether the number of German troops so engaged had exceeded 100,000.

MARSHALL FOCH replied in the negative.

PRESIDENT WILSON said that in putting his question he had in mind such isolated places as East Prussia, which adjoined Russia.

MR. LLOYD GEORGE pointed out that the province of East Prussia

---

[2] The individual articles in Annexure "A" are printed here at the points where they were read and discussed in the meeting.

would have no direct contact with Russia, as Lithuania intervened.

MARSHAL FOCH said that in the whole of Eastern Germany, the number of German troops did not exceed 28,000 to 30,000 men.

(Article 2 was approved.)

Article 3.

Divisions and Army Corps Headquarters staffs shall be organised in accordance with Table No. I. annexed hereto.[3]

The number and strengths of the units of infantry, artillery, engineers, technical services and troops laid down in the Table constitute maxima which must never be exceeded.

The following units may each have their own depot:

An infantry regiment;

A cavalry regiment;

A regiment of Field Artillery;

A battalion of Pioneers.

PRESIDENT WILSON called attention to the use of the word "never" in the second paragraph of Article 3. In his opinion, that word would cover all future time, and if that were intended, some permanent machinery would have to be set up to ensure the execution of the conditions therein set forth.

MR. BALFOUR suggested that President Wilson's point would be met by substituting the word "not" for "never."

(It was agreed that paragraph 2 of Article 3 should read: "The number and strengths of the units of infantry * * * constitute maxima which must not be exceeded.")

Article 4.

The divisions must not be grouped under more than two army corps headquarter staffs.

The maintenance or formation of forces differently grouped or of other organisations for the command of troops or for preparation for war is forbidden.

The Great German General Staff and all similar organisations shall be dissolved and may not be reconstituted in any form.

The officers, or persons in the positions of officers, in the Ministries of War in the different States in Germany and in the Administrations attached to them, must not exceed three hundred in number and are included in the maximum strength laid down in Article 2, 2nd paragraph, of the present stipulations.

---

[3] "Table No. 1, STATE AND ESTABLISHMENT OF ARMY CORPS HEADQUARTER STAFFS AND OF INFANTRY AND CAVALRY DIVISIONS." It provided for two army corps headquarters, each with no more than thirty officers and 150 other ranks; for infantry divisions, each with no more than 410 officers and 10,830 other ranks; and for cavalry divisions, each with no more than 275 officers and 5,250 other ranks. The numbers, types, and maximum permitted strength of regiments, battalions, squadrons, and other units per division were also specified.

Article 5.

Army administrative services consisting of civilian personnel not included in the number of effectives prescribed by the present stipulations will have such personnel reduced in each class to one-tenth of that laid down in the Budget of 1913.

Articles 4 & 5 (Were read and accepted.)

Article 6.

(Reserved by the Supreme War Council.)

M. CLEMENCEAU said that Marshal Foch had proposed the following text in substitution of the one which had been previously reserved by the Supreme War Council: "The number of Employés or Officials of the German States, such as Customs House Officers, Forest Guards, Coastguards, must not exceed that of the employés or officials functioning in 1913. The number of gendarmes and employés or officials of the local or municipal police, may only be increased to an extent corresponding to the increase of population since 1913 in the districts of municipalities in which they are employed. These employés and officials shall never be assembled for military training."

MR. BALFOUR suggested that the word "not" should, as in the previous Article, be substituted for "never" in the last paragraph.

(This was agreed to.)

MR. BALFOUR, continuing, said that if the Peace Conference were to decide that the territory on the Western bank of the Rhine should be administratively severed from the rest of Germany, the eastern section would, under this article, still be authorised to have the number of employés formerly needed by the entire German Empire.

PRESIDENT WILSON said that this question had better be postponed for the present, as it could not be settled until a decision had been reached on the territorial question itself.

(Clause 6 was accepted, subject to such modifications as might be required when the territorial question relating to the future constitution of German territories on the Western bank of the Rhine came to be settled.)

Chapter II. Armament, Munitions and Material.

Article 7.

At the expiration of two months from the signature of the present stipulations the German army must not possess an armament greater than the amounts fixed in Table No. 2,[4] with the exception of an optional increase not exceeding one-twenty fifth part for small arms

---

[4] "*Table No.* 2, TABULAR STATEMENT OF ARMAMENT ESTABLISHMENT FOR A MAXIMUM OF 7 INFANTRY DIVISIONS, 3 CAVALRY DIVISIONS AND 2 ARMY CORPS HEADQUARTER STAFFS." It provided altogether for 84,000 rifles, 18,000 carbines, 1,926 heavy and light machine guns, 252 trench mortars, 204 7.7 cm. guns, and 84 10.5 cm. howitzers.

and one-fiftieth part for guns, which shall be exclusively used to provide for such eventual replacements as may be necessary.

Article 8.

At the expiration of two months from the signature of the present stipulations, the stock of munitions which the German army may have at its disposal shall not exceed the amounts fixed in Table No. 3.[5]

Within the same period the German Government will store these stocks at points to be notified to the Allied and Associated Governments. The German Government is forbidden to establish any other stocks, depots or reserves of munitions.

Articles 7 & 8 (Were read and accepted.)

Article 9.

The number and calibre of the guns constituting, at the date of the signature of the present stipulations, the armament of the fortified works, fortresses, and land or coast forts which Germany is allowed to retain, will be immediately notified by the German Government to the Allied and Associated Governments, and will constitute maximum amounts which may never be exceeded.

Within two months from the signature of the present stipulations, the maximum stock of ammunition for these guns will be reduced to, and maintained at, the following uniform rates: 1,500 rounds per piece for those the calibre of which is 10.5 cm. and under: 500 rounds per piece for those of higher calibre.

PRESIDENT WILSON suggested that the word "not" should be substituted for the word "never" in the last line of the first paragraph.

(This was agreed to.)

(Article 9 was accepted, as amended.)

Article 10.

The manufacture of arms, munitions, or any war material, shall only be carried out in factories or works, the location of which shall be communicated to the Allied and Associated Governments, and the number of which they retain the right to restrict. All orders shall be notified to the Allied and Associated Governments, and may not be carried out until after such notification.

Within three months from the signature of the present stipulations, all other establishments for the manufacture, preparation, storage or design of arms, munitions, or any war material whatever shall be closed. The same applies to all arsenals except those used as depots for the authorised stocks of munitions. Within the same period the personnel of these arsenals will be dismissed.

---

[5] *"Table No. 3,* MAXIMUM STOCKS AUTHORISED." It provided for 40,800,000 rounds of rifle and carbine ammunition, 15,408,000 rounds for machine guns, 176,400 rounds for trench mortars, 204,000 rounds for 7.7 cm. guns, and 67,000 rounds for howitzers.

PRESIDENT WILSON called attention to the very great scope and difficulty of the second sentence of this Article, namely:

"All orders shall be notified to the Allied and Associated Governments, and may not be carried out until after such notification."
No limiting time was given, and no provisions were made to set up a permanent machinery for receiving the notification therein referred to, and for granting permits. In his opinion, the execution of that sentence was not feasible, and he proposed that it should be deleted from the text. It would be impossible to introduce a guarantee of that nature without setting up an instrumentality permanently limiting the sovereignty of Germany. The only other alternative would be to reserve the right of going to war with Germany in the event of her failing to make the notification therein referred to.

M. CLEMENCEAU pointed out that the same difficulty would arise if Germany were to set up an army of 200,000 men in place of the 100,000 allowed her.

PRESIDENT WILSON agreed. He pointed out that in the Convention provisions had been made for the setting up of Inter-Allied Commissions of Control, but no time limit of any kind had been given. He quite agreed to the setting up of these Commissions during the definite time required for carrying out the necessary disarmament. But all these Commissions of Control had been made instrumentalities of the Inter-Allied High Command, which, in his opinion, meant an indefinite continuation of that Command, and of the Allied and Associated armies. In his opinion, if the Allied armies were to be maintained for ever in order to control the carrying out of the Peace Terms; not peace, but Allied armed domination would have been established. His Government would never agree to enter into such an arrangement and, were he to enter into such an agreement, he would be far exceeding his authority under the United States Constitution.

MR. LLOYD GEORGE expressed the view that there was very great force in what President Wilson had said. In his opinion, Article 10 was the sort of clause which would be a perpetual source of irritation and humiliation to any country; whilst, on the other hand, it would not ensure the purpose intended. For instance, if in 1870 the Germans had imposed on France a condition to limit her army, that would have been a reasonable proposition. But if Germany had, in addition, imposed a condition that France was not to order a single rifle without asking her permission, that would have been intolerable. In 40 years' time, when Germany might have recovered her self-respect, should she require to order anything to replace the armaments permitted to her, she would have to give notice separately to France, Great Britain, America, Italy and Japan. He did not know what the Germans were made of, but he certainly knew what France and Great Britain would have felt about it. In his opinion, such a condition would constitute a constant source of insult, whilst, on the other hand, it did not really serve any useful purpose. Should the Germans mean to evade it, they would merely refrain from making the required notification. The first part of Article 10, which President Wilson was ready to accept, was merely a treaty obligation, whereas the second part of the first paragraph was merely intended to check that obligation. In his opinion, however, it did not succeed in doing that, and the Allied and Associated Governments would obviously be thrown back on the ordinary means which Governments possess of checking the doings of other countries. Although diplomatically the Allies had been taken by surprise when Germany declared war, and especially in regard to the use that might be made of the guns, the number of men and the number of guns possessed by Germany had been fully and accurately known. The construction of guns and the training of men could not be carried out clandestinely. Should there be a clause in the League of Nations requiring each member to notify to the others its programme of armaments and stocks of war material, that would be in no way humiliating, as every country would be bound to do the same thing.

PRESIDENT WILSON pointed out that a condition to that effect already practically existed in the League of Nations Covenant.

MR. LLOYD GEORGE, continuing, said that the clause as it now stood would merely be making for trouble. Should some German Minister say that he would defy the Allies and refuse to give the information required: would the Allies be prepared to go to war? That might be done should Germany proceed to order rifles or war material greatly in excess of the quantities prescribed; but not otherwise. His military advisers took substantially the same view as President Wilson, namely, that the conditions objected to could never in reality be enforced, and, in his opinion, it was inexpedient to put into a treaty a number of conditions that the enemy would be bound to evade. In his opinion, that was not a good plan, as the continual evasion of a multitude of small points would eventually lead to the document itself becoming a mere scrap of paper. He wished, therefore, strongly to support President Wilson's objection.

MARSHAL FOCH held that there were two objects to be attained in regard to the control to be exercised over the execution of the clause. One control would have to be set up in order to follow the immediate application of the conditions dealing with the surrender and destruction of armaments and other war materials in excess of the quantity prescribed. The work of that control would naturally come to an end as soon as the material in question had been surrendered. But, in regard to the application of the other conditions, no provisions had been made for setting up a special control and the only control possible would be that which would, under ordinary circumstances, be exercised by Military Attachés and other similar agencies. Should the Supreme War Council, however, hold the opinion that the condition in question would cause unnecessary humiliation to the enemy, he agreed to its suppression.

(It was agreed to accept Article 10, with the omission of the following sentence: "All orders shall be notified to the Allied and Associated Governments and may not be carried out until after such notification.")

Article 11.

Within two months from the signature of the present stipulations, German arms, munitions and war material, including anti-aircraft material, existing in Germany in excess of the quantities allowed, will be surrendered to the Allied and Associated Governments to be destroyed or rendered useless. This will also apply to special plants intended for the manufacture of military material, except such as may be recognised as necessary for manufacture which is authorised.

The surrender in question will be effected at such points in German territory as may be selected by the Allied and Associated Governments.

Within the same period arms, munitions and war material, including anti-aircraft material, of origin other than German in whatever state they may be, will be delivered to the Allied and Associated Governments, who will decide as to their disposal.

PRESIDENT WILSON proposed that the last sentence of the first paragraph of Article 11 should read as follows:

"This will also apply to any special plant intended for the manufacture of military material, except such as may be recognised as necessary for the manufacture which is authorised."

(This was agreed to.)

Article 12.

Importation into Germany of arms, munitions and war material of every kind is strictly prohibited.

The same applies to the manufacture for and export of arms, munitions and war material of every kind to foreign countries.

PRESIDENT WILSON pointed out that Article 12, in effect, established a limitation on the activities of other countries than Germany. One of the outstanding difficulties of the present war had been the question of ensuring that goods shipped to neutral countries did not find their way to Germany. This clause would have the effect of limiting sales by other countries to Germany. As far as he was concerned, he would be content to oblige Germany to manufacture her own armaments, if possible. But that involved a supervision of exports and imports from and into Germany, and he did not see how that could be done without setting up very complicated machinery. The United States of America had tried to do that on the Mexican frontier but with little success, because the power of smuggling was very great and required a minuteness of supervision which was not practicable. It had been agreed to set up a League of Nations which made it obligatory for each member to notify its stock of war material.

MR. LLOYD GEORGE enquired whether that would not be the answer to President Wilson's criticisms.

PRESIDENT WILSON, continuing, said that the League of Nations by itself would not be sufficient, because the application of Article 12 involved a perpetual and permament supervision. In accordance with the Covenant of the League of Nations, the members would only be required to disclose the war material possessed by them and not whence it came, whereas the Article under consideration required an investigation into the origin of supplies, not only in Germany, but in other countries also. If suitable inoffensive machinery could be set up, he would be prepared to accept the Article in question, but in the place of an illusive process of that nature he would prefer merely to judge by results. In order to give effect to his proposal, he would suggest that Article 12 should be made to read:

"Germany shall strictly prohibit the import of arms, munitions and war materials of every kind, and shall also prohibit the export of the same to foreign countries."

The treaty obligation to enforce the provisions of the Article would thus be placed upon Germany.

MR. LLOYD GEORGE said that, in his opinion, Article 12 should be accepted as it stood, as, under the Covenant of the League of Nations, it had been laid down that the manufacture of arms, munitions and war material should become a State undertaking.

PRESIDENT WILSON said that the procedure mentioned by Mr. Lloyd George had only been accepted in principle.

MR. LLOYD GEORGE, continuing, said that his argument was thereby somewhat weakened. Nevertheless, if the Article as originally drafted were included as a part of the Treaty, any member of the League of Nations selling arms to Germany would be guilty of a breach of the League's Covenant.

PRESIDENT WILSON said that, under the circumstances, he was prepared to withdraw his objection.

MR. BALFOUR pointed out that the French and English drafts did not correspond, in that the English version read:

"Importation into Germany of arms, munitions and war material of every kind *is* strictly prohibited," whereas the French text read:

"Importation into Germany of arms, munitions and war materials of every kind *shall be* strictly prohibited."

(Article 12, with the following amendment, was accepted:

"Importation into Germany of arms, munitions and war material of every kind shall be strictly prohibited. The same applies to the manufacture for and export of arms, munitions and war materials of every kind to foreign countries.")

Article 13.

The use of asphyxiating, poisonous or other gases and all analogous liquids, materials or devices being prohibited, their manufacture and importation are strictly forbidden in Germany.

The same applies to materials for the manufacture, storage and use of the said products or devices.

The manufacture and the importation into Germany of armoured cars, tanks and all similar constructions suitable for use in war are also prohibited.

MR BALFOUR enquired how it would be possible to forbid the importation of materials required for the manufacture of asphyxiating gases, as many of these were innocent chemicals which were eventually perverted to these nefarious uses.

MARSHAL FOCH suggested, in order to meet Mr. Balfour's criticism, that the second paragraph of Article 13 might be altered to read:

"The same applies to materials specially intended for the manufacture, storage and use of the said products or devices."

(This was agreed to.)

(Article 13, as amended, was accepted.)

Chapter III. Recruiting and Military Training
Article 14.

Universal compulsory military service shall be abolished in Germany.

The German Army may only be constituted and recruited by means of voluntary enlistment.

Article 14 was read and accepted.

Article 15.

The period of enlistment for non-commissioned officers and privates must be twelve consecutive years.

Until the expiration of his period of enlistment no non-commissioned officer or private may leave the Army except for reasons of health and after having been first finally discharged as unfit for service.

The proportion of men so discharged must not exceed in any year five per cent of the total effectives fixed by Article 2, second paragraph, of the present stipulations.

MR BALFOUR called attention to the second paragraph which laid down that "Until the expiration of his period of enlistment, no non-commissioned officer or private may leave the army except for reasons of health and after having been first finally discharged as unfit for service." That condition would require the retention in the Army of men, for instance, who had committed every crime in the calendar. In his opinion, the imposition of such a condition would be inherently impossible.

PRESIDENT WILSON agreed. He thought that for pure reasons of humanity, it might be desirable to omit such a condition.

MR LLOYD GEORGE suggested that the second paragraph in question should be omitted, and that the third paragraph should be made to read:

"The proportion of men discharged for any reason must not exceed in any year 5 per cent, etc."

PRESIDENT WILSON said that the words "before expiration of period of their enlistment" should be added after the words "for any reason."

(Article 15, as amended, was approved, namely:

"The period of enlistment for non-commissioned officers and privates must be 12 consecutive years.

The proportion of men discharged for any reason before expiration of the period of their enlistment must not exceed in any year 5 per cent of the total effectives fixed by the second paragraph of Article 2 of the present stipulations.")

Article 16.

The officers who are retained in the Army must undertake the obligation to serve in it up to the age of forty-five years at least.

Officers newly appointed must undertake to serve on the active list for twenty-five consecutive years at least.

Officers who have previously belonged to any formations whatever of the Army, and who are not retained in the units allowed to be maintained, must not take part in any military exercise whether theoretical or practical, and will not be under any military obligations whatever.

No officer may leave the Army except for reasons of health and after having been first finally discharged as unfit for service.

The proportion of officers so discharged must not exceed in any year five per cent of the total effectives of officers provided by Article 2, third paragraph, of the present stipulations.

MR BALFOUR pointed out that a corresponding correction to that made in Article 15 would also have to be made in Article 16, by the omission of paragraph 4 and by making paragraph 5 read:

"The proportion of officers discharged for any reason must not exceed in any year 5 per cent, etc."

(This was agreed to.)

Article 17.

On the expiration of two months from the signature of the present stipulations there must only exist in Germany the number of military schools which is absolutely indispensable for the recruitment of the officers of the units allowed. These schools will be exclusively intended for the recruitment of officers of each arm, in the proportion of one school per arm.

The number of pupils admitted to attend the courses of the said schools will be strictly in proportion to the vacancies to be filled in the cadres of officers. The pupils and the cadres will be reckoned in the effectives fixed by Article 2, second and third paragraphs, of the present stipulations.

Consequently, and during the period fixed above, all military academies or similar institutions of the German States as well as the different military schools for officers, student officers ("Aspiranten"), cadets, non-commissioned officers or student non-commissioned officers ("Aspiranten"), other than the schools above provided for, will be abolished.

(Article 17 was read and approved.)

Article 18.

Educational establishments, the universities, societies of discharged soldiers, shooting or touring clubs, and generally speaking associations of every description, whatever be the age of their members, must not occupy themselves with any military matters. In particular they will be forbidden to instruct or exercise their members, or to allow them to be instructed or exercised, in the profession or use of arms.

These societies, associations, educational establishments and universities must have no connection with the Ministries of War or any other military authority.

(Article 18 was read and approved.)

Article 19.

All measures of mobilisation or appertaining to mobilisation are forbidden.

In no case must formations, administrative services or General Staffs include supplementary cadres.

PRESIDENT WILSON asked to be told for his own information what was technically included under "Mobilisation." Would it, for instance, prevent the whole of the 100,000 men being assembled in one place?

MARSHAL FOCH explained that by "Measures of Mobilisation" was understood any steps taken to increase the number of men, or the number of animals, forming part of an army, by the calling up of reserves.

(Article 19 was accepted.)

Chapter IV. Fortifications.
Article 20.

Within three months of the date of the signature of the present stipulations all fortified works, fortresses and field works situated on German territory to the west of a line drawn fifty miles to the east of the Rhine will be disarmed and dismantled.

The construction of any new fortification, whatever its nature and importance, is forbidden in this zone. The fortified works of the southern and eastern frontiers of Germany will be maintained in their existing state.

PRESIDENT WILSON observed that he quite agreed with the provisions contained in Article 20 in regard to the Western frontiers of Germany. In regard to the Eastern frontiers, however, Germany would now be faced with much weaker Powers, owing to the creation of a number of new States, such as, Poland, Czecho-Slovakia, Hungary, a new Roumania, a modified Serbia, and a Turkey broken up into a score of parts, from which the stronger units would have disappeared. It must not be forgotten that Germany's ambitions had always leant towards the South and the East, and he would like to enquire whether sufficient thought had been given towards ensuring the safety of those regions against future German aggression. He was particularly concerned that nothing should be done to revive those ambitions, either by permitting Germany to attach to herself the newly created States, or by permitting her to retain as formidable a front on that side as heretofore.

MR LLOYD GEORGE drew attention to the answer given by General Degoutte at a previous meeting, which would appear to cover President Wilson's objections. General Degoutte had then stated that Germany only had two fortresses which were situated less than 50 miles from the Eastern and Southern frontiers.

PRESIDENT WILSON accepted this explanation and withdrew his objections as being more theoretical than practical.

M. CLEMENCEAU said that he understood a large number of railway sidings existed along the Franco-German frontier. He enquired from Marshal Foch whether he placed any importance on their existence.

MARSHAL FOCH replied in the negative.

(Article 20 was accepted without amendment.)

SECTION II. *Naval Clauses.*
Article 21.
After the expiration of a period of two months from the signature of the present stipulations the German naval forces in commission must not exceed

6 battleships of the "Deutschland" or "Lothringen" type,

6 light-cruisers,

12 destroyers,

12 torpedo boats, or an equal number of ships constructed to replace them as provided in Article 30.

No submarines are to be included.

All other warships, except where there is provision to the contrary in the present stipulations, must be placed in reserve or devoted to commercial purposes.

(Article 21 was read and accepted.)
Article 22.
Until the completion of the minesweeping prescribed by the present stipulations (Article 33) Germany will keep in commission such number of minesweeping vessels as may be fixed by the Allies and the United States of America.

(Article 22 was read and accepted.)
Article 23.
After the expiration of a period of two months the total personnel of the German navy, including the manning of the fleet, coast defences, signal stations, administration and other land services, must not exceed 15,000, including officers and men of all grades and corps. The total strength of officers and warrant officers must not exceed 1,500.

Within two months from the signature of the present stipulations, the personnel in excess of the above strength shall be demobilised.

No naval or military corps or reserve force in connection with the navy may be organised without being included in the above strength.

(Article 23 was read and accepted.)
Article 24.
From the date of the present stipulations all the German surface warships which are not in German ports cease to belong to Germany, who renounces all rights over them.

Vessels which, in compliance with the armistice, are now interned in the ports of the Allies, are declared to be finally surrendered.

Vessels which are now interned in neutral ports will be there surrendered to the Governments of the Allies and the United States of America. The German Government must address a notification to that effect to the neutral Powers on the signature of the present stipulations. (All these vessels will be destroyed or broken up.)

M. LEYGUES suggested that the last sentence of Article 24, which states that "all these vessels will be destroyed or broken up" should be omitted, as the question was purely one which affected the Allied and Associated Governments, and a decision would be reached among themselves.

(This was agreed to.)

MR LANSING pointed out that in the Military Clauses the expression "Allied and Associated Governments" had been employed, whereas in the Naval Clauses the expression "Governments of the Allies and the United States of America" had been used. He assumed that would be put right when the text came to be edited.

MR. BALFOUR thought it was important to decide which of these expressions should be employed. The expression "Governments of the Allies and the United States of America" had been deliberately used in the Article in question in order that no other Associated Government should participate in the possible distribution of the ships to be surrendered.

BARON SONNINO pointed out that the word "Government" appeared in the singular in connection with the word "Associated" in the French text.

PRESIDENT WILSON said that he preferred that the present text be retained.

(Article 24 was approved, the last sentence being deleted, namely: "All those vessels will be destroyed or broken up.")

Article 25 (reserved).

Within a period of two months from the date of the present stipulations, the German surface warships enumerated below will be sunk.

These warships will have been disarmed as provided in Article 23 of the Armistice dated 11 November, 1918. Nevertheless they must have all their guns on board.

These vessels will be sunk in the presence and under the control of representatives of the Governments of the Allies and of the United States of America and in such place as shall be fixed by the said Governments.

Battleships

Oldenburg	Posen
Thüringen	Westfalen
Ostfriesland	Rheinland
Helgoland	Nassau

Light-Cruisers

Stettin	Strassburg
Danzig	Augsburg

| München | Kolberg |
| Lübeck | Stuttgart |

and in addition forty-two modern destroyers and fifty modern torpedo boats, as chosen by the Governments of the Allies and of the United States of America.

(Article 25 was reserved for further consideration.)

Article 26

On the signature of the present stipulations the German Government must undertake, under the supervision of the Governments of the Allies and of the United States of America, the breaking-up of all the German surface warships now under construction.

(Article 26 was read and accepted.)

Article 27.

The German auxiliary cruisers and Fleet auxiliaries, of which the list is annexed to the present section,[6] will be disarmed and treated as merchant ships.

(Article 27 was read and accepted.)

Article 28.

On the expiration of one month from the date of the present stipulations all German submarines, submarine salvage vessels and docks for submarines, including the tubular dock, must have been handed over to the Governments of the Allies and of the United States of America.

Such of these submarines, vessels and docks as are considered by the Governments of the Allies and of the United States of America to be fit to proceed under their own power or to be towed shall be taken by the German Government into such Allied ports as have been indicated (there to be destroyed or broken up). (reserved)

The remainder, and also those in course of construction, shall be broken up entirely by the German Government under the supervision of the Governments of the Allies and of the United States of America. The breaking-up must be completed within three months at the most after the signature of the present stipulations.

(Article 28 was read and accepted.)

Article 29.

Articles, machinery and material arising from the breaking-up of German warships of all kinds, whether surface vessels or submarines, may not be used except for purely industrial and commercial purposes. They may not be sold or disposed of to foreign countries.

(Article 29 was read and accepted.)

Article 30.

Germany is forbidden to construct or acquire any warships other

---

[6] "GERMAN AUXILIARY CRUISERS AND FLEET AUXILIARIES," a list of four ships interned in neutral countries and twenty-eight ships in Germany, which was included in Annexure "A" as an annex following Article 40.

than those intended to replace the units in commission provided for in Article 21 of the present stipulations.

The vessels-of-war intended for replacement purposes as above shall not exceed the following displacement:

Armoured ships	10,000 tons
Light-cruisers	6,000 "
Destroyers	800 "
Torpedo boats	200 "

Except where a ship has been lost, units of the different classes shall only be replaced at the end of a period of 20 years in the case of battleships and cruisers, 15 years for destroyers and torpedo boats, counting from the launching of the ship.

(Article 30 was read and accepted.)

Article 31

The construction and acquisition of any submarine, even for commercial purposes, shall be forbidden in Germany.

PRESIDENT WILSON enquired what the term "in Germany" was intended to mean. Did it mean that the construction and acquisition of any submarines would be forbidden both to the German Government and to private individuals?

MARSHAL FOCH replied in the affirmative.

(Article 31 was accepted.)

Article 32.

The vessels-of-war in commission of the German fleet must only have on board or in reserve the allowance of arms, munitions and war materials fixed by the Governments of the Allies and the United States of America.

Within a month from the fixing of the quantities as above, arms, munitions and war material of all kinds, including mines and torpedoes, now in the hands of the German Government and in excess of the said quantities, shall be surrendered to the Governments of the Allies and of the United States of America at places to be indicated by them. (Such arms, munitions and war material will be destroyed or rendered useless.) (reserved)

All other stocks, depots or reserves of arms, munitions or naval war material of all kinds are forbidden.

The manufacture and the exports of these articles to foreign countries shall be forbidden in German territory.

PRESIDENT WILSON suggested that the last words of the last paragraph, namely: "in German territory" should be omitted.

(This was agreed to.)

(Article 32 was accepted, with the omission of the last three words: "in German territory.")

Article 33.

On the signature of the present stipulations, Germany will forthwith sweep up the mines in the following areas in the North Sea to the eastward of longitude 4°00'E. of Greenwich:

(a) between parallels of latitude 53°00'N. and 59°00'N.

(b) to the northward of latitude 60°30'N.

Germany must keep these areas free from mines.

Germany must also sweep and keep free from mines such areas in the Baltic as may ultimately be notified by the Governments of the Allies and of the United States of America.

BARON SONNINO pointed out that in the last paragraph of Article 33 the French word "Ultérieurement" had been translated as "ultimately." He suggested that a better translation would be "subsequently."

(This was agreed to.)

(Article 33 was accepted, the word "ultimately" in the last paragraph being altered to "subsequently.")

Article 34

(1) The personnel of the German navy shall be recruited entirely by voluntary engagement entered into for a minimum period of

25 consecutive years for officers and warrant officers,

12 consecutive years for petty officers and men.

The number engaged to replace those discharged on account of ill-health must not exceed five per cent per annum of the totals laid down in this section (Article 23).

(2) The personnel discharged from the Navy must not receive any kind of naval or military training or undertake any further service in the Navy or Army.

(3) Officers belonging at the date of the signature of the present stipulations to the German Navy and not demobilised must engage to serve till the age of 45, unless discharged on account of ill-health.

(4) No officer or man of the German Mercantile Marine shall receive any training in the Navy.

PRESIDENT WILSON suggested that the words "on account of ill-health" should be omitted in para. (1) and para. (3) of Article 34. The concluding sentence of para. (3) being made to read: "* * * must engage to serve to the age of 45, unless discharged *for sufficient reasons.*"

(This was agreed to.)

(Article 34 as amended was accepted.)

Additional Articles

Article 35

Heligoland.

The fortifications, military establishments, and harbours of the

Islands of Heligoland and Dune shall be destroyed under the supervision of the Allied Governments, by German labour and at the expense of Germany, within a period to be determined by the Allied Governments.

The term "harbours" shall include the north-east mole; the west wall; the outer and inner breakwaters and reclamation works within them; and all naval and military works, fortifications and buildings, constructed or under construction, between lines connecting the following positions taken from British Admiralty chart No. 120 of 19 April, 1918:

    (a) lat. 54°10′49″N., long. 7°53′39″E.
    (b)   54°10′35″N.,   7°54′18″E.
    (c)   54°10′14″N.,   7°54′00″E.
    (d)   54°10′17″N.,   7°53′37″E.
    (e)   54°10′44″N.,   7″53′26″E.

PRESIDENT WILSON said he was entirely in sympathy with the destruction of the fortifications on the Islands of Heligoland and Dune, but he thought the destruction of break-waters was rather a serious matter from a humane point of view, as those formed havens for fishermen in case of storms in the North Sea. If the destruction of the fortifications could be assured, he could see no real justification for destroying harbours. No doubt the works had been undertaken for military reasons, but they were there now, and were extremely useful as fishing harbours.

MR. LLOYD GEORGE pointed out that the fishing harbours were quite different and separate from the Naval harbours. No fishing boats had ever been allowed into the Naval harbours.

MR. BALFOUR thought that the Clause was not well expressed. What was meant was that only certain harbours, that is to say, that only purely Naval harbours, should be destroyed. But that was not clearly stated in the Article in question, as the use of the word "included" gave the sentence too wide an interpretation.

ADMIRAL DE BON said that in Heligoland two kinds of harbours existed, harbours for fishermen and harbours constructed as Naval Bases. After Germany had obtained possession of these islands she had built ports purely as Naval bases, and the latter were alone intended for destruction in the Article in question. That destruction was absolutely necessary in order to prevent Heligoland again becoming useful as a base for military operations.

PRESIDENT WILSON pointed out that Germany's Naval Establishment had under the Naval Convention been reduced to a minimum. The Naval Service had also been reduced to a minimum; and in addition the fortifications were all to be destroyed. Consequently, his contention was that the artificial harbours were useful places of refuge. It would be noticed that the destruction of these harbours was to be carried out "under the supervision of the Allied Governments," since the United States of America did not wish to take part in a destruction which was not considered to be necessary from a purely military point of view.

MR. LLOYD GEORGE said that after President Wilson's statement he would rather like to look further into the question, and he suggested that this Article be reserved for future consideration.

(It was agreed that Article 35 should be reserved for future consideration.)

Article 36
Routes Into the Baltic

In order to ensure free passage into the Baltic to all nations, Germany shall not erect any fortifications in the area comprised between latitudes 55°27′N. and 54°00′N. and longitudes 9°00′E. and 16°00′E. of the meridian of Greenwich, nor instal any guns commanding the maritime routes between the North Sea and the Baltic. The fortifications now existing in this area shall be demolished and the guns removed under the supervision of the Allied Governments and in periods to be fixed by them.

The German Government shall place at the disposal of the Allies and of the United States of America all hydrographical information now in its possession concerning the channels and adjoining waters between the Baltic and the North Sea.

(Article 36 was read and accepted.)

Article 37
Coast Defences

All fortified works and fortifications, other than those mentioned in Articles 35 and 36, now established within fifty kilometres of the German coast or on German islands off that coast shall be considered as of a defensive nature and may remain in their existing condition. No new fortifications shall be constructed within these limits.

The armament of these defences shall not exceed, as regards the number and calibre of guns, those in position at the date of the signature of the present stipulations. The German Government shall communicate forthwith particulars thereof to the Governments of the Allies and the United States of America.

On the expiration of a period of two months from the signature of the present stipulations the stocks of ammunition for these guns shall be reduced to and maintained at a maximum figure of:

Rounds per piece	Calibre
1,500	for 3-inch and under
500	for over 3-inch.

PRESIDENT WILSON pointed out that the second paragraph of Article 37 made it incumbent on Germany to notify to the Governments of the Allies and the United States of America the strength of the armaments of the coast defences. In his opinion, that was a question in which all European countries were particularly interested. He proposed, therefore, that the second sentence of Paragraph 2 should read: "The German Government shall communicate forthwith particulars thereof to all European Governments."

MR. BALFOUR enquired whether it would not be preferable to say straight away that the League of Nations should be informed.

PRESIDENT WILSON replied that the League of Nations should be regarded as something more than an alliance to enforce this Peace Treaty. In his opinion the United States of America could be omitted from this clause, since it was not more entitled to have the information therein set forth than Japan or any other Asiatic Government.

MR. BALFOUR thought that Article 37 should be compared with Article 9 in which it was clearly stated that the number and calibre of the guns constituting the armament of fortified works, etc., would have to be notified by the German Government to the Allied and Associated Governments. He thought the two articles should be placed in the same framework and, consequently, America should not be left out of Article 37.

PRESIDENT WILSON admitted the force of Mr. Balfour's contention. On the other hand, Article 37 dealt with local fortifications which could not be transported to the United States of America or elsewhere.

BARON SONNINO enquired whether the Allied and Associated Governments could not be made responsible for giving the necessary information to other Governments.

PRESIDENT WILSON replied that that would place Germany under the perpetual obligation of notifying a particular group of States as to her doings; a condition, which he considered exceedingly humiliating to her.

(Article 37 was approved; the last sentence of Paragraph 2 being made to read: "The German Government shall communicate forthwith particulars thereof to all the European Governments.")

Article 38
Kiel Canal.
(Reserved)

M. LEYGUES said that the Sub-Commission appointed by the Supreme War Council at the meeting held on March 6th, 1919, to report on the future regime of the Kiel Canal had unanimously agreed that the following clause should be inserted in the preliminary Treaty of Peace, on the assumption that the canal should remain entirely within German territory and without prejudice to any guarantees of a military nature which might be stipulated:

"The Kiel Canal shall remain under the sovereignty of Germany with the reservation that the rules, which shall ultimately be formulated in regard to the international regime of navigable waterways shall be applied to this Canal and its approaches, in particular those rules which concern freedom of navigation for the subjects, goods, and flags of all nations at peace with Germany in such manner that no distinction shall be made between the subjects, goods, and flags of Germany, and of all other States at peace with her. This provision shall apply not only to merchant ships, but also to ships of war."

M. LEYGUES continuing, said that two questions arose in connection with the text submitted by the Sub-Commission. In the first place, the proposal had been made that the Canal should be placed under the sovereignty of Germany. In the past that arrangement had permitted the hegemony of Germany, and enabled it to make the Baltic a German lake, both economically and militarily. He did not think the Allies were going to allow Germany to reconstitute that power; but the use of the word "sovereignty" meant the grant of full power to Germany to do what she liked. Should the Allied and Associated Governments wish to assure a normal existence to the new Baltic nationalities, such as Finland, Poland, Esthonia, Lithuania, free access to the sea must be assured. Now, the Baltic was not a free sea since all channels had been mined by Germany with the exception of the Kiel Canal, which was reserved for her own use. The Belt[7] was not practicable, on account of the dangers to navigation, and there remained only the Sound[8] which was too shallow, being less than 7 metres deep, for the passage of large ships. Therefore, the Kiel Canal could not in justice be placed under the sovereignty of Germany; it must be subjected to a regime, which would allow its free use to all countries for the passage both of commercial and military ships. The Canal was accessible to the larger ships: it had a surface width of 100 metres, a bottom width of 31 metres, and a depth of 11 metres. Therefore, unless the Kiel Canal were opened, the Baltic countries would only be able to keep ships below a certain size owing to the shallowness of the only other

[7] Actually, there are two "Belts": Great Belt ("Store Baelt" in Danish) and Little Belt ("Lille Baelt"). They are straits situated to the east and west, respectively, of Fyn Island, Denmark. Both connect the Baltic Sea with the Kattegat, another strait which connects with the Skagerrak, an arm of the North Sea.

[8] "Øresund" in Danish: still another strait, situated between the Danish island of Zealand ("Sjaelland" in Danish) and Sweden, which forms the only other access from the Baltic Sea to the Kattegat, and thus to the North Sea.

available channel, the Sound. In his opinion, therefore, two things were necessary, namely: firstly, German sovereignty over the Kiel Canal must not be proclaimed and, secondly, the regime to be enforced should allow free access to the Baltic through the Kiel Canal to the ships of all countries, and especially to the ships of those Baltic countries whose independence and autonomy it has been decided to recognise so that their means of existence might be ensured to them.

PRESIDENT WILSON said that he was quite prepared to discuss any proposal that would make the Kiel Canal a free International waterway. But the draft text under consideration merely stated that the rules, which might ultimately be formulated in regard to the International régime of waterways should be applied to this Canal. In his opinion, that statement was extremely vague as the unknown rules formed the essence of the system to be applied. Had it been proposed to give to the Kiel Canal the same status as the Suez or Panama Canal, that would constitute a definite proposal. But the clause as now drafted merely prescribed the application of an un-named and undefined system. He inquired, therefore, whether it would not be sufficient to say that the régime to be applied to the Kiel Canal should be the same as that applied to the Suez Canal.

M. LEYGUES said that the Admirals who had first considered the question, had proposed the following text: "The Kiel Canal shall be opened at all times to all commercial and war ships of all nations. No nation will be given favoured treatment and no class ships shall be excluded." He suggested that the Conference should accept that text.

MR. LLOYD GEORGE enquired when the Report of the Commission on International Ports, Waterways and Railways could be expected. He did not think that Germany should be treated in any different way to other countries in connection with the public waterways passing through her territory. He invited attention to the International régime applied, for instance, to the Danube.

PRESIDENT WILSON thought that a distinction should be drawn between the Kiel Canal and other International waterways, in that the Kiel Canal was an artificial waterway running altogether through Germany, and created by her; whereas great rivers, like the Danube, constituted the boundaries of nations, or passed through one national territory and continued in another.

MR. BALFOUR pointed out that the Conference was now discussing how to limit Germany's military and naval power. The use of the Kiel Canal in time of war gave Germany an enormous advantage, and it was in the public interest that the Kiel Canal should not be used for purely military purposes. From a commercial point of view, he was told, the Kiel Canal was not of much importance; consequently, unless the fortifications in connection with the Canal could be destroyed, it was of little use to take any other action. He proposed that the whole question should be referred to the Inter-Allied Commission on International Ports, Waterways and Railways.

PRESIDENT WILSON agreed that the question should be left to the Commission on International Ports, Waterways and Railways because it constituted, in reality, a purely commercial question and, he thought, the same general policy ought to apply to the Kiel Canal as to other International waterways.

MR. LLOYD GEORGE expressed the view that the Sub-Commission which had considered the question of the Kiel Canal had accepted that principle. On the other hand, it would be difficult to avoid the Kiel Canal remaining under the sovereignty of Germany.

MR. BALFOUR thought that measures should nevertheless be taken to prevent its being fortified.

ADMIRAL DE BON said, in reference to Mr. Balfour's statement in regard to the employment of the Kiel Canal for military purposes, that the destruction of all fortifications had been prescribed. The French representatives had, in fact, drawn up the following text for inclusion in Article 38:

"In view of ensuring free passage through the Kiel Canal, from the North Sea into the Baltic, Germany will neither erect any fortification nor instal any gun, in the islands or on its territory, within 30 miles from the Elbe Mouth and the Kiel Canal.

The fortifications now in existence will be demolished and the guns removed, within three months.

The same will apply to the torpedo-tube batteries, the mine-stores, and obstruction material sheds."

This text had, however, not yet been accepted by the Allied Naval experts.

MR. LLOYD GEORGE proposed that the further consideration of Article 38 should be postponed until the Report of the Inter-Allied Commission on International Ports, Waterways and Railways had been received. He understood their Report might shortly be expected.

BARON SONNINO said that if he were correctly informed, the work of the Commission on International Ports, Waterways and Railways was being held up pending a decision being reached on certain territorial questions. Consequently, this particular question should be referred to that Commission as a special thing, requiring immediate decision. Otherwise the Conference by referring questions from one Commission to another would be entering into a vicious circle.

PRESIDENT WILSON drew attention to the fact that in a previous Article provisions had been made for the disarmament of the coasts of Germany, which would obviously include the armaments in the neighbourhood of the Kiel Canal. Therefore, there would be no great objection in omitting Article 38 altogether. The Convention was, in his opinion, quite complete without that Article, which could, eventually, find a place in some other document.

M. CLEMENCEAU agreed on the clear understanding that the Article should form part of the Preliminaries of Peace.

(It was agreed to reserve Article 38 for further consideration.)

Article 39.
Wireless Telegraphy.

Until the Treaty of Peace the German high-power W/T stations at Nauen, Hannover and Berlin shall not be used for the transmission of messages relative to naval, military or political affairs in Germany, or any State which has been allied to Germany in the war, without the assent of the Governments of the Allies and the United States of America. These stations may be used for commercial purposes, but only under the supervision of the Allies and the United States of America, who will decide the wave length to be used.

Until the Treaty of Peace Germany shall not build any more high-power W/T stations in her own territory or that of Austria-Hungary, Bulgaria or Turkey.

(Article 39 was read and agreed.)

Article 40.
Submarine Cables.
(Reserved.)

M. CLEMENCEAU said that a Report relating to submarine cables had been submitted by the Judicial Commission to which the question had been referred, but it had not yet been circulated.

PRESIDENT WILSON submitted that the question was not a military or a naval one at all, except in a very restricted measure.

M. LEYGUES suggested that the consideration of this question should be adjourned to a later date as the Report of the Commission relating thereto had not yet been distributed.

(Article 40 was reserved for further consideration.)

SECTION III. Air Clauses.
Article 41.

The armed forces of Germany must not include any military or naval air forces.

Germany may, during a period not extending beyond October 1st, 1919, maintain a maximum number of one hundred seaplanes or flying boats, which shall be exclusively employed in searching for submarine mines, shall be furnished with the necessary equipment for this purpose, and shall in no case carry arms, munitions or bombs of any nature whatever. In addition to the engines installed in the seaplanes or flying boats above mentioned, one spare engine may be provided for each engine of each of these craft.

No dirigible shall be kept.

(Article 41 was read and approved)

Article 42.

Within one month from the signature of the present stipulations the personnel of the air forces on the rolls of the German land and sea forces shall be demobilised. Up to the 1st October, 1919, however, Germany may keep and maintain a total number of one thousand men including officers, for the whole of the cadres and personnel, flying and non-flying, of all formations and establishments.

(Article 42 was approved. The English text being altered to read: "within *two* months from the signature of the present stipulation. * * *")

Article 43.

No aviation ground or shed for dirigibles will be maintained or established:

(1) to the east of the Rhine, within a distance of 150 kilometres from that river;

(2) to the west of the eastern frontier of Germany, within a distance of 150 kilometres from that frontier;

(3) to the north of the southern frontier of Germany within a distance of 150 kilometres from the frontiers of Italy and Czecho-Slovakia.

All aviation grounds now existing in the zones defined above will be immediately put out of use. The sheds will be dismantled and the earth ploughed up. The work of putting these out of use must be completed within one month from the signature of the present stipulations.

(Article 43 was read and approved.)

Article 44 (Reserved).

Germany will allow to all Allied aircraft free passage through the air, free transit, and the right to land on her territory, until the complete evacuation of German territory by the troops of the Allied and Associated Powers.

(The following text of Article 44 was approved:

"Until the complete evacuation of German territory by the Allied and Associated troops, the aircraft of the Allied and Associated Powers shall enjoy in Germany freedom of passage through the air, freedom of transit and of landing.")

Article 45.

The manufacture and importation of aeroplanes, parts of aircraft, seaplanes, flying boats or dirigibles, and of engines for aeroplanes, shall be forbidden in all German territory until the signature of the final Treaty of Peace.

GENERAL DUVAL pointed out that in drafting Article 45 the British, Italian, Japanese, and French Representatives had asked for the addition of the following words at the end of Article 45, viz:

"And after the signature of the Treaty of Peace during a period to be fixed by the Treaty of Peace."

This proposal had been opposed by the American representative.

PRESIDENT WILSON said that he could not accept any such additional condition. He thought the Article should stand as at present drafted.

GENERAL DUVAL explained that the Commission had asked for the addition of the words in question for the reason fully set forth in the following report of the Aeronautical Commission on the question referred by the Supreme War Council of the Peace Conference:

"It was thereupon ruled that the questions to be answered were four in number, viz:

1st Question. Can civil aeroplanes and airships be easily transformed into weapons of war?

2nd Question. Should all aviation and all aeronautical fabrication continue to be forbidden, in Germany and all other enemy States, until the signature of the Treaty of Peace?

3rd Question. After the Treaty of Peace and in view of the easy transformation of commercial aircraft into weapons of war, will it be necessary to prohibit civilian aviation in Germany and all other enemy States?

4th Question. Arising out of the preceding questions is it necessary to suggest alterations in the Regulations concerning the Air Terms imposed on Germany until a signature of the Treaty of Peace?

I. In answer to Question 1 the Commission unanimously replied:

YES Commercial aeroplanes and airships can be very easily and quickly transformed into weapons of war.

II. In answer to Question 2, the Commission unanimously replied:

YES (question quoted)

III. In reply to Question 3 (quoted), Great Britain replied as follows:

YES, for a period long enough to dissipate the very extensive air industry now existing in Germany and all States which became our enemies by reason of the war. This period should not, in its opinion, be less than from two to five years.

France replied as follows:

YES, for 20 to 30 years, a period required for the destruction of all existing flying material and dispersion of personnel, for it is impossible to foresee the progress of flying in the immediate future. Even now:

1 aeroplane can carry 1 *ton* of explosives a distance of 300 kilometres.

1000 *aeroplanes* can carry 1000 *tons* of explosives a distance of 300 *kilometres* (or more than has been dropped during a whole year of war). In order to have 1000 *aeroplanes* ready for use at any time, it is sufficient for the factories to turn them out at the rate of 100 *a month*.

Italy replied as follows:

YES; for a long period, since Germany and all enemy States deserve to be penalised and the Allies are entitled to take precautions. Japan replied:

YES, (agreeing with the majority).

The United States replied:

NO, considering all such restrictions of the entire flying activity of Germany and her Allies after the signature of the Treaty of Peace to be neither wise nor practicable.

IV. In accordance with the answers given to the above questions, and after extensive study of the Regulations relating to the Air Terms imposed on Germany until the signature of the Treaty of Peace, the Commission recommended that the following amendments be made to such Regulations, viz:

1. That Article 45 be completed as follows:

"And after signature of the Treaty of Peace during a period to be fixed by the Treaty of Peace."

This was carried by a majority of votes.

The United States reserve their opinion as regards this addition.

2. That the whole of Article 50 be omitted.

This was carried unanimously.

PRESIDENT WILSON said that the Military Units of aircraft had already been regulated by other Articles. The addition proposed was an excursion into other realms. Railroad trains could be used to carry guns, should the manufacture of trains therefore be limited? Some types of ships could be readily converted for military use, should the construction of ships be limited on this account? The amount of military equipment authorised had already been limited, and personally he was not willing to go any further in that direction.

(Article 45 was accepted without amendment.)

Article 46.

On the signature of the present stipulations, all military and naval aeronautical material, except the machines mentioned in Article 1, second and third paragraphs, must be delivered to the Allied and

Associated Governments. Delivery must be effected at such places as the Allied and Associated Governments may select and must be completed within three months.

In particular there will be included in this material:

Complete aeroplanes and seaplanes, as well as those being manufactured, repaired or assembled.

Dirigibles able to take the air, being manufactured, repaired or assembled. Plants for the manufacture of hydrogen. Dirigible sheds and shelters of every sort for aeroplanes.

Pending their delivery, dirigibles will, at the expense of Germany, be maintained inflated with hydrogen; the plants for the manufacture of hydrogen, as well as the sheds for dirigibles, may, at the discretion of the Allied and Associated Powers, be left to Germany until the time when the dirigibles are handed over.

Engines for aeroplanes.

Nacelles and fuselages.

Armament (guns, machine guns, light machine guns, bomb dropping apparatus, torpedo dropping apparatus, synchronization apparatus, aiming apparatus).

Munitions (cartridges, shells, bombs, loaded or unloaded, stocks or explosives or material for their manufacture).

Instruments for use on aircraft.

Wireless apparatus, and photographic or cinematograph apparatus for use on aircraft.

Detached parts connected with any of the preceding categories.

The material referred to above shall not be removed without special permission from the Allied and Associated Governments.

PRESIDENT WILSON asked the Commission that formulated Article 46 to say whether all the materials specified constituted military material or not.

GENERAL DUVAL replied in the affirmative.

PRESIDENT WILSON enquired whether plants for the manufacture of hydrogen necessarily constituted military material?

GENERAL DUVAL replied that the proviso in question related only to hydrogen plants in military Aviation Parks.

PRESIDENT WILSON thought that had not been specifically stated.

GENERAL DUVAL pointed out that the commencement of Article 46 clearly stated that "on the signature of the present stipulations, all military and naval aeronautical material * * * must be delivered to the Allied and Associated Governments."

PRESIDENT WILSON said that if the first paragraph were strictly interpreted and applied it would be sufficient. He was perfectly satisfied with all military material, but he did not think that it was clear that only this was intended. He had another observation to make, namely, that it was not definitely stated whether this material should be destroyed or turned over. If turned over, it must either be stored or divided. In case the latter method were adopted, would it be put to the credit of Germany on the balance sheet or not? He thought many complicated questions might arise from this paragraph.

GENERAL DUVAL stated that there had not been full unanimity as to what disposition should be made of the materials surrendered; but in any case it was not considered that this disposition should be specified in the terms agreed to with the Germans. There was entire unanimity about this and about the fact that the material should be surrendered.

MR. BALFOUR said that the question under consideration formed a parallel case with that relating to the surrender of ships, and the disposition of the aircraft should be decided on the same principles. · He was informed by his experts that all aircraft and aircraft appliances and sheds, now in Germany, were military, as Germany had no commercial aircraft as yet.

M. SONNINO proposed that the third paragraph should be made to read as follows:

"In particular, there will be included the following military and naval material."

PRESIDENT WILSON, subsequently, proposed that the following phraseology should be accepted for the third paragraph of Article 46:

"In particular, the material to be handed over will include all items under the following heads which are or have been in use or designed for military or naval aeronautical purposes."

(This was agreed to.)

(Article 46 was adopted, paragraph 3 being altered to read:

"In particular, the material to be handed over will include all items under the following heads which are or have been in use or designed for military or naval aeronautical purposes.")

SECTION IV. *General Articles.*

Article 47.

After the expiration of a period of three months from the signature of the present stipulations the German laws must have been modified and shall be maintained in conformity with the preceding articles. Within the same period all the administrative or other measures relating to the execution of the present stipulations must have been taken.

PRESIDENT WILSON expressed his willingness to accept Article 47, but the German Government was in an unstable equilibrium, and supposing it were upset within three months, then the Allied and Associated Governments would presumably have to set up a new Government in Germany.

M. CLEMENCEAU thought that the same remark would apply to all the Articles of the Convention.

M. FROMAGEOT[9] asked for a ruling as to the character of the document that the Conference wished to present to the Germans. If the Convention under discussion were to be considered merely as a set of military clauses for immediate execution by the Germans, and not as a Treaty of Peace, it was to be feared that when the Treaty of Peace was presented to Germany, she would argue that the clauses previously accepted had not been Peace conditions, and consequently were open to fresh discussions. On the other hand, if the Articles under consideration were to be considered as final Peace conditions, then it would be necessary for them to be ratified by the legislators of the various countries, parties to the agreement, and in that case he would suggest that Article 47 be made to read:

"After the expiration of a period of three months from the date of exchange of ratifications of present stipulations for German laws, etc."

PRESIDENT WILSON remarked that the same question arose in regard to Article 48, and asked that that Article be read before the whole question came under discussion.

(Article 48 was then read.)

Article 48

The Armistice of November 11, 1918, and the Conventions subsequent thereto remain in force so far as they are not inconsistent with the present stipulations.

PRESIDENT WILSON, continuing, said that the paragraph as it now read indicated that these terms would be part of the Armistice. But if they were to constitute the Preliminary Treaty of Peace, the wording was not correct. In this matter he found himself in considerable difficulty, and he would be compelled to seek legal advice. He had assumed that this preliminary Convention would only be temporary until the complete Treaty was prepared, and that it would have the character of a sort of exalted armistice, the terms being re-included in the formal Treaty. If this Preliminary Convention should have to be submitted to the Senate for a general discussion there, he knew from the usual slow processes of legislatures that it would be several months before it could be ratified.

MR. BALFOUR expressed the view that the statements made by President Wilson were most important and serious. As he understood the situation, the policy accepted was that a Preliminary Peace

---

[9] Henri Auguste Fromageot, legal adviser to the French Ministry of Foreign Affairs.

should be made, each clause of which should be a part of the final Act, so that by the settlement of the Preliminary Peace a great part of the final permanent Peace would actually have been conquered [completed?]. It now appeared, however, that the American Constitution made that full programme impracticable.

PRESIDENT WILSON said he did not feel quite sure of his ground, and he proposed that the question be postponed until he could consult the Constitutional lawyers, in whose opinion he had more confidence than in his own. For the present, it appeared to him that they would have to use the alternative phraseology proposed by M. Fromageot, namely: "After the expiration of a period of three months from the date of exchange of ratifications of present stipulations for German laws, etc."

(Articles 47 and 48 were reserved for further consideration.)

SECTION V. *Inter-Allied Commissions of Control.*

Article 49.

The military, naval, and air clauses contained in the present stipulations shall be executed by Germany under the Control of Inter-Allied Commissions specially appointed for this purpose by the Allied and Associated Governments.

MR. BALFOUR drew attention to the footnote of Article 49, and expressed the view that the note was not really relevant, as no express time limit had been fixed.

PRESIDENT WILSON said that while it was not specifically stated that any of the Commissions provided should have an indefinite duration, he thought it would be advisable to add a statement including the explanation made by Marshal Foch that these Commissions would not continue more than three months.

MARSHAL FOCH stated that it appeared to him unnecessary to undertake such a contract with the Germans. They could agree to this among themselves.

MR. BALFOUR called attention to the fact that some of the operations might take more than three months, such as the destruction of the naval works at Heligoland harbour. It appeared to him that provision would have to be made for supervision during an indefinite, not an eternal, period.

M. CLEMENCEAU thought that some definite conclusions should be reached.

MR. BALFOUR enquired whether it would not be necessary to continue to exercise supervision over the German Army and its armaments in order to ensure their maintenance in the status stipulated.

PRESIDENT WILSON held that supervision of that nature would become endless. He thought that the Allies should agree among themselves that these Commissions would cease to function when the terms had once been carried out; for example, as soon as the army had been actually reduced to 100,000 men.

MARSHAL FOCH maintained that Articles 49 and 50 mutually explained one another.

MR. BALFOUR thought that Article 49 included in general all the terms, and was not specifically limited by Article 50.

M. ORLANDO thought that a very important point had been raised and it was necessary that a distinction should be made. First of all, there were clauses the execution of which could be completed within a definite period, and it had been unanimously agreed that the Commissions of Control over the execution of these clauses would last during the time necessary for their execution. But there were also clauses the execution of which would extend over an indefinite period, and the most important of these seemed to be that Germany should not have an army exceeding 100,000 men. It was necessary, then, to know what control the Allies would establish to supervise the carrying out of these clauses operating during an indefinite period. Marshal Foch had said that the control of the Commissions would not be applied to the clauses having an indefinite period of execution. Article 49 should, therefore, be modified to conform with this interpretation and to make the distinction between the two kinds of stipulations clear. It remained, then, to determine what guarantee the Allies would have for the execution of the other stipulations. Commissions could not be charged with this duty, as Germany would, as a result, always remain under the control of such Commissions. He personally would not object to such a proposal, but he did not think it would be accepted. What guarantee would there then be? The League of Nations might be considered. One of the Allied Powers alone could not be charged with this duty since Germany had taken engagements towards all the Allies conjointly. Some Inter-Allied agency would, therefore, have to be constituted. He feared he might be accused of raising difficulties, but it seemed to him that these were questions which must be considered.

M. CLEMENCEAU agreed that the question raised by M. Orlando was a very important one, but he thought that they were digressing from the question under consideration.

PRESIDENT WILSON suggested that "*All* Military, Naval and Air Clauses" should be substituted for "*The* Military, Naval and Air Clauses."

(This was agreed to.)

(Article 49 as amended was approved, to read as follows:

"All Military, Naval and Air Clauses contained in the present stipulations for which a time limit is fixed, shall be executed by

Germany under the control of Inter-Allied Commissions specially appointed for this purpose by the Allied and Associated Governments.")

Article 50.

The Inter-Allied Commissions of Control will be specially charged with the duty of seeing to the complete execution of the works of destruction, demolition and rendering things useless to be carried out at the expense of the German Government in accordance with the present stipulation.

They will communicate to the German authorities the decisions which the Allied and Associated Governments have reserved the right to take, or which the execution of the military, naval and air clauses may necessitate.

(Article 50 was read and approved.)

Article 51.

The Inter-Allied Commissions of Control may establish their organisations at the seat of the central German Government.

They shall be entitled as often as they think desirable to proceed to any point whatever in German territory, or to send Sub-Commissions, or to authorise one or more of their members to go to any such point.

(Article 51 was read and approved.)

Article 52.

The German Government must give all necessary facilities for the accomplishment of their missions to the Inter-Allied Commissions of Control and to their members.

It shall attach a qualified representative to each Inter-Allied Commission of Control, for the purpose of receiving the communications which the Commission may have to address to the German Government and to supply or procure for the Commission all information or documents which may be required.

The German Government must in all cases furnish at its own cost all labour and material required to effect the deliveries and the works of destruction, demolition, dismantling and of rendering things useless provided for in the present stipulations.

(Article 52 was read and approved.)

Article 53.

The cost of maintenance of the Inter-Allied Commission of Control, and the expenditure incurred by them in the execution of their duties, shall be borne by Germany.

(Article 53 was read and approved.)

MILITARY INTER-ALLIED COMMISSION OF CONTROL.

Article 54.

The Military Inter-Allied Commission of Control will represent the Inter-Allied High Command in dealing with the German Government in all matters concerning the execution of the military clauses. In particular it will be charged with the duty of receiving from the German Government the notifications relating to the location of the stocks and depots of munitions, the armament of the fortified works, fortresses, and forts which Germany is allowed to retain, and the location of the works or factories for the production of arms, munitions and war material and their operations.

It will take delivery of the arms, munitions, and war material, will select the points where such delivery is to be effected, and will supervise the works of destruction, demolition and rendering things useless to be carried out in accordance with the present stipulations.

The German Government must furnish to the Military Inter-Allied Commission of Control all such information and documents as the latter may deem necessary to ensure the complete execution of the military clauses, and in particular all legislative and administrative documents and regulations.

NAVAL INTER-ALLIED COMMISSION OF CONTROL.

Article 55.

The Naval Inter-Allied Commission of Control will represent the Admiralties of the Allied Governments and the United States in dealing with the German Government in all matters concerning the execution of the Naval Clauses.

In particular it will be its special duty to proceed to the building yards and to supervise the breaking up of the ships which are under construction there, to take delivery of all surface ships or submarines, salvage ships, docks and the tubular dock, and to supervise the destruction and breaking up provided for.

The German Government must furnish to the Naval Inter-Allied Commission of Control all such information and documents as the Commission may deem necessary to ensure the complete execution of the Naval Articles, in particular the designs of the war ships, the composition of their armaments, the details and models of the guns, munitions, torpedoes, mines, explosives, wireless telegraphic apparatus and in general, everything relating to Naval War Material, as well as all legislative or administrative documents or regulations.

AERONAUTICAL INTER-ALLIED COMMISSION OF CONTROL.

Article 56.

The Aeronautical Inter-Allied Commission of Control will represent the Inter-Allied High Command in dealing with the German Government in all matters concerning the execution of the Air Clauses.

In particular it will be charged with making an inventory of the aeronautical material existing in German territory, of inspecting aeroplane, balloon and motor manufactories, and factories producing arms, munitions and explosives capable of being used by aircraft and visiting all aerodromes, sheds, landing grounds, parks and depôts, of authorising, where necessary, a removal of material and of taking delivery of such materials.

The German Government must furnish to the Aeronautical Inter-Allied Commission of Control, all such information and legislative administrative or other documents which the Commission may consider necessary to ensure the complete execution of the Air Clauses, and in particular a list of the personnel belonging to all the German Air Services, and of the existing material, as well as of that in process of manufacture or on order, and a list of all establishments working for aviation, of their positions, and of all sheds and landing grounds.

PRESIDENT WILSON said that these Articles [54, 55, and 56], as at present drafted, contemplated the continuation of the Inter-Allied High Command during a period of three or four months after the signing of the Peace Preliminaries. He wished to enquire why the High Command should be continued when Commissions had been created whose function it would be to supervise the complete execution of the stipulations of the Treaty. He proposed, therefore, that the Military Inter-Allied Commissions of Control should represent the Allied and Associated Governments. The same remark applied to Article 55, where the words: "Allied and Associated Governments," should be substituted for "Admiralties of the Allied Governments and the United States."

(It was agreed:

(1) That Article 54 should read: "The Military Inter-Allied Commission of Control will represent the Allied and Associated Governments in dealing with * * * *"

(2) That Article 55 should read: "The Naval Inter-Allied Commission of Control will represent the Allied Governments and the United States in dealing with * * * *"

(3) That Article 56 should read: "The Aerial Inter-Allied Commission of Control will represent the Allied and Associated Governments in dealing with * * * *")

(The Military, Naval and Aerial Terms of Peace were accepted, subject to the following amendments and reservations: . . .)

[Here follow the texts of the amendments and reservations listed by articles above.]

2. MARSHAL FOCH asked permission to draw the attention of the Conference to the situation in Poland. On the 22nd of January last the Allied and Associated Governments had decided to send to Poland a Mission[10] to report on the situation and on the needs of

[10] See the minutes of the Supreme War Council printed at Jan. 22, 1919, Vol. 54. The members of the commission were Joseph Noulens and Gen. Henri Albert Niessel for

that country. Mr. Noulens, in despatches dated the 5th, 8th, 11th
and 12th March had, in the name of the Mission, drawn attention
to the actual situation existing in Poland. The gravity of the situation
was such that the very existence of this nation, which the Allied
and Associated Governments had decided to recognise, to reconstitute and to assist, was in question. The most imminent danger
related to the town of Lemberg which was infested by the Ukrainians, and whose fall would entail that of the Polish Government.
Such an eventuality threatened to draw into anarchy a country
menaced on three sides by the Germans, Bolsheviks and by the
Ukrainians. It was, therefore, absolutely necessary to take immediate action, and the Allied and Associated Governments could no
longer delay in arriving at a decision in order to ward off the grave
peril which threatened Poland. Assistance must at once be sent to
Lemberg. The possible measures included the transport to Lemberg
of a part of the Polish troops at Odessa if the situation in that region
made this possible; and the transport to Lemberg of one Polish
regiment from France. The transport of those troops would be carried out over the Roumanian, Italian and Austrian railways and for
this purpose an understanding would have to be reached by the
Allied General Staffs. The force thus made available would, however, [be] largely strengthened by the support of the Roumanian
Army, for which purpose a force of ten to twelve divisions at least
could be obtained of good physique and good moral[e]. The Roumanian Government had, in principle, agreed to participate in the
prepared operations on the condition that the Allied and Associated
Governments would furnish the material which was lacking, namely:
clothing, equipment and food. The assistance of the Roumanian
Army should be accepted without delay and without hesitation on
account of its great value and on account of the proximity of Roumania to the theatre of operations. It was of the utmost importance
that Roumania should be given, without delay, the assistance required, but in order to bring together the necessary resources con-
certed action between the Allied General Staffs was again necessary.

To sum up, the two countries, Poland and Roumania with whom
the Allies were tied, offered sufficient forces for the purpose required, provided that these troops received guidance and material
assistance. Their combined action would constitute a most solid

France, Brig. Gen. Adrian Carton de Wiart and Sir Esme William Howard for Great
Britain, and Maj. Gen. Francis Joseph Kernan and Robert Howard Lord for the United
States. For the activities of this commission in Poland up to this time, see Kay Lundgreen-
Nielsen, *The Polish Problem at the Paris Peace Conference: A Study of the Policies of
the Great Powers and the Poles, 1918-1919*, trans. Alison Borch-Johansen (Odense,
Denmark, 1979), pp. 170-73, 180-93.

barrier against Bolshevism, which would otherwise triumph. The object in view would be realised as soon as the Allied Governments decided on a resolute policy, affirming their resolve to stop the progress of Bolshevism, and constituting for the purpose an Allied High Command, charged with the duty of supplying to Poland and to Roumania (and eventually to the other Governments in a position to act, such as Finland etc.) the necessary material aid, and with the duty of co-ordinating the action of these various Governments.

MR. LLOYD GEORGE hoped the Conference would not accede to the proposals contained in the statement read by Marshal Foch as, he thought, it would merely mean giving support to the perpetration of a great mischief. The proposal at bottom merely meant the setting up of a great army for the eventual invasion of Russia. It would be agreed that Roumania had nothing whatever to do with Lemberg, but it was hoped that, once the Roumanian troops had been brought to that place, they would be available for operations against Russia. He was entirely opposed to any such operations which could only be carried out at the expense of the Allies. Even supposing the policy was correct, who was going to pay? Roumania could not finance their own justifiable military operations. The Poles were starving and unable to defend Lemberg against an untrained mob of Ukrainian rebels, unless they were organised, furnished with supplies, and paid by the Allies. He, therefore, personally would have nothing to do with the proposal which merely, being interpreted, meant that in the first place the Roumanians and the Poles would be assembled in Galicia and under the guise of relieving Lemberg, Russia would be invaded. Furthermore, the proposal suggested the transfer of troops from Odessa. Did the Conference fully realise what was happening in that region? It had been said that the Ukrainians possessed a powerful army, that they did not want the Bolsheviks, that they would be able in effect to roll the Bolsheviks back to Moscow. As a matter of fact, it appeared that the Allied troops, as well as the anti-Bolshevik Ukrainian troops, had actually been driven back to a narrow fringe in the south of the country. Kerson[11] had been lost and the Bolsheviks were pressing on towards Odessa; the whole of that grain district had, in fact, fallen into the hands of the Bolsheviks. In the face of that situation, it was now proposed to take all the forces from Odessa in order to take part in some quarrel at Lemberg. In his opinion, these proposals merely meant giving help to the Bolsheviks, since Petlura[12]

[11] That is, the Ukrainian city of Kherson.
[12] That is, Symon Vasyl'ovych Petliura, about whom see I. J. Paderewski to EMH, Jan. 12, 1919, n. 7, Vol. 54. He was at this time the chief military leader of the beleaguered Ukrainian Directory.

was fighting against the Bolsheviks and now it was proposed to destroy him.

In regard to the question of Lemberg, he would enquire whether any decision had been reached that the town should belong to Poland. In his opinion no decision had been reached by the Committee appointed to enquire into the frontiers of Poland. Why, therefore, should the Conference decide the question in favour of the Poles and against the Ukrainians before the question had been properly examined? Had the Poles felt very strongly on this question he thought they would have been able to defend themselves.

To sum up, he was entirely in favour of using all sources of persuasion in order to bring about the temporary settlement of the dispute between the Poles and the Ukrainians in the same way as had been done in the case of Teschen. But he was absolutely opposed to the idea of organising armies, to the idea of sending Roumanians at the Allies' expense to Lemberg, and to the idea of sending Haller's Army,[13] which was required to defend Poland, to Lemberg to fight questions of this kind. Consequently, he suggested that the proposal made by Marshal Foch should be negatived in so far as it related to military operations, and that persuasion should, in the meantime, be used pending a decision on the question of the frontiers of Poland. Apparently the Poles had a quarrel with the Ukrainians and an attempt was being made by them to grasp territory from the Ruthenians. No doubt the Polish troops would march against Lemberg, provided they were fed and paid by the Allies, but he personally would never agree to such a proposal.

MARSHAL FOCH asked that the discussion should be brought back to the particular question under consideration. Today was the 17th March, a month in which the enemy generally prepared his offensive, a fact which was evidenced by the experience of previous years. Therefore, if the Conference would that day merely consider the Allied situation, and not that of the enemy which was unknown, the following conclusions would be reached.

In accordance with M. Noulens' report, it would be admitted that the situation in Poland was very grave. Lemberg was about to fall, and if Lemberg fell the Polish Government would fall with it. That is to say, the Government would be wrecked at its birth, and the country, which it had been intended to re-constitute, would be threatened, by Germans, Bolsheviks and Ukrainians with the result that the creation of the Allies might only live a few days. To prevent the occurrence of this catastrophe, the Commission sent to Poland by the Allied and Associated Governments had proposed that the

---

[13] About which, see I. J. Paderewski to EMH, Feb. 4, 1919, n. 4, Vol. 54. The army was still in France at this time. See Lundgreen-Nielsen, pp. 225-26.

Polish troops at Odessa and in France should be sent to Lemberg without delay. And, as Allied Commander-in-Chief, he had put forward proposals to give effect to the demands made by the Commission. He had accordingly proposed that arrangements should forthwith be made by the Allied General Staffs for the transportation of the above Polish troops across various territories, in order to assist in the defence of Lemberg, which would otherwise fall. The Commission had also reported that assistance could be given by Roumanian troops, who were only too anxious to give the help required, provided an understanding were reached between the Roumanian and Polish Governments. He (Marshal Foch) still took, as the basis of his proposals, the suggestions made by the Inter-Allied Commissions which had been sent to Poland; and, in order to give effect to the recommendations of the Commission, he had merely formulated a scheme having as its object the continuation of the policy hitherto followed, namely: the creation of an independent Poland, and its support when threatened. The Roumanian Government, which was fighting on the Allied side, had agreed to send troops to Lemberg on condition of its receiving some assistance. The scheme he had proposed was a very moderate and restricted one; it was based on the recommendations made by the Polish Commission and it would work out successfully with the employment of only small military means, without great expense, and without undertaking any imprudent engagements. By the application of this scheme, a nucleus of resistance against the Bolsheviks would be created, and time would be gained for a further study of the situation. At the present moment, it was undeniable that the Bolsheviks were gaining ground everywhere in South Russia, and they were preparing a big attack on the Lower Dniester. Consequently, measures should forthwith be taken to put up a resistance to prevent the wings of the anti-Bolshevik armies being rolled up and the centre being pierced. It was with that object in view that he had proposed to constitute here an Inter-Allied staff to deal with this question with a view to the utilisation of all available means.

M. PICHON drew attention to the fact that the Polish Commission, which had dealt with this particular question, had put forward certain definite proposals, which would appear to agree with what Mr. Lloyd George had said. Paragraph 3 of the Commission's proposal, dated 14th March, 1919, read as follows:

"3. Lastly, with the object of making a simultaneous diplomatic attempt to save Lemberg, it submits to the Supreme Council the proposal to enjoin the Ukrainian Government, through the intermediary of the Warsaw Commission to accept an armistice.

If this attempt is to have any chance of success, the armistice conditions should, generally speaking, take the present situation into account, and more particularly in regard to the present possession of the oilfields."

In his opinion, in the manner above suggested, a solution might best be obtained. He thought if the Ukrainians were given the oilfields, they would be likely to accept an armistice. That was the proposal which had been put forward by General Barthélemy, and General Carton de Wiart, and had been accepted by all the experts, except Marshal Foch.

M. CAMBON said that he was President of the Committee for Polish Affairs. Having heard General Barthélemy and General Carton de Wiart and Lieutenant Foster,[14] his Committee had decided to adopt the recommendation just read by M. Pichon, which included the idea of an armistice. The Commission in Poland had recently visited General Petlura and had been somewhat badly received. In consequence the conclusion had been reached that the proposal for an armistice by itself would not in all probability satisfy the Ukrainians, unless some advantages were at the same time granted to them, such as the temporary cession of the oilfields. In addition, in order to make the acceptance of an armistice more certain, it would be necessary for Poland to be able to put forward some show of force. For that reason, in his opinion, the necessary help should be given to Poland by the immediate return of the Polish troops now in France.

M. CLEMENCEAU enquired by what route the troops would be sent from France to Poland. He thought there would be some difficulty in sending them via Dantzig.

MR. LLOYD GEORGE pointed out that the difficulty was one of shipping. No ships were available unless each of the Allies agreed to make a contribution, as it was a question of withdrawing ships which would otherwise be employed for the transportation of Australian or American troops from France.

PRESIDENT WILSON enquired as to the advisability of communicating with the Allied Maritime Transport Council with a view to hastening the matter.

[14] First Lt. Reginald Candler Foster, a former artillery officer, at this time the representative of the Coolidge mission in Poland. The American Commission to Negotiate Peace on December 26, 1918, had ordered Archibald Cary Coolidge, Professor of History and Director of the Library of Harvard College and a leading member of The Inquiry, to proceed to Vienna to investigate and report on conditions in the former Austro-Hungarian Empire. He and a party of other American observers, including Foster, arrived in Vienna on January 5 and began work immediately. For the origins and early history of the Coolidge mission, see *PPC*, II, 218-37; Harold Jefferson Coolidge and Robert Howard Lord, *Archibald Cary Coolidge: Life and Letters* (Boston and New York, 1932), pp. 192-98; and Robert F. Byrnes, *Awakening American Education to The World: The Role of Archibald Cary Coolidge, 1866-1928* (Notre Dame, Ind., 1982), pp. 165-77.

MR. LLOYD GEORGE pointed out that the shipping question was one which would have to be settled by the Governments concerned as matters of policy were involved, which the Allied Maritime Council could not settle. There was no spare shipping and consequently the ships required for Polish troops could only be obtained by the temporary withdrawal of ships at present employed for the transport of Allied and American homeward bound troops.

PRESIDENT WILSON enquired whether the Allied Maritime Council could not be asked to submit a memorandum showing what each country was required to do, that is to say, to submit a scheme giving a definite quota of contribution.

(This was agreed to.)

M. CLEMENCEAU summing up, said that the proposal made by the Committee for Polish Affairs which read as follows should at present be accepted:

"With the object of making a simultaneous diplomatic attempt to save Lemberg, it submits to the Supreme Council the proposal to enjoin the Ukrainian Government, through the intermediary of the Warsaw Commission to accept an armistice. If this attempt is to have any chance of success, the armistice conditions should, generally speaking, take the present situation into account, and more particularly in regard to the present possession of the oil-fields."

(This was agreed to.)

MARSHALL FOCH proposed that the question of the transport of Polish troops from France and Odessa to Poland should be studied by an Allied General Staff. He also proposed, with the consent of the Conference, to study the possible utilisation of the Roumanian troops in Poland.

M. CLEMENCEAU thought that the question to be settled was chiefly a financial one, as the employment of the Roumanian army would entail considerable expense.

MARSHAL FOCH pressed for a definite answer to his proposal. He asked, in the event of its acceptance, that a representative of each Government should be appointed.

MR. LLOYD GEORGE said that he agreed to accept the first part of Marshal Foch's proposal, relating to the study of the question of the transport of Polish troops from France and Odessa to Poland; but he declined to agree to the study of the second proposition to which he was entirely opposed in principle. He could not agree to instruct the Allied Commander-in-Chief to study the question of attacking the Ukrainians at Lemberg, whilst at the same time, General Franchet d'Esperey was being instructed to do all he could to help the Ukrainians to fight against the Bolsheviks at Odessa.

PRESIDENT WILSON expressed his agreement with Mr. Lloyd George's views.

M. ORLANDO said that he would also accept Marshal Foch's first proposal.

(It was agreed:

(1) To call upon the Allied Maritime Transport Council to submit a scheme showing what should be the contribution in shipping of each of the Allied and Associated Governments for the transport of General Haller's troops from France to Dantzig.

(2) To enjoin the Ukrainian Government through the intermediary of the Warsaw Commission to accept an armistice. The armistice conditions should, generally speaking, take the present situation into account and more particularly in regard to the present possession of the oilfields.

(3) To authorise Marshal Foch to study the possibility of the transport of Polish troops to Poland from France and Odessa.)

(The meeting then adjourned.)

T MS (SDR, RG 256, 180.03101/59, DNA).

A Draft of a Letter to David Lloyd George

> The President wrote this at my suggestion
> & that of Sir Wm. [Wiseman]
> E M House
> Paris, March 17/19.[1]

[Paris, March 17, 1919]

It seems to us imperative in order that the world may wait no longer for peace than is actually unavoidable that you should remain in Paris until the chief questions connected with the peace are settled and we earnestly beg that you will do so If you can arrange to remain for another two weeks we hope and believe that this all important result can be attained

We write this with a full comprehension of the very urgent matters that are calling you to England and with a vivid consciousness of the sacrifice we are asking you to make[2]

WWhw (E. M. House Papers, CtY).
[1] EMHhw.
[2] There is a TC of this letter in the E. M. House Papers, CtY.

To Joseph Patrick Tumulty

[Paris, c. March 17, 1919]

In reply to yours of March 15,[1] appreciate Mr. Taft's offer of suggestions and would welcome them. The sooner they are sent the better. You need give yourself no uneasiness about my yielding anything with regard to the embodiment of the Covenant in the treaty.   Woodrow Wilson

T telegram (WP, DLC).
[1] He meant JPT to WW, March 16, 1919 (second telegram of that date), Vol. 55.

From Frederick Henry Lynch

My Dear Mr President   [London] March 17, 1919

Since I came over to London—about six weeks ago—I have been meeting many prominent Englishmen, addressing a good many meetings, and last week took part in the League of Nations conference here. I have everywhere found a great desire to have Mr. Taft come to England just as there is a considerable desire in America to have Mr. Asquith come to our shores. This desire springs I think mostly from a growing desire to cement the ties already existing between the United States and the British Empire.

This desire has grown so rapidly during the last few weeks that it has at last taken formal shape in a joint invitation, which the English-Speaking Union[1] (of which Mr Balfour is President) the British Committee on Exchange between the British and American Churches (which has such eminent church leaders as the Lord Bishop of Oxford[2] and Sir Albert Spicer[3] on its list) and the League of Nations Union (of which Viscount Grey is President) have formulated and which also has the names of many leading Englishmen upon it. They have this invitation ready to send to Mr. Taft if it meets with your approval.

They have asked me to lay the matter before you, and I am glad to add a word. I remember that the last time the matter came up you did not feel that it would be wise for Mr Taft to go at that time. I think you were wise to decide as you did. But from pretty intimate conversations with many people during the last month, I have come to think that it would be one of the best things that could happen if Mr. Taft could spend two months here speaking on the closer union of the English Speaking peoples. There is a sentiment here just now toward America which offers an unusual opportunity to deepen the appreciation of each country for the other and to strengthen the strong bonds already existing and make them permanent.

There has already been some exchange of eminent clergymen. I have been very closely connected with it and I am sure it has worked great good. I believe an exchange now of great statesmen would do equal, if not greater good. It would be hoped that Mr Taft might come in May or June, if you feel that the project is wise.

Yours very sincerely   Frederick Lynch

ALS (WP, DLC).
[1] Organized in London on June 28, 1918.
[2] That is, the Rt. Rev. Charles Gore.
[3] Paper manufacturer of London, former M.P., active in many religious and business organizations.

From the Diary of David Hunter Miller

Monday, March 17th [1919]

The President was in Colonel House's rooms, and just as I was leaving, Colonel House came in and said he wanted to speak to me. He said that he had spoken to the President about my suggestion of a protocol, and said this: "The President is concerned about making a separate peace with Germany before making peace with Austria, etc., in the thought that Germany may be a necessary party to that peace," and asking what I could suggest. I told him that yesterday with Dr. Young[1] I had dictated a clause which would untangle Germany from the other Central Powers, and that with a clause added to that which would bind Germany to consent to any treaty of peace that we made with the other Central Powers and to become a party to such clauses of it as we required them to become a party to, the matter would be settled and we could proceed to make peace with Germany. He asked me if I would like to talk to Mr. Gregory about it and I said that I would. Colonel House told me to be at his office at 12 o'clock tomorrow in case I should be needed at his conference with Lord Robert Cecil. . . .

While I was at the Meurice I had a telephone call from Mr. Lansing's office asking me to be there at 10 o'clock to give my opinion on a constitutional question. The message was from Mr. Kirk who said that Major Scott[2] would be present.

At ten o'clock P.M. I went to Mr. Lansing's office and met at the door Doctor Scott, who had two or three books under his arm, including Crandall on Treaties and one volume of Malloy.[3] Doctor Scott mentioned that the question involved was ratification of the Preliminaries of Peace.

We went in to see Mr. Lansing and he said that the President had advanced the idea that afternoon that the Preliminary Treaty of Peace need not be ratified by the Senate and that he, Mr. Lansing, had been shocked at the idea and told him that that was impossible, and that the President had said to consult the legal advisors.[4]

Mr. Lansing asked me my opinion, and I said that I did not think it was debatable; that the status of war could not be changed into the status of peace, so far as the United States was concerned, except by a treaty ratified by the Senate. Doctor Scott was entirely of the same opinion and cited several cases to that effect, including one in the war between Great Britain and us in 1813, one after the Mexican War, and one after the Spanish War.

Mr. Lansing was in accord with these views and instructed Doctor Scott and myself to prepare a short opinion on the matter, which, after we went out, I asked Doctor Scott to write.

David Hunter Miller, *My Diary at the Conference of Paris, with Documents* (21 vols., New York, 1924), I, 174-76.

[1] That is, Allyn Abbott Young.

[2] That is, Alexander Comstock Kirk, Second Secretary of the embassy in Paris, and James Brown Scott, who had been commissioned as a judge advocate.

[3] Samuel Benjamin Crandall, *Treaties, Their Making and Enforcement*, 2d edn. (Washington, 1916); and William M. Malloy, comp., *Treaties, Conventions, International Acts, Protocols and Agreements between the United States of America and Other Powers* (2 vols., Washington, 1910).

[4] If the minutes of the Supreme War Council may be trusted, Lansing misunderstood what Wilson said. Moreover, Wilson's position on this question is stated with great clarity in the following entry from the Grayson Diary. Finally, the reader will recall that House had earlier proposed to put the League of Nations into practical operation (EMH to WW, Feb. 27, 1919 [first telegram of that date], Vol. 55), and that Wilson had vetoed the plan on the ground that he could not make any such arrangement without the consent of the Senate (WW to EMH, March 3, 1919 [second telegram of that date], *ibid.*).

From the Diary of Dr. Grayson

Tuesday, March 18, 1919.

This morning while the President was working in his study I went in and he turned to me and said: "You seem to have effectively smoked Pichon out." The President told me that Pichon had called him up on the phone to tell him that his remarks had been entirely misunderstood and misinterpreted, and that, as a matter of fact, he had never desired to be recorded as believing that the League of Nations constitution could be deferred and kept out of the preliminary peace treaty. It was a distinct victory for American publicity.

Today marked the end of suggestions that the League of Nations constitution could be considered by itself. Lloyd-George took occasion to tell the British newspapermen that the British attitude now was to believe that the League must be part of any and all peace treaties. Clemenceau and Orlando said the same thing. The Japanese position was rather peculiar. They had raised the question of equal rights of immigration when the original draft of the League constitution was made. Last night in the United States Ambassador Ishii had made an address in which he said that the Japanese government was prepared now to insist that this equality of immigration should be made a part of any constitution of any League of Nations.[1] The French government saw fit to have a complete draft of Ishii's speech brought forward and spread broadcast among the correspondents. However, when the Japanese delegates here learned of this they immediately got into touch with Colonel House and told him that this speech did not represent their views. They said that they would reserve the right to propose equality of immigration in any discussion of the League constitution but that they would not go to the extent of declaring their willingness to blockade the constitution simply for that purpose. Instead, they would simply go on record as reserving their rights to bring the matter up at a future day, and probably to ask the Executive Council of the League to pass upon it. This ended the Japanese opposition, and it was possible as a result of statements issued by practically all of the peace delegations to arrive at a general knowledge of what the new plan really was. It was to be as follows: The League of Nations would be an absolute integral part of the peace treaty. The peace treaty would not be a preliminary treaty; it would be an initial treaty, in every way binding and enforceable. It would include the settlement of all questions involving Germany in so far as they could be directly settled by the German delegates themselves and by the new German government. It would include all outside matters dealing with territorial problems where they could be completely disposed of and where they could not, they would be referred to the League of Nations committee, which would have power to settle them. The outstanding difficulties which were causing delay were not questions growing out of the League of Nations, it developed, but the big problems of reparations, personal responsibilities for personal guilt, and the disposal of the French claims, dealing with the buffer state along the Rhine. When these had been settled, the League of Nations problem would be easy.

Today Clemenceau and Colonel House had a lengthy conference as a result of which Clemenceau suggested to Colonel House that they "wipe the slate clean" on the Rhinish Province question, and ask each other what could best be done. Clemenceau told the Colonel that he absolutely believed it necessary for France's safety that a buffer republic be created to extend from the left bank of the Rhine as far as the Alsace-Lorraine boundary. However, he said he was still willing to be convinced that the safety necessary could be afforded by the prohibition of all fortified areas within that same territory and the prohibition of any fortifications at any Rhine bridgehead or within fifty miles of the river itself. Such a plan would mean that Germany's western boundary would be absolutely unguarded by permanent fortifications. The matter was to be settled by conferences to be held later on.

During the morning Secretary Lansing also talked with a number of neutral delegates who had been sent on to talk over the League of Nations with the President if they could, and he arranged for a conference to be held on Thursday, at which a sub-committee of the full committee of the League of Nations would listen to any suggestions from the neutrals dealing with proposed amendments to strengthen the constitution. The various committees to whom had been assigned the work of finding out what must be included under the sub-heads in the treaty of peace were all notified to have their majority and minority reports prepared in such form that whichever was accepted by the Council of Ten would be ready for immediate incorporation, thus doing away with any revamping and hastening the clerical work. This was a good piece of work inasmuch as it was designed to make possible the winding up of the initial treaty within twelve days, so that an agreement could be arrived at by the Allied governments, and then Germany notified what she could expect. The initial treaty which it was now expected would be ready for the signatures of the Allies and the German delegates by the first week in April would be a permanent document rather than a preliminary one. That is to say, it would include everything that could be settled at this time and would be subject to ratification by all of the states. It would remain effective until another treaty was arranged, which need not be for months, nor until Germany had rehabilitated herself sufficiently so that she could ask for membership in the League of Nations. With the League of Nations made the first part of the proposed treaty, if present plans are carried through to consummation, it would be possible to refer many knotty problems to the League itself and its executive committees, and would greatly expedite the work of putting the world back on a peace basis. Had only a preliminary treaty been agreed upon as was originally proposed when the President landed, it would be a stop-gap which would have no real effect and would mean that months would have to pass before the actual treaty could be made effective. It was because he knew that it was a race "between the forces of anarchy and the forces of law and order" that the President took the strong position against a preliminary treaty and insisted on an initial treaty that would be to all intents and purposes a real treaty of peace.

The President walked alone across the street and called on Lloyd-George in his apartment. He spent the morning in his study with the exception of this call on the British Premier. This afternoon the President, Mrs. Wilson, Miss Margaret and I walked down to the Crillon Hotel, where the President had a conference with Lloyd-George and Clemenceau.

This evening the President had Lord Robert Cecil and Colonel and Mrs. House for dinner. After dinner the conversation, after being somewhat general, drifted to Earl Grey,[2] and the President expressed the deepest regret that he had lost his eyesight. Lord Robert Cecil told the President that Earl Grey's chief hobby was fishing and birds, and that he had written books on both subjects.[3] The President said he knew this, because the Earl had sent him both books, and he had the greatest admiration for Grey himself. This drew the talk to Mr. Balfour, and Lord Robert Cecil said that Balfour had two hobbies: the first was music and the second was golf; all other things in life were incidental to him. The President laughingly stated that he himself enjoyed music very much and that when he was in school he sang in a church choir and he had some pretense then of having a good tenor voice. Lord Cecil asked how the President had enjoyed the French Opera, which he attended,[4] and especially how the voice of the leading soprano[5] had sounded. The President smiled and said: "Only her very high notes caused pain." Lord Robert asked the President what he thought of Alexander Hamilton, and the President said that he was convinced that Hamilton was the greatest constructive statesman of his time. The conversation drifted to Clemenceau and the President likened him to one of Earl Grey's game trouts, which, when you have hooked him, you first draw in a little, then give liberty to the line, then draw him back, finally wear him out, break him down and land him. The President said he had been trying to show Clemenceau that the real reason that the people of the world had rallied towards France was because they believed she had been wronged by Germany. "Now if the policies are to be carried out which you are advocating," he told Clemenceau, "and which wrong the German people, the world must naturally turn against you and France, and through sympathy alone it may be likely to forget Germany's crimes." The President expressed the belief that Clemenceau's only present thought seemed to be a desire to build up a defensive league against Germany.

[1] Actually, Ishii had spoken at a dinner meeting of the Japan Society at the Hotel Astor in New York on March 14. While he made a strong plea for the inclusion of a provision against racial discrimination in the Covenant of the League of Nations and indicated clearly that this was the policy of his government, he did not state or even imply that his government would "insist" on "equality of immigration," as Grayson says here. For a report of and extracts from Ishii's speech, see "Ishii Looks to End of Race Prejudice," *New York Times*, March 15, 1919.
[2] That is, Viscount Grey of Fallodon, not Earl Grey.

³ The book on fishing was Edward Grey, *Fly Fishing* (London, 1899). However, bcth Cecil and Wilson were confused about the book on birds. Grey may have produced a manuscript study of birds by this time, but his only book on the subject, *The Charm of Birds*, was first published in London in 1927.

⁴ The Wilsons, along with many other dignitaries, attended a presentation of Jean-Philippe Rameau's *Castor et Pollux* at the Paris Opera on January 25, 1919. For an account of this gala affair, see Paris *Le Temps*, Jan. 26, 1919.

⁵ Germaine Lubin.

To Edward Mandell House

My dear House: Paris, 18 March, 1919.

Won't you be kind enough to give me your opinion on the enclosed about Dr. Moton?¹

Affectionately yours,   Woodrow Wilson

TLS (E. M. House Papers, CtY).
¹ See NDB to WW, Feb. 28, 1919, Vol. 55.

To George Lansbury

My dear Mr. Lansbury: Paris, 18 March, 1919.

Your letter of March 14th¹ was entirely welcome, and I beg that you will pardon me for not having replied sooner.

I find myself very much in sympathy with all that you urge in your letter and shall very much enjoy a conversation with you. I notice from your letter that the first issue of the Daily Herald will come out on March 31st. I assume that it would not be possible for you to come next week, when you will be in the midst of preparations for its issue, and yet things are moving a little faster here now and it is desirable that our interview should occur as soon as possible. I wonder if you could make it possible to see me at say noon on Tuesday of next week, a week from today, which will be the twenty-fifth.

Cordially and sincerely yours,   [Woodrow Wilson]

CCL (WP, DLC).
¹ G. Lansbury to WW, March 14, 1919, Vol. 55.

To Howard Duryee Wheeler

My dear Mr. Wheeler: Paris, 18 March, 1919.

Thank you for your letter of March sixth.¹ I do not know how the idea got started that I was intending to write a history of my own Administration. I would not dream of undertaking anything of the kind. I shall be entirely too near the events to give an account of them, and moreover I have not the least idea what my opportunities for writing will be after I lay down the duties of my present office.

I am very much obliged to you for your kind letter but feel obliged to make this frank response.

I sincerely hope that Mrs. Wheeler is making a successful and rapid recovery.   Sincerely yours,   [Woodrow Wilson]

CCL (WP, DLC).
  [1] H. D. Wheeler to WW, March 6, 1919, Vol. 55.

To Auguste Schaffner[1]

My dear Pastor Schaffner: Paris, 18 March, 1919.

It is with genuine regret that I find it my duty to say that I cannot be personally present at the meeting on Sunday next,[2] but I am sure that both you and all who are associated with you will understand that it is only from imperative considerations of public duty that I am led to absent myself.

Inasmuch as I cannot be personally present, will you not be good enough to convey to the meeting not only my very cordial greetings but an expression of my sincere interest in all that concerns the great issues of religion which those who have arranged the meeting have at heart? I wish that I might have had an opportunity to personally express my belief in the great matters of inspiration and Divine Providence, whose renewed revelation to the whole world seems to me at present to be of such vital and permanent consequence.   Sincerely yours,   [Woodrow Wilson]

CCL (WP, DLC).
  [1] President of the Society of Sunday Schools of France.
  [2] Wilson was replying to A. Schaffner to WW, March 18, 1919, TLS (WP, DLC).

From Thomas Nelson Page

Confidential

My dear Mr. President: Rome, March 18, 1919.

I sent Colonel House by our Military Attaché, Colonel M. C. Buckey,[1] Saturday evening, a letter about the increasing press propaganda here to fortify the steadily expanding Italian claims which I asked might be shown you.[2] I now write you directly because there is going on here so evidently a press campaign to frustrate your effecting your plans for the League of Nations as the basis of the Peace Treaty that I feel you should be in possession of all the facts touching this new propaganda, as far as I have them.

I have just sent a telegram[3] which I hope you will see stating that the instigation of this campaign apparently comes from Paris. The telegrams in the press received here from Paris are giving a sort of key note in their references to the opposition which the American—your plan—is encountering not only on the part of the French but now, according to report, by the British. Also, the op- position in America to your plan is being very much played up with the manifest intention of diminishing public confidence here in you and, as I believe, of preparing the public to stand for a more ve- hement campaign against you than has hitherto been started. I have a conviction that this campaign has its origin in Paris. I have heard that "the word has gone out that the press is to start a cam- paign of depreciation of you and of your plans," and I at least feel sure that this campaign would not have been inaugurated unless it had been believed that it would be acceptable to Baron Sonnino. For several days there have been suggestions that France and Italy would stand by each other and make joint common cause in the determination to have accorded to them the full extent of their several territorial claims or aspirations in Europe. To-day's press states, based on telegrams from Paris, that France and Italy have actually come to an accord as to this, and the note in the Italian press is much bolder than hitherto.

A day or two since there were conjectures that your visits to the Italian headquarters at the Hotel Edward VII were evidence of sympathy between you and Orlando and of an approaching un- derstanding between you. To-day's press, however, takes a different note, conjecturing that there is not the accord which has hitherto been hoped for and declaring that France and Italy are in accord and England becoming critical of you; that your plan is to push forward to a Peace Treaty with Germany first, basing this on your League of Nations and deferring the settlement of Italy's claims as one of the matters to be settled hereafter under the Peace Treaty by the League of Nations.

This the Italians resent and there is a hot editorial in one of the papers this morning declaring that Italy has established her position as one of the great powers and the peer of her Allies and of America and will never consent to be placed by them on a par with the lesser nations. Another paper simply has a note that if the suggestion, which is said to be that of the American Delegation, has any basis of fact Italy will not sign the Peace Treaty. All of this is based on telegrams from Paris to the papers here. Unfortunately, I do not know what is going on in Paris except as I get it from the press—

Italian, French or English, so I am left to work out for myself how much basis there is in these reports. Undoubtedly, however, the propaganda will have a marked effect on Italy and on her attitude towards America.

Sonnino's hand has been tremendously strengthened and apparently he is growing stronger all the time—that is according to the reports he is growing stronger in Paris and, consequently, he is growing stronger in Italy. My conviction is that unless something be done in Paris to open his eyes to the danger of losing the friendship of America for Italy and to the unhappy consequences of cutting Italy off from one of the most fruitful sources of supply for her he will continue his policy of refusing any compromise with results which may be disastrous to the League of Nations.

They are evidently preparing to isolate America, as far as possible, and encouraged by the opposition of the Republicans in America, to break up the League of Nations plan. Sonnino has never given adhesion to the idea further than he was obliged to do and if he believes in it at all it is only academically. It is not unnatural that he should wish to extend the boundaries of Italy to lines which he believes will not only render her strong and safe and take in all her hitherto unredeemed people but will add to her future greatness; inasmuch as the lines now laid down are likely to remain fixed for at least an indeterminate period. But he will certainly claim more than he expects to get and he will relinquish nothing unless it be made plain to him that he cannot get it. When he knows that he cannot get it I think he will accept the situation, but only at the end. Meantime, I feel sure that every effort is being made by him to guard against America's having too much influence both now and in the future. I feel that there is much secret work going on in Paris, and that the sooner the final decision is arrived at the better the chance for the League of Nations and for the permanent character of the Treaty of Peace which you will bring about. I should be greatly disturbed if I did not believe confidently that you will be able to accomplish your high design and overcome all the opposition of those who oppose it, whether openly or in secret.

Always, my dear Mr. President,

Yours most sincerely,   Thos. Nelson Page

TLS (WP, DLC).

[1] That is, Mervyn Chandos Buckey.

[2] T. N. Page to EMH, March 15, 1919, TLS (E. M. House Papers, CtY), which repeats a good deal of Page's letter to Wilson.

[3] T. N. Page to A.C.N.P., March 18, 1919, T telegram (WP, DLC).

A Memorandum by William Shepherd Benson

MEMORANDUM   Paris 18 March 1919.

For: The President.

Articles 21 and 23, limiting German Naval strength in men and ships, are indefinite in their terms as regards duration of restrictions.

Articles 30, 31, 32

and 34 place limitations of indefinite duration upon the German Government as to future construction, as to supplies and munitions to be carried and as to length of service of personnel.

Agreement to the above articles makes the United States a member of a continuing alliance to curtail the sovereignty of Germany, and hampers the application of the principle of the League of Nations to Germany later on.

It is believed that the President may not have realized this feature of these articles, as he was assured that *supervision* would continue only for a limited period.

The same principle is involved in the terms limiting the German Military and Air forces.   W. S. Benson

TS MS (WP, DLC).

A Memorandum by David Hunter Miller and James Brown Scott

18 March, 1919.

From: David Hunter Miller and Major James Brown Scott.

To: The Commissioners Plenipotentiary.

The question submitted to the Technical Advisors for their opinion is whether a preliminary treaty of peace negotiated by the President would bind the Government of the United States from the date of its signature or whether it would require the advice and consent of the Senate to its ratification, and only bind the Government upon and from the latter date.

In providing that the President "shall have power, by and with the advice and consent of the Senate, to make treaties," (Art. 2, Sec. 2), the Constitution makes no distinction between classes of treaties which are subject to the advice and consent of the Senate, and in determining whether an instrument is or is not a treaty within the constitutional provisions the name given to it is not essential; it must be construed according to its purposes and objects.

As Commander in Chief of the Army of the United States, the President has the authority to conclude an armistice and incorporate therein such terms of a military nature as the exigencies of the situation may seem to him to require. Of such a nature was the "Protocol of agreement embodying the terms of a basis for the establishment of peace" between the United States and Spain signed on August 12, 1898, which was not submitted to the advice and consent of the Senate. This protocol suspended hostilities upon its signature, embodied a promise on the part of Spain to relinquish her sovereignty over Cuba and to cede Porto Rico and certain other islands to the United States, and made provision for their evacuation by the Spanish troops. It provided for the occupation of Manila by American forces "pending the conclusion of a treaty of peace" and for the appointment of "commissioners to treat of peace."

In the case of the Preliminary Treaty of Peace between France and Germany signed at Versailles on Feb. 26, 1871, ratification by both parties, namely, the Emperor of Germany and the French National Assembly, was expressly stipulated. (Art. X.) The same is true of a number of other important preliminary peace treaties. (See Phillipson,[1] op. cit. p. 99.)

The declaration of war by the United States Congress on April 6, 1917 created a status of war which may only be terminated by a treaty of peace equally as valid as the law of the land with the declaration of April 6, 1917, and "as in the case of other treaties, a treaty of peace is not definitively binding until the exchange of ratifications; and a state of war in the technical sense continued until the date of the exchange." (Crandall: ["]Treaties, Their Making and Enforcement," p. 352, citing several decisions of the Supreme Court.)

The legal effect of the protocol between the United States and Spain of August 12, 1898 was judicially passed upon in the case of Hijo v. United States, in which the United States District Court held that "The protocol and proclamation did not end the war. The protocol worked a mere truce. The President had not the power to terminate the war by treaty without the advice or consent of the Senate of the United States." In confirming this decision, Mr. Justice Harlan, speaking for the Supreme Court, declared that "a state of war did not in law cease until the ratification in April 1899 of the treaty of peace." (1943 U.S. pp. 317 and 323.)

It is therefore submitted that a preliminary agreement signed by the President, but not ratified by the Senate, can have no legal effect, so far as ending the war is concerned, and can operate only as a truce; and that if it is desired in the preliminary agreement, by whatever name it may be called, to effect the legal transition from the state of war to a state of peace, this may only be accomplished by submitting it to the Senate for its advice and consent according to the constitutional provision.

James Brown Scott.
David Hunter Miller

TS MS (WP, DLC).
[1] Coleman Phillipson, *Termination of War and Treaties of Peace* (New York, 1916).

A Memorandum on Reparations by Baron Sumner of Ibstone[1]

18th March 1919

The conditions of this problem are stringent; the data are scanty; the conclusions can only be matter of forecast and of opinion.

It is imperative not to under-estimate Germany's capacity for it will certainly fall short of her liability, and any under-estimate would result in her rapidly paying off the sum imposed upon her, as France did after 1871, thus winning a brilliant financial victory and also palpably escaping the just consequence of her aggression. This would produce intense and widespread political resentment in all the Allied countries.

It is necessary also not to over-estimate her capacity. Two grounds are urged for this: (1) that it might lead Germany to prefer the continuance of a state of war to the conclusion of such a peace; (2) that if the sum demanded plainly exceeded her capacity to pay, the German bonds would be no foundation for credit and an early repudiation might be feared.

To (1) we can only say that we know of no substantial sum, of which, for bargaining purposes, the Germans will not allege that it is beyond their capacity, but that we believe the pressure of a state of war and the continued severance of trading relations, which it involves, to say nothing of the blockade, will eventually bring them to sign. That Germany will permanently accept Bolshevism, repudiate all obligations and renounce all trade prospects does not accord with what is known of Germans.

[1] John Andrew Hamilton, Baron Sumner of Ibstone, a Lord of Appeal in Ordinary, considered to be one of the great English judges of his time. He was an adviser on legal questions in the British delegation and a member of the Reparation Commission. The grim visaged Sumner was a spokesman for the vast majority of M.P.s who were crying, "Hang the Kaiser and make Germany pay!" He and his crony on the Reparation Commission, Walter Cunliffe, 1st Baron Cunliffe of Headley, were commonly referred to as "the heavenly twins" by their colleagues at the peace conference, presumably because their greed extended even to heaven.

As to (2) we think that between a sum which can be paid, though with effort, and a sum which clearly cannot be found at all, there is a very wide margin, on which we have tried not to trench.

The Economic data are of two kinds, Germany's natural resources and Germany's pre-war trading. The first are largely immutable and can only be valued vaguely. Their value depends on the industry of those who use them. The second are an index now of a state of society and of industry which not merely will pass away as a result of the war but to a large extent has passed away already. The sums raised by Germany during the war would have passed all belief in 1913 but with the same effort and organisation almost equally great results may be looked for in the prospect of a return of peaceful prosperity.

To be on the safe side we have assumed that Germany may lose not only Alsace Lorraine but also the Saar Valley, Posen, and the industrial parts of Upper Silesia; nor do we assume that her loss of population will be made good by the adherence of German Austria. We note also that this loss of territory involves not only a loss of natural resources, but also of many going concerns, which it will take time to replace elsewhere. Should these assumptions not be realised the argument is strengthened.

On the other hand we take account of the following facts. The former German war expenditure will almost disappear. Military training will no longer withdraw masses of men from industry. Secret service and propaganda outlays will cease. The internal war debt cannot be allowed to compete with our claim. That sum Germany staked in the war and lost, we have won. Her pre-war debt is also mainly held at home and might be postponed to our claim. Thus Germany is free to impose large taxation to pay our interest in the first instance. As it is, the German debt per head stands far below the British debt per head. The cost of war pensions and compensations will steadily diminish.

It is not the case that Germany cannot export raw material or even food. Her enormous Westphalian coalfield is very far from exhaustion and in coal, timber, potash and beet sugar she has a large natural export capacity. Her factories are full of machinery; her industrial processes have been improved by new discoveries during the war; her coal exports command large ore imports from Scandinavia; and Russia, if she recover, presents one enormous field to German enterprise, which the Allies cannot close to her for they cannot occupy it themselves.

No doubt Germany must pay in exports direct or indirect and a flow of manufactured exports cannot be indefinitely maintained unless the necessary raw materials are regularly paid for by corresponding exports. Payment of our claims in exports may seem to displace our internal manufactures and payment of very large claims seems to postulate a very large increase of German exports. Still Germany can make no substantial payment without exporting something, which might have been produced in England; the choice lies between giving some manufacturers a grievance, which is inevitable and leaving all the taxpayers, the commerce, and the finance of the country to bear, unaided, the present load of debt if it can. As to the second point, German exports before the war paid for many imports, which were not indispensable. Germany was then rich and disposed to 'do herself well'; she must now do with as little as possible at home, dispense with everything except strict necessaries, try to live on home-grown produce and devote her exports, after purchase of necessary raw materials, to paying her debts. Payment, even of very large sums, by means of exports after the war does not therefore involve the huge expansion of her turnover that might be supposed. Before the war she worked hard and lived well; now she has to work harder and live hard too.

There are two methods of obtaining compensation from Germany; either, if pressed to extremity, excludes the other, but they may be reconciled. The first is to take what she has now and so leave her; the second is to take her promises in future. If the first were thoroughly done Germany could never start business again, but unfortunately her debts would only have begun to be paid. The second plan alone will not suffice, for reconstruction of the devastated districts demands immediate deliveries of certain commodities in kind.

Accordingly, our suggestion falls into two parts. The first consists of a lump sum payment, valued at £1,000,000,000 which, as it must mainly be made in commodities, will not be completed for a year and a half or two years. Some gold, all ships over about 1,500 tons, all foreign securities that can be got at, coal, timber, potash, machinery, chemicals, dyes and other commodities will thus be handed over. The Sub-Commission has received a large body of evidence contributed by the delegations of states bordering on Germany and dealing fully with her resources and has examined such further information as it could get and is unanimous in thinking that such a payment is obtainable, though it recognises that the full amount above given may not be ontained [obtained].

The second part consists of an annual payment for interest and sinking fund extending over a second series of years to commence at the conclusion of the above-named first period, say in 1921. By that time it may be expected that the Allies need no longer feed Germany, that the cost of the Army of Occupation will be much reduced, and that German trade will have obtained sufficient foreign credits for her initial supplies of raw material and can begin exportation. To ease the situation we proposed that this annual payment should involve no sinking fund till 1926, and should be at rates of interest only rising to 5% in that year, say 4, 4¼, 4½, 4⅝, 4⅞, 5. This [Thus] in 1926 the annual payment will rise to a nominal £600,000,000, which we believe it will then be practicable to obtain from Germany provided that it is paid in the following way.

The £600,000,000 consists of £100,000,000 sinking fund and £500,000,000 interest: the sinking fund and half of the interest is to be payable each year in gold marks; the other half of the interest is to be payable in German paper currency at the rate of exchange of to-day. We shall thus fix from the outset how much each payment will amount to, but Germany should have the right, if the rate moves in her favour, of paying more than half in gold marks so as not to have to pay the old number of marks after her credit has improved. The annual burden will thus be £350,000,000 payable in the equivalent of gold; the residue will consist of internal paper currency, which must not be demonetised or varied and we shall have to take our chance of selling it or borrowing on it as best we may. As Germany returns to normal conditions this chance will improve and we shall have the means of making lucrative investments in Germany as well. In this connection one must bear in mind the effect on international trade if Germany pays her labour in very depreciated currency.

From 1921 to 1925 inclusive the annual sum will be payable as interest only. Though we suggest 1% for the annual sinking fund in order to obtain an early amortization of the debt, we think it is really a question of politics whether a longer or a shorter term of payment off should be fixed and whether accordingly a lower or a higher percentage should be taken for the sinking fund. If Germany can pay for a series of years at all, her capacity to go on paying will increase and not diminish with every year; the nearer she gets to the end of the term, the better it will be worth her while to win the financial prestige which will come from continuing the payments to the end.

5% is not likely to be a high rate of interest for a long time to come and a longer term might in some ways favour the debtor country. In any case she should always have the option of paying off her debt at a faster rate than the fixed sinking fund rate and of providing a higher proportion of gold marks than of currency, if she finds it to her advantage to do so.

The debt should take the following form. At or before the conclusion of the first period before mentioned Germany will deposit with the Allies an issue of bearer bonds with half-yearly or quarterly coupons attached, in order to provide the machinery for the payment of the whole funded debt and interest. As each instalment of sinking fund is realised a corresponding drawing of the bonds will take place.

The importance of this issue of bearer bonds is that the Allies must not hold them but must make it their business to distribute them as widely among neutrals and among raw material countries as possible. This is worth while even at the cost of a large discount. Germany might risk repudiating an issue chiefly held by her old enemies but if it were largely held by her customers and her money lenders she would think twice about it.

Apart from such matters as the right to inspect the accounts of Customs, Railways and State monopolies and to object to diminution and different[i]ation in traffic rates we think a valuable additional security can be obtained as follows.

Along with the issue of the bearer bonds Germany should deliver, as collateral security, a large amount of her Private Bank note currency, say £250,000,000, consisting of notes of all the private issuing banks in Germany in proportion to the total amounts of their issues. If, owing to her default this collateral should ever be resorted to and depleted, she should be bound forthwith to make it up. The utility of this collateral is not of course that it adds much directly to the money value of the bonds, and in itself it will only involve the cost of printing. The notes are only further promises to pay. The object is to enlist Germany's need for maintaining her internal as well as her external credit on the side of the service of her debt. To throw this paper on the market in case of default would produce such an effect on Germany's foreign credit and exchanges and on the credit of the private banks as well as would powerfully contribute to bringing her to reason. In the Allies' own interests the[y] would be slow to use these weapons; they might even seek at times to support German credit, but the knowledge that the weapon could be used would operate to keep up the service of the debt so long as Germany had any credit, either at home or abroad, which either the German State or its merchants or its banks thought worth preserving. This is in addition to the value, such as it is, of the threat of presenting to the Reichsbank such an amount of its own bank notes at any time as would compel it formally to declare that it could not cash its own currency notes.

We advisedly do not base out [our] estimate of the annual sum which Germany can pay on statistics nor do we offer estimates in support of it. Statistics are of use and have been examined with regard to the sum obtainable in the first two years. For a period of years beginning thereafter and for conditions, of which nothing can be declared with certainty, except that they will differ from those of the past, no statistics can really avail. As an estimate the sum named is below the mean of the estimates advanced by the various persons, members of the sub-Commission and others, so far as we know them. We can see no answer to the proposition that, of [if] Germany can (as it is agreed she can) furnish nearly £1,000,000,000 in two years or less, she can, with time and the graduated rates above provided, furnish fully £350,000,000 in gold marks per annum from 1926 onwards, as well as the £250,000,000 per annum in currency notes. The value of the payment in German currency is admittedly problematical nor do we suppose that for several years the mark can possibly approach gold parity, but it is what may be called a 'legitimate' speculation. If Germany makes money, the paper will be worth money in time; the one thing that we find it impossible to believe is that the Germans, as hitherto known, will not manage to make money somehow. If that is accepted, the real problem is to make them make money for us.

Under this head the argument rests upon human nature. We assume that peace will be assured for one or two generations. The German people are industrious, orderly and educated. They will ardently desire to be rich. They are organised and equipped industrially and commercially and the money-lenders and the raw material men of the world are eager to find customers among them. Nothing that we can do will prevent Germans from competing with us, but the competition will be less keen, if every sovereign of profit that they make is made part for us and part for themselves, than it would be if they could exploit and supply the whole world themselves; they have neither the capital nor the labour to make good the waste of war and to annex all foreign markets as well. The world will need vast quantities of goods for the next fifty years. There will be room for all and nothing can prevent Germany from getting a good share of the trade, unless Germans become quite unlike what they have hitherto been.

It will thus be seen that, as regards the future, our opinion is mere opinion, though we believe it is sound. Fortunately it rests on grounds which others can judge of as well as we can ourselves, nor do we think that as regards the future anything is possible but a reasoned opinion founded on consideration of the kind above set out.

T MS (WP, DLC).

From the Diary of David Hunter Miller

Tuesday, March 18th [1919]

Then Mr. Gregory came in and told me that he had seen Mr. Lansing last night at 11 o'clock, and that the subject of the discussion had been the same as at the previous conference I had had with Mr. Lansing and Doctor Scott. I described this conference to Mr. Gregory and he entirely agreed with the view expressed. I showed him the protocol with Spain and the Peace Treaty with Spain, in which he was very much interested, saying he had not seen them before. He mentioned that Mr. Lansing had asked him to see the President on the subject, but Mr. Gregory said that he had not been in the Cabinet for four and a half years without knowing that if the President wanted his opinion he would ask for it.

Going in to lunch Mr. Rappard[1] came up to me and said that the Swiss would like that no definite figure be put in the amount to be paid to Germany on the St. Gothard Tunnel matter. I suggested that perhaps there might be put in such amount as may be due or may be found to be due by the League of Nations, and I repeated this suggestion to Mr. Hudson[2] a little later.

I had a conference with Mr. Finch[3] regarding the opinion on the Preliminaries of Peace and the constitutional question involved, and I suggested some omissions. The opinion was drawn up later, adopting my suggestions, and signed by me, and I suppose it was later signed by Doctor Scott. . . .

At 6 o'clock Mr. Auchincloss telephoned me that Colonel House wished me to be at the President's house at 8 o'clock. Accordingly, I gathered together some papers regarding the League of Nations and reached the President's house a little before 8 o'clock. I waited some time, when he came down from dinner with Colonel House and Lord Robert Cecil, and I went with them into his library.

We first went through certain amendments proposed by Lord Robert Cecil.[4] He had the Covenant in the form reported, in three

[1] That is, William Emmanuel Rappard, who was acting as a "liaison agent" (*Verbindungsagent*) of the Swiss government to the American and British delegations to the peace conference. See Heinz K. Meier, *Friendship Under Stress: U. S.-Swiss Relations, 1900-1950* (Bern, 1970), pp. 114-15.

[2] That is, Manley Ottmer Hudson, at this time a technical adviser on legal questions in the A.C.N.P.

[3] George Augustus Finch, lawyer, an assistant technical adviser on legal questions in the A.C.N.P.

[4] For these amendments, which Cecil introduced, see the minutes of the Commission on the League of Nations printed at March 22, 24, and 26, 1919. There is a printed copy of the Covenant embodying Cecil's amendments in Wilson's and Miller's handwriting and also in typewriting in WP, DLC. There is also a printed copy in WP, DLC, in parallel columns of the text of the unamended Covenant and of the Covenant with Cecil's changes. Miller, *My Diary at the Conference of Paris*, I, 180-88, annotates all the changes.

copies, marked with the proposed changes in red ink. One of these he gave to the President and one to Colonel House. At first I sat beside the President and attempted to take note of the amendments, but Colonel House asked me to sit beside him, and handed me his copy.

Cecil stated that the first change in the Preamble was simply for euphony, the words "secure" and "security" coming close together.

The second change in the Preamble is intended to have Germany agree to the Covenant although not a member of the League. For this reason it was agreed that the expression "States Members of the League" should be used throughout instead of "High Contracting Parties" after the Preamble, and this change first occurs in Article I.

In connection with Article III Cecil explained that the purpose of his amendment was to provide for an addition to the Executive Council. The President said perhaps that could be left to the Body of Delegates; to which Cecil replied that they might swamp it, and the President agreed that they might. Cecil said that really the Great Powers had to be the essential factor and that he was thinking of the future participation of Germany and even of Russia. In answer to French objections it could be said that France would be on the Executive Council and could prevent any addition. Cecil thought, however, that if Germany became a really great Power the pressure to have her added would be very great. The President said that Germany would be a great Power after a few years except in a military sense but that, however, it was better not to go farther than the proposed amendment in view of sentiment now which had to be taken into consideration.

The amendment to Article IV was stated by Cecil and admitted to be nothing more than a statement of what the Covenant would mean if it was not contained in it, but was put in to satisfy sentiment. It was at first suggested to leave out the words "at the meeting" but after some consideration it was thought that they had better be in any way to prevent one State from stopping the Body of delegates from meeting, or possibly be not able to be represented.

At Article V the President asked if there had been any discussion of a place for the seat of the League. Colonel House said that the Swiss had been around talking to everybody about it and were perfectly willing to have the League take any territory it wanted, either at Geneva or Lausanne. He said that he had had the climatic conditions looked into and they would be about the same; Geneva would be more convenient and that the property which the Swiss were willing to give and which it would probably be necessary to take over was worth ten million francs; that he did not think that the countries of the world should accept that from a comparatively poor Power. Cecil agreed to this, although he said, laughingly, it would be a very good investment for them to give it away for that purpose.

There was also some discussion of Swiss neutrality, and the President said that in the Swiss constitution neutrality was a part thereof and that the whole canton in which the seat of the League was situated will be given to the League for that purpose, and that neutrality of the whole State of Switzerland will be recognized by the League. It was agreed tentatively to put Geneva or Lausanne in the blank in Article V, so that it might come up for discussion. Cecil said that nearly everybody, for one reason or another, was opposed to Belgium and that the Belgians as a matter of fact were rather hard to get on with.

Cecil explained Article VII as partly necessary because of the assent of Germany in the absence of membership, and that otherwise it was changed so as to make the language positive and not negative. The requisite for a two-thirds majority for the Body of Delegates was retained, after some discussion, in order to please the French.

As to Article VIII, Cecil explained that the changes were in the way of simplification in drafting, except the proposal to change the word "permission" to the word "notice." He said this was wished by the British Admiralty, and the President said he did not see how it could be accepted. Cecil then said that he would not press it but he wished the President would understand that he had various amendments of the Admiralty and it would be understood that he had pressed them very seriously, but as this was the weakest of the lot and the President had not accepted it, it was not worth while mentioning the others.

There was some little discussion of Article X. Cecil's proposed amendment he said he did not think made any difference in the meaning. The President said that this was the one Article on which the French relied and he did not see how it could be weakened.

The President agreed to the amendment to Article XI without any particular discussion, although it seemed to me that it was quite important.

Similarly, the amendment to Article XIV did not lead to any particular discussion, although it seems to me to be in the direction of compulsory arbitration.

There was some discussion on the proposed amendment to the second paragraph of Article XV. The President said he had thought of the matter a good deal. Cecil said he had proposed the amendment in order to clear up the ambiguity suggested by the President in a case where a recommendation was not satisfactory to either party to the dispute. The President spoke of the hypothetical case urged in the Senate Committee on Foreign Relations, that the Japanese might acquire a harbor for a naval base in Magdalena Bay; that if the matter was submitted to the Executive Council, with Japan and the United States not voting, possibly because of some ill feeling against the United States, the other powers might decide unanimously that the fears of the United States were not well founded and that it would be an insult to Japan to suppose that she acquired the harbor for anything except commercial purposes. He said that all this seemed highly improbable to him but it was a perfectly fair answer for the Senate to say that that was only his opinion. What, under those circumstances, would the Executive Council propose? Following the discussion the President suggested that the amendment be dropped and that the words in the third sentence of the paragraph, after the word "recommendation" where it first occurs be stricken out.

The amendments to Article XVII were accepted as merely preventing ambiguity, substituting the Executive Council for the League as to what modifications, if any, would be necessary in *ad hoc* membership.

The next amendment was to combine Articles XVIII, XX, and XXI in a new article numbered XIX. The President suggested one change in this, namely, to strike out the word "any" before the word "conventions," and insert after that word "hereafter to be," so as to make it clear that those conventions were for the future. Colonel House suggested, which was accepted, to insert the words "communications and" before the word "transit" in Article XXI which becomes Article XIX(c).

A suggestion for a Financial Commission was hardly more than mentioned and disapproved.

It was not mentioned that the last five articles would have to be renumbered. The discussion of the amendment of the last article brought up the whole question of withdrawal. The result was to disapprove the amendment and to suggest a tentative amendment permitting withdrawal, to see how it would be received, although it was admitted that the French would be very much opposed to it. The President stated that the majority of the delegates, led by Orlando, had said that a State had the right to withdraw from the League under the Covenant as now drafted. Cecil said that was not his understanding at all; the President asking my opinion, I told him that except under the doctrine of changed conditions, which was known as the doctrine of *rebus sic stantibus*, my opinion was that a State did not have the right to withdraw from the Treaty;

that the doctrine of changed conditions had been used to satisfy almost any violation of a treaty; that in modern times treaties had usually been drawn to continue for a certain period, with a clause permitting denunciation thereafter, and that this was true even of treaties of alliance, such as the triple alliance, for say a twelve-year period. The President said that when he had lectured on international law he had thought that a State had the power to denounce any treaty. I said in reply that that was not my opinion as to the legal right, although as to the power I did not question that a State has power to denounce a treaty. Lord Robert Cecil said that he agreed with my statement of the law.

The question then came up as to the insertion of an Article that domestic affairs of a State should not be within the province of the League. This led to the discussion of the Japanese and Irish questions. The President said that it was his opinion as a constitutional lawyer that the treaty power was extensive enough to override State laws about land, and that if it did so in California the question would be one between California and the United States on that, and not between the United States and Japan. He said this was purely a hypothetical case, of course; the Senate would never ratify such a treaty. He then spoke of the Irish question and said that he had been made very angry by a delegation of the Irish who had visited him while in the United States and had asked him to promise to ask the Peace Conference to make Ireland independent.[5] Of course he had refused to promise anything about it. He had decided then to go to Mr. Lloyd George and tell him what the situation was in the United States and ask him whether he wanted nothing done, in which case he would do nothing, but if he wanted something done, what it was; but to tell him the situation and that the question might be raised in the United States by the Irish making a campaign against the League on this ground, and that this would raise a racial and religious question which would have far-reaching consequences. Of course, he said, it would be overwhelmingly defeated by the Irish and would insure the success of the League, and that his first impulse had been, from his fighting blood getting up, that he had wanted to tell them (the Irish) to go to hell, but he realized that while that might give some personal satisfaction it would not be the act of wisdom or the act of a statesman. He said, however, turning to Lord Robert Cecil, that it might get to such a state that its discussion in the League of Nations would be inevitable, and Cecil said that he quite agreed with this. The President said that the attitude of the Irish was that they would create such a dis-

[5] For the fullest account of this meeting, see the extract from the Grayson Diary printed at March 4, 1919, Vol. 55.

turbance so continuously as to compel international notice to be taken of them; if an article was put in against interference in domestic affairs, it would be said by the Irish to be put in directly as a shot at them. This would start the sort of campaign that he had mentioned. Colonel House suggested that the President might say this to the Senate Committee on Foreign Relations as they were urging the insertion of such an Article.

An addition to the former Article XIX was written out by Cecil on the suggestion of the President that there was some contention in the United States that a State might be compelled to be a mandatary.

After some discussion of the proposed new Article XXVII it was agreed by my suggestion that this should be left out as there would undoubtedly be a general clause as to when the treaty should take effect, and that this would include the Covenant.

The Japanese question was only incidentally discussed, but when it was mentioned I handed to Colonel House a copy of the dispatch regarding the Ishii speech of March 14th.[6] He said that he had seen it, but he read it over again.

There was some discussion of the Monroe Doctrine. The President alluded to the fact that the Monroe Doctrine had never been defined and that the Senate did not want it defined. He spoke of the question with Mexico after the Civil War. He alluded to the fact that the Monroe Doctrine had permitted force to be used, or at least threatened, against the South American republics. He said that the Doctrine as originally launched had been to prevent the extension of the European System to the American continents. I then handed him an extract from the text of President Monroe, which he said he had overlooked and that in addition to that the Doctrine was pointed against European colonization. It was agreed that it would be impossible to put in the Covenant a reservation of the Monroe Doctrine without a similar reservation of an Asiatic doctrine of the Japanese, and accordingly the idea was disapproved.

The President endeavored in vain to find a copy of Senator Hitchcock's letter to him,[7] and discussed it from memory. He spoke of his difficulty on the withdrawal question in view of what he had told the Senate Committee on Foreign Relations; that there could be withdrawal at any time, based on what Orlando and the others had said.

Then the question came up about the printing and I told the

[6] FLP to A.C.N.P., March 15, 1919, T telegram (WP, DLC), printed in Miller, *My Diary*, VI, 441-42. About this speech, see n. 1 to the extract from the Grayson Diary, March 18, 1919.
[7] See G. M. Hitchcock to WW, March 4, 1919, Vol. 55.

President the matter could be printed so as to show the amendments, and possibly in the Congressional form with a line struck through what was stricken out and new matter italicized.

Various meetings were spoken of; first, of the Neutrals on March 20th at 3 o'clock, and probably the next day, and the meeting of the full commission was agreed to be called for March 22 at 10 A.M.

In the course of the discussion Cecil said that the Japanese were talking to Hughes about some clause for racial equality and said they were getting on very well with them.

I spoke to Miss Wilson and Miss Benham on the way out and went to the Meurice to dinner at quarter to eleven.

I then came back to the office and wrote a letter to Lord Robert Cecil, sending him his copy of the Covenant, which Colonel House had asked him to give me, and mark it and be sure that mine was conformed.

I also wrote a letter to Colonel House on the two amendments to Articles XI and XIV, which I think will make more difficulty in the Senate.

I also corrected proof for the printer and finished about half past two.

Miller, *My Diary at the Conference of Paris*, I, 179-88.

From the Diary of Lord Robert Cecil

March 18 [1919].

Dined with the President at seven. No one there except House and his wife, Dr. Grayson, his A.D.C., Mrs. Wilson and his two daughters.[1] The President was very pleasant, telling stories, and keeping up the conversation himself. After dinner he came and sat by me while he was drinking coffee and again bore the brunt of the conversation, telling me of his great irritation with the French; that it was intolerable talking to them; it was like pressing your finger into an indiarubber ball. You tried to make an impression but as soon as you moved your finger the ball was as round as ever. He said that nothing would induce him to consent to the division of the country on the left bank of the Rhine from Germany, but he was prepared to agree to something in the nature of an alliance between England and America and France to protect her against sudden aggression, in addition to the protection which she would already have by the League of Nations. But he appears to have rather spoiled the effect of this conversation by pointing out to

Clemenceau that it really amounted to very little more than Article
10 of the Covenant.

Then we went to work on the amendments of the Covenant. I
found him in a very different and far more malleable frame of mind.
He assented to the greater part of the suggestions which I made,
and even admitted this time what he had indignantly repudiated
on Sunday—namely, some kind of concession to the Monroe Doctrine. I said frankly that I did not like it, but going away with House
I agreed to try and draft something in that direction, which I did
and sent down to him this morning.

T MS (R. Cecil Papers, Add. MSS, 51071-551157, PRO).
  ¹ Margaret Wilson was present. Cecil must have thought that Miss Benham was
Wilson's daughter.

From the Diary of Colonel House

March 18, 1919.

Lord Robert Cecil and I had a long session concerning the amendments which we think the League of Nations might profitably add
to the different articles of the Covenant. This meeting was preparatory to the after dinner conference which we had with the President tonight. David Miller was also present. We dined with the
President at the early hour of seven. I suspect that Cecil went
without his usual tea and took the dinner as a substitute.

Our meeting was fairly successful. We agreed upon a number
of changes. I found the President more reasonable than he was the
other day as to meeting the wishes of the Senate, but we found it
nearly impossible to write what the Senate desires into the Covenant, and for reasons which are entirely sufficient. We are perfectly
willing to adopt them if the balance of the world would accept them,
and if they do not cause more difficulties than they cure. If a special
reservation of the Monroe Doctrine is made, Japan may want a
reservation made regarding a sphere of influence in Asia, and other
nations will ask for similar concessions, and there is no telling
where it would end. If a statement is made that is not intended to
interfere in domestic affairs, this would please our Senators from
the Pacific Slope, but it would displease all the Senators of pro-
Irish tendencies, for they would declare that it was done at the
instance of the English in order to keep the Irish question forever
out of the League of Nations.

We are not trying to act in an arbitrary way but are sincerely
desirous of meeting the views of those Senators who really have
serious objections, but who do not understand our difficulties. No

one can understand them without being here to formulate a Covenant as we have.

To Carter Glass

Paris, 18 March, 1919.

Cannot give any assurance of the calling of Congress by May first but in the meantime am glad to authorize the allotment of $2,368,000 returned to security fund by the War and Navy Departments to the War Risk Bureau for the purposes stated in your cable of March 15.[1]   Woodrow Wilson.

T telegram (WP, DLC).
[1] C. Glass to WW, March 15, 1919, Vol. 55.

From William Howard Taft

[Washington] 18 March, 1919.

[No. 19] Following from Wm. H. Taft:

"If you bring back the treaty with the League of Nations in it, make more specific reservation of the Monroe Doctrine, fix a term for the duration of the League and the limit of armament, require expressly unanimity of action in Executive Council and Body of Delegates, and add to Article XV a provision that where the Executive Council of the Body of Delegates finds the difference to grow out of an exclusively domestic policy, it shall recommend no settlement, the ground will be completely cut from under the opponents of the League in the Senate. Addition to Article XV will answer objection as to Japanese immigration as well as tariffs under Article XXI. Reservation of the Monroe Doctrine might be as follows:

Any American State or States may protect the integrity of American territory and the independence of the government whose territory it is, whether a member of the League or not, and may, in the interests of American peace, object to and prevent the further transfer of American territory or sovereignty to any European or non-American power.

Monroe Doctrine reservation alone would probably carry the treaty but others would make it certain.   Wm. H. Taft."
          Tumulty.

T telegram (WP, DLC).

From Herbert Clark Hoover

My dear Mr. President: Paris, March 18, 1919.

I enclose herewith draft of Proclamation releasing the meat packers from license.[1]

As you are aware the stabilization of the price came to an end on March 1st, and there appears to be no reason why the same policy could not now be followed in this case as has already been adopted with respect to practically all the other food trades.

I should be greatly obliged if you would sign the Proclamation and return to me either the original or enclosed copy.

Faithfully yours,   Herbert Hoover

TLS (WP, DLC).
[1] [H. C. Hoover], CC MS (WP, DLC).

From Charles Evans Hughes

Sir: New York, March 18, 1919.

The Union League Club of the City of New York, pursuant to a resolution unanimously adopted at its regular meeting held on the thirteenth day of March, nineteen hundred and nineteen, respectfully presents this petition urging Your Excellency promptly to convene the Senate of the United States in extraordinary session, to the end that its members may consider and discuss the form and substance of the proposed covenants to establish a League of Nations as submitted by the Committee of the Peace Conference sitting in Paris and any amendments or revision thereof, and thereupon give the President the benefit of the advice of the Senate as contemplated and provided in the Constitution of the United States.

The Union League Club of the City of New York, as stated in its resolution, earnestly urges that in the judgment of this Club the calling of an extra session of the United States Senate would tend to allay objectionable public agitation and to promote a better realization of the difficulties involved, a wiser solution of the great problem of how to enforce peace throughout the world, and particularly a truer understanding by the people of the United States of the nature and extent of the obligations which it is proposed they shall assume and be called upon to perform in the future and which they cannot be expected to perform unless they rest under such a sense of moral duty and pledged faith as can arise only if their duly constituted representatives in the Senate are consulted before any such obligations are undertaken in their name and on their behalf.

A copy of the resolution adopted by the Club is annexed hereto.[1]
All of which is respectfully submitted.

The Union League Club of the City of New York,

By Charles E. Hughes President.

Attest: Henry C. Quinby[2] Secretary.

TLS (SDR, RG 59, 763.72119/4218, DNA).
 [1] Resolution of the Union League Club, March 13, 1919, T MS (SDR, RG 59, 763.72119/4218, DNA).
 [2] Henry Cole Quinby, lawyer of New York.

From the Diary of Dr. Grayson

Wednesday, March 19, 1919.

In the morning the President worked in his study for a while, and then went across the street to Lloyd-George's house, where Clemenceau joined them. The absolute necessity for speeding up the Peace Conference work was now so plain that the three men, who after all were compelled to settle these problems, must devote all of the time possible to conferring together. There was no apparent slight to either the Italian or Japanese delegations, but their interests were neither potent nor personal, and if the "big three" could reach an agreement it was obvious that the others would fall in line. Because of the absolute necessity that there be no premature publication or premature discussion of the matters being debated by the President and Premiers Clemenceau and Lloyd-George all agreed to withhold any intimation on the subject. While this had the effect of allowing various erroneous stories to be printed and was responsible for the inauguration of an organized campaign of abuse upon the President by the opposition, in British papers, it was one of the things for which there was no immediate remedy. It was understood that among the subjects under discussion were the questions of reparation, indemnities, personal responsibility, and the recreation of a Western frontier for Germany. The conference between the three Premiers was the big feature of today's business and a good part of the President's waking hours were devoted to it and to disposing of a number of important documents.

Yesterday morning the President called me in and said that he was suffering from a great deal of pain in his left eye and nose. Upon examination I found an abscess developing in his left nostril. The nose condition yielded to treatment and he said today that he felt a great relief from the intense pain of yesterday.

An incident came up today recalling the President's visit to Rome. One of the ladies-in-waiting of the Queen told me while there of a

complication that had arisen concerning the Queen accompanying
the King to the railroad station to see the President and Mrs. Wilson
off. For her to do so would break a rule or custom of long-standing.
There was great consternation as to what she should do in the
matter. Finally, after discussing the matter with Queen Marguerita
and the Queen-Mother,[1] they concluded to break this rule and
establish a precedent, saying that they would not do so but for the
fact that Queen Mary had set the example; and she did it only
because she (The Queen of Italy) felt it would be more diplomatic
for her to do so, notwithstanding the fact that such a thing had
never been heard of before in Italy.

Tonight the President had Ambassador and Mrs. Sharp as dinner
guests. This dinner was arranged so that the President could talk
over some French matters with Ambassador Sharp, and in order to
have him present, the President absented himself from a formal
dinner and reception given at the Hotel Crillon by Colonel and Mrs.
House. The fact that the President was not at the dinner of Colonel
House caused considerable comment, and for a time rumors that
there was an actual break between the President and his long-time
adviser were given circulation in State Department circles. It was
not until well along the next day that the Hotel Crillon representatives learned the real reason why the President was not present.

Ambassador Sharp warned the President against Tardieu and
explained to him that the movements of Tardieu while he was
French High Commissioner in the United States had been checked
up and it was found that he was in almost constant communication
while he was over there with all of the intense partisan Republican
opponents of the President. The Ambassador did not know how
much Pichon was in contact with Tardieu and his crowd, but he
was rather of the opinion that Pichon hardly had enough "savvy"
to get away with this successful intrigue. The President was rather
amused at this comment and said that Clemenceau and the political
ring that surrounded him were to him like a rubber ball: You make
a dent in it only so long as you keep the pressure on, but the moment
the pressure is released it bounces back to its original position.
Inasmuch as Tardieu was and is Clemenceau's chief leader of intrigue and his personal selection for President of France this comment was very apt.

The President said that it was his belief that the rank and file of
the French people themselves are all right, but that they are under
the absolute domination of the political element, and that as a result
of it they have nothing whatever to say in the affairs of their own
government. Given the proper opportunity the President believed

that the French people would be all right in every way. The President said that it was due entirely to the machinations of the French politicians that the British had been able to become the best international friends of the Americans. It was due entirely to the fact that the French politicians had permitted so many apparent discriminations against Americans that the rank and file of the people of the United States had turned from being pro-French to being pro-British. And the President also said that the British seemed to be playing the game nobly and loyally.

Theodore Roosevelt became a subject for discussion, and the President said that the Colonel had appealed to him for permission to go to France in command of a division of volunteers, which he desired to raise. At that time Clemenceau had expressed the belief that it would be a very good plan to have Roosevelt come over-seas to show the American flag for the purpose of capitalizing the prestige of the former President and raising the morale of the French soldiers in that way. Clemenceau thought there would only be a few thousand soldiers sent over anyhow and that they would be practically useless except to display the fact that America really was a participant in the war. Roosevelt came to Washington, went to the White House to see the President, and he told him that he would like very much to command a division of reserves in France.[2] The President asked him whether he thought he had sufficient military training to justify his being placed in the command of a body of men and be responsible for their lives. Roosevelt said that he would select, and in fact, he told the President that he already had the promise of all the best officers of the Regular Army, that they would accompany him and pilot him, in order that there would be no cause for fear because of his lack of military training. The President told Colonel Roosevelt that it was his viewpoint that this was the very reason why he ought not be sent to France inasmuch as these very officers would be badly needed to train the vast army of soldiers that the United States must raise in order to take its proper part in the winning of the war.

Taking up William Jennings Bryan, former Secretary of State, the President said that so far as Mr. Bryan was concerned he was at all times more interested in the argument than he was in the fact. As an illustration of this, the President called attention to the fact that in one of the earlier notes between Germany and the United States the declaration was made by Germany that "war in itself was wrong," and Mr. Bryan promptly seized upon that as justification for argument. He contended that the thing to do was to have Germany quit the war by arguing her out of it rather than by using force to compel her to stop. The President said that he believed that if Bryan had been an evangelist he would have been the greatest evangelist the world had ever known.

After dinner the President said to me that General Allenby, Commander-in-Chief of the British Armies in Palestine and Jerusalem, who was responsible for the complete defeat of the Turks, had called to see him in the morning. Speaking of the British General, the President said: "Allenby to my mind is the best looking officer I have ever seen."

---

¹ Grayson was confused. The Queen Mother, that is, the mother of Vittorio Emanuele III, and Queen Margherita were one and the same person.

² About this meeting, see EMH to WW, April 10, 1917, n. 1, and the extract from the Diary of Thomas W. Brahany printed at April 10, 1917, both in Vol. 42.

Hankey's Notes of a Meeting of the Council of Ten[1]

BC-53   Quai d'Orsay, March 19, 1919, 3 p.m.

[After some discussion of the means of establishing an armistice between the Poles and the Ukrainians in eastern Galicia, in which Wilson took little part, the council turned to the subject of the borders between Germany and Poland.]

3. M. CAMBON[2] said that he had received a telegram from M. Noulens to the effect that the Germans wished to discuss the question of the landing of Polish troops at Dantzig at Spa, instead of with the Inter-Allied Commission in Poland. A draft telegram had been prepared for the approval of the Council in answer to this message.

GENERAL WEYGAND explained that Marshal Foch had given orders to the Armistice Commission at Spa that any discussion on this subject should be refused, and that the Germans should be referred to the Inter-Allied Commission in Poland. A copy of this order had been sent to M. Noulens for his information.

(There was a short adjournment.)

4. M. CAMBON referring to the map accompanying the report[3] explained that the red line represented the claims of the Poles, and the blue line the frontier proposed by the Committee. There were in these regions no natural frontiers. The population was very mixed as was usual in central and eastern Europe. The Committee had followed as far as possible the ethnological principle, but it had been impossible to draw any lines that did not include alien populations. Economic and strategic requirements had also been taken

---

¹ The complete text of these minutes is printed in PPC, IV, 404-22.

² That is, Jules Cambon.

³ "Report No. 1 of the Commission on Polish Affairs: Frontier Between Poland and Germany, March 12, 1919," printed document (WP, DLC); printed in Miller, My Diary at the Conference of Paris, VI, 350-66.

into account, in order that the new State should be so delimited as to be capable of life. At all points save one, the frontier adopted by the Committee gave the Poles less than they asked for. The exception was in the region of the river Bartsch. The reason in this case was of a military nature. Without this line of frontier Posen would be exposed, at the very outbreak of war with Germany, to be surrounded and captured at once. It was to render its defence possible that the Committee had placed the frontier further west than the Poles themselves had suggested. Further north the Committee had adopted a line considerably more to the east than the Poles. This region was sparsely populated and was the scene of the intense German colonization that had been pursued of late years. In 1908, Prince Bülow, who was then Chancellor, had obtained legislation for the forcible expropriation of the Poles in this region. Not only could no land or houses be sold to Poles but they were prevented from building or even repairing their houses. He had himself seen Poles living in abandoned trucks and omnibuses and then evicted from them because they had placed stoves inside them which the Germans represented as repairs. It was commonly supposed that the Russians had persecuted the Poles more than the Germans. This was not the case. German persecution penetrated into private life in a manner unknown to the Russians. This had led to the emigration of Poles on a large scale. Still further north the Committee had adopted a line following the Lakes up to the sea. This line had been drawn in accordance with statistics of school attendance.

In order to give Poland access to the sea, the Committee had attributed to Poland a strip of territory enclosing Dantzig. There was another Port east of this, namely, Elbing, which had once been Polish, but which the Committee had decided to leave in Eastern Prussia. Dantzig had been Polish until the first partition, and its possession was a matter of life and death to Poland. Discussions at present proceeding regarding the transport of Polish troops to Poland through Dantzig indicated the importance of that Port. Without access to the sea, Poland would be stifled. There were commercial and economic reasons as well as military reasons to justify the attribute of Dantzig to the Poles. Since its annexation by Germany, Dantzig had diminished in importance. It was true that the townspeople themselves were mostly of German race, but the surrounding population was Polish. Dantzig had communication with the interior by two railways, one leading to Thorn and the other to Mlawa. The Committee proposed to give both these lines to Poland.

East Prussia was doubtless the most Prussian part of Germany, and its capital, Königsberg, was a holy place of Prussianism. In the southern part of the Province, notably in the district of Allenstein, the people were Polish, but the Poles here, unlike the majority of their countrymen, were Protestants, and had been very largely Germanized. They spoke German as much as Polish. The Committee therefore, proposed that these people be consulted concerning their future allegiance, and that a plebiscite be held there.

MR. LLOYD GEORGE said that the bulk of the recommendations of the Committee represented views that had secured general agreement. He would suggest that only controversial questions should be discussed, and that M. Cambon be asked to give replies to any points that might be raised on questions that might appear still open to discussion. He himself, had one general question to put. He noted that the number of Germans to be included in the future Polish State as drawn up by the Committee was not less than 2,132,000. This was a considerable figure, and might spell serious trouble for Poland in the future. The Germans moreover might hesitate to sign any Treaty containing such a provision. Any terms that no delegate and no Government were likely to sign should make the Council hesitate. The present German Government had gained a temporary victory,[4] but was not very strong. It was said that another rising was likely to take place in 6 weeks. The Government might not be able to withstand it. If the Allies should present a document requiring from Germany huge indemnities and the cession of a large German population to Poland, the German Government might collapse. The Poles, as it was, had not a high reputation as administrators. He wished to ask if the Committee could not restrict the Polish claims in such a way as to diminish the German population assigned to Poland. In the Dantzig district alone 412,000 Germans were assigned to Poland. Was it necessary to assign so much German territory, together with the port of Dantzig? There was another district in which a German majority was being attributed to Poland, namely that of Marienwerder. He would ask whether this could not be avoided.

M. CAMBON said that in his general explanation he had pointed out that it was very difficult to make a frontier on purely ethnological lines. The same difficulty would be encountered in dealing with the frontiers of Greece and other countries in the east of Europe,

---

[4] That is, in the defeat of the various Communist uprisings in Germany since January by units of the *Freikorps*. For the earliest of these incidents, see n. 4 to the Enclosure printed with S. E. Mezes to WW, Jan. 16, 1919, Vol. 54. Since that time, numerous other attempted Communist takeovers had been put down in various parts of Germany, most notably in Bremen, Mühlheim, and Halle. These battles between the forces of the left and right had culminated in a second Spartacist uprising in Berlin, beginning on March 3. Several *Freikorps* organizations suppressed this rising with great bloodshed; the struggle was over by March 13. See Robert G. L. Waite, *Vanguard of Nazism: The Free Corps Movement in Postwar Germany, 1918-1923* (Cambridge, Mass., 1952), pp. 66-79.

where the population was very mixed. Economic and strategic reasons therefore must be given weight. In the case of Marienwerder, for instance, if this place were left to Prussia, all the lines from Warsaw to the sea would pass through Prussian territory, and Poland would practically be cut off from the sea.

MR. LLOYD GEORGE agreed that it was hardly possible to draw any line that would not have Germans on both sides of it, but he thought it was very dangerous to assign two million Germans to Poland. This was a considerable population, not less than that of Alsace-Lorraine in 1870. He would point out that the Germans had been accorded communication between East and West Prussia across Polish territory. Why was a similar arrangement not possible in favour of the Poles? To hand over millions of people to a distasteful allegiance merely because of a railway was, he thought, a mistake.

PRESIDENT WILSON drew attention to the very special effort made in late years by the German Government to colonise the very region to which Mr. Lloyd George had drawn attention. The Germans had sought to make a German cordon from Schneidemühl to Marienwerder in order to isolate Dantzig from Poland. Hence, this was actually a region of political colonization.

MR. LLOYD GEORGE said that he referred less to Marienwerder itself than to the country East of it, which was historically German.

M. CAMBON said that he regarded it as essential for Poland to have free access to the sea. This region afforded the best corridor from the mainland to Dantzig. He thought that a large number of the German population which was of recent importation would emigrate to other parts of Germany when the Polish State was constituted.

MR. LLOYD GEORGE said that he raised no objection in respect to the regions lately colonized by Germany, but he did not feel that he could assent to the delivery of areas whose whole history was German.

PRESIDENT WILSON said that this would only be justified by reciprocity. Many Poles in areas historically Polish were to be left within Germany.

MR. LLOYD GEORGE asked whether the Council proposed to define the frontiers of Germany finally on ex parte evidence alone. The other side had not been heard. It was not only a question of fairness to Germany but of establishing a lasting peace in Europe. It was neither fair nor prudent, because of a railway, to hand over large populations to a Government they disliked.

M. CAMBON said that it was quite true the Committee had only heard the Poles. It had not been commissioned to listen to the Germans. It had been asked to examine the means of setting up a

Polish State with some prospect of continued life. The Committee had tried to approximate to the Polish State as it existed before the first partition. After examination they had made recommendations of a far more modest character. What had caused the death of Poland was not merely its faulty political system, but principally its lack of communication with the sea. The end of Poland might be considered to have occurred in the year 1743, when Dantzig fell. Without it, Poland could not live. By it alone could Poland have contact with the liberal Powers in the West. It was no use to set up a Poland deprived of access to the sea as it would inevitably be the prey of Germany or Russia. Not only must Poland have a sea-board, but full and free communication with Dantzig. If he had to choose between protecting German populations largely imported since the 18th Century, and protecting the Poles, he preferred the latter alternative. There was no comparison between the need of the Germans for communication between East and West Prussia and that of the Poles for communication between Warsaw and Dantzig. East Prussia had very little railway traffic with Western Prussia. Nine tenths of its exports—chiefly wood—went by sea. The products of East Prussia, by reason of the cost of land transport, at the present time went by sea. The council need therefore feel no anxiety about the land communication between East and West Prussia. On the other hand, the two railways linking Warsaw to Dantzig were absolutely essential to Poland.

M. TARDIEU said that he wished to draw attention to two points. One was that the Committee set up to co-ordinate recommendations as to boundaries had unanimously approved the report of the Polish Committee. Secondly, the situation which Mr. Lloyd George wished to avoid was bound to recur everywhere. The Conference had set out to revive ancient States subjected for a number of years or centuries to alien domination. In every instance inevitably some of the dominating race would be found settled in these areas. With the best will in the world it would not be possible to settle frontiers on ethnological grounds alone. If the submerged nations were to be revived a mixed population must be included in them.

M. CAMBON added that the Polish Committee had also reached unanimous conclusions.

MR. LLOYD GEORGE said that though the British delegates had adopted the conclusions, they had done so reluctantly. They regarded them as a departure from the principles of the Fourteen Points which had been adopted by the Allies. In some parts of the territory assigned to Poland the argument of political colonisation did not apply. We were told, moreover, that a region colonised with Germans as far back as the 18th Century should be restored to

Poland. But because fifty years ago some capitalists had built a railway that was convenient to the Poles, the area surrounding it must be ascribed to Poland, in spite of the undoubted German nationality of the population. M. Cambon had said that a corridor to the sea was necessary to Poland. He had nothing to say against this. The Vistula was a navigable river, and must remain the principal artery for commerce. There were, moreover, other railways. A railway could be removed, but a long-settled population was not removed with the same ease. He thought that in accepting these proposals the Council would be abandoning its principles and making trouble, not only for Poland, but for the world. Wherever it could be shown that the policy aimed at reversing the German policy of Polish expropriation the decision might be accepted by the Germans, but the areas he had in mind would be represented as "Germania Irredenta" and would be the seed of future war. Should the populations of these areas rise against the Poles, and should their fellow-countrymen wish to go to their assistance, would France, Great Britain and the United States go to war to maintain Polish rule over them? He felt bound to make this protest against what he considered to be a most dangerous proposal.

PRESIDENT WILSON said that the discussion had brought out a difficulty which, it had been said, would be met in many cases, and he had not reached a definite conclusion in his own mind on the particular point under discussion. He hoped that the discussion would be carried far enough to bring out all its elements. Everywhere in Europe blocks of foreign people would be found whose possession of the country could be justified by historic, commercial and similar arguments. He acknowledged that the inclusion of two million Germans in Poland was a violation of one principle; but Germany had been notified that free and safe access to the sea for Poland would be insisted upon. The Allied and Associated Powers were therefore not open to the reproach that they were doing this merely because they had the power to do it. This was one of the things they had fought for. The difficulty was to arrive at a balance between conflicting considerations. He thought Mr. Lloyd George was misinformed in saying that the river carried the largest proportion of the commerce. He would find that the railroad along the river carried the greater, or at least an equal amount, of the traffic.

MR. LLOYD GEORGE pointed out that he was referring not to the railroad along the river, but to the one further to the East.

PRESIDENT WILSON said that the proposal would, however, leave in German hands territories abutting on the westerly railroad at several points.

M. CAMBON said that the direct line to Warsaw through Mlawa

was quite near the frontier proposed by the Committee. Mr. Lloyd George had mentioned the Vistula as the main artery of traffic. Marienwerder dominated the Vistula as well as the railway lines, and anyone holding that place commanded the valley.

M. PICHON pointed out that there were only two lines of railroads from Dantzig to supply twenty millions of people. One of these was through Thorn and the other through Mlawa. The latter passed East of Marienwerder, this was the one referred to by Mr. Lloyd George. Both were indispensable to the economic life of Poland.

MR. LLOYD GEORGE admitted that the line from Mlawa was important, but did not regard it as essential for access of Poland to the sea.

PRESIDENT WILSON said that it must be realised the Allies were creating a new and weak state, weak not only because historically it had failed to govern itself, but because it was sure in future to be divided into factions, more especially as religious differences were an element in the situation. It was therefore necessary to consider not only the economic but the strategic needs of this state, which would have to cope with Germany on both sides of it, the Eastern fragment of Germany being one of a most aggressive character. There was bound to be a mixture of hostile populations included in either state. The Council would have to decide which mixture promised the best prospect of security. He was afraid himself of drawing the line as near the Dantzig-Thorn railway line as Mr. Lloyd George suggested. He, however, felt the same anxieties as Mr. Lloyd George. The desire might arise among the Germans to rescue German populations from Polish rule, and this desire would be hard to resist. It was a question of balancing antagonistic considerations. He had wished to bring out the other elements in the problem.

MR. BALFOUR said that he agreed with President Wilson that a balance must be attained, and that it was necessary to admit that ethnological considerations must in many cases be qualified. The line under discussion was that joining the port and the capital of Poland. It might be presumed that no circuitous line was likely to be built which could compete with the direct line. If the ethnological frontier were adhered to this line would cut German territory twice— at Soldau and Riesenburg. This was doubtless inconvenient; but he would like to ask the experts if Poland could be given such rights over this line as would preserve its character as a Polish line, in spite of crossing German territory at these two points.

PRESIDENT WILSON suggested that the Committee should consider the ancient boundary of the province of East Prussia as it existed in 1772. This line was in some cases intermediate between the line recommended by the Committee and the ethnological line advocated by Mr. Lloyd George. It would not cut the railway between Dantzig and Mlawa and its adoption might offer a sentimental justification to Germany for the loss of some German population.

MR. LLOYD GEORGE agreed that this might be considered with advantage. He proposed that the report on the boundaries of Poland should be referred back to the Committee for reconsideration with a view of a readjustment of the boundaries of East Prussia in such a manner as to exclude from the new Polish State territory historically as well as ethnologically Prussian, while ensuring to Poland secure access to the sea.

PRESIDENT WILSON suggested that the Committee be merely asked to reconsider its recommendations in the light of the discussion.

(It was agreed to refer to the report on the boundaries of Poland back to the Committee for reconsideration in the light of the foregoing discussion.)

(The Meeting then adjourned.)

T MS (SDR, RG 256, 180.03101/60, DNA).

From William Jennings Bryan

New York March 19 [1919]

Knowing as I do your very deep interest in the welfare of Armenia I am taking the liberty as a member of the American Committee for the Independence of Armenia to appeal to you once more on a subject connected with Armenia period We learn with deep concern state Cilicia may be taken away from the proposed Armenian state period It is evident that this arrangement would place Armenia even with a Black Sea port in a worse position than even Serbia was in nineteen fourteen since Armenian neighbors are practically all non Christians period. Having in view the terrible suffering Armenians have gone through it is extremely difficult to believe that the nations now assembled at Versailles to mete out justice would permit a fresh act of injustice against Armenia period.

William Jennings Bryan.

T telegram (WP, DLC).

To William Jennings Bryan

Paris, 19 March, 1919.

Your cable received. Beg to assure you that my interest in Armenia is identical with your own.   Woodrow Wilson.

CC telegram (WP, DLC).

To Robert Lansing

My dear Lansing: Paris, 19 March, 1919.

Will you not be kind enough to ask our Consul at Dublin[1] to call upon the Lord Mayor of Dublin[2] in person and acknowledge with my appreciation the receipt of the invitation to visit Dublin and receive the freedom of the city,[3] apologize for the delay in replying, and express my regret that it will not be possible for me to visit Dublin because of the constant pressure of my engagements, which the Lord Mayor will realize are of the first consequence. I would be obliged if you would ask the Consul to do this with as much formality as possible.

Sincerely yours,   [Woodrow Wilson]

CCL (WP, DLC).
  [1] Edward Le Grand Adams.
  [2] Laurence O'Neill.
  [3] L. O'Neill to WW, Dec. 28, 1918, TLS (WP, DLC).

Gilbert Fairchild Close to Robert Lansing

My dear Mr. Secretary: Paris, 19 March, 1919.

The President has asked me to hurry this memorandum to you in order to ask your advice. He hesitates to receive Mr. Sidoresko,[1] Minister of Roads and Communications of the Ukrainian Republic because so far as he remembers our government has not recognized the Ukrainian Republic, and yet it would seem that to see these gentlemen would afford a useful opportunity to give them a warning about Lemburg. He asks whether you would think it wise yourself or wise for the members of the American Delegation to have an interview with these gentlemen.

Sincerely yours,   [Gilbert F. Close]

CCL (WP, DLC).
  [1] Actually, Gregory Sydorenko, who was at this time the head of the delegation of the Ukrainian Republic in Paris.

Alexander Comstock Kirk to Gilbert Fairchild Close

My dear Mr. Close: Paris, March 19, 1919.

The Secretary directs me to acknowledge the receipt of your letter of March 19th, regarding an appointment with Mr. Sidoresko, a representative of the Ukrainian Republic, and to inform you that he agrees with the President that it does not seem desirable to meet Mr. Sidoresko officially at the present moment.

Mr. Lansing has received a similar request from a representative of the Ukrainian Delegation and has referred the entire matter to Professor Lord, the member of the American Mission who has recently returned from Warsaw and Lemberg.

Very sincerely yours,   Alexander Kirk.
Secretary to Mr. Lansing

TLS (WP, DLC).

A Memorandum by Robert Lansing

STRANGE IDEA OF PRESIDENT AS
TO PRELIMINARIES OF PEACE.
MARCH 19, 1919.

During a session of the Council of Ten which took place on the 17th, I was astounded at certain statements made by the President concerning "preliminaries of peace."

We were at the long green table in the Salle de la Horloge, to which we had adjourned from M. Pichon's tapestried office, because of the large number of persons in attendance. I should say that there were fully seventy-five in the room, most of whom were military and naval officers, as we were discussing the military, naval and air terms to be presented to Germany. These, as well as the many civilians, were chiefly French. It is always safe to assume that there are three times as many French as there are persons of other nationalities at our meetings. It is one of the penalties of meeting in Paris.

The question arose as to certain time limits imposed by the report. I suggested that "ratification" rather than "signature" of the Treaty should be the basis of computation. To this M. Fromageot of the Drafting Committee agreed. I then said that I thought that "exchange of ratifications" would be even better. M. Fromageot said that was his opinion.

At this point the President leaned toward me and said in low voice: "You to [do] not mean to say that all these preliminaries have to be ratified by our Senate?" I replied, "Why of course they have to be Mr. President. They contain permanent undertakings, and many other terms which are not military in character will have to go into the document."

"You surprise me," the President said, "I had not thought it necessary. I never thought of anything but the final treaty as needing ratification. It makes it difficult."

I explained that it made no difference what we called the document. We might term it an armistice, an agreement or a protocol, but it would nevertheless be a treaty and have to be sent to the Senate. I continued, "We can't have peace and continue a state of war. If we change the status from war to peace it has to be by a ratified treaty. There is no other way, save by a joint resolution of Congress."

The President was evidently much disturbed. "Why," he said, "that may take till December." I replied, "Possibly, but there is no other way."[1]

He then asked me to get the opinion of our legal advisers in regard to this, and I told him that I would.

The same evening I called in Scott and Miller and laid the case before them. They agreed with my opinion and promised a memorandum to be given to the President. Later, about eleven, Gregory came in and I told him of the extraordinary idea which the President had and what I had told him. Gregory said that I was absolutely right and that he would see the President and tell him so.

At the meeting of the Council of Ten today I gave the President the memorandum. He remarked without looking at it: "Well, I suppose there is no other way." There the matter ended.

I suppose the President had planned to put everything into the "preliminaries," League of Nations and all with an agreement that they would go into the final treaty. Then we would have peace in fact by the preliminaries. Clever but faulty.

T MS (R. Lansing Papers, DLC).
  [1] We leave it to the reader to determine, in the light shed by preceding documents, to come to his or her own conclusion concerning the accuracy of this narative. Lansing, *The Peace Negotiations: A Personal Narrative* (Boston and New York, 1921). pp. 206-208, repeats his account. Kurt Wimer, "Woodrow Wilson's Plans to Enter The League of Nations through an Executive Agreement," *Western Political Quarterly*, XI (Dec. 1958), 800-12, largely relies upon Lansing for his evidence.

From Thomas William Lamont, with Enclosure

Dear Mr. President: Paris, March 19, 1919.

I am so intensely interested in supporting the League of Nations idea in America—and before my departure for Paris I gave so much of my time to the matter—that I cannot help feeling you may be interested to let me give you briefly, in person, some reports that I have received by cable from New York as to the situation there.

Of course we cannot for a moment admit the possibility of any lasting objection on the part of the Senate to the confirmation of a treaty which contains the League of Nations idea. At the same time, I am impressed with the desirability of removing in advance, so far as may be possible, the obstacles to prompt action by the Senate. To this end I cabled one of my discreet partners in New York, who is very much committed to the idea of the League, to secure privately an idea as to what concrete objections are being offered by those who may be, in all sincerity, opposing the present Covenant. I wanted to see for myself whether such objections were worthy of consideration, and whether, without in any way deranging the present scheme of the League, they could be considered here by you in any minor changes that may be made between now and the date of the preliminary Peace.

Mr. Morgan and Mr. Morrow,[1] my partners, have replied to my cable by securing briefly Senator Root's views, and I attach a copy of Mr. Morgan's cable herewith. Senator Root is likely to represent, I think, an intelligent and sincere opinion, and I think it is politically important to get his mind working with ours on this whole matter.

If you could possibly spare me even a moment I think I might lay before you one or two other points in the hope that they might prove helpful to you in this matter, upon your solution of which the whole world must depend.

Meanwhile, I have conferred with Colonel House and at his suggestion left with him a copy of this cable and have given a copy to Mr. David Hunter Miller.

With great respect, my dear Mr. President, I am,

Very sincerely yours,   Thomas W. Lamont

TLS (WP, DLC).
[1] That is, John Pierpont Morgan, Jr., and Dwight Whitney Morrow.

ENCLOSURE

Senator Elihu Root stated that he was giving careful study to the documents in the light of the historical difficulties which complicated the task of the Peace Commission and did not want to express any opinion until he had matured his judgment. (stop) We did not ask him for any authority to state his present personal views of the Covenant. (stop) He talked however with us very frankly and from his (?) talk we gathered:

1. That he fully appreciates the very great difficulty of the Com-

mission in getting a large number of States to agree upon anything that is reasonable.

2. That he thinks there are many commendable features in the plan notably the great step forward that is made in insuring common counsel on political disputes before war is entered upon.

On the other hand he regretted:

"A." The failure to create a court and the apparent breaking down of the distinction that has been growing up in the last generation between justiciable and political questions.

"B." The guarantee of political boundaries in Article 10 which he felt committed the various nations including the U. S. of America to intervention in many boundary disputes with which they were not concerned. (stop) He mentioned particularly the long time dispute between Chili and Peru on the boundary line in the Arica district and asked on which side of this controversy the guarantee of the United States would be enforced.

"C" He took a very broad view of the whole problem of the Monroe Doctrine feeling that we very properly had an interest in world affairs, as the (?) war itself had disclosed, but that our interest in European affairs was only to the extent that they threatened to become world questions, that our force should be put back of (?) European disputes only when required to protect world order and that conversely the eastern hemisphere should not come into the western except under the same conditions. (stop) Without attempting to technically state his views it seemed to us that he substantially took the position that while we had an (?) interest and responsibility in European affairs it was a secondary (?) interest and responsibility and that their position in the eastern hemisphere was similar to ours in the western.

"D." That the provisions as to voting needed clearing up; that if the proposed organs of the league were merely international conferences the rule as expressed by Lord Robert Cecil in his speech, that unanimity was required except where the contrary was provided, might prevail. (stop) However it was not clear from the instrument whether the bodies created (?) would merely be conferences or whether the league would be a union or even a confederation and that it might well be urged later that questions would be decided by majority vote except where the contrary is specifically stated.

We found Senator Elihu Root's whole attitude toward the documents temperate and constructive. (stop) He plainly indicated his hope that the discussion should not be along partisan lines, the issues involved being so great. (stop)

T MS (WP, DLC).

Gilbert Fairchild Close to Herbert Clark Hoover

My dear Mr. Hoover: Paris, 19 March, 1919.

The President has asked me to send you the enclosed proclamation releasing the meat packers from license which you forwarded with your letter of March 14th.[1] You will note that the
President has signed the proclamation and I am forwarding a copy
of it to the White House at Washington for their record.

Sincerely yours,   [Gilbert F. Close]

CCL (WP, DLC).
[1] HCH to WW, March 14, 1919, Vol. 55.

From Robert Lansing, with Enclosure

My dear Mr. President: Paris. 19th March, 1919.

I am enclosing herewith a copy of a telegram which I have received from Mr. Polk in which he raises the question of a recess
appointment in the case of Mr. Norman Hapgood who as you know
has been appointed Minister to Denmark and I shall be glad to
communicate to Mr. Polk any views which you may wish to express
on the matter.   Faithfully yours,   Robert Lansing

TLS (R. Lansing Papers, DLC).

E N C L O S U R E

Washington. March 7, 1919.

CONFIDENTIAL, for Secretary Lansing.

Norman Hapgood's appointment failed, after having confirmation
[hearings]. Senator Hitchcock advises me that some objection was
raised by committee. In the circumstances am somewhat doubtful
as to what President desires to do, whether he wishes to make
recess appointment, or to await reassembling of Congress. Am in
touch with Hapgood and have told him that I would endeavor to
ascertain the President's wishes. Please take up the matter with
Colonel House.

I could probably find out what the sentiment of the Republicans
will be, but hesitate to do so unless President will hold up recess
appointment. In case the sentiment is against Hapgood, if after
finding out that the Republicans probably will not confirm Hapgood's nomination, appointment should be made, and Hapgood go
to his post; it would be a reason for more irritation on the part of
the Republican Senators.   Polk, Acting.

T telegram (R. Lansing Papers, DLC).

From Herbert Clark Hoover

Dear Mr. President: Paris, 19 March 1919.

I understand that Secretary Houston is cabling you recommending a plan for the handling of the next wheat crop. I hope that you will take occasion to consult me before coming to a decision on the matter, as it necessarily involves the present situation.

Faithfully yours,   Herbert Hoover

TLS (WP, DLC).

From the Diary of Dr. Grayson

Thursday, March 20, 1919.

While I was treating the President this morning, the subject of trusts came up, and the President asked me if I had ever heard the late Tom Reed's (of Maine) definition of what a trust really was. I had not, and the President said: "A trust," Reed said, "was a small body of very rich men surrounded by a large number of very able lawyers."

The condition he had been suffering from has yielded very fully to treatment and all pain has disappeared. The President is not now suffering any inconvenience and, as he expressed it today, except when he pressed on the point he could not feel any twinges of pain.

The President, Clemenceau and Lloyd-George again conferred at Lloyd-George's home in the Rue Nitot. One of the subjects that was taken up was the question of Syria, where England and France have clashed so far as the predominance in trade was concerned. Lloyd-George made it plain that so far as he was concerned, he was very anxious that all the British forces now in Palestine be removed and brought home as quickly as possible, and he also said that in no case would Great Britain accept a mandate for either Syria or Armenia. The President took no part in deciding this question, which he held was one for France and England to dispose of between themselves.

While the President was conferring with the two Premiers, representatives of thirteen neutral countries met with Lord Robert Cecil, Leon Bourgeois of France, M. Hymans of Belgium, Venizelos of Greece, and M. Pashich of Servia, in Colonel House's rooms in the Hotel Crillon. The neutrals had been called in to make suggestions from their viewpoint of amendments to the constitution of the League of Nations, and they managed to get through two-thirds of the constitution before the conference broke up. A rather clever trick had been worked in dealing with the neutrals by getting them altogether instead of permitting them to come in and individually present their views. This expedited matters very much, and the fact that outside of Colonel House and Lord Robert Cecil the other members of the sub-committee were more or less obstructionists, helped out to a great extent, inasmuch as they found themselves compelled to be listeners instead of in their usual role of talkers. It was apparent that the neutrals were fully convinced that the League of Nations is to be a permanent institution, this being proven by the fact that Holland asked for the establishment of permanent headquarters for the League at The Hague, Switzerland asked for it for Geneva, and several of the other envoys said they would be very glad to welcome the League to their shores.

Tonight the President and I after dinner went for a walk, which lasted for an hour. It was raining but with umbrellas, over-shoes, and overcoats it was possible to get exercise, which the President needed very badly to counteract the strain of the hard work he is doing. We walked all through the crowds of Paris but no one recognized him.

From the Diary of Ray Stannard Baker

Paris Thursday the 20 [March 1919].

An undeniable tone of pessimism prevails here. It seems to be a race of peace with anarchy. Very bad news from Germany (I dined to-night with Villard, just back from there). The industrial situation in England is acute & from America we hear of bitter attacks on Wilson & the L of N. In the meantime everyone connected with the peace conference is rushing at full speed to get the treaty ready next week. The President was at Lloyd George's house (just across the street from the new "White House" in the Place des Etats-Unis[)] this after noon conferring with Lloyd George, Clemenceau and Orlando, assisted by Balfour, Pichon, Allenby & Diaz in regard to the situation in Syria, & Asiatic Turkey. I went up just after the meeting was over with the Admiral.[1] It was the first time I had been in the new house. It is much less gorgeous than the Murat hotel but more homelike. The Admiral has his office in the Nursery! While waiting for the President the lights went out & we stumbled along hallways & down stairs, quite lost in the President's house— still new even to the Admiral. I had quite a talk with the President in his study. He is in fine form & told me fully what had taken place at the conference, but desired that only the main points be made public at present. It seems that it began with quite a discussion between the French & British—the Italians breaking in—

as to their rights in Asia Minor & in Turkey under old treaties. Finally the President said: "If the position in Syria is to be discussed only upon the basis of previous understandings between France, G.B. & Italy, then of course I have nothing to do with it, & can see no reason for taking part in it. It is only upon the understanding that the whole problem is on the peace table without reference to old understandings, and with the clear purpose of not forcing mandatories upon any of the peoples concerned, without consulting their desires, that I can be of any assistance." The trend of the discussion immediately took the new form & it was decided to send an inter-allied commission to Syria to make an investigation of the exact situation. The President asked me if I could not suggest some one. "I want the ablest American now in France!"

The President said of General Allenby that he was one of the handsomest men he had ever seen.

Hw MS (R. S. Baker Papers, DLC).
  [1] That is, Dr. Grayson.

Hankey's Notes of a Meeting of the Council of Four[1]

I.C.-163A.   Prime Minister's Flat at 23 Rue Nitot, Paris, on
                 THURSDAY, MARCH 20, 1919, at 3 p.m.
                 SYRIA AND TURKEY.

M. CLEMENCEAU suggested that M. Pichon should open the discussion.

M. PICHON began by explaining that the origin of this question was the agreement of May 1916 (Sykes-Picot)[2] concluded between Great Britain and France in regard to Mesopotamia, Syria, and the adjoining regions. This agreement had two objects. First, to detach the Arabs from the Turks; second, to decide the claims of Great Britain and France. He then proceeded to explain the principles of the dispositions made on a map. The agreement fixed a zone coloured blue within which France would exercise direct administration, and a zone coloured red in which England would exercise direct administration. In addition, there was a zone coloured white enclosed by a blue line within which France should exercise indirect administration, known as zone A. and a corresponding zone

  [1] As previous documents, particularly the Grayson Diary, have revealed, Wilson, Lloyd George, Clemenceau, and Orlando agreed to meet privately, but often with advisers, in order to speed up the work of the peace conference. The meeting of March 20 was in fact the first meeting of what would soon be called the Council of Four. The minutes of this meeting are printed in *PPC*, V, 1-14.
  [2] See A. J. Balfour to WW, May 18, 1917, n. 1, Vol. 42, and n. 7 to the minutes of the Council of Ten printed at Feb. 6, 1919, Vol. 54.

enclosed in a red line within which Great Britain would exercise indirect administration (Zone B). At this stage it was unnecessary to say anything of the subsequent agreement with Italy. Within the A. and B. zones it was intended to favour the creation of an independent Arab State or Confederation of Arab States. In area A. France, and area B. Great Britain should alone supply advisers or foreign functionaries at the request of the Arab State or Confederation of Arab States. In addition Great Britain was to be accorded the ports of Haifa and Acre. Haifa was to be a free port as regards the trade of France, and there was to be freedom of transit for French goods through Haifa by the British railway, for which facilities were to be given. Alexandretta, which fell in the blue area, was to be a free port as regards the trade of the British Empire, and there was to be freedom of traffic for British goods through Alexandretta by railway through the blue area. In addition, there were certain customs and political stipulations. Such were the general dispositions of 1916 which he emphasised were designed:

(1) To favour the establishment of an Arab State or Confederation of States and to detach the Arabs from Turkey:

and

(2) To decide between the claims of Great Britain and France. The above agreement confirmed, by an exchange of Notes between M. Paul Cambon and Sir Edward Grey (Lord Grey), declarations which had been made by Great Britain as early as 1912, in which Great Britain had disinterested herself and recognised the rights of France in Syria, subject only to Great Britain's insistence on keeping untouched her economic rights. In short, Great Britain had declared she had no political claims, but that her economic rights must remain intact in Syria.

Since the conclusion of the Agreement of 1916 there had been a long further correspondence and an exchange of many Notes between France and Great Britain concerning particularly various local interests. This brought us to the most recent period in which the French made, he would not say a protest against, but a series of observations in regard to, the British attitude in Syria. The whole series of these had recently been handed by the President of the Council to Lord Milner.

The incidents referred to in this correspondence were chiefly due to the disproportion in the relative contingents furnished by Great Britain and France to the campaign in Syria. It had only been possible for France to send a very small number of troops to Syria in consequence of the large demands made on her for the protection of French soil and to the prominent part played by her armies in Salonica. Great Britain, however, had interested herself far more in the Turkish campaigns, and had sent many troops which had been led by General Allenby. From that disproportion there resulted a great many incidents. Eventually, the President of the Council had thought it right to bring them before the British Government with a view to putting an end to the factions and the friction which now existed.

From all the declarations made by the British and French Governments he only wanted to quote one, namely, that of November 9, 1918. This was particularly important as showing the disinterested attitude of both Governments towards the Arabs. This declaration had been communicated shortly after its issue by the French Ambassador in Washington to President Wilson.

MR LLOYD GEORGE interpolated at this point that this announcement, which was the latest expression of policy by the two Governments, was more important than all the old agreements.

M. PICHON then read the declaration of November 9, 1918, as follows:

"The aim which France and Great Britain have in view in prosecuting in the East the war let loose by German ambition is the complete and final liberation of the peoples so long oppressed by the Turks, and the establishment of national governments and administrations deriving their authority from the initiative and free choice of the native populations.

"In order to give effect to these intentions, France and Great Britain have agreed to encourage and assist the establishment of native governments and administrations in Syria and Mesopotamia already liberated by the Allies, and in the territories which they are proceeding to liberate, and they have agreed to recognise such governments as soon as they are effectively established. So far from desiring to impose specific institutions upon the populations of these regions, their sole object is to ensure, by their support and effective assistance, that the governments and administrations adopted by these regions of their own free will shall be exercised in the normal way. The function which the two Allied Governments claim for themselves in the liberated territories is to ensure impartial and equal justice for all; to facilitate the economic development of the country by encouraging local initiative; to promote the diffusion of education; and to put an end to the divisions too long exploited by Turkish policy."

As the difficulties between the two Governments continued, and as the French Government particularly did not wish them to reach a point where ultimate agreement would be compromised, the President of the Council, on his visit to London in December 1918, had asked Mr. Lloyd George to confirm the agreement between the two countries. Mr. Lloyd George had replied that he saw no difficulty about the rights of France in Syria and Cilicia, but he made demands for certain places which he thought should be included in the British zone, and which, under the 1916 agreement, were in the French zone of influence, namely, Mosul. He also asked for Palestine. M. Clemenceau had, on his return to Paris, been desirous that this suggestion should be examined in the most favourable spirit. In consequence, he had ordered a scheme of agreement to be prepared, with the inclusion of Mosul in the British zone of influence, and this had been handed to the British Government on the 15th February, 1919. The letter which accompanied this proposal had asked for a recognition of the historic and traditional case for including the regions claimed in the French zone. It had pointed out that there was no Government in the world which had such a position as France in the regions claimed. It had given an exposition of the historic rights of France dating from the time of Louis XIV.

M. PICHON continued by pointing out that French intervention in Syria had been frequent, the last instance being the case of the expedition organised in Syria and Lebanon in 1860, which had resulted in the establishment of the status of the Lebanon. France, he pointed out, had a great number of hospitals in Syria. There were a great number of schools in many villages, and some 50,000 children were educated in French primary schools. There were also a number of secondary schools and one great university in Beyrout.[3] Moreover, the railway system of Syria was French, and included the Beyrout to Damascus line, and the Tripoli-Homs line, which latter it was proposed to prolong to the Euphrates and to unite with the Bagdad system. Altogether it was contemplated to have a system of 1,233 kilometres, of which 683 kilometres had already been constructed. Beyrout was entirely a French port. The gas and electricity works were French, and the same applied to the lighting along the coast. This was not the limit of French enterprise, for France had perfected the agriculture and the viticulture of Syria and had established many facories. No other country had anything like so complete a development in these regions. Hence, France could not abandon her rights. Moreover, France strongly protested against any idea of dividing Syria. Syria had geographical and historic unity. The French Government frankly avowed that they did not want the responsibility of administering Palestine, though they would prefer to see it under an international administration. What they asked was:

(1) That the whole Syrian region should be treated as a unit: and

3 The University of St. Joseph, a French Jesuit institution.

(2) That France should become the mandatory of the League of Nations of this region.

On January 30 of this year Mr. Lloyd George had urged the Conference to reconsider the distribution of troops in Turkey and the Caucasus with the object of lightening the heavy burden which fell on Great Britain. As a result, the Military Representatives had been asked to prepare a plan.[4] The scheme of the Military Representatives provided for:

The occupation by France of Syria and Cilicia, with 2 divisions and 1 cavalry brigade:

The occupation by Great Britain of Mesopotamia, including Mosul, by 2 divisions and 1 cavalry brigade:

The occupation by Italy of the Caucasus and Konia.[5]

The economy which Great Britain would achieve by this plan would have amounted to 10 divisions of infantry and 4 divisions of cavalry. The plan of the Military Representatives had been placed on the Agenda Paper of the Conference, but at Lord Milner's request the subject had been adjourned and had never been discussed.

About this time a Conversation had taken place between M. Clemenceau and M. Pichon and Mr. Lloyd George and Mr. Balfour, as a result of which Sir Maurice Hankey had handed M. Pichon a map containing a British counter proposal to the French proposal of February 15. This scheme provided for a great limitation of the territory to come under French influence, both on the east and on the south as regards the Jebel Druse.[6] The French Government was quite unable to take this project into consideration. Recently Lord Milner had left a map with M. Clemenceau containing yet another project, which M. PICHON proceeded to explain, and which, he added, greatly circumscribed the French area. It was evident that the French Government could not look at this scheme either, even though they had the greatest desire to reach an agreement. No one felt more deeply than he what Great Britain and France owed to each other, and no one had a greater desire to reach an agreement. It was, however, quite impossible to accept a proposal such as that put forward by Lord Milner. It would be absolutely indefensible in the Chamber. It was enough for the Chamber to know that the Government were in negotiation with Great Britain for the handing over of Mosul to create a movement that had resulted in a proposal in the Budget Committee for a diminution of

[4] See the memorandum by T. H. Bliss printed at Feb. 8, 1919, and the discussion of the report included in the minutes of the meeting of the Supreme War Council printed at Feb. 10, 1919, both in Vol. 55.

[5] A city in southwest central Turkey.

[6] A mountainous province in southern Syria.

credits for Syria. This had not been a mere budget trick, but represented a real movement of public opinion. French opinion would not admit that France could be even partly excluded after the sacrifices she had made in the War, even if she had not been able to play a great part in the Syrian campaign. In consequence, the minimum that France could accept was what had been put forward in the French Government's Note to Mr. Lloyd George, the object of which had been to give satisfaction to his desire for the inclusion of Mosul in the British zone.

MR LLOYD GEORGE said that M. Pichon had opened as though the question of the mandate for Syria was one between Great Britain and France. There was, in fact, no such question so far as Great Britain was concerned. He wished to say at once that just as we had disinterested ourselves in 1912, so we now disinterested ourselves in 1919. If the Conference asked us to take Syria, we should reply in the negative. The British Government had definitely decided this because otherwise it would be said afterwards in France that they had created disturbances in order to keep the French out. Hence, the British Government definitely intended to have nothing to do with Syria. The question of the extent to which Great Britain and France were concerned was cleared up in the interview he had had with M. Clemenceau in London, and at which he had said that he wanted Mosul with the adjacent regions and Palestine.

As there was no question between France and Great Britain in regard to Syria, we could examine the question in as disinterested a spirit as we could a Carpathian boundary to be decided in accordance with the general principles accepted by the Conference. He wished to make this clear before General Allenby said what he had to say. In regard to Mosul, he wished to acknowledge the cordial spirit in which M. Pichon had met our desires.

But if there was a French public opinion there was also a British public opinion, and it must be remembered that the whole burden of the Syrian campaign had fallen upon Great Britain. The number of French troops taking part in the campaign had been so small as to make no difference. Sometimes they had been helpful, but not on all occasions. The British Empire and India had maintained from 900,000 to 1,000,000 troops in Turkey and the Caucasus. Their casualties had amounted to 125,000, the campaign had cost hundreds of millions of pounds. He himself had done his best to induce M. Clemenceau's predecessors to take part in the campaign. He had also pressed Marshal Foch on the subject, and to this day he had in his possession a rough plan drawn up by Marshal Foch during an air raid at Boulogne. He had begged the French Government to co-operate, and had pointed out to them that it would enable them to occupy Syria, although, at the time, the British troops had not yet occupied Gaza. This had occurred in 1917 and 1918, at a time when the heaviest casualties in France also were being incurred by British troops. From that time onwards most of the heavy and continuous fighting in France had been done by British troops, although Marshal Pétain had made a number of valuable smaller attacks. This was one of the reasons why he had felt justified in asking Marshal Foch for troops. He had referred to this in order to show that the reason we had fought so hard in Palestine was not because we had not been fighting in France. M. Pichon seemed to think that we were departing from the 1916 agreement in other respects, as well as in respect to Mosul and Palestine. In fact, we were not. M. Pichon had omitted in his lucid statement to explain that the blue area in which France was "allowed to establish such direct or indirect administration or control as they may desire and as they may think fit to arrange with the Arab State or Confederation of Arab States" did not include Damascus, Homs, Hama, or Aleppo. In area A. France was "prepared to recognise and uphold an independent Arab State or Confederation of Arab States * * * under the suzerainty of an Arab Chief." Also in area A. France would "have priority of right of enterprise and local loans * * * and * * * shall alone supply advisers or foreign functionaries at the request of the Arab State or Confederation of Arab States." Was France prepared to accept that? This, however, was not a question between Great Britain and France. It was a question between France and an agreement which we had signed with King Hussein.

(*At this point* M. ORLANDO *and* GENERAL DIAZ *entered.*)

M. PICHON said he wished to say one word. In the new arrangements which were contemplated no direct administration whatsoever was claimed by France. Since the Agreement of 1916, the whole mandatory system had been adopted. If a mandate were granted by the League of Nations over these territories, all that he asked was that France should have that part put aside for her.

MR LLOYD GEORGE said that we could not do that. The League of Nations could not be used for putting aside our bargain with King Hussein.[7] He asked if M. Pichon intended to occupy Damas-

---

[7] That is, the agreement of 1915 between Hussein ibn Ali al-Hashimi and Sir Arthur Henry McMahon (or M'Mahon), the British High Commissioner in Egypt, the most important document of which is quoted extensively by Lloyd George immediately below.

For more information on this diplomatic exchange, see Howard M. Sachar, *The Emergence of the Middle East, 1914-1924* (New York, 1969), pp. 126-29, and Elie Kedourie, *In the Anglo-Arab Labyrinth: The McMahon-Husayn Correspondence and its Interpretations, 1914-1939* (Cambridge, 1976). The complete Hussein-McMahon correspondence from August 30, 1915, to March 10, 1916, is printed in J. C. Hurewitz, comp., trans., and ed., *The Middle East and North Africa in World Politics: A Documentary Record*, 2d edn. (2 vols., New Haven, Conn., 1975-79), II, 48-56.

cus with French troops? If he did, it would clearly be a violation of the Treaty with the Arabs.[8]

M. PICHON said that France had no convention with King Hussein.

MR LLOYD GEORGE said that the whole of the agreement of 1916 (Sykes-Picot), was based on a letter from Sir Henry McMahon to King Hussein from which he quoted the following extracts:

"The districts of Mersina and Alexandretta, and portions of Syria lying to the west of the districts of Damascus, Homs, Hama, and Aleppo, cannot be said to be purely Arab, and should be excluded from the proposed limits of boundaries. With the above modifications, and without prejudice to our existing treaties with Arab Chiefs, we accept these limits of boundaries; and in regard to those portions of the territories therein in which Great Britain is free to act without detriment to the interests of her ally France, I am empowered, in the name of the Government of Great Britain, to give the following assurances and make the following reply to your letter:

'Subject to the above modifications Great Britain is prepared to recognise and support the independence of the Arabs within territories included in the limits of boundaries proposed by the Sherif of Mecca.'

(*Extract from a letter from Sir H. McMahon to King Hussein, Oct. 24, 14*)."[9]

M. PICHON said that this undertaking had been made by Great Britain (Angleterre) alone. France had never seen it until a few weeks before when Sir Maurice Hankey had handed him a copy.

MR LLOYD GEORGE said the agreement might have been made by England (Angleterre) alone, but it was England (Angleterre) who had organised the whole of the Syrian campaign. There would have been no question of Syria but for England (Angleterre). Great Britain had put from 900,000 to 1,000,000 men in the field against Turkey, but Arab help had been essential; that was a point on which General Allenby could speak.

GENERAL ALLENBY said it had been invaluable.

MR LLOYD GEORGE, continuing, said that it was on the basis of the above quoted letter that King Hussein had put all his resources into the field which had helped us most materially to win the victory. France had for practical purposes accepted our undertaking to King Hussein in signing the 1916 agreement. This had not been M. Pichon, but his predecessors. He was bound to say that if the British Government now agreed that Damascus, Homs, Hama, and Aleppo

---

[8] That is, the agreement discussed in n. 7 above. It was actually in the form of an exchange of diplomatic notes, rather than a treaty.

[9] *Sic.* The correct date of McMahon's letter is October 24, 1915.

should be included in the sphere of direct French influence, they would be breaking faith with the Arabs, and they could not face this. He was particularly anxious for M. Clemenceau to follow this. The agreement of 1916 had been signed subsequent to the letter to King Hussein. In the following extract from the agreement of 1916 France recognised Arab independence:

"It is accordingly understood between the French and British Governments:

(1) That France and Great Britain are prepared to recognise and uphold an independent Arab State or Confederation of Arab States in the areas A. and B. marked on the annexed map under the suzerainty of an Arab Chief."

Hence, France, by this act, practically recognised our agreement with King Hussein by excluding Damascus, Homs, Hama, and Aleppo from the blue zone of direct administration, for the map attached to the agreement showed that Damascus, Homs, Hama and Aleppo were included, not in the zone of direct administration, but in the independent Arab State.

M. PICHON said that this had never been contested, but how could France be bound by an agreement the very existence of which was unknown to her at the time when the 1916 agreement was signed? In the 1916 agreement France had not in any way recognised the Hedjaz. She had undertaken to uphold "an independent Arab State or Confederation of Arab States," but not the King of the Hedjaz. If France was promised a mandate for Syria, she would undertake to do nothing except in agreement with the Arab State or Confederation of States. This is the *role* which France demanded in Syria. If Great Britain would only promise her good offices, he believed that France could reach an understanding with Feisal.

PRESIDENT WILSON said that he would now seek to establish his place in the Conference. Up to the present he had had none. He could only be here, like his colleague M. Orlando, as one of the representatives assembled to establish the peace of the world. This was his only interest, although, of course, he was a friend of both parties to the controversy. He was not indifferent to the understanding which had been reached between the British and French Governments, and was interested to know about the undertakings to King Hussein and the 1916 agreement, but it was not permissible for him to express an opinion thereon. He would, however, like to point out that one of the parties to the 1916 agreement had been Russia, and Russia had now disappeared. Hence, the partnership of interest had been dissolved, since one of the parties had gone out. This seemed to him to alter the basis of the agreement. The point of view of the United States of America was, however, indifferent to the claims both of Great Britain and France over peoples unless those peoples wanted them. One of the fundamental principles to which the United States of America adhered was the consent of the governed. This was ingrained in the United States of America thought. Hence, the only idea from the United States of America point of view was as to whether France would be agreeable to the Syrians. The same applied as to whether Great Britain would be agreeable to the inhabitants of Mesopotamia. It might not be his business, but if the question was made his business, owing to the fact that it was brought before the Conference, the only way to deal with it was to discover the desires of the population of these regions. He recalled that, in the Council of Ten, Resolutions had been adopted in regard to mandatories, and they contained a very carefully thought out graduation of different stages of mandate according to the civilisation of the peoples concerned. One of the elements in those mandates was the desire of the people over whom the mandate was to be exercised. The present controversy broadened out into very important questions. Cilicia, for example, from its geographical position, cut Armenia off from the Mediterranean. If there was one mandatory in the south, and another in the north of Armenia, there would be a great danger of friction, since the troublesome population lived in the south. Hence, the controversy broadened into a case affecting the peace of the whole world in this region. He hoped, therefore, that the question would be discussed from this point of view. If this were agreed to, he hoped that he might ask General Allenby certain questions. If the participation of M. Orlando and himself were recognised as a matter of right and not of courtesy, the question he wanted to know was whether the undertaking to King Hussein, and the 1916 agreement, provided an arrangement which would work. If not, and you asked his opinion, he would reply that we ought to ask what is the opinion of the people in the part of the world concerned. He was told that, if France insisted on occupying Damascus and Aleppo, there would be instant war. Feisal had said that he could not say how many men he had had in the field at one time, as it had been a fluctuating figure, but from first to last he had probably had 100,000 men.

GENERAL ALLENBY said that he had never had so many at one time.

PRESIDENT WILSON said that, nevertheless, from first to last France would have to count on having 100,000 troops against her. This would mean that France must send a large number of troops. He was greatly concerned in a fight between friends, since he was the friend of France and the friend of Feisal. He was very concerned to know if a "scrap" was developing. Hence, he asked that it might be taken for granted that this question was on the Council table, since it was one of interest to the peace of the world, and that it was not merely a question of agreement between France and Great Britain. The Turkish Empire at the present time was as much in solution as though it were made of quicksilver. Austria, at any rate, had been broken into pieces, and the pieces remained, but the Turkish Empire was in complete solution. The councils of the world would have to take care of it. For his part, he was quite disinterested, since the United States of America did not want anything in Turkey. They would be only too delighted if France and Great Britain would undertake the responsibility. Lately, however, it had been put to him that he must approach his own people on this matter, and he intended to try, although it would mean some very good talking on his part. He admitted that the United States of America must take the responsibilities, as well as the benefits, of the League of Nations. Nevertheless, there was great antipathy in the United States of America to the assumption of these responsibilities. Even the Philippines were regarded as something hot in the hand that they would like to drop. If we said to the French Government "Occupy this region," what would happen? He had a method to propose of finding out, which he would develop later.

MR LLOYD GEORGE suggested that General Allenby should be questioned at this point.

PRESIDENT WILSON asked the following question:

If before we arrive at a permanent settlement under the League of Nations we invite France to occupy the region of Syria, even as narrowly defined, what would the result be?

GENERAL ALLENBY said there would be the strongest possible opposition by the whole of the Moslems, and especially by the Arabs. Shortly after the capture of Damascus, Feisal had been allowed to occupy and administer the city. He had said that he would like to be helped in the administration. A little later, after the setting up of the military administration in these regions, General Allenby had put French administrators in the blue area. When they arrived Emir Feisal had said that he could not retain the command of the Arab Army if France occupied the ports. He had said it meant that he was occupying a house without a door, and it would be said that he had broken faith with the Arab nation. Feisal had originally asked if he could occupy Beyrout and the ports. GENERAL ALLENBY had replied in the affirmative, but had told him that he must withdraw when the Allied Armies came along, and he had done so. To Feisal's protests against the occupation by the French of places in the blue zone, GENERAL ALLENBY had replied that he himself was in charge of the administration, as Commander-in-Chief; and that the French officers appointed as administrators must be regarded not as French officers, but as Allied military officers. Feisal had then said that he would admit it for the present, but would it last for ever? GENERAL ALLENBY had replied that the League of Nations intended to give the small nations the right of self-determination. Feisal had insisted that "if put under French control" he would oppose to the uttermost. GENERAL ALLENBY had replied that at present there was no French control, but only the control of the Allies, and that eventually Feisal's rights would be considered. Soon afterwards he had visited Beyrout, and there and in other places deputations had come to protest against the French administration. These had included various Christians, Orthodox and Protestants, as well as Musulmans. GENERAL ALLENBY had again replied that it was not a French administration, but merely officers put in by himself as Allied Commander-in-Chief. Every time he had been in that country he had found the greatest opposition to French admin-istration. He had done his utmost to make a *rapprochement* among the Arabs and the French, but without success. The French liaison officers did not get on well with the Arabs. M. Picot[10] had been with him to Damascus and Aleppo and was perfectly conversant with the situation. M. Picot would say that General Allenby had done his best to create good feeling. Lately, Sir Mark Sykes[11] had been to Beyrout, Aleppo, and Damascus with M. Picot and had done his best. Nevertheless, the misunderstanding continued. If the French were given a mandate in Syria, there would be serious trouble and probably war. If Feisal undertook the direction of op-erations there might be a huge war covering the whole area, and the Arabs of the Hedjaz would join. This would necessitate the employment of a very large force. This would probably involve Great Britain also if they were in Palestine. It might even involve them in Egypt, and the consequences would be incalculable.

He had gone with M. Picot to Damascus and had seen there Ali Riza el Rikaby Pasha, the Governor of the territory to the east of Damascus. The administration had not been doing well. There was practically no Budget, and it had been necessary to give him ad-visers. GENERAL ALLENBY had given him two British advisers, Ma-jors Cornwallis and Stirling.[12] M. Picot had subsequently sent a very good man named Captain Cousse,[13] to replace a liaison officer

[10] Charles François Georges Picot, former French Consul General in Beirut, at this time a special adviser on middle eastern affairs to the French Ministry of Foreign Affairs.

[11] Lt. Col. Sir Mark Sykes, M.P., an adviser to the Foreign Office on middle eastern policy. He had died in Paris on February 16, 1919.

[12] Kinahan Cornwallis, director of the Arab Bureau in Cairo and assistant chief political officer with the Egyptian Expeditionary Force under Gen. Allenby, and Walter Francis Stirling, formerly chief of staff to Thomas Edward Lawrence.

[13] Probably Édouard Sylvain Cousse.

(Captain Mercier)[14] who had been there before who had not got on with the Arabs because he had stood too much on his dignity. Even Captain Cousse, however, had not been able to get on well. Afterwards, General Allenby had sent a British financial expert, and had invited M. Picot to send a French financial expert. The British adviser, Colonel Graves,[15] had cooperated with M. Moulin,[16] the French adviser. They reported very badly on the finance. There had practically been no Budget. Then GENERAL ALLENBY had withdrawn Colonel Graves. M. Moulin was still there, but was meeting great difficulties owing to Ali Riza el Rikaby's dislike of the French administration. GENERAL ALLENBY had visited Damascus with M. Picot and had there interviewed Riza el Rikaby Pasha. GENERAL ALLENBY produced at the Conference a document containing the gist of the communication made by him to Riza el Rikaby Pasha. A copy of this document in Arabic and English had been left with Riza el Rikaby Pasha.

In reply to Mr. Lloyd George he said that at Damascus there was a bridge of infantry and two regiments of cavalry. The Sherifian troops[17] were only used for police purposes, since the Sherifian Army was still in process of formation.

(*At this point there was an adjournment.*)

PRESIDENT WILSON suggested that the fittest men that could be obtained should be selected to form an Inter-Allied Commission to go to Syria, extending their inquiries, if they led them, beyond the confines of Syria. Their object should be to elucidate the state of opinion and the soil to be worked on by any mandatory. They should be asked to come back and tell the Conference what they found with regard to these matters. He made this suggestion, not because he lacked confidence in the experts whose view he had heard, such as Dr. Howard Bliss and General Allenby. These, however, had been involved in some way with the population, with special objects either educational or military. If we were to send a Commission of men with no previous contact with Syria, it would, at any rate, convince the world that the Conference had tried to do all it could to find the most scientific basis possible for a settlement. The Commission should be composed of an equal number of French, British, Italian and American representatives. He would send it with *carte blanche* to tell the facts as they found them.

M. CLEMENCEAU said he adhered in principle to an inquiry, but

---

[14] He cannot be further identified.
[15] Lt. Col. Robert Windham Graves, former financial adviser to the Ottoman and Egyptian governments and deputy chief political officer with the Egyptian Expeditionary Force.
[16] He cannot be further identified.
[17] That is, the troops of King Hussein who, prior to becoming King of the Hedjaz, was best known under his other title of Sharif of Mecca and Medina.

it was necessary to have certain guarantees. The inquiry must not confine itself to Syria. Mandates were required for Palestine, Mesopotamia, and Armenia, and other parts of the Turkish Empire as well as Syria. The peoples of these districts were not isolated. They were all connected by historical and religious and other links, including mutual feuds and old quarrels [which] existed between all of them. Without contesting what General Allenby had said, he wished it to be recorded, if there were a proces verbal, that many Syrians were not Arab, and that if the Syrians were put under the Arabs they would revolt. He knew quite well the great share taken by Feisal in the Syrian campaign, and he thought that the British were also a little afraid of it. The whole inquiry would be an extremely delicate one. Orientals were very timid and afraid to say what was at the back of their minds. It was very difficult to get the real feelings of the people. It was very important, therefore, that the inquiry should not be merely superficial. Hence, he would ask for twenty-four hours of reflection before setting up the Commission. He might like to send some French Arabs there, as Feisal only represented one side of the Arab race. Moreover, Feisal was practically a soldier of England. That was a fact that all the world knew. He said he would revolt if the French were at Damascus, but, as a matter of fact, French artillery had recently been sent there and had been received quite well. He had made every effort to bring himself to agree with the principles propounded by President Wilson, but something must be said for the historical claims and for the efforts that nations had made in different regions. For example, insistence on an Arab outlet to the sea would destroy the claim of one nation in that part of the world. The members of the Commission must be very carefully selected, and they must inquire into every Turkish mandate. Subject to these provisions he was prepared to accept President Wilson's proposal in principle.

MR LLOYD GEORGE said he had no objection to an inquiry into Palestine and Mesopotamia, which were the regions in which the British Empire were principally concerned. Neither would he object to an inquiry into Armenia, in which they were not so closely concerned.

PRESIDENT WILSON said he saw advantages in a unified inquiry into Turkish mandates.

MR LLOYD GEORGE said if this extension was to be given to the Commission it was essential it should get to work at once, as the burden of military forces in Turkey fell mainly on the British.

MR BALFOUR said he felt these proposals might postpone the making of peace.

PRESIDENT WILSON said this was not so. For the purposes of peace all that was necessary to tell Turkey was that she would have nothing.

MR LLOYD GEORGE said that Turkey was entitled to know who would be the mandatory for Turkish territory.

PRESIDENT WILSON said it was rather that they ought to know how much was to remain Turkish.

MR LLOYD GEORGE said that the question of who was to be the mandatory of Anatolia would make all the difference for the arrangements for Turkey.

PRESIDENT WILSON said that Turkey was entitled to know if she was to have territory of her own, and that other parts of Turkey were to be placed under the League of Nations. Subsequently she would be informed who would be her next-door neighbours.

MR LLOYD GEORGE said he supposed that if the evidence were so overwhelming that, for example, the British Empire was ruled out of Mesopotamia they would be free to consider whether they could take a mandate elsewhere in Turkey?

PRESIDENT WILSON said this was an administrative matter and not one of sovereignty. Turkey was entitled to knowledge on all questions affecting the sovereignty.

M. PICHON suggested that, in order to avoid delay, the Commission might divide into Sub-Commissions working in different sections.

MR BALFOUR asked whether it would be wise to include Western Anatolia in the purview of the Commission. Constantinople was mainly a military question—(President Wilson said a strategic question)—but south of the region which went with Constantinople came regions to which the Greeks laid claim.

MR LLOYD GEORGE said there was no suggestion that the Commission was to travel beyond Armenia.

At Mr. Lloyd George's request:

President Wilson undertook to draft a Terms of Reference to the Commission.[18]

POLAND.

M. CLEMENCEAU read a despatch from General Nudant at Spa to the effect that General Dupont,[19] who had just returned to Berlin, telephoned that negotiations at Posen had broken down. After a series of confused notes he had received a definite intimation from the Germans which amounted to this:

(1) That they would not allow the disembarkation of Polish troops at Dantzig:

(2) That they would not allow the Allied Commission at Warsaw to go into German territories east of the Vistula.

---

[18] See Wilson's memorandum printed at March 25, 1919.
[19] Gen. Charles Joseph Dupont, president of the Inter-Allied Commission at Berlin.

MR BALFOUR said that this was contrary to the terms of the armistice.

PRESIDENT WILSON said the Germans would probably stand on the technical point that the terms referred only to Allied troops, and the Poles were not Allies.

It was agreed that:

The question should be discussed first on the following day.

T MS (SDR, RG 256, 180.0341/101, DNA).

To Robert Lansing

My dear Lansing: Paris, 20 March, 1919.

There was such confusion yesterday as to who was to carry out the decisions of the Conference that I am taking the liberty of suggesting that we take no chances and that you yourself find means to communicate to the groups of gentlemen representing Ukrania and Poland here in Paris the whole purpose and temper of the discussion yesterday with regard to Lemberg, particularly impressing upon them the impossibility of getting their claims properly considered if this fighting is not stopped.

Faithfully yours,   Woodrow Wilson

Communicated to Dr. Lord who saw Polish & Ukrainia Representatives. March 20 1919.[1]

TLS (R. Lansing Papers, DLC).
[1] RLhw.

To Henry Pomeroy Davison

My dear Mr. Davison: Paris, 20 March, 1919.

I have had time to read your important letter of March 14th[1] but not time yet to seek an interview with you, which I must have in order to discuss the matter a little more fully, and therefore this is just an acknowledgement and a promise that I will go into the whole thing with you at the earliest possible moment.

In the meantime thank you for the letter.

Sincerely yours,   Woodrow Wilson

TLS (DARC).
[1] H. P. Davison to WW, March 14, 1919, Vol. 55.

To Edward Mandell House

My dear House: Paris, 20 March, 1919.

I wish you would read this letter and let me have your comments upon it.[1]   Affectionately yours,   Woodrow Wilson

TLS (E. M. House Papers, CtY).
   [1] That is, H. P. Davison to WW, March 14, 1919, Vol. 55.

To Homer Hosea Johnson[1]

My dear Mr. Johnson: Paris, 20 March, 1919.

Thank you for your letter of March 19th.[2] The suggestion which it contains was one which was fully discussed by the Commission that formulated the Covenant for the League of Nations and I think I can say that it was the unanimous opinion of the Commission that we must be careful *not* to preclude the right of revolution which most free peoples in common with our own have always held to be a sacred and indefeasible right.

I think that you will agree with me that it would be a very questionable policy to attempt immediately to bind the world together in any such intimate way as is presupposed in the provision of our Constitution to which you refer.

May I not thank you very warmly for your words of approval of what we are attempting to do? It is hard work but in every way worth while.

                    Cordially and sincerely yours,   [Woodrow Wilson]

CCL (WP, DLC).
   [1] Lawyer of Cleveland, at this time a member of the United States Liquidation Commission of the War Department in Paris.
   [2] H. H. Johnson to WW, March 19, 1919, TLS (WP, DLC). Johnson recommended that Article X of the proposed Covenant of the League of Nations be amended to include "the remainder of Article 4, Section 4, of the Constitution of the United States not now covered by it [Article 10], to wit: The guaranty to every developed nation of a republican form of government and freedom from domestic violence."

To Frederick Henry Lynch

My dear Doctor Lynch: Paris, 20 March, 1919.

My answer to your recent letter of March 17th is that I do not think that Mr. Taft can be spared from the United States just now. It is in my judgment very much more serviceable that he should continue the work he is doing than that he should interrupt it for the purpose of visiting England, much as I should like to see him do the latter.

Of course this is only my individual judgment, but I hold it very distinctly and am fresh from the impressions I gained at home.

In unavoidable haste,

Cordially and sincerely yours,   [Woodrow Wilson]

CCL (WP, DLC).

From George Davis Herron

Dear Mr. President,   Geneva, Switzerland March 20th, 1919.

I am sending to you, through the courtesy of Minister Stovall, a letter addressed to me by the President of the Council of State of the ancient Republic of Geneva.[1] The letter was presented to me with the urgent request that it be placed personally in your hands.

May I add my emphatic and urgent endorsement to the plea of the Genevese Republic for the location of the seat of the League of Nations here? Historically speaking, Geneva seems to me the logical place for the League to assemble.

It is out of this city that both religious liberty and political democracy have gone forth to the world. Because of their quiet and conservative way, because of the high seriousness and spiritual dignity of the old Genevese citizenry, there is little understanding of how much the modern world owes to this ancient city. It is to John Calvin, and not to Martin Luther, that the birth of the Scot[t]ish Covenanters and the English Puritans must be traced. Geneva is the real parent of New England. And it is Rousseau—who is after all a true child of Calvin—who is the author of our Declaration of Independence. Albert Gallatin, our early great minister, who was also the first great Pacifist and advocator of international arbitration, was born in Geneva. John Knox, like many of the Scotch and English reformers, sat for two years at the feet of Calvin. We are in the bounds of historic truth when we say that the Puritan Revolution, the French Revolution, the American Revolution, all had their springs in Geneva.

The idea of a federate world, for which you so sublimely stand and under the inspiration of which you led America into the war, has its historical source here.

All in all, it seems to me no place upon our planet has such fitting claims to be the meeting place of the League of Nations as Geneva—unless it be Jerusalem.

And the property which the Council of State offers to the League, on the banks of the lake here, is superbly located and uniquely beautiful. Geneva would spare no expense towards supplying the League with harmonious surroundings and a fitting home.

May I beg you, as one who in some sense has kinship with Geneva, to give Geneva's claims most serious, and if possible affirmative, consideration.

Most faithfully yours,   George D. Herron

TLS (WP, DLC).
[1] John Louis Gignoux to G. D. Herron, March 19, 1919, HwLS (WP, DLC).

Gilbert Fairchild Close to Mohammed Abd Hamid El Kadi[1]

My dear Sir: Paris, 20 March 1919.

I am writing to acknowledge receipt of the letters and telegram which you addressed to the President,[2] and to say that they have been brought to his personal attention.

Sincerely yours,   [Gilbert F. Close]

CCL (WP, DLC).
[1] Student in economics and politics at the Victoria University of Manchester.
[2] M. A. H. Kadi to WW, March 13, 1919, T telegram; March 13, 1919, TLS; and March 14, 1919, TLS, all in WP, DLC. On behalf of "the Egyptians in Manchester," all three communications protested against the arrest and deportation from Egypt to Malta by the British government of Sa'd Zaghlul and three other Egyptian nationalist leaders on March 9. Zaghlul and his colleagues had proposed to go to London and/or Paris to urge greater autonomy, if not complete independence, for Egypt. The arrest and deportation, initiated by Sir Milne Cheetham, the acting British High Commissioner in Egypt, led to widespread rioting and destruction of property in Egypt. In response, Lloyd George and Balfour announced on March 20 the appointment of Gen. Allenby as Special High Commissioner in Egypt. For a detailed discussion of this complex incident, see Elie Kedourie, *The Chatham House Version and other Middle-Eastern Studies*, new edn. (Hanover, N. H., and London, 1984), pp. 82-110.

From Robert Lansing and Others

Dear Mr. President: Paris, March 20, 1919.

In the Diplomatic and Consular Appropriation Bill, passed and signed on March 4, 1919, provision was made for Legations and Ministers Plenipotentiary at Prague, Warsaw, Belgrade and Sofia. The missions at Belgrade and Sofia are at present filled by Chargés d'Affaires. Legations at Prague and Warsaw have not yet been established.

As regards Prague we wish respectfully to call to your attention the fact that England, France and Italy have already maintained Ministers at those points for several months, the United States being still diplomatically unrepresented. The Czecho-Slovak Government and people seem to have assumed that we would be the first country to send them a Minister and they were frankly disappointed when they saw the other great powers establishing legations at Prague without any sign from us, which appears to them an indication that we lack interest in their welfare. They do not realize that, unlike other countries, we required Congressional action, but now that this difficulty has been removed it would seem desirable to give them no excuse for the continuance of this unfortunate impression.[1]

The American Relief Administration is undertaking considerable activities in Czecho-Slovakia, involving great operations in food, finance, railroad transport and shipping. There will necessarily be numbers of American officials dealing with various branches of the Czecho-Slovak Government whose important work can best be facilitated and coordinated by a Minister representing the American Government as a whole.

Reports from the Czecho Slovak countries indicate that the next few months will be fraught with difficulty for the maintenance of orderly democratic government. In this situation an American Minister could exert a helpful influence that could be wielded by no one else. This influence should be used now when it can be most productive of good.

As regards Warsaw, now that the United States Government has recognized the Polish Government, it is highly important that a Minister should be appointed with the least possible delay as a demonstration to the Polish people of the friendship and support of the United States. Many things which have happened since the Armistice have unavoidably produced the impression in Poland that the Allies and the Associated Governments are indifferent or even unfriendly to the Polish cause and a widespread and insidious campaign has been carried on from certain quarters to spread the idea that our Government in particular has altogether changed its attitude towards Poland. Much might be done to dispel such impressions or to refute such slanders through the presence of an American Minister in Warsaw.

The Polish Government is in need of friendly counsel and it is particularly disposed to defer to the advice of the United States. That Government is faced by internal and external problems of great difficulty; it runs some danger of being deflected from its course by agitated public opinion; it is exposed to certain influences from outside which need to be counteracted. It is important that other powers should not establish an exclusive influence over the Government at Warsaw, and that that government should not be left without such measure of steadying and disinterested guidance as the United States can give.

The American members of the Interallied Commission to Poland will probably return to Paris before the end of this month. Therefore it is strongly recommended that an American Minister to Poland should be appointed before the first of April, and should be sent to Warsaw as quickly as possible in order that there may be no considerable interval during which we should be without representation in Poland.[2]

In making these recommendations we feel most earnestly that the men chosen for these posts should be democratic and truly representative Americans, with breadth of view and sound judgment, and that they should be so equipped by temperament and knowledge that they may win the confidence and sympathy of the Governments and people of these newly created states, sensitive as they are in the knowledge of their yet incomplete development.

We feel that upon the early selection and the personality of these two original Ministers will depend in large measure the future sympathetic relationship between the United States and these two countries.

We are, Mr. President,

Very sincerely yours, Robert Lansing.
Henry White
Tasker H. Bliss.
E. M. House

TLS (WP, DLC).
[1] Richard Crane was appointed Minister to Czechoslovakia on April 23, 1919.
[2] Hugh Simons Gibson was appointed Minister to Poland on April 16, 1919.

To George Creel

My dear Creel: Paris, 20 March, 1919.

I was very glad to find your letter of the first of March[1] awaiting me here in Paris, and heartily sorry that I did not have another chance to see you before you left this side of the water. The suggestions of your letter are very valuable indeed, and you may be sure will remain in my mind.

I wanted to tell you in person, but find I must now tell you by letter, how deeply I have appreciated the work you have done as Chairman of the Committee on Public Information. The work has been well done, admirably well done, and your inspiration and guidance have been the chief motive power in it all. I have followed what you have done throughout and have approved it, and I want you to know how truly grateful I am.

Your personal consideration of myself and your constant thoughtfulness have been a source of pleasure to me all the way through, and I feel that I now know beyond peradventure the high motives by which you are governed. It is with real emotion, therefore, that I sign myself,   Your sincere friend,   Woodrow Wilson

TLS (G. Creel Papers, DLC).
  [1] G. Creel to WW, March 1, 1919, Vol. 55.

To E. de Mohrenschildt[1]

My dear Miss de Mohrenschildt: Paris, 20 March, 1919.

Allow me to acknowledge the receipt of your letter of March 16th.[2]

Unhappily Mrs. Wilson and I have very little more knowledge of the circumstances of your brother's death[3] than you have. He died just as we were leaving the United States and all that we learned was that the cause of his death was a very severe attack of the influenza which very rapidly developed and very promptly proved fatal. We also learned that his death occurred just about two days after the birth of a little child, I am not sure whether a son or a daughter, and that therefore his wife[4] was in a very weak condition. Her father, Mr. McAdoo, was at the time in California but immediately upon receipt of the news hastened east. It would have taken him at least four days to accomplish the journey and I am sorry to say that I have not heard any further particulars since we left America, and therefore do not know in what condition he found his daughter and the little child when he reached New York, but I am quite confident from the fact that we have had no news at all that they are probably all right.[5]

This is the extent of our information, but if it would be of any service to your brother[6] to see me or Mrs. Wilson, if he would be kind enough to communicate with us I am sure he can see one or the other.

Our hearts go out to you in very deep and sincere sympathy upon the loss of a brother who was in every way so promising. It is indeed a very tragical thing.

Sincerely yours,   [Woodrow Wilson]

CCL (WP, DLC).
  [1] She described herself in the letter cited in n. 2 below as a "Protestant sister" (*soeur protestante*), working at the Hospice de Saint Jean de Caen, a home for the aged in Caen, France. The Editors have been unable to learn her given name or names. She was a sister-in-law of Nona Hazlehurst McAdoo (Mrs. Ferdinand) de Mohrenschildt.
  [2] E. de Mohrenschildt to WW, March 16, 1919, ALS (WP, DLC).
  [3] That is, Ferdinand de Mohrenschildt, about whose death, see n. 1 to the extract from the Grayson Diary printed at March 5, 1919, Vol. 55.
  [4] That is, Nona de Mohrenschildt.
  [5] Nona de Mohrenschildt did survive, but none of the few available sources says anything whatever about the child or its fate.
  [6] The letter cited in n. 2 above states that this brother was the proprietor of a "Chateau" in Libourne, France, but neither it nor any other available source reveals his name.

From the Diary of Colonel House

March 20, 1919.

Perhaps the most interesting feature of the day was my going with André Tardieu to call on Clemenceau at his request. He had had a meeting with Lloyd George and the President all the afternoon, and I did not call at the Ministry of War until 6.30. I asked how they had gotten on in the afternoon. "Splendidly, we disagreed about everything." When he told me they had agreed to adopt the President's suggestion to send a commission to Syria to report upon conditions and the wishes of the people as to what nation should become mandatory for them, I congratulated him. I told him Lloyd George did not want to settle the questions purely French, which relate to the Treaty with Germany, until after the Syrian question had been settled. This was a new phase of the situation to Clemenceau and one which he appreciated for the first time. He asked me to come to see him for the purpose of talking about the better security of France. I had written during the day a resolution[1] which I thought might be signed by France, Great Britain and the United States, provided Lloyd George and the President thought the American and British people would sustain such action.

Clemenceau read it with keen delight and substituted but one word which was "attack" instead of "invasion." I append a copy of the resolution. I have my doubts as to the Senate accepting such a treaty but that is to be seen. Meanwhile, it satisfies Clemenceau and we can get on with the real business of the Conference. It is practically promising only what we promise to do in the League of Nations, but since Clemenceau does not believe in the League of Nations, it may be necessary to give him a treaty on the outside. When he read it he said: "A monument ought to be erected to you."

---

[1] It reads as follows: "Because of the havoc which Germany has brought upon the world by her attack upon France and Belgium in 1914, and in order to prevent as far as ⟨humanly⟩ possible such another disaster to humanity, we hereby solemnly pledge to one another our immediate military, financial, economic and moral support of and to one another in the event Germany should at any time make a like unprovoked and unwarranted ⟨invasion of⟩ *attack against* the territories of either one or more of the subscribing powers." T MS (E. M. House Papers, CtY). Words in angle brackets deleted by House; words in italics added by him.

From the Diary of Dr. Grayson

Friday, March 21, 1919.

This morning the President sent me down to see Secretary Lansing to arrange for the bringing through as speedily as possible of a Ukrainian delegate who has been called for by the Council of Ten to confer with them and find out the best method of reconciling the serious differences between the new Republic of Poland and the Ukrainian Republic. The situation there resulted in a direct appeal having been made by the Council of Ten a few days ago to both the Poles and Ukrainians to make suggestions covering boundaries and exchange of trade which would prevent war between the two countries.[1] After explaining what the President wanted, Secretary Lansing, whom I found devoting a little time to bringing his diary up to date, asked me to urge the President to have an interview with Oswald Garrison Villard, who has just returned from Germany. Villard had been over there for about four weeks and had related to Mr. Lansing this morning a very harrowing story in which he told of terrible suffering for lack of food among German people. When I brought the matter to the President's attention he said he would very gladly see Villard if he thought that by doing so it would get food into Germany any quicker, but he said that ever since he had arrived in Paris he had been fighting with all his power to get food to the starving Germans and that ever since December the Republicans at home had been endeavoring to defeat the asked-for appropriations. He said, as a matter of fact, that food was now on the way and more was coming as quickly as transportation could be arranged; therefore, it would be unnecessary to listen to what Villard had to say as it would merely be a recital of details of facts already well-known to the President.

The President made the statement: Bolshevism has overwhelmed Poland, has overwhelmed Russia, engulfed Poland, and is poisoning Germany, and is spreading Westward. Force cannot stop it, but food can!

The President spent the morning in his study and went to the Quai D'Orsay at three o'clock this afternoon, where the Council of Ten[2] was in session considering the report of the Polish Commission.

It developed at the meeting of the Supreme War Council that there was a very wide difference of opinion between the American and British representatives on the one side and the French, Italian and Japanese on the other concerning the boundaries of the Polish Republic. The boundary commission which had reported on the subject had practically proposed that a good part of East Prussia be annexed to Poland, carrying with it the port of Danzig. As a result the entire afternoon was practically wasted, and the whole program arranged by the President was more or less knocked in the head. He had expected to dispose of the Polish Boundary question so that he would have all day Saturday clear to devote to the meeting of the full committee on the League of Nations constitution. It was necessary, however, to have the War Council meet again the next day.

The President remained indoors after dinner.

[1] At its meeting on March 19, the Council of Ten had decided to send identic telegrams to the commanders of the Polish and Ukrainian forces confronting each other near Lemberg, demanding an immediate truce between them. The telegrams also declared the willingness of the council to have delegates from Poland and the Ukraine present their territorial claims to the peace conference with a view to changing the truce into an armistice. For the text of the telegram and the discussion leading thereto, see *PPC*, IV, 405-12.

[2] Actually, the Supreme War Council.

From the Diary of Ray Stannard Baker

Friday the 21st [March 1919]

More pessimism. The Committee of Ten & the War Council talked for hours on the Polish question & got nowhere. Col. House continues to be optimistic & predicts a speedy settlement, but a great wave of criticism is now arising all over the world & most of it specifically directed at Pres. Wilson. The London Express & Globe are particularly bitter. Many good judges here think that Germany will not sign the treaty when it is presented & ask "what then?" In the meantime Bolshevism spreads & an enormous industrial & social unrest.

I had quite a talk with the President to-day & came over from the Quai d'Orsay with him in his motor. Just as we were getting in he called attention to the number on it "1921." I spoke of it as symbolic. "Of what?" he laughed. He has a sly strain of superstition in him—like all stern men of religious minds. He has always played with the "13" & Friday myths.

He told me at length of the difficulties & talk at to-days session. He grows very impatient with the constant obstruction & underhanded practice of the French. To-day's session stranded on Foch's pride & the bitter desire of the French to punish Germany. The French use their press—secretly informed as to what goes on inside—to push their contentions.

Hankey's Notes of a Meeting of the Supreme War Council[1]

BC-54, SWC-19   Quai d'Orsay, March 21, 1919, 3 p.m.

M. CLEMENCEAU having declared the meeting open, called on Marshal Foch to make a statement in connection with the transport of General Haller's army to Poland.

MARSHAL FOCH said that the question of the transportation of General Haller's army to Poland by rail had been studied, and the conclusion had been reached that it could be carried out as soon as the Conference gave the necessary authority, five or six days only being required in order to get the rolling stock together. By the land route one or two trains could be despatched daily; but conversations in regard to details were still taking place between the general staffs of the Allied Powers concerned.

The transport of the troops by sea, via Dantzig, had also received consideration, and a conclusion had been reached in regard to the tonnage which would be required.

The carriage by rail would only give very feeble results; consequently, it should be supplemented by the sea route, provided an agreement could be reached in regard to the disembarkation of the troops at the Port of Dantzig, and their transportation thence over the railway lines, under proper guarantees.

M. CLEMENCEAU asked Marshal Foch to make some statement about the views taken by the Germans in regard to the passage of the Polish troops through Dantzig.

MARSHAL FOCH replied that all he knew on this subject was contained in the telegrams received from M. Noulens and General Dupont, copies of which had been circulated.

M. CLEMENCEAU drew Marshal Foch's attention to the recommendation contained in M. Noulens' telegram of the 18th March, 1919, to the effect that the Inter-Allied Commission at Warsaw considered it necessary that the Naval forces of the Entente should immediately make a considerable demonstration opposite Dantzig, and enquired whether that proposal had Marshal Foch's approval.

MARSHAL FOCH said that with the information at his disposal, he could express no opinion. The Supreme War Council alone could determine the object to be attained; it would then be possible to determine the means of securing the end desired.

MR. LLOYD GEORGE enquired from Marshal Foch what it was that he wished the Conference to decide. It had been definitely settled that General Haller's army should be sent to Poland, provided the

[1] The complete text of these minutes is printed in PPC, IV, 423-42.

necessary tonnage could be made available. He failed therefore to understand what else was in Marshal Foch's mind.

MARSHAL FOCH pointed out that in accordance with the decision taken by the Supreme War Council on the 17th March, 1919, he had been merely authorised "to study the possibility of the transport of Polish troops to Poland from France." He wished to know, therefore, whether the Conference agreed to the transport of the troops by rail to Poland.

MR. LLOYD GEORGE said that as far as the Conference was concerned, the decision had been reached that General Haller's army should be sent to Poland; and the only question left to be considered was the means of transport. In other words, the principle of the transport of the Polish troops was decided, the only question in doubt was the method of transportation. The latter obviously was a question which should be decided by the specialists; it could not be decided by the Conference.

MARSHAL FOCH pointed out that the transport of the Polish troops by rail could be started at once, but as this method would be very slow, he proposed that transport by sea should continue to be studied by the Allied Maritime Transport Council, to whom the question had been referred by the Supreme War Council on the 17th March last.

In connection with the sea route, another question however, required to be settled, namely, whether the troops could be landed at Dantzig. This operation at the moment, seemed somewhat doubtful.

MR. LLOYD GEORGE enquired to what place the troops sent by rail were to be taken.

MARSHAL FOCH replied that the troops could be railed either to Lemberg, or to Cracow, or to any other part of Poland.

MR. LLOYD GEORGE again asserted that the question was not one which the Conference could be called upon to decide; the Allied Maritime Transport Council alone was competent to furnish the necessary information. A decision had already been reached by the Conference that the troops should be sent provided tonnage could be made available, as would appear from the Resolution taken at the meeting held on 17th March last, namely:

"To call upon the Allied Maritime Transport Council to submit a scheme showing what should be the contribution in shipping of each of the Allied and Associated Governments for the transport of General Haller's troops from France to Dantzig."

MARSHAL FOCH pointed out that he sought the sanction of the Conference to both routes being used, namely, the rail route and the sea route; and enquired whether that proposal was approved by the Conference.

MR. LLOYD GEORGE thought that the reply should be in the negative. The land route was extremely long, and complicated by the situation at Lemberg. The Conference had merely agreed to the transport by sea, because it was anxious not to appear to take sides in the quarrel which was taking place at Lemberg.

MARSHAL FOCH enquired whether under those conditions the land route was ruled out.

President Wilson, Mr. Lloyd George and M. Clemenceau replied in the affirmative.

MARSHAL FOCH continuing, said that the sea route then alone remained. A transport scheme had been worked out and could forthwith be brought into operation. Only two questions remained to be considered, namely, the possibility of landing at Dantzig, and the transportation by rail from Dantzig to Thorn.

MR. LLOYD GEORGE said that he was not altogether satisfied with the manner in which the negotiations had been conducted in Poland. He could not bring himself to believe that the Germans would in reality point blank refuse to carry out one of the conditions of the armistice, and, as a matter of fact, it was not clear from the information available that the Germans had actually done so. It was not quite clear what had occurred at Posen, and whether the Germans had really refused to carry out the accepted conditions of the armistice. Under those circumstances, he thought the best solution of the difficulty would be for Marshal Foch to put the question to the German representatives at Spa, particularly as a military operation was involved. Marshal Foch should, in his opinion, be authorised to tell the German delegates that the Allied and Associated Governments had decided to send troops to Poland through Dantzig in accordance with the provisions of Clause XVI of the armistice. He did not think the Germans would ever refuse compliance.

PRESIDENT WILSON drew attention to the fact that Clause XVI of the armistice stated that the troops of the Allies should have free access to Poland through Dantzig. A technical question might be raised as to whether the Polish troops could be defined as "troops of the Allies." In his opinion, the answer would be in the affirmative since those troops had been raised in France and America to fight on the side of the Allies. Nevertheless that was a matter which would have to be explained to the Germans.

MARSHAL FOCH pointed out that Clause XVI of the armistice of 11th November 1918, read as follows:

"The Allies shall have free access to the territories evacuated by

the Germans on their Eastern frontier, either through Dantzig or by the Vistula, in order to convey supplies to the populations of those territories or for the purpose of maintaining order."
That was all it contained. Had troops been dispatched shortly after the signature of the armistice, the Germans would undoubtedly have allowed them free passage; but today the Germans would undoubtedly maintain that, since perfect order prevailed in Poland, it was unnecessary to send troops for the purpose of maintaining order and that the line could only be employed to convey supplies to the population. Furthermore, he would invite attention to the instructions sent to M. Noulens on the 25th February 1919, that the Germans should guarantee the proposed disembarkation of troops at Dantzig, and their transit thence by rail to Poland. It was necessary that the guarantee in question should be obtained, otherwise great risks would be run. In his opinion, that constituted a new condition, which could not be considered to form part of Clause XVI of the armistice of November 1918.

MR. LLOYD GEORGE said he could not agree with the view taken by Marshal Foch. His information went to show that Haller's army was essential for the maintenance of order in Poland, and to prevent the spread of Bolshevism. If those troops were not required to maintain order, he did not understand why they should be sent at all. They certainly were not required to fight against the Germans or anyone else: a definite ruling on that point had been given by the Conference at a previous meeting.

MARSHAL FOCH pointed out that Clause XVI stated that: "The Allies shall have free access, etc." He did not know whether the Poles were "Allies": but, even so, it was certain that without proper guarantees, it would not be safe to convey troops over a railway line whose two extremities (Thorn-Dantzig) were fortified and held by the enemy, without taking other measures to secure the safety of the line.

M. CLEMENCEAU asked Marshal Foch to put forward his own proposals.

MARSHAL FOCH said that on the 11th January 1919, the Military High Command had suggested to the Supreme War Council the occupation by Allied contingents of the railway line in question, but the proposal had been rejected. Again, on the 24th February 1919, he had suggested that the only possible solution of the question appeared to be that the Eastern boundaries of Germany should forthwith be determined, and that the Germans should be required to accept that frontier line, and to withdraw their troops behind it. In that way, free transit over the Dantzig line would be obtained. In his opinion, as long as the railway line remained in the hands of the Germans, there could be no guarantee even if a verbal promise were given by them—a thing which, as a matter of fact, they had so far refused to do. He would again ask the Conference to consider the railway route to Poland, as by that route troops could be taken to any place desired. The traffic capacity of the line, as he had already stated, was very poor, but the troops would reach Poland eventually, whereas by the northern sea route, in his opinion, they would never get there. It would not be necessary for the troops to go to Lemberg, if taken by the land route. They could be sent wherever required, either to Cracow or to Warsaw.

PRESIDENT WILSON said it was not clear to him from the telegrams, which had been circulated, that the Germans had denied their obligations under Article XVI of the Armistice of November 1918. It appeared to him that they merely wanted to discuss the question at Spa at a meeting with the military authorities, just as had been done in the case of other similar matters. In his opinion, the Conference was taking a great deal for granted when it assumed that the Germans would attack the troops when passing over the Dantzig-Thorn railway line, since that would mean a renewal of the war. He had been told that General Haller considered that an escort of Allied troops would not be necessary; merely a few officers were required to superintend the process of transportation. Consequently, if his information were correct, the Germans had not denied their obligations under the Armistice. On the contrary, it would appear from messages received from Poland that they actually admitted their obligations. In this connection he would point out that Marshal Foch had stated that all his information in regard to the unwillingness of the Germans to comply with the demands of the Allies had been obtained from M. Noulens' messages. Now, M. Noulens was the head of a Commission that had been sent by the Allied and Associated Governments to Poland, and it was highly probable that the Germans might imagine that the Commission would naturally act in the interests of the Poles. Therefore, he could not help thinking that when the matter came to be dealt with by the Allied High Command at Spa, as suggested, the question would assume a different aspect in the minds of the Germans.

MARSHAL FOCH drew attention to a very precise message dated Spa, 20th. March, 1919, in which the following statement occurred, namely:

"In confirmation of these incidents, the German Commission communicated to me this morning a note which amounts to a clear and categorical refusal (1) to let Poles land at Dantzig; (2) to authorise Officers of Warsaw Mission to proceed to territory occupied by the Germans to the east of the Vistula."

MR. LLOYD GEORGE said he entirely shared President Wilson's views. He did not know what had really occurred at Posen, but if Marshal Foch was satisfied that General Haller's troops should be sent to Poland, provided tonnage could be set free for the purpose, then he would suggest that the Marshal should himself without delay interview the German representatives at Spa so that all necessary arrangements might be made. He could not believe that the Germans would refuse to allow the troops free passage along the Dantzig-Thorn railway line; and the idea that the Germans would cut them off was most unlikely. What object would the Germans have in doing so? Even if a whole brigade were cut up, it would not reduce the strength of the Allied Forces in any way, whereas such an outrage would lead at once to the Allied troops marching into Germany, or to the renewal of a strict blockade. He was not surprised to hear that General Haller himself had no apprehensions from that side.

In conclusion, he proposed definitely that Marshal Foch should be authorised to proceed to Spa to take the matter up with the German representatives there with a view to making a formal demand and the necessary arrangements.

MARSHAL FOCH pointed out that Germany had already given, according to General Dupont, a point blank refusal. Under those conditions, it was a question whether negotiations should now be reopened. Certainly he could go to Spa and say to the Germans that they must either allow the passage of the troops or he would wring their necks. It might be a moot point whether the question to be put to the Germans did or did not constitute a new demand; but if he went to Spa, he must go there fully authorised to tell the Germans that they must comply with the demands of the Allies, failing which hostilities would be renewed.

MR. LLOYD GEORGE suggested that Marshal Foch should first put forward his demand in exactly the same way as other similar conditions had previously been put forward, that is to say, tactfully but firmly. He could see no difference between the demand, now to be delivered, and those previously made.

PRESIDENT WILSON thought that the chief advantage of discussing the matter at Spa was that Marshal Foch would be able to explain, firstly, that the demand was made in execution of Clause XVI of the Armistice; secondly, that the troops to be transported were actually Allied troops; thirdly, that they were required for the maintenance of order in Poland; and fourthly, that there was no idea of using them against Germany. This explanation would relieve the Germans of any suspicions that might exist in their minds. He hoped Marshal Foch would give a frank and open explanation to the Germans and tell them that they were expected to yield in good faith to the conditions of the Armistice; there was no necessity to say what the consequences of a refusal would be.

MARSHAL FOCH called attention to the character of the conversation which he had previously held with the Germans. In each case, he had had to deal with the renewal of an Armistice, which expired on a fixed date. That is to say, a refusal by the Germans to accept the terms to be imposed as a condition of the renewal of the Armistice by the date given naturally entailed the breaking of the Armistice, and the renewal of hostilities. Consequently, the Germans had no choice in the matter. Similarly, if on this occasion he did proceed to Spa to communicate the decision of the Supreme War Council to the Germans, he could not be expected to remain there indefinitely to await an answer.

M. PICHON expressed the view that Marshal Foch's proposals should be accepted, otherwise the Allied and Associated Governments would find themselves in a difficult and delicate position in view of the fact that the Germans had already given a categorical refusal to allow the Poles to land at Dantzig. Should Marshal Foch, therefore, simply ask for the enforcement of Clause XVI of the Armistice without being empowered to give an ultimatum, the effect would be merely to encourage the growing tendency of the Germans to resist the demands of the Allies. Therefore, he asked the Conference to authorise Marshal Foch to insist on an immediate compliance with the conditions of the Armistice. Public opinion was already much exercised by the fact that the Germans had apparently been able with impunity to confront the Allies with a refusal. He, therefore, very strongly seconded Marshal Foch's proposal. If he correctly understood the telegram received from General Nudant at Spa, it was the German Peace Commission that had notified to the representative of the Allied and Associated Governments at Spa, the clear and categorical refusal of the German Government to allow the Poles to land at Dantzig, since the message in question had been given officially to General Nudant, Marshal Foch's representative at Spa. Under those conditions he did not think Marshal Foch could be asked to proceed to Spa without giving him at the same time full authority to compel the Germans to submit.

PRESIDENT WILSON thought that if it were considered that a question of dignity was involved, he would like to ask whether it was more undignified to make sure that the Germans understood what was wanted, than it would be to send troops by another route, as proposed by Marshal Foch. In his opinion, to send troops by another route than Dantzig would constitute an entire yielding to German demands. He thought, therefore, it would be far more dignified to renew conversations with the Germans.

MR. LLOYD GEORGE said that to bring the discussion to a point he proposed, definitely, that Marshal Foch should be authorised to place the demands of the Allied and Associated Governments before the German Delegates, calling upon them to comply with the conditions of Clause XVI of the Armistice, the correct interpretation of which would be set forth. He quite agreed that Marshal Foch should not be asked to make a demand, which the Allied and Associated Governments were not prepared to impose; but if the Germans refused to comply with the just interpretation of the terms of the Armistice, that would naturally constitute a serious matter. He thought most of the difficulties which had been raised by the Germans had reference to the occupation of the port of Dantzig. Marshal Foch treated the question of the passage of the troops between Dantzig and Thorn as a march through an enemy country, where bases and lines of communication would have to be held. Clause XVI of the Armistice, however, merely stipulated "free passage" and, therefore, Marshal Foch's demands should be restricted to the free passage of troops from Dantzig to Poland, and the port of Dantzig should not be held any longer than was required for the troops to pass through. In his opinion it was possible that the Germans thought that the demands of the Allied and the Associated Governments merely constituted a method of prejudging the question of the ownership of Dantzig in favour of Poland. The Allies and Associated Governments, however, were entitled to the use of this route, and Marshal Foch should make it quite clear to the Germans that if free passage were not allowed, that would constitute a breach of the armistice, and he would return to Paris to consult with the Supreme War Council in regard to the further measures to be taken.

MARSHAL FOCH argued that a clear and categorical refusal had already been given to the question he had been asked to put to the Germans. Suppose he agreed to repeat the question and met with the same reply, he could then hardly tell the Germans that he would proceed to Paris to consider what should be done. He felt that if he agreed to go to Spa he should have full discretion to take the necessary measures, should he meet with a refusal.

MR. LLOYD GEORGE thought his proposal had not been fully understood by Marshal Foch. In his opinion, in the event of the Germans declining to accede to his demands, Marshal Foch should be authorised forthwith to tell the Germans that their refusal constituted a breach of the armistice, and that he would proceed to Paris merely to decide what means should be taken to enforce his demands, namely, whether troops would be marched into Germany, or whether economic restrictions would be imposed.

He drew attention, however, to the fact that he did not know exactly what demands had been put forward by the Polish Commission to the Germans. The Conference had seen General Nudant's telegram giving the reply of the German Commission, but no information was given in regard to the question put to the Germans.

PRESIDENT WILSON agreed with Mr. Lloyd George that General Nudant's telegram gave the reply to demands which had been made by the Allies, but it was not known what those demands were.

MARSHAL FOCH expressed the view that if the Conference considered that the terms of the armistice established the right of free passage through Dantzig, it would be sufficient for the Supreme War Council to inform the German Government of its intention to apply Article XVI of the Armistice and the necessary steps could then be taken to enforce compliance. It would not be necessary, therefore, for him to proceed to Spa.

MR LLOYD GEORGE said that someone would have to present the demand to the Germans.

M. CLEMENCEAU suggested a written document could be delivered by Marshal Foch.

MR. LLOYD GEORGE agreed to M. Clemenceau's proposal, provided it were made perfectly clear in the document that an occupation of Dantzig was not intended, but merely a free passage through Dantzig.

M. CLEMENCEAU said he understood that Marshal Foch's proposal was accepted, namely, that the Supreme War Council would draft its demands and Marshal Foch would proceed to Spa to present the document to the German Delegates.

MARSHAL FOCH agreed that he would transmit the document to Spa, stating that the Supreme War Council demanded the execution of Clause XVI of the Armistice. At the same time, in reference to Mr. Lloyd George's argument, it would be necessary to establish a base at Dantzig in order to supervise the embarkation and entrainment of the Polish troops. He thought, therefore, that the document should contain a statement to the effect that provisions should be made by the Germans for the landing of the troops, housing and transport.

M. CLEMENCEAU understood that Marshal Foch would himself take the document to Spa.

MARSHAL FOCH said that he would telegraph the document to his representative, General Nudant, at Spa, since it was not intended that he should discuss the question with the German Delegates, and General Nudant was there to see to the execution of the clauses of the armistice. He would, therefore, merely tell General Nudant to insist on the execution of the conditions contained in Clause XVI of the Armistice which conditions had been held in abeyance.

MR. LLOYD GEORGE said he would ask the Conference to accept the following resolution:

"It is agreed: That Marshal Foch shall receive full authority to demand from the Germans that Clause XVI of the Armistice of November 11th shall be so interpreted as to permit the free passage of General Haller's army, as part of the Allied army, to Poland through Dantzig, to maintain order in Poland. That he will inform them that this passage does not involve a permanent occupation of the port of Dantzig and that a refusal to accede to this demand will be interpreted as a breach of the armistice by Germany. In the event of a refusal on the part of the Germans to accede to this demand Marshal Foch will inform them that the armistice has been broken and that he is returning to Paris to take the instructions of the Allied and Associated Governments as to the action to be taken."

MARSHAL FOCH maintained that if the intention were merely to apply Clause XVI of the armistice, it would only be necessary to call on the Germans to execute its provisions.

MR. LLOYD GEORGE said that it would be necessary to insist on the Germans interpreting Clause XVI to mean that General Haller's Army must be given free passage through Dantzig in order to proceed to Poland for the purpose of maintaining order, and that the passage asked for did not mean the occupation of Dantzig.

MARSHAL FOCH called attention to the fact that Mr. Lloyd George's resolution contained a statement to the effect that the free passage of General Haller's Army to Poland did not involve the occupation of the port of Dantzig. In his opinion, no such undertaking could be given since it would be necessary to constitute a temporary base at Dantzig in order to supervise the disembarkation and entrainment of the troops, operations which might continue for two or three months, if five or six divisions were to be transferred.

MR. LLOYD GEORGE expressed the view that such temporary establishments could not be defined as an occupation. Nevertheless, if the Conference preferred he would suggest adding the words: "that every facility must be given for the temporary accommodation of the troops passing through the port."

PRESIDENT WILSON said he did not like to force on Marshal Foch an unacceptable mission. If Marshal Foch's judgment were against this, the Conference should not urge him to undertake it, and should he so desire, some other channel of communication should be sought. He could see that the mission was extremely distasteful to Marshal Foch, and he did not wish to insist on his carrying out a work against his wishes. As an alternative, he would therefore suggest that the Supreme War Council should draw up its demands in writing to be conveyed in a formal manner to the German Delegates through General Nudant at Spa. That would be a less impressive way than the delivery of the message by Marshal Foch in person; but this method might have to be taken if the Marshal did not like to undertake the duty himself.

MR. LLOYD GEORGE agreed that it might be necessary to find some other channel of communication; but he did not think the proposal to transmit the message through General Nudant was a good one.

PRESIDENT WILSON said he would read, for the information of the Conference, a portion of M. Noulens' despatch dated Posen, 18th March, 1919:

"The following conclusions have been reported by the Commission which returned to Warsaw on March 15th, after having been instructed to go to Dantzig to examine the possibilities of disembarking Polish troops: this operation will be very easy, for the wharfs, in particular those of Kaiserhafen, are large and well-suited for unloading several large steamers. The apparatus for unloading is sufficient. There are also two large empty warehouses for the housing of troops, and accommodation and sheds for material and provisions. The railways connect the quays with the principal lines; in a word, all facilities exist for a fairly extensive disembarkation of troops. Colonel Marshall and Intendant Gruet[2] started for Paris on Sunday, and will give all detailed information with a view to effecting as soon as possible the despatch of General Haller's troops, the urgency of which is felt more and more."

M. CLEMENCEAU said that, putting aside altogether his own personal opinions, which by the way coincided with those of M. Pichon, he would allow himself to ask Marshal Foch whether he would not subordinate his own personal feelings and inclinations, in order to remain the mouthpiece of the Allies—and they were Allies. It was essential that no dissensions should appear among the Allies on the eve of taking a decision which might lead to very serious consequences, even to a renewal of hostilities. Marshal Foch had been the Commander-in-Chief of the Allied Armies and had led them magnificently to victory. He had thus acquired great influence, and unless he were the Allied spokesman on this occasion, the Germans would be led to believe that serious differences existed among the Allies, and these imaginary differences would be taken to explain the delays which had occurred, even though he and his colleagues

[2] Neither can be further identified.

knew that a delay was unavoidable, owing to the inherent difficulties of the questions to be settled. Nevertheless, the Germans
would take this as further evidence that disagreements existed
between the Allies and would draw therefrom additional encouragement. He trusted that such an unfortunate incident would be
avoided and that a formula would be found, which would meet
Marshal Foch's objections. With this object in view, Mr. Lloyd
George had proposed the following amended resolution:

"It is agreed: That Marshal Foch shall receive full authority to
demand from the Germans that under Clause 16 of the Armistice
of November 11th, they shall permit the free passage of General
Haller's army, as part of the Allied Army, to Poland through Dantzig
to maintain order in Poland. That he shall inform them that this
passage does not involve the occupation of the port of Dantzig,
although every facility must be given for the temporary accommodation of the troops passing through the port. That he shall notify
the Germans that a refusal to accede to this demand will be interpreted as a breach of the armistice by Germany. In the event of a
refusal on the part of the Germans to accede to this demand, Marshal Foch is instructed to take counsel with the Supreme War
Council as to the action to be taken."

MARSHAL FOCH thought there existed a contradiction in the resolution just read. On the one hand, he was given full authority to
make demands, whilst on the other hand, he was told to come back
for further instructions. In other words, he was authorised to speak,
but not to act.

M. CLEMENCEAU explained that it would only be necessary for
Marshal Foch to consult with the Supreme War Council as to the
particular action to be taken in the event of a refusal. In his opinion,
Marshal Foch should merely deliver the message to the German
delegates at Spa, and then return immediately to Paris. On receipt
of the Germans' reply, the Marshal would then consult the Council
as to the further measures to be taken.

MARSHAL FOCH said that he did not think it necessary that he
should go to Spa merely to deliver a letter.

M. CLEMENCEAU replied that the Council placed considerable
importance on the delivery of the message by Marshal Foch in
person.

MARSHAL FOCH called attention to the fact that he would find no-
one at Spa, except General Hammerstein,[3] who would say he had
no authority; he was merely a letter-box and he himself also had
a letter-box, a representative at Spa, in the person of General Nudant.

[3] Gen. Hans, Baron von Hammerstein, military representative on the German Armistice
Commission.

MR LLOYD GEORGE enquired whether no means existed for informing the Germans that Marshal Foch would come to Spa to lay an ultimatum before them on the subject of the transport of troops to Poland, and that a delegate should be sent to receive that message. In that case the question would not be left to General Hammerstein.

MARSHAL FOCH agreed that if a German Plenipotentiary were sent to receive the message he would go; but otherwise he did not see what useful purpose would be gained by his proceeding to Spa.

PRESIDENT WILSON thought that Marshal Foch clearly regarded this Mission, for some reason which he could not understand, as humiliating to himself. He (President Wilson) was the last man to propose anything that was humiliating to a man he so much admired as Marshal Foch. Therefore, he would ask Marshal Foch to suggest a solution of the difficulty.

MARSHAL FOCH saw nothing humiliating to himself in the proposal under consideration. He only saw in the proposal a violation of the principle which had so far governed his relations with the Germans. In other words, he was now asked to talk and argue with the Germans, whereas his strength had so far lain in silence. In reply to President Wilson's question, he proposed that a telegram to the following effect should be sent:

"The Supreme War Council calls the attention of the German Government to Article XVI of the Armistice and demands its immediate execution in regard to the disembarkation and free passage of troops from Dantzig to Thorn, and the grant of all facilities for the transport of the Polish forces. Guarantees shall be given for the complete execution of the conditions contained in that clause. Refusal to comply with the demands herein contained shall constitute a breach of the Armistice, leading to immediate renewal of hostilities."

PRESIDENT WILSON enquired whether any means existed for communicating with the Authorities in Berlin, who might be informed that the Supreme War Council had received a message from General Nudant, which was not understood. The German Authorities would at the same time be informed that the Allied and Associated Governments had decided to send the Polish troops through Dantzig to Poland, and they desired the Berlin Authorities to give the necessary instructions to their military authorities on this point. He should be glad to know whether there was any direct or indirect channel of communication with Berlin.

MR LLOYD GEORGE thought that no other means of communication existed, except through Spa.

PRESIDENT WILSON suggested that no decision should be taken until General Nudant's promised reports had been received, so that the Conference might know exactly what demands had been put forward by M. Noulens, and whether those demands were consistent with the terms of the Armistice.

MR LLOYD GEORGE thought that the proposals put forward by M. Noulens might have been inconsistent with the letter of Article XVI. In this connection he called attention to the following extract from the Minutes of the Conference held on the 19th March:

"M. CAMBON said that he had received a telegram from M. Noulens to the effect that the Germans wished to discuss the question of the landing of Polish troops at Dantzig at Spa instead of with the Inter-Allied Commission in Poland. A draft telegram had been prepared for the approval of the Council in answer to this message.

GENERAL WEYGAND explained that Marshal Foch had given orders to the Armistice Commission at Spa that any discussion on this subject should be refused, and that the Germans should be referred to the Inter-Allied Commission in Poland. A copy of this information had been sent to M. Noulens for his information."

PRESIDENT WILSON called attention to the fact that the Warsaw Commission had been instructed to arrange for the receipt and transportation of the Polish troops at Dantzig. The Germans, on the other hand, had asked to have the discussion transferred to Spa, and the Council had been told that this request had been refused. The Germans then refused to discuss the matter further. This might be a perfectly proper refusal, and he suggested that M. Cambon be called on to furnish all the correspondence on the subject, so that the Council should know exactly what M. Noulens' Commission had asked and what had been refused.

M. CAMBON explained that the Secretariat-General of the Peace Conference had from time to time forwarded to him, as Chairman of the Committee on Polish Affairs, all the documents received from M. Noulens in order to keep him fully advised. The day before yesterday the following telegram, dated Posen March 18th, 1919, received from M. Noulens, had been communicated to him:

"The Inter-Allied Commission has taken note of the declaration according to which the Berlin Government guarantees the safety of transport on German territory, but the Commission protests against the inadequacy of the reply on the other points of detail set forth by the Commission at the Conference held at Kreutz on March 5th.

"As a matter of fact, the German Government is seeking all possible ways of escape in order to delay and avoid the landing of Polish troops at Dantzig.

"We have proof of this in intercepted telegrams. If the Allied Governments do not rush things through and demand the complete execution of Article XVI of the Armistice, the Germans will manoeuvre between the Commission of Spa and that of Warsaw in order to delay all decisions.

"As the Allied Governments have instructed the Warsaw Commission to find a solution to this question we demand that the Berlin Government should be once more informed of the matter officially, and that the Commission at Spa should force the Germans to address themselves to us and insist on their submitting, without delay, in all the measures of detail which the Inter-Allied Military Commission may have to require. Further, the Inter-Allied Commission at Warsaw holds it necessary that the Naval Forces of the Entente should immediately make a considerable demonstration opposite Dantzig. This will be the way to prevent the Germans stirring up troubles on the day before that when the port will be opened to the troops of General Haller, and assigned according to the wireless messages to Poland."

A draft telegram had been prepared by him for the approval of the Council in answer to this message; but General Weygand had explained to the Meeting that Marshal Foch had already, in reply to a similar telegram, received by him, given orders to the Armistice Commission at Spa that any discussion on this subject should be refused, and that the Germans should be referred to the Inter-Allied Commission in Poland. A copy of this order had also been sent to M. Noulens for his information. Consequently, there was nothing more to be said.

MR. LLOYD GEORGE drew attention to a previous telegram of the same date, signed by M. Noulens, which read as follows:

"The pourparlers with the German Delegation are almost ended. As a result of our demand with regard to the disembarkation of Polish troops at Dantzig, von Rechenberg[4] has just written to say that the German Delegation had no authority to consider this point, and that his Government had the right, and also the duty, of approaching the Armistice Commission at Spa, as the exact interpretation of Article XVI was not fixed. He added, 'My Government authorises me to say that, in the event of an eventual disembarkation at Dantzig, it would doubtless reserve the right to discuss the application of the principle set up by the Agreement of the 11th November, but that it was able to guarantee the safety of transport on German territory.'

"Finally, as the Commission complained some time ago that orders had not been given to the local authorities at Dantzig when our Mission arrived there, von Rechenberg says that it will be necessary to be informed in advance of the time fixed for disembar-

---

[4] Albrecht, Baron von Rechenberg, a former Consul General in Warsaw, at this time a member of a German delegation to implement the German-Polish armistice.

kation, the numbers and composition of the expeditionary corps, and the length of time it will stay in Dantzig."

In his opinion, the requests made by the German Delegation were very reasonable and there was nothing contained therein which would justify the renewal of hostilities.

In regard to the reply sent by General Weygand to the telegram read by M. Cambon, he regretted that the question had not first been referred to the Supreme War Council.

GENERAL WEYGAND explained that he had sent the telegram on his own responsibility, because the Supreme War Council had authorised the Commission in Poland to take all necessary action.

PRESIDENT WILSON said that the Conference was still ignorant as to the demands made by M. Noulens to the German Government. That is to say, the Conference did not know what their Commission had demanded and what had been refused.

M. CAMBON said that the following telegram sent by M. Noulens on the 16th March, 1919, gave some indication as to the demands made by him to the German Government:

"On account of the frequent bombardment of the Polish front by the Germans, the Inter-Allied Commission at Posen has thought it necessary to impose on both the parties the obligation to withdraw their artillery to a distance of 20 kilometres on either side of the line of demarcation. This condition, which had at first been accepted by the Germans at Kreutz, has subsequently been put in question by them. They state to-day that the German High Command refuses to withdraw the artillery to a greater distance than 6 kilometres from the line.

"As regards Dantzig, after having declared that they awaited instructions, and thereby delayed a solution of the question, the German Delegates state to-day that their Government wished to discuss the question at Spa. This request is put forward in the hope that different views may be taken by the various Missions representing the Allied Governments. It is necessary that the German answer should be given to the Commission charged with the study of the question of the debarkation of Polish troops at Dantzig. The local authorities at Dantzig have been given permission to the Mission of Lt.-Col. Marshall to study the available resources for this operation, but they have refrained from giving any assistance and from taking any engagements on the pretext that they had received no instructions from their Government. We have therefore actually no guarantees that the disembarkation can be carried out with safety. The Inter-Allied Commission considers it indispensable in order to put an end to the dilatory proceedings of the German

Delegation that the wishes of the Allied Governments should be communicated to Berlin by the Allied High Command."

It was on the strength of that telegram that he had drafted a reply for the approval of the Supreme War Council, informing M. Noulens that negotiations would not be transferred to Spa and should be continued by him at Posen.

PRESIDENT WILSON said that the telegrams which had been read showed that everything was approaching a satisfactory conclusion on the 17th and 18th, while on the 20th everything was exploded. In that connection he would again invite attention to the fact that General Dupont had telegraphed to General Nudant from Berlin that negotiations at Posen had been broken off for reasons given by M. Noulens. General Nudant, in forwarding that message had said:

"In confirmation of these incidents, the German Commission after sending several vague notes has communicated to me this morning a note which amounts to a clear and categorical refusal (1) to let Poles land at Dantzig, (2) to authorise officers of Warsaw Mission to proceed to territory occupied by the Germans to the east of the Vistula."

He again wished to draw attention to the fact that the Conference did not know what the "vague notes" referred to by General Nudant were, nor what it was that had been categorically refused by the Germans.

GENERAL WEYGAND explained that the telegram from General Nudant, just read by President Wilson, had been despatched at 14 hours 15 the previous afternoon. At the same time, the papers relating thereto had been sent by special messenger, but they could not reach Paris before tomorrow, the 22nd March.

MR. LLOYD GEORGE suggested that what was interpreted as "a clear and categorical refusal" would probably be found to be due to the refusal given to the Germans to discuss the question at Spa. It was probable that the German delegates at Posen were not authorised by the German Government to carry out the necessary negotiations relating to Armistice Conditions, which had invariably been carried out at Spa. He sincerely regretted the fact that General Weygand had sent his reply without first consulting the Supreme War Council, especially as the telegram was one which might have led to very serious results, including the resumption of hostilities.

GENERAL WEYGAND explained that the telegram from M. Noulens to which he had replied was one dated the 12th March 1919, which read as follows:

"The Inter-Allied Commission of Warsaw learns from intercepted telegrams that the German Government were inclined to refuse to grant passes to Allied officers to study the preparatory measures to be taken in connection with the transport of troops through Dantzig, stating that a request had already been forwarded to Marshal Foch requesting that the troops should be disembarked at Königsberg and at Libau. That proposal would put aside the decision taken by the Inter-Allied Commission to insist on the enforcement of Article XVI of the Armistice of November last. Should another port be approved by the Allied Governments, the Germans would take that condition to imply a disavowal of the Commission; inevitable complications would delay the transportation of the troops; and lastly, the fear of insurrections which the Germans invoked as a reason for keeping the troops away from Dantzig would certainly take place, whereas it was hoped that the early arrival of Haller's Division and the authority which that event would give us to reason with the Poles, were likely to prevent the occurrence of any disturbances."

General Weygand, continuing, said that he had forthwith replied to that telegram, because he knew that the Germans, if unable to get what they wanted in one way always tried to get it by other means. In this case again their intention had been to complicate the issue and to create dissensions. Had he given any other reply to the Germans, they would have taken it as a disavowal of the Commission, to whom the Council had given full powers to settle this question. Thus, M. Noulens having been given full authority, the Germans appealed to Spa, and Dantzig having been selected as the port of debarkation, the Germans offered Königsberg or Libau. Consequently, he had felt justified in replying at once to M. Noulens to allow him to continue his negotiations.

M. CLEMENCEAU suggested that under the circumstances the meeting should be adjourned to await the receipt of General Nudant's reports from Spa. A telegram should also be despatched forthwith to M. Noulens asking him to report in clear and precise terms what demands had been made to the Germans. He regretted that an adjournment until Monday should be necessary; but that was unavoidable even though the Germans might thereby gain confidence from a knowledge of the fact that no decision had been reached.

MR. LLOYD GEORGE suggested that a copy of the exact answer given by the German Delegation should also be obtained.

M. PICHON proposed sending the following telegram to M. Noulens at Warsaw:

"You are requested to telegraph immediately the exact terms of your demands to the German Commission to permit Allied Polish troops to disembark to Dantzig and their free passage on the railway line to Thorn: also the precise replies made by the Germans."

MR. LLOYD GEORGE requested that the reports received from General Nudant should forthwith be circulated.

MARSHAL FOCH enquired whether, pending further decision, the transportation of troops by rail to Poland was duly authorized.

The transportation of troops by that route would be extremely slow, but still some results would be obtained.

MR. LLOYD GEORGE thought that President Wilson's comment on that subject was irrefutable. Should the Allied and Associated Governments agree to send the Polish troops to Cracow by that route after the Germans had refused passage through Dantzig, it would mean yielding to the German pretensions.

PRESIDENT WILSON suggested that in the interval preparations for the expedition of the troops to Dantzig should be completed.

M. PICHON enquired, in view of the fact that an adjournment had been agreed to, whether the fact should not be published that the Supreme War Council had decided upon the transportation of the Polish troops via Dantzig.

MR. LLOYD GEORGE thought it would be advisable to wait before publishing anything on the subject.

MR. BALFOUR pointed out that considerable difficulty existed in connection with the supply of the required tonnage for the transport of troops via Dantzig. He was informed by the experts that passenger ships would alone be suitable for this work, and that none were available, unless ships at present employed for the transport of British and American troops were temporarily withdrawn for the purpose.

PRESIDENT WILSON pointed out that the Allied Maritime Transport Council had already been called upon, in accordance with a decision taken on the 17th March last, to submit a scheme showing what should be the contribution in shipping of each of the Allied and Associated Governments for the transport of General Haller's troops from France to Dantzig.

MR. LLOYD GEORGE thought it would be extremely unwise under these circumstances to publish the fact that the Supreme War Council had decided to send General Haller's Army to Poland by sea, because considerable difficulties existed in regard to tonnage, the withdrawal of which would seriously affect the shipping programme relating to Australian troops.

(It was agreed:

(1) To send the following telegram to M. Noulens at Warsaw:

"You are requested to telegraph immediately the exact terms of your demands to the German Commission to permit Allied Polish troops to disembark at Dantzig and their free passage on the railway line to Thorn also the precise replies made by the Germans."

(2) To adjourn further consideration of the question pending receipt and circulation of reports to be received from General Nudant for M. Noulens.

(3) To obtain report from the Allied Maritime Council, in accordance with the decision taken on 17th March, 1919.)

(The Meeting then adjourned.)

T MS (SDR, RG 256, 180.03101/61, DNA).

Hankey's Notes of a Meeting of the Council of Ten[1]

BC-55   Quai d'Orsay, March 21, 1919, 6 p.m.

MR. LLOYD GEORGE said that he raised the following question with considerable disinclination. It would be in the recollection of the Conference that on Tuesday last[2] a discussion took place on the subject of Poland. It was necessary that at these meetings the members should express themselves quite freely and quite clearly. He was therefore surprised on the following morning to find in the French papers not only a full report of the Committee's finding illustrated by secret maps; but, in addition, a garbled account of what he himself had said in the Council.[3] The account contained actual quotations of the words used by him between quotation marks. Had a verbatim report been given, he would not have objected so strongly. But the report gave a very wrong impression of what he had said, and the distortion permitted an opportunity for violent attacks against him. He did not mind the personal attacks, except in so far as they did undoubtedly tend to create ill-feeling, more especially as England itself was abused for its action in Syria.

The Conference would recollect that President Wilson had on a previous occasion drawn the attention of the Council to a similar occurrence.[4] The report then complained of had also been a very garbled version of what had actually taken place at the meeting. There had been sufficient evidence to justify the conclusion that the information must have come from British sources and had probably been supplied by someone who had been present at the meeting. Feeling that the honour of the British Delegation was thereby involved, he had directed that measures be taken in order

---

[1] The complete text of these minutes is printed in PPC, IV, 443-47.
[2] He meant Wednesday, March 19.
[3] For a brief discussion of these articles, see Noble, Policies and Opinions at Paris, 1919, pp. 309, 346n38.
[4] See the minutes of the meeting of the Council of Ten printed at Jan. 30, 1919, 11 a.m., Vol. 54.

to discover the offender. The case was tracked down, with the result that not only was the person concerned dealt with as far as possible, but also the newspaper correspondent responsible was sent away from Paris. He was afraid from internal evidence that the incident now complained of had come from French sources, for reasons which he could give. It was most unfortunate that such disclosures should be made, and he felt sure that the French delegates would not resent his taking notice of the matter. That very afternoon General Bliss had told him that an American gentleman just returned from Berlin stated that the disclosures which were daily appearing in the papers in connection with the peace negotiations were causing the greatest harm in Germany. From what this witness had seen and heard in Germany, he felt convinced that if the whole peace terms, however stiff, were at once presented, they would be accepted. But the disclosure of one condition at a time had the effect of driving the Germans to desperation, especially as each new thing was published to the world with the suggestion that the Allies were not agreed among themselves. He wished to speak quite plainly, and to say that if similar disclosures were to be repeated, he would much prefer not to take any further part in the discussions, and to put off expressing his views until the final Conference took place. A perusal of the articles complained of would make it clear that someone who had been present in the room was responsible for the disclosure, and his colleagues would agree that it would be impossible to continue these discussions if such incidents were likely to recur.

It would be in the recollection of some of his colleagues that he had hesitated to agree to the Peace Conference meeting in a capital, because he was afraid that the local press would take an undue part in the proceedings, and attempt to influence decisions by an injudicious criticism of the delegates of other countries. The mere fact that the Peace Conference was meeting in Paris should transform the city for the moment from a French into an international capital.

It would be unnecessary for him to lay stress on the fact that the occurrence of such incidents only tended to encourage the Germans to give the public the wrong impression that the Allies were only fighting each other for individual advantages. Consequently, such incidents must be put a stop to; strong action must be taken to prevent the possibility of their recurrence; otherwise, that Conference would become absolutely futile.

M. CLEMENCEAU said that he could only thank Mr. Lloyd George for his statement, which he accepted in the spirit in which it was made. Mr. Lloyd George would recognise how difficult it was to supervise the press. The pressmen had entry into all Government offices, and it was impossible to prevent leakage occurring. He could only express his deep regret that the articles referred to had found their way in the press, and he promised to take every possible measure to prevent a recurrence of the incidents complained of. Here, in France, the press censorship still functioned; but the Government did not dare to enforce it too rigorously. Nevertheless, he would do his best to stop the publication of such harmful articles. He agreed word for word with everything that Mr. Lloyd George had said. Nothing had done more to put the Allies in the wrong light with the Germans than the indiscretions of the press. He promised to do his best to prevent a repetition of such indiscretions. But he could hardly guarantee that nothing of the kind would ever occur again.

MR. LLOYD GEORGE drew attention to the fact that the articles complained of had been published in the "Temps," the "Journal," and the "Echo de Paris." As was well known, the "Temps" was, at any rate, supposed to be in close touch with the Government, so that the article in question became doubly mischievous. His complaint, however, was not directed against the press. His chief point was that someone sitting in that room had deliberately given the information complained of to the press with a definite purpose. He fully agreed with M. Clemenceau that it was impossible to control the press, but it should be possible to prevent responsible officials from giving away such information, especially when the information so given was deliberately altered in order to make it the ground for a violent attack on one of the Allied countries.

M. CLEMENCEAU said he would make very serious protests to the directors of the "Temps." At the same time he would point out that in France a press censorship still existed which did not exist in Great Britain and America, consequently measures could be taken for its proper application.

PRESIDENT WILSON enquired whether in M. Clemenceau's opinion a severe enquiry could not be instituted to discover who had given out the information about Poland.

MR. LLOYD GEORGE explained that the British authorities had in the previous case instituted a stern inquiry, with the result that the offender had been discovered. He thought that if the French Government were to make a stern and persistent enquiry, the culprit in this case would also be found. In his opinion, the culprit ought to be tracked down, otherwise discussion here would become impossible.

M. CLEMENCEAU agreed.

MR. BALFOUR invited attention to another aspect of the same case.

The same leakage was taking place in regard to Commissions and Committees, with the result that the members who had expressed an opinion on any question were subsequently lectured by outside parties. For instance, he himself had mentioned at one of the meetings that the port of Dantzig constituted a difficult problem. In consequence, M. Dmowski had called on him and talked to him for a considerable time on his supposed anti-Polish feelings; though, as a matter of fact, he was a great supporter of the Poles. The point, however, was this, namely, that as a result of his having made a remark at a secret meeting, an outside diplomat had forthwith been sent to him to discuss the whole question.

PRESIDENT WILSON said he could confirm Mr. Balfour's statement, because he himself had first learnt of the decisions about to be reached by Commissions from outside parties against whom the decision was going to be given. In his opinion, every member of the Delegations should take steps to ensure that no one connected with his Delegation was to blame.

M. CLEMENCEAU enquired whether, to begin with, a notice should not be circulated to all members of the Peace Conference, enjoining strict secrecy.

MR. LANSING pointed out that the whole of the military and naval terms had been published in the press.

M. SONNINO said that whilst all were agreed in regard to the question of the Press, the proceedings of Committees and Commissions presented a greater difficulty. In his opinion, a circular should be issued to all members of the Commissions impressing on them the necessity for reticence. He thought a great many people talked almost unconsciously; therefore, a circular might be useful.

MR. LLOYD GEORGE expressed the view that whoever was responsible for giving the information should not be allowed in the Council Chamber. The incident to which he had called attention presented the same characteristics as the previous case, that is, it contained a communication in inverted commas, which could only have been given by someone who had been present in the room.

M. PICHON said that he agreed with all that had been said by M. Clemenceau. He merely wished to add that severe instructions had been given to the Press, and daily a great number of articles and paragraphs were suppressed by the press censor. An enquiry would, however, be carried out as suggested by Mr. Lloyd George.

(It was agreed:

(1) That a strict and severe enquiry should be instituted by the French Authorities in order to discover, if possible, the name of the person who had given information to the Press in regard to the Conversation held at the Quai d'Orsay about Poland.

(2) That a circular should be issued by the Secretariat General to members of the Peace Conference impressing on them the necessity for strict reticence in regard to the proceedings of the Conference.)

(The Meeting then adjourned.)

T MS (SDR, RG 256, 180.03101/62, DNA).

From Robert Lansing

My dear Mr. President: Paris, March 21, 1919.

Mr. Polk has asked me to take up with you the directions he should issue to the Secretary of War in reference to the policy and orders under which General Graves should act in Siberia.[1] The situation is extremely complex on account of the bitterness between Russian factions. General Graves feels unable to support either the Reactionary or Liberal parties, and so incurs criticism by both. He would like to know whether his policy of considering the Bolshevik trouble in Siberia as an internal trouble, in which he should take no part, conforms with the policy of the Department.

Mr. Polk recommends that General Graves make clear to the various Russian military authorities that reactionary methods on the part of such commanders will paralyze United States assistance to Russia and create a strong contra public sentiment in America; and further, that General Graves be instructed to use the prestige of his forces, without assisting one Russian faction against another, to influence all to a policy of moderation, accompanying such policy with a statement that the United States will not lend itself to measures savoring of counter-revolution or reaction. Mr. Polk feels that the support that General Graves is to lend Mr. Stevens will require him, not only to use his good offices to prevent factional conflicts, but to use force where communications or the safety of our men is threatened. An added element is that perhaps General Graves has not the necessary diplomatic and political ability to steer safely a difficult middle course and further, that it may be hard to come to a co-operative agreement with the Japanese to follow out such a policy, moderate in purpose but broad in its scope.

I feel that our general policy in Siberia is to favor economic rehabilitation, divorced as far as possible from internal politics. Our particular effort is to keep the Siberian and Chinese Eastern Railway open, and free from one nation and one faction control; and the present purpose and duty of General Graves' forces is to protect such operation of the railroad. I fear that due to the complexity of the situation, and inexperience of General Graves in such matters, general instructions to him to use the prestige of his forces to prevent factional quarrels, in light of the Japanese attitude, would be dangerous, offer small chance of success and might involve very dubious results. The following policy would seem preferable and is agreed to by General Bliss and Mr. Williams.[2] Instruct General Graves that the United States favors economic rehabilitation of the country and feels strongly that a policy of political moderation among the several Russian factions is a necessary condition. In particular General Graves should be told that his mission is to insure, in cooperation with his Allies, uninterrupted operation of the Siberian and Chinese Eastern Railway; and that, in a zone to be limited say to three miles on either side of the Railroad, his instructions should be to exercise definite police power, and to prevent any disturbances whatsoever which might interfere with the operation of the Railroad. Positive instructions of such a character, while involving possible use of force, would be strictly limited in territorial scope and be carried out under a definite purpose easily understood by General Graves, unequivocal in nature and difficult to misrepresent. Such policy should have a certain appeal to the different factions and offers a point of agreement. If strongly followed it would accomplish definite good, would tend to have the support of home public opinion and would avoid pitfalls.

If this course should be agreed to by the other powers having military forces in Siberia it might be advisable to issue a general notice to all concerned that the Interallied Committee will not permit any disorder within the railway zone and will use the forces at its disposal to preserve the peace.

I should appreciate an expression of your opinion for the guidance of Mr. Polk in his instructions to the War Department.

Faithfully yours,   Robert Lansing.

TLS (SDR, RG 256, 861.00/391A, DNA).
  [1] FLP to RL and V. C. McCormick, March 13, 1919, Vol. 55.
  [2] That is, Edward Thomas Williams, head of the Far Eastern Division of the State Department.

From Robert Lansing, with Enclosure

My dear Mr. President: Paris, March 21, 1919.

I am enclosing a copy of a telegram which has just been received from Mr. Gary, American Diplomatic Agent in Cairo,[1] in which he outlines the critical condition now prevailing in Egypt and suggests the advisability of discussing the matter with the British Government which, it appears, does not fully appreciate the gravity of the situation.

This question is extremely delicate and accordingly I am not inclined to send any information to the Department of State or to Mr. Gary, for his guidance, until you have communicated to me your views on the matter.

Very sincerely yours,   Robert Lansing

TLS (WP, DLC).
   [1] Hampson Gary, also Consul General in Egypt.

E   N   C   L   O   S   U   R   E

Cairo, March 18, 1919.

URGENT. Please forward the following telegram to the Department and American Peace Commission. 588 March 18, 4:00 p.m. Referring to my cable of March 16, 7:00 p.m.[1] The situation in Egypt is now exceedingly grave. The disturbance is losing its character as a political demonstration and is rapidly developing into Bolshevism in which law and order are being overborne by the worst element of the population and the movement is showing indications of an animus against all foreigners and their property. The civil and military authorities, and even the leaders of the Nationalists Party who instigated the original demonstrations, have become alarmed. The Nationalists leaders have lost control over their peoples and are now trying to help the British restore order. The military authorities hesitate to infuriate the country further by employing force to quell the uprisings throughout Egypt nor indeed have they a sufficient force here to do so.

The Acting High Commissioner[2] sent for me today. He outlined the situation and stated that at no time since the Araby rebellion in 1862[3] has the state of (omission) been so critical. He told me that he has fully informed London of all the facts but is unable to elicit instructions and he intimated that he desires me to report the serious conditions to my Government in the hope that it would exert promptly some influence upon his own Government and thus make them appreciate the gravity of the situation. He said that he might have to call upon me to assist in the restoration of order, undoubtedly realizing that on account of the warm relationship that all Egyptians feel for the United States an announcement by the American representative here would have great influence and perhaps prevent the destruction of life and property of foreigners.

The situation is hourly growing worse. Cairo is cut off from the rest of Egypt and the outside world except by aeroplane and wire-less. The Acting High Commissioner has called me to the residency to tell me that the situation is getting beyond control and to ask if I will be prepared to help in the matter if there is a possibility worst comes. I venture to suggest that the Acting High Commissioner's conversation as reported above should be considered confidential and not disclosed to his government.

I respectfully recommend that our Government promptly exert its good offices with the British Government and I ask for any particular instructions the Department may desire to give me. Please send instructions by cable wireless.

Gary,   American Diplomatic Agent.

T telegram (WP, DLC).
    [1] H. Gary to Amembassy, Paris, March 16, 1919, T telegram (WP, DLC). Gary reported on the spreading violence occasioned by the arrest and deportation of Sa'd Zaghlul and his colleagues, about which see G. F. Close to M. A. H. Kadi, March 20, 1919, n. 2. Gary warned that the "spirit of disorder" might soon spread to the Egyptian "peasantry," and that this in turn might threaten the lives and property of American missionaries. "I believe," he wrote, "that one of the Chief causes of the present unrest is the indef-initeness of the political status of the country and the failure to make announcement more clearly defining the British protectorate and the degree of autonomy Egyptians may expect thereunder."
    [2] That is, Sir Milne Cheetham.
    [3] He meant the so-called rebellion of 1882, not 1862, which centered around the Egyptian Minister of War, Ahmed Arabi. For the complicated history of this affair, which led directly to the British military occupation of Egypt in the summer of 1882, see John Marlowe, *Anglo-Egyptian Relations, 1800-1956*, 2d edn. (London, 1965), pp. 112-29.

From Ray Stannard Baker

My dear Mr. President: [Paris] March 21, 1919.

I have been thinking about the question which you asked me last night in regard to possible American members of the Syrian Commission.

Have you thought of Mr. George Rublee? He is at present prac-tically unoccupied and his experience with men and affairs I believe would make him a valuable man to consider. President Henry Churchill King of Oberlin College is in France. He may be a pos-sibility. He commands very high respect and esteem in America and is a man of liberal spirit.

I think you know both of these men well. Either would do for the principal member of the Commission. As for the expert on the affairs of Asia Minor, I have been very favorably impressed with what I have seen here of Mr. Westerman, who is the expert on this subject in our Peace Commission. He not only has a thoroughgoing knowledge of the affairs of Asiatic Turkey, but is a firm believer in the right of human beings to decide their own destiny.

There [These] are merely suggestions. If I can be of further assistance, in this matter, please command me.

Very sincerely yours,   Ray Stannard Baker

TLS (WP, DLC).

From George Lansbury

My dear President Wilson: London E.C 4 March 21st 1919.

Many thanks for your note. I have wired you to-day that I hope to be able to call on you at 12 o'clock on Tuesday next—25th March. I will call in at the Crillon and see Mr. Baker before doing so in order that I may know for certain where I shall find you.

Again thanking you,   Yours sincerely,   G Lansbury

TLS (WP, DLC).

To Joseph Patrick Tumulty

[Paris, c. March 21, 1919]

World poll of the newspapers has appeared in the papers over here.[1] Very useful. Please thank Mr. Taft for his message[2] and say that I expect it to be very useful. Best wishes from us.

T transcript of CLSsh (WP, DLC).

[1] The New York *World* had asked its correspondents in all parts of the United States to determine, as accurately as possible, the division of newspaper editorial opinion on the proposed League of Nations in their respective states. The *World*, on March 17, printed summaries of some fifty telegrams sent in reply, grouping them under five regional headings: East, South, Middle West, Northwest, and West. The *World* summarized the results as follows:

"A majority of the leading newspapers in the United States, which have declared themselves one way or another on the question, is in favor of the League of Nations.

"This statement applies generally to all sections of the country, from Maine to Texas, and from Georgia to Oregon, and is based upon dispatches from World correspondents who were asked to ascertain definitely the editorial opinions of the newspapers in their respective States.

"In answer to its inquiry, The World received nearly fifty telegrams from all sections of the country. In not one of these telegrams was the statement made that a majority of the dailies in any particular State openly opposed the league.

"Furthermore, very many of the correspondents reported that not only were the Democratic papers supporting President Wilson but that many of the Republican newspapers are openly advocating the President's policy. Some even go so far as to criticise Republican Senators for their opposition to the President.

"In some sections of the country there is a demand from the newspapers for more definite information; and those which oppose the league make it clear that modifications and amendments aimed to insure the future integrity of the Monroe Doctrine would meet their objections.

"In some instances correspondents found it impossible to state the exact number of papers in the State for or against the league. In such cases, without exception, information obtainable showed that by far the greater number of dailies favor the league, even eliminating those who have not declared themselves one way or the other."

For the complete results of the survey, which also revealed some significant regional variations of sentiment on the subject, see the New York *World*, March 17, 1919.

[2] That is, W. H. Taft to WW, March 18, 1919.

From William Howard Taft

[The White House] 21 March 1919

Number 24. The following letter from Hon. Wm. H. Taft: "I have thought perhaps it might help more if I was somewhat more specific than I was in the memorandum note I sent you yesterday,[1] and I therefore enclose another memorandum."

Duration of the Covenant.

Add to the Preamble the following:

"from the obligations of which any member of the League may withdraw after July 1, 1929, by two years' notice in writing, duly filed with the Secretary General of the League."

Explanation.

I have no doubt that the construction put upon the agreement would be what I understand the President has already said it should be, namely that any nation may withdraw from it upon reasonable notice, which perhaps would be a year. I think, however, it might strengthen the Covenant if there was a fixed duration. It would completely remove the objection that it is perpetual in its operation.

Duration of Armament Limit.

Add to the first paragraph of Article VIII, the following:

"At the end of every five years, such limits of armament for the several governments shall be reexamined by the Executive Council, and agreed upon by them as in the first instance."

Explanation.

The duration of the obligation to limit armament which now may only be changed by consent of the Executive Council, has come in for criticism. I should think this might be thus avoided, without in any way injuring the Covenant. Perhaps three years is enough, but I should think five years would be better.

Unanimous action by the Executive Council or Body of Delegates.

Insert in Article IV, after the first paragraph, the following:

"Other action taken or recommendations made by the Executive Council or the Body of Delegates shall be by the unanimous vote of the countries represented by the members or delegates, unless otherwise specifically stated."

Explanation.

Great objection is made to the power of the Executive Council by a majority of the members and the Body of Delegates to do the things which they are authorized to do in the Covenant. In view of the specific provision that the Executive Council and the Body of Delegates may act by a majority of its members as to their procedure, I feel confident that, except in cases where otherwise provided, both bodies can only act by unanimous vote of the countries represented. If that be the right construction, then there can be no objection to have it specifically stated, and it will remove emphatic objection already made on this ground. It is a complete safeguard against involving the United States primarily in small distant wars to which the United States has no immediate relation, for the reason that the plan for taking care of such a war, to be recommended or advised by the Executive Council, must be approved by a representative of the United States on the Board.

Monroe Doctrine.

Add to Article X.

(a) "A state or states of America, a member or members of the League, and competent to fulfill this obligation in respect to American territory or independence, may, in event of the aggression actual or threatened, expressly assume the obligation and relieve the European or non-American members of the League from it until they shall be advised by such American state or states of the need for their aid."

(b) "Any such American state or states may protect the integrity of any American territory and the sovereignty of the government whose territory it is, whether a member of the League or not, and may, in the interest of American peace, object to and prevent the further transfer of American territory or sovereignty to any European or non-American power."

Explanation

Objection has been made that under Article X, European governments would come to America with force and be concerned in matters from which heretofore the United States has excluded them. This is not true, because Spain fought Chili, in Seward's time, without objection from the United States, and also Germany and England instituted a blockade against Venezuela in Roosevelt's time. This fear could be removed, however, by the first of the above paragraphs.

Paragraph (b) is the Monroe Doctrine pure and simple. I forwarded this in my first memorandum.

It will be observed that Article X only covers the integrity and independence of members of the League. There may be some American countries, which are not sufficiently responsible to make it wise to invite them into the League. This second paragraph covers them. The expression "European or non-American" is inserted for the purpose of indicating that Great Britain, though it has American dominion, is not to acquire further territory or sovereignty.

Japanese Immigration and Tariffs.

Add to Article XV:

"If the difference between the parties shall be found by the Executive Council or the Body of Delegates to be a question

which by international law is solely within the domestic jurisdiction and polity of one of the parties, it shall so report and not
recommend a settlement of the dispute."

Explanation.

Objection is made to Article XV that under its terms the United
States would be bound by unanimous recommendation for settlement of a dispute in respect to any issue foreign or domestic; that
it therefore might be affected seriously and unjustly by recommendation against the exclusion of Japanese or Chinese, or by
recommendations forbidding tariffs on importations. In my judgment, we could rely on the public opinion of the world evidenced
by the Body of Delegates, not to interfere with our domestic legislation and action. Nor do I think that under the League as it is,
we covenant to abide by a unanimous recommendation. But if there
is a specific exception made in respect to matters completely within
the domestic jurisdiction and legislation of a country, the whole
criticism is removed. The Republican Senators are trying to stir up
anxiety among Republicans, lest this is to be a limitation upon our
tariff. The President has already specifically met the objection as
to limitation upon the tariff when the fourteen points were under
discussion. Nevertheless, in respect to the present language of the
Covenant, it would help much to meet and remove objections, and
cut the ground under Senatorial obstruction.

Prospect of Ratification.

My impression is that if the one article already sent, on the Monroe Doctrine, be inserted in the treat[y], sufficient Republicans who
signed the Round Robin would probably retreat from their position
and vote for ratification so that it would carry. If the other suggestions were adopted, I feel confident that all but a few who oppose
any League at all would be driven to accept them and to stand for
the League. (End letter)

T telegram (WP, DLC).
¹ That is, W. H. Taft to WW, March 18, 1919.

Frank Lyon Polk to Robert Lansing and Vance Criswell McCormick

Washington. March 21st, 1919.

URGENT 1232. For Lansing and McCormick.

Owing to his more pressing engagements I had no opportunity
to discuss with the President the question of the status of the
Russian Embassy and the funds and accumulated materials which
the Embassy controls. The situation, which is pressing, is as follows,

figures being given in round numbers: Cash standing to
Ambassador's[1] credit in City Bank $3,400,000; owed Ambassador
by Shipping Board for charter of Russian steamships of the volunteer fleet 1,400,000; owed Ambassador by War Department, rails
purchased, 3,000,000, together with lesser items the aggregate ap-
proximates 8,000,000. Cash materials constitute additional assets
as follows: military supplies as follows: boots 8,500,000; sole leather
3,500,000; horse shoes 200,000; total $12,200,000, railway supplies
including 137 locomotives and 4,400 cars, $11,000,000; miscella-
neous 2,000,000, $25,200,000; aggregate assets of cash and ma-
terials, $33,300,000. Against these assets of $8,000,000 cash and
$25,200,000 materials there are the following major liabilities: 1st,
Interest on government loans. Interest on demand obligations of
Russia held by the United States is as follows: Unpaid and past
due $4,000,000, due May 15, 1919, 4,700,000, total $9,100,000.
2nd. Obligations of Russian Government from private sources as
follows: Russian Treasury notes maturing May 1, 1919, held by
National City and other banks $11,000,000, interest thereon se-
cured by confirmed credit due May 1, 1919, $336,000. Six and one
half per cent credit advanced to Russia by City Bank in 1916,
payable June 18, 1919, $50,000,000 interest thereon due June 18,
1919, $1,625,000; commission due April 10, 1919, 125,000; com-
mission due June 18, 1919, $125,000; five year note payable 1921,
$25,000,000; interest on these notes due June 1, 1919, 687,000;
total $97,992,000. It is obvious that if the United States or the
private creditors, principally the City Bank, collect their indebtedness when due the Embassy will be bankrupt in May or June.
Furthermore, the supplies of boots, leather, and railway materials
so urgently needed for economic relief of Russia may be attached,
and possibly sold. The situation seems to me to require decision as
to certain principles before we can decide what measures it may
be necessary to take, as follows:

1. Does the President desire Russian assets of cash and railway
supplies, boots, etc., to be protected and used for the purpose for
which they were originally obtained by the Russian Government,
namely, for assistance to Russia?

2. Does the President desire Russian diplomatic and consular
officials to continue to function in this country?

3. If so, does he desire Department to lend its good offices to
assist the Russian Ambassador in safeguarding Russian cash assets
adequate for that purpose, say until July 1st, 1920, in case such
assistance proves requisite?

4. Does the President desire to postpone collection of interest on
Russian obligations held by Treasury Department? This will be my
understanding if he approves 1 and 2 above. I am ascertaining just

how we can effect the above. If the President approves, as a last resort, I believe the following procedure would be justified:

1. Have the War Department requisition all military and railway supplies not shipped to Russia and arrange with the War Trade Board, Russian Bureau Incorporated, for their shipment to Russia and disposal for the best advantage of Russia.

2. That the cash assets of the Russian Ambassador be disposed of as follows: part deposited with the United States Shipping Board as advance payment of sea freights for Russian supplies remaining in this country and available for shipment to Russia; a second part deposited with the Railway Administration of the United States as advance payment for railway freight charges for above supplies, and a third part to be deposited with the War Trade Board, Russian Bureau Incorporated, or such other agency as the President may designate, for payment in full and to defray charges and expenses incurred by the Russian Ambassador and approved by the Department of State, including maintenance and upkeep of Russian officials in this country.

The foregoing procedure is suggested as a last resort. I am hopeful that other arrangements may prove possible. In the meanwhile, however, I can take no effective action until the President approves the general question of principle which I have outlined.

Polk,   Acting.

T telegram (WP, DLC).
[1] That is, Boris Aleksandrovich Bakhmet'ev.

Frank Lyon Polk to the American Commissioners

Washington, March 21st, 1919.

1214. URGENT. Phillips had conversation with President Lowell morning following Lodge-Lowell debate.[1] Lowell asked to have his views of the situation transmitted to the President. Lowell believes that Lodge and his colleagues have committed themselves to such an extent against the present covenant that it will be practically impossible for them to back down unless an opportunity is given for them to do so. Lowell feels that if following three amendments, which he roughly drafted himself, are introduced into the covenant, the principal objections raised by Lodge will be overcome in the minds of the public, which in turn would have its immediate affect on Lodge's attitude.

|"|(One) No foreign power shall acquire by conquest, purchase, or in any other way, any possession on the American continent, or the Islands adjacent thereto.

(Two.) After a period of ten years from the date of the signature

of the treaty pledging ourselves members of the League, may withdraw therefrom on giving two months notice, provided that all its
obligations have been fulfilled up to the date when it withdraws.

(Three.) Questions of purely internal national policy such as the
right to restrict immigration, to impose customs duties, shall be
treated as under the authority of the several states, and shall not
be the subject of inquiry by the executive council or the body of
delegates."

Mr. Lowell has accompanied ex-President Taft on his speaking
tour through the country. He is in sympathy with the principles of
the covenant, and has been doing, and is continuing to do his
utmost to explain them to the public. Mayor Peters, Judge Anderson[2]
of Boston, among other prominent Democrats, share President
Lowell's views of the situation and concur in the suggestions which
he has made, quoted above.   Polk,   Acting.

T telegram (WP, DLC).
  [1] Senator Lodge and Abbott Lawrence Lowell had participated in a well-publicized
debate on the proposed League of Nations before an overflowing crowd at Symphony
Hall in Boston on the evening of March 19. Lodge professed to favor a league of nations
in some form but strongly criticized the Covenant presented by the drafting committee
at Paris. Lowell admitted that the draft Covenant was defective in many points of style
and substance but argued that a mildly amended version should be adopted and accepted
by the United States. In response to questions from Lowell, Lodge stated that he would
"support" a league which would bring "no injury or injustice" to the United States, but
that only the Senate could suggest amendments to the proposed Covenant which would
bring about this result. He also castigated Wilson for not having consulted the Senate
about the document. See John A. Garraty, *Henry Cabot Lodge: A Biography* (New York,
1953), pp. 359-61, and the New York *Evening Post*, March 20, 1919. Full texts of the
debate appear in the *New York Times*, March 20, 1919, and in "Joint Debate on the
Covenant of Paris," World Peace Foundation, *League of Nations* (6 vols., Boston, 1919-
23), II, 49-97.
  [2] That is, George Weston Anderson.

Ellery Sedgwick to Joseph Patrick Tumulty

Dear Mr. Tumulty: Boston March 21, 1919

The Lodge-Lowell debate has cleared the air, and I am altogether
mistaken if it is not now possible to secure an expression of dominant political opinion in this section of the country. I have also
recently returned from a trip through the Middle West, and I believe
that the country is about ready to make up its mind with definiteness. A large majority of voters favor the League, but they have
been sufficiently impressed by the opposition to demand certain
amendments, and it does not need the soul of a prophet to foresee
that if certain alterations are not made in the draft at Paris, a far
more radical revision of the treaty will be made in Washington in
the interests not of the world, nor of the country, but of the Republican party.

The changes demanded are (1) a general clarification of the wording, (2) explicit recognition of the Monroe Doctrine, (3) classification of tariff and immigration questions as domestic problems, (4) proper provision to enable a signatory to withdraw, either after a term of years or upon reasonable notice.

I have talked on this subject with many friends of the President in this locality, and with a number of his more reasonable opponents, and I feel some confidence in this diagnosis.

The President was not in this country long enough, perhaps, to gain a perfectly just impression of the state of public opinion. Cannot the situation be now conveyed to him ·with great definiteness? You will excuse the liberty I take in writing to you, which is owing to my keen interest in the formation of the League and in the success of the administration in continuing and completing its programme.   Yours very truly,   Ellery Sedgwick.

TLS (WP, DLC).

From the Diary of Dr. Grayson

Saturday, March 22, 1919.

The President worked on his correspondence this morning proceeding to the Quai d'Orsay shortly before 11:00 o'clock, accompanied by Mrs. Wilson and myself. As a result of his timely warnings to his colleagues the day before, the Polish question was speeded up and material progress made. It was decided, however, that the general boundary question would be deferred until a complete report dealing with all of the Polish Republic boundaries had been disposed of. As a matter of fact, a great deal of the trouble in the Supreme War Council over Poland has been because of a desire on the part of the French and of the military officials to save General Foch's pride. The General took a determined stand regarding the sending of the Polish Legion to Poland, vetoing the proposition. Later it appeared that this was an erroneous position and the result has been serious trouble and much talk. This talk has interfered very greatly with the progress toward peace, and it also has resulted in wide-spread criticism of dilatory tactics which has been distinctly unfair so far as President Wilson was concerned.

The President went home for lunch, returning to the Hotel Crillon at 3:30 o'clock, where the full committee on the League of Nations constitution met with him. He presided over the session and all of the amendments that had been suggested to the constitution, including those which were fathered by the neutrals, were taken up.

There were 37 amendments under consideration, and every one of them was considered pertinent. There was a desire to amend each of the 26 articles, but it was generally agreed that only such amendments as carried changes of a desired character would be voted on. The big question was securing clearer interpretation of certain clauses of the covenant. Two very important amendments were tabled. The first was the French proposal, fathered by M. Léon Bourgeois, which provided there should be in the covenant the creation of an inter-allied staff whose duty it would be to study mobilization and stra-tegical plans for carrying out with speed and effect any military action which might be considered necessary in the future by the League of Nations to coerce other members or frustrate sudden aggression. The Japanese proposal was designed to declare in the preamble of the constitution that there should be no interference with equality so far as the various nations concerned were affected. The Japanese proposal had been made in several different forms, and finally their representatives declared they would be satisfied to have it made plain that it in no way was designed to enable Japanese immigrants to proceed indiscriminately to any other country with-out regard to existing laws and covenants. This apparent concession was made by the Japanese because of their knowledge that the Pacific Coast States were unalterably opposed to any proposition which would seem to permit Asiatic immigration into the United States. It was claimed that the amendment as finally framed would meet that situation. However, it was not necessary for the United States to take a stand in this connection because the British Gov-ernment, backing the opposition of Australia and New Zealand, declared they could not accept any such plan, and the Japanese allowed the tabling of the proposed amendment, reserving their right to renew the suggestion after the League of Nations was formed if not at the Plenary Session, which would be called to ratify the constitution.

The President remained with the committee until after seven o'clock, when he returned to the temporary White House very much fatigued with the arduous labors of the day. It had been a very hard task and he was very, very tired. After talking with Mrs. Wilson and myself until nearly ten o'clock, the President played Canfield for a little while to get the larger problems of state out of his mind before retiring.

From the time dinner was finished for an hour and twenty min-utes, the President sat quietly saying nothing. At last he took out his watch and said: "For an hour and twenty minutes now I have said nothing at all about the meeting. It is hard to keep one's temper when the world is on fire and we find delegates, such as those of the French, blocking all of the proceedings in a most stubborn manner simply by talking and without producing a single constructive idea designed to help remedy the serious situation existing. The French delegates seem absolutely impossible. This is especially marked in the League of Nations deliberations. Bourgeois apparently has no thought further than to aid Clemenceau and his followers in building up a League against Germany. They seem to have not the slightest idea of the value or the preciousness of time at this very moment. They talk and talk and talk and desire constantly to reiterate points that have been already thoroughly thrashed out and completely disposed of. This entire afternoon has been about wasted because of the stupidity of the French delegates. It is bad enough to waste time just talking but these men give us no constructive suggestions whatever. They simply talk."

Hankey's Notes of a Meeting of the Council of Ten[1]

BC-56   Quai d'Orsay, March 22, 1919, 11 a.m.

1. M. CLEMENCEAU opened the Meeting by asking M. Jules Cambon to address the Council.

M. CAMBON said that he proposed to read the note prepared for the Council by the Committee on Polish Affairs in accordance with the instruction received to re-examine the proposals concerning the western frontier of East Prussia in the light of the exchange of views in the Council on the 19th March.

MR. LLOYD GEORGE expressed the opinion that as this note had been communicated to all the representatives, it would be unnecessary to read it.

M. CLEMENCEAU said that the conclusion of the note was that the Committee on Polish Affairs, after reconsidering the problem, maintained its previous proposals.

(For text see Annexure "A")[2]

MR. LLOYD GEORGE said that as he had taken an active part in the discussion of the first Report of the Polish Committee and as

---

[1] The complete text of these minutes is printed in *PPC*, IV, 448-58.

[2] The Commission on Polish Affairs reported that, as instructed by the Council of Ten, it had reconsidered its recommendation as to the western frontier of East Prussia, particularly in response to the objection that the number of Germans to be included in the new Polish state was excessive. The commission summarized the conflicting claims and said that it remained of the opinion that "the importance to Poland of retaining complete control over the Danzig-Mlawa-Warsaw railway overrides the historical and ethnographical arguments in favour of Germany in this area." It was clear, the report continued, that the unavoidably large number of Germans assigned to Poland was "primarily the result of the nature of the intimate racial distribution in this part of Europe, and not of any neglect on the part of the Commission to consider ethnographical facts." The text of the report, dated March 20, 1919, is printed in *ibid.*, pp. 452-54.

he had raised objections to the inclusion within Poland of two million Germans, he felt he must add a few comments on this second Report. He was still somewhat alarmed by the effect the Report would produce. He was not as convinced as at the previous meeting that this effect could be avoided. He did not wish to criticise the Polish Committee which had worked in a perfect spirit of impartiality and which had had to solve serious difficulties. Poland had to be given a corridor to the sea with every guarantee of security. The Committee had come to the conclusion that this could not be done without subjecting to Poland a large German population. He feared that this demand, added to many others which would have to be made from Germany, would produce deplorable results on German public opinion. The Allies should not run the risk of driving the country to such desperation that no Government would dare to sign the terms. At the present time the Government at Weimar was not very stable and all the currents of German life went on their way without taking much notice of its existence. It was tolerated, however, as there was nothing put in its place. The Conference must avoid presenting such a Treaty that no Government would dare sign it, or such as would cause the immediate collapse of any government that undertook the responsibility of accepting it. These observations were not levelled at the Committee on Polish Affairs, but the recommendations of that Committee were a considerable element in the difficulty just mentioned. He was inclined to accept, provisionally, the solution proposed by the Committee and to do likewise with all similar proposals by other Committees, with the clear understanding that the Supreme Council reserved the right of revision when it came to consider the total effect of all these proposals.

M. CAMBON said that he had only a word to add. He agreed that the Germans in general and the Prussians in particular would be extremely sensitive in regard to the destruction of the cherished enterprise of Prussia pursued for so many years. They had hoped to link Eastern and Western Prussia along the coast of the Baltic. The Committee, however, had been charged with the constitution of a Polish State with some chance of survival. The Committee had considered that to do this, wide access to the sea was necessary.

PRESIDENT WILSON said that he thought the procedure proposed by Mr. Lloyd George was wise, and he was prepared to accept it. He did not, however, quite see how the Public would be made to understand that the Council had provisionally accepted frontiers for Poland.

MR. LLOYD GEORGE pointed out that when the matter of communications to the Press had been dicussed, it had been decided that no information should be given regarding territorial questions. It would, therefore, be enough to inform the Press that an agreement had been reached, without any details.

PRESIDENT WILSON said that the Public might be informed that the Committee's Report had been received and reserved for further examination together with the whole group of territorial questions. He would suggest the following formula:

"The new Report of the Commission on Polish Affairs was received and discussed and reserved for final examination in connection with subsequent boundary determinations affecting Germany."

(This text was adopted.)

2. M. CLEMENCEAU caused to be read to the Council four telegrams lately received relating to the rupture of negotiations.

(See Annexure "B" (a), (b), (c) and (d).)[3]

MR. BALFOUR said that two questions arose. The first, which was the more important, was to determine whether the demands addressed by the Allies to the Germans were in conformity with the clauses of the Armistice. For his part he thought they were and that the Germans were attempting to evade their execution. If the

---

[3] The four telegrams dealt with the proposed disembarkation of Polish troops at Danzig. In the first, dated March 7, 1919, Hammerstein called Nudant's attention to the danger of "fresh bloodshed" and recommended that, if the Allies thought it necessary to bring Polish troops to Poland by the Baltic Sea, other ports be used. In the second telegram, dated March 8, Hammerstein questioned the authority of the Inter-Allied Commission to settle the question of sending Polish troops through Danzig, an operation which was not provided for in the Armistice conventions. In the third telegram, dated March 18, Foch reminded Hammerstein that the Allied governments had given the Inter-Allied Commission at Warsaw "full powers to settle the conditions of the application of Article 16 of the Armistice" of November 11, 1918, and that, consequently, it was "for the Commission alone to lay down these conditions." Hammerstein's reply, in the fourth telegram, dated March 20, reiterated the legal arguments and concluded as follows:

"3. ... The German Government can in no way lend itself to the passage of enemy troops through a country where nationalities are mixed, in a case where the right is so plainly on its side. Neither is it possible to suppose that the Allied Governments wish to act contrary to the assurances which they have repeatedly given and in accordance to which they have no other intention in the East than to maintain order, and avoid further bloodshed. The German Government can declare that quiet prevails in the region in question. Unhappily it cannot but fear that the appearance of Polish Troops would mean an attempt at the violent and flagrant oppression of the Germans who are undoubtedly in a majority in West Prussia.

"4. In these conditions, the German Government cannot be expected to yield to the demand that it should allow Allied Officers, and among them Polish Officers, to move about in the region to the East of the Vistula, without restriction as regards their journeys, and without supervision. No paragraph of the Convention obliges the German Government to consent to this. In view of its experience with Mr. Paderewski and Colonel Wade in a similar case, it has now to be doubly prudent. The Government however is disposed, in this instance also, to do all it possibly can. It will willingly examine, in each particular case, whether it can allow these journeys for special objects, without threatening public order, and in what conditions."

These four telegrams are printed in *ibid.*, pp. 455-58. Concerning the incidents in Posen in December 1918 involving the Paderewskis, who were accompanied by Lt. Col. Harry Amyas Leigh Herschel Wade, the British Military Attaché at Copenhagen, see *ibid.*, II, 422-24. See also I. J. Paderewski to EMH, Jan. 12, 1919, Vol. 54.

Council shared his opinion he thought that the application of the terms of the Armistice should be vigorously pursued through the instrumentality of Marshal Foch at Spa. The second question raised by the Germans was whether it was more convenient to land troops at Königsberg or at Libau. This was a question of convenience which might be examined.

MR. LLOYD GEORGE pointed out that disembarkation might be carried out at all three ports.

MR. LANSING enquired whether the whole correspondence relating to disembarkation was now available.

PRESIDENT WILSON observed that M. Noulens' note to the Germans[4] was not yet before the Council. According to the terms of General von Hammerstein's telegrams it would seem that M. Noulens had asked for free passage for *Polish* troops and not for Allied troops. If so, the request would not be in agreement with the terms of the Armistice. Polish soldiers could, if need be, be represented as Allied troops if they had been enlisted in the French or American armies, but, if the Germans were required to give passage to Polish troops as such, the Allies might be putting themselves ostensively in the wrong. This point, therefore, should be made clear, and once our rights had been established, the Council might enquire whether it was more expedient to disembark at Königsberg or at Libau than at Dantzig, in order to avoid crossing German territory.

BARON SONNINO observed that this would entail crossing Bolshevik territory.

PRESIDENT WILSON said that if the Polish troops were disembarked at Königsberg it was not quite clear how they would avoid crossing German territory. It must be remembered that this question was closely related in the minds of the Germans to the ultimate fate of Dantzig. An impression would be produced on the population of Dantzig that the Poles had come to take possession of the town. This impression might perhaps only last for a few days during the passage of the troops, but it might be strong enough to provoke disorder. It had been declared that the decisions of the Conference must not be prejudged by military operations. A bad example should therefore not be set. It was therefore very desirable to know exactly in what terms M. Noulens had addressed the Germans.

MR. LLOYD GEORGE thought that it would be advantageous to use all three routes. This would doubtless hasten the realisation of our plans and facilitate the importation of food into the country. The idea of disembarking at Dantzig should, however, not be abandoned, as this would look like a surrender of our position.

4 Not found.

He also wished to draw attention to the wording of Clause 34 of the Armistice:

"To secure the execution of the present Convention under the most favourable conditions the principle of a Permanent International Commission of Armistice is accepted. This Commission shall operate under the supreme authority of the Chief Command of the Naval and Military Forces of the Allies." Consequently, it appeared to him that the Germans were within their rights in demanding that the negotiations should be conducted at Spa and not at Posen.

M. CLEMENCEAU agreed.

MR. BALFOUR observed that the Germans suggested the disembarkation of Polish troops at Königsberg or Libau. As regards Königsberg, Marshal Foch might be asked to furnish a report, but as to Libau, he wished to point out that this port was in Courland, in a zone claimed by the Lithuanians. Lithuanians and Poles were not on the best of terms.

PRESIDENT WILSON remarked that the same difficulty arose in respect to Memel.

M. CLEMENCEAU proposed as a result of the discussion that Marshal Foch be requested to furnish the Council with all documents not at present before it; to prepare a report on the subject of a possible disembarkation at Königsberg, and to meet the heads of Governments at a private meeting, on Monday, 24th March, at 3 p.m.

(This proposal was accepted.)

Following on proposals by President Wilson and Mr. Balfour, it was decided that the Secretary General should draw up a list of all questions ready for immediate discussion, giving priority to such as concerned Preliminaries of Peace with Germany.

It was further decided that the two following questions should be considered at the next Meeting of the Council on Monday, 24th March, 1919, at 4 p.m.:

(1) Submarine Cables.

(2) Teschen.

(The Meeting then adjourned.)

T MS (SDR, RG 256, 180.03101/63, DNA).

From Felix Ludwig Calonder

Mr. President,   Paris, 22nd of March 1919,

At the close of the non-official conference summoned to allow the representatives of the neutral nations to present their views on the League Covenant, Lord Robert Cecil declared that all the States which had been invited would be welcome in the League of Nations.

I avail myself of this opportunity to inform you that Switzerland would count it a great honor to be allowed to offer the hospitality of her territory, in case the League of Nations wished to establish its seat in our country.

The government and the people of Switzerland would be happy and proud thereby to manifest their ardent desire to coöperate in the work of world pacification undertaken by the authors of the Covenant. The political and humanitarian traditions of the Helvetic Confederation, its democratic institutions, and its geographic position seem to recommend it to the choice of the commission of which you are chairman.

I can assure you that the federal, cantonal, and municipal authorities would be very glad to offer to the League all the facilities and advantages which it might desire.

I may add that a similar note is being addressed to Mr. Clemenceau, President of the Peace Conference.

Allow me, Mr. President, to assure you of my highest esteem.

Calonder.

TLS (WP, DLC).

Minutes of a Meeting of the League of Nations Commission

ELEVENTH MEETING, MARCH 22, 1919, AT [3:30 P.M.]
President WILSON *in the Chair*.

At the request of President Wilson, *Lord Robert Cecil* explained that two meetings had been held under his chairmanship, at which views had been exchanged with the representatives of 13 neutral Governments.[1] The neutrals had seemed to show general approval of the Covenant. In accordance with the desire of an illustr[i]ous member of the Peace Conference, he proposed that any suggestions made by, or intended to satisfy, the neutrals should be put forward as coming from members of the Commission. This was agreed to.

[1] A subcommittee of the Commission on the League of Nations had met with representatives of thirteen neutral nations on March 20 and 21. The subcommittee included, besides Cecil as chairman, Colonel House, Léon Bourgeois, Paul Hymans, Milenko R. Vesnić, and Eleuthérios Vénisélos. The thirteen nations represented were Argentina, Chile, Colombia, Denmark, the Netherlands, Norway, Paraguay, Persia, El Salvador, Spain, Sweden, Switzerland, and Venezuela. The proposed Covenant of the League of Nations was discussed article by article, and numerous amendments were proposed by the neutrals. See David Hunter Miller, *The Drafting of the Covenant* (2 vols., New York and London, 1928), I, 303-309. The minutes of these meetings and full texts of all amendments proposed are printed in both French and English in *ibid.*, II, 592-645.

President Wilson said the Commission would now resume the consideration of the Covenant.[2]

Preamble.

Lord Robert Cecil pointed out a difficulty in the present phrasing. It was intended that the Covenant should form part of the Peace Treaty, which was to be signed by the Germans. Consequently Germany would be one of the High Contracting Parties. In this case the present wording would make Germany a member of the League. He proposed a method by which Germany might be made to agree to the Covenant without becoming a member of the League. The end of the Preamble should run: "The High Contracting Parties agree to the following Covenant as the constitution of the League of Nations" and "States members of the League" should be substituted for "High Contracting Parties" in the body of the Covenant. This was agreed to.

Mr. Hymans said that he had a number of amendments to propose which, however, were amendments of form only. He asked that he might be allowed to submit them as a whole to the Drafting Committee.

This was agreed to by the Commission.

It was further agreed that the Drafting Committee which would be required later should have orders to make no changes of meaning: when the Committee had finished its work, the revised draft should be circulated to members of the Commission; if anyone objected, the old wording should stand.

ARTICLE I.

Mr. Larnaude suggested that the French equivalents of the words "meetings of" and "meetings at more frequent intervals of" seemed to destroy continuity of action on the part of the League, and to give it a casual character. On his motion, therefore, these words were struck out.

ARTICLE 2.

Lord Robert Cecil proposed an amendment to the effect that the proceedings of the Body of Delegates should be public except when otherwise determined.

The Commission felt, however, that this statement would probably not give to the general public the reassurance hoped for by Lord Robert Cecil and that it was, after all, a matter of procedure which could best be regulated by the Delegates themselves. The amendment was withdrawn.

The draft under discussion is printed as part of Wilson's address to the Third Plenary Session of the peace conference at Feb. 14, 1919, Vol. 55.

ARTICLE 3.

In order to meet criticism that the League was dominated by the five Great Powers, *Lord Robert Cecil* moved to insert after the words "think fit" in the first paragraph the words "The representatives of States not [*sic*] permanently represented on the Council shall not participate in this selection."

The amendment was withdrawn in deference to the opinion of *Mr. Vesnitch* and *Mr. Hymans*, who believed that more suitable representatives of the smaller Powers would be chosen if the larger Powers participated in their election.

Lord Robert Cecil moved the following amendment as a second paragraph of the Article: "The Executive Council may, subject to the approval of the majority of the Body of Delegates, co-opt on to the Council representatives of States other than those specified above, provided that in any such increase due regard shall be had to just proportional representation of States not permanently represented on the Council." He pointed out that this change would make it possible for the Executive Council to enlarge its own membership without the necessity of a formal amendment to the Covenant. Such a provision would tend to make the League more attractive to newcomers as well as to the smaller States.

This amendment was adopted.

Mr. Hymans proposed an amendment as follows:

"The Executive Council shall be composed of nine members to be elected by the Body of Delegates from among its number. These nine members shall be chosen as from nine separate States, but they shall always include a citizen of the United States, the British Empire, France, Italy and Japan.["]

He said that the election of the members of the Council by the Body of Delegates would increase their prestige and would be an international recognition of their distinguished character.

Lord Robert Cecil remarked that the decisions of the Council would lose a great deal of necessary authority if the representatives of the Great Powers were not directly appointed by the Powers themselves.

This amendment was thereupon withdrawn.

Mr. Hymans proposed an amendment suggesting that a distinction should be drawn between the functions of the Executive Council and those of the Body of Delegates.

President Wilson said that such a distinction would probably be interpreted as a limitation on the power of the Body of Delegates. He added that the Executive Council would by its nature be better fitted for action, but that this action might be the subject of discussion by the Body of Delegates.

After discussion, *Mr. Hymans* expressed his satisfaction with President Wilson's explanation, and withdrew his proposal.

Lord Robert Cecil moved an amendment to the last paragraph after the words "to attend" so as to run "and sit as a member at any meeting of the Council at which matters directly affecting its interest are to be discussed." This amendment represented a return to an earlier wording of the Covenant and was brought forward again in order to avoid ambiguity. The amendment was adopted.

ARTICLE 4.

Lord Robert Cecil moved the following amendment:

"Except where otherwise expressly provided in the present Covenant, decisions at any meeting of the Body of Delegates or of the Executive Council require the agreement of all the States represented at the meeting."

He said that this amendment was merely a specific statement of a fundamental principle of the League; but that its statement would clear away many misapprehensions. The amendment was adopted.

ARTICLE 5.

President Wilson read a letter from the Swiss Government, offering the hospitality of Switzerland to the League.

Mr. Hymans then spoke as follows:

"I have heard from several quarters that there is talk of establishing the Seat of the League in some neutral country.

"At a previous meeting I expressed the desire that Brussels should be made the Seat of the League, and President Wilson was kind enough to say that he and all the members of the Commission had listened to my words with sympathy. I think it my duty to remind the Commission at this time of the proposals officially placed before the Allied Powers by the Belgian Government, proposals which have the entire support of Belgian opinion.

"For any country to be chosen as the Seat of the League will be a signal and precious honour, and Belgium thinks that she is entitled to ask for that glory by way of compensation.

"Whatever may be the decision, the Belgian nation will be cruelly disappointed if the choice should fall upon some country which has not borne its share of the sufferings of the war which led to this final triumph of justice. If such a decision were made, public opinion would lose its faith and its hopes in the League.

"Brussels is a great centre of intellectual and legal life. It is in easy communication with the world.

"The Commission should not forget that through all this war Belgium has been the very symbol of the cause of Right, and has rendered to that cause services which have made her the admiration of all mankind.

"Such are the motives behind our aspirations. I lay them before the opinion of the Allied and Associated countries."

President Wilson then suggested that he should appoint a small committee to consider where the Seat of the League should be. This suggestion was agreed to.

Lord Robert Cecil moved to amend the first paragraph of the Article to read after the words "Secretary-General of the League," "The first Secretary-General shall be the person named in the protocol hereto and his successors shall be chosen by the Body of Delegates on the nomination of the Executive Council." This amendment was suggested in order that the work of the League might begin at the earliest possible moment. The amendment was adopted.

ARTICLE 6.

Mr. Larnaude proposed to substitute the word "inviolability" as a more accurate expression than the word "extraterritoriality." This suggested change was referred to the Drafting Committee for examination.

ARTICLE 7.

Lord Robert Cecil moved to amend this Article to read as follows:

"The original members of the League shall be those States which are named in the Protocol hereto. Any fully self-governing State, including dominions and colonies, may become a member of the League if its admission is agreed to by a two-thirds majority of the Body of Delegates, provided that it is able to give effective guarantees of its sincere intention to observe its international obligations, and shall accept such regulations as may be prescribed by the League in regard to its Naval and Military forces and armaments."

The purpose of this amendment was to give a more ready welcome to newcomers by substituting a positive for a negative form of wording. Only a slight modification in the form of the Article was necessary in order to change its spirit.

President Wilson asked whether there would be any objection to changing the two-thirds majority in the Assembly of Delegates now required for the admission of a new adherent into a simple majority, in order to carry out further the ideas expressed by Lord Robert Cecil.

Mr. Reis suggested that the Allied States should be the original members of the League and that the other States should be invited subsequently to participate.

Mr. Larnaude recalled a distinction which had previously been drawn by Lord Robert Cecil between the neutrals which should be immediately admitted into the League and those which should subsequently be admitted after fulfilling the conditions laid down in Article 7.

Mr. Hymans said the original idea of the Commission had been that the names of those neutrals which were to be invited should be contained in a protocol to take effect only after the signature of peace.

Lord Robert Cecil said that though all States without exception might not be immediately admitted into the League, certain of them deserved to be admitted at its very foundation, and that the protocol might take effect after the signature of the Treaty of peace and before its ratification.

Mr. Bourgeois reserved the right to consult his Government before expressing an opinion upon the question whether the League of Nations should be incorporated in the Treaty of peace at the time of its signature or at the time of its ratification.

Mr. Reis made a similar reservation.

Lord Robert Cecil stated that there was nothing at issue except a simple question of form, and that the Conference might take any action it thought fit with regard to the protocol. The latter might contain the names of all the neutrals, some of the neutrals or no neutrals at all.

Mr. Hymans thought that the honour of having been the founders of the League of Nations should be reserved for those States which had participated in the war.

President Wilson believed that it was best to avoid giving to the League the appearance of an alliance between victorious belligerents, in the first place because it was a world league; in the second place, because such a policy would lead to a too exclusive spirit in considering the claims to admission of new members.

Lord Robert Cecil agreed with President Wilson.

Mr. Hymans agreed that it would be right to admit certain neutral States into the League at the earliest possible moment, but they could not be admitted at the time when the Treaty of Peace was signed. The protocol to be drawn up could not take effect until after the signature of peace.

Mr. Reis agreed with Mr. Hymans, adding that only those nations which had taken part in the war had the power to establish a lasting peace.

Mr. Bourgeois said that he had always contemplated three successive stages in the formation of the League; first, its actual formation by the belligerent Powers, in connection with a Treaty of peace to which the neutrals could naturally not be a party. Second, an invitation to certain neutrals to accede to the constitution of the League. Third, the subsequent admission of further States who should have to secure a two-thirds majority as required by the present Article.

Mr. Vesnitch shared the opinion of President Wilson and Lord Robert Cecil in believing that the neutrals should be admitted at the earliest possible moment and upon a footing of equality. It was not necessary that the victory of the Allies over Germany should be perpetuated in the creation of the League. All the world would know, as an historical fact, that the League could not have been founded without the victory of the Allies.

Mr. Orlando thought that the only difference between the new text and the old was that, under the old text, there was a logical interval between the formation of the League and the admission of neutral States. Under the new wording, this logical interval disappeared. He thought that this difference was of sentimental rather than of practical importance, and that it was better to establish the League from its inception upon the broadest basis possible.

President Wilson suggested that Lord Robert Cecil's amendment should be modified to read as follows:

"The original members of the League shall be those of the signatories named in the schedule annexed to the Covenant, and also those other Powers named in the schedule who are hereby invited subsequently to accede to the Covenant."

After an exchange of views between Mr. Hymans, Mr. Kramar, Mr. Bourgeois and Mr. Diamandy, the amendment suggested by Lord Robert Cecil and the modification proposed by President Wilson were referred to the Drafting Committee for examination. President Wilson's amendment, providing that the two-thirds vote should be reduced to a simple majority, was withdrawn.

ARTICLE 8.

Lord Robert Cecil proposed to modify the first paragraph as follows:

After the words "for effecting such reduction" add the words "for the consideration and action of the several Governments." Strike out the first part of the second sentence of the first paragraph down to the word "disarmament," and make a new sentence to read as follows: "These limits, when adopted, shall not be exceeded without permission of the Executive Council."

This amendment was adopted subject to reference to the Drafting Committee.

Baron Makino moved to place a comma after the word "formulate" in paragraph 1 and to insert the following words: "subject to reconsideration and revision every ten years."

President Wilson suggested to insert "at least" after "revision." This amendment, as thus altered, was adopted.

Lord Robert Cecil proposed to modify the last paragraph to read:

"The States members of the League undertake that there shall be full and frank interchange of information as to the scale of their armaments, their military and naval programmes and the condition of such of their industries as are capable of being adapted to warlike purposes."

This amendment was adopted.

Mr. Bourgeois again proposed the amendment which he had suggested at the time of the first and second readings of the Covenant.[3] He reported that this amendment had been unanimously adopted at the recent international meeting of League of Nations societies in London.

He repeated that the object of the verification which he proposed was to prevent States of bad faith from acting in a way which would endanger international peace. The important thing in his opinion was to admit the principle of verification. Afterwards, the form which it should take might be determined in a way which would not offend the susceptibilities of any State.

Mr. Veniselos asked whether Mr. Bourgeois would be satisfied to substitute for the words "will form a commission whose duty it shall be to make the necessary investigation," the words "authorise the Executive Council to undertake the necessary investigation."

Mr. Bourgeois said that it made very little difference whether the examination were conducted by the Executive Council itself or by a commission, provided that the examination would actually be made, and provided also that the principle should be unequivocally laid down in the Covenant.

President Wilson said that in view of the principles upon which the League was to be established, such a commission would seriously offend the susceptibilities of sovereign States. A commission to discover whether nations were keeping faith or not would certainly be unwelcome in many countries.

Mr. Veniselos asked whether it was understood that the Executive Council had the right to call to account a Government which did not observe its obligations regarding the limitation of armaments.

President Wilson replied in the affirmative.

After further discussion in which *Mr. Larnaude, Mr. Bourgeois* and *Mr. Kramar* took part, *Mr. Veniselos* observed that the introduction of such an amendment would obviously compromise the fate of the League of Nations in many countries, and notably in America.

[3] See Bourgeois' proposed amendments to Article VIII in the minutes of the meeting of the Commission on the League of Nations printed at Feb. 11, 1919, Vol. 55.

On the other hand, he understood the interest which public opinion in France took in the proposed amendment. Nevertheless, he felt that the last paragraph of Article 7 which required, for the admission of new States, a two-thirds majority together with the acceptance of all the other conditions imposed upon the League, would give the people of France all the assurance which they required.

Mr. Bourgeois, however, persisted in his amendment, reserving the right to present it again before the Commission and before the plenary session of the Conference.

The next meeting of the Commission was fixed for March 24, at 8:30 P.M.

(The Meeting adjourned at 7 P.M.)

Printed copy (WP, DLC).

From the Diary of Lord Robert Cecil

March 22 [1919]

Saturday morning we were to have had a meeting of the League of Nations Commission, but it was put off till the afternoon, which was a nuisance, as it clashed with the further meeting of the Economic Council, so I went to the Economic Council at 2.30, and then straight on to the League of Nations Commission from 3.0 till 7.0 p.m. Not a bad meeting, the President being very friendly to me, so that we practically carried through most of the things we wanted. Unfortunately I insulted Bourgeois by telling him that one of his amendments was absurd, which apparently is regarded in French as very offensive. Hymans also made a violent speech against the admission of neutrals to the League, at any rate at its early stages. To which I replied by saying that that showed how impossible it would be to have the seat of the League at Brussels, so that altogether I did not make myself very popular.

From the Diary of David Hunter Miller

Saturday, March 22nd [1919]

At this meeting of the Commission it was agreed that amendments proposed by the Neutrals as such should not be considered, but only if proposed by one of the Powers there represented. This, Lord Robert Cecil explained, was due to a request from a very important personage whom he did not name but who was M. Clemenceau, as he told me.

The meeting lasted until after 7 o'clock and went as far as Article VIII, inclusive. The French amendment to Article VIII was reserved after being proposed again and debated at great length. Cecil said to me after the meeting that he thought he had been very badly treated by the French in their insistence on this amendment because Clemenceau had told him that they cared nothing about it. Both the President and Lord Robert Cecil spoke very earnestly against this amendment and Cecil in particular spoke of its uselessness and of the danger to the success of the Covenant which it would create by making feeling in the United States. Mr. Auchincloss told me after the meeting that Colonel House was not particularly opposed to it, but I told him that anything that would make opposition in the United States, which this amendment certainly would, should not be added, as the difficulty was great enough now.

Miller, *My Diary at the Conference of Paris*, I, 197-98.

From the Diary of Ray Stannard Baker

Saturday 22nd March [1919]

Whirling day. Two big meetings: Big Ten in morning and L. of N at Crillon in afternoon: but the air is full of nervous tension. While these men talk the world is falling apart. I went down to the President's House this evening & suggested some form of statement which would urge hurry. The President himself is growing very impatient especially with the French who are delaying & objecting at every point. The French as a nation are suffering from a kind of "shell-shock"—& think only of their own security, their own money; & wish to crush the Germans. The same report comes from every committee—"the French are holding us back: the French are talking us to death!"

Dined with Attorney General Gregory.

The president has accepted my suggestion for the appointment of President Henry Churchill King to the Syrian Mission. I am to get in touch with him.

From the Diary of Colonel House

March 22, 1919.

I got the President to see Hoover after the meeting and approve a telegram which Hoover desired him to send in regard to tonnage for food.[1] The President looked worn and tired. He does so much unnecessary work. There was no need for him to sit in the Committee this afternoon. I could have done it for him. He[,] Cecil and I decided the other night upon our amendments and it was a sheer waste of time and energy for him to preside. I am discouraged at the outlook. We are not moving as rapidly now that the President and Lloyd George are back as we did before. I have no authority to decided [decide] questions on my own initiative as I did while the President was away. Lloyd George never does anything until a crisis is upon him, then he moves swiftly. From the look of things the crisis will soon be here. I hear rumblings of discontent every day. The people want peace. Bolshevism is gaining ground everywhere. Hungary has just succumbed.[2] We are sitting upon an open powder magazine, and some day a spark may ignite it.

I feel, too, that the President's prestige is trembling in the balance and that his future place in history is in jeopardy. He is taking terrible chances by frittering away his time and opportunity. If the world were not in such a fluid state I should not object to matters going as deliberately as they have been going, but under present conditions, I cannot but feel that we are gambling each day with the situation.

[1] That is, WW to NDB and E. N. Hurley, March 22, 1919.
[2] See n. 1 to the memorandum by R. Lansing printed below.

From the Diary of Vance Criswell McCormick

March 22 (Saturday) [1919]

Meeting of advisers to meet President at 6.00 P.M. He was tied up in long session of League of Nations Committee. Hoover and I waited in outer room until he came out. Got his approval of reference to Supreme War Council and Hoover got his approval of strong cable to Shipping Board and Treasury Department concerning great need of ships for immediate supply of food, for Europe. Predicted no food here June unless gets 500,000 tons of shipping immediately.

President asked me if I could go to Syria to report to him upon the preference of the people there as to mandatory. Told him I would think it over as Blockade work not yet quite finished here. President told me he had promised the Allies to try to get our country to agree to act on mandatory for Armenia and Constantinople. Could not guarantee they would do it, however. Suggested Charles R. Crane might go with me to Syria. Might be interesting trip but think I will decline until economic control entirely cleared up. . . .

In talk with President he told me of program for next day, including appointment with Lloyd George, Clemenceau and himself to call upon Foch, who was very peeved and angry about not having his plan concerning Polish borders accepted. The President was furious that such a thing was necessary yet amused at the whole proceeding. Foch is just like a child and must be humored or his feelings are hurt so the meeting of the five great powers was held up until the Prime Minister and the President placate the old Marshal.

Printed copy (V. C. McCormick Papers, CtY).

From the Diary of Edith Benham

March 22, 1919

Last night the President came in tired out. He said he had been so much with his colleagues—"The Big Four"—that he knew just what they were going to say before they opened their mouths. The French are behaving so badly and he says he really thinks they want to begin the war again. They want to do just what Germany did in '70, annex some of Germany and then stir up the same bad feeling there was after the Annexation of Alsace and Lorraine.

A curious thing came up. The Germans had been asked to allow the passage of allied troops to Poland to establish order among the Poles. Foch stated he had been refused, so a meeting was called yesterday afternoon to determine what should be done, for it was a queer situation and looked as though a resumption of the fighting would be necessary if Germany refused. They considered all afternoon methods of procedure. Finally nearing the end of the meeting the President asked for the written statement from Germany. They replied there was none and all that had been asked was the elucidation of certain points about carrying out the transportation of the troops and absolutely no refusal. The French are always trying to make such situations. They are in a perfect panic and yet one can't blame them after these four years and the treachery of the Germans.

T MS (Edith B. Helm Papers, DLC).

A Memorandum by Robert Lansing

March 22, 1919.

URGENT

Memorandum for the President from Mr. Lansing

Your attention is called to the two telegrams quoted below which have just been received from Professor Coolidge of the American Mission in Vienna:

"March 21. Budapest telephones newspapers not coming out; rebellion apparently getting upper hand. Board sitting; Karolyi said to have left."

"March 21, 10 A.M. Karolyi Government resigned. Boehm, Kunfi, Pogany, Bela Kuhn now in power.[1] No fighting so far reported. General mobilization has been ordered."

Of the four men mentioned in the second telegram the first two are the leading and more radical Social Democrats in the Hungarian Cabinet; the third is the leader of the Soldiers' Councils (Soldaten-räte) of Hungary; and the fourth, Bela Kuhn, is the Bolshevist leader who was imprisoned by order of the Government in the latter part of February.

T MS (WP, DLC).

[1] The provisional government of President Mihály Károlyi had suffered from mounting economic chaos, social unrest, and external aggression from Czechoslovakia and Rumania since November 1918. However, the catalyst for the fall of the Károlyi regime was a diplomatic note from the peace conference which was presented to Károlyi on March 20 by Lt. Col. Ferdinand Vix, the French representative of the Entente in Budapest. The note demanded that Hungary immediately withdraw its troops behind a new zone of neutrality which it had proclaimed in Transylvania, which in effect permitted Rumania to take over much new territory in an area long claimed by Hungary. Károlyi concluded that the Allies proposed to dismember Hungary, and he declared that no government could accept such an ultimatum and survive. Károlyi's own party and the other moderate parties immediately withdrew from the governing coalition, leaving the field to the Social Democratic party. The Social Democratic leaders in turn immediately began negotiations with Béla Kun and other Communist party figures, then in jail in Budapest as the result of an attempted uprising in February. The outcome of these talks was a fusion of the Social Democrats and the Communists on March 21 and the proclamation of the Hungarian Soviet Republic on March 22. Kun, a former Socialist party functionary and political journalist who had only recently returned from Soviet Russia, became People's Commissar for Foreign Affairs and the real leader of the new soviet government. Vilmos Böhm, the Minister of Defense in the Károlyi government, became Commisar for Socialization; Zsigmond Kunfi, the former Minister of Welfare, became Commissar of Public Education; and József Pogány, former Commissioner for the Soldiers' Councils, became Commissar of National Defense.

For the various aspects of the complex story of the decline and fall of the Károlyi government and the rise of the Hungarian Soviet Republic of Béla Kun, see Peter Pastor, *Hungary Between Wilson and Lenin: The Hungarian Revolution of 1918-1919 and the Big Three* (Boulder, Colo., 1976); Francis Deák, *Hungary at the Paris Peace Conference: The Diplomatic History of the Treaty of Trianon* (New York, 1942), pp. 3-58, 355-410; Arno J. Mayer, *Politics and Diplomacy of Peacemaking; Containment and Counterrevolution at Versailles, 1918-1919* (New York, 1967), pp. 521-55; Rudolf L. Tökés, *Béla Kun and the Hungarian Soviet Republic: The Origins and Role of the Communist Party of Hungary in the Revolutions of 1918-1919* (New York, 1967), pp. 1-136; and Iván Völgyes, ed., *Hungary in Revolution, 1918-19: Nine Essays* (Lincoln, Neb., 1971), pp. 31-60. The most extensive biographical studies of Béla Kun in English are in Völgyes, pp. 170-207, and in Tökés, *passim.*

Gilbert Fairchild Close to Wen Pin Wei[1]

My dear Mr. Wei: Paris, 22 March, 1919.

With reference to your two notes of March 21st to Mr. Hoover[2] the President asks me to say that he would be glad to meet Doctor Koo and the gentleman whom he wishes to present to the President at two o'clock on Monday, March 24 at 11 Place des Etats Unis.[3] I hope it will be possible for Doctor Koo to combine both appointments which he requested for the same time.

Sincerely yours,   [Gilbert F. Close]

CCL (WP, DLC).
  [1] Third Secretary of the Chinese legation in Washington; at this time a secretary in the Chinese delegation to the peace conference.
  [2] W. P. Wei to I. H. Hoover, March 21, 1919 (two letters), TLS (WP, DLC).
  [3] Koo's memorandum of their conversation is printed as an Addendum in Vol. 57.

Gilbert Fairchild Close to Arthur Hugh Frazier[1]

My dear Mr. Frazier: Paris, 22 March, 1919.

The President has asked me to refer to you the enclosed memorandum with regard to a desire of a society of industrial workmen to give its association the title of "The Wilsonian."[2] The President is inclined to accept their "homage." He does not wish to ask the advice of the French Government but would like to be sure that the organization is steady and reliable. Can you give him some advice in the matter?[3]   Sincerely yours,   Gilbert F. Close

TLS (WP, DLC).
  [1] At this time Counselor of Embassy at the American embassy in Paris and one of the secretaries of the A.C.N.P.
  [2] It is missing but, as later correspondence reveals, the memorandum was from one M[onsieur?] Lelong, who asked Wilson's permission to name the society "La Wilsonnienne." M. Lelong to WW, May 12, 1919, ALS (WP, DLC).
  [3] Frazier replied saying that investigation revealed that the society was "small and unimportant," but that he saw no "serious reason" why it should not be allowed to call itself "La Wilsonnienne." A. H. Frazier to G. F. Close, March 26, 1919, TL (WP, DLC). The letterhead of the letter cited in n. 2 above reveals that it did so.

Robert Lansing to Frank Lyon Polk

[Paris] March 22nd 1919.

1273, URGENT. March 22, 7 PM. STRICTLY CONFIDENTIAL.
Bullitt is on way to Paris via Stockholm and London. Lynch and Steffens are with him. He reports courteous treatment. He requested permission to send Pettitt[1] back to Petrograd since he had established an unofficial courier service to Helsingfors but Mission has telegraphed disapproving of Pettitt's remaining Petrograd and instructing him to leave Russia. Lansing. 1273.

T telegram (WP, DLC).
  [1] That is, Capt. Walter William Pettit.

From Robert Lansing, with Enclosures

Dear Mr. President: [Paris] March 22, 1919

With further reference to the policy and orders under which General Graves should operate in Siberia, concerning which I wrote you on March 21st, I am sending you enclosed herein a copy of a telegram from the Commander-in-Chief of the Asiatic Squadron[1] to the Navy Department reporting a conference with General Graves and his own views of the rather serious situation in Siberia.

I send also a paraphrase of a confidential telegram sent to the British War Office by General Knox, who commands the British contingent in Siberia. The telegram makes unfavorable criticism of General Graves' conduct.

Reports received today from the American consuls at various places in Siberia seem, however, to confirm on the whole General Graves opinion of Japanese activities as intended to aid the reactionary party and as conducted with a view to the eventual domination of Eastern Siberia by Japan.

In view of the rather strained relations between the American and Japanese military forces in Siberia it seems urgent that definite instructions be given to General Graves.

As regards the Admiral's recommendation that a special battleship fleet be sent to the Pacific, I understand from Admiral Benson that in less than two months in the natural order of events as prescribed in naval orders a substantial fleet will be in the Pacific or ready to proceed there. To specially order a fleet to the Pacific at this time, when the friction is just developing, would seem to tend to aggravate and intensify the situation for all concerned rather than help matters.   Faithfully yours,   Robert Lansing

TLS (WP, DLC).
    [1] Rear Adm. William Ledyard Rodgers, who had replaced Austin M. Knight in early December 1918.

E N C L O S U R E   I

Cablegram received 21 March 1919
Serial No. [blank] Mission 320.
Origin: Washington
To: Amnavpar, Paris.

Following message received from Commander in Chief Asiatic: Quote. Following message from Kane Marguard Pekin[1] China: "Report from Tientsin, China, states trouble between Japanese and American soldiers night eleventh and twelfth resulted in serious injury to several Americans and also Japanese.[2] Reported that American consul was stoned and the Japanese Consul General[3] injured in the riot. Any further information will be forwarded later. Kane."

Nearly all of this information published Vladivostok News Items Reuter Service March 15th. Have conferred with Graves, and it is anticipated that similar disturbances will occur between the armed forces Japan and United States as soon as troops are placed along railroads, especially at Chita where Seminoff[4] and Japanese troops both stationed. Increasing indication of Japanese intrigue leads to believe Japanese military party willing to strain relations before sacrificing hope for retaining control of China eastern railroads and with it territory of Eastern Siberia. Doubt whether military government wants war, but its action and report as stated by Japanese press may arouse popular feeling beyond control of government.

The Hara Ministry in Japan is apparently governing the activity of the military government, but the military authorities in command of the Japanese forces in Siberia are apparently disregarding obeying orders and wishes of Ministry. Japanese military authorities Vladivostok admit they are supporting Ivanoff Rinof.[5] This was confirmed by fact Japanese troops guarded trains occupied by Rinof following recent arbitrary arrests made by his orders and alleging further, in that Japanese troops guarded car in which prisoners were deported. Local conditions Vladivostok and vicinity as follows: Members of Center Party excited and may arise in self-protection against oppression by Cossack reactionaries. This will not be a Bolsheviki demonstration. If this uprising should occur it will endanger lives and property of American citizens. Both Graves and Flag[6] are without explicit instructions as to interfering between parties in preservation local order for protection American interests under these conditions. Local friction becomes minor importance compared to development Siberian policy between Tokyo and Washington. In view of general condition in the Far East, increasing friction and tense international situation Siberia recommend early application is made Department's recently announced plans to maintain battleship fleet on Pacific and believe such action would have beneficial effect on diplomatic situation in Far East with reference to Japanese local authorities. Request information as to attitude of Department in view of Japanese American situation. Copies this sent to American Ambassador Tokyo. 216. Commander in Chief Asiatic. Unquote. 12020.

T telegram (WP, DLC).
[1] Col. Theodore Porter Kane, commander of the American Legation Marine Guard in Peking.

² Even after extensive investigation, Japanese and American diplomats were unable to agree upon the exact causes and course of this minor fracas between Japanese and American soldiers in Tientsin, China, on March 11, 12, and 13. For the Japanese and American official reports of the affair, see R. S. Morris to F. L. Polk, March 23, 1919, and F. L. Polk to R. S. Morris, April 4, 1919, *FR 1919*, II, 422-26. For the lengthy diplomatic correspondence on the incident, see *ibid.*, pp. 426-44, and *FR 1920*, III, 21-27.

³ The American Consul General in Tientsin, Percival Stewart Heintzleman, was stoned but not injured as he drove through the Japanese area in Tientsin on March 12. Neither the Japanese nor American reports, cited in n. 2 above, indicate that the Japanese Consul, or Acting Consul, one Kamei, was injured.

⁴ That is, Grigorii Mikhailovich Semenov.

⁵ That is, Pavel Pavlovich Ivanov-Rinov.

⁶ That is, Adm. Rodgers.

E N C L O S U R E I I

General Knox, of the British Army, reported to the British War Office from Vladivostok on March 8th in a telegram which became known to the Mission on March 20th that General Graves had changed his mind and "now refuses to forward a representative to an interallied mission of enquiry into alleged atrocities in the Olginsk district."¹ He is said to have agreed that the (people) would not tell the truth. Knox told Graves that Bolsheviki were claiming America as pro-Bolshevik and that this endangered the solidarity and safety of the allied detachments and asked Graves to take steps to contradict it. Knox asked Graves to join in supporting constituted authority. Graves replied that the anti-Bolsheviki were doing more propaganda work than the pro-Bolsheviki. Knox reports Wanov² as saying that reports in circulation said Americans were supplying funds and arms to the rebels. Sakharov and Romanovski³ said they would be delighted if Americans left Siberia, since they were not helping the Russians. Knox says also that Russians contrast the attitude of Americans with that of the Japanese. The latter send troops to suppress disorders. Among the educated classes hatred of America increases every day and Japan gains in popularity. He adds: "The tendency among foreigners who understand Bolshevism is to draw nearer to the Japanese standpoint."

T MS (WP, DLC).

¹ The Editors have been unable to discover anything about this alleged incident. Olginsk is a small village in the extreme eastern corner of the present Amur Oblast of Siberia.

² Probably a garbled version of "Ivanov": that is, Pavel Pavlovich Ivanov-Rinov.

³ Gen. Konstantin Viacheslavovich Sakharov and Gen. B. S. Romanovskii, both serving with the military forces of Adm. Kolchak.

Frank Lyon Polk to the American Commissioners

Washington. March 22nd, 1919.

1248. David Lawrence-Ishii interview printed yesterday WASH-
INGTON STAR, NEW YORK EVENING POST,—submitted to Ishii, who,
Lawrence says, approved quoted parts. Lawrence, pointing out frankly
course in international relations, said Ishii, as true exponent new
diplomacy, discussed relations with Japan with candor that marks
distinct advance methods of diplomats at Washington.

"What is your version reports from Peking of quarrel between
American and Japanese soldiers stationed at Tientsin"[1] asked Lawrence? Ambassador replied:

"While it was a most regrettable occurrence and I sincerely believe a thorough investigation will be made to determine who was
at fault, the incident is local in importance and does not reflect any
general feeling as between the American and Japanese troops in
the far East. Whenever large bodies of troops are gathered together
there are bound to be brawls. Even in France there have been
occasional mixups between individuals in the different Allied armies, and I am confident that, if our soldiers have been the cause
of it, they will be punished just as I am sure the military commanders of the American forces would discipline the American
troops, should they be found in the wrong. But again I emphasize
that the incident is purely local in importance."

Lawrence asked, "What of stories that have been coming to the
United States of independent [independence] movement in Korea."[2] Viscount Ishii replied;

"The disturbances in Korea have been the work of several young
Korean students. Most of them were educated in Japan where they
got many of their ideas of parliamentary ideals and democracy.
When they returned home naturally they seek to set up a government of their own making. Really we Japanese are proud of our
administration in Korea. We submit that under our supervision the
Korean people have been better governed than they ever have been,
and I earnestly believe that a majority of the people in Korea would
bear out that assertion. Unrest, however, is not confined to Korea.
It is running through many nationalities, who aspire to self-determination. Undoubtedly the Korean will be gradually given more
share in the government."

"What is the real meaning of discussion at this time by Japan of
question of racial discrimination and what is sought at Peace Conference on that point," asked Lawrence. Ishii's answer was: "I am
sorry that some Senators and others in this country have misunderstood that portion of my speech in New York last week in which

I referred to this point.[3] As a matter of fact I had no particular instructions from my government to make that address but the subject is so close to the heart of every Japanese that I merely reflected Japanese public opinion. Briefly, Japan is in favor of a League of Nations and wants to do her share to make that League a preventive of war which we all abhor. But if we are to prevent wars we must go to the source of all friction between peoples and do the best we can toward removing such differences. Indeed what Japan seeks is largely sentimental. It would involve for example no change in status of our relations with United States. I said nothing in my New York speech which would give anybody basis to believe Japan intended to have the gates open to unrestricted flow Japanese immigrants to United States. Quite the contrary is true. Few men perhaps know this immigration question between the United States and Japan better than I for it fell, my dear sir, to me while in Japan as head of the Consular bureau actually to execute the provisions of the gentlemens agreement[4] entered into between the U.S. and Japan whereby Japan herself agreed to impose restrictions on exodus of Japanese laborers to your country. We are satisfied with the gentlemens agreement. Indeed if we had intended to raise the question of our right to enter United States there is a treaty between the two countries which gives us that right.[5] But while we cherish that right nevertheless in the interest of friendly relations we also recognize the economic problems which make it desirable to exercise strict measures of restriction upon immigration of labor into your country and I doubt if any international agreement has been more punc[t]iliously kept than the arrangement whereby we promised to prevent the exit of Japanese to the United States. I would not give the impression that Japan wants to instruct her people leave her shores and go to other countries yet every nation likes to feel that when her nationals travel anywhere in the world they shall not be subject to discrimination. Did not the United States abrogate a treaty with Russia at one time because Russia refused to give passports to American citizens of certain religious faiths.[6] What Japanese agreement asks is largely sentimental rather than substantial.

"The gentlemens agreement on immigration is working so splendidly between the U. S. and Japan that practically there is now no question of labor as between the two countries but this is not true of other countries and my conviction is that somehow there should be incorporated in the League of Nations constitution, general principles which underline the question and which led the United States and Japan while recognizing the reciprocal rights of the nationals of either country to free entry nevertheless took steps to protect the economic interests of each. A declaration of race equality would be like a declaration that government ought to rest on consent of the governed, a matter of simple justice. Japan has accepted the principle of League of Nations and will fulfill her pledged word in that respect as she has in the past.

"Japanese interest in the effective operation of the League of Nations however will be greater, Japanese enthusiasm for it as a real measure to prevent war and to enable us all to work out our own destinies in this new age, reason will be more intense and the Japanese people will co-operate with happier heart if they feel that the great principle of a brotherhood of nations as enunciated by President Wilson becomes in fact an association of powers seeking to remove sources of German policy of discrimination that cause ill feeling between peoples. Certainly if a discrimination tax is a proper subject for narrowest concern a discrimination not against property but against persons is an even more vital matter. Again let me say I look for the friendly settlement of this question when it is fully understood on all sides."

Lawrence asked significance so called secret treaties between Japanese Cabinet and China.[7] Ishii replied: "There are no more secret treaties. All have been published. When China published some of them[8] she did so without Japan's consent. As there had been an agreement not to make them public without one the other like the famous treaty box of Chinese fable in which, when the treaties were published, there was a surprise for they did not contain anything strikingly new or anything infringing upon the rights of other nations."[9] Lawrence closed interview with this statement. "To ensure absolute accuracy I asked the Ambassador to verify the above quotations after they were transcribed which he did in the interest of the new way to thrash out delicate points between countries, absolute frankness and open diplomacy."   Polk.

T telegram (WP, DLC).
   [1] See n. 2 to Enclosure I printed with RL to WW, March 22, 1919.
   [2] Korean nationalists, both in Korea and abroad, had organized a demonstration for Korean independence from Japan which was timed to coincide with the funeral ceremonies, set for March 3, for Kojong, the former Korean Emperor, who had died on January 22. The reading of a declaration of Korean independence in Seoul on March 1 set off demonstrations in many parts of the country. Although the organizers had intended that the movement should be peaceable, its suppression by the Japanese led to many incidents of violence. Official Japanese reports covering the period from March 1 to April 30 stated that 587,641 persons were involved in the outbreaks, of whom 26,713 were arrested, and that 553 Koreans and nine Japanese were killed and 1,409 Koreans and 186 Japanese were injured. The affair, which came to be known as the "March First Movement," became the great symbol of independence for the Korean nation. See Chong-sik Lee, *The Politics of Korean Nationalism* (Berkeley and Los Angeles, 1963), pp. 101-26.
   [3] About this address, see n. 1 to the extract from the Grayson Diary printed at March 18, 1919.
   Senators George E. Chamberlain, Miles Poindexter, Wesley L. Jones, and William H.

King, on March 15, 1919, all issued statements strongly critical of Ishii's speech and of the Japanese drive for the inclusion of a nondiscrimination clause in the Covenant of the League of Nations. All the senators said that they believed that Ishii's remarks reflected the official position of the Japanese government. King summed up the senators' attitude in one comment: "If Japan insists upon equality for her citizens in immigration, that simply means that either Japan or the United States will not be a signatory to the League of Nations compact." See "Ishii's Plea Stirs Western Senators," *New York Times*, March 16, 1919.

⁴ The agreement reached between Japan and the United States in February 1907, revised in February 1908, by which Japan agreed to restrict the migration of Japanese laborers to Hawaii and the United States. See Charles E. Neu, *An Uncertain Friendship: Theodore Roosevelt and Japan, 1906-1909* (Cambridge, Mass., 1967), pp. 20-88, 163-80.

⁵ That is, the Japanese-American Commercial Treaty of 1911.

⁶ About the abrogation of the Russian-American Commercial Treaty of 1832, see WW to H. Bernstein, July 6, 1911, n. 2, Vol. 23.

⁷ About which see RL to FLP, Feb. 26, 1919, n. 1, Vol. 55.

⁸ There had been much discussion in the American press about secret treaties between China and Japan, and China had published at least one of them to this point. There are numerous documents in Volume 57 relating to this matter.

⁹ *Sic.* The version of this and the preceding sentences printed in the New York *Evening Post*, March 21, reads as follows: "When China published some of them, she did so without Japan's consent, as there had been an agreement not to make them public without one notifying the other. Like the famous treasure box of Chinese fable, however, when the treaties were published there was a surprise, for they did not contain anything strikingly new or anything infringing upon the rights of other nations."

To Newton Diehl Baker and Edward Nash Hurley

[Paris] March 22, 1919.

URGENT. PRIORITY A.

Please deliver following message from the President to Secretary of War Baker and Hurley, Chairman of the Shipping Board. "A review of the food situation in Europe shows that it is essential that transportation asked for by Hoover for April loading shall be furnished without fail. The human, political and military issues that revolve upon any failure of delivery of this program are incalculable. I therefore desire that the Shipping Board shall find the tonnage necessary and am confident that they may count upon the War Department to share the burden to the point of sacrificing all but the most absolutely necessary services. While it is probable that British Government has considerable duty in this direction, there seems little hope of their undertaking much service by April loading of ships and therefore we must take no risks and carry the burden for that Month. I feel sure that a realization by our people of this, a service second only to the mission of our Army in Europe, will reconcile them to any sacrifices that is necessary for its execution. I am informed that the burden upon us will rapidly relax after the end of April and therefore the sacrifice is of temporary duration.   Woodrow Wilson."

T telegram (WP, DLC).

To Robert Lansing

My dear Mr. Secretary: Paris, 22 March, 1919.

I would prefer in this case to make a recess appointment on my own responsibility without waiting to ascertain the sentiments of the Senators towards Mr. Hapgood, unless indeed Hapgood would prefer that I should wait.[1]

Cordially and faithfully yours,   Woodrow Wilson

TLS (R. Lansing Papers, DLC).
[1] Wilson did give Hapgood a recess appointment as Minister to Denmark.

To Joseph Patrick Tumulty

Paris (Received March 22, 1919, 830 am)

Please convey following message to Mrs. Catt at St. Louis. Best wishes for convention.[1] I earnestly hope suffrage amendment will soon be adopted.   Woodrow Wilson.

T telegram (J. P. Tumulty Papers, DLC).
[1] The annual convention of the National American Woman Suffrage Association was to be held in St. Louis from March 23 to March 29. Wilson's message was read to the convention on March 27. See the *New York Times*, March 24-30, 1919, *passim*.

To the Very Reverend Hardwicke Drummond Rawnsley

My dear Canon Rawnsley: Paris, 22 March, 1919.

I have been beyond measure distressed at the news of Fred Yates' death.[1] After receiving a letter from him written just before the operation, I wrote to him[2] and I am afraid the letter will distress Mrs. Yates rather than cheer her because it was full of expectation that he would recover. I shall be very glad indeed to contribute to the fund which you and other friends are raising to buy an annuity for Mrs. Yates and would be very much obliged if you would tell me in what form to send you the money. You may be sure that I will contribute to the utmost of my means.

Cordially and sincerely yours,   [Woodrow Wilson]

CCL (WP, DLC).
[1] Wilson was replying to H. D. Rawnsley to WW, March 2, 1919, Vol. 55, and a printed form letter from Canon Rawnsley and others (WP, DLC), dated "March 1919."
[2] WW to F. Yates, Feb. 26, 1919, Vol. 55.

From Joseph Patrick Tumulty

The White House, March 22, 1919

#25. It has been suggested by many that it would be a wise, humane and just act for you, directly or through Secretary Baker, to appoint a commission of very eminent men, mostly civilian, to investigate and report to Secretary Baker on all court-martial sentences imposed during the war. This would satisfy public opinion, which has been agitated into the belief that some extreme and even cruel and inhuman sentences were imposed for trivial offenses. In announcing the appointment of this commission, Secretary Baker could state that during the war when this nation was fighting for its existence there was neither time nor opportunity to relax the strict law of military discipline; that it was a case of enforcing military rule and winning the war first; that individuals' rights had to yield to the common good, the preservation of the whole people; but now that the war has been won and peace is assured, there is time and opportunity to review all cases, and wherever a sentence seems disproportionate to the offense to adjust the same through executive clemency. In the spirit of American justice and humanity, wherever a wrong has been inflicted during the war conditions, it certainly should be remedied in times of peace to accord with the American sense of justice; that when the report of these commissioners shall be made to him, he will make a report and recommendation to the President so that the American people may be assured that justice was administered in every instance.

This action, it is suggested, would allay propaganda that hostile partisanship is spreading and would pull the teeth of any investigation by the next Congress. There is appearing a studied and adroit campaign throughout the press to arouse the sympathetic over the alleged inhumanity of some of the sentences. It is suggested that in the selection of these men it would be very wise if a high and fair class of Republicans should predominate upon it. At the present time an investigation is being conducted by the Secretary of War himself through the Judge Advocate General's department. In my opinion, no matter what the findings may be, the country will not be satisfied, an investigation of this kind lacking independence. You remember how public opinion was satisfied when you appointed Justice Hughes in the aircraft investigation. I am afraid that the Secretary of War does not realize the seriousness of this situation. Therefore aggressive action on your part is necessary. The Democrats are raising Cain with Reed in Missouri.[1] Our friends just beginning to fight.   Tumulty

T telegram (WP, DLC).
  [1] Senator Reed had addressed a joint session of the Missouri State Senate and House of Representatives on March 18. His attacks upon Wilson and the League of Nations so incensed sixteen Democratic representatives that they left the hall in protest. On March 19, a conference of fifty of the sixty-seven Democratic members of the Missouri House of Representatives passed resolutions calling upon Reed to resign his Senate seat and run for reelection in order to determine public sentiment on his views. They also affirmed their support of Wilson and his conduct of foreign affairs. On March 21, the fifty Democrats offered to resign and run for reelection themselves on the issue of the League of Nations if Reed would do so also. Alternatively, they proposed that the Democratic State Committee "call a convention of representative Democrats from every county in the State, to give endorsement to the President and his aims, to denounce Senator Reed, and to bring about a reorganization of the party in the State if conditions are found to justify it." Reed denied that his speech had been disrespectful of Wilson and dismissed the actions of the representatives as being intended solely to embarrass him. *New York Times*, March 19-22, 1919; see also E. F. Goltra to WW, April 5, 1919.

From Herbert Clark Hoover

My dear Mr. President: Paris, France. March 22, 1919.

The need for clothing in the various liberated regions of Europe is almost beyond description. The large surplus supplies of Army clothing have been placed in the hands of the United States Liquidation Board, of which Judge Parker[1] is Chairman, to be sold. The Liquidation Board have large powers in the matter and are entirely sympathetic towards realizing the material on fair terms and extending credit for its payment. In order to get a rapid execution, it is necessary for someone to take responsibilities in the determination of prices and values. I am perfectly willing to take my share of these responsibilities. In order for the Board to take action in this direction, they desire to have from you an indication that you are in agreement with this policy, and we have jointly drafted the attached letter, which, if you could see your way to address to Judge Parker, would put the matter in motion.[2]

                          Yours faithfully,   Herbert Hoover

TLS (WP, DLC).
  [1] That is, Edwin Brewington Parker.
  [2] See WW to E. B. Parker, March 24, 1919.

From Walker Downer Hines

                              Washington, March 22, 1919.

#27. The Peek Committee[1] submitted late yesterday its report as to basic prices for steel and iron commodities. stop. The report is having careful consideration by the Railroad Administration Division of Purchases and also by its Advisory Committee on Purchases. stop. I am proceeding on the assumption that the questions are so

important as to justify careful consideration before finally committing the Railroad Administration to purchasing at the price suggested in this report.   Walker D. Hines.

T telegram (WP, DLC).
    [1] That is, the Industrial Board of the Department of Commerce, about which see WCR
to WW, Feb. 6, 1919, ns. 1 and 2, and WCR to WW, Feb. 7, 1919, both in Vol. 54, and
WW to WCR, Feb. 13, 1919, Vol. 55.

From Joseph Bartlett Eastman[1]

My dear Mr. President: Washington March 22, 1919

    I want you to know my deep appreciation of the confidence which
you have reposed in me by appointing me a member of this Commission. You may be sure that I shall do my best to be worthy of
it and to administer the office in the public interest.

    This letter will, I fear, seem somewhat belated, but I refrained
from writing before because of your absence abroad and the feeling
that even a note like this might be an additional and unnecessary
burden. One who knows you better than I, however, assures me
to the contrary. I have, I think, some faint realization of the load
you are now carrying. Permit me to say, also, that I believe you are
struggling bravely and wisely to serve the best interests of mankind,
that this is now appreciated by the mass of the people, and that it
will be even more generally appreciated when history is written.

                Most respectfully yours,   Joseph B. Eastman.

ALS (WP, DLC).
    [1] Former member of the Massachusetts Public Service Commission. Wilson had nom-
inated him as a member of the Interstate Commerce Commission on December 19,
1918. The Senate had confirmed him on January 24, 1919.

From the Diary of Dr. Grayson

                                    Sunday, March 23, 1919.

    We spent the day visiting the battle-front section. We left the
temporary White House at eight o'clock in the morning, returning
at eight in the evening. The official statement covering the trip,
which was made public following our return, was as follows:

    The President, accompanied by Mrs. Wilson, Miss Benham,
    and Admiral Grayson, spent the day visiting Soissons, the Chemin
    des Dames, Coucy le Chateau, Chauny, Noyon, Montdidier, and
    the neighboring regions, following with the greatest interest the
    movement of arms in those regions and getting a very vivid
    impression of the havoc that had been wrought there. On his
    return he said:

"The day has been very instructive to me. It has been in many ways exceedingly painful, because what I saw was deeply distressing, but it has enabled me to have a fuller conception than ever of the extraordinary sufferings and hardships of the people of France in the baptism of cruel fire through which they have passed."

At Saint Maxence a very pleasant little incident occurred. The President's car stopped to get oil, and a little group of the people of the village, together with some who had been driven out of Montdidier, gathered about the car and chatted, giving Mrs. Wilson and the President two or three very pretty bouquets of flowers brought by little children. The party had lunch at a little half-repaired inn at Soissons, where a great crowd of poilus gathered to greet the President.

There were, of course, many very intimate points of human interest that could not be covered in the official statement because of the necessity of refraining from any over-extravagance in the public account.

The President was unaccompanied by the numerous military aides who have been conspicuous in all previous trips. The result was that he was able to get into the human character the entire day, was able to talk as he pleased with the people whom he met by the roadside, and was able to spend a Sunday untrammeled by form and pomp, which is extremely distasteful to him. The party was made up simply of the President, Mrs. Wilson, Miss Benham and myself, and the necessary secret service guard. The pilot of the day was Sergeant Doughty,[1] who was familiar with this entire section, as he had gone over it for three years as an American ambulance driver. It was a beautiful day, the sun shining, although the usual French spring drizzle overtook us just as we arrived back home at about eight o'clock.

The first of the trip carried us through familiar ground which had been covered on the initial trip to Rheims, passing through Vaux and by way of Chateau Thierry. The first real objective of the trip was the big gun emplacement at Coincy. Here an emplacement was erected upon which the Germans had installed one of their so-called super-cannon. The majority of the French believe that it was this cannon that was used for the long-distance bombardment of Paris, while some of our artillery experts and most of the British dispute this. However, there is no question that it was a base for a super-cannon. In appearance it resembles very much the average railway turn-table at a railway terminal in the United States. The

---

[1] He cannot be further identified.

whole thing was very heavily camouflaged, and in the railway switches leading to the gun emplacement proper, provision had been made whereby trees could be stuck in in order to disguise the rails from aviators flying overhead. While the emplacement itself had been dynamited by the Germans in an effort completely to destroy it, yet there was sufficient left in order to permit one to reconstruct the whole thing in their mind. When the gun was in use it must have resembled an enormous turret such as is on battle-ships. The President went all around, over every section, at one place picking up a small tree and placing it in the hole across the track so he could get an idea of just how the camouflage was worked. He also went down into the great pits underneath the emplacement where the Germans kept the ammunition stored. We picked up a large number of bolts and other little souvenirs in this vicinity. We remained at this point for about twenty minutes getting a good view of the gun emplacement itself and everything in that locality. The President and I tried to surmise to ourselves how the gun was pointed, and what distance the projectile ascended in the air, and the calculations for lack of resistance at certain heights. The President wondered what the length of time was from the moment of discharge from the gun to the landing of the projectile in Paris. The President and I both made guesses based purely on observation and in no way on any scientific knowledge of what had actually transpired. The gun emplacement is entirely 110 kilome-ters from Paris as the crow flies.

Leaving the gun emplacement we proceeded northward, and following the enemy's line of retreat in August, 1918, as far as Soissons, which we reached at exactly 12:10. It was rather re-markable, and I took a little personal pride in the fact, that Colonel Jones[2] and myself had figured out the schedule and had arranged on it to reach the city at 12:10, and we did so to the second.

Soissons is one of the great points of history in the war. It was destroyed chiefly during the engagements of May, 1918, when for several days street fighting took place. From the time of the battle of the Marne in 1914, when the German retreat took place, the enemy lines had been practically at the gates of the city. For all of that period Soissons was under daily bombardment, yet the people or at least a great many of them remained in their homes, living in their cellars, and refusing to run away.

We rode through Soissons proper and had pointed out to us the various places where street barricades were erected and house to house fighting took place, the points where the French and the

[2] Identified in the second paragraph below.

Germans exchanged rifle and shell fire across the Aisne River, finally winding up in a half-ruined inn, where we had lunch. Colonel Percy L. Jones, Chief of the American Ambulance Corps, had arranged for the luncheon for the party and was awaiting us upon our arrival. Even before the luncheon was placed on the table the news that the President was in town had spread and soon a crowd of natives and French soldiers began to gather about the entrances to the inn courtyard. They were very much interested and all were trying to get a look at the President of the United States.

As we were about to partake of lunch, the President called my attention to Bernard M. Baruch, the head of the War Industries Board, who seemed to be trying to push his way through the crowd to enter the inn. The President asked me to go out and ask Mr. Baruch to join him at luncheon. I went out and found that Mr. Baruch had been denied entrance to the inn because of the fact that the President was there. I repeated the invitation of the President to Mr. Baruch, but he said he did not desire to intrude. He seemed distinctly and decidedly embarrassed, but I told him that the President had directed me to convey the invitation, and then Mr. Baruch blushingly admitted that he was not alone, but that he was accompanied by a very beautiful French lady and a French officer. All three were invited to the luncheon. But Mr. Baruch was still distinctly embarrassed, and while he did remember to introduce the lady to the President and Mrs. Wilson, he forgot entirely to introduce the officer, and when I rallied him about it he took refuge in the excuse that he had forgotten the name.

During the progress of the lunch a terrific explosion took place apparently from the northward. The concussion had sufficient force to rattle the dishes on the table, and it developed when we went outside that the explosion was at an ammunition dump, less than a mile outside of Soissons, which had been on fire for two days. It was impossible, of course, to do anything to check the fire, so all that the French authorities had been doing was to keep people from going too close, leaving the shells and high explosives stored there to burn themselves out without danger to any one.

We passed northward from Soissons en route to the region which forms the western extremity of the Chemin des Dames. Before we had gone very far we came to a little bridge guarded by soldiers, and a large number of soldiers not on duty. They moved over in front of the car and stopped it, appealing to us to go no further in that direction as we were even then under shell-fire from the exploded projectiles in the burning dump to the north. We halted and I returned to the inn to consult with Colonel Jones about the situation. I found Colonel Jones surrounded by a number of French soldiers and non-commissioned officers, who had watched us. They were addressing him and one, explaining their position in English, asked him to convey a message to the President. This spokesman was a French officer, and he said that he and his colleagues wanted the President to furnish France with the sort of peace he (the President) stood for. The officer told Colonel Jones that the soldiers wanted the President to know that they were back of him and his plans of peace, and they did not want him to allow France to get a kind of peace that Clemenceau and the members of the French Commission at the Quai d'Orsay were desirous of having made. They declared that the Clemenceau peace would be a peace designed to favor the capitalists in every way, while they had such faith and trust in the President of the United States that they knew that he would give them a peace that would be just to all.

Colonel Jones and I proceeded to the bridge and went across it to determine just what the situation was. We found that it would be impossible to go on over to the right as was originally our plan, as a soldier and a woman had already been wounded just shortly before by being struck by an exploding missile. We saw them being conveyed away in a motor truck, so it was decided that we would bear our road away to the left, which we did at high speed.

We passed on through the region west of Chemin des Dames, crossing the village of Coucy, which had been entirely destroyed. We visited the famous Moulin de Laffaux, which was before the war one of the most noted points of interest in all of northern France, and which is now simply a mass of ruins and broken stone. This territory is distinctly historic as during the entire war almost daily engagements had been fought. Here it was also that in September, 1918, the American troops conducted themselves most heroically during the advance, which culminated in the taking of Laon.

The road from here on branched to the west crossing the region known as the Massif de St. Gobin, which formed one of the strongest of the enemy's positions. The road led on through Anizy and Coucy de Chateau. The latter place contained a very famous old chateau which was destroyed by the Germans in their retreat in 1916. The President after looking at the lamentable ruins of this wonderful old historic structure, shook his head and said: "What a pity that a place like this should be destroyed when there was no military or other advantage to be gained—only wantonness."

We reached the Oise River at Chauny, and then took the road which follows the river as far as Noyon. Chauny is nothing but a mass of powdered stone and filled cellars, bearing no resemblance to the city it once was. Noyon was the next point of interest.

Before reaching there we encountered a party of German officers who were out taking their daily exercise. Under the laws of war these officers cannot be worked as our other prisoners but are messed separately and are allowed to take exercise at stated periods. They were a jaunty appearing crowd, most of them carrying canes or swagger sticks, and when the claxon on the car sounded, they shuffled slowly to the side of the road, apparently in no way concerned by the fact that the President of the United States, the man who more than any other human was responsible for their present predicament, was passing by. As a matter of fact, while they gazed at us and we slowed down, it is doubtful whether a single person in the line of prisoners knew who was in the big black cars going by. From casual observation it seemed as though these officers were not guarded but farther along we came upon some French guards. However, the officer prisoners in the north of France are not very closely guarded by the French, as there has been no real incentive for them to desire to escape to Germany under present conditions.

Noyon had suffered very greatly from the bombardments and engagements during the war. It was recaptured by the French in 1917, only to be lost again in March, 1918, and finally retaken by direct assault in September, 1918. For many weeks after the Germans retreated the explosion of delayed mines continued to wreck the city, and it was a long time before it was possible to come back into the city.

Leaving Noyon, and while we were crossing over a shell-hole the chauffeur was unable to slow the car down sufficiently to prevent a terrific jar, and the President was thrown from the cushion striking his head hard on the bow of the top, slightly breaking the skin and causing a contusion, as well as giving the President a terrific headache. It was, however, an absolutely unavoidable accident, due entirely to the broken nature of the road.

We continued west beyond Lassigny to Montdidier, which was taken by the Germans during the great attack on the 24th of March, 1918, and all along this section the American troops took a most heroic part.

At the little town of St. Maxence a very large crowd of people gathered around the President's car while we were taking on oil and gas. Some could speak English, and included in the group were old men and old women, French soldiers, a number of whom were on horseback, and many little children. They acclaimed the President as the savior of the world and the savior of the nation, and appealed to him to stand by the common people of France and bring about a peace which would be a peace for the people. They told him very warmly that they did not believe in their own government, declaring that Clemenceau and his associates were interested not in the common people of France but in the capitalists of France, and shouted that if the politicians in Paris were given their way the aristocrats and the rich would gain everything and the people would get nothing.

From Montdidier we proceeded by way of Claremont directly to Paris, reaching home just after eight o'clock.

From Vance Criswell McCormick

My dear Mr. President   [Paris] March 23' 1919

I am grateful to you for having suggested my name for the Syrian Mission and shall of course do anything you desire in the matter, if it helps you during these difficult days but I wonder if I could not accomplish more by remaining at my present work as Chairman of the Inter-Allied Blockade Council, a member of the Supreme Economic Council and one of the U. S. delegates on the Reparation Committee. I am particularly anxious to see the blockade removed as soon as possible and all economic barriers pulled down and I feel I can help in bringing this about in an orderly manner due to my two years experience in economic control and to my close personal relationship with many of the representatives of the Allied Governments.

While I am greatly interested in this work yet I want you to understand that I am ready to go at once to Syria if you still feel under all the circumstances I should do so. I know you will be perfectly frank with me in this matter as my only desire is to help you and do the thing that is of the greatest service.

Faithfully yours   Vance C. McCormick

ALS (WP, DLC).

From Charles Homer Haskins

Dear President Wilson,   Paris 23 March 1919.

I enclose herewith an advance copy of the report on Schleswig,[1] which still lacks the maps being printed by the French. You may wish to look it over before to-morrow.

Very truly yours,   Charles H. Haskins

ALS (WP, DLC).
[1] Paris Peace Conference, Committee on Danish Affairs, *Report . . . Presented to the Supreme Council of the Allies,* n.d., printed report with T and Hw additions (WP, DLC). This report presented the committee's recommendations for a three-stage plebiscite of the inhabitants of the province of Schleswig to determine whether all or part of that area should come under the sovereignty of Denmark or remain under that of Germany.

A Memorandum by Robert Lansing, with Enclosure

[c. March 23, 1919]

1. The French demand some physical protection from a sudden attack by Germany. Various proposals have been made such as the creation of a Rheinish Republic of German territory on the left bank of the Rhine. In the paper handed Colonel House by M. Tardieu annexed hereto and marked exhibit "A," the zone of protection is stated to be "delimited by a line running fifty kilometers to the east of the Rhine." It is desired that any military operations whatever within this zone shall be prohibited and that any violation of this prohibition on the part of Germany should be deemed to be an hostile act against France. It is only fair to provide that any violation of this prohibition on the part of France or any of her allies should be deemed to be an hostile act against Germany. In other words military operations within this zone should be prohibited to all alike.

2. The Military terms to be presented to Germany (Article XX, first paragraph) provide that all fortresses, etc. within the zone mentioned must be dismantled and disarmed within three months after the date of the signature of the treaty of peace. In order that the desired situation as set forth in one supra may be attained it is necessary that the terms of peace should be amplified.

3. It is suggested that the terms of peace should frankly state the situation somewhat as follows:

(a) Because of the aggression of Germany in 1870 and again in 1914 the territorial integrity of France has twice within the past fifty years been seriously threatened. The unprovoked and unwarranted invasion of France and Belgium in 1914 by Germany plunged the entire world into unprecedented disaster. The violence and the suddeness of Germany's attack placed France in an extraordinarily precarious situation and threatened the capture of her capitol before her Allies could render her assistance. The signatories of the present treaty are determined that such a situation shall not again be permitted to arise, and accordingly are prepared to establish physical arrangements under which the danger of military aggression against France of a character calculated to plunge the entire world into war shall be as far as possible eliminated.

(b) It is recognized that the zone hereinafter referred to is inhabited almost exclusively by German nationals. It is further recognized that the Rhine is the principal natural and physical barrier against any sudden military aggression on the part of Germany against France.

(c) Having in mind the considerations mentioned in (a) and

(b) supra, the signatories to the present treaty unite in agreeing that:

1. Within three months after the date of the signature of the present stipulations all fortified works, fortresses and field works situated on German territory to the west of a line drawn fifty kilometers to [t]he east of the Rhine will be disarmed and dismantled. The construction of any new fortification whatever its nature and importance is forbidden in this zone. (Article XX of present military terms.)

2. Within the zone above mentioned there shall not be maintained or introduced any armed or military organization. Materials of war shall not be manufactured within said zone. (This is the substance of point 1 of appendix "A.")

3. A commission will be designated by the British & French & Belgian Governments to report jointly to the several governments respecting the fulfillment of these engagements. Said Commission shall be accorded complete facilities for inspection within the zone above referred to. (This is Article 2 of Appendix "A.") (If it is thought best this provision can be left out and the duty of reporting on conditions in the zone assigned to consuls, military attaches, etc.)

4. Any violation of the above engagements shall be considered as an hostile act directed against the signatories of the present Treaty and such act shall be regarded as calculated to disturb the peace of the world. (This is the substance of Article 3 of appendix "A.")

ENCLOSURE

"A"

1. In the zone delimited by a line running fifty kilometers to the east of the Rhine, Germany shall not maintain either armed or military organization or keep up or construct fortifications, and shall not manufacture materials of war.

2. A Franco-Anglo-Belgian Commission shall have the right to assure itself on the spot that these engagements are fulfilled.

3. The entrance or attempted entrance of all or a part of the German army into the zone delimited by Article 1 shall be considered an aggression.

4. If the Commission invisaged [envisaged] by Article 2 observes a violation by Germany of the engagements under Article 1 or of the military air and naval clauses of the Peace, France shall have the right to occupy the line of the Rhine with bridgeheads necessary for the defence of this line.

T MSS (WP, DLC).

A Memorandum by Arthur James Balfour

PARIS. MARCH 23RD, 1919.

I made some observations yesterday to President Wilson and the
Prime Minister, with regard to the inclusion of Palestine and Cilicia
in the sphere of operations to be covered by the Commissioners
who are going to investigate the Eastern portions of the former
Turkish Empire. They did not think the arguments I used were
sufficiently strong to justify any alteration in the draft already sanctioned,[1] and I do not propose formally to reopen the subject. Inasmuch, however, as a great deal of time must elapse before the
Commission can set to work in Palestine and Armenia—and much
may happen in the interval—it is as well to put on record my objections to the inclusion of Palestine within the area of investigation.

If anybody will read attentively the documents quoted in the
instructions to the Commissioners, they will, I think, see that the
Commissioners are directed to frame their advice upon the wishes
of the *existing* inhabitants of the countries they are going to visit.
They are to advise, for example, on the establishment of "national
Governments and administrations, deriving their authority from the
initiative and free choice of the native population"; and the Conference declares that it is obliged to make itself acquainted "as
intimately as possible with the sentiments of the people in these
regions with regard to the future administration of their affairs."

I submit that, with these instructions before them, the Commission will have no choice but to find out from the population of
Palestine what sort of "national Government and administration"
they desire to see established, and what are the sentiments of the
people now inhabiting that country with regard to the future administration of their affairs. If they carry out these instructions, I can
hardly doubt that their report will contain a statement to the effect
that the present inhabitants of Palestine, who in a large majority
are Arab, do not desire to see the administration of the country so
conducted as to encourage the relative increase of the Jewish population and influence. If I am right, and they do so report, the task
of countries which, like England and America, are anxious to promote Zionism will be greatly embarrassed; and if either of them
becomes the Mandatory for this part of the Turkish Empire, it will
find that the difficulties of carrying out a Zionist policy have been
much increased. To that policy, however, they have publicly declared their adhesion; and though the task of carrying it out will
in any case be hard of accomplishment, it cannot now be abandoned

without giving a shock to Jewish opinion throughout the world, which cannot but have most unhappy results. Somewhat similar arguments apply, though in a fainter degree, to Armenia, but I need not elaborate them here.   (Sgd.)   A.J.B.

TC MS (Balfour Papers, Add. MSS 49751, British Library).
    [1] Wilson's memorandum printed at March 25, 1919.

A News Release

American Red Cross
Washington, D. C.
Released for Morning Papers of March 23, 1919.

It may now be definitely stated that as a sheep-raiser Woodrow Wilson also is a success. The White House flock, after less than a year of residence on the grounds of the executive mansion, is not only in the best of health and nearly ready to surrender another good-sized wool clip, but also is growing. Seven tumbly black-legged, black-muzzled lambs have already taken their place in the flock and more are expected.

Of course President Wilson doesn't personally shepherd the White House sheep but he has taken a lively interest in their welfare. This interest is shared by the rest of the country because the last wool clip given up by the original flock of eighteen brought probably the highest price of any ever sheared. It was donated, it will be remembered, by President Wilson to the American Red Cross and auctioned off in small lots throughout the country, adding over $30,000 to the war fund of the organization.[1]

The rich grass of the White House grounds that is practically the only fodder the sheep get has made them all "fat as butter" and now that they are fully acclimated to Washington it is seen that sheep-raising in the heart of a great city is easily possible.

The flock now numbers 26, and is increasing.

T MS (RSB Coll., DLC).
    [1] See K. Neville to WW, May 28, 1918, n. 3, Vol. 48.

From Charles Lee Swem

Dear Mr. President: [Paris] March 23, 1919

I know how much time is saved by a note rather than by trying to see you personally during these busy days, and I therefore adopt this odd method (for me) of asking your advice.

In view of the fact that the Peace Commission has encouraged the civilian members and clerks, at their own expense, to bring their wives to Paris, I have thought of the possibility of having Mrs. Swem[1] with me for a week or two. I would not think seriously of sending for her without first asking your permission. Will you tell me frankly whether you have any objection?

Cordially and respectfully,   Chas. L. Swem

TLS (C. L. Swem Coll., NjP).
 [1] Daisy Bunting Swem.

From the Diary of Dr. Grayson

Monday, March 24, 1919.

In the morning news arrived of the Soviet uprising in Hungary, which had centered at Budapest. As a result an emergency meeting of the President, and Premiers Lloyd-George, Clemenceau and Orlando was held, which preceded the meeting of the Council of Ten. The Council of Ten held its last meeting today. It had developed that it was unwieldy and that it was impossible to make any real speed with the open discussions that took place, generally aided and abetted by the French representatives. As a matter of fact, the name "Council of Ten" was a misnomer, inasmuch as, with secretaries, interpreters and other necessary attendants, the number was never less than thirty. This made it impossible for the use of the plain and direct language that has been required to reach any decision up to the present time. As a result, following today's Council of Ten meeting, it was decided that hereafter the decisions would be promulgated by the President and Premiers Clemenceau, Orlando and Lloyd-George. The reason that the Japanese representatives were not included was that they had no direct interest in any of the matters now to be settled growing entirely out of the war in Europe itself. Japan's interests, as well as her participation in the war, have been entirely in the Pacific, and those matters already have been practically disposed of. The Council of Ten debated before it went out of existence today the question of the German cables and the reports on the Teschen Basin.

The President today saw George Lansbury, the British labor leader, who discussed rather frankly with the President the exact conditions prevailing in Great Britain. He told the President that the labor crisis had not been in any way exaggerated. It was most serious because the Railway Workers Union and the Coal Miners believe that they have not been given a square deal by the present government. Mr. Lansbury told the President that one of the great troubles so far as British labor and Lloyd-George were concerned was that labor distrusted the Premier because he had failed to keep many of his promises and also because he had a reputation of failing to maintain his position after publicly announcing it and stating what it would be. Lansbury told the President that he intended to tell Premier Lloyd-George so as a friend in order that he might know just what they were thinking in England and take such steps as he might desire to remedy the condition. Because of the extremely chaotic conditions which prevail in England, Mr. Lansbury told the President that a majority of the British workers looked to the President more than anywhere else for an adjustment which would bring about a permanent peace and speedily restore normal conditions to the British Isles.

In the evening the President presided over the 12th meeting of the League of Nations commission. This has been the second meeting at which amendments to the draft covenant were considered, and the amendments affecting Articles 9 to 16 were read over and carefully considered. Good progress was made, although there were two or three rather knotty problems which presented themselves. However, the President managed to prevent the usual outburst of oratory on the part of the French and Belgian representatives.

During the evening the French plan providing for the creation of a League of Nations International Police Force to be made up of an allied Army and Navy was definitely laid away. No vote was taken on it. The French representatives agreed, after solving [sensing?] the sentiment of the commission, to permit it to be tabled without a record vote.

I asked the President afterward what progress he had made. He said they were getting along well but that if he could get rid of Bourgeois and the Belgian representative half of the time could be saved.

From the Diary of Colonel House

March 24, 1919.

This has been one of the most fruitful days I have had for a long while. I determined this morning to give the President a talk which would bring some action. The evidence is overwhelming that the public everywhere is getting weary of what is being done in Paris. It is not that we are taking too much time for normal conditions, but since the world is crumbling about us, it is necessary to act with a celerity commensurate with the dangers that confront us.
. . .

I saw the President for nearly an hour at his residence and pointed out the necessity of forcing the Conference out of the rut into which it has fallen. He asked what I had to suggest. I said it was necessary to tell George, Clemenceau and Orlando that immediate peace was not only imperative, but if we did not make it in a reasonable time we would find ourselves with a peace treaty and no one excepting ourselves to sign it. Hungary went over to Bolshevism yesterday, and other states are tottering while we sit here trying to satisfy the greed and fears of certain of our Allies. I urged him to settle once and for all the question as to whether the League of Nations was to go into the Peace Treaty. He, Cecil and I wanted it in and I thought it would go in. George and Clemenceau do not want it in and have intimated that it would not be in. I advised a showdown.

In making the argument, I suggested that he tell them that the Covenant for the League of Nations would either be written into the Treaty of Peace or we would have none of it; that the only excuse we could give for meddling in European or world affairs was a league of nations through which we hope to prevent wars. If that was not to be, then we would not care to mix again in their difficulties.

The other three questions I thought should be put to the Prime Ministers were:

1. The amount of reparation;
2. What was necessary to satisfy France and safeguard her future;
3. What should be the boundary lines between the old Austria-Hungary and Italy.

I advised doing away with the Quai d'Orsay meetings and for him to meet with the Prime Ministers in continuous session until these three essentials to peace had been determined. He said he would do it, and he did do it after a fashion; not as thoroughly as it should be, but still the Quai d'Orsay meetings are at an end for the present, and the Prime Ministers and himself meet tomorrow at eleven to get at grips with the questions I have outlined.

The President again insisted that all the treaties should be made at once, that is the one with Germany, the one with the remains of Austria Hungary, the one with Bulgaria and the one with Turkey. I undertook to get these matters in shape in time to cause no delay. It is evident that we know as much about what the proper boundaries should be now as we shall know in six months hence. We have had thorough preparation, not only since we have been in Paris, but for months before we came here.

After I left the President, I sent for Mezes and Miller and asked them to get to work and draft a treaty with the boundary lines that were recommended by our experts. I have the thing moving now in the right direction and I hope there will be no further delay.

I arranged with the President about the Syrian Interallied Commission. We also tentatively arranged for Ministers to Poland and Slovakia. I submitted to him a draft which Gordon drew as a solution of the French desires. I had already submitted this to our Commissioners and they accepted it without reserve, excepting Bliss who made a tentative reservation. I spoke to the President about seeing our Commissioners. I have the greatest difficulty in making them feel that I am as much in the dark as to his movements and intentions as they are. They are becoming sensitive and it will be necessary for the President to see them. He promised to do so tomorrow.

He asked me to keep in touch with our financial experts and not let them agree to the absurd figures which some of the French and British financiers still have in mind. Lloyd George told Lamont and Davis Saturday that he thought twen[ty]-five billion dollars was the maximum figure that Germany could pay, but that his financial advisers such as Lord Cunliffe thought that a sum of fifty-five billion dollars should be asked. Lloyd George asked our men to undertake to get them down. George appointed these men when he had great flights in regard to this matter and now he cannot control them. Montagu and Keynes[1] agree with our people, but George believes he will be crucified at home if his original experts are not also brought down to reasonable figures.

I advised Davis and Lamont and Straus[s] not to go beyond thirty-five billions, and to agree to such an amount only in the event that a large part of it could be paid in depreciated marks, and a commission appointed with authority to make reductions in the event it was later considered necessary.

[1] Edward Samuel Montagu, M.P., Secretary of State for India, plenipotentiary delegate for India at the peace conference; and John Maynard Keynes, Fellow of King's College, Cambridge, Acting Principal Secretary of the Treasury and its principal representative at the peace conference.

Mantoux's Notes of a Meeting of the Council of Four

March 24, 1919, 3 p.m.

Wilson. At this moment there is a veritable race between peace and anarchy, and the public is beginning to show its impatience. Yesterday, amid the ruins of Soissons, a woman, speaking to me, said to me: "When will you give us peace?"

I am of the opinion that we should take in hand the most difficult and urgent questions among the four of us, questions such as reparations, the protection of France against aggression, and the Italian frontier along the Adriatic coast. Once the most important and difficult questions have been settled, the road will be cleared and the rest will go quickly.

Clemenceau. I would add to your list the fate of German Austria.

Lloyd George. I support President Wilson's suggestion, especially regarding the question of reparations, which is the most difficult of all. This method is the only one which can extricate us from our difficulties. Our experts will never come to an agreement. The problem is two-fold: we must know what the Germans will be able to pay, and how we will distribute it among ourselves. The experts will never extricate themselves unless we agree on a common course and assume the risk of our decision. I propose then, along with President Wilson, that we have a meeting of heads of government twice a day if necessary, in order to proceed more quickly, and that we begin tomorrow.

Clemenceau. I join in this suggestion, and I believe as you do that it will allow us to expedite the march of affairs.

Paul Mantoux, *Les Délibérations du Conseil des Quatre* (2 vols., Paris, 1955), I, 13; used with the approval of Mme. Paul Mantoux, Philippe Mantoux, and Jacques Mantoux.

Hankey's Notes of a Meeting of the Council of Ten[1]

BC-57   Quai d'Orsay, March 24, 1919, 4 p.m.

(1) (See Annexure "A.")[2]

(2) M. CLEMENCEAU called on M. Fromageot to give a summary of the report of the Committee on Submarine Cables.

M. FROMAGEOT said that at a meeting of the Supreme War Council held at the Quai d'Orsay, on Friday, March 7th, 1919, the following resolution was accepted:

"(1) Is it right under the rules or principles of International law

[1] The complete text of these minutes is printed in *PPC*, IV, 459-75.

[2] This "Annex to Procès Verbal" reads as follows:

"In the course of a meeting which took place at 3 p.m. on Monday, March 24th, 1919, in M. Pichon's Room at the Quai d'Orsay between M. Clemenceau, President Wilson, Mr. Lloyd George, M. Orlando, and Marshal Foch with M. Mantoux as Interpreter, the following Conclusions were reached on the subject of the transport of General Haller's Army to Dantzig:

"1 The negotiations shall be taken up at Spa, under Clause 34 of the Armistice of November 11th, 1918.

"2 Marshal Foch shall demand that under Clause 16 of the Armistice of November 11th, 1918, the Germans shall permit the free passage of General Haller's Army as part of the Allied Army, through Dantzig to Poland, for the purpose of maintaining order in that country. They must also undertake to give every facility for the temporary accommodation of the troops passing through the port. Any refusal to accede to this demand will be interpreted as a breach of the Armistice by Germany.

"3 In the event of a refusal by the Germans to accede to this demand, Marshal Foch shall confer with the Supreme War Council as to the action to be taken.

"4 This decision shall be notified by the Secretary-General to the Warsaw Commission."

to treat as capture or prize submarine telegraph cables of an enemy cut or taken possession of by naval operations?

(2) Is it right under the rules or principles of International law for a Government whose naval forces have cut or taken possession of a submarine telegraph cable of an enemy to retain such cable by way of reparation?

(3) In the event that the cut or captured cable of an enemy is landed on the territory of another nation, what right and authority does such nation possess under contracts or permits granted to the enemy to cancel the same or to control the use of the cable?"

To these questions the Committee had submitted the following replies:

"*On the first and second questions.*

(1) The Committee is unanimous in thinking that military necessity is a justification for the cutting of enemy cables.

(2) On the question as to whether the enemy cables can or cannot be the subject of capture or prize the Delegates of the British Empire, France and Japan think that the capture and confiscation of enemy cables are legally justified by the general principle of the right of capture of enemy property at sea. The delegates of the United States and of Italy consider, on the other hand, that in the present state of international law this opinion is not well founded, the property in enemy cables cannot be assimilated to property subject to capture at sea.

(3) In these circumstances the Committee is unanimous in considering that in the absence of a special rule, recognising the right of confiscation of enemy submarine cables, the treaty of peace must decide the disposal of these cables.

On the third question.

The Committee is unanimous in considering that the answer depends upon the terms of the contracts entered into between the owner of the cable and the third Power on whose territory such cable is landed, and that, in all cases, these contracts are, as regards the belligerents who have cut or seized the cable, a *res inter alios acta.*"

MR. BALFOUR said that as far as he had been able to make himself acquainted with the report of the Committee, he did not think it gave as much assistance as had been hoped for. The question would, therefore, have to be discussed in full conference. In the first place, he thought that two points should be sharply distinguished, namely: a first question, which was relevant to peace with Germany, and a second question, which would have to be left to be settled after peace had been concluded. The latter question was this: "Ought world-arrangements to be made for the regulation of

submarine cables?" It might well be that the movement to inter-
nationalise waterways, great rivers, straits, certain railways, etc.,
would have to be extended to cables, which were of the utmost
value for commercial purposes. That question, however, could well
be postponed.

The other question to be decided was this: "Had Germany any
right over cables which had been cut and diverted? Had Germany
any right to complain and, if so, what principle should be asserted?"
In his opinion Germany had no right to complain of the action
which had been taken; and the Allied and Associated Governments
had a right to appropriate cables in exactly the same manner as
ships captured at sea. That view, he admitted, had not received
unanimous acceptance: it had been accepted by the French, Japanese and British members, and rejected by the American and
Italian representatives. Consequently, a difference of opinion existed, and it was difficult for a man who was not a lawyer to argue
where lawyers disagreed. He maintained, however, that the question had been settled during the Spanish-American War, when the
United States Courts had decreed that belligerents had no claims
in regard to cables cut during the War. He did not think that the
Germans could, with reason, complain if the Allies seized the cables
which, though constructed by private enterprise, had been heavily
subventioned by the enemy Governments and used by them for
strategic and warlike purposes, until destroyed. Therefore, in his
opinion, if the right to appropriate any property at all were admitted,
the right to appropriate cables undoubtedly existed. He did not wish
to make any pronouncement in regard to the regulation of cables
throughout the world. That world-problem could not be discussed
during the present conferences, and the consideration of that question would have to be postponed to a more favourable occasion.
That was all he wished to say on the subject for the moment and
he would like to hear the case argued on the other side before
saying anything more.

ADMIRAL DE BON said that at the Meeting of the Supreme War
Council held on March 6th, 1919, when the question of the disposal
of German cables first came under discussion, he had expressed
the view that submarine cables undoubtedly formed instruments
of war, since they were used for the transmission of enemy messages and, since ships had been lost in cutting enemy submarine
cables, the latter must be considered to be war material and fair
prize, resulting from war operations. At that meeting, the view
appeared to have been accepted by all parties that Germany could
have no pretensions in regard to the future disposal of her submarine cables. Furthermore, when the matter came to be referred

to the Judicial Commission, the conclusion reached was that International Law contained nothing which would upset the views expressed by the Military Authorities. In regard to the principle involved, two points of view had been expressed by the legal experts, which clearly proved that the problem could not be solved on purely legal grounds. The British, French and Japanese experts held that the Allied and Associated Governments had full right to appropriate the cables in question, while the American and Italian experts held the opposite view without having any established principles on which to base their conclusions. In other words, the views expressed were not based on International Law. In this connection he wished, however, to point out that the views expressed by the American Members of the Committee were not shared by other American experts, such as Mr. Grafton Wilson and Admiral Stockton.[3]

He agreed with Mr. Balfour that the question to be answered was this: "Could the Allied and Associated Governments appropriate cables without giving Germany just cause of complaint?" He thought the Conference was entitled to accept the recommendations made by their Military experts since the legal experts had been unable to produce any ruling against such procedure. In other words, the Allied and Associated Governments should decide to keep the cables in question. In regard to the regulation of cables throughout the world, he agreed that the question should form the subject of future study, since it did not appertain to the immediate problem under consideration.

MR. LANSING said that he had listened with interest to the arguments advanced in favour of retaining possession of the cables seized by France and Great Britain during the war, and he quite agreed with Mr. Balfour that the matter of internationalising cables should be taken up as soon as possible so that there should be no monopoly of cables. In the case under consideration, he thought the report submitted by the Committee was excellent in that it did not attempt to solve what had not been solved. The Committee had, it was true, unanimously admitted the right to cut cables as a war measure; but he (Mr. Lansing) denied the fact that the cutting of cables as a war measure gave the right of possession. In his opinion there was a very great difference between the capture of ships at sea and the seizure of cables. Cables were attached to a submarine region, which was not in the sovereignty of any nation. The cutting

---

[3] George Grafton Wilson, Professor of International Law at Harvard University, and Rear Adm. Charles Herbert Stockton, U.S.N., Ret., most recently President of the George Washington University, also a specialist on international law.

of a cable was merely an expedient of war; and, in his opinion, it was wrong that such a cable should continue in the possession of the nation, who cut it, after hostilities were over. Furthermore, cables could not be considered as belonging wholly to one country since they crossed other territorial waters and terminated in other countries. Consequently, to divert such cables to other uses and to deprive their use to former owners would constitute a dangerous precedent. The basis of capture on the high seas was that the ship could be brought within the jurisdiction of the captor, where it could be reduced to possession. This could not be done with submarine cables. Cables were the result of private enterprise and represented investments of money by individuals or companies. If it were argued that the keeping of cables deprived individuals of all ownership, no individuals would hereafter invest money in cables, to the great detriment of mankind. Admiral de Bon had given expression to the opinion held by certain naval authorities; but he would invite attention to the fact that there was not unanimity on the subject among naval experts. To sum up, in his opinion, since no basis in law existed for the guidance of the Conference, he thought it would be most impolitic to take over as spoils of war cables useful to all the world and to convert them into the State property of the captors. Such action would be contrary to American opinion as it involved acceptance of the principle that the conqueror could deal with the conquered as he wished.

MR. BALFOUR enquired whether Mr. Lansing wished to suggest that cables were less useful to mankind because removed from the property of Germans.

MR. LANSING replied that his contention was that it would make more of an monopoly.

MR. BALFOUR said that he himself was no lover of monopolies, but he thought the word was somewhat out of place in connection with the question under investigation. As far as the connection between the United States of America and Europe was concerned, he would admit that the majority, but not all the cables passed through Great Britain. He believed 13 cables passed through Great Britain; but all of them were owned or controlled by American capital. He quite agreed that a cable landing in a country would be subject to the laws of that country, and in war-time it was only natural that restrictions would be put on the use of such cables, as national interests might require. As a result, cases had occurred when Great Britain had been obliged to take over the control of all the 13 cables just mentioned. But in addition to the 13 American cables to Europe, which passed through Great Britain, there were

3 other cables which went through France and did not touch British soil. Consequently, he thought the word monopoly was somewhat excessive.

In regard to the question of sparing private property amid the horrors of war, he would invite attention to the fact that the United States of America had itself, during the war, put in a claim for acquiring 600 miles of German cables and the British Government had given its consent. He was ignorant, however, whether the United States had used those 600 miles of cable or not. But, at any rate, the American Government had not driven to its extreme logical conclusion the principle which Mr. Lansing had laid down, the justice of which he himself fully recognised. He thought that the case had been very fairly presented on both sides. He quite felt that the question of international communications would have to be dealt with sooner or later; but all were agreed that it could not form part of the problem under consideration.

MR. LANSING enquired whether the Conference thought it would be advisable to submit to a Prize Court the question of the right to the appropriation of the cables in question.

MR. BALFOUR said he would wish, in the first place, to consult with his experts. He feared, however, that a Prize Court would refuse to give any judgment as no actual precedent existed.

PRESIDENT WILSON said he had experienced great difficulty in coming to a conclusion. In the first place he would have hesitated to discuss the question from a legal point of view, but as no legal point of view existed he felt warranted in expressing an opinion. It was true that the problem to be solved contained two parts, namely: (1) Was Germany to be deprived of the ownership of the cables, and (2) what was to be done with them in regard to their use as indispensable means of communication? Up to now the Conference had only considered the question from the point of view of depriving the Germans of the ownership of the cables as a result of the war; but it should not be overlooked that the question also affected the whole commercial world. For that reason he was unable to agree with Admiral de Bon that the cables could be appropriated solely on the ground that they formed instrumentalities of war; for it was evident, that cables were also indispensable instruments of commerce, and indispensable to the pacific intercourse of nations. He thought, therefore, the cables must be regarded as property from the point of view of habitual use, that is to say, from a peace point of view. As a consequence, it would be impossible to contemplate embarrassing their use as means for re-establishing the ordinary courses and processes of trade, to which the commercial world had become accustomed in times of peace. Furthermore, the Allied and

Associated Governments expected Germany to pay heavy sums as reparation, and she could only do that by establishing favourable international balances to herself; otherwise she would be compelled to pay in her own currencies, which would be of little value to the Allies. It followed, therefore, that the question of the ownership of the cables must also be looked at from the German trade point of view. Four cables existed with one end in Germany itself, namely: the Emden-Vigo, Emden-Brest, Emden-Teneriffe, and Emden-Azores lines. These formed means of communication between Germany and the rest of the commercial world, and, in his opinion, it would be agreed that it made a great difference whether they were administered by one instrument or various.

Reference had been made to the decision reached by the United States Courts in the Spanish-American war, when it had been decided that damages could not be claimed for what had been done to cables during the period of hostilities. That decision related merely to the responsibility of the Government towards the owners of enemy property. Similarly, in his opinion, the cables now under consideration were really enemy private property, unless it could be established that the Government was the only owner. Consequently, the question of the disposal of the cables was one which could only be dealt with in connection with the disposal of other enemy property, since all countries had during the war taken temporary possession of enemy alien property within its borders. He thought the question would have to be considered from that point of view. Those familiar with International Conferences on the Rights of Nations maintained that the United States of America had never willingly assented to the principle of the capture of private property at sea. He would, therefore, hesitate to agree to the appropriation of the cables in question, even if cables could be considered to be private property, captured at sea. Hence he shared the views of the American representatives on the Committee. In his opinion, no analogy could be drawn between cables, which consisted of fixed lines uniting two shores, and ships, which were built to move from place to place and which could be converted into possession when carried into the harbours of the captors. He begged the Conference to proceed very slowly in deciding to do something, the basis of which had never been discussed in time of peace when a careful and unbiased decision could have been reached. In his opinion, it would be extremely unwise to establish a principle of law as a war measure.

MR. BALFOUR said he wished to make one observation of a practical character without adding anything more to the theory of the principles involved. The Conference had discussed the question of restoring these cables to Germany in order that she might resume her economic existence. That was an error because the belligerents besides cutting the cables had also diverted them. The point, therefore, was that though it would be possible to relay the cables at the expense of the Allies, it would not be possible to hand over the cables as they were before the war. Fortunately, or unfortunately, the necessities of war and the pressure of events had compelled France and Great Britain to divert these cables. Therefore, nothing could be done except to relay them in order to revert to the *status quo ante bellum*.

PRESIDENT WILSON enquired whether a list of the cables which had so been diverted could be given.

(Mr. Balfour then read a list of the cables which had been diverted.)

PRESIDENT WILSON enquired whether by diversion was merely meant that the cable had been cut, and the cut end being attached to a new cable which went in the new direction required.

MR. BALFOUR explained that for the purpose of diverting the cables whole sections had been taken up and placed in an altogether different position.

M. CLEMENCEAU said he found some difficulty in arriving at a definite conclusion. He had at first thought that the suggestion made by Mr. Lansing to refer the question to a Prize Court would have found acceptance. But he was now given to understand that the Prize Courts both of Great Britain and France would be compelled to rule that the question fell outside their jurisdiction because no precedent existed.

In his opinion a distinction would have to be made between the question of right, which could only be settled by law, and the question of fact. He had been much struck by the statement made by Mr. Balfour that the cables having been rightly diverted as an act of war, could not be restored to their former position, and the act of war constituted an accomplished fact. The question of right could however be referred to a legal committee.

BARON MAKINO said that the cables mentioned in today's programme comprised two links in which Japan was interested. The Japanese view, as expressed by her experts, coincided with the opinions expressed by Great Britain and France. In regard to the two cables seized by Japan, the one belonged entirely to the German Government; the other was private, but had been heavily subsidized by the German Government out of all proportion to its importance. Both cables had been employed to promote Germany's "Welt Politik" as well as her economic domination. He did not wish to discuss the legal aspect of the case; but from the point of view of preventing military domination and economic abuses Japan was opposed to the return of the cables to Germany, since they might again be used for the same purposes. In conclusion he would add that the two cables in question had also been taken up and diverted for war purposes, and in that respect the situation in Japan was the same as that of Great Britain and France.

PRESIDENT WILSON asked Baron Makino to name the two lines he had referred to.

BARON MAKINO replied that the two lines in question were:

(1) Chifu-Tsingtau-Shanghai.

(2) { Yap-Shanghai.
     { Yap-Menado.

M. ORLANDO said that there were evidently two questions involved; the question of law and the question of fact. In regard to the legal aspect of the case he had always maintained that law was not a mystical science and, consequently, any one possessed with an atom of common sense had a right to express an opinion. From a common sense point of view he thought the Conference could not talk of applying to cables the Clauses of International law applicable to ships, since the two cases were quite different: the law applicable to ships was inapplicable to cables.

Next in regard to the possibility of appropriating a particular thing. If the thing were private property, even enemy property, it could not, in accordance with the rules of international law, be appropriated. In his opinion the two principles which he had just expressed must be accepted, namely: the impossibility of applying the rules relating to the capture of ships to the seizure of cables and, secondly, the illegality of appropriating private enemy property. He would add, however, with equal frankness, that the question of fact put forward by M. Balfour had made a great impression on him because, whilst international law could not be applied, the dictum that "what is done is done" could be accepted. In regard to the diversion of the cables it would be necessary to decide whether such action was permissible under the rules of war. That question had been unanimously decided in the affirmative, that is to say, a permissible act of war had been accomplished. Secondly, it was evident that the cables in question could not be restored to Germany, and either an indemnity would have to be paid to Germany or something would have to be done to put the cables back in the position in which they were before the war. In his opinion, to do this would be to admit that what had been done had not been right. He regretted that the fact relating to the diversion of the cables had not been raised before the question had been referred to the special commission, because, in his opinion, that fact altered the whole situation. On the legal aspect of the case he was in complete agreement, with the views expressed by the American and Italian representatives, but if the facts were as stated by Mr. Balfour, that is to say, if the Allied and Associated Governments were faced with an accomplished act which had been carried out in strict accordance with the admitted rules of war, then the thing had been done, and there was really no question for discussion.

M. TARDIEU thought that the Conference was faced with a question of fact which could not be undone, and a question of law relating to the disposal of private enemy property. Under these conditions he suggested that all the German Government's cables should be appropriated, and the private cables should be kept, their value being entered on the list of reparations, the German Government being charged with the duty of indemnifying private owners.

PRESIDENT WILSON said that the principle he was seeking to go on was this. He was interested in seeing that there should be an entirely just Peace, rather than that advantages should be gained by any Country from a material point of view. The decisions embodied in the Peace Treaty should be such that they could hereafter be accepted as precedents. Thus, while he understood that the right to cut cables had been established by law, he was doubtful whether the same right existed to divert cables to other termini, that is to say, to appropriate private property to public uses. On that question he would be glad to have an expert ruling.

MR. BALFOUR said that he did not pretend to have sufficient authority to deal with the question of law. Nevertheless, Mr. Wilson said that the right to cut cables in time of war had been established. In his opinion, that right had only been established because the United States of America had done it, that was apparently the only justification.

PRESIDENT WILSON explained that the question had been referred for decision to a Commission.

MR. BALFOUR, continuing, said that so far as his opinion went the United States of America had cut a cable, the British Government had complained, the question had then been taken to a Court and tried by the regular machinery, which had justified the action taken by the American Government by ruling that private owners had no right to compensation in the case. President Wilson now made a distinction between destroying private property and appropriating private property. In his opinion, if the destruction of private property were admissible its appropriation, after diversion, could not be denied.

PRESIDENT WILSON explained that, in his opinion, it was permissible to destroy certain property for purposes of war but it was not permissible to use the same continuously for purposes of Peace.

MR. BALFOUR suggested that the German Government should be informed that so much of their property in cables still remained under the sea and so much had been diverted. The Government could be permitted to resume possession of the part lying in its old bed which could be put in order. He thought that would be a solution of the problem.

MR. LANSING pointed out that Great Britain had so far never recognised the fact that the cutting of a cable gave the right to its appropriation.

MR. BALFOUR said that he had just been reminded that an important distinction existed between the case of the Spanish American cable, to which reference had previously been made, and the present case. The Spanish American cable had been a *neutral* cable, whereas the present cable was an *enemy* cable.

MR. LANSING agreed. He pointed out, however, that the cable in question had been used by the Spanish, and Great Britain had then declared that she would not allow its use unless both belligerents were granted equal rights to usage.

M. ORLANDO thought the observations just made still further confirmed the view he had previously taken. To be quite frank, he thought the whole question turned on whether by diverting the cables anything had been done contrary to the laws of war. If an Army were to occupy enemy territory, it was entitled to damage communications, railway lines, tunnels, and bridges. No indemnity would be due for such damage, because the destruction of the enemy railway lines constituted a regular act of war. But it was not permitted to remove the rails as an act of war. In his opinion, exactly the same argument applied to cables. In the present case, however, the property in question had not been destroyed; it had been diverted. Consequently, though he, himself, was not a great believer in Commissions, he thought the whole question was so very complicated that it could only be settled on grounds of equity. On that account, it should be referred to a special Commission.

MR. BALFOUR said that he had a suggestion to make which he thought would meet the general views. He wished to propose the following resolution:

"The Treaty of Peace should not debar Germany from repairing at her own expense the submarine cables cut by Allied and Associated Powers during the war, nor from replacing at her expense any parts which have been cut out from such cables, or which without having been cut are now in use by any of those Powers."

MR. BALFOUR, continuing, said that since drafting his resolution, his attention had been drawn to the fact that certain of the cables taken by the Japanese and Italian Governments were purely Government cables. That question had been overlooked in his draft resolution. He thought that point should be considered by the Drafting Committee in preparing the necessary clause.

ADMIRAL THAON DI REVEL[4] explained that no enemy Government cables had been appropriated by the Italian Government. In the North Adriatic there was one cable which had been cut. In the Lower Adriatic there were two cables, one between San Giovanni di Medua and Taranto and the other between Otranto and Corfu. Both had been cut, and the latter had been diverted by the British Government.

BARON MAKINO enquired whether the resolution as drafted might not be interpreted to mean that all cables might be returned to Germany.

M. CLEMENCEAU explained that the whole question had merely been referred to the Drafting Committee and would be reconsidered when the Report of that Committee was received.

(It was agreed to refer the following resolution to the Drafting Committee for early submission of a draft clause for inclusion in the Treaty of Peace:

The Treaty of Peace should not debar Germany from repairing at her own expense the submarine cables cut by Allied and Associated Powers during the war, nor from replacing at her expense any parts which have been cut out from such cables, or which without having been cut are now in use by any of those Powers.)

(3) DR. LORD said that the proposal laid before the Supreme War Council (see Annexure "B"),[5] was designed to render more effective the work of the Commission at Teschen. That Commission had been established with the object of putting an end to the fighting between the Poles and the Czechs, and to regulate other contentious questions. The Commission, accordingly, had taken up its duties in February last and had endeavoured to work along the lines of their mandate; but without success, because the powers accorded were not sufficient to enable effective action to be taken. The great difficulty was due to the fact that the role allotted to the Commission was only that of adviser and counsellor, to make suggestions to the Czech and Polish Governments. In every case, the questions to be settled had to be referred to the Governments at Warsaw or Prague with the result that great delays invariably ensued. The most important question related to the supply of coal to Poland and the Commission had not so far succeeded in getting a

---

[4] That is, Adm. Paolo Thaon di Revel.
[5] For the text of this "Proposal for Rendering Effective the Work of the Teschen Commission," March 21, 1919, see PPC, IV, 473-75.

single ton of coal to Poland, because it was unable to put through its wishes. It was now proposed that the four Great Powers, represented on the Inter-Allied Teschen Commission, should request the Czecho-Slovak and Polish Governments to accept the principle that, within the limits of the original mandate, the decisions of the Inter-Allied Teschen Commission should become effective the moment they were promulgated, without requiring the assent of the Governments of Prague and Warsaw. It was understood, however, that the Czecho-Slovak and Polish Governments would reserve the liberty of presenting their objections to the Inter-Allied Teschen Commission or of appealing to the Conference, but in any case the decisions of the Inter-Allied Teschen Commission would be binding until revoked by that Commission or countermanded by the Conference.

PRESIDENT WILSON enquired whether the Teschen Commission thought that those proposals would be effective.

DR. LORD explained that he did not speak on behalf of the Teschen Commission as a whole. The proposals he had put forward had the support of the American Representatives of that Commission who were now in Paris; but he believed that the proposals represented roughly the views of the whole of the Teschen Commission.

MR. BALFOUR said that he could answer President Wilson's question as far as the British Government was concerned. Colonel Coulson,[6] the British Representative on the Teschen Commission had made a proposal substantially identical to that put forward by Dr. Lord.

M. CAMBON explained that a copy of Dr. Lord's proposals had been forwarded to him and in consequence he had, that morning, called together the Commission on Czecho-Slovak questions. The American Representative on that Commission[7] had, however, expressed his inability to throw any light on the question and in consequence the meeting had been adjourned to a later date.

DR. LORD explained that the proposal put forward by the United States Delegation did not come officially from the Teschen Commission. It had been put forward by himself and Dr. Bowman, but he believed it agreed with the views of the Commission.

M. CAMBON, continuing, said he personally had no objections to offer to the proposal made, but the question had not been examined by his Commission. He was, however, quite prepared to accept the proposal on behalf both of the Commission on Czecho-Slovak questions and of the Polish Commission.

---

[6] Lt. Col. B.J.B. Coulson, a technical adviser on political and diplomatic questions in the British delegation to the peace conference.

[7] Allen Welsh Dulles, former Second Secretary of the American Legation in Bern, at this time a technical adviser on political and diplomatic questions in the A.C.N.P.

BARON SONNINO enquired whether the Czecho-Slovak and Polish Governments would accept the proposal.

DR. LORD explained that the resolution had merely been submitted in order that the principle might be accepted by the Supreme War Council, whose duty it would then be to obtain the acceptance of the proposals therein contained by the Governments of Czecho-Slovakia and Poland.

(It was agreed:

1. That the four Great Powers represented on the Inter-Allied Teschen Commission request the Czecho-Slovak and Polish Governments to accept the principle that within the limits of the original mandate of this Conference (February 3, 1919)[8] the decisions of the Inter-Allied Teschen Commission are to become effective the moment they are promulgated, without requiring the assent of the Governments of Prague and Warsaw.

It is understood that the said Governments may reserve the liberty of presenting their objections to the Inter-Allied Teschen Commission or of appealing to the Conference, but in any case, the decisions of the Inter-Allied Teschen Commission will be binding until revoked by that Commission or countermanded by the Conference. The Inter-Allied Teschen Commission is requested to report its proceedings to the General Secretariat of the Peace Conference for review by the Paris Commission on Polish Affairs.

2. To telegraph to the Governments of Poland and of Czecho-Slovakia an identic note to give effect to the preceding.)

(For text of telegram to be sent see Annexure "B"; paragraph IV.)[9]

(The meeting then adjourned.)

T MS (SDR, RG 256, 180.03101/64, DNA).

[8] The text of this mandate is printed in *PPC*, IV, 473.

[9] This paragraph reads as follows:

"IV. To make the foregoing resolutions effective, the following telegrams are proposed.

"(1) *To the Interallied Teschen Commission*:

Recognizing the importance of quick and effective decisions in the administration of the powers entrusted to the Interallied Teschen Commission, the Conference has sent an identic note to the Governments of Poland and of Czecho-Slovakia requesting them to instruct the local authorities of the Duchy of Teschen that they are to accept the decision of the Interallied Teschen Commission without waiting for the assent of their respective Governments.

"The local authorities will keep their respective Governments fully informed of the decisions of the Interallied Teschen Commission and should either of the Governments concerned protest the decisions of the Commission, due attention should be given to such protestation.

"The two Governments may reserve the right to appeal to the Peace Conference should they be unwilling to accept any decision of the Interallied Teschen Commission, but, in each instance, pending a final decision, the local authorities shall follow the mandate of the Interallied Teschen Commission. A resolution of the Conference requires your Commission to report its proceedings to the general secretariat of the Peace Conference for review by the Commission on Polish Affairs.

"(2) *Identic note to the Governments of Poland and of Czecho-Slovakia.*

"In order to ensure the administration of the Teschen agreement of February 3rd in a more effective manner, the Peace Conference requests your Government to consent to the following arrangement. It proposes that the principle should be established that the decisions of the Interallied Teschen Commission are in each case to become effective as soon as they are announced, without requiring the local authorities to await the agreement of the Governments of Poland or of Czecho-Slovakia.

"Should your Government desire to do so, it may reserve the liberty of presenting any objections to these decisions either to the Conference at Paris or to the Interallied Teschen Commission, but it is proposed that, pending a reply, the decisions of the Interallied Teschen Commission should be binding. An identic note to this effect is being sent to the Government of Poland (Czecho-Slovakia). Should your Government accept this principle it is requested that immediate notification be sent to all the local authorities and to the Conference at Paris."

From the Diary of David Hunter Miller

Monday, March 24th [1919]

At 2:30 P.M. Mr. Close, The President's secretary, came down and handed me three amendments written on the President's type-writer,[1] and said the President wanted this ready for the meeting, in English and French, with the three amendments on one sheet of paper. I at once had them put into French by Mr. Warrin,[2] and mimeographed in English and French.

Miller, *My Diary at the Conference of Paris*, I, 199-200.
[1] There are WWT copies of these amendments in WP, DLC. Two of them are reproduced in the minutes of the League of Nations Commission printed at March 24 and 26, 1919. The third one, an amendment to Article X concerning the Monroe Doctrine, is reproduced in revised form in the minutes of the League of Nations Commission printed at April 10, 1919.
[2] Frank Lord Warrin, Jr., lawyer of New York, at this time a secretary for territorial questions in the A.C.N.P.

Minutes of a Meeting of the League of Nations Commission

TWELFTH MEETING, MARCH 24, 1919, AT 8.30 P.M.
President WILSON *in the Chair.*

President Wilson read a letter from the International Council of Women asking that they might present to the Commission certain important matters which had a bearing upon the claims of women.[1] After a discussion of this request, it was agreed that the Commission should receive a delegation from the Inter-Allied Council of Women for half an hour before the last meeting.

ARTICLE 9.

Mr. Bourgeois proposed a new amendment (Annex 1)[2] which was intended to anticipate and prepare for military or naval oper-

[1] This letter from Lady Aberdeen of March 22, 1919 (see Miller, *The Drafting of the Covenant*, I, 324), is missing. She was Ishbel Maria Marjoribanks Gordon, Marchioness of Aberdeen and Temair, wife of John Campbell Gordon, Marquess of Aberdeen and Temair. Both were well known advocates of liberal causes, and she was also active in the international peace movement.
[2] The Annexures are printed below.

ations and to secure their immediate and effective performance. He thought that it was necessary to make an explanation with regard to his proposal because of certain interpretations which the Press had placed upon the French amendments. It had been said that these amendments proposed the creation of a permanent international force on the frontiers of France and all other countries in a particularly dangerous position. This interpretation was entirely incorrect. It had been said also that the permanent organism which was contemplated by the amendments would have of itself a power of making decisions. Such a statement likewise was erroneous, for the Executive Council, upon whose authority this Council depended, would alone be able to give instructions and orders whenever peace was threatened.

The essential idea of the French amendments was to give to the Executive Council adequate information as well as a methodical and considered plan of action from the military and naval point of view, so that, if a danger should arise, if a sudden attack should be launched, the Executive Council would be ready to take immediate decision relying upon the programme of the permanent organ. It was not only a matter of protecting the French frontier, but of protecting every frontier which might be in a dangerous geographical position; and this fact was true of a great number of frontiers in the world. The precautions to be taken, therefore, were of great importance to all peaceful nations.

The machinery contemplated by the French amendments would be the following: the permanent organ would concern itself with preparing the plan of military and naval action in such a way that, in case of necessity, each one of the Governments, retaining sovereignty, might immediately advise its constitutional authority and submit to it a definite plan for meeting a threatened attack or any danger of a warlike character. The Parliaments of the respective Governments could only decide upon the amount of credits to be established and upon the order for mobilisation if their responsible Governments were ready to furnish them with exact information as to the extent of the military action required by the League of Nations. The French proposal, instead of causing any anxiety to constitutional authorities, was on the contrary calculated to give them all necessary guarantees concerning the extent of the effort which each country might be called upon to make. Such explanations as these would make clear the meaning of the French amendments and defeat such objections as an incorrect interpretation had provoked. The Allied Associations represented at London, which unanimously adopted the text of the French amendments, had been thoroughly convinced.

The President of the United States had recently been good enough to visit the devastated areas of France and of Belgium. It was to prevent the reappearance of such terrible destruction that the amendment proposed to Article 9 had been conceived. Its object was to eliminate the surprise which allowed such an invasion, and to give to the action of the League of Nations the greatest possible effect. Any form of words which would permit of the realisation of this object would be acceptable to the French Delegation.

Mr. Larnaude had only a word to add to the comprehensive explanation of the first French Delegate. History showed that all recent wars had begun with a sudden attack. Such was the necessity of modern war; war could not succeed unless it was unexpected and crushing. In order to create a feeling of security such as was required by the people of the invaded districts to permit them to rebuild their homes and their industries, they must be assured that the attack whose victims they had been could not be repeated, and that the League of Nations presented some new and effective safeguard for their existence.

President Wilson said that he had read the French proposal with a great deal of care. Article 9 of the Covenant made provision for a permanent Commission which should "advise the League of Nations on military and naval questions generally." The Executive Council would therefore be entirely free to direct all the necessary researches of this Commission. Inasmuch as France had a member on the Executive Council, she would be able, in case of need, to give the danger signal and insist upon the drafting of a plan of action, or of co-operation, which appeared indispensable to her. The amendment of the French Delegation did not appear to add anything important to the present text, since the latter placed no restriction upon the scope and the kind of advice which the Executive Council might ask of the Permanent Commission. Its competence was not limited and was quite broad enough to relieve all the anxieties which had been so clearly set forth by Mr. Bourgeois.

Mr. Bourgeois said that inasmuch as it was understood that Article 9 left it open to the Commission to study the protective guarantees which he asked for, there could be no objection to using a form of words which would be acceptable to public opinion. The Executive Council would remain master of the situation; but it was important that technical advice should be asked beforehand from experts of various countries and that they should have a position recognised in the Covenant itself. If they formed one of the sections of the League of Nations, they would give to the study of military questions a continuity which it would not have if their position were less clearly defined.

President Wilson observed that every definition constituted a limitation and that it was frequently preferable to adopt a larger and more elastic formula adaptable to all kinds of circumstances.

Lord Robert Cecil said that the present text of Article 9 as it stood was the result of a compromise between the original Article and the French amendment, and that it would seem difficult to change its terms further.

Mr. Kramar could not see that there was any difference between the French amendment and the text of Article 9. One might add a reference to Article 7 and change the word "League" to the words "Executive Council." In this way the control exercised by the Executive Council would be more clearly defined.

Mr. Bourgeois and *Mr. Larnaude* held to the text of the French amendment, which seemed to them to be more precise. In such a matter precision was essential.

Mr. Hymans tried to reconcile the two views by proposing a text drafted as follows:

"A permanent Commission shall be constituted to advise the Executive Council on the execution of the provisions of Articles 7 and 8 and on the military and naval means by which the obligations imposed by the present Covenant upon the High Contracting Parties shall be fulfilled."

He added that if a *procès-verbal* of the discussion were added to the Covenant, it would be an enlightening commentary upon the meaning of the text.

Mr. Orlando was of opinion that a form of words could hardly be found wider in scope than those of Article 9, and that the amendment of Mr. Hymans would only serve to limit the scope of the text. The word "organisme" signified something quite different from "commission." It carried with it the idea of an independent will.

Thereupon, *Mr. Hymans* withdrew his suggestion, and the two changes suggested by Mr. Kramar were adopted.

The French Delegation made a reservation with regard to its amendment.

ARTICLE 10.

President Wilson said that he intended subsequently to draft a proposed amendment to Article 10. There being no other amendments, the Article was passed, President Wilson reserving the right to bring forward his amendment at a later time.

ARTICLE 11.

The amendment of the British Delegation to substitute for the words "the High Contracting Parties reserve the right to" the words "the League shall" was adopted.

Mr. Larnaude proposed to add to this Article an amendment

which had earlier been proposed by the French Delegation with respect to Article 3, and which was intended to permit the immediate convocation of the Executive Council in a crisis. The text, which was to constitute a third paragraph to Article 11, would be as follows:

"Moreover in case of any occurrence calculated to imperil the maintenance of peace, the Secretary-General shall, at the request of any one of the Associated Governments, convoke the Executive Council immediately."

This amendment was adopted in principle, subject to reference to the Drafting Committee.

ARTICLE 12.

Mr. Larnaude proposed an amendment (Annex 2) intended to indicate more clearly the obligation of the members of the League to submit any difference in the first instance to inquiry or to arbitration. This amendment was referred to the Drafting Committee, together with an amendment, proposed by the British Delegation, to delete the words after "Executive Council" in the first paragraph, sixth line, as far as the end of the sentence, and substitute therefor "as hereinafter provided."

Baron Makino proposed to add the following words at the end of the second paragraph:

"From the time a dispute is submitted to arbitration or to inquiry by the Executive Council, and until the lapse of the aforesaid term of three months, the parties to the dispute shall refrain from making any military preparations."

This amendment was intended to permit the League to examine the matter submitted to it without being distracted by the fact of military preparations, and in order that it might have time to make its decision with every sense of security.

President Wilson suggested that the Japanese amendment should appear as a separate Article which would provisionally be called 12A.

Subject to these changes and reference to the Drafting Committee, the Article was adopted.

ARTICLE 13.

Lord Robert Cecil read an amendment (Annex 3) which was intended to draw a distinction between justiciable and non-justiciable disputes.

President Wilson suggested that the text of the British amendment should be revised so as to make clear that the cases enumerated therein were only mentioned as examples, and that the States members of the League might have recourse to arbitration in many other cases not expressly defined.

After an exchange of views between *Mr. Larnaude, Lord Robert Cecil*, and *Mr. Vesnitch*, the amendment of the British Delegation was referred to the Drafting Committee in order that President Wilson's suggestion might be utilised.

Mr. Hymans proposed another modification to this Article (Annex 4).

After discussion the amendment was adopted in principle and referred to the Drafting Committee.

ARTICLE 14.

Lord Robert Cecil proposed an amendment on behalf of the British Delegation (Annex 5) which was adopted.

Mr. Larnaude read an amendment (Annex 6) whose object was to define the jurisdiction of the Permanent Court of Justice and entrust it particularly with questions relative to the interpretation of the Covenant. He added that his proposal was based upon the American Constitution, according to which the Supreme Court had jurisdiction over questions of a constitutional nature.

Mr. Orlando thought that this definition of functions would be dangerous, and that it was preferable to leave to the Executive Council, who applied the Covenant, the duty of resolving questions of interpretation.

Lord Robert Cecil shared the opinion expressed by Mr. Orlando, and thought that paragraph "B" of the French amendment might be cut out.

After an exchange of views between *Mr. Bourgeois, Baron Makino* and *Lord Robert Cecil*, the French amendment was adopted in principle, with paragraph "B" omitted and paragraph "C" altered by cutting out the words "one of the parties" and substituting therefor the words "both parties." It was referred to the Drafting Committee for incorporation in the text, together with the British amendment, which proposed to add at the end of the article the words "and also any issue referred to it by the Executive Council or Body of Delegates."

Mr. Hymans read an amendment (Annex 7) which was intended as a new Article. The object of this amendment was to strengthen the principle of arbitration.

Mr. Orlando proposed that the Court should settle the question which the Belgian Delegation had in mind; this would avoid the creation of the machinery of a new tribunal.

Lord Robert Cecil remarked that the only case in which the Belgian amendment would apply would be that in which one of the parties should consent to go before the Court while the other party refused. This assumption raised an important political question which it would be difficult to settle by means of compulsory arbitration.

Mr. Larnaude believed that if both parties had agreed to a "*compromis*" it would be because they believed that their dispute was of a justiciable nature.

Lord Robert Cecil remarked that there were certain general Conventions of arbitration which were not of the nature of "*compromis*," whereas the amendment referred only to Conventions.

After a discussion between *Mr. Orlando* and *Mr. Hymans*, the amendment was withdrawn.

ARTICLE 15.

Lord Robert Cecil proposed a British drafting amendment in the third line to delete the semi-colon and substitute a full stop, and to substitute "any" for "either"; this was adopted and referred to the Drafting Committee.

In the second paragraph, *President Wilson* proposed to omit the words following "recommendation" in line 10 to the end of the sentence. This was adopted, subject to reference to the Drafting Committee.

Lord Robert Cecil proposed on behalf of the Greek Delegation an amendment (Annex 8) which was accepted in principle and likewise referred to the Drafting Committee.

President Wilson proposed the following amendment:

"If the difference between the parties shall be found by the Executive Council or by the Body of Delegates to be a question which by international law is solely within the domestic legislative jurisdiction of one of the parties, it shall so report, and shall make no recommendation as to its settlement."

It was agreed that the word "legislative" should be omitted.

Mr. Koo proposed to add at the end of the amendment proposed by President Wilson the words "unless a recommendation is requested by the party or parties within whose exclusive domestic jurisdiction the subject-matter lies."

The amendment of the United States Delegation together with the additional clause proposed by the Chinese Delegation was referred to the Drafting Committee.

The French amendment (Annex 9) was likewise referred to the consideration of the Drafting Committee.

Mr. Hymans read an amendment (Annex 10) the object of which was to sanction the establishment of special Conventions, by which certain States might bind themselves to accept the decisions of a simple majority of the Executive Council.

President Wilson remarked that this amendment was consistent with the general spirit of the Covenant, which authorised special Conventions of a kind calculated to support the guarantees accorded by the League of Nations.

Mr. Hymans explained that his object had been to enable the small States to agree to accept a decision reached by a simple majority. This would be one way of diminishing the chance of war.

Mr. Orlando thought that the Belgian amendment conflicted with the spirit of the Covenant. A State which had concluded special Conventions with another State might some time find itself obliged to take part in a war which the League of Nations was conducting against that State, and so there would be a conflict between its general obligation toward the League of Nations and its particular obligation to an individual State.

President Wilson observed that it had been understood that the terms of the Covenant allowed the conclusion of special Conventions intended to diminish the risk of war.

Lord Robert Cecil did not think that the League would guarantee particular conventions.

Mr. Hymans noted President Wilson's statement on the subject of the possibility of concluding special Conventions, and felt that, under these circumstances, the object of his amendment was sufficiently safeguarded without the necessity of adding a change in the text. The amendment was withdrawn.

Lord Robert Cecil read a proposed new Article 15A (Annex 11).

This amendment, which provided for commissions of conciliation, would make it possible for the members of the Executive Council, whose time would be otherwise very much engaged, to establish commissions composed of capable men to whom they would entrust the examination of certain cases. The neutral countries had expressed a great desire that the League should contain some conciliatory organ of a non-political character.

President Wilson remarked that the Executive Council was already competent to name such commissions inasmuch as it had the right to suggest methods of conciliation.

So long as this power was expressly recognised as inhering in the Executive Council, *Lord Robert Cecil* was willing not to press his amendment.

ARTICLE 16.

The French Delegation proposed an amendment which was intended to bring under the sanctions of Article 16 not only Article 12, but Articles 8, 13 and 15 as well.

Lord Robert Cecil agreed that it would be well to include a reference to Article 15 in this connection, but considered that it would be unfortunate to bring any other article within its scope, particularly Article 8, wherein the only obligation laid down was the obligation to exchange information. It would be very severe to call into play *ipso facto* the sanctions provided by Article 16 merely because a State had not produced the information asked for.

Mr. Bourgeois yielded to the objection so far as Article 8 was concerned. As for the reference to Article 13, it seemed clear that the failure to execute a decision of the Executive Council would be a grave offence. On the other hand, it might not be advisable to lay down precisely the measures by which this Article would be rendered effective, inasmuch as it might be impossible to put the decision into execution, and one could not very well punish a State which had shown evidence of malicious intent. Refusal alone should be considered as a violation of the Covenant, and the application of the penalties should be proposed only in that event.

After an exchange of views between *Lord Robert Cecil, Mr. Bourgeois* and *President Wilson*, the French amendment was accepted with reference to Article 15 only.

Two amendments of the British Delegation were adopted: to insert after the word "recommend" the words "to the several Governments concerned," and in paragraph 3, line 6, to insert after the word "will" the words "take the necessary steps to." It was decided to continue the examination on March 26 at 8.30 P.M.

(The meeting adjourned at 11 P.M.)

Annexes to Minutes of Twelfth Meeting.

Annex 1.

Add:

A permanent organism shall be established to concert and prepare in advance the necessary military and naval measures for fulfilling the obligations imposed on the High Contracting Parties by this Covenant, and to ensure that they shall be immediately effective in any case of emergency.

Annex 2.

Substitute for the present text:

The High Contracting Parties agree that, should there arise between them any dispute which cannot be settled by the ordinary methods of diplomacy, they will submit the matter to inquiry by the Executive Council or to arbitration.

They will in no case resort to war against a member of the League which complies with the award of the arbitrators or with the recommendation of the Executive Council.

Annex 3.

Delete the first sentence and substitute the following:

If a dispute should arise between the States members of the League as to the interpretation of a Treaty, as to any question of international law, as to the existence of any fact which, if established, would constitute a breach of any international obligation, or as to the extent and nature of the reparation to be made for any such breach, if such dispute cannot be satisfactorily settled by diplomacy, the States members of the League recognise arbitration to be the most effective and at the same time the most equitable means of settling the dispute; and they agree to submit to arbitration any dispute which they recognise to be of this nature. For this purpose the Court * * * etc.

Annex 4.

Substitute for "which they recognise to be" the words "which is, according to any Convention existing between them, or which they agree to be."

Annex 5.

In the third line, after the word "determine" insert "any dispute or difference of an international character including."

Annex 6.

Substitute for the present text:

The Executive Council shall formulate a plan for the establishment of a Permanent Court of International Justice: this Court shall, when established, be competent to hear and determine:

(*a*) any matter which is submitted to it by the Body of Delegates or the Executive Council,

(*b*) any matter arising out of the interpretation of the Covenant establishing the League,

(*c*) any dispute which, with the consent of the Court and the Executive Council, any of the parties may wish to have submitted to it.

Annex 7.

Insert as Article 14A:

In the event of the parties to a dispute not agreeing on the interpretation to be given to an arbitration Convention between them, the question shall be referred to a special tribunal composed as follows: each party shall nominate one member of the Executive Council and one member of the Permanent Court of International Justice; two members shall be nominated by the above Court from among its own members; an additional member shall be selected by the Executive Council from among its members; this tribunal shall nominate its own president from among those of its members belonging to the Permanent Court of International Justice.

Annex 8.

The Executive Council may, in any case under this Article, refer the dispute to the Body of Delegates at the request of any party to the dispute, provided that such request be made within 14 days after the submission of the dispute to the Council. In this case, a recommendation made by the Body of Delegates shall have the force of an unanimous recommendation by the Executive Council, provided that such recommendation is supported by all the States represented in the Executive Council and a majority of the other States represented in the Body of Delegates.

Annex 9.

Add:

The dispute shall be referred to the Body of Delegates in any case in which the Executive Council has failed to come to a decision.

Annex 10.

Fourth paragraph, add:

It shall be lawful for States to conclude special Conventions intended to eliminate any possibility of war between them, whether by agreeing to accept the decisions of a simple majority of the Executive Council, or by agreeing to any other mode of settling disputes.

Annex 11.

The Executive Council may formulate plans for the establishment of a system of commissions of conciliation and may make recommendations as to the method of employing such commissions in the settlement of such disputes as are not recognised by the parties as suitable for arbitration.

Printed copy (WP, DLC).

To Thomas William Lamont

My dear Mr. Lamont: Paris, 24 March, 1919.

I sincerely value your letter of March 19th enclosing the copy of the cable you have received from your partners with regard to Mr. Root's views on the League of Nations.

I am glad to tell you in the meantime that in the conferences the Commission on the League of Nations is again holding there is a very good prospect that some of the chief difficulties which are apparently in Mr. Root's mind and which have been very definitely expressed by others may be removed by amendment or clarification of the Covenant.

I shall certainly hope to have a word with you personally about this matter, though I am daily being disappointed by being kept so long in conference that nothing of the day is left.

Cordially and sincerely yours,   Woodrow Wilson

TLS (T. W. Lamont Papers, MH-BA).

To Felix Ludwig Calonder

My dear Mr. Calonder: Paris, 24 March, 1919.

I received your communication of the 22nd of March in which you make official offer to the League of Nations of the hospitality of Switzerland and invite the League to establish its seat in Switzerland. On Saturday I had the pleasure of reading your letter to the members of the Commission on the League of Nations which is sitting under the authority of the Peace Conference. No discussion of the matter took place but I was authorized to appoint a small committee to take the whole matter of the determination of the seat of the League under careful consideration, and I shall take real pleasure in placing your letter in the hands of that committee.

In the meantime may I not express warm appreciation of this generous offer on the part of the Swiss Government and people?

Cordially and sincerely yours,   [Woodrow Wilson]

CCL (WP, DLC).

To Edwin Brewington Parker

My dear Judge Parker: Paris, 24 March, 1919.

Mr. Hoover has represented to me the critical clothing conditions in the liberated countries.[1] He has also presented to me the fact that the War Department is possessed of enormous stocks, not only of new clothing but of renovated materials. It must be obvious that these renovated materials can have but little value in the world markets and that the unused materials, purchased and manufactured under war conditions, will soon be heavily depreciated by the return of commerce to more normal prices. It would appear, therefore, that it is desirable to liquidate these stocks at the earliest possible moment.

It would appear that but little market could be found for such large quantities of clothing and shoes and similar articles, except through some such relief agency as that conducted by Mr. Hoover and, to some extent, this agency may be of value in the distribution of the unused material. The sympathetic interest which the American people must have in the alleviation of misery amongst the liberated peoples should lead us to entertain the most sympathetic view as to prices and terms upon which this material is disposed of to them. I would be glad, therefore, if the Commission could accept as its guiding principle in these negotiations the fact that it is not only securing a rapid liquidation of materials that may otherwise prove practically unsalable, but also that it has an opportunity to perform a fine human service by approaching the matter in the most sympathetic mind, and I would be glad if the Commission could see its way to very largely accept[ing] Mr. Hoover's views as to the terms upon which dealings should be undertaken with the liberated peoples.   Faithfully yours,   [Woodrow Wilson]

CCL (WP, DLC).
[1] HCH to WW, March 22, 1919.

Two Letters to Robert Lansing

My dear Lansing: Paris, 24 March, 1919.

I am disturbed to hear that the members of the civilian staff of our delegation are being allowed to bring their wives over. I do not know what permission they have been given or by whom, but it seems to me to be sure to constitute a basis for the most serious and perhaps for justified criticism.

It is clearly not feasible for them literally and in all respects to bring their wives over "at their own expense" particularly if their wives are permitted to come over on transports (which I think they ought not to be) and to lodge with them at the Crillon.

I am so anxious about this matter that I am taking the liberty to ask you to post me as to the facts. If this has been done I hope with all my heart that the permission will be rescinded.

Faithfully yours,   [Woodrow Wilson]

My dear Lansing: Paris, 24 March, 1919.

Before I answer your letter herewith returned[1] I wish you would read the enclosed letter from General Graves[2] which I received from Baker the other day and then let me know whether that changes your view or not. I would be obliged if you would let General Bliss also see the letter.

Please enjoin your Secretary not to forget to return General Graves' letter and also your own enclosed.

Faithfully yours,   Woodrow Wilson

TLS (SDR, RG 256, 861.00/392, DNA).
[1] RL to WW, March 21, 1919 (first letter of that date).
[2] It is printed as an Enclosure with NDB to WW, March 3, 1919, Vol. 55.

From Henry Mauris Robinson,[1] with Enclosure

My dear Mr. President: [Paris] 24 March 1919

The work of the Commission on International Legislation for Labor has been completed and, as I understand it, the formal report will go to the Peace Commission tomorrow.[2]

In order to put you in possession of the information, I am passing to you herewith the following:

(a) A copy of the Draft Convention for the Permanent Conference for International Legislation for Labor.[3]

(b) The substitute for Article 19 in the printed draft.[4]

(c) Copy of a protocol to Article 19.[5]

(d) Copy of the draft of principles for a labor charter for action by the Peace Commission.

(e) Copy of a statement by Andrew Furuseth and Edward P. Flynn,[6] and additional memorandum of statement signed by Andrew Furuseth under date of March 22[7] which would show that the protocol to Article 19 appears to satisfy his objections to the draft convention.

In passing this to you I wish to reiterate the statement of the opinion that it would have been and still is preferable from the point of view of the United States if the States themselves had had the right to treat draft conventions as recommendations, and it is entirely possible that the American Peace Commission will reach this conclusion. However, it is the fact that the European delegates to the Labor Commission and European labor generally had dreamed that the proposed organization would be put in a position, in an international way, to legislate for labor, and the draft convention as it now stands will not be entirely acceptable to European labor. In fact, M. Jouhaux,[8] the head of the Federation of Labor of France, has written into the record a letter that, inasmuch as this draft convention does not set up definite international legislative powers, it is not satisfactory to the Federation of Labor of France. This is some indication of the attitude of European labor.

If you care to discuss the matter, I am at your service.

Very truly yours,   Henry M. Robinson

TLS (WP, DLC).

[1] At this time he was officially an alternate representative of the United States on the Commission on International Labour Legislation.

[2] The Council of Ten, at the instigation of Lloyd George, had established this commission on January 23. See the minutes of the Council of Ten printed at that date in Vol. 54. Samuel Gompers and Edward N. Hurley were appointed as the American representatives on the commission, but Robinson replaced Hurley after the first meeting. The commission began its deliberations on February 1, and Gompers was chosen as its president on the nomination of the French Minister of Labor, Pierre Colliard. The commission held thirty-five meetings between February 1 and March 24, with a hiatus between February 28 and March 11. The members worked with a draft plan for an

international labor organization prepared by the British delegation. For a detailed summary of the work of the commission, see James T. Shotwell, ed., *The Origins of the International Labor Organization* (2 vols., New York, 1934), I, 105-98. The complete minutes of the meetings of the commission are printed in *ibid.*, II, 149-322.

3 Commission on International Labour Legislation, A DRAFT CONVENTION CREATING A PERMANENT ORGANIZATION FOR THE PROMOTION OF THE INTERNATIONAL REGULATION OF LABOUR CONDITIONS, printed texts in English and French (WP, DLC). Both texts are printed in Shotwell, I, 373-421. This document provided for the establishment, under the auspices of the League of Nations, of an International Labour Conference, to meet at least once a year and empowered to propose international conventions on subjects affecting labor or to propose needed labor legislation to the nations which were members of the league. It also established an International Labour Office to collect data on the conditions of labor and, under the direction of a Governing Body, to act as an executive agency for the Conference. The remainder of the document spelled out in detail the powers and functions of the two bodies.

4 "New Article XIX" and "New Article XX," T MS (WP, DLC). The subject matter of Article XIX (Article XVIII in the original British draft mentioned in n. 2 above) had inspired a prolonged dispute between the delegates of the United States and those of the other nations represented on the Commission on International Labour Legislation. The British draft had provided that the proposals of the International Labour Conference should be embodied solely in international conventions, which each nation belonging to the League of Nations was to ratify and enforce unless a particular convention was disapproved by its national legislature. The American delegates objected that this provision was unacceptable under the American federal system, in which the state legislatures had the final authority over labor legislation. The resulting impasse in the commission was resolved only in late March through an elaborate compromise draft of Article XIX and XX under which the International Labour Conference might embody its recommendations in either conventions or recommendations for legislation to be submitted to the member nations, and those nations with a federal system might choose to regard a proposed convention as in fact a recommendation for legislation. For a thorough discussion of this complex issue, see Shotwell, I, 145-63.

5 Its text follows: "In no case shall any of the High Contracting Powers be asked or required through the adoption by the Conference of any recommendation or draft convention to diminish the protection afforded by its existing legislation to the workers concerned." T MS (WP, DLC).

6 A. Furuseth and E. P. Flynn, "*Memorandum* On the Constitution of the Conference on Labor Legislation in Relation to the Seamen's Act of America," n.d., T MS (WP, DLC), also printed in Shotwell, II, 357-58. On behalf of the seamen of the world, Furuseth and Flynn protested against the whole draft convention submitted by the Commission on International Labour Legislation on the ground that it infringed upon the protections to seamen guaranteed by the Seamen's Act of 1915 (about which see the index references in Vols. 27-32 of this series). Great Britain, they charged, had dominated the commission and had thus put through a draft convention favorable to its maritime interests. Only if the so-called "Labor Charter" (that is, the clauses for insertion in the treaty of peace printed as the Enclosure with the above document) was adopted could the seamen accept the proposed convention. The Editors have been unable to identify Edward P. Flynn.

7 A. Furuseth, "*Supplemental Memorandum*," March 22, 1919, T MS (WP, DLC). The substance of this document is conveyed in A. Furuseth to WW, March 26, 1919.

8 That is, Léon Jouhaux.

E N C L O S U R E

CLAUSES PROPOSED FOR INSERTION IN THE TREATY OF PEACE

The High Contracting Parties declare their acceptance of the following principles and engage to take all necessary steps to secure their realisation in accordance with the recommendations to be made by the International Labour Conference as to their practical application:

1. In right and in fact the labour of a human being should not be treated as merchandise or an article of commerce.

2. Employers and workers should be allowed the right of association for all lawful purposes.

3. No child should be permitted to be employed in industry or commerce before the age of fourteen years in order that every child may be ensured reasonable opportunities for mental and physical education.
   Between the years of fourteen and eighteen young persons of either sex may only be employed on work which is not harmful to their physical development and on condition that the continuation of their technical or general education is ensured.

4. Every worker has a right to a wage adequate to maintain a reasonable standard of life having regard to the civilization of his time and country.

5. Equal pay should be given to women and to men for work of equal value in quantity and quality.

6. A weekly rest including Sunday or its equivalent for all workers.

7. Limitation of the hours of work in industry on the basis of eight hours a day or forty-eight hours a week subject to an exception for countries in which climatic conditions, the imperfect development of industrial organisation or other special circumstances render the industrial efficiency of the workers substantially different.
   The International Labour Conference will recommend a basis approximately equivalent to the above for adoption in such countries.

8. In all matters concerning their status as workers and social insurance foreign workmen lawfully admitted to any country and their families should be ensured the same treatment as the nationals of that country.

9. All States should institute a system of inspection in which women should take part, in order to ensure the enforcement of the laws and regulations for the protection of the workers.

T MS (WP, DLC).

From Robert Lansing, with Enclosures

My dear Mr. President: Paris, March 24, 1919.

I beg to call your attention to the enclosed copies of telegrams regarding the present situation in Budapest. There is also enclosed a memorandum which has been drawn up by one of the technical advisors on Austro-Hungarian affairs, containing certain recommendations of policy in regard to this situation. I am of the opinion that the suggestions of this memorandum deserve serious consideration in view of the present emergency.

Faithfully yours,   Robert Lansing

TLS (WP, DLC).

ENCLOSURE   I

Paris March 24, 1919

The Present Situation in Hungary—Action Recommended.

According to telegraphic and newspaper reports, a Communist Revolution has broken out in Hungary. The leaders of the Revolution call upon the Hungarian proletariat to rise against the Hungarian land-holder and against the Czechs and Rumanians, appealing both to feelings of class and feelings of nationalism. A call for help has allegedly been sent to the Moscow Soviet Government and the Austrian proletariat is especially invited to follow Hungary's example "to break definitely with Paris and to ally itself with Moscow." The leaders of the new Hungarian Government are Bela Kun, a notorious communist, and Pogany, who has control of all the Workmen's and Soldiers' Councils and of what remains of Hungary's Army (approximately six divisions).

The situation in Hungary calls for the following action:

I. *Measures should be taken to isolate the Hungarian revolution from Russia and prevent its spread to neighboring countries*:

(a) The Czechs and Rumanians should be allowed to occupy the passes of the Carpathian Mountains and the railway connecting Czecho-Slovakia with Rumania, south of these passes.

(b) The Servians or the French should be permitted to occupy a strip of territory to connect the Slovene territory with the Danube near Pressburg, now held by the Czechs.

(c) The Czechs should be granted the necessary railway connections along their present line of occupation in Slovakia.

II. *Measures should be taken to endeavor to control the situation in Budapest.*

(a) A number of small gunboats or monitors might be sent to Budapest. It is understood that the British have one gunboat there at present. More could probably be sent from the Black Sea.

(b) Food supplies should be sent to Hungary under the condition that ordered distribution is assured. In any case a trial shipment should be sent as a proof of good faith in this matter. (The failure to deliver certain shipments of fats apparently promised to Hungary is one of the causes of the present trouble.)

(c) If possible a statement of policy regarding Hungary should be made. Tell the Hungarians the truth about the dismemberment of their country but give them some hope of economic and food assistance and fair treatment within the boundaries which are granted them, as well as a speedy peace if an organized government is established.

III. *Measures should be taken to prevent a repetition of the mistakes which have brought about the present situation in Hungary.*

(a) Faulty coordination between Paris and Entente representatives in Austria and Hungary is to some extent responsible for Hungary's revolution. If the Peace Conference had fully realized the situation it might not have put into effect the new armistice line (which brought the crash in Budapest)—nor would the Conference have permitted the British naval authorities to issue an order turning over all Danube shipping to the Czechs, which made the Hungarians desperate. To prevent similar mistakes in the future it is suggested that the Inter-Allied Commission, which should be the final Allied authority in Austria and Hungary, should be sent to Vienna. This Commission should act on instructions from Paris. This would tend to eliminate the ill-advised initiative of various Entente military officials in this part of the world. Representatives of the Allies already in Vienna might constitute this Commission and avoid creation of new machinery.

(b) Foodstuffs should be hastened to Austria and Bohemia in every possible way. The situation, both social and economic, is most serious in both these countries and it is hard to foresee what effect the action of Hungary may have upon either the Austrian or the Czech Government.

(c) Every effort should be made to have a treaty ready for Austria and Hungary at the same time as for Germany. The people in these countries might not understand added delay in their case.

A. W. Dulles

TS MS (WP, DLC).

E N C L O S U R E   I I

Fiume, March 23, 1919.

For Tyler.[1] URGENT

Left Budapest 9 P.M., March 22nd on special train given American Food Mission. Situation generally quiet, government having preserved order energetically. Order issued condemning to death any person offering armed resistance to the Soviet Government and condemning to death any person robbing or plundering. Second order punishes with fine of 50,000 kronen the sale of alcoholic liquor and 10,000 kronen for drinking it. Bela Kun empowered Zerkowitz[2] to control foreign mission[s] and Vaga[3] assured me government would permit no harm to English or American. Safety of French questioned owing to bitter resentment of populace. Two British monitors arrived 6 p.m., 22nd, having been fired on while coming up. No definite decision on departure of Allied Missions when I left. Shortly after six government returned parts of engine of British sub-chaser previously removed and offered apologies for incident.

In proclamation of the government it is stated that only socialism the creation of communism is capable of preserving the country from the anarchy of disruption. Speaking of foreign policy, a proclamation said, "The Hungarian revolution is confronted with a complete catastrophe in regard to foreign politics. Paris Conference decided military occupation of almost entire Hungarian territory and considers occupation line final political frontier, thereby making impossible alimentation and coal supply of revolutionary Hungary. In this situation the Hungarian revolution has only one means of salvation, namely dictatorship of proletarians, the reign of the laborers and the agricultural proletariat." It adds that an army of the proletariat is being raised against Hungarian capitalism and large landowners as well as against Roumanian guards and Czech Bougevi [bourgeoisie?] and adds, "It declares its unrestricted ideal and spiritual unity with the Mission [Moscow?] Soviet Government and offers an armed balance to the prolitarians of Russia." Pod[4] states Karoly morning of 22nd in close touch with new Government. General rumors of rapid advance of Bolshevik armies on northern Hungary. General impression that nationalists have resorted to Bolshevism in hopes of being able to preserve integrity of country. Public opinion apparently favors armed aggression towards neighbors.   Roosevelt.[5]

[1] Maj. Royall Tyler, U.S.A., in charge of field observers in the Secretariat of the A.C.N.P. under the Secretary General, Joseph C. Grew.

[2] Probably Emil Zerkowitz, former banker, immigration agent, and journalist, who had spent some time in the United States prior to the war and who spoke English fluently.

[3] Actually, Béla Vágó, People's Commissar for Internal Affairs in the regime of Béla Kun.

[4] A garbled word. Perhaps the correct word was "Podmaniczky," that is, the Baron Podmaniczky mentioned in a similar context in the Enclosure printed with RL to WW, March 27, 1919.

[5] Capt. Nicholas Roosevelt, U.S.A., recently a representative of the Coolidge Mission in Hungary.

E N C L O S U R E   I I I

Berne, March 23, 1919.

489. With reference to report in press concerning situation in Hungary, I learn following respecting new ministry from Sigray:[1]

1. Garbai,[2] president, is a workman. Was at first Moderate Socialist, but has now moved to Left. Uneducated but intelligent.

2. Pogony, Minister of War, was formerly President of Soldatenrat. Was an orderly in second army and was punished for indiscretion about army affairs. Very intelligent Jew, violent and hates Bourgeoisie. He has done everything to prevent forming effective army. Is reported to have knowledge of Tiszas death.[3]

3. Brelsford, H. M.,[4] formerly Minister of War, now Commissioner for Social affairs, has lately gone to the Left.

4. Bela Kun, Minister Foreign Affairs, is pupil of Trotsky and his Aid-de-Camp in Russia for four years. He is described as Bolshevist of most dangerous type.

Sigaraz[5] says that the situation can only be saved by the immediate sending of United States or Allied troops. Department informed in my 6793 of today.   Stovall.

T telegrams (WP, DLC).
    [1] Antal, Count Sigray, diplomatic agent of the Károlyi government in Bern.
    [2] Sándor Garbai, chairman of the Revolutionary Governing Council of the Hungarian Soviet Republic.
    [3] István, Count Tisza, had been murdered by soldiers at his home in Budapest on October 31, 1918.
    [4] Garbled. As has been said, the Minister of Defense in the Károlyi government who became Commissar for Socialization in the Kun regime was Vilmos Böhm.
    [5] That is, Count Sigray.

A Memorandum by Béla Kun

Budapest, March the 24th 1919.

AIDE-MEMOIRE FOR PRINCE BORGHESE[1]

The New Government of Hungary, the Council of the Commissioners of the People, recognise the validity of the Treaty of Armistice signed by the former Government and do not think that the non-acceptance of the note presented by Colonel Vix[2] has infringed it.

By asking Russia to enter an alliance with the Republic of the Councils of Hungary, the Government has not thought that this step might be interpreted as an expression of its desire to break all diplomatic intercourse with the Powers of the Entente, and still less as a declaration of war on the Entente. The alliance with Russia is not a formal diplomatic alliance, it is at the most—if we may use the expression—an "entente cordiale," a natural friendship justified by the identical construction of their respective constitutions, which, in the thought of the Hungarian Government, does not in any way imply an aggressive combination. The new Hungarian Republic, on the contrary, has a firm desire to live in peace with all the other Nations and to devote its activities to the peaceful social re-organisation of its country.

The Hungarian Socialist Party has been driven by the force of the events to take hold of the executive power. It wishes to organise a new social State, a State in which every man will live of his own work, but this social State will not be hostile to other Nations. It wishes on the contrary to cooperate for the great human solidarity.

The Government of the Republic of the Councils of Hungary declare themselves ready to negotiate territorial questions on the basis of the principle of self-determination of the People, and they view territorial integrity solely as in conformity with that principle.

They would gladly welcome a civil and diplomatic mission of the Entente in Budapest and would guarantee to it the right of extra-territoriality and undertake to provide for its absolute safety.

Bela Kuhn,
Commissioner of the People
for Foreign Affairs.

T MS (WP, DLC).
  [1] Prince Luca Livio Borghese had gone to Belgrade in early March as the new Italian Minister to Serbia. The Belgrade government had refused to accept his letter of accreditation because it was not addressed to the King of the Serbs, Croats, and Slovenes. Borghese left Belgrade and arrived in Budapest on March 17, on his way back to Italy. He was approached on March 22 by a representative of Béla Kun, who wished to use him as a medium to open relations with the Allied governments. See the memorandum by V. E. Orlando printed at March 25, 1919.
  [2] See n. 1 to the memorandum by Lansing printed at March 22, 1919.

A Translation of a Letter from Prince Faisal

Dear Mr President   Paris, March 24, 1919.

The fortunate issue just obtained for the Arab peoples,[1] giving them a means of expressing their own purposes and ideals for their national future, has been won for them by the new principles whose first defender you are. Otherwise it would have been difficult, if not impossible, for our people, so long under the yoke of a barbarous militarism, to have made their voices heard above the cries of success raised by the victors of this terrible war.

In consequence I cannot find words in which to show our gratitude to you, and our realisation of the debt we owe to the nation which speaks through you. Perhaps this very feeling of the impossibility of thanking you shows how much we feel. I hope you will acquit me of the importunity if, on the eve of my departure for Syria, I venture to ask you to continue to encourage us forward on the path of moral and material development. I leave Paris probably on Friday and I would esteem it the greatest honour if you could find time, in the midst of your many engagements, to give me an opportunity of thanking you personally.

Believe me dear Mr President

Yours most respectful and grateful   Faisal[2]

T MS (WP, DLC).

[1] That is, the decision by the Council of Four on March 20 to send an inter-Allied commission to Syria to ascertain the opinions of the Arab peoples as to their future status, about which see the minutes of the Council of Four printed at March 20, 1919.

[2] The ALS, in Arabic, is in WP, DLC.

From the Diary of Edith Benham

March 24, 1919

Coming out from luncheon we had quite a curious experience. A large crowd of "poilus" blocked the street and they called to the President, "Give us peace, Mr. President, give us your peace; it is on you we count," and Colonel Jones, who stayed behind to settle up, etc., said they got a spokesman who delivered a regular address to him in English saying that they wanted the President's terms of peace, that the people at the Quai d'Orsay (Foreign Office) did not represent them, that they understood them and they wanted the President to know they were behind him. Unfortunately this can't be published, but it is significant, for no one knew we were coming and the crowd gathered while we were at luncheon which took some time, and this straw shows clearly the fact that the people understand the efforts made by the politicians to block peace and that the Government does not represent the French people.

To Newton Diehl Baker

Paris, 24 March, 1919.

For Secretary Baker: I know that you are having the court martial sentences of the war reviewed by the Judge Advocate General but do you not think it would be wise in view of the systematically stimulated public criticism of the matter to associate with the Judge Advocate General as I associated Hughes with Gregory in the aircraft investigation a committee of civilians chiefly Republicans of high standing in order that we might have a report which could not in the least be suspected of being a defense of the Administration? I would very much like your judgment about this.

Woodrow Wilson.

T telegram (WP, DLC).

To Albert Sidney Burleson

Paris, 24 March, 1919.

For Postmaster General. Repeated suggestions come to me about the removal of the cable censorship on our part. I understood before I left home that it had been entirely removed so far as we are concerned and that no cable censorship was exercised between the United States and Europe except by the French and British Governments. Am I right or what are the facts.

Woodrow Wilson.

T telegram (WP, DLC).

From Francis Patrick Walsh and Others

The White House, March 24, 1919

#28 Quote. The conviction of Eugene Debs under one of the war statutes has been affirmed by the Supreme Court and within thirty days he must begin to serve his sentence of ten years. We most respectfully and earnestly request that a respite may be granted in his case and in the others that are like his until we can have a chance to present to your consideration certain facts and circumstances that we are sure you will deem of important bearing. Frank P. Walsh, Allan L. Benson, Charles Edward Russell. Unquote. I am sending you foregoing at request of Charles Edward Russell. He has been your friend and has done much to stem the tide of bolshevism in this country.   Tumulty.

T telegram (WP, DLC).

From Edward Nash Hurley

My dear Mr. President: Washington March 24, 1919.

In reply to your letter of March 1st,[1] concerning the disposition of housing facilities, permit me to say that the Emergency Fleet Corporation will be very glad to consult with the Secretary of Labor concerning the restrictions and safeguards which should be made in the transfer of any property now in our hands, so as to preserve ideal living conditions in these industrial communities.

The Emergency Fleet Corporation decided not to build an ideal industrial community in Philadelphia, because of the length of time it would take to construct such an operation, but it commandeered something like 500 houses that were under construction in fairly close proximity to the shipyard and completed these. All of the other houses in Philadelphia which the Fleet Corporation built followed the lines of the standard Philadelphia workmen's cottage. The Fleet Corporation is now disposing of the 500 houses which it commandeered, and these, in spite of the extra expense incurred to expedite their completion, are sold at a net loss by the Fleet Corporation of between six and seven per cent. These are the only sales that the Fleet Corporation has as yet undertaken, and we shall consult with the Secretary of Labor before continuing the disposition even of the remaining houses in Philadelphia.[2]

Faithfully yours,   Edward N. Hurley

TLS (WP, DLC).
    [1] WW to E. N. Hurley, March 1, 1919, Vol. 55.
    [2] About this subject and its sequel, see Roy Lubove, "Homes and 'A Few Well-Placed Fruit Trees': An Object Lesson in Federal Housing," *Social Research*, XXVII (Jan. 1961), 469-86.

From the Diary of Dr. Grayson

Tuesday, March 25, 1919.

The four heads of the Peace Conference took full charge of the preparation of the Peace Treaty today. Lloyd-George, Clemenceau and Orlando met with the President in the temporary White House for the purpose of disposing of the very troublesome question of indemnities. It had been arranged beforehand that all would have their figures ready so that it could be seen whether they could be adjusted along a fair, average line and worked out in a manner which would meet the wishes of all concerned. The President furnished the figures for the United States, being the first to lay them upon the table. Lloyd-George followed with those of Great Britain; then came Orlando's turn. The trio then waited for Clemenceau to present France's figures, inasmuch as Clemenceau objected to the size of the amounts fixed by each of the three. He took the position that they were far too small, and so he was asked to furnish those which he had prepared for France. It then developed that the French plan of delay was still working overtime. Not only did Clemenceau have no figures, but he apparently had no definite knowledge of what he wanted. He said that he would have to get France's estimates from his Minister of Finance, but the Minister of Finance was not there. The result of this maneuver on the part of the French Premier was absolutely to nullify the effect of the morning conference, and still further to waste the time of the President and the other Peace Commissioners, despite the fact that the situation was growing more and more critical throughout Europe. When the President found that this time had been wasted, he talked very frankly, addressing his remarks chiefly to Premier Clemenceau, declaring that it was a crime to waste time when every hour meant so much to the settlement of world conditions along proper lines. He declared that the world was on fire and that it now was a race between law and order and anarchy, and that every minute lost assisted the forces of unrest.

The President said that there were many things in the Bolshevik program that he could almost agree to. Of course, he declared, their campaign of murder, confiscation and complete disregard for law, merits the utmost condemnation. However, some of their doctrines have been developed entirely through the pressure of the capitalists, who have disregarded the rights of the workers everywhere, and he warned all of his colleagues that if the Bolshevikis should become sane and agree to a policy of law and order they would soon spread all over Europe, overturning existing governments.

The President told Premier Clemenceau that his demands were impossible, inasmuch as in order to meet them Germany would be forced to put into effect a taxation that could hardly be paid. He said that the German people could be expected not to stand for a burden that would grind them down for fifty years, and then be a legacy to be passed on to their children. Rather than do that they would turn to anything—Bolshevism, or something which would promise them relief. He said that he believed Germany should be made to pay as much as it was possible for her to pay, but that she would have to have her status retained and be permitted to continue as a nation.

"Don't you see," the President asked Clemenceau, "that the very program that you propose to impose, carrying with it an excessive burden of taxation for generations, would be the greatest encouragement that could be held out to the German people to go over to Bolshevism? Your very program if put forth simply plays into the hands of the Bolsheviki leaders, and, frankly, I cannot say that I would blame the German people, who are being slowly poisoned by the circulation of Bolshevist doctrines, if they would go over to Bolshevism as an alternative from a burden of unjust taxation which could not be paid." The President explained to Premier Clemenceau that he sympathized very deeply with the French people and with the position of the Clemenceau government. He said that he had visited the devastated region and had seen with his own eyes the very distressing scenes there, which he characterized as distressing beyond expression, but he pointed out that it was the duty of himself and his colleagues at the present time to endeavor to bring about permanent peace conditions which will be for the benefit of the entire world. He said that it was not wise to see red because of the distress of those who had suffered in the past but that it was clearly the duty of the commission as members delegated to carry on a great task to establish justice and right upon which the future peace of the world could rest. He pointed out they were sitting as judges and that they agreed that the past had been dreadful. However, he let it be known that if they were to make horrible conditions again they would simply bring back the very conditions which had made for the war and all that went with it. If Germany was to be completely crushed the result must be that a condition of sympathy would be created for her which later on would result in the same conditions prevailing so far as Germany was concerned that prevailed for France before the present war, and naturally would result in another war.

In the afternoon the Big Four went to the Quai d'Orsay, where they received first-hand reports on the actual conditions prevailing in Russia. General Thwaites[1] of the British Army and Field Marshal Foch presented their latest reports showing exactly the disposition of the Bolshevist armies at the strategical points where they could be utilized in any effort to aid hunger where the Soviets had assumed control.

I had luncheon Tuesday with Frank H. Hitchcock,[2] former Chairman of the Republican National Committee, and former Postmaster General under President Taft. Mr. Hitchcock and I were old friends and he talked rather frankly of conditions in the United States, and especially of the Republican opposition to the League of Nations. Mr. Hitchcock was entirely out of sympathy with the Republican opposition. Taking up the manner in which it was being handled by the present Republican Chairman, he said that he (Hitchcock) had been in part responsible for the selection of Mr. Will Hays, but that Mr. Hays had been raised in a small town and had lived in that small town the greater part of his life and grown to it. When he left the small town for the larger city just a few years ago, he retained his native town growth. As a matter of fact, Mr. Hitchcock's position was that any man who put party politics before the welfare of their country, or who would utilize party politics to prevent the country taking its proper place in history was not a very good citizen. Hitchcock said that Mr. Hays' position was a deep disappointment to him, and he attributed it more or less to provincialism. He said that apparently Mr. Hays wanted a policy of nationalism rather than internationalism, and this was due entirely to his failure to realize the broad questions involved at the present time. He said the President by the masterly way in which he has been handling the great problems of the Peace Conference was entitled to the patriotic support of every loyal American. He said that every American should want to see the United States take the broad place to which it is entitled in history at the present time, and that he considered it very poor politics to oppose the President merely for political reasons at the present moment.

The President remained home tonight and he and I talked at some length. Discussing styles of oratory, I asked the President whether he himself had adopted any particular style or any special rule for public speaking. He said that he had made it his plan to follow the ornament of construction rather than the construction of ornament in all of his speeches. In other words, by the ornament of construction he tried to put his facts in plain, concise, simple and direct language so that any man listening could grasp his meaning quickly and understand all that he was trying to say. He said that he had found this method by far more efficacious than through the construction of ornament plan, which depended for its effectiveness on the use of beautiful, flowery language. He said that the construction of ornament class carrying with it flowing speech based rather upon beautiful words and phrases than upon actual logic was not particularly effective. He likened it to the odor of a sweet flower which soon passes away in the atmosphere. Such speech not being lasting to the ear could hardly be impressive to the mind.

[1] That is, Maj. Gen. William Thwaites.
[2] That is, Frank Harris Hitchcock.

Mantoux's Notes of Two Meetings of the Council of Four

March 25, 1919, 11 a.m.

President Wilson explains the reasons for including the document concerning the League of Nations in the preliminaries of peace. It would be very easy to get this text approved, along with that of the treaty, if the two only were part of the whole. Otherwise, the discussion on the League of Nations in the American Senate will cause prolonged debates and perhaps difficulties.

Clemenceau. If the Germans are not admitted to the League of Nations, and this is out of the question, how can the clauses relevant to the Covenant of this League be included in the preliminaries of peace which the Germans will have to sign?

President Wilson comments that, even if the Germans are not admitted to the League of Nations at the beginning, the fact that this League must be mentioned in more than one article of the treaty, and that it will be employed to enforce a number of measures which the Germans must accept, suffices to justify joining the two documents.

Clemenceau. I accept, if it is well understood that this can be accomplished without the Germans being admitted at the start to the League of Nations.

Lloyd George. For my part, I would rather see the Germans in the League of Nations than outside it. That would give us a stronger hold over them. But I understand M. Clemenceau's objection and the public sentiment behind it.

Orlando. It seems to me necessary to join the two documents, since the existence and functioning of the League of Nations is taken for granted in our requirements concerning the administration of colonies under mandates, the mutual territorial guarantee which members of the League will enjoy against all aggression, and, finally, disarmament. On the last point, Germany, being obliged to disarm, might hesitate to sign without a guarantee of the League of Nations against unjustified aggression.

President Wilson's proposal is accepted.

M. Clemenceau maintains his objection to the proposed text creating the League of Nations, as it has been drafted. He would like to see it completed by clauses establishing (1) the control of German armaments; and (2) a military sanction. If this sanction does not exist, there will have to be other guarantees for us.

Wilson. In determining Germany's capacity to pay, we must avoid pushing our demands to a point which would permit no German government to sign the peace treaty. We must also take into account the fact that Germany's capacity to pay is reduced, due to her loss of important and economically very valuable territories, such as Lorraine with its mines.

Our financial advisers have not been able up to now to agree on the figures, and there are great divergences among the estimates.

Mr. Lloyd George believes that M. Loucheur agrees with Mr. Norman Davis on the sum of seven billion pounds as representing the present value of what Germany would be able to pay.

M. Clemenceau declares that M. Loucheur said nothing of the kind to him. Confusion must be avoided. What M. Loucheur accepted was a system to reduce the annual payments for a certain number of years.

President Wilson examines the figures submitted to him. The minimum estimate gives 8.7 billion pounds sterling as the total sum of annual payments, which corresponds to an actual present value of five billion pounds sterling if interest and amortization are taken into account. The maximum corresponding estimates are thirteen billion pounds and seven billion pounds.

Wilson. The report[1] that I have before me expresses doubts as to the duration of payment; it may not be in the interest of the

---

[1] See the memorandum by N. H. Davis printed at March 25, 1919, and n. 4 thereto.

Allies to prolong it. It indicates the present value of what Germany can pay to be a maximum figure of thirty-five billion dollars and a minimum figure of twenty-five billion. Each year a commission would determine the sum to be paid, between the maximum and the minimum, and would also decide the proportion payable in marks. There remains a great degree of uncertainty in all these figures.

Lloyd George. On the subject of distribution—a much more difficult question, because here there is not agreement but competition among our interests, and because we have to consider our public opinions—I refer to the letter which we jointly addressed to President Wilson before the signing of the Armistice.[2] We declared that we would demand reparations for property and for damages suffered by persons in the civilian populations.

On this last point, we can take as a base figure each state's costs for pensions granted to families of men killed or disabled by the war. Under this procedure, we must be careful not to allow the figures to rise beyond what is strictly justifiable. Belgium, for example—where, even though the enemy deprived the country of much of its industrial equipment, direct devastation was limited—presents to us very exaggerated claims. She includes, notably, losses sustained by commercial establishments. It is impossible to allow claims of this type, since it would raise all our figures to unbelievable proportions.

As for France, no one doubts that in strict justice the most complete possible reparation is due her; but the figures presented in her name seem to us excessive. After all, the area of land devastated is very limited in relation to all of her territory, nor does it include any very large cities. Lille, Valenciennes, etc., were occupied and more or less pillaged but not destroyed. The figure the French financiers have arrived at is so high that it approaches the total national capital in 1908, which cannot be admitted.

I propose to settle the question based on a simple distribution between us and France. What Germany can pay being represented by 100, I propose that France receive 50, and Great Britain 30, 20 being reserved for the other powers. This proportion would give France a very marked advantage; but I could not, in the face of British public opinion, go below the proportion which I propose to reserve for Great Britain.

Clemenceau. I enter my strong reservations on the observations just presented, and I ask that the figures be compared and submitted, if that is necessary, to a new examination.

[2] He referred to the "Memorandum of observations by the Allied Governments on the correspondence which has passed between the President and the German Government," embodied in EMH to WW, Nov. 4, 1918 (first telegram of that date), Vol. 51.

Wilson. Another important question is that of the interdependence of claims. Do Italy and Serbia have a claim against Germany? Certainly Austria-Hungary, having been dissolved, cannot indemnify them.

M. Orlando observes that, without abandoning the principle of the responsibility of the successor states of the Austro-Hungarian Empire, he sees no solution to the problem unless there is an interdependence among all who are to pay and among all who are to receive. The principle of interdependence cannot be rejected, both for a factual and a moral reason. In fact, German artillery bombarded Italian cities, and submarines in the Mediterranean were more often German than Austrian. From a moral point of view, it is impossible to admit that Italy be without remedy simply because its debtor has disappeared.

M. Orlando concludes by noting that Italy is the nation which bears the highest war costs in proportion to its total prewar wealth.

Mr. Lloyd George asks for information about the Italian war debt and the cost of pensions.

Orlando. The debt is eighty billion lire, national capital before the war having been 140 billion; and the annual amount of pensions will be 560 million lire.

Mr. Lloyd George returns to the proposal to allot 50 per cent of the payments to France, 30 per cent to Great Britain, and 20 per cent to Italy, Serbia, and Belgium.

Orlando. We must have a clear definition of what will be allowed as reparation.

Lloyd George. I believe that we are agreed on this point: reparation should be understood to mean compensation for property destroyed and losses suffered by civilians through death or mutilation of their next of kin.

March 25, 1919, 3:30 p.m.

Clemenceau. We have three questions for immediate examination: (1) revictualling Odessa; (2) aid to be given to the Poles by way of Danzig—but this might be considered settled; (3) help to give the Rumanians who, threatened by the appearance of Bolshevism in Hungary, ask us to furnish them with equipment for their troops. On the Odessa question, I suggest we hear General Alby.

General Alby is introduced.

Alby. A series of telegrams from Generals Berthelot and Franchet d'Espérey discuss the issue of provisions for Odessa.

In his telegram of March 12, General Berthelot indicates that the loss of the resources of the southern Ukraine forces us to find another way to feed a million people in Odessa and the surrounding area. If we cannot do this, it is useless to dream of holding Odessa.

Responding to a question asked by Mr. Lloyd George about the total Allied effectives at Odessa, General Alby answers that there are approximately 25,000 men.

Clemenceau. This very morning General d'Espérey asked that Polish troops be sent to him from Italy for Odessa.

Alby. Italy is prepared to send 7,000 Poles; there are approximately 25,000 in Italy.

A second telegram from General Berthelot, dated March 17, notifies us that the Russian authorities in Odessa are asking for 1,000 tons of bread per week. Another telegram of the same day warns us that the city of Odessa has only fifteen days of flour, five days of meat, etc. Fifteen thousand tons of coal per month are absolutely necessary; without it, the danger of a popular revolt would be very great.

A telegram from General d'Espérey, dated March 22, asks that the Allies send to Odessa fifteen thousand tons of wheat per month and at least ten thousand tons of coal, as well as manufactured goods which could be used, at the end of two months, to obtain, by exchange, wheat from the Kuban[3] to replace the wheat sent by the Allies.

Clemenceau. This question is in the hands of the Food Commission.

M. Clemenceau asks General Alby to discuss the situation in Rumania.

Alby. Regarding the aid to be furnished to Rumania, we have a telegram from General Berthelot of March 12, which asks for the Rumanians 300,000 clothing kits and 400,000 pairs of shoes, harnesses, etc. If the Rumanian army was sufficiently equipped, it could put ten divisions on the Dniester, for whose support two Allied divisions would suffice.

General Franchet d'Espérey telegraphs on March 19 that the Army of the East could not furnish the articles requested for the Rumanian army, and that, consequently, they must be sent from France. On March 14, a note verbale presented by the Rumanian Minister in Paris[4] asked the Allies to furnish the means to combat the Russian and Ukrainian Bolshevik offensive and warned of a possible agreement between the Bolsheviks and the Hungarians.

General Alby shows a map indicating the disposition of troops in Rumania.

Alby. Without the equipment the Rumanians request of us, they cannot effectively use their own manpower, which is adequate.

Wilson. Our situation is difficult to define. Nominally, we are friends of the Hungarians and even better friends of the Rumanians. What exactly is our position with regard to the Bolsheviks?

[3] A region in the northern Caucasus.   [4] Victor Antonescu.

No one can say. We have tried to prevent conflict between the Rumanians and the Hungarians by tracing a line and declaring that whoever crosses it would prejudice his own claims; it does not seem that this method has given us the desired result.

Clemenceau. The Hungarians are not our friends but our enemies. While the other peoples of the Austro-Hungarian Empire have fought us despite themselves and, whenever they could, have fought on our side, the Hungarians have been our resolute enemies and their leaders, like Tisza, are among those responsible for the war.

The boundary drawn in Transylvania is short of the border promised the Rumanians in 1916, and the imposition of this line was enough to induce the Károlyi government to give way to the Bolsheviks.

Wilson. I am struck to see Rumania asking for the same material which she has always said that she lacked in earlier circumstances.

Lloyd George. Since it is France which has taken particular responsibility for this region, I propose that she let us know the limit of what she can furnish and what she will ask of us to furnish as a supplement. We for our part take the same responsibility for that part of Russia occupied by Denikin's troops.

Wilson. In the dispatches which have been read to us, I am struck by these words: "The population of Odessa is hostile to us." If this is the case, we might wonder about the wisdom of preserving this encircled island, nearly submerged in Bolshevism. This confirms me in my policy, which is to leave Russia to the Bolsheviks—they will stew in their own juice until circumstances will have made the Russians wiser—and confine our efforts to keeping Bolshevism from invading other parts of Europe.

Lloyd George. Recently I heard M. Brătianu state what he considers the most important order of business in Rumania: (1) to feed the people; (2) to equip the army; (3) to give land to the peasants. These are intelligent and efficacious means to preserve Rumania from Bolshevism. But should we persist in defending Odessa, when its population will rise as soon as the Bolsheviks make their appearance? It would be better to concentrate on the defense of Rumania and to establish there our barrier against Bolshevism.

General Thwaites is introduced at Mr. Lloyd George's request and gives details about what England can send to General Denikin. It is proposed to divert to Rumania 100,000 clothing kits.

Questioned about Denikin's situation and that of the other anti-Bolshevik chieftains, the General replies that Denikin is holding his position, despite the loss of the salient of Tsaritsyn. Kolchak's troops have retaken Ufa.

Lloyd George. It seems then that the Bolsheviks are weak in eastern Russia.

Kisch.[5] They have concentrated on the Ukraine, where they have around 180,000 men.

Lloyd George. Is the Siberian population favorable to Kolchak or not?

Thwaites. Kolchak seems to be supported by the population; but an opposition movement and a tendency toward Bolshevism are developing in the region occupied by the Japanese.

Lloyd George. If Odessa falls, what will happen?

Thwaites. The Bolsheviks will immediately attack Rumania.

Lloyd George. What would it be better to do? Defend Odessa or concentrate our forces in Rumania?

Kisch. According to a witness who has lived in Russia for a long time, the occupation of Odessa by the Bolsheviks will give Russia the impression of a great victory by them over the Allies. Thus the event would be important from the point of view of morale. But that is the only serious reason we have for defending Odessa.

Lloyd George. If it was necessary to choose between Odessa and Rumania in shipments of food and equipment, which they ask us, which would you choose?

Thwaites. Of the two, Rumania is the more important, if a choice must be made.

Marshal Foch, summoned by the heads of governments, is introduced.

M. Clemenceau informs him of the subject under discussion and asks him the following question: do you believe that the danger is very pressing for Rumania? If we possess only limited means, would it be better to use them to support Odessa, or to send them to Rumania?

Foch. Everything depends upon the intentions of the governments: what do they wish to do?

Clemenceau. It is rather a question of knowing what we can do.

Marshal Foch shows a map indicating the situation between the Black Sea and the Baltic.

Foch. The Bolshevik peril now extends toward the south and toward Hungary; it will continue to expand as long as it is not stopped; we must stop it at Odessa and at Lemberg. From the second point, the Bolsheviks plan to break through toward Hungary. We have to close the door at Lemberg and hold on to the area of Odessa. Are the governments considering the necessity of linking these operations, and in what measure can they participate in them? The Allied forces in this region are rather small; it will be easiest to use the Rumanian army, but only if it is equipped.

---

[5] Lt. Col. Frederick Hermann Kisch, technical expert in the British delegation on military questions pertaining to Russia, China, and Japan.

Do we want a comprehensive solution? Without it, we will be attacked on one side just as we have succeeded in stopping danger on another point.

Clemenceau. How would you plan to build a continuous barrier?

Foch. It should be done by reorganizing the Polish and Rumanian armies, while holding on to Odessa.

Clemenceau. What is the importance of Odessa itself?

Foch. Odessa has no importance, except from the point of view of morale.

Lloyd George. What would you do, if, as far as supplies are concerned, you had to choose between Odessa and Rumania?

Foch. I would try to keep both as long as possible. I would not cut off my left arm because I value my right arm more. But we need to send a general to Rumania to take command of the Rumanian army, whose mission it is to defend the entire Rumanian front and to look for a way to effect its junction with the Poles.

Lloyd George. Are there enough Rumanians to defend their front?

Foch. They have twelve divisions which, admittedly, lack equipment and shoes. If they are equipped, they could organize up to sixteen or eighteen divisions.

Wilson. Is it essential to send thirty thousand tons of coal and wheat per month to Odessa, if Rumania needs them at the same time?

Foch. No, Odessa is not a starting point.

Lloyd George. The French, because it is they who are responsible for Rumania, will see what they can supply to this country and what they must ask of us ourselves to furnish. I am convinced that we must not waste our resources in maintaining a precarious and hopeless position at Odessa. We should recall to Rumania the twenty-five thousand men now surrounding this city and also send to Rumania the thirty thousand tons that Odessa would require.

Foch. To abandon Odessa is to abandon southern Russia; but, to tell the truth, it is already lost, and we cannot lose it a second time.

Clemenceau. We take it that the 100,000 clothing kits originally intended for General Denikin will be rerouted to Rumania.

Foch. Whatever is sent to General Denikin is lost. I do not attach a great importance to Denikin's army, because armies do not exist by themselves. There must be a government, laws, an organized country behind them. It would even be better to have a government without an army than an army without a government. This is why I tell you: build upon Rumania, because there you have not only an army, but also a government and a people. An army should not be vegetation which springs spontaneously from artificial soil.

Clemenceau. If we have to evacuate Odessa, may I emphasize that it is important that nothing be said about this in advance. Any indiscretion could endanger this delicate operation. I would ask Marshal Foch if he can give us the name of the general to assume command of the Rumanian army.

Foch. I would have several names: Mangin, Guillaumat, Degoutte.[6] But whatever man is chosen, we must not clip his wings by placing him under the command of Franchet d'Espérey; he must have complete freedom of action.

Lloyd George. I propose that Marshal Foch prepare a plan for us which we will read carefully before deciding. We can immediately order to Constanta the 100,000 units of equipment destined for General Denikin.

Mantoux, I, 14-23.
  [6] That is, Gen. Charles Marie Emmanuel Mangin, commander of the French Tenth Army; Gen. Louis Guillaumat; and Gen. Jean Joseph Marie Degoutte.

From Robert Lansing

My dear Mr. President: Paris, March 25, 1919.

I enclose a letter which I have just received through our Legation at Berne from Professor Lammasch of the University of Vienna[1] who is one of the great students of political history of his country and whom I knew through his being a member of an international tribunal which sat at The Hague in 1910 on the Northeast Fisheries Arbitration, with Great Britain.

Doctor Lammasch is a man of the highest motives and I believe is to be credited with all sincerity in what he suggests. I therefore think you will find his letter very well worth reading, and his suggestions worth considering.

Would you be good enough to return the letter to me after you have read it, in order that I may lay it before some of our specialists?
                  Faithfully yours,   Robert Lansing.

TLS (WP, DLC).
  [1] H. Lammasch to RL, March 19, 1919, ALS (WP, DLC). Lammasch disclaimed any official backing but said that he spoke for many of his compatriots. He wished to call Lansing's and Wilson's attention to three problems connected with the future of Austria. First, he argued that the South Tyrol was predominantly German both in language and character and therefore should remain Austrian rather than become part of Italy. Second, he admitted that the situation was different in the lands comprising the new state of Czechoslovakia, where the Germans made up about one third of the population. However, he warned that there would be great potential for "dangerous ferment" unless the three million German-speaking inhabitants of the region were allowed to express their wishes as to their future status in an internationally supervised plebiscite. Even if a majority voted for union with the Czechs, they would have to be granted "a complete national autonomy under international guaranties."
  Lammasch wrote at greater length, both in his letter and in a "continuation," or

postscript, about the third problem of whether or not the so-called Alpine districts of German Austria should be united with Germany or become a separate, independent state. By the Alpine districts, he apparently meant most of present-day Austria beyond the immediate region around Vienna. Here again, he said that there should be a plebiscite to determine the peoples' wishes, although he predicted that the result would be against union with Germany. He also warned that an independent Alpine Austrian state would be viable only if it included certain border areas of Hungary, Bohemia, Moravia, and Bavaria.

About Heinrich Lammasch, see H. R. Wilson to RL, Jan. 1, 1918, n. 1, Vol. 46.

A Translation of a Letter from Désiré-Joseph Cardinal Mercier

Mr. President,   Malines, March 25, 1919.

For some months I have aspired to the honor of meeting you and of asking for a brief interview. King Albert, in January last, led me to hope for the good fortune of seeing you in the Palace at Brussels, but your voyage to the United States deprived me of that honor. I have decided, consequently, to present to you in written form what would have been the principal object of my oral communication.

It is not possible that such solemn sessions as those of the peace conference could come to a close without rendering some public religious homage to God. The delegates at the conference are believers or they represent a nation in which religion is honored. Each year, the United States of America, by celebrating their "Thanksgiving Day," gives to the world an example of national recognition to the Divine One.

I am confidently asking M. Clemenceau, president of the conference, to invite Cardinals Gibbons of Baltimore, Bourne of Westminster, Richelmy of Turin, Amette of Paris,[1] and Mercier of Malines, to a religious ceremony in the Church of Nôtre Dame in Paris on the occasion of the signing of the preliminaries of peace or on some other date which the president of the conference might propose to us.

Filled with admiration for the beneficial role that Providence has bestowed on you in the world at this time, Mr. President, I dare to beg you to be insistent with your colleagues, if necessary, so that my request will be granted and satisfaction will be given to the Catholic conscience, or better, to the religious conscience of humanity.

M. Clemenceau is a statesman, has a broad conception of liberty, and he will understand you.

Accept, Mr. President, the assurance of my sentiments of profound esteem and grateful devotion.

+ D. J. Card. Mercier, Arch. of Malines.[2]

T MS (WC, NjP).
  [1] Francis Cardinal Bourne, Archbishop of Westminster; Agostino Cardinal Richelmy, Archbishop of Turin; and Léon Adolphe Cardinal Amette, Archbishop of Paris.
  [2] The ALS is in WP, DLC.

A Memorandum by David Lloyd George[1]

SECRET   Paris. March 25, 1919.
          Some considerations for the Peace Conference
               before they finally draft their terms.

[I] When nations are exhausted by wars in which they have put forth all their strength and which leave them tired, bleeding and broken, it is not difficult to patch up a peace that may last until the generation which experienced the horrors of the war has passed away. Pictures of heroism and triumph only tempt those who know nothing of the sufferings and terrors of war. It is therefore comparatively easy to patch up a peace which will last for 30 years.

What is difficult, however, is to draw up a peace which will not provoke a fresh struggle when those who have had practical experience of what war means have passed away. History has proved that a peace which has been hailed by a victorious nation as a triumph of diplomatic skill and statesmanship, even of moderation in the long run has proved itself to be shortsighted and charged with danger to the victor. The peace of 1871 was believed by Germany to ensure not only her security but her permanent supremacy. The facts have shown exactly the contrary. France itself has demonstrated that those who say you can make Germany so feeble that she will never be able to hit back are utterly wrong. Year by year France became numerically weaker in comparison with her victorious neighbour, but in reality she became ever more powerful. She kept watch on Europe; she made alliance with those whom Germany had wronged or menaced; she never ceased to warn the world of its danger and ultimately she was able to secure the overthrow of the far mightier power which had trampled so brutally

  [1] Lloyd George, Henry Hughes Wilson, Philip Henry Kerr, Maurice P. A. Hankey, and Edwin Samuel Montagu had gone to a hotel in the forest of Fontainebleau for the weekend of March 22-23 in order to evaluate the status of the peace conference and to work out a program to expedite its proceedings. After some sightseeing, they settled down to lengthy discussions, including some role-playing, in which Wilson spoke first for the Germans and then for the French, while Hankey spoke for the average Englishman. Kerr first took extensive notes and then drafted a memorandum. This document was discussed and revised on March 24. The result was the following document, often referred to as "the Fontainebleau Memorandum," which was sent to Clemenceau, as well as to Wilson, on March 25. See Mayer, *Politics and Diplomacy of Peacemaking*, pp. 518-20, 579-84; Maurice P. A. Hankey, *The Supreme Control at the Paris Peace Conference 1919: A Commentary* (London, 1963), pp. 97-102; and Peter Rowland, *Lloyd George* (London, 1975), pp. 484-86.

upon her. You may strip Germany of her colonies, reduce her armaments to a mere police force and her navy to that of a fifth rate power; all the same in the end if she feels that she has been unjustly treated in the peace of 1919 she will find means of exacting retribution from her conquerers. The impression, the deep impression, made upon the human heart by four years of unexampled slaughter will disappear with the hearts upon which it has been marked by the terrible sword of the great war. The maintenance of peace will then depend upon there being no causes of exasperation constantly stirring up the spirit of patriotism, of justice or of fair play to achieve redress. Our terms may be severe, they may be stern and even ruthless but at the same time they can be so just that the country on which they are imposed will feel in its heart that it has no right to complain. But injustice, arrogance, displayed in the hour of triumph will never be forgotten or forgiven.

For these reasons I am, therefore, strongly averse to transferring more Germans from German rule to the rule of some other nation than can possibly be helped. I cannot conceive any greater cause of future war than that the German people, who have certainly proved themselves one of the most vigorous and powerful races in the world should be surrounded by a number of small states, many of them consisting of people who have never previously set up a stable government for themselves, but each of them containing large masses of Germans clamouring for reunion with their native land. The proposal of the Polish Commission that we should place 2,100,000 Germans, under the control of a people which is of a different religion and which has never proved its capacity for stable self-government throughout its history must, in my judgment, lead sooner or later to a new war in the East of Europe. What I have said about the Germans is equally true of the Magyars. There will never be peace in South Eastern Europe if every little state now coming into being is to have a large Magyar Irredenta within its borders. I would therefore take as a guiding principle of the peace that as far as is humanly possible the different races should be allocated to their motherlands, and that this human criterion should have precedence over considerations of strategy or economics or communications which can usually be adjusted by other means. Secondly, I would say that the duration for the payments of reparation ought to disappear if possible with the generation which made the war.

But there is a consideration in favour of a long-sighted peace which influences me even more than the desire to leave no causes justifying a fresh outbreak 30 years hence. There is one element in the present condition of nations which differentiates it from the situation as it was in 1815. In the Napoleonic war the countries were equally exhausted but the revolutionary spirit had spent its force in the country of its birth and Germany had satisfied the legitimate popular demands for the time being by a series of economic changes which were inspired by courage, foresight and high statesmanship. Even in Russia the Czar had effected great reforms which were probably at that time even too advanced for the half savage population. The situation is very different now. The revolution is still in its infancy. The extreme figures of the Terror are still in command in Russia. The whole of Europe is filled with the spirit of revolution. There is a deep sense not only of discontent, but of anger and revolt amongst the workmen against pre-war conditions. The whole existing order in its political, social and economic aspects is questioned by the masses of the population from one end of Europe to the other. In some countries, like Germany and Russia, the unrest takes the form of open rebellion, in others like France, Great Britain and Italy it takes the shape of strikes and of general disinclination to settle down to work, symptoms which are just as much concerned with the desire for political and social change as with wage demands.

Much of this unrest is healthy. We shall never make a lasting peace by attempting to restore the conditions of 1914. But there is a danger that we may throw the masses of the population throughout Europe into the arms of the extremists whose only idea for regenerating mankind is to destroy utterly the whole existing fabric of society. These men have triumphed in Russia. They have done so at a terrible price. Hundreds and thousands of the population have perished. The Railways, the roads, the towns, the whole structural organisation of Russia has been almost destroyed, but somehow or other they seem to have managed to keep their hold upon the masses of the Russian people, and what is much more significant, they have succeeded in creating a large army which is apparently well directed and well disciplined, and is, as to a great part of it prepared to die for its ideals. In another year Russia, inspired by a new enthusiasm may have recovered from her passion for peace and have at her command the only army eager to fight, because it is the only army that believes that it has any cause to fight for.

The greatest danger that I see in the present situation is that Germany may throw in her lot with Bolshevism and place her resources, her brains, her vast organising power at the disposal of the revolutionary fanatics whose dream it is to conquer the world for Bolshevism by force of arms. This danger is no mere chimera. The present government in Germany is weak; it has no prestige;

its authority is challenged; it lingers merely because there is no alternative but the spartacists, and Germany is not ready for spartacism, as yet. But the argument which the spartacists are using with great effect at this very time is that they alone can save Germany from the intolerable conditions which have been bequeathed her by the war. They offer to free the German people from indebtedness to the Allies and indebtedness to their own richer classes. They offer them complete control of their own affairs and the prospect of a new heaven and earth. It is true that the price will be heavy. There will be two or three years of anarchy, perhaps of bloodshed, but at the end the land will remain, the people will remain, the greater part of the houses and the factories will remain, and the railways and the roads will remain, and Germany, having thrown off her burdens, will be able to make a fresh start.

If Germany goes over to the spartacists it is inevitable that she should throw in her lot with the Russian Bolshevists. Once that happens all Eastern Europe will be swept into the orbit of the Bolshevik revolution and within a year we may witness the spectacle of nearly three hundred million people organised into a vast red army under German instructors and German generals equipped with German cannon and German machine guns and prepared for a renewal of the attack on Western Europe. This is a prospect which no one can face with equanimity. Yet the news which came from Hungary yesterday shows only too clearly that this danger is no fantasy. And what are the reasons alleged for this decision? They are mainly the belief that large numbers of Magyars are to be handed over to the control of others. If we are wise, we shall offer to Germany a peace, which, while just, will be preferable for all sensible men to the alternative of Bolshevism. I would, therefore, put it in the forefront of the peace that once she accepts our terms, especially reparation, we will open to her the raw materials and markets of the world on equal terms with ourselves, and will do everything possible to enable the German people to get upon their legs again. We cannot both cripple her and expect her to pay.

Finally, we must offer terms which a responsible Government in Germany can expect to be able to carry out. If we present terms to Germany which are unjust, or excessively onerous, no responsible Government will sign them; certainly the present weak administration will not. If it did, I am told that it would be swept away within 24 hours. Yet if we can find nobody in Germany who will put his hand to a peace treaty, what will be the position? A large army of occupation for an indefinite period is out of the question. Germany would not mind it. A very large number of people in that country would welcome it as it would be the only hope of preserving the existing order of things. The objection would not come from Germany, but from our own countries. Neither the British Empire nor America would agree to occupy Germany. France by itself could not bear the burden of occupation. We should therefore be driven back on the policy of blockading the country. That would inevitably mean spartacism from the Urals to the Rhine, with its inevitable consequence of a huge red army attempting to cross the Rhine. As a matter of fact, I am doubtful whether public opinion would allow us deliberately to starve Germany. If the only difference between Germany and ourselves were between onerous terms and moderate terms, I very much doubt if public opinion would tolerate the deliberate condemnation of millions of women and children to death by starvation. If so the Allies would have incurred the moral defeat of having attempted to impose terms on Germany which Germany had successfully resisted.

From every point of view, therefore, it seems to me that we ought to endeavour to draw up a peace settlement as if we were impartial arbiters, forgetful of the passions of the war. This settlement ought to have three ends in view. First of all it must do justice to the Allies, by taking into account Germany's responsibility for the origin of the war, and for the way in which it was fought. Secondly, it must be a settlement which a responsible German Government can sign in the belief that it can fulfil the obligations it incurs. Thirdly, it must be a settlement which will contain in itself no provocations for future wars, and which will constitute an alternative to Bolshevism, because it will commend itself to all reasonable opinion as a fair settlement of the European problem.

II. It is not, however, enough to draw up a just and far-sighted peace with Germany. If we are to offer Europe an alternative to Bolshevism we must make the League of Nations into something which will be both a safeguard to those nations who are prepared for fair dealing with their neighbours, and a menace to those who would trespass on the rights of their neighbours, whether they are imperialist empires or imperialist Bolshevists. An essential element, therefore, in the peace settlement is the constitution of the League of Nations as the effective guardian of international right and international liberty throughout the world. If this is to happen the first thing to do is that the leading members of the League of Nations should arrive at an understanding between themselves in regard to armaments. To my mind it is idle to endeavour to impose a permanent limitation of armaments upon Germany unless we are prepared similarly to impose a limitation upon ourselves. I recognise that until Germany has settled down and given practical proof that she has abandoned her imperialist ambitions, and until Russia has also given proof that she does not intend to embark upon a military crusade against her neighbours, it is essential that the leading members of the League of Nations should maintain considerable forces both by land and sea in order to preserve liberty in the world. But if they are to present an united front to the forces both of reaction and revolution, they must arrive at such an agreement in regard to armaments among themselves as would make it impossible for suspicion to arise between the members of the League of Nations in regard to their intentions towards one another. If the League is to do its work for the world it will only be because the members of the League trust it themselves and because there are no rivalries and jealousies in the matter of armaments between them. The first condition of success for the League of Nations is, therefore, a firm understanding between the British Empire and the United States of America and France and Italy that there will be no competitive building up of fleets or armies between them. Unless this is arrived at before the Covenant is signed the League of Nations will be a sham and a mockery. It will be regarded, and rightly regarded as a proof that its principal promoters and patrons repose no confidence in its efficacy. But once the leading members of the League have made it clear that they have reached an understanding which will both secure to the League of Nations the strength which is necessary to enable it to protect its members and which at the same time will make misunderstanding and suspicion with regard to competitive armaments impossible between them its future and its authority will be ensured. It will then be able to ensure as an essential condition of peace that not only Germany, but all the smaller States of Europe undertake to limit their armaments and abolish conscription. If the small nations are permitted to organise and maintain conscript armies running each to hundreds of thousands, boundary wars will be inevitable and all Europe will be drawn in. Unless we secure this universal limitation we shall achieve neither lasting peace, nor the permanent observance of the limitation of German armaments which we now seek to impose.

I should like to ask why Germany, if she accepts the terms we consider just and fair, should not be admitted to the League of Nations, at any rate as soon as she has established a stable and democratic Government. Would it not be an inducement to her both to sign the terms and to resist Bolshevism? Might it not be safer that she should be inside the League than that she should be outside it?

Finally, I believe that until the authority and effectiveness of the League of Nations has been demonstrated, the British Empire and the United States ought to give to France a guarantee against the possibility of a new German aggression. France has special reasons for asking for such a guarantee. She has twice been attacked and twice invaded by Germany in half a century. She has been so attacked because she has been the principal guardian of liberal and democratic civilisation against Central European autocracy on the continent of Europe. It is right that the other great Western democracies should enter into an undertaking which will ensure that they stand by her side in time to protect her against invasion, should Germany ever threaten her again or until the League of Nations has proved its capacity to preserve the peace and liberty of the world.

III. If, however, the peace conference is really to secure peace and prove to the world a complete plan of settlement which all reasonable men will recognise as an alternative preferable to anarchy, it must deal with the Russian situation. Bolshevik imperialism does not merely menace the states on Russia's borders. It threatens the whole of Asia and is as near to America as it is to France. It is idle to think that the Peace Conference can separate, however sound a peace it may have arranged with Germany, if it leaves Russia as it is today. I do not propose, however, to complicate the question of the peace with Germany by introducing a discussion of the Russian problem. I mention it simply in order to remind ourselves of the importance of dealing with it as soon as possible.

OUTLINE OF PEACE TERMS.

PART I.

Termination of State of War.

War, i.e., the state of belligerency cannot be brought to an end more than once. If the forthcoming treaty is to enable the transition of the Allied countries to a peace footing to be carried through, and demobilisation to be completed, it should put an end to the state of War.

PART II.

The League of Nations.

(1) All high contracting parties, as part of the Treaty of Peace, to become members of the League of Nations, the Covenant of which will be signed as a separate Treaty by those Powers that are admitted, subject to acceptance of the following conditions:

(i) An agreement between the principal members of the League of Nations in regard to armaments which will put an end to competition between them.

(ii) The lesser members of the League of Nations to accept the limitation of armaments and the abolition of conscription.

(iii) An agreement to be made between all members of the

League of Nations for the purpose of securing equal and improved conditions of labour in their respective countries.

PART III. *Political.*

A. *Cession of territory by Germany and the consequential arrangements.*

Eastern
Boundaries
of Germany.

Western
Boundaries
of Germany.

(1) Poland to be given a corridor to Dantzig, but this to be drawn irrespective of strategic or transportation considerations so as to embrace the smallest possible number of Germans.

(2) Rectification of Bohemian frontier. (Still to be decided after hearing Report of Czecho-Slovak Commission.)

(3) No attempt to be made to separate the Rhenish Provinces from the rest of Germany. These Provinces to be demilitarised; that is to say, the inhabitants of this territory will not be permitted to bear arms or receive any military training, or to be incorporated in any military organisation either on a voluntary or compulsory basis, and no fortifications, depots, establishments, railway construction, or works of any kind adapted to military purposes will be permitted to exist within the area. No troops to be sent into this area for any purpose whatsoever without previous notification to the League of Nations. As France is naturally anxious about a neighbour who has twice within living memory invaded and devastated her land with surprising rapidity, the British Empire and the United States of America undertake to come to the assistance of France with their whole strength in the event of Germany moving her troops across the Rhine without the consent of the Council of the League of Nations. This guarantee to last until the League of Nations has proved itself to be an adequate security.

(4) Germany to cede Alsace-Lorraine to France.

(5) Germany to cede to France the 1814 frontier, or, in the alternative, in order to compensate France for the destruction of her coalfields, the present Alsace-Lorraine frontier with the

use of the coal mines in the Saar Valley for a period of 10 years. Germany to undertake, after the expiration of 10 years, to put no obstacle on the export of the produce of these coal mines to France.

(6) Abrogation of Customs Union with Luxembourg and other Luxembourg questions. (Still to be decided.)

(7) Germany to cede to Belgium Malmedy and Moresnet.

Northern Boundaries of Germany.
German Over-Sea Possessions and Rights.

(8) Heligoland and Dune. (Still to be decided.)

(9) Germany to cede certain portions of Schleswig to Denmark as provided by the Danish Commission.

(10) Germany to cede all rights in the ex-German Colonies and in the leased territory of Kiauchow.

B. *Recognition of New States which receive no German territory.*

C. *Russian Section.*

(1) Germany to renounce all rights under Brest-Litovsk Treaty.

(2) Germany to renounce all rights under Treaty of Bukarest.

(3) Germany to renounce all arrangements by Allied and Associated Governments with reference to previous Russian territory, including special agreements with new States.

D. *Turkish Section.*

(1) Germany to recognise the cession by Turkey of the whole of her territory to mandatories responsible to the League of Nations. As far as Germany is concerned mandates to be settled by the Allied and Associated Powers.

NOTE: Included in the Turkish Section also will be a number of provisions arising out of the Report of the Financial Commission, the Commission on the Breaches of the Laws of War, e.g., the surrender of Turks hiding in Germany, with their property, as well as an undertaking by Germany to be bound by terms of the treaty of peace with Turkey and a recognition of the British Protectorate over Egypt with renunciation of extra-territorial privileges and recognition of transfer to His Majesty's Government of the Sultan's rights under the Suez Canal Convention.

E. *Miscellaneous.*

   (1) Acceptance by Germany of Arms Convention.

   (2) Waiver of rights under Berlin and Brussels Acts[2] and acceptance if desired of new instrument to replace them.

   (3) Acceptance of new regime replacing Treaty of 1839 as to Belgium.
(Otherwise the claims of Belgium against Holland to be disregarded.)[3]

   (4) Opening of Kiel Canal to ships of all nations.

   (5) Special arrangements for control of Rhine, Oder, Vistula, Niemen, Elbe.

   (6) Rhine-Danube Canal.

   (7) St. Gotthard Railway.

   (8) Acceptance of new arrangements as to European Commission of Danube.

   (9) Other political multilateral treaties; acceptance of abrogation (if so desired by Allies).

  (10) Waiver of all *pre-war* claims against Allied and Associated Powers on behalf of either Governments or individuals.

  (11) Acceptance of all Allied Prize Court decisions and orders.

PART IV.

Reduction of Armaments.

Preamble explaining that the disarmament of Germany is the first step in the limitation of the armaments of all nations.

(a) Military terms ⎫
(b) Naval terms   ⎬ as already agreed on.
(c) Air terms.   ⎭

(d) Questions as to restoration of prisoners of war and interned persons.

(e) Waiver by Germany of all claims on behalf of prisoners of war and interned persons.

---

[2] For the Berlin Act of 1885, see n. 2 to the minutes of the Council of Ten printed at Jan. 28, 1919, 11 a.m., Vol. 54. A second international conference held in Brussels between November 1889 and July 1890 produced numerous modifications in the original agreement which came to be known collectively as the Brussels Act. The most important provisions of the new document concerned the suppression of the slave trade, restrictions on trade in liquors and firearms, and the right of the powers to impose import duties in their respective colonial possessions. See Arthur Berriedale Keith, *The Belgian Congo and the Berlin Act* (Oxford, 1919), pp. 77-80.

[3] About which, see C. H. Haskins to WW, Feb. 11, 1919, Vol. 55.

PART V.
Reparation.

(1) Germany to undertake to pay full reparation to the Allies. It is difficult to assess the amount chargeable against Germany under this head. It certainly greatly exceeds what, on any calculation, Germany is capable of paying. It is, therefore, suggested that Germany should pay an annual sum for a stated number of years. This sum to be agreed among the Allied and Associated Powers. Germany to be allowed a number of years within which to work up to payment of the full annual amount.

It has been suggested that a Permanent Commission should be set up to which Germany should be able to appeal for permission to postpone some portion of the annual payment for adequate reasons shown. This Commission would be entitled to cancel the payment of interest on postponed payments during the first few years. The amount received from Germany to be distributed in the following proportions:

50 per cent. to France:

30 per cent. to the British Empire:

20 per cent. to other nations.

Part of the German payments to be used to liquidate debts owed by the Allies to one another.

(2) Return of relics, &c., taken by the Turks from Medina and handed over to Germany.

(3) Return of objects of native veneration removed from German East Africa.

PART VI.
Breaches of the Laws of War.

(1) Demand and surrender of the Kaiser and all individuals responsible for the War, and also of all individuals responsible for inhuman breaches of the laws of war:

(2) Creation of Court.

(3) Jurisdiction and procedure:

(4) Punishment of offenders.

PART VII.
Economic.

Germany to be given full access to raw materials and markets of the world on same terms as Allies directly she signs the peace. The Allied and Associated Powers to do all they can to put her upon her legs once more. In addition we await the report of Economic and Financial Commissions but will include the following:

(1) Settlement of pre-war private debts;—scheme of a clearing house.

(2) Regulation of pre-war contracts between Allied and enemy individuals.

(3) Settlement of claims arising out of businesses, &c., liquidated, sold, &c.

(4) Revival of Economic Treaties.

(5) Provisions as to Industrial Property, (Patents, Trademarks, &c.)

(6) Provisions as to Freedom of Transit.

(7) Provisions as to international use of railways, ports, and waterways, if of general application.

(8) Acceptance of the draft commercial clauses. (Economic Section's draft A. of March 6, 1919.)[4]

(9) Enforcement of Customs Control (if necessary).

10) Undertaking to ratify and enforce the Opium Convention.[5]

T MS (WP, DLC).
    [4] Not found.
    [5] The International Opium Convention, signed at The Hague on January 23, 1912, which was designed to regulate and limit the international traffic in opium and other narcotics. By March 1919, some nations, notably Turkey, still had not signed the convention, many had not ratified it, and only the United States, China, the Netherlands, Honduras, and Norway had actually put it into effect. For the negotiation of the convention and for subsequent events relating to it through the Paris Peace Conference, see Arnold H. Taylor, *American Diplomacy and the Narcotics Traffic, 1900-1939: A Study in International Humanitarian Reform* (Durham, N. C., 1969), pp. 82-145. A full text of the convention in English is printed in Westel Woodbury Willoughby, *Opium as an International Problem: The Geneva Conferences* (Baltimore, 1925), pp. 483-92.

A Memorandum by Norman Hezekiah Davis

Memorandum for The President:					March 25, 1919.

As you will recall, after Messrs. Loucheur, Montague, and myself had agreed upon and submitted a report to you and the two Prime Ministers as to the amount which Germany might be called upon to pay,[1] Mr. Lloyd George, in the absence of Mr. Montague, called into the last meeting Lord Sumner, one of the British representatives on the Reparation Committee, and Mr. Keynes of the British Treasury. In an endeavor to arrive at a unanimous report by reconciling the views which had been previously submitted by Lord Sumner, we have had several meetings. We have agreed substantially upon the form for the Peace Treaty and upon the plan for its execution, but we have been unable to arrive at any agreement with Lords Sumner and Cunliffe (who was called in by Lord Sumner), because these two gentlemen still stand upon their original estimate of eleven billion pounds. Mr. Lloyd George told Mr. Lamont and myself last Saturday that he thought five billion pounds would be all right and that it would be quite acceptable to him, provided we could get Lords Sumner and Cunliffe to agree to this amount, which he would like to have them do for his own protection and justification. We have handed our proposed wording to Colonel House who, I understand, has transmitted it to you,[2] with the various schedules of figures which may be used after you agree with the two Prime Ministers upon the exact sum which shall be taken.

In our opinion it is very essential to have Sub-committee No. 2 of the Reparations Committee[3] (which is to report on the amount which Germany can pay and how it may be paid) make its report and get out of the way. As Lord Cunliffe is the British representative on this Sub-committee, it is apparently going to be impossible to make a unanimous report; and, even if it were possible, it is, as I understand, your view as well as that of Mr. Lloyd George and Mr. Clemenceau that it would be inadvisable now to have any fixed amount reported by that Sub-committee even if they could agree upon it.

I therefore suggest the advisability of having this Sub-committee make a report to the General Committee, in general as follows:

I. It is impossible to estimate with any accuracy just how much Germany can pay, but the Sub-committee estimates that Germany could pay, over a series of years, anywhere from one hundred billion to two hundred fifty-five billion marks, depending upon various factors, such as: (a) the amount of territory which may be taken from Germany; (b) the number of years over which payment can be exacted; (c) the extent to which German commerce may be expanded without detriment to the creditor nations.

II. That a Commission be provided for in the Peace Treaty which shall have power, within certain limits, to determine what can and should be paid during certain periods by Germany.

III. Or we suggest, as an alternative plan, that, instead of having any estimate made by the Sub-committee, they state in substance that, in view of the uncertain elements involved and until it is known what Germany will be left with, it is impossible to make any accurate estimate, and it is therefore recommended that the Sub-committee be dissolved and that the representatives of the respective Governments report directly to their chiefs from time to time during the negotiations as to what, in their opinion, might be collected from Germany.

Under such a general form of report, the embarrassment of the present situation could be avoided, and you and the two Prime Ministers could then appoint independently a representative each to conduct the negotiations and agree upon something more concrete and constructive, because it is impossible to handle such a delicate matter as this in so large a committee.

The foregoing is dictated hastily, but we are preparing for submission to you today a more carefully prepared plan of the whole situation. This is now ready and is submitted herewith.[4]

Norman H. Davis.

P.S. I have shown this to Col. House who approves.   NHD

TS MS (WP, DLC).
[1] Printed at March 15, 1919, Vol. 55.
[2] This was the so-called "Third Revise" of the provisions regarding reparations to be included in the peace treaty with Germany. It was enclosed in T. W. Lamont to EMH, March 24, 1919. Both documents are printed in Philip M. Burnett, *Reparation at the Paris Peace Conference: From the Standpoint of the American Delegation* (2 vols., New York, 1940), I, 704-707. The draft provisions included statements about the total war loss and damage for which the Central Powers were responsible, the portion of this total which those nations would be obliged to pay in reparations, a schedule of payments of the sums agreed upon, and the establishment of a commission representing the Allied and Associated governments which would oversee the payment of reparations. No total amount of reparations was included in the draft provisions since the Allied and Associated powers had thus far been unable to agree on what it should be. Lamont's covering letter to House emphasized the importance of establishing the commission to oversee the payment of reparations, because it would have "very considerable powers to modify, extend, &c." over a period of many years to come.
[3] The members of this subcommittee were Norman H. Davis, Baron Cunliffe, Louis Loucheur, Antonio Salandra, Konojo Tatsumi of Japan, George Danielopol of Rumania, Kosta Stojanović of Serbia, and Zygmunt Chamiec of Poland.
[4] N. H. Davis, Albert Strauss, and T. W. Lamont, "Reparation," T MS (WP, DLC), printed in Burnett, I, 713-19. This document also stressed the importance of establishing the commission to supervise reparation payments and included proposals for the establishment, composition, and powers of that body, as well as suggestions for instructions to be given to it by the peace conference. The memorandum also included American, French, and English proposals for the total amount of reparations to be paid by Germany. The American proposal suggested a minimum figure of $25 billion and a maximum of $35 billion; the French, a minimum of $31 billion and a maximum of $47 billion; and the English, a single figure of £11 billion, or $55 billion.

A Memorandum[1]

SECRET   25th, March, 1919.
Future Administration of Certain Portions
of the Turkish Empire under the Mandatory System.

Instructions for Commissioners from the Peace Conference to make enquiries in certain portions of the Turkish Empire[2] which are to be permanently separated from Turkey and put under the guidance of Governments acting as Mandatories for the League of Nations.

(Agreed to by President Wilson, Mr. Lloyd George, M. Clemenceau and M. Orlando.)

It is the purpose of the Conference to separate from the Turkish Empire certain areas comprising, for example, Palestine, Syria, the Arab countries to the east of Palestine and Syria, Mesopotamia, Armenia, Cilicia, and perhaps additional areas in Asia Minor, and to put the development of their people under the guidance of Governments which are to act as Mandatories of the League of Nations. It is expected that this will be done in accordance with the following resolutions adopted by the Representatives of the United States, Great Britain, France, Italy and Japan at a conference held at the Quai d'Orsay on January 30th, 1919.

"1. Having regard to the record of the German administration in the colonies formerly part of the German Empire, and to the menace which the possession by Germany of submarine bases in many parts of the world would necessarily constitute to the freedom and security of all nations, the Allied and Associated Powers are agreed that in no circumstances should any of the German Colonies be restored to Germany.

"2. For similar reasons, and more particularly because of the historical mis-government by the Turks of subject peoples and the terrible massacres of Armenians and others in recent years, the Allied and Associated Powers are agreed that Armenia, Syria, Mesopotamia, Palestine and Arabia must be completely severed from the Turkish Empire. This is without prejudice to the settlement of other parts of the Turkish Empire.

"3. The Allied and Associated Powers are agreed that advantage should be taken of the opportunity afforded by the necessity of disposing of these colonies and territories formerly belonging to Germany and Turkey which are inhabited by peoples not yet able to stand by themselves under the strenuous conditions of the modern world, to apply to these territories the principle that the wellbeing and development of such peoples form a sacred trust of civilization and that securities for the performance of this trust should be embodied in the constitution of the League of Nations.

"4. After careful study they are satisfied that the best method of giving practical effect to this principle is that the tutelage of such peoples should be entrusted to advanced nations who, by reason of their resources, their experience or their geographical positions, can best undertake this responsibility, and that this tutelage should be exercised by them as mandatories on behalf of the League of Nations.

"5. The Allied and Associated Powers are of opinion that the character of the mandate must differ according to the stage of development of the people, the geographical situation of the territory, its economic conditions, and other similar circumstances.

"6. They consider that certain communities formerly belonging to the Turkish Empire have reached a stage of development where their existence as independent nations can be provisionally recognized, subject to the rendering of administrative advice and assistance by a mandatory power until such time as they are able to stand alone. The wishes of those communities must be a principal consideration in the selection of the mandatory power.

"7. They further consider that other peoples, especially those of Central Africa, are at such a stage that the mandatory must be responsible for the administration of the territory subject to conditions which will guarantee the prohibition of abuses such as the slave trade, the arms traffic and the liquor traffic, and the prevention of the military training of the natives for other than police purposes, and the establishment of fortifications or military and naval bases, and will also secure equal opportunities for the trade and commerce of other members of the League of Nations.

"8. Finally, they consider that there are territories, such as South-West Africa and certain of the Islands in the South Pacific, which, owing to the sparseness of their population, or their small size, or their remoteness from the centres of civilisation, or their geographical contiguity to the mandatory state, and other circumstances, can be best administered under the laws of the mandatory state as integral portions thereof, subject to the safeguards above-mentioned in the interests of the indigenous populations.

"In every case of mandate, the mandatory state shall render to the League of Nations an annual report in reference to the territory committed to its charge."

And it is agreed that the administration of these mandates shall be in the spirit of the following document which was formally presented to the President of the United States on behalf of the Governments of Great Britain and France:

"Anglo-French Declaration, November 9, 1918.

"The aim which France and Great Britain have in view in prosecuting in the East the war let loose by German ambition is the complete and final liberation of the peoples so long oppressed by the Turks and the establishment of national governments and administrations deriving their authority from the initiative and free choice of the native populations.

"In order to give effect to these intentions, France and Great Britain have agreed to encourage and assist the establishment of native governments and administrations in Syria and Mesopotamia already liberated by the Allies, and in the territories which they are proceeding to liberate, and they have agreed to recognise such governments as soon as they are effectively established. So far from desiring to impose specific institutions upon the populations of these regions, their sole object is to ensure, by their support and effective assistance, that the governments and administrations adopted by these regions of their own free will shall be exercised in the normal way. The function which the two Allied Governments claim for themselves in the liberated territories is to ensure impartial and equal justice for all; to facilitate the economic development of the country by encouraging local initiative; to promote the diffusion of education; and to put an end to the divisions too long exploited by Turkish policy."

The Conference therefore feels obliged to acquaint itself as intimately as possible with the sentiments of the people of these regions with regard to the future administration of their affairs. You are requested, accordingly, to visit these regions to acquaint yourselves as fully as possible with the state of opinion there with regard to these matters, with the social, racial, and economic conditions, a knowledge of which might serve to guide the judgment of the Conference, and to form as definite an opinion as the circumstances and the time at your disposal will permit, of the divisions of territory and assignment of mandates which will be most likely to promote the order, peace, and development of those peoples and countries.

T MS (WP, DLC).
    [1] Drafted by Wilson, or under his direction, at the request of the Council of Four on March 20, 1919.
    [2] What became the exclusively American commission of inquiry, the so-called King-Crane Commission, headed by Henry Churchill King and Charles Richard Crane. The standard work on this subject is Harry N. Howard, *The King-Crane Commission* (Beirut, 1963).

A Memorandum by Vittorio Emanuele Orlando

SECRET.   [c. March 25, 1919]

Prince Livio BORGHESE, recalled from Belgrade as the result of the refusal of the Serbian Government to recognize his credentials because they had not been addressed to the King of the Serbs, Croates and Slovenians, returned to Italy by way of Budapest, arriving on the 17th of March.

On the 25th of March he addressed me the following letter:

"I had intended leaving Budapest on the 24th, when on the 21st, the change of government came about. On the 22nd of March I was approached by an intermediary who proposed to me, in the name of the new Popular Government, that I should have an interview with the substitute of the Commissioner of the People for Foreign Affairs (Under Secretary of State).[1] He assured me that it was a matter of extreme importance, which might perhaps save the situation. Thereupon I went that same evening to the house of a private individual, where the first interview took place.

With the Under Secretary of State for Foreign Affairs, Professor

    [1] Peter Ágoston, formerly *Privatdozent* of Law at Kolozsvar University (now Cluj University in present-day Rumania).

Agostom, there was Professor Szasz,[2] employed in the Ministry of Public Construction and confidential man of Mr. Kunly.[3] These gentlemen assured me that while this (change of government) had been planned for a long time on account of the absolute lack of results obtained by the late government, and in consequence of the development of communistic ideas, the fact which precipitated these happenings was without any doubt the ultimatum presented by Colonel Vix to the Government on the 20th of March, demanding, (1) That all Hungarian Troops should be retired from the Eastern Frontier, (2) That a neutral zone should be established between Hungary and Roumania, and (3) Imposing an excessive reduction in territories, etc. He was coming to me as a last resort and begged me to be their intermediary with the Entente. In the course of the conversation they complained bitterly of the manner in which the Entente had acted towards Hungary, the injustice done Hungary in taking away from her for the benefit of the Czechs, Roumanians and Serbs, territories which were entirely Hungarian, and especially the fact that Hungarian representatives had never been allowed to meet and discuss matters with the Entente delegates, as Austrian representatives had been allowed to do. They added, that the actual government, in spite of the negative answer given to the ultimatum of Colonel Vix, and in spite of appeals to the Russians and the masses all over the world, eagerly desired not to break off relations with the Entente, and hoped to be able to renew them under better conditions.

I explained my situation to them and told them that I had no official position, being in Budapest by chance and almost as a tourist. They answered that this was no obstacle and that as I was there I could carry to the Entente the wishes of Hungary in an impartial way. It was, they assured me, the last attempt to save the situation and not to break completely with the Entente. If this attempt failed, Hungary, not being able to remain isolated, would be forced to appeal to the East, confident of the support of the Russian Troops who are now advancing towards the Carpathians, and to break away entirely from the Powers of the Entente. The general situation would be much aggravated; difficulties and even dangers would result, and a peace which the entire world hoped for would be delayed without doubt. Again stating that I had no official position, I told them that I would repeat what they had just told me, on condition that the communication which they begged me to make to Your Excellency was discussed and approved by the entire Government and that while waiting for Your Excellency's answer that they should

[2] He cannot be further identified.
[3] He apparently referred to Zsigmund Kunfi.

respect foreign missions and their flags and the properties and subjects of Entente Nations.

Yesterday, the 24th, after the first conversation which I have just detailed, Mr. Kunly asked to see me. He is considered here as being the most intelligent and strongest man of the present Government, with very liberal ideas and representing a relatively moderate element. As a matter of fact, he is recognized as the head of the Nationalist Party in Hungary. During the conversation that I had with him the same things were gone over in a general way. I told him that I considered the appeal to the Russians for union and solidarity a very grave error which might burn the last bridges still remaining between Hungary and the Entente, and that certainly this must be the interpretation given to this step in the West. He wanted to explain to me that the general impression here was that of having been abandoned by the Entente, which as far as Hungary was concerned, had followed a different line of action than that taken towards other countries, and almost in opposition to the principles laid down by President Wilson. Then, exasperated by the ultimatum of Colonel Vix, the Hungarians were forced to take this decision. Mr. Kunly also told me that the actual Government was not Bolshevist, but only Socialist, Radical and Popular, and that, as a matter of fact, the control of the Government, in spite of its union with the Communists, remained in the hands of the Socialistic Party, the only one really well-organized in Hungary.

As a result of the conversation with Mr. Kunly, the Plenary Council of the Commissioners of The People met yesterday afternoon (the 24th) and discussed at length all the questions concerning this attempt to reopen relations with the Entente, and with the complete assent of the entire Government, a memoire reserved for my exclusive use was drawn up, which was sent to me "brevi-manu" late in the afternoon.

In agreement with the actual Government, I am sending herewith to Your Excellency, a copy of this memoire,[4] signed by the Commissioner (Minister) of Foreign Affairs, and also a short resume. The documents will go via Vienna, the only route which is still fairly safe, as well as being the quickest.

My impressions of these days, arrived at after having spoken with several of these gentlemen, can be summed up as follows:

This enormous evolution, or revolution if it can be called that, has been very well organized and very well carried out.

With the exception of certain instances, very few in number, from the very first hour it may be said that almost complete order

[4] See the memorandum by Béla Kun printed at March 24, 1919.

has reigned in the city, and from what I hear, also in the country districts. Here in Budapest a state of siege has been declared from the first moment under very strict conditions.

The more moderate element in the new Government has decided to maintain order, and up to the present time has succeeded in keeping in control of events and dominating the extreme element whose excessive ideas it has been able to moderate.

The Government absolutely desires to establish, as soon as possible, relations with the Entente, but altogether outside military missions.

If this is not refused by the Entente, the Government wishes, in the first place, to obtain permission for its Hungarian Delegates to confer with those of the Entente, either in Paris or in Switzerland or elsewhere, as has been done with Austria. In the matter of the choice of delegates I feel that I can give my assurances that the Government would take the wishes of the Entente into consideration.

In regard to the question of territorial integrity, the Government will be disposed to discuss this matter and to arrive at an understanding.

It understands that certain sections could be ceded without inconvenience, but it believes that territory where Hungarians (which also includes Germans) are in a majority should remain Hungarian. In effect, it believes that the homogeneousness of the different sections is indispensable in order to continue or make possible the independent existence of Hungary. On this point the country would be willing and ready to resist by force, even at the risk of ruin, rather than agree to amputations which would make life impossible.

I am not concealing the fact that the situation is very serious and very grave, and that in spite of the energy, order and strength demonstrated up to the present time by the new Government, it (the situation) may become irreparable at any moment, with the dangerous consequences that this might carry with it, even for the other states of Europe.

It is because of this very seriousness of the present situation and the consequences which might follow, that I have taken the responsibility of communicating to you the preceding.

I believe that it is my duty to add that if any action is decided on it is necessary that it be done without delay by finding an effectual way at least in the form of effacing the deep feeling of injustice which here is believed to have been shown in all the acts of the Entente towards Hungary during the last months.

I also believe that it is absolutely necessary, in order to help the

Government to maintain order, to send food at once, as it is already scarce and might soon lack altogether."

T MS (WP, DLC).

William Phillips to Robert Lansing

Washington, March 25th, 1919.

1280. Referring Archangel Embassy's 606 and 607 to Mission.[1] Does President still desire that this Government shall participate in financing Government for Northern region Russia? If so, what funds are available? Phillips Acting.

T telegram (WP, DLC).
[1] Actually, the telegrams numbered 66 and 67: D. C. Poole, Jr., to Ammission, Paris, March 22, 1919, T telegram (SDR, RG 59, 861.51/30½, DNA), and D. C. Poole, Jr., to Ammission, Paris, March 23, 1919, T telegram (SDR, RG 59, 861.51/32, DNA). Poole reported in the first telegram that the British government had agreed to furnish five million rubles per month for the first six months of 1919, half of which was to be contributed in the name of France, to finance the anti-Bolshevik government of North Russia in Archangel. Britain in turn intended to request the governments of the United States and Italy to contribute two and one-half million rubles each per month to make up a total of ten million. In the second telegram Poole made the following suggestion: "It is urgently recommended that if we consent to participate in the project for temporarily financing the provisional government our quarter share be paid to the Government directly by this Embassy and not through British channels. Complete control of our contribution is necessary in order to enforce our policies and to assure for American merchants who may rely in [on] this market the means, now almost altogether absent, of converting the roubles realized into foreign exchange."

From the Diary of Colonel House

March 25, 1919.

This has been rather a quiet day, although a number of people have called without there being any special significance to their visits. I have been in close touch with the President over the telephone.

Nothing was done either at the morning or afternoon meetings of the Prime Ministers, Clemenceau claiming not to be ready. The matter under discussion was reparations. It seems almost grotesque that Clemenceau should have made such an assertion after all these weeks of discussion. However, there it is. It is the usual thing, first one excuse and then another to evade the issue.

Bullitt got back tonight from Russia. His story is interesting and at last I can see a way out of that vexatious problem, that is, if we can get action by the Prime Ministers and the President. I cautioned Bullitt against telling all he told me. Russia, according to him, is orderly but starving, and if relations are not opened with the outside world, anarchy will be prevalent, for the man without bread will steal and murder for it. That part of his story I told him must be for my ears alone. Most of the Allies, I regret to chronicle, would just as soon have the people starve as not. They were willing to allow the people of the Central Empires [to] starve, and they are just as willing to have Russia go the same way. It is fear that will bring about a Russian settlement, not pity. Most of the world seems to have lost its sense of compassion.

While Bullitt was talking I was maturing plans which I shall begin to put in execution tomorrow.

To Charles Mills Galloway

My dear Mr. Galloway: Paris, 25 March, 1919.

I have your letter of March 7th[1] and beg to assure you that you are under an entire misapprehension. I did not request your resignation because of ill conduct or anything such as you very naturally would wish investigated, but solely because I knew from yourself as well as from others that the counsels of the Commission have been very much divided, that a great deal of feeling had been generated, and that this division of feeling had embarrassed a great deal the work of the Board. I thought it was wise therefore to follow the course that I have more than once followed in such circumstances and reconstitute the Board entirely. It is seldom possible after such experiences to reestablish the work of a commission on a basis of quiet harmony and undisturbed routine, and you may be sure that I have neither the wish nor the right to cast any reflection upon your character or conduct.

Cordially and sincerely yours,   [Woodrow Wilson]

CCL (WP, DLC).
[1] C. M. Galloway to WW, March 7, 1919, Vol. 55.

To Henry van Dyke

My dear Doctor van Dyke: Paris, 25 March, 1919.

I have read with the greatest interest your letter[1] suggesting Mr. Robert Underwood Johnson to succeed Mr. Thomas Nelson Page, should Page withdraw at Rome. I know Mr. Johnson and have the highest esteem for him.

Thank you also for your little book of verses "Golden Stars." I have already dipped into it enough to know its fine flavor and have read with great happiness the last page.[2]

In unavoidable haste,
Cordially and sincerely yours,   [Woodrow Wilson]

CCL (WP, DLC).
¹ H. van Dyke to WW, March 7, 1919, TLS (WP, DLC).
² Henry van Dyke, *Golden Stars, and Other Verses, Following "The Red Flower"* (New York, 1919). There is a copy of this book in the Wilson Library, DLC. The last page (p. 27) contains the final stanza of "Golden Stars," an ode written for a memorial service held at Princeton University on December 15, 1918. It reads as follows:

> "Come, let us gird our loins and lift our load,
> Companions who are left on life's rough road,
> And bravely take the way that we must tread
> To keep true faith with our beloved dead.
> To conquer war they dared their lives to give,
> To safeguard peace our hearts must learn to live.
> Help us, dear God, our forward faith to hold!
> We want a better world than that of old.
> Lead us on paths of high endeavor,
> Toiling upward, climbing ever,
> Ready to suffer for the right,
> Until at last we gain a loftier height,
> More worthy to behold
> Our guiding stars, our hero-stars of gold."

From Herbert Clark Hoover

My dear Mr. President: Paris, 25 March 1919.

The determination of the method of administration of the 1919 wheat crop requires an early decision. I have the feeling that with the completion of this harvest year the great call for relief work in Europe will have been completed and before this time the Food Administration will have ceased legally to exist, except so far as it is necessary to carry on outstanding contracts in the 1918 wheat crop and in connection with sugar purchases. I believe that the completion of the harvest year, therefore, offers a proper opportunity for me to retire after five years of public service.

The handling of the 1919 wheat crops, however, is a matter of extreme importance and I am convinced that the world demand for wheat would be such that if it is capably carried out there need not necessarily be a single dollar lost to the government. The only reason why, on present prospects, any loss should be incurred, would be amateur handling of a matter of extreme technical and financial complexity or, alternatively, of deliberate desire of the government to subsidize the price of flour for economic reasons. The addition of this latter function would, in any event, be one that could only be carried out by the very highest experience and skill.

I am convinced that the only man in the nation today who is capable of carrying through this difficult operation is Mr. Julius Barnes, who, as you know, has had charge of this work for the last two years. He has, directly and indirectly, handled nearly two billions of dollars of money, has not cost the government a penny of loss, and there has never been even a suggestion of either incapacity or of bad faith in his work. His recent announcement that he felt that he would retire with the harvest year has brought a storm of protest throughout the nation, both from the farming community and the trades, as they feel that his administration has been not only capable but just, as between the conflicting interests concerned. I have also received urgent telegrams from many different quarters, including even Senators, urging that he should be continued as a matter of national importance. Mr. Barnes is, I believe, nominally a Republican, but his principal politics consist of great personal devotion to yourself. I have inquired of him by cable whether he would be willing to continue for another year to direct this matter and I believe he could be induced to accept it but with one reservation, that is, that he should be placed directly under yourself, without the intervention of any other government department. He is that type of man who requires a considerable latitude of action, but, of course, would accept entirely your direction.

In order to carry out the guarantee in the light of the new legislation, it will be necessary to make some legal changes in the present United States Food Administration Grain Corporation to adapt it to the legislation. I would suggest that these changes should be made some time in June, that a complete statement be made of its operations, prepared up to July 1st as marking the end of its Food Administration association and that the name be changed to the United States Wheat Corporation. Under these plans, Mr. Barnes, as President of the corporation, would become at that date directly responsible to you instead of to myself as Chairman.

As the whole problem is one of our greatest national liquidation problems, I believe that the same direct association with yourself that I have enjoyed is of the utmost importance.

Faithfully yours,   Herbert Hoover

TLS (WP, DLC).

From Charles Edward Russell and Others

New York Mar 25 1919

We respectfully petition for full pardon for Eugene Debs on ground of advanced years high moral character and long years of devoted service to cause of human freedom notwithstanding his violation of law. We also respectfully urge pardon or amnesty for all sentenced to imprisonment for honest expressions of opinion against America's course in the war as distinguished from those who defied the law or purposely aided enemy. America we feel can afford to be generous to honest opponents of her course now that victory has been achieved.

Charles Edward Russell, Henry L. Slobodin, J. G. Phelps Stokes, John Spargo, Ben Wilson, Upton Sinclair, W J Ghent, Mila Tupper Maynard, J. I. Sheppard, Chester M. Wright, Charlotte Perkins Gilman, Louise Adams Grout, C. G. Hoag, Gertrude Breslau Fuller, James Mackaye, William Edlin, Rev E. E. Carr, Frederick Almy, Floyd J. Melvin, Herman Simpson, Nicholas Klein.[1]

T telegram (WP, DLC).

[1] Those persons not heretofore identified in this series were the Rev. Mila Tupper (Mrs. Rezin Augustus) Maynard, of Denver, former Unitarian minister, active as a lecturer for the United States Reclamation Service; Chester Whitney Wright, Professor of Political Economy at the University of Chicago; Clarence Gilbert Hoag, of Philadelphia, general secretary and treasurer of the American Proportional Representation League; James Mackaye, of Boston, writer and lecturer on scientific ethics and political engineering; William Edlin, editor in chief of *The Day*, a Jewish daily newspaper of New York; Frederic Almy, social worker of Buffalo and secretary of the Charity Organization Society; Floyd J. Melvin, a teacher in New York; Herman Simpson, writer of New York, former editor of the New York *Call*; and Nicholas Klein, lawyer of Cincinnati, widely known as a counsel for labor unions. Wilson, Sheppard, Grout, Fuller, and Carr cannot be identified.

From the Diary of Dr. Grayson

Wednesday, March 26, 1919.

This was probably the hardest day the President has had since he has been in France. In the morning he had a long session of the Big Four at his house; in the afternoon the meeting was continued at the residence of Lloyd-George; while in the evening the President conferred with and presided over the meeting of the committee on the League of Nations—not returning home until half past eleven o'clock.

The morning session of the Big Four was devoted again to the question of reparations. The President was endeavoring to bring about an agreement on the amount of indemnity that is to be exacted from Germany, and it developed today that he has the support along this line of both Lloyd-George and Orlando.

Today Lloyd-George told the President he believed that when they considered the time that had been lost he was convinced something must shortly be done to speed everything up. He called the President's attention to the fact that he (the President) had been responsible for the unity of military command, and wondered whether it would not be a good idea to have a unity of diplomatic command. There has been a growing disposition on the part of both the British and the Italians lately to propose that the President himself formulate the complete program and put it across in his own way. They argue that inasmuch as the President will be held more or less responsible for the results, it is only fair that he should frame the program himself.

The Big Four at both morning and afternoon sessions made what was described as "substantial" progress in their work to establish the foundations for a peace that would be founded on the sound principles of justice, and which would be acceptable to Germany herself. Inasmuch as there has been some talk that Germany might not sign when the peace treaty was finally submitted to her, there has been discussion in peace conference circles over what could be done should that refusal come. The general opinion, however, was that if the President's plans were followed out the treaty, while stern, would not be so harsh that it would not finally receive approval from the Central Powers. It had been about decided that the treaty when completed will be a blanket treaty dealing with all of the Central Powers, instead of following out the original program, which was to make separate treaties with Germany, Austria-Hungary, Bulgaria and Turkey.

I asked the President what would be the outcome if the Germans refused to sign the peace treaty. He heaved a sigh and said: "God knows." "Of course," he said, "it would mean that it would be necessary for the Allies to intervene by arms and this would be an awful thing to contemplate, but something of this kind would have to be done. What we must do, however, is what I have been contending for all along, and that is to prepare a peace that will be founded on justice. We must bear in mind all of the time that the peace must be one which Germany can sign. If we do that and our terms are based entirely on justice, should Germany refuse to sign, then the entire opinion of the world will be against her and it will simplify the task of dealing with her."

At the night session of the League of Nations committee the entire constitution of the League was definitely approved and referred to a committee to be passed upon as to legal phraseology. This committee was made up of Lord Robert Cecil, Colonel House, Venizelos and Larnaude, the French Jurist. It was stated that the committee would probably have the complete re-drafted treaty ready for consideration by the full committee within a day or two. All of the amendments which had been approved and the original draft of the treaty were turned over to the committee, whose duty it was to clarify all ambiguous language and to reduce the textual size of the document as much as possible.

The biggest concession made to public opinion at home was to set forth in unmistakeable language the right of a nation to withdraw from the League should a contingency arise which would make such action desirable. In discussing this point before the committee the President said that he was prepared to say that so far as the United States was concerned it never would withdraw from the League unless a situation arose which would imperil its national honor. Should the time ever come when it did withdraw, the President said the world would unanimously approve its action, and he could not see a situation arising which would compel such action.

Afterward the League of Nations committee assured the President and Colonel House at a ten-minute conference, at which Colonel House reported to him the result of his (House) conference with Premier Orlando earlier in the day.

Lloyd-George called the President's attention to the fact that more than a majority of the members of the British Parliament had signed a memorial setting forth that he (the Premier) must stand for the infliction upon Germany of an assessment for war claims that would compel the payment of Germany's last cent.[1] He said that he had been warned if he did not stand out for such a program the opposition would have a vote of lack of confidence, and as they had the votes would remove him as Premier and force the downfall of the present Cabinet. The President did not seem to consider this in the nature of a catastrophe if it should come and told Lloyd-George that nothing would be finer than to be put out of office during a crisis of this kind for doing what was right. Should some one succeed him and discover that he had assumed a task which could not be accomplished, the roof of the temple would fall about his head, swallowing him, and history would give him (Lloyd-George) the fine distinction of standing for what was right and for not being awed by the opinion of the majority who were in the wrong. The President added: "I could not wish a more magnificent place in history."

Another very interesting development which tended to show the British and American viewpoint regarding the question of excessive indemnity came today when Lord Sumner called at the temporary White House to present to Lloyd-George figures arrived at by the British experts, and which covered the British indemnity claims.[2] These figures were very excessive and a sharp colloquy between the President and Lord Sumner developed. The President said that if the demands which Lord Sumner had presented were to be enforced they would inevitably lead to Bolshevism throughout all Germany. In reply the British representative said that they (Germany) would be cutting its own throat. To which the President responded that it would be inhuman for any normal being to contribute to anything that would lead to the murder of a nation; in other words, the President said: "You would be willing to have Germany murder itself rather than give up the indemnity. Any man who would express an opinion like this should not be permitted to participate in a peace settlement."

[1] Grayson must have misunderstood Wilson, or Wilson must have incorrectly reported Lloyd George's remarks (cf. the minutes of the meeting of the Council of Four, March 26, 1919, 11 a.m., printed below). Although a majority of the members of Parliament, during the election campaign of December 1918, had vowed to fight for the exaction of a full indemnity from Germany, they had not yet presented Lloyd George with any formal statement of their views. It was not until April 8, 1919, that 370 M.P.s reminded Lloyd George in a strongly-worded telegram that they expected him to carry out his election promises "to present the Bill in full, to make Germany acknowledge the debts and then to discuss ways and means of obtaining the payment." Lloyd George's remarks at this time were probably based upon a speech in the House of Commons by Lt. Col. Claude Lowther, Conservative M.P. from Lancashire, who, on March 17, 1919, had demanded assurances that the government had not "departed from the Prime Minister's electioneering pledge . . . that the whole of this war bill" would be presented to Germany. "It must be remembered," Lowther stated, "that there are some 400, I am not certain there are not more, Members of this House, . . . who are solemnly pledged to do all they can in their power to exact from Germany the very last farthing that she can be reasonably called on to pay." *Parliamentary Debates*, Fifth Series, Vol. 113, House of Commons, Cols. 1870-72. For a detailed discussion, see Mayer, *Politics and Diplomacy of Peacemaking*, pp. 151-58, 623-32; Robert E. Bunselmeyer, *The Cost of the War 1914-1919: British Economic War Aims and the Origins of Reparations* (Hamden, Conn., 1975), pp. 75-184; and, particularly, A. Lentin, *Lloyd George, Woodrow Wilson and the Guilt of Germany* (Baton Rouge, La., 1984), pp. 30-53.

[2] See the memorandum by Norman H. Davis printed at March 25, 1919.

Mantoux's Notes of Two Meetings of the Council of Four

March 26, 1919, 11 a.m.

Wilson. We would like to question M. Loucheur about Germany's capacity to pay. I thought I understood, at a meeting which took place at my residence, that Mr. Davis and M. Loucheur had reached an agreement.

Loucheur. On the principle, but not on the figures. At our meeting yesterday, Lord Sumner, Mr. Davis and I agreed on the principle of a maximum and a minimum annual payment. As for the figures, Mr. Norman Davis arrives, as a minimum, at twenty-five billion dollars—total present value—and, as a maximum, at thirty-five billion dollars. But these figures were not accepted by the French and English delegates. The French figures are thirty billion dollars minimum and fifty billions maximum. Our minimum figure is based on what I sincerely believe to be Germany's capacity to pay, and it corresponds approximately to reparation for material damages. The figure of fifty billion dollars would cover not only material damages, but also pensions, calculated at a uniform rate for all countries. It is not absurd to think that Germany can manage to pay this maximum figure.

Concerning the fixing of annual payments, we agree on the establishment of a commission which will determine each year a figure between the maximum and the minimum and which will also fix the proportion to be paid in exportable securities.

President Wilson observes that the national capital of France in 1908 was estimated at fifty billion dollars.

Loucheur. Sixty billion dollars would be closer to the truth. But we should not forget about the change in prices since the war. The prices upon which we have to base our estimates for reconstruction are two and a half or three times higher than those of 1914.

Wilson. Agreed. But how can we believe that Germany can pay such amounts?

Loucheur. Before the war, according to Helfferich,[1] Germany put aside between eight and ten billion marks each year. Now, the average annual installment corresponding to the figures I have given would vary between ten and fifteen billion francs, that is eight and twelve billion marks. It is true that Germany will have lost the productive capacity of Lorraine and Silesia. But the depreciation of the currency reduces appreciably the sum of what we are asking. Besides, we are ready to grant Germany a several years' grace period for recovery. From 1921 to 1926, we envisage only substantially reduced payments.

Lloyd George. If, during this transitional period, you require less of Germany, will you carry forward the unpaid balance to the following years, which could make the burden too heavy?

Loucheur. What we propose is to make Germany pay 200 million pounds sterling in 1921, this sum gradually increasing to 400 million pounds in 1926. We have provided that, if Germany cannot pay the total required during these six years, the deficit would be distributed over the total thirty-five-year payment period, without interest. The British, American, and French delegates agree entirely that Germany's recovery should be facilitated during this transitional period.

Lloyd George. What is the estimated normal figure?

Loucheur. Six hundred million pounds maximum and 400 million pounds minimum. Also, the commission could grant Germany the option of paying up to 50 per cent of the sum due in paper marks at an agreed rate.

Lloyd George. Suppose that France had to find 150 million pounds sterling each year in gold or in foreign currencies, or in exports. Could you come up with this sum? We certainly could not do it if we had to pay 150 million pounds a year to America.

[1] That is, Karl Theodor Helfferich.

Loucheur. We have given our attention to the matter of how Germany can pay. Unless we know that, in effect, everything else is useless speculation. I estimate that, since the price of the materials Germany can export has risen permanently, more than the price of her imports, it will be possible for her to improve her commercial balance in the future. For example, instead of exporting forty million tons of coal worth 500 million francs, she can receive 2.5 billion francs for fifty million tons exported after the war. I do not think that the price of coal will fall.

Wilson. There is a variable factor here. In the United States, it is the price of coal which will fall and the price of wheat that has a chance to remain steady. But do you not believe it is unduly optimistic to think that Germany, considering all that we will take from her, will find herself in a more favorable position regarding exports?

Lloyd George. We are taking from her six or seven million inhabitants, three quarters of her iron, one third of her coal, and 20 per cent of her potash. France has grounds for hoping to take her place in the metallurgical industries. Add to this the probability of reduced work hours in Germany, as elsewhere. Can it be imagined that, in these conditions, Germany could increase her production enough to raise the surplus of her balance of payments from the prewar figure of fifty million pounds to 200 million pounds?

Loucheur. Taking lignite into account, we are taking only one seventh of Germany's exportable coal, and we must also take into account price inflation. Moreover, we must recognize that it is difficult to know how much Germany can pay; that is why we must allow considerable latitude to the commission responsible for determining the annual payments.

Lloyd George. Prices will not remain at triple the former prices.

Loucheur. Yes they will, at least for coal. For the other items, they will remain at least double.

Lloyd George. I ask M. Loucheur to answer this question as a statesman as much as a great businessman. Suppose that the Germans share the point of view of the American experts and refuse to accept responsibility for paying beyond a certain maximum amount. Has M. Loucheur considered the consequences of a refusal to sign the treaty?

Wilson. And what would we have to do in such a case?

Loucheur. Without our concern to repair damages, according to the solemn obligation we have undertaken toward our peoples, I would have accepted the American minimum. But I must repeat that it does not permit us to repair all damage to persons and to property; what will our people say if this is confessed to them? As for knowing what must be done if they refuse to sign, this is not a question peculiar to the financial problem.

Lloyd George. We must face this possibility of a refusal to sign. According to my latest information, what the Germans are most concerned about, in addition to the left bank of the Rhine, are the questions of Danzig, Silesia, and the payment of reparations. If the German leaders conclude that it is best for them to imitate Hungary and ally themselves with the Bolsheviks, if they prefer the risk of several years of anarchy to thirty-five years of servitude, what shall we do? Lands such as Danzig and Silesia can be occupied militarily; but as for money, how will we make them pay?

Loucheur. In that case I would occupy the basin of the Ruhr. This region and the left bank of the Rhine could yield four to five billion marks per year. This involves risks, and I am not proposing it as a firm solution. Like you, I am convinced that we must be moderate in order to avoid as far as we can the danger of a refusal.

Lloyd George. I am surprised at the figure which M. Loucheur has just given. The total annual profit of Great Britain's coal mines is twenty million pounds sterling. I fear, moreover, that the German miners will not work hard if they know that they are only working for their enemies.

Loucheur. I did not mean that mining profits would be four or five billions per year, but that, in the part of Germany that we would occupy, it would be possible to obtain an annual sum of four or five billions, which would be added to the German payments. A domestic debt of 100 billion marks at the end of thirty-five years would constitute for Germany a budget that her people could perfectly support.

Lloyd George. This leads us beyond the limits of good sense. At this time, we are holding only bridgeheads on the Rhine, Germany is putting up no resistance, and this occupation costs 350 million pounds sterling per year. If we had to occupy a very populous region, like Westphalia, while Germany, all around us, is in revolt or agitated by contagious Bolshevism, what then would be our expenses and our risks? And do you believe that we could maintain that situation until we received 100 billion marks?

It will be as difficult for me as for M. Clemenceau to dispel the illusions which surround the subject of reparations. Four hundred members of the British Parliament have sworn to extract from Germany the very last penny to which we are entitled; I will have to answer to them face to face. But our duty is to serve our nation in the best way we can. If I am defeated because I did not do the impossible, my successor, whoever he may be, will not be able to do better; one year later, if he has made extravagant promises without keeping them, everyone will say that he was foolish and that we were right.

I am convinced that the Germans will not sign the proposals we envisage. In their place, I would not sign. Germany will turn to Bolshevism. Europe will remain mobilized, our industries halted, our states will go bankrupt; it will be said rightly that we are to blame because we did not know how to make peace. We must decide to act wisely, whatever your opposition and our opposition will think.

Wilson. I can only express my admiration for the spirit shown in the words of Mr. Lloyd George. There is nothing more honorable than to be turned out of power because one was right.

We must look at this financial problem from a political point of view. Those who have studied the question have too often based their calculations on prewar Germany. That Germany rested upon a powerful organization, that is, a rich, enterprising government determined to lead Germany to economic mastery of the world. That Germany no longer exists. We are reducing its territory. The Weimar government has no credit. If it cannot stay in power, it will be replaced by a government we will be unable to deal with.

We can only hope that a disorganized and demoralized Germany will do as much as prewar Germany, which might have taken pride in satisfying our demands. We owe it to the peace of the world not to tempt Germany to plunge into Bolshevism; we know only too well the relations of the Bolshevik leaders with Germany.

I believe that if we offer reasonable proposals and take care to explain them, not a parliament in the world would dare to blame us. We must not ask ourselves too often what we have the right to demand because of our losses, but rather what it would be possible and wise to demand. We can receive what we demand only if we can do it without crushing Germany for thirty-five years.

This question is more difficult to solve than that of Danzig. We can say: we will occupy Danzig. But we cannot militarily occupy fifty billion dollars. Besides, Germany could pay very large sums only by taking an even larger share of world markets than before the war. Is that in our interest? Would it not be better to try to gain this money ourselves in the markets, instead of encouraging Germany to take them from us?

Clemenceau. I basically agree with Mr. Lloyd George and Mr. Wilson, but I do not believe that they disagree with M. Loucheur who, as an experienced businessman, would carefully avoid killing the goose that lays the golden egg.

I have no fear of affronting Parliament; but I cannot forget the document which we signed and sent to President Wilson about reparation for war damages. If we admit that such reparation is impossible, we must frankly say so; but we should only say it if we are certain that it is impossible.

I propose that we submit figures for damages suffered by each of our nations to a small arbitration commission; in cases where its members could not agree, President Wilson could decide. Fortunately, we do not have to discuss today the question of distribution. What concerns us is to notify Germany what she will have to pay. I am impressed by the ingenuity of the system of a permanent commission proposed by our financial delegates. It permits us to deal with the circumstances. The commission will act freely within certain limits; but the governments would be able to reserve the right to reduce or even to abolish the minimum. I do not believe that one could find anything more flexible.

What impresses me in M. Loucheur's lucid report is how close we are to an understanding. The only possible difficulty is in the distribution. Hence my suggestion of an arbitration commission; any one of us who presents exaggerated figures would dishonor himself. Frankly, I would agree to discuss the amount to pay with the Germans themselves. If they can show me good reasons why we should lower our figures, I am ready to listen to them.

What we must avoid is going to the other extreme and, because we fear demanding too much, not to demand enough. Can we proclaim the principle of payment of war damages and establish a minimum and maximum rate of annual payment without indicating a total amount due? At the same time, we would create the commission I referred to. I believe that public opinion would support us.

I shall ask our experts to try harder to come to an agreement taking into account the political point of view which we are adopting. We might ask them to give us their solution within forty-eight hours. When we have adopted it, the hardest question will be settled, and we will be able to resolve many other questions during the following week.

This solution is necessary. It is necessary because of the condition in which Europe, which the war has left in shreds, finds itself; it is rendered necessary by the universal desire to demobilize the armies and to resume normal life. From all sides are heard complaints about the slow pace of the work of the conference. I do not pretend that we have done our job very rapidly; but, if we consider the crushing weight of its task and the complexity of the problems to be resolved, our conference will bear comparison with any other human assembly.

We know that public opinion demands an early peace. President Wilson has repeated to us the words of the woman from Soissons asking him to "make peace very quickly." I am ready to hasten a conclusion by asking, from the financial point of view, what is just and possible and nothing more. We can ask our financial advisers to assist us in finishing within forty-eight hours.

Wilson. I believe that our experts have already done what they can to come to an agreement, and some will not budge from their positions. I agree with everything that M. Clemenceau has said; but we have not yet found a way to avoid specifying in the treaty the total figure of payment that we will demand. If we limit ourselves to demanding annual payments, they will ask us this question: "For how long?" If we limit ourselves to saying that a commission will be able to regulate the payment according to the situation in Germany, I fear that this will not satisfy public opinion, which has no confidence in the good faith of the Germans. I agree with you that we should permit them to discuss it, but we cannot avoid saying what they will have to pay.

Loucheur. We still have the option of not fixing the figure definitively before discussing it with the Germans at Versailles.

Lloyd George. It seems useless to have our specialists meet yet again. My own are competent but obstinate people. When I spoke to Lord Sumner, who is an eminent judge and a man of great character, about the Bolshevik danger in Germany, if we go too far in our demands, Lord Sumner answered me: "In that case the Germans will be cutting their own throats, and I would like nothing better." It is a waste of time to argue with a man of that opinion. Lord Cunliffe is more tractable, despite much innate stubbornness; but he is under the influence of Lord Sumner, who never leaves his side.

Our experts have made their stand and will not change. Would it not be better to ask them to supply us with figures representing damages caused to the civilian populations, both to property and to persons? We must limit the definition so as to exclude failure to earn by business firms, etc. We must also consider price inflation; I think, with M. Loucheur, that prices should be calculated at a rate at least double the prewar rate.

There is a difficulty with regard to persons. Pension payments are different for us and for France, for ourselves and for our dominions. I propose to ask our specialists to give us only the figures such as they are, and to leave to us the responsibility of determining the principle of division.

March 26, 1919, 3:30 p.m.

Lloyd George. The subject of our conversation is not the German capacity to pay, but compensation owed for damages to persons and property. Concerning property, what is due for reparation is equivalent to the cost of replacement. We agree to consider prices to have doubled, at least if one considers a period of several years; for if everything had to be replaced on this very day, the difference would be greater. We also agree to leave aside all indirect losses, such as failure to earn by business firms. Great Britain, moreover, has never included these indirect losses in its accounting.

As for persons, there are two ways to treat this question. We can take the figures covering war pensions to be paid by each state. The objection, presented by France in particular, is that pensions are calculated at different rates in different countries, and that, by purely and simply registering each state's budget figures, injustice would be done to those which give the lowest pensions. But it may be said in response that any intermediate figure between these two rates would give an advantage to states which have fixed pensions at the lowest level.

Let us begin the discussion by examining property damages.

Loucheur. I have a preliminary remark to make. Mr. Lloyd George said that it was necessary to calculate repairs at double the prewar price; that is true for the reconstruction of houses, but not for the replacement of raw materials stolen or destroyed. Wool requisitioned by the Germans at Roubaix can only be replaced at five times the price of 1914. I would accept the ratio of 1 to 2 as a basis, but with this reservation.

I reviewed carefully the statistics prepared by the different French ministries, and I have eliminated all indirect damages. We arrive at the following figures:

Buildings and furnishings	35,000,000,000.
Agricultural damage	16,000,000,000.
Industrial damage	19,300,000,000.
Public works	5,150,000,000.
Post offices and telegraphs	135,000,000.
Merchant marine	
(at forty pounds sterling per ton)	1,610,000,000.
Value of cargoes	500,000,000.
Education and fine arts	1,000,000,000.
War levies paid to the Germans	1,414,000,000.
Total	80,109,000,000.

Lloyd George. If this figure represents damages done to such a limited part of French territory, France must be far richer than we would have imagined.

Loucheur. France does not intend to receive one dollar more than what is due her. She is ready to accept any audit of the figures she presents. But you would be greatly mistaken if you believed that such an examination would yield a noticeable reduction. I made a study of what would be necessary to restore merely the mines of northern France: it could not be done for less than two billions.

Lloyd George. The value of all the coal mines of Great Britain before the war was estimated at 130 million pounds sterling, and, according to you, these mines, inferior by comparison, would require eighty million pounds sterling for their repair? How can that be justified? The distribution of reparations must be made equitably; and, also, in presenting our bill to Germany, we should not give the impression that we demand from her a payment double or triple what it ought to be. I assert to M. Loucheur that if he were charged with spending the money that he claims for the reconstruction of the devastated lands of northern France, he would not be able to spend it. The national capital of France in 1908 was estimated at 250 billion francs, and you are asking one third of that for your repairs, when such a small part of France was devastated.

Loucheur. The figure which you cite comes from a book by M. Edmond Théry,[2] and I attach no kind of value to it. The true figure, if it was possible to calculate it, would be much higher. Consider the value of buildings in Paris alone and everything they contain. I cannot accept the observation just stated, and I simply repeat that what France asks is the cost of the reconstruction of her pillaged or devastated regions. She does not want one sou more.

Wilson. Don't you have official statistics on the total wealth of France?

Loucheur. I have only one reliable figure, which is that of the negotiable securities belonging to France before the war: they amounted to 120 billion francs.

Wilson. The United States and, I believe England, have official estimates of national capital.

Loucheur. I do not believe that we have calculated it and, in any case, I was not able to procure it. As for the estimates I present, I ask only that you have them examined by whomever you wish; but I repeat that it would be an error to believe that they could be reduced seriously.

Lloyd George. In England we have the income tax, which permits us to know rather exactly the national wealth, and the total at which we have arrived permits me to judge that the present figure I have quoted for France, given the relative position of the two countries, must not be far from the mark. If this is so, then, what France is asking for the reconstruction of a limited region is necessarily very exaggerated. France would not be able to spend on reconstruction all that she claims.

[2] Edmond Amédée Théry, *La Fortune publique de la France* (Paris, 1911).

Loucheur. We think that reconstruction will require ten years and one million men. In the urban area of Lens alone, which includes Courrières, there are 12,000 houses to rebuild, each costing 5,000 francs before the war and worth 15,000 today.

Lloyd George. These high prices will not continue.

Loucheur. Let us say that they will cost an average of 10,000 francs, which makes 120,000,000 merely for this very limited reconstruction.

Lloyd George. When we calculate the total wealth of a country like France, we include the value of the land. Now, in the invaded regions, the land did not disappear, however much it was damaged in certain spots. But even if you sold the Chemin des Dames[3] you would find a buyer.

Wilson. To examine figures such as those which are presented to us, it is necessary to be able to make comparisons.

Lloyd George. For what concerns us, it is very simple: we demand compensation for our sunken ships, so much per tons; we have to pay pensions, and we know the exact amount. It is this figure we claim. The rate of our pensions is intermediate between that of France and that of the United States.

Loucheur. What we are asking is that pensions be calculated on a common basis, corresponding to the rate of pensions in the country paying the lowest schedule. Otherwise, it would be too easy to double the rate of our pensions in order to claim this among the damages of war.

Lloyd George. To fix a uniform scale at the lowest rate would not be fair to England. The English public would not understand why the entire cost of each destroyed chimney in France would be compensated, but not that of lost lives by England.

Loucheur. We cannot admit that the price of a human life is different in different countries except if it is based on the price of consumer goods.

Norman H. Davis. To avoid some of these arguments and unfortunate comparisons, could we not agree purely and simply on the proportion of the payment to which each country has a right?

Lloyd George. That would be much better. I proposed an arrangement according to which, out of 100 pounds sterling received from Germany, fifty would be given to France and thirty to Great Britain; France has not accepted.

The great advantage of this system is that we could avoid entering into these disagreeable details. What France claims is not fair to her allies. If M. Loucheur wants to accept this proportion, which

[3] A portion of the western front, totally devastated after years of fighting.

I consider a very generous offer, it will become pointless to examine the figures. This examination is not without danger. If we do not agree among ourselves here, that will lead to a public examination, and, if the figures which we have just heard are published and compared to what we know about the total wealth of France, that will produce a very unfortunate impression.

Loucheur. I am distressed to seem to be demanding more for France than she deserves. France has the most solemnly recognized right to reparations, after her sufferings and sacrifices. What she demands is reparation for damages conforming to the principles accepted by the American delegation. If I acted other than I do, I would be acting against the interest and rights of my country.

Mr. Lloyd George speaks of the disadvantages of a public debate; we do not fear it at all, and we fear even less a comparison of our figures with those which result from the arbitrary studies of more or less qualified economists. No one today can make an absolutely certain estimate of the total reparations due. It is easy when it is a question of sunken ships; we know that these ships are worth so much per ton. It is more difficult, if not impossible, when it is a question of an entire region devastated and ruined.

France only asks what it will cost to repair the damages suffered. I regret to appear to be defending a cause which is not absolutely just, and I believe that it is this impression which does an injustice to my country.

Lloyd George. Does M. Loucheur not agree to discuss the principle of proportional distribution?

Davis. M. Loucheur seemed so disposed in our conversations.

Lloyd George. In that case, it would be better for our specialists to meet again and resume this discussion.

Wilson. The maximum figure must be not only moderate, but reasonable; that is to say, it must take political necessities into account. That is why it seems to me that we should inform our specialists of our desire to do nothing which would have the consequence of completely destroying Germany and of preventing her from accepting our terms.

Lloyd George. My impression is that the figures which have been furnished us are beyond what Germany can pay. I am much less interested in these figures than in the proportion according to which the distribution is to be made.

The heads of government withdraw and leave M. Loucheur and the financial experts to confer.

Mantoux, I, 24-40.

From the Diary of Lord Robert Cecil

March 26 [1919]

Then I talked to the Prime Minister. . . . Finally I approached the question of protecting the Monroe doctrine in the League of Nations Covenant. We argued it a little, and then he said that he could not accept the responsibility of introducing such a change without consulting the British Delegation; to which I replied that I knew he was very afraid of taking responsibility, which pleased him mightily. He then admitted that his real reason for resisting it was that he wanted to have something to bargain with, and he was anxious to induce the Americans to give up their plan of building ships against the British. I told him that I did not believe there would be any difficulty in inducing the Americans to do this; that I did not think it would help him to try to use a means of pressure which was really quite irrelevant to the discussion, and which would, I believe, only enrage the Americans without making them amenable; that the bargaining plan did very well with the French, but was bad with the Americans. However I altogether failed to move him, and it was left that I should tell the President that he had better discuss the matter with Lloyd George. . . .

I dined with Eddy Hartington[1] alone, and went on to the League of Nations Commission. A highly successful meeting, at which there was quite an interesting discussion as to whether the States should be allowed to withdraw from the League, the President advocating it in a really fine speech, on the ground that in the end it would make the League stronger if people had the right to withdraw from it, and it being resisted by Larnaude on the ground that it would cast an air of insecurity over the whole structure. Ultimately we passed the clause, as indeed we pass all clauses really urged upon us by the President. As a matter of fact, as the Conference goes on the dominating position of America becomes more and more evident. The great want of the future is money, and the only one of the Associated Governments that has money at its command is the United States.

[1] Edward William Spencer Cavendish, Marquess of Hartington.

Minutes of a Meeting of the League of Nations Commission

THIRTEENTH MEETING, MARCH 26, 1919, AT 8:30 P.M.

On the motion of *President Wilson* a Committee consisting of:
Mr. Orlando,
General Smuts,
Baron Makino,
Colonel House,
was appointed to enquire into the question of the locality of the Seat of the League.

ARTICLE 17.

On the motion of *Lord Robert Cecil* the following British amendments were adopted:

In the 6th line delete "above" and insert after "provisions of Articles 12 and 16 inclusive."

In the 8th line delete "League" and substitute "Executive Council."

ARTICLE 18.

The British amendments:

"Present Article 19 to become Article 18," and in the second paragraph, line 3:

After "responsibility" insert "and who are willing to accept it," were adopted.

Certain other drafting amendments were referred to the Committee on Revision.

NEW ARTICLE 19.

The following British Amendment was discussed:

Present Articles 18, 20, and 21 to be put together in a new Article to read as follows:

"In accordance with the provision of international Conventions hereafter to be agreed upon for the purposes hereinafter stated, the States members of the League

"(a.) Will endeavour to secure and maintain fair and humane conditions of labour for men and women and children both in their own countries and in all countries to which their commercial and industrial relations extend.

"(b.) Engage to secure just treatment of the native inhabitants of the territories under their control.

"(c.) Entrust the League with the general supervision over the execution of such agreements as shall have been jointly come to with regard to the traffic in women and children and the traffic in opium and other dangerous drugs.

"(d.) Agree that the League shall be entrusted with the general supervision of the trade in arms and ammunition with the countries in which the control of this traffic is necessary in the common interest.

"(e.) Agree that provision shall be made to secure and maintain freedom of communications and transit and equitable treatment for the commerce of all States members of the League, having in mind, among other things, special arrangements with regard to the necessities of the regions devastated during the war of 1914-1918."

Lord Robert Cecil explained that he thought that Articles 18, 20 and 21 in the original draft might with advantage be combined.

President Wilson, in reply to a question by *Mr. Vesnitch*, explained that by the words "and all countries to which their commercial and industrial relations extend" in paragraph (*a*), influence only on a friendly and legitimate scale, and not intervention, was meant.

Mr. Reis said that he thought that the words "general supervision" in paragraph (*d*) were too strong.

Lord Robert Cecil explained that the supervision was to depend upon subsequent international agreements.

Article 19 was accepted as amended, except in the matter of the insertion in paragraph (*a*) of the words "by means of an international Bureau" after "endeavour" which were to be the subject of discussion by the Drafting Committee.

ARTICLE 20.

The following British amendments were proposed:

(1.) After the word "bureaux" insert "or Commissions for the regulation of matters of international interest."

(2.) Add a second paragraph as follows:

"In all matters of international interest which are regulated by general Conventions but which are not placed under the control of special international bureaux or commissions, the Secretariat of the League shall act as central organisation for the collection and distribution of information and for securing the effective observance of such Conventions if the States thereto consent."

(3.) Add a new paragraph as follows:

"The expenses of all such bureaux and commissions, including those provided for by this Covenant, may, with the consent of the Executive Council, be treated as part of the expenses of the Permanent Secretariat of the League."

Mr. Hymans said that he thought that in the second paragraph now proposed the words "and for securing * * *" to the end should be struck out as involving the Secretariat in too extensive a task.

This suggestion was accepted, and the first and second British amendments were adopted.

It was decided that the third paragraph should be adopted subject to examination by the Drafting Committee to determine whether its provisions conflicted with present arrangements concerning the Postal Union.

ARTICLE 19.

Two amendments were proposed by the French Delegation: the first looking towards the establishment of a Financial Commission, the other establishing an International Bureau of Labour.

After some discussion, the amendments were withdrawn.

The French delegation proposed the addition of Article 21 *bis*, as follows:

"Il y a lieu de créer une section économique de la Société des Nations en vue d'étudier et de réaliser dans l'intérêt de la civilisation les grandes entreprises économiques d'ordre international."

President Wilson said that he thought that the proposed new clause admitted a most dangerous principle which was known in his country as the principle that "the flag follows the dollar." The League should be on its guard against accepting principles of this kind.

The amendment was thereupon withdrawn.

Mr. Hymans proposed a new amendment, that the States members of the League should endeavour to intensify agricultural production and should appoint a permanent Agricultural Commission.

The amendment was withdrawn on the ground that the work was already done by the Institut de Rome: it had already been agreed that all existing international organisations might pass to the League.

The Article was adopted without amendment.

Articles 21, 22 and 23 were adopted without discussion.

ARTICLE 24.

Lord Robert Cecil proposed an amendment as follows:

Line 2, delete "three-quarters" and substitute "a majority." He considered that the proposed amendment would make no great difference, but that it would remove the impression which existed that the Covenant was to be unalterable.

Mr. Veniselos considered that the amendment exposed the smaller Powers to the risk of losing still more of their authority. The feelings of neutral States should be considered.

At this point, *President Wilson* said that he thought that the subject under discussion depended upon an amendment of his own which he asked leave to introduce.

Lord Robert Cecil accordingly agreed that the discussion of his amendment should be deferred.

With reference to his [Wilson's] amendment, which read as follows:

"After the expiration of ten years from the ratification of the Treaty of Peace, of which this Covenant forms a part, any State member of the League may, after giving one year's notice of its intention, withdraw from the League, provided all its international obligations and all its obligations under this Covenant shall have been fulfilled at the time of its withdrawal."[1]

President Wilson stated that he thought that if the League were successful it would be morally impossible for a State to withdraw.

Mr. Larnaude said that the world demanded something definite: the essence of the idea of the League was that it was to be a permanent thing. The placing of a ten years' time limit would give the idea that the success of the League was not hoped for.

President Wilson said that he had no idea of limiting the duration of the League, but sovereign States could not permanently be bound.

Lord Robert Cecil said that he had been much impressed by Mr. Larnaude's argument, but that it was foolish to suppose that any Treaty could be permanent. He doubted, however, whether ten years sufficed. The effects of the war would only be beginning to pass off in ten years: he suggested twenty or fifteen years. If, however, a period of less than twenty years was fixed, then two years' notice ought to be given: he would prefer, however, twenty years.

Mr. Orlando said he thought that the possibility of withdrawal might be left; he considered that the time limit should be abandoned, but that two years' notice should be given.

President Wilson said that he was willing to abandon the time limit and substitute two years' notice.

Mr. Larnaude was not convinced. He stated that for some time past national sovereignty had been a fiction. He wanted not to make a Treaty on the old lines, but to strike out on new lines and provide a substitute for the old order of international relations. He thought that the giving of notice by a Great Power would throw the League into confusion. If a League were to be established at all, the foundation should be firm.

President Wilson said that he did not entertain the smallest fear that any State would take advantage of the proposed clause. Any State which did so would become an outlaw. The sovereignty of their own country was the fetish of many public men. If they entered into a permanent arrangement they would feel that they were

---

[1] There is a WWT draft of this amendment in WP, DLC.

surrendering this sovereignty. America valued her sovereignty more highly than most nations. Americans would have to be assured that they were not giving up the sovereignty of their State. He thought that the clause would have no practical effects, while its omission might have very serious results. It was necessary to avoid such consequences by making concessions to existing prejudices and thus avoiding these risks. The time would come when men would be just as eager partisans of the sovereignty of mankind as they were now of their own national sovereignty. He himself would be in a very awkward position if the amendment was not passed, since in the earlier sessions of the Commission he alone had been anti-secessionist, and had reluctantly acquiesced in the opinion of the Commission that the right to withdraw should exist. No State would have a moral right to withdraw. States would have a legal right, that was all that he proposed to admit. He was afraid that the Senate would not agree to come in if the right to withdraw did not somewhere exist. He had frequently stated this understanding in America.

Mr. Bourgeois said he thought that there should be a negative rather than a positive formula. This would leave the right to withdraw and would also ensure that States might not do so except on terms that would not damage the League.

Mr. Larnaude said that the question of the cessation of military service was one which was keenly discussed all over France. If the people of France thought that the League was to last 10 years only they would think that it had already failed. He repeated his assertion that it was not a question of a private compact or of an ordinary meeting. It was a question of founding a new system of international relations. If this idea of his was that of an idealist, it resembled the conceptions of President Wilson.

Mr. Vesnitch thought that the constitution of the League should be as elastic as possible, so that the principle of liberty might be protected.

Mr. Reis said that the Commission had already been widely accused of having laid violent hands upon national independence. They should do all that they could to remove that impression, but they had already made great sacrifices to the sovereignty of States in not having established the principle of obligatory arbitration, which he considered essential.

Mr. Orlando said that the Commission was in agreement that the general delay should be abolished.

Mr. Veniselos said that the Commission did not agree; he wanted a term of 20 years fixed, but he would accept 15 or even 10. The essential thing was that some security should be obtained.

Mr. Orlando thought that as a matter of psychology the League would be better supported by popular opinion if the specific time limit were cut out, but States were left the option of withdrawing or giving two years' notice. It was not so much actual liberty as theoretical liberty that was valuable to people's minds. If States had the power of withdrawing, they would probably not want to use it.

Mr. Larnaude thought that nations leaving the League should be compelled to render an explanation.

The amendment was adopted in the following form:

"Any State a member of the League may, after giving two years' notice of its intention, withdraw from the League, provided all its international obligations and all its obligations under this Covenant shall have been fulfilled at the time of its withdrawal."

Lord Robert Cecil asked whether his amendment to the previous Article was agreed to.

The amendment was adopted.

Lord Robert Cecil moved a new Article providing that:

"All bodies formed under or in connection with the League, including the Secretariat, may comprise women as well as men."

The amendment was adopted.

President Wilson said that the work of revision was now to be undertaken by a Committee on Revision, consisting of Lord Robert Cecil, Mr. Larnaude, Mr. Veniselos and Colonel House.

Lord Robert Cecil urged that a small Committee on Organisation should be appointed at once to consider questions such as the Housing of the League, Secretariat, etc.

It was agreed that the Chairman should appoint such a Committee.

Mr. Bourgeois asked whether the Commission would have another opportunity of going into the question of the limitation of armaments.

The discussion of this matter was deferred until the next meeting.

(The Commission then adjourned.)

Printed copy (WP, DLC).

To Sidney Edward Mezes

My dear Doctor Mezes: Paris, 26 March, 1919.

If I knew which of the group of gentlemen associated with you were studying the questions to which the enclosed papers[1] refer I would not trouble you but send the papers directly to them, but I do not know and am therefore taking the liberty of begging that you will put the papers in the proper hands in order that they may be carefully read and considered in connection with the questions they affect. I would be very much obliged if I might have a very brief resume of the conclusions of our expert colleagues with regard to these difficult matters.

Cordially and sincerely yours,   Woodrow Wilson

TLS (E. M. House Papers, CtY).
¹ The Editors have been unable to identify these "papers." However, Wilson probably sent to Mezes the memoranda and maps cited in n. 1 to the memorandum by W. E. Lunt *et al.*, April 4, 1919, and other materials relating to Fiume and the Adriatic question.

To Sir Horace Plunkett

My dear Sir Horace: Paris, 26 March, 1919.

I sincerely value your letter of March 2nd¹ forwarded to me by Mr. Polk and wish that I had time for more than this line of appreciation. I am very glad indeed to have your guidance in a most perplexing matter.

I hope that you are rapidly getting to feel like yourself again.

Cordially and sincerely yours,   [Woodrow Wilson]

CCL (WP, DLC).
¹ H. Plunkett to WW, March 2, 1919, printed as an Enclosure with FLP to WW, March 6, 1919, Vol. 55.

From Robert Lansing

My dear Mr. President: Paris, March 26, 1919.

I have carefully considered the letter to [from] General Graves which you enclose in your letter of March 24th,¹ and have gone over the matter with General Bliss and Mr. McCormick. I see nothing in the letter which changes the views expressed in my letter of March 21st. General Bliss and Mr. McCormick are in accord with me in these views. I feel that General Graves will be able to carry out efficiently the mission outlined unless future developments show that some other man might be able to gain more cordial co-operation from Generals Knox and Janin.²

Faithfully yours,   Robert Lansing

TLS (SDR, RG 256, 861.00/392, DNA).
¹ That is, WW to RL, March 24, 1919 (second letter of that date).
² That is, Pierre Thiébaut Charles Maurice (Maurice) Janin, commander of the Czech forces in Siberia.

From Tasker Howard Bliss

My dear Mr. President: Paris, March 26th, 1919.

Referring to the queries which you put to me yesterday evening in regard to the practicability of furnishing supplies to the Roumanian Army, I beg to say that on my return to the Hotel de Crillon, I found a letter from Marshal Foch stating that this question of supply of material and equipment to the Roumanian Army would be taken up by his Committee at 11 o'clock this morning, and asking me to send a representative to the meeting. I assigned Colonel Browning[1] of my staff for this work and he is now with that Committee.

Meanwhile, shortly after 9 o'clock last night I had a long interview with Mr. Norman Davis on the general subject. I learned from him certain things which caused me to telephone to your secretary asking that you should, if possible, have an interview with Mr. Davis before this subject came up again in the Council of the Heads of Governments. It is a more or less complicated financial question which he alone can explain to you, and he told me that a ten or fifteen minutes interview with you would probably save you two or three hours of discussion.

Mr. Davis told me that some five days ago Mr. Bratiano, the Roumanian Prime Minister, came to him with the request that the United States give a credit to Roumania to enable the latter to purchase railway material,—locomotives, cars, rails, repair-shop tools and machinery, etc.,—which the American Army would leave here in France. Mr. Bratiano said that the credit would also be for the purchase of shirts, shoes and underclothing for the civil population of Roumania, but added that a small part of this clothing might have to be used for the army. This latter statement led Mr. Davis to broach the subject of the supply and maintenance of the Roumanian Army, saying that he apprehended difficulty in securing assistance from the United States for this purpose. Mr. Bratiano then informed him that he had no need of assistance with respect to the army; that he had completed an agreement with Great Britain and France by which the latter governments were to finance a Roumanian Army of 260,000 to 280,000 men, together with all of its material and equipment.

Thus, it would appear that several days before General Barthelot's [Berthelot's] telegrams about the situation in Odessa were brought to your attention yesterday, the British and French Governments had, for some purposes of their own, completed an agreement for the maintenance of the Roumanian Army. It seems fair to assume that when the telegrams about the Odessa situation were received and in general connection with the Bolshevik propaganda, the French and the British concluded that they could transfer a part of the expense of the maintenance of the Roumanian Army to the United States.

Mr. Davis informs me that the United States is now supplying credit to Roumania in the amount of $5,000,000 per month for food. This, however, is not a credit of indefinite continuance. France and Great Britain have contributed nothing for this purpose except a diversion made by England, under pressure of Mr. Hoover, of some $2,000,000 worth of food. I am also informed that since December 1, 1918, the United States has contributed $200,000,000 (Mr. Davis thinks that it may amount to $250,000,000) for the relief of Europe, as against $25,000,000 from other Powers.

Mr. Davis informs me that we can establish a credit in favor of Roumania for the purchase of surplus army material up to the limit of the balance of the original appropriation. This balance, however, will have many drafts made upon it for other purposes in Europe. We have no authority to give a credit to Roumania for payment of troops or purchase of material other than that of the United States.

In regard to the practicability of furnishing United States army supplies to Roumania, in case a credit can be properly arranged, I am informed by the officer in charge of this matter in Paris that the only supplies which he has available for such disposition is a limited amount of army rations, all of which he is turning over to Mr. Hoover for his relief work. He further informs me that information as to the possibility of obtaining other material for the Roumanian Army must be obtained from General Harbord[2] at Tours, to whom I am now telegraphing for this information.

After my conversation with Mr. Norman Davis last night, I came to the conclusion that, if my advice were asked, I would suggest that you say to the Prime Ministers that the United States is doing, apparently, some eight times more for the checking of Bolshevism by general relief work in Europe than the other Powers combined; that, inasmuch as we can continue this relief work without the embarrassment that would probably result from having to ask Congress for authority to engage directly or indirectly in operations of war in Eastern Europe, it would be better if they were to agree that we should continue to furnish assistance in this way and let them charge themselves with the equipment and maintenance of armies. To my mind, any nation which takes upon itself expenditures for military operations intended to check the universal revolutionary tendency in Europe, will be assuming a burden that will last for indefinite years. If we are once committed to it, in any degree, it will be difficult to withdraw. We may easily find ourselves tied up in a military situation which will subsequently demand the sending of our troops. Notwithstanding all of the talk of the withdrawal of the Archangel expedition, I think that it is not improbable that the Allies will make a demand upon us for further considerable reinforcements to that expedition. When we once engage ourselves in that sort of adventure, a thousand unforeseen reasons crop up for our continuing in it and for engaging ourselves in it more deeply than before. The Allies want to engage in extensive military operations, but they are afraid to do so on account of expense and the unwillingness of their own peoples. Nevertheless, they appear to be unwilling to face the alternative, which is a complete cessation of such operations. The assistance which we are asked to give in Roumania and Poland brings us face to face with the final and positive determination of our future policy in European affairs. You must remember that the request made of us to furnish supplies to the Roumanian Army is a continuing request of indefinite continuance. If we take the first step which commits us to this policy, we shall have to continue in that course. And that will commit us to what may be perhaps a long series of wars for the purpose of throttling the revolutionary movement in Europe. The long-continued Napoleonic Wars resulted in the unchaining of these forces of revolution which the Holy Alliance attempted to combat. In the same way, this horrible war, which concentrated in itself all of and more than the energies of destruction of twenty-five years of Napoleonic Wars, has again broken up all of the founts of the great political deep. I cannot convince myself that it is wise, from any point of view, for the United States to engage in the work of combating these new forces of revolution.

Very sincerely,   Tasker H. Bliss.

P.S. Colonel Browning has at this moment returned from Marshal Foch's Committee and reports to me that, in addition to any contributions of food, equipment and material that we may make to the Roumanian Army, all of the expenses of the other governments for the maintenance of that Army will be put into a pool, of which we shall be expected to pay our share.

Colonel Browning tells us that General Weygand appears to have the idea that it was agreed at the meeting yesterday that all of the four Powers should participate in the expense of equipping and maintaining the Roumanian Army, and he expects Colonel Browning to inform him to-morrow morning of just what the contribution of the United States will be. I understood from you yesterday evening that you had not formulated any positive decision.

T.H.B.

TLS (WP, DLC).
¹ Col. William Stacy Browning.   ² That is, Maj. Gen. James Guthrie Harbord.

From Andrew Furuseth

My dear Mr. President,   London. 26th March, 1919.

Busy and overburdened as you must necessarily be, I feel that I would not be doing my duty to you if I failed to send you this letter.

The representatives from the United States to the Convention on International Labor Legislation submitted two clauses for the proposed Labor Charter dealing with human freedom.

1. Neither Slavery nor involuntary servitude except as a penalty for crime or [of] which a person shall have been duly convicted shall exist.

This was voted down. The representative from Great Britain leading the opposition.

2. A Seaman shall not be punished by imprisonment for leaving his vessel in a safe harbour nor shall he be arrested, detained and surrendered to his vessel.

This was also voted down, America and Cuba voted "Aye," all the others voted "No" under the leadership of Great Britain. If this had been adopted the several powers would have been debarred from imprisoning any seaman who might return to his own country after having deserted his vessel in some other country.

After a tremendous struggle the following was adopted as a protocol to be read in connection with Article 19 of the Constitution of the Conference on International Labor Legislation:

"In no case shall any of the High Contracting Powers be asked or required, as a result of the adoption by the Conference of any recommendation or draft Convention, to diminish the protection afforded by its existing legislation to the workers concerned."

Since my arrival here I have submitted these matters to some English Labor Leaders. They were astounded and shocked.

It is my deliberate judgment that failure to write these two propositions into the Labor Charter will rouse, not only the working people of America, but the working people of the world against this Constitution and against the League of Nations. I do not charge that this was the intention, but considering the expressions from Labor Leaders here, it would look somewhat like that. With reference to the proviso or protocol, the men with whom I have spoken promptly caught the word "existing" and then said: "This is crystalisation."

I do not know if it be possible for you to write these two defeated Clauses into the Labor Charter. I feel that you would desire to. I feel that I would be lacking in my duty if I did not furnish you with this information. I shall expect no answer.

Most respectfully and faithfully yours,   Andrew Furuseth.

TLS (WP, DLC).

From the Diary of Colonel House

March 26, 1929.

Orlando called by appointment at ten o'clock and remained for an hour. I tried the Russian plan out on him and it succeeded admirably. What I told him was that Russia had become orderly and wanted to resume relations with the outside world. If we met her in a reasonable way she would agree to leave the boundary lines as they stand today; to stop all fighting on all fronts, and to agree not to use any propaganda in any of the Allies countries, provided propaganda was not used by them in Russia. That they have about 1,200,000 well armed men that would fight in the event peace was not made. That food was scarce and the army could be augumented [augmented] to any number of men the Russian authorities desired, because the army would always be fed. If we did not make terms with them, it was certain that as soon as we made peace with Germany, Russia and Germany would link up together, thereby realizing my prophecy that, sooner or later, everything east of the Rhine would be arrayed against the Western Powers. If we did come to terms, the general Russian dislike for Germany would give the Entente a dominating influence in Russia.

It seemed to me footless to say we preferred some other plan. As far as I could see, there was no other. It was either reckon with the De facto Government, or remain in a state of war, or semi-war. We cannot intervene, everyone admits that, because we cannot get troops to go into Russia and fight.

I suggested that we proceed to draw up a treaty with Russia, practically upon our own terms, provided they were just, and send this treaty to Moscow for their signatures, promising to sign it ourselves in the event it was agreed upon there. I did not think we should make another Prinkipo proposal or try to have a meeting in some neutral country.

Orlando agreed with this and said I could count upon his cooperation. I am having Gordon and David Miller look into the matter of such a treaty. In the meantime, I have telephoned the President, but as usual find that his "one track mind" is against taking up this question at present. I would have preferred to have taken it up first with the President, but since he is not in a frame of mind to do so, I shall take it up with Lloyd George and see whether I cannot commit him as I have Orlando. If peace is to come to the world, the Russian settlement must be a part of it. I told Orlando, as I shall tell George, that a settlement with Russia will enable us to treat with Germany in a much more positive and satisfactory way.

Secretary Daniels came in just before and remained to lunch. I submitted to him the amendments we have in mind to made [make] to the Covenant in order to appease the recalcitrants in the Senate. He thought well of what I had in mind.

Felix Frankfurter was an excited afternoon caller. The Jews have it that the Interallied Commission which is to be sent to Syria is about to cheat Jewry of Palestine. I assured him there was no such intention and gave him the real situation so he might take it to his fellow Hebrews.

I asked President King of Oberlin College to come. He has been at Coblentz doing some Y.M.C.A. work. I wanted to look him over and find whether he was suitable timber for the Syrian mission. The other man whom the President has decided upon is Charles R. Crane. I found King an intelligent vigorous fellow and arranged with him that he should go. I am telegraphing to Oberlin College about the matter and the cable is attached.

To Joseph Patrick Tumulty

Paris, 26 March, 1919.

If the Attorney General consents I am willing to grant a respite in the case of Eugene Debs and the others as suggested by Walsh, Benson and Russell, but I doubt the wisdom and public effect of such an action and hope that you will discuss it in the most serious way with Palmer and let me know the results of the conference before I act.   Woodrow Wilson

T telegram (WP, DLC).

From the Very Reverend Hardwicke Drummond Rawnsley

Dear Mr President   Grasmere. March 26, 1919.

Thank you sincerely for your promise of help to the Yates Fund. We are getting along with it well. We have I think close on £1400 *to date*, that has come in in sums from £100 to £1. As to your own kind offer of a subscription it can be sent to me in any way that suits you. *Either by cheque* or *in Dollar Notes* which I could get turned into British cash at the Bank, or by a Draft on your Bank, just as you will.

We are feeling the sorrow of his going away all the more by reason of the extraordinary beauty of the snow & sunlight on the hills & the purples in the woodland by the Mere he loved so well.

Yours gratefully   H D Rawnsley.

We are each day remembering you in our prayers. The task seems superhuman. I can only hope your health will stand the strain. My wife[1] sends her kind regards & wishes to be remembered to your wife & your daughter if she is with you. Remember there is asylum here for you or any of your family if you can take a few days rest in this furious time. I am hoping the Danzig difficulty may be got over by Right of Free Port I dont want to see another Alsace & Lorraine for the Baltic, but I speak as a fool.

ALS (WP, DLC).
[1] Edith Fletcher Rawnsley.

James Patrick Noonan and Julia S. O'Connor to Joseph Patrick Tumulty

My dear Mr. Tumulty: Washington, D. C., March 26, 1919

We are enclosing as per your suggestion cable which we desire to send to the President.[1]

Any suggestions from yourself relative to change therein will be appreciated.

Thanking you for considerations, we are, with very best wishes,
Respectfully yours,   International Brotherhood of
Electrical Workers
Jas. P. Noonan Acting Int. Pres.
Julia S O Connor Pres. Telephone
Operators Dept.

TLS (WP, DLC).
[1] J. P. Noonan and Julia S. O'Connor to WW, March 26, 1919, TS MS (WP, DLC). The authors outlined the plight of the organized telephone workers of the United States since the telephone and telegraph lines of the country had been taken over by the Post Office Department in August 1918. Since they were now employed by the federal government, the workers no longer had a recognized right to organize and bargain collectively. The writers asserted that the requests of the telephone operators for wage increases had been ignored by the Post Office Department and that many of these workers received wages upon which they could not live. The department had no adequate machinery for adjusting wages or remedying burdensome working conditions. Moreover, many officials of telephone companies now under governmental control were taking advantage of the present situation to conduct campaigns of discrimination and persecution against union members. The authors stated that the members had repeatedly petitioned their leaders to authorize a strike, but that the leaders, in a spirit of moderation and patriotism, had so far refused. They appealed to Wilson "as the final authority in this matter to avert the tying up of the telephone communications of the country by the simple expedient of reaffirming on behalf of the telephone workers now employed by the Government of the United States, those splendid principles enunciated by yourself and reiterated by the War Labor Board; the right to organize and the right to bargain collectively."

From the Diary of Dr. Grayson

Thursday, March 27, 1919.

The President met with the Council of Four at 11:00 o'clock in the morning at the temporary White House, and in the afternoon at the office of the French Minister for War. He also issued a statement dealing with the League of Nations covenant and correcting the erroneous impression that discussion of the League of Nations subject had delayed the final formulation of the Peace Treaty. The statement is as follows: . . .[1]

The situation continued extremely complicated because of the fact that the French were maintaining an attitude of bitter obstruction to the program suggested by the President, which had for its basis the payment by Germany only of a reasonable indemnity and did not carry with it annexation of the Saar Valley. The French were demanding the Saar Valley despite the fact that its 500,000 inhabitants are entirely German and have no sympathy whatever with France.

At the end of the morning meeting I asked: "How are you feeling, Mr. President?" He replied: "I feel terribly disappointed. After arguing with Clemenceau for two hours and pushing him along, he practically agreed to everything, and just as he was leaving he swung back to where we had begun. It seems impossible to get him to realize the value of time and the need for results. I laid the facts down to him very plainly and said that if he was going to continue to act in this way the other three of us would write out our views of the peace terms, and if his (Clemenceau's) government did not accept them, they could take the consequences and we would go home." Lloyd-George concurred with the President in his ultimatum, and so did Orlando.

The afternoon session developed into a discussion of the problems of the Supreme War Council, and especially as to the question of sending additional troops to the Odessa district. The President was in favor of the withdrawing of troops from Odessa and from Russia. He expressed himself as believing that to maintain a small body of troops in Russia was entirely worthless so far as any advantage being secured by the Allies was concerned. In expressing this view he said that he did not believe in using one finger to cover a situation where the entire hand was needed.

The Polish question also was discussed and the question of giving Poland a 200-mile corridor from Dantzig to Poland proper came up. Although there are 2,000,000 Germans in this particular section, Orlando, Lloyd-George and Clemenceau all three favored its being seized and made a part of Poland. This the President would not stand for. He told them very definitely that any such action would simply sow the seed for a further war and engender bitterness that would be hard to overcome later on. He said that his colleagues did not realize that the whole object is not only to settle the immediate question but to establish a condition that will make for a permanent peace. All that Clemenceau wanted to do, it appeared, was to put a barrier between France and Germany—he did not seem to have any vision for the rest of the world.

In the evening the President worked in his study.

¹ Here follows the text of the statement printed as the next document.

A Statement

March 27, 1919.

In view of the very surprising impression which seems to exist in some quarters that it is the discussions of the Commission on the League of Nations that are delaying the final formulation of peace, I am very glad to take the opportunity of reporting that the conclusions of this commission were the first to be laid before the Plenary Conference. They were reported on February 14th, and the world has had a full month in which to discuss every feature of the draft covenant then submitted. During the last few days the commission has been engaged in an effort to take advantage of the criticisms which the publication of the Covenant has fortunately drawn out. A committee of the Commission has also had the advantage of a conference with representatives of the neutral nations, who are evidencing a very deep interest and a practically unanimous desire to align themselves with the League. The revised Covenant is now practically finished. It is in the hands of a committee for the final process of drafting and will almost immediately be presented a second time to the public.

The Conferences of the Commission have invariably been held at times when they could not interfere with the consultation of those who have undertaken to formulate the general conclusions of the Conference with regard to the many other complicated problems of peace, so that the members of the commission congratulate themselves on the fact that no part of their conferences has ever interposed any form of delay.

T MS (WP, DLC).

A Memorandum by Marshal Foch

March 27th, 1919

NOTE

I

The situation is known: between Roumania and Poland, through the breach of Lemberg, Bolchevism has just penetrated into Hungary, thus creating a redoubtable menace on the very rear of the barrier which we must oppose to it, and having, via Vienna, an open field for its march towards Western Europe.

II

In order to block the way of Bolchevism, the following line of conduct seems to be the right one:

1 Reinforce the framework of this barrier, by upholding Poland and Roumania;

? Ensure its continuity by closing up the breach of Lemberg;

Purify the rear-areas by extinguishing the blaze alight in Hungary;

? Ensure the Allied communications at Vienna.

III

Up to the present, the Governments have decided to help Poland by sending her the Polish Army; the transportation scheme is settled; it will be carried out as soon as the result of the conversations at SPA has been obtained.

The Governments have likewise decided to uphold Roumania by giving the Roumanian Army the requisite material help, in clothing, equipement and food.

Certain arrangements are already being carried out: diverting on to Roumania of 150,000 sets of clothing and equipements which England had previously designed for General DENIKINE (these sets are being loaded). It seems probable that the complement of items asked for will be easily and promptly obtained; the Interallied Staffs are engaged in looking out for them.

IV

It is around Roumania that the Bolchevist danger is the most pressing:

Russian danger (at Odessa and on the Dniester), in the East.

Hungarian danger in the West.

It is therefore on these two fronts that it is necessary to act at first.

On these fronts, we have forces, in suitable numbers, but for the precise use of which, the Higher Command must be organised.

It is necessary to organise:

facing Russia: an Army comprising   3 French Divisions
                                     3 Greek   "
                                     3 Roumanian "
                                     1 Polish   "
under the command of General [blank]
facing Hungary: an Army comprising 2 French Divisions
                                     3 Servian   "
                                     4 Roumanian   "
under the command of General [blank]

Each of these Armies having its own Chief and its own objective will draw from a common source, viz. Roumania, whose forces it will be necessary to transport towards the Russian or the Hungarian front, according to circumstances. These forces must therefore be put under a higher command, that of General [blank]

Besides, the organization of this higher command will be subject to subsequent changes, when, quiet having been restored in Hungary, it will only be necessary to face eastwards, and when it will be especially necessary to coordinate the action of Poles and Roumanians.

V

Communications are in danger of being cut off at Vienna, to the detriment of Poles, Tchecs, Roumanians. It is indispensable to pro-
? tect them against the bolchevist peril, by occupying Vienna.

So as to demonstrate the disinterested nature of this occupation, the sole object of which is to ensure order in view of general intere[s]ts of the highest importance, it would be advantageous to have this occupation carried out by an interallied force, under an American Command. The Governments would have to decide on the strength which each Nation would supply.

VI

It is therefore proposed:

1°) to go on with the transportation of the Haller Army to Dantzig;

2°) to go on with the organization and the supplying of the Roumanian Army;

3°) to organise the higher command in Hungary and in Roumania on the lines shown above;

4°) to occupy Vienna.

Marshal FOCH, aided by the Allied Staffs which are already with him, is intrusted therewith.

T MS (WP, DLC).
[1] Wilson's question marks.

Mantoux's Notes of Two Meetings
of the Council of Four

March 27, 1919, 11 a.m.

Lloyd George. Have you read the memorandum which I sent you regarding the general conditions of the peace?

Clemenceau. I intend to respond to it in writing; but it must first be translated into French for the President of the Republic.

Wilson. I hope that you agree in principle with Mr. Lloyd George on the moderation which it is necessary to show toward Germany. We neither wish to destroy Germany, nor could we do so; our greatest error would be to give her powerful reasons for one day wishing to take revenge. Excessive demands would most certainly sow the seeds of war.

Everywhere we are obliged to modify frontiers and to change national sovereignties. There is nothing which involves greater danger, for these changes run contrary to long-established customs and change the very life of populations while, at the same time, they affect their sentiments. We must avoid giving our enemies even the impression of injustice. I do not fear future wars brought about by the secret plottings of governments, but rather conflicts created by popular discontent. If we show ourselves guilty of injustice, this discontent is inevitable, with the consequences which it entails. Hence our desire to negotiate with moderation and equity.

Lloyd George. I have an historical precedent to cite. In 1814, after the defeat of Napoleon, Prussia, whose chief representative in this was Blücher, wanted to impose crushing terms upon France. Wellington, who had good sense, took an opposite attitude and was supported by Castlereagh, who had earlier been one of France's most bitter enemies. Both felt that it would be a great error to seek to destroy France, whose presence was necessary for civilization and for European order. Such was the attitude taken by the representatives of England toward France; and if their opinion had not prevailed, France would have been half destroyed, with no other result than to deliver all of Europe to the Germanic powers.

Germany has learned a lesson as hard as any in history. The fall of the Napoleonic empire in 1814 cannot be compared, for the campaign in France was a glorious conclusion to Napoleon's wars; while last November the Germans capitulated without even attempting a last stand.

Clemenceau. I said yesterday that I agree completely with Mr. Lloyd George and President Wilson about the manner in which to treat Germany; we must not abuse our victory; we must treat peoples with consideration and fear provoking a surge of national consciousness.

But I venture a fundamental objection. Mr. Lloyd George is excessively afraid of the consequences of a possible resistance of the Germans in refusing to sign the treaty. I remind you that the Germans surrendered without even waiting for our troops to enter Germany, fearing no doubt the atrocious reprisals of which we were incapable. This time we must expect them to resist: they will argue, they will dispute every point, they will talk of refusing to sign, they will play up incidents such as the one which has just taken place in Budapest and those which may occur tomorrow in Vienna; they will contest or refuse all that they can refuse. You were able to read in yesterday's newspapers the interview with Count Bernstorff:[1] he speaks with the arrogance of a victor. But we must not fear them any more than is necessary. We must be aware of possible danger; but we must also, after having obtained victory at the price of so many sacrifices, assure ourselves of its fruits.

After all, the resistance of the Germans has not always been what we expected. You took their entire war fleet from them; still, they were very proud of it, and their Emperor had told them, "Our future is on the sea." We had envisaged the possibility of a desperate resistance on the part of the Germans once they were deprived of their fleet; you remember the observations made by Marshal Foch on this subject when we were drafting the terms of the Armistice. In fact, nothing happened. We are now seizing their merchant fleet—in order to feed them, it is true. But they have foreseen the possibility that they would not be fed, for the *Berliner Tageblatt* reports today that, in that case, Germany would manage to live despite the blockade.

I come to President Wilson's precept, which I accept, but which

[1] The interview was with the Berlin correspondent of *Le Temps* and was printed in that newspaper on March 26, 1919, under the headline, "L'Allemagne et la paix: Déclarations du Comte Bernstorff." The tone of his remarks is well conveyed in the following extracts printed in English translation in the New York *Evening Post*, March 26, 1919. Commenting generally on a peace settlement, Bernstorff said: "The armistice of November 11 was signed when all the Powers interested had accepted the programme of peace proposed by President Wilson. Germany is determined to keep to this agreement, which history will regard, in a way, as the conclusion of a preliminary peace. She herself is ready to submit to the conditions arising from it, and she expects all the interested Powers to do the same. If these essential conditions of the Wilson programme should be violated or neglected, and especially if conditions are imposed which go beyond the programme, the German delegates would unfortunately find themselves in a position of, say, *non possumus*." On the subject of indemnities, Bernstorff stated: "Germany's attitude on indemnities is fixed by her acceptance of the note of November 15, 1918, whereby reparation is accorded for all damage done to the civil populations of France and Belgium by German aggression. This note admits of the payment of no other indemnities." Asked what the consequences would be of the failure to sign a peace, Bernstorff replied: "I am no prophet, but Bolshevism would gain immensely. The liberal world, which has seen salvation for humanity in President Wilson's principles, would be terribly disappointed if peace were not made. Even the higher classes would be driven to despair. Remember that, since the Middle Ages, no idea has aroused the world's enthusiasm like a League of Nations based on peace and justice, and who will dare to cause the idea to miscarry at the first test? I hope that a league of all the nations of the world will make common cause against the spectre of Bolshevism and triumph over it." In addition to these observations, Bernstorff also advocated plebiscites to determine the future of Alsace-Lorraine and German-speaking Austria.

I apply to the Germans only with certain reservations. We must not—says President Wilson—give the Germans a sense of injustice. Agreed, but what we find fair here in this chamber will not necessarily be accepted as such by the Germans.

There is surprise that France is opposed to the immediate admission of Germany to the League of Nations. Just yesterday, I received a new report on the atrocities committed in France. Unfortunately, we have come to know the Germans at our own expense; and we know that they are a people who submit themselves to force in order to impose their own force upon the world. I remind Mr. Lloyd George of a conversation I had with him at Carlsbad seven or eight years ago: I imparted to him my uneasiness over the future of Europe, and I mentioned the German threat. Mr. Lloyd George hoped that Germany would be wise; unfortunately, he has had his eyes opened.

The Germans are a servile people who need force to sustain an argument. Napoleon said before his death: "Nothing permanent is founded upon force." I am sure of that; for it suffices to look at the great nations of Europe and the United States itself to have doubts. What is true is that force cannot establish anything solid unless it is in the service of justice. We must do everything we can to be just to the Germans; but, as for persuading them that we are just toward them, that is another matter. I believe we can do something to spare the world from German aggression for a long time; but the German spirit will not change so quickly. Look at the German Social Democrats, who called themselves the brothers of our Socialists and yours: we have seen them in the service of the Imperial government, and today they serve Scheidemann, surrounded by the old Imperial bureaucracy, with Rantzau at its head.

Notice that no one in Germany makes a distinction between just and unjust demands by the Allies. There is no resistance stronger than that exhibited against assigning Danzig to Poland. However, to compensate for the historical crime committed against the Polish nation, we are obliged, in bringing that country back to life, to give her the means to live. We must not forget the crimes committed in particular by Germany against Poland, following the great crime of her partition, in the nineteenth century, and by so-to-speak scientific methods. We remember the children whipped for having prayed to God in Polish, peasants expropriated, driven from their lands, to make room for tenants of the Germanic race.

Perhaps each of us has similar expropriations on his conscience, in a more or less distant past; but here we have facts which took place under our very eyes, and those who have committed them are before us. The Social Democrats are among them, for they supported their government during four years of war.

I pay tribute to Mr. Lloyd George's spirit of equity, when he expresses the desire to give Poland as few German subjects as possible. But I do not accept the sentence in which he says that, on the question of communications between Danzig and the interior, we must leave aside all strategic considerations. If we followed this advice, we would leave a sad legacy for our successors. We must accept the fact that there are inevitable difficulties with the principle of the right of peoples to self-determination, if we wish to safeguard this very principle.

An example haunts me: that of Austria. We speak of everyone disarming: I want it very much; believe me, the spirit of conquest which was once that of the French people is dead forever. But if we reduce our armaments, and if, at the same time, Austria adds seven million inhabitants to the population of Germany, the power of our German neighbors will increase in a manner very threatening to us. Is it a flagrant insult to the rights of peoples to say to the Austrians: "We only ask you to remain independent. Do what you wish with this independence; but you must not enter into a German bloc and participate in a plan for German revenge"?

My principles are the same as yours; I am only arguing about their application. May I say to President Wilson: do not believe that the principles of justice which satisfy us will also satisfy the Germans. I know them; since 1871 I have compelled myself to go to Germany nearly every year. I wanted to know the Germans, and, at certain times, I hoped that mutual understanding could be reached between our two peoples. I can tell you that their idea of justice is not ours.

After the greatest effort and the greatest sacrifices of bloodshed that history has ever seen, we must not compromise the result of our victory. The League of Nations is offered to us as a means of giving us the security which we need. I accept this instrumentality, but if the League of Nations will not be able to give military sanctions to its decrees, that sanction would have to be found from another quarter. I note that, on the sea, this sanction is already in effect: Germany has no more fleet. We must have an equivalent on land. I do not have preconceived opinions about the means to employ. I implore you to understand my feelings about this, just as I am making an effort to understand yours. America is far away, protected by the ocean. Not even Napoleon himself could touch England. You are both sheltered; we are not.

No man is further than I am from the militaristic spirit. I am ready to do anything to arrive at a solution which would be better than the military solution. But we cannot forget that, in our great crisis, the military did much to save us. Do not make the error of not accepting their advice at a moment like this. On the day of danger and of trial, they would say to us: "It was not our fault if you did not listen to us."

One last word. We are right to fear Bolshevism among the enemy and to avoid provoking its development; but we must not spread it among ourselves. There is a sense of justice among allies which must be recognized. If this sentiment was violently opposed, either in France or in England, great danger could result. To wish to spare the conquered is a good thing; but we must not lose sight of the victors. If a revolutionary movement was to appear somewhere because our solutions appear unjust, let it not be in our own countries. I wish only to give here a simple indication.

Lloyd George. I am in agreement on many points with M. Clemenceau, but certain of the positions he takes seem to me full of peril. I know something about the Bolshevik danger in our countries; I have fought it myself for several weeks now, and I congratulate my colleagues for having had less trouble with it than I do. I combat Bolshevism, not by force, but by searching for a means to satisfy legitimate aspirations which have given birth to it.

The result is that trade unionists like Smillie, the secretary-general of the miners,[2] who could have become fearsome, end up by helping us to avoid a conflict. The English capitalists—thank God—are frightened, and that makes them reasonable. But concerning the conditions of peace, what could provoke an explosion of Bolshevism in England would not be the reproach of having asked too little from the enemy, but of having asked too much. The English worker does not want to crush the German people with excessive demands. Rather, it is among the upper classes that you find an unlimited hatred of the German. Moreover, a marked change of attitude has taken place in this matter since Germany renounced its old political regime. If our terms seem too moderate, I will have great difficulties in Parliament, but they will not come from the common people.

I do not agree with what M. Clemenceau has said about the opinions of the military. Their assistance is essential in time of war. But in matters of state, they are the last people I would consult. I admire and very much like Marshal Foch; but in the matter of political questions he is a child. I would not take his advice about the manner in which to assure the greatest possible security to nations. Let us remember that Moltke, who was undoubtedly an eminent military leader, perhaps led Bismarck in 1871 further than he would have gone himself. In the end, Germany fell victim to the idea of a strategic frontier, which led it to multilate France.

Likewise we have had a school of officers who sought to give the

---

[2] Robert Smillie, actually president of the Miners' Federation of Great Britain.

Indian Empire what was called a scientific frontier. Gladstone did not believe in scientific frontiers. But Disraeli, in the name of this doctrine, allowed the occupation of Afghanistan, from which we were eventually obliged to withdraw under disastrous conditions. Since then, Afghanistan, respected by us, has become a most useful buffer state. This leads us to the discussion between Wellington and Blücher about which I spoke a moment ago.

I received a letter from General Smuts,[3] who is an impartial spirit and whose loyalty to us I wish to recall. He is one of the best generals who fought against us in the Boer War. He invaded the Cape Colony with several hundred men; he had thousands at the time he surrendered to us. During the present war, I have only to recall the role which he played in assisting us to check the uprisings fomented by Germany in South Africa.

His letter, as he himself says, is unpleasant. He talks much about Danzig; he believes that the conditions which we wish to impose are contrary to those which a statesman should impose. I admit my own grave fears concerning Danzig. We are going to give Poland two million Germans. The Poles will govern badly and will take a long time to conduct business in the western manner. There will be disturbances; the Germans in Poland, if they revolt, will be defeated. If Germany wishes to intervene, will you send troops to keep the Germans of Poland under the yoke? The Poles, it is true, will tell us: what good is it to have given us these territories if you do not help us to defend them? I am certain that public opinion neither in America nor in England would support us if we intervened in such conditions. The League of Nations, the treaty which we will sign, will be equally flouted. I do not believe in a treaty whose future execution could not be assured. If you are not determined to assure the execution of this clause, what good is it to place it in your treaty?

Whatever happens, we are going to impose upon Germany a very hard peace: she will have no more colonies, no more fleet; she will lose six or seven million inhabitants, a great part of her natural resources: nearly all her iron, a notable portion of her coal. Militarily, we are reducing her to the status of Greece and, from a naval point of view, to that of the Argentine Republic. And on all these points, we are entirely in agreement. Moreover, she will pay, according to the estimates, five or ten billion pounds sterling. Setting our conditions at the lowest level, they will be such as no civilized nation has ever been obliged to accept. If you add to that secondary conditions which could be considered unjust, that will perhaps be the straw that breaks the camel's back.

[3] See the minutes of the Council of Four, March 29, 1919, 3 p.m., n. 11.

What did France resent the most: the loss of Alsace-Lorraine or the obligation to pay five billions in indemnity? I already know your answer. What struck me most on my first trip to Paris was the statue of Strasbourg in mourning. Germany must not be able to erect such statues in her cities on account of our failure.

Clemenceau. Nor do I want that.

Lloyd George. The Germans have certain fine qualities of character. They fought very bravely. I believe that they will accept everything else, including a very heavy indemnity; but what will wound them the most is the idea of abandoning millions of Germans to Polish domination. It has been very painful for France to see Frenchmen pass under German domination; but the French would at least consider the Germans their equals. It is not the same with the Poles in the mind of the Germans. It is this type of sentiment which might prevent them from signing the peace treaty.

I would prefer a solution making Danzig a free port, and leaving the Poles in Poland and the Germans in Germany. General Smuts writes very aptly: "Poland cannot exist without the good will of Germany and of Russia." When we all go home, the Poles will stay there by themselves, isolated in the middle of enemies who surround them on all sides.

Clemenceau. What is your conclusion?

Lloyd George. My conclusion is that we must not create a Poland alienated from the time of its birth from its most civilized neighbor by an unforgettable quarrel.

Do not believe that our most extreme democrats do not understand the necessities of the present situation. In a conversation I had yesterday with Lansbury, one of our most notorious pacifists, I told him that I would be ready to promise France that, in case of German aggression, we would place all our forces at her disposal. Lansbury told me that he approved. But we ourselves must avoid sowing the seeds of war.

The letter from General Smuts is read. He greatly fears the imposition on Germany of excessive conditions and is alarmed about what is being said about Danzig and the left bank of the Rhine, as well as the figures for indemnities, and maintaining that it is in collaboration with Germany, and not against her, that it will be possible to keep alive new nations such as Poland and Bohemia: "Germany," writes General Smuts, "will remain despite everything a dominant element in continental Europe, and it would be a folly to believe that we will be able to reconstruct the world without her assistance."

Clemenceau. I am willing to believe that General Smuts, who has proved his loyalty to England, does not speak solely as a friend of Germany. But I want the French point of view also to be taken into account.

March 27, 1919, 3:30 p.m.

Lloyd George. I have a few words to say about our plan to send a commission to Ottoman Asia. I just spoke with one of our administrators in Mesopotamia, whose views are rather different from those of General Alby concerning Arab sentiment toward France. He also believes that it is better not to stir up trouble in that whole region by sending a commission there. It would only be able to collect insufficient information, since oriental people are wary and do not open up to newcomers from the start.

Wilson. Despite everything, I would prefer an inquiry conducted impartially. If we fear delaying the definitive reestablishment of peace by too lengthy an inquiry, we can instruct the members of the commission so as to limit their task precisely.

Lloyd George. The Emir Faisal also seems to have changed his attitude. We received a petition from the inhabitants of Iraq, to whom we offered the possibility of being ruled by an Arab emir. They responded with polite oriental phrases, that, while they were very grateful, they preferred the direct administration of Europeans.

Wilson. I insist that we adhere to our decision about the inquiry. Doctor Bliss,[4] who has seen these people close up for a number of years, and who, for that reason, identifies with them, tells me that the inquiry will make a good impression upon them.

Clemenceau. I agree with President Wilson, at the same time wishing that the inquiry be carried out without wasting time. Could we now take up the question of the left bank of the Rhine?

Wilson. It seems to me that we have already come much nearer on this question. We agree to forbid all military installations, not only on the left bank of the Rhine, but also within a zone of fifty kilometers on the opposite bank. We can extend this stipulation to include strategic railroads and forbid the assembling of armed forces in the entire region, even for maneuvers; and we could add that any violation of these provisions would be considered a hostile act. If we add to that a military guarantee by Great Britain and, I hope, the United States, acting under the authority of the League of Nations, to come to the immediate assistance of France in case of aggression committed without provocation by Germany against France, it seems to me that you will have satisfaction.

Clemenceau. What Mr. Lloyd George has already said to me on this subject satisfies me, and if others are not of my opinion, that

---

[4] That is, Howard Sweetser Bliss. For his statement to the Council of Ten, see the minutes of that body printed at Feb. 13, 1919, Vol. 55.

will not prevent me from following my path. But what I could not accept would be a temporary guarantee.

Wilson. We have sought to avoid a formula which, by substituting on a permanent basis the action of a group of states for that of the League of Nations, would seem to admit that the guarantee of the latter would always remain insufficient. But, in our mind, this problem is closely linked to that of the effective action of the League of Nations.

Clemenceau. Could we not write the guarantee which you offer into the pact of the League of Nations?

Wilson. We cannot insert into a pact which sets forth general principles, clauses aimed at one nation in particular. But we are ready to do what is necessary so that, while awaiting the action provided for by the Executive Council in case of unjustified aggression against a member of the League, two or more nations would be authorized to act without delay. The plans of action could even be examined in advance.

Clemenceau. I am ready to accept, if aggression is defined as entry of German forces into the zone of fifty kilometers beyond the Rhine.

Tardieu. In case of aggression, we must have the right to transport our troops up to the Rhine, which is our line of defense.

Wilson. What must be feared is a state of nervousness, which will probably last for a generation or more, and the danger of a premature action. On the frontier between the United States and Canada, following our agreement to leave it without fortification of any kind, incidents occurred for years.

Clemenceau. That is why we have proposed the establishment of a Franco-Anglo-American commission, which would establish the fact of aggression.

Wilson. Mr. Lloyd George has proposed to entrust this task to the Executive Council of the League of Nations.

Clemenceau. I fear that this would only lead to delays.

Lloyd George. We are ready to give to France a promise of immediate and unlimited support in case of aggression. Here it would be necessary to review the correspondence exchanged before the war between M. Paul Cambon and Sir Edward Grey, which foresaw and, it seems to me, promised cooperation of this kind if France was attacked without provocation.

Marshal Foch and Generals Bliss, Sir Henry Wilson, and Diaz are introduced.

Foch. We received a telegram from General Nudant on the reception by the German representatives at Spa of our communication about transporting Polish troops by way of Danzig. (The telegram is read.)

Wilson. I would have liked this communication to have been delivered directly by Marshal Foch, and I had understood that that was what would be done; that would have given it much more solemnity and weight.

Lloyd George. I agree with the President here.

Foch. General Nudant is my executive agent in Spa. It is through him that I transmit to the German government all communications from the Allies. I could not go to Spa simply to hand a piece of paper to a subordinate.

Wilson. Is it not yet time to ask the Germans to send a plenipotentiary to Spa who would meet with Marshal Foch? I believed that would be the procedure.

Clemenceau. We can send a telegram worded as follows: "In order to hasten the solution, Marshal Foch, under instructions from the Associated Governments, invites the German government to send a plenipotentiary to Spa to examine with him the execution of the measure decided upon."

Wilson. We must at the same time clearly indicate to the Germans that we are not today settling the fate of Danzig. Today we only wish to avail ourselves of the right, which belongs to us according to the Armistice, to send Polish troops, considered as Allied troops, into Poland by way of Danzig.

Clemenceau. I ask Marshal Foch to keep this point well in mind. Since the question of Danzig has not yet been finally decided upon at the conference, it is essential to tell the Germans that for the moment, in using the port of Danzig, we only wish to treat the question of transporting Polish troops.

I now ask Marshal Foch to present to us his report on the question, which we examined the day before yesterday, of the aid to be furnished to Rumania.

Reading of the document (summary): To stop the Bolshevik infiltration, it is necessary to create a barrier in Poland and in Rumania, closing the breach at Lemberg, and to cleanse the points behind it which could be infected, such as Hungary, while assuring the maintenance of communications by way of Vienna.

Concerning Rumania specifically, the necessary measures are planned in detail to send to her army supplies and equipment which it lacks. This army will be placed under the command of a French general. Vienna would be occupied by Allied troops under American command.

Wilson. Part of this plan refers to what we discussed the other day; but the whole plan seems to aim at something more. It is essential to distinguish between the two proposals.

We agree on the assistance to be given the Rumanian army and on the evacuation of Odessa, which is linked to our action in Rumania. But this document goes very much further. There is the question of Lemberg. In the quarrel between the Ukrainians and the Poles, it is difficult for us to intervene without having a better understanding of our position vis-à-vis the Ukrainians or the Bolsheviks who are besieging Lemberg. "To close the breach at Lemberg" at this time means to take the part of the Poles against the Ruthenians.

As for the idea of effecting a junction between Polish and Rumanian forces to face eastward, this is the prelude to a march toward the East, and that leads us to the question of a military intervention in Russia. We have examined this question more than once, and each time we have arrived at the same conclusion: that we must not consider a military intervention.

As for the occupation of Vienna, it seems to me that nothing in the Armistice gives us the right to do that.

Sir Henry Wilson. The Armistice gives us the right to occupy all strategic points in Austria-Hungary, as we see fit.

Wilson. Undoubtedly, but we are to occupy them to assure execution of the Armistice and not for an aim outside the Armistice, such as this one. Can we not limit ourselves to the immediate object which we had in view the day before yesterday, that is, to measures necessary to strengthen Rumania, without preparing an offensive action against anyone? The phrase used by Marshal Foch was: "The Rumanian citadel must be reinforced." The evacuation of Odessa was considered as the means of transferring resources, whose use at Odessa could not lead to any satisfactory result, to Rumania in order to bring her means of defense up to strength.

Lloyd George. I would ask Marshal Foch if, when he speaks of establishing a barrier, he wishes to take precautions against a military danger from the Bolsheviks, or against danger of another kind.

Foch. Against an epidemic disease, we create a *cordon sanitaire*: one places a customs officer every 200 meters, and they prevent people from crossing. Moreover, if we fear an armed invasion, we create a stronger barrier. My advice is that we create a barrier against both dangers, which does not mean preparing an offensive.

Orlando. I ask permission to read two telegrams which we have from our Italian commissioner in Vienna about the situation. The first informs us that a dispatch from the revolutionary government of Budapest has been received in Vienna, inviting the Viennese proletariat to follow the example of the Hungarians. The Viennese revolutionaries have decided to form a workers' council, all set to take power; demonstrations have taken place in front of the city hall and in the streets of Vienna.

In Budapest, the business establishments have been closed by order of the government, and it is forbidden to remove merchandise from them on penalty of death. It is possible to save the situation only by an occupation of Budapest by Allied troops, on the condition that these troops do not include Czechs, Rumanians, or Poles.

The moderate elements in Vienna fear Bolshevism and are making overtures to us in favor of the occupation of Vienna by Italian troops.

The second telegram reports a conversation with a member of the government who is not a Socialist: he considers Bolshevik infiltration as probable if the people's army is not disarmed. The government is weak; but in order to stabilize the situation, it would suffice to send to Vienna two American regiments, which would be greeted with relief by the great majority of the population. A declaration by the Allies on the subject of revictualing would produce a useful effect, but would serve no purpose if it followed a Bolshevik triumph.

Diaz. Bolshevism is a popular movement which appears everywhere where food is lacking and where central authority is weak. It spreads along lines of communication, where small cells are formed and soon grow and join together. Its progress appears to be linked to the present success of the Russian Bolshevik movement. Sending troops without holding on to lines of communication would be very unwise, since these troops could be cut off from their base and placed in a most dangerous situation.

The fermentation now taking place is not happening only in Vienna, but even as far away as the Slovene regions—everywhere, in a word, where the population suffers lack of foodstuffs. By occupying Vienna in strength, one holds the lines of communication and stops this threatening advance. What is necessary is to give the people the impression that we bring food, order, and security. Without that, they will throw themselves instinctively on the side of disorder.

If Vienna is occupied, since it is Italy which fought against Austria, I ask that Italian troops be charged with this mission.

Sir Henry Wilson. The statesmen should decide whether or not they wish a military action against Bolshevism. If this decision is taken, the plan presented by Marshal Foch is the best we have. The longer we delay, the more difficult the solution to the problem will become. The Bolshevik incursion into Hungary has already lengthened the frontier to be patrolled by several hundred kilometers.

Bliss. The word "Bolshevik" comes up so often in these debates that it obviously sets the tone for all that has just been said. If we replaced it by the word "revolutionary," perhaps that would be clearer. Bolshevism is the form the revolutionary movement takes in backward countries which have suffered particularly. Furthermore, we hear it said sometimes that Russian Bolshevism is a German product, at other times that it is an essentially Russian movement which comes to invade Europe from the East. If it was certain that it comes from Russia, obviously it is there that it must be killed. But the problem is more difficult.

A *cordon sanitaire* could stop the Bolsheviks, but not Bolshevism; to create a true barrier, it would be necessary to deploy very considerable forces all the way from the Baltic to the Black Sea. I do not believe this route should be taken without being sure that there is no other means of action. I see two other routes: peace, with a determination of frontiers, since uncertainty about them causes much trouble and agitation among people; and in the second place, lifting the blockade and thereby allowing the entire world to go back to work.

Marshal Foch repeats his proposals: the occupation of Vienna is absolutely necessary to maintain our communications with Bohemia, Poland, and Rumania.

Foch. The entire system which I submit to you tends to organize a barrier against Bolshevism; this is not a question of an offensive, but a defensive barrier, behind which the necessary cleansing will be done.

Marshal Foch and Generals Bliss, Diaz, and Sir Henry Wilson retire.

Wilson. We again find ourselves on familiar ground; is it not a question of knowing whether it is possible to organize armed resistance against Bolshevism, which means: have we not only the required troops, but also the material means and the public sentiment to support us?

The word "Bolshevik" covers many different things. In my opinion, to try to stop a revolutionary movement with ordinary armies is like using a broom to sweep back a great sea. The armies, moreover, can be impregnated by the very Bolshevism which they would be charged to combat. A germ of sympathy exists between the forces that one would wish to oppose the one against the other. The sole means of acting against Bolshevism is to make its causes disappear. Moreover, it is a formidable enterprise; we do not even quite know what the causes are.

In any case, one of the causes is the uncertainty of populations about their future frontiers and the governments which they will have to obey, and at the same time their distress about lack of food, transportation, and the means of work. The only way to kill Bolshevism is to establish the frontiers and to open all the doors to commerce.

As for the occupation of Vienna by American troops, that is impossible, because I believe that the Armistice does not give us the right to send our troops to Vienna. I am steadfastly opposed to the reconstitution of an eastern front, which is being proposed to us once again.

The question which we wished to examine was much more limited: that of revictualing Odessa. We had asked Marshal Foch if it would be better to transfer to Rumania those resources which maintaining our troops at Odessa would require, without any hope of a favorable outcome. We receive as a reply to this question a plan which envisages the establishment of a continuous line from the Baltic to the Black Sea. One speaks to us about "cleansing" Hungary, which is to say crushing Hungarian Bolshevism. If this Bolshevism remains within its frontiers, that is not our concern. The only problem which we intended to solve today was that of sending assistance to Rumania.

Orlando. This question is in fact different from that of intervention in Russia. We had to choose, in Russia, between two equally logical and defensible politics. The first is that of intervention: to go as far as Moscow if necessary and to crush Bolshevism by force. The second is to regard Bolshevism as a *de facto* government and to establish relations with it, which would be, if not cordial, then at least more or less normal. We have done neither, and thus we have suffered the most distressing consequences of both policies at once. Without making war, we are in a state of war with Russia. So far, when all is said and done, the Russian or Ukrainian Bolsheviks are only defending their own territory.

I will not comment on the question of Lemberg, which might be either a Ruthenian or a Polish city. At this moment, it is not a question of intervening in Russia, but of defending our allies and assuring our communications with them. Since, from a political point of view, we agree about our duty to support our allies, the only problem left to solve is a military one. We must defend Rumania: the question may arise tomorrow with regard to the Czechs. The occupation of Vienna may become a military necessity. It would not be justified for purely political reasons; but if our military advisers tell us that Vienna is indispensable to assure our communications with the Rumanians and the Czechs, I personally believe that we would take on a great responsibility by refusing to go to Vienna. Moreover, I picture the occupation of this city as an inter-Allied enterprise; and I do not support the opinion expressed by

General Diaz. I repeat only that, if this is a military necessity, we would incur a great responsibility if we refused.

Clemenceau. President Wilson has expressed my opinion. I am asked to equip or rebuild the Rumanian army; this is the question to which we must limit ourselves.

Lloyd George. There has been talk of suppressing the revolution in Hungary. I do not see why we should do that: there are few countries so much in need of a revolution. Just yesterday I had a conversation with someone who visited Hungary and who knows her well; he tells me that this is the country which has the worst system of landholding in Europe. The peasants there are as oppressed as they were in the Middle Ages, and manorial law still exists there.

After an exchange of observations, it is decided that Marshal Foch will be asked to limit his proposals to the measures necessary for the reinforcement of the Rumanian army, including the evacuation of Odessa and the sending to Rumania of the provisions destined for this city.

Mantoux, I, 41-57.

From Tasker Howard Bliss, with Enclosure

My dear Mr. President: Paris, March 27th, 1919.

I enclose, herewith, telegram received by me for you from Mr. Secretary Baker. Should you so desire, I will transmit to him any reply you desire to make.

Sincerely yours,   Tasker H. Bliss

Telegram returned to General Bliss, with President's approval. 3/29/19

TLS (WP, DLC).

ENCLOSURE

[Washington] March 27, 1919.

PARAGRAPH ONE. Prior to the receipt of your message March twentieth with regard to courtmartial sentences I had asked the American Bar Association to appoint a committee of distinguished lawyers to examine into the whole question of military law and courtmartial procedure. The committee has just arrived in Washington and I have placed all of the records of the department at its disposal. The members are men of great distinction and their recommendations will be most helpful. I am taking other action by way of clemency to reduce excessive sentences and believe the whole controversy now clarifying.

PARAGRAPH TWO. I have just returned from a visit to the Pacific Coast. Made some twelve stops to inspect army camps, incidentally addressing large audiences under auspices of chambers of commerce. League of Nations plan almost unanimously approved. Genuine enthusiasm for it. Also found business conditions throughout the country good. A very obvious industrial and commercial revival is in progress. In Iowa, Oregon, California, as well as in southern states like Texas, men are back of you without distinction of party.

PARAGRAPH THREE. My present plan is to leave here April sixth for a brief trip to France unless in your judgment I should postpone it.   Newton D. Baker

TC telegram (N. D. Baker Papers, DLC).

From Robert Lansing, with Enclosure

My dear Mr. President: Paris, March 27, 1919.

I beg to enclose herewith an interesting report of the revolution in Hungary, prepared by an American officer[1] who left that city thirty-six hours after the new Government came into power.
                    Faithfully yours,   Robert Lansing.

TLS (WP, DLC).
[1] That is, Capt. Nicholas Roosevelt.

E N C L O S U R E

THE HUNGARIAN REVOLUTION

The following summary of conditions in Hungary is presented by Captain Roosevelt who left Budapest about 8:P.M., March 22nd, thirty-six hours after the outbreak of the revolution. The information published in the papers since then throws no new significant light on the subject.

1. The revolution in Hungary was primarily nationalistic in character. The Hungarians who are united in their conviction that Hungary must not be dismembered, have made use of Bolshevism as a last desperate resort to preserve the integrity of their country, and have openly defied the Allies, and set a precedent for Germany to follow.

2. The revolution was precipitated by the presentation to the Hungarian government on the morning of March 20 of a decision of the Peace Conference concerning the demarcation line in Transylvania and the temporary creation of a neutral zone to be occupied

by Interallied troops. This note was presented by Colonel Vix of the French Mission at the direction of General de Lobbit,[1] the French commander at Belgrade. The new line of demarcation follows closely the ethnic boundary between the Roumanians and Hungarians in Transylvania and was therefore taken by the Hungarian government to be the indication of the intention of the Peace Conference to give the whole of Transylvania to Roumania. Furthermore, the withdrawal of Hungarian troops to the westward of the neutral zone provided for in this decision meant that the Hungarians would have to abandon virtually half their territory to enemy occupation.

3. The revolution was accomplished with comparative quiet. During the night of the 21st there was a good deal of shooting in Budapest but only a few casualties and only a small amount of plundering. On the 22nd the government issued orders punishing with death any persons carrying arms, offering armed resistance to the new government, robbing, or plundering, and punishing with a 50,000 kronen fine the sale of alcoholic liquor. The effect of these measures was good. As far as the political aspect is concerned, the revolution was brought about apparently through a common understanding between the old government and the various elements which have constituted the new government. Baron Podmanicsky,[2] who presented to Colonel Vix the answer of President Karolyi, informed me that it had first been decided to maintain Karolyi as President, but with an ultra radical cabinet and with an understanding with the Russian Soviet government. The members of the Communist party including Bela Kuhn favored this, but the members of the Laborers' party insisted on a complete change and on the establishment of the rule of the proletariat. This was done. Karolyi accepted the resignation of his government and himself resigned, turning the government over to the proletariat, and appealing to the proletariat of the world to come to the rescue of Hungary. The new government, which is based on the Russian Soviet model, is a combination of the Communists and the left wing of the Socialists and includes Bela Kuhn and others who were previously arrested as Bolshevik agitators. In a manifesto the new government proclaimed its adherence to the Russian Soviet government.

4. There were also rumors which I was unable to substantiate but which it is my belief are true;—to the effect that there is some sort of an understanding with the Germans. Major Pentamalli,[3] the Chief of the Italian Mission, informed me that he had been in close touch with Kunfi, one of the strongest men of the new cabinet, and that Kunfi while at the Berne Socialist Conference had come to an understanding with the Russians and Germans about this

very matter. It is interesting to note that in my last interview with Karolyi on March 18 he showed keen interest in the question of the rate of return of American troops in France and asked what the attitude of the United States would be towards having American troops police Europe.

5. In this connection it is important to note that Major Pentamalli told me he had tried "to soften the blow" for Karolyi, and when I saw Prince Borghese, the rejected Italian Minister to Servia, who is in Budapest, (tho he states it is in no official capacity) Prince Borghese volunteered the opinion that the Allies would make a great mistake if they failed to give the new government a chance to make good, and he added that in his opinion it was advantageous that a "neutral person" should remain if the Allied Mission left, and keep in touch with the situation. He suggested that he might be such a "neutral person" and said if he remained he would of course keep his government informed of conditions. It is my opinion, tho here again I can adduce no definite proof, that the Italians were not altogether ignorant of this revolutionary movement. It appears from what Major Pentamalli said that the Italians would be willing to consider occupying Hungary. The only reason I can see for this is their policy of gaining power over a strengthened Hungary at the expense of Yugo Slavia.

6. The general opinion in Hungary as far as I was able to ascertain from newspapers, and from talking with persons of various classes, as well as from the reports of the Hungarian-American Lieutenant who was with me, is one of welcome for this revolutionary move. All classes seem to consider it as a step in the right direction, and as a probably successful method of preserving the integrity of their country. It is therefore essentially nationalistic, making use of Bolshevism for national ends—in this particular case against the Czechs and the Roumanians who have occupied parts of Hungary and for whom there is a bitter hatred. When it comes to a question of Hungarian integrity all parties are in accord.

7. The grave significance of this revolution is that this, the first important decision of the Peace Conference made known to one of the Central Powers has been met by open defiance. Hungary has refused to comply, and is holding the club of Bolshevism over the Allies and asking "What are you going to do about it?" The precedent set by this action will offer an encouragement to the Germans which may be disastrous.

8. The immediate results to be expected are military activities against the Czechs and the Roumanians. The hatred is perhaps more bitter against the Czechs because they are stronger from a military point of view, but the bulk of the best troops are concen-

trated in the Transylvanian section. The American Military Attache in Bucharest[4] informed me on March 12th that according to his information the Hungarians were in a position to put about ten divisions into Transylvania at short notice. The greatest handicap to any military operations by the Hungarians is the lack of coal, which has crippled their transportation.

9. The following alternatives have been suggested as possible measures of relief:

(1) Ordering the Czechs and Roumanians to advance and occupy Hungary. Owing to the intenseness of hatred against these people such an action would only result in the worst kind of bloody war. Furthermore it is questionable whether the military organizations of these two countries are in a position to carry out such operations.

(2) Occupation by Allied troops. This was advocated by the Italian and British missions in Budapest, the last word of the Chief of the British Mission[5] to me being that 10,000 troops would be sufficient. This number is probably too small and might suffice for Budapest alone. If, however, the feeling of the country continues to be of as strong a nationalistic character as it is at present, occupation by any troops will surely be met with resistance.

(3) If the Peace Conference desires to enforce its decision regarding the Transylvanian armistice line, a blockade is a practical weapon, but it would not prove really effective for about two months, when the food situation will become desperate, without imports.

10. The conclusion of the matter is that unless immediate and vigorous action is taken the Allies will be met with a disastrous state of affairs in Central Europe which it may take years to straighten out. Hungary has defied the Peace Conference and allied herself with the Bolsheviki. It is Germany's turn next.

T MS (WP, DLC).

[1] Gen. Paul Joseph Jean Hector de Lobit (not Lobbit).

[2] Baron Tibor Podmaniczky, Counselor to the Ministry of Foreign Affairs in the Károlyi government.

[3] The correct form of the surname is Pentimalli. The Editors have been unable to learn his given name or names.

[4] Col. Halsey Edward Yates.

[5] The chief of the British mission in Budapest was a Col. Baker. The Editors have been unable to learn his given names.

From the Diary of Colonel House

March 27, 1919.

Just before the meeting last night of the League of Nations Committee, I had a talk with Venizelos in my study and told him I would like to take up the Greek question with him in a few days and try and delineate the boundaries.

I had the President also in my room for a few minutes before the meeting. It was to tell him that the draft for the article on the Monroe Doctrine, which Balfour, Cecil and I had agreed upon, was refused by Lloyd George, therefore Cecil asked me to urge him not to present it, or to bring up the matter at last night's meeting. Lloyd George told Cecil that he had no intention of having the the [sic] Covenant in the Peace Treaty, and that he did not intend to sign any Covenant for a League of Nations until he had had a complete understanding with the President concerning the United States Naval building program.

I was surprised to see how calmly the President took this information. He declared he was willing to take the chances with the Senate without putting in a clause on the Monroe Doctrine. I combatted this complacent attitude and insisted that he force Lloyd George to come to our way of thinking. He asked if I would not see him myself. I was willing but thought it would be much more effective if he would have it out with him personally. I called his attention to the many concessions we had made to Great Britain in the drafting of the Covenant and asked him to remind George that on their part they had made none. This is not literally true, but the weight of the argument is on our side.

The President insisted upon having me go on the committee for the selection of a site for the home of the League. The other members which I made out for him were, Orlando, Smuts and Makino.

To show what a nimble mind the President has, it amused those of us near him last night to hear him state that he would appoint "the old drafting committee." When he reached this point in the sentence, I slipped a memorandum under his eye giving a new drafting committee which Cecil and I had just agreed upon and which did not include any of the old committee, excepting Cecil. The President glanced at the memorandum and continued his sentence without a halt, "but I think it would be an imposition to ask them to serve again, therefore I shall name the following." He then looked down the list and read it as we had prepared it. I wondered how many had seen this little byplay, and I wondered how many saw the inconsistency of his remarks when Lord Robert Cecil was included in the new list, he having been on the old.

I put myself in merely in order to get David Miller to serve as my proxy. The meeting did not break up until 11.30, but I had a few minutes talk with the President concerning the interview which he is to have with the Prime Ministers tomorrow and at which the question of the western boundaries and the security of France will probably come up. He surprised me by saying that he was willing to guarantee with Great Britain that we should come to France's rescue in the event of an attack by Germany. I had not shown him the memorandum on this subject which I had drafted, and which Lloyd George, Balfour and Clemenceau had accepted. This draft reads as follows:

"Because of the havoc which Germany has brought upon the world by her attacks upon Belgium and France in 1914, and in order to prevent as far as possible such another disaster to humanity, we hereby solemnly pledge to one another our immediate military, financial, economic and moral support of and to one another in the event Germany should at any time make a like unprovoked and unwarranted attack against either one or more of the subscribing powers."

George and Balfour accepted this without change. I had first written "Unwarranted invasion" and Clemenceau suggested "attack" which is better. In thinking about this matter today, I thought I ought to call the President's attention to the perils of such a treaty. I told him among other things that I thought it would be looked upon as a direct blow at the League of Nations. The League is supposed to do just what this treaty proposed, and if it were necessary for the nations to make such treaties, then why the League of Nations? I did not shake him for in a moment of enthusiasm he committed himself to Clemenceau and he does not wish to withdraw his promise, a position which I thoroughly commend.

I told him that George was saying, in spite of the fact that he had promised yesterday his willingness to have the Covenant go into the Peace Treaty that he had made no such promise. In reply to this the President said, "then he lies, for he not only agreed but he agreed in the presence of both Orlando and Clemenceau who will bear witness."

After lunch today the President called me over the telephone to tell me he had had it out with Lloyd George again, and George had said that his conversation with Cecil had been before he had made the promise, which of course is not true. I think the President is beginning to realize how unreliable George is. George is so clever and has so much charm, and is so quick and humerous that I do not wonder the President was deceived.

I have taken up actively with the President today the Russian question. I am trying to think something out that is workable. It is very difficult because no one wanted to deal with such as Lenine and Trotsky. The President suggested that I talk to Hoover and Robinson[1] of the Shipping Board and see whether we could get ships and food to Russia in the event we wished to do so. Hoover thought we could, Robinson thought that it would be sixty to ninety days before anything effective could be done.

Hoover was anxious for the President to send another cablegram to Hurley asking for more ships to supply Europe with necessary food. He wants 500 000 tons for April and Hurley declares he can give him only 300 000. I dictated a cable for the President to O.K. which insists that Hurley take over the necessary tonnage to make the 500 000 tond [tons] that Hoover thinks necessary.[2] I shall try and enlist Hoover actively in the Russian question and together I hope we may be able to reach some sort of solution. . . .

I suggested to the President that he make a statement regarding the Covenant and to say something which would refute the general belief which George and others have fostered that peace was being delayed because the President wished to have the League of Nations included in the Peace Treaty.

The President came by the Crillon and picked me up, and he, Ray Stannard Baker and I went to his house where together we formulated a statement to be given to the press tomorrow.

[1] That is, Henry Mauris Robinson.
[2] WW to E. N. Hurley, March 28, 1919.

From the Diary of Ray Stannard Baker

Thursday the 27th [March 1919]

What whirling days! Every moment from early morning until late at night occupied. President King came on & I introduced him to Col. House & he has been appointed delegate to Syria. I spent a good deal of the day working out a proposed statement by the President to head off the criticism that the L. of N. was holding up the peace settlement, but it was spoiled by tinkering in Col. House's office. After his afternoon conference at the War office the President came down to the Crillon & Col. House & I got in with him & rode up to his house in the Place des Etats-Unis where he revised the statement & dictated it to Mr. Close & we got it out this evening. He showed me the pictures in his library—very interesting old Rembran[d]ts, a Delacroix, a Hobemas [Hobbemas] & several Goyas. He looks tired but is very vigorous. Has a cut on the top of his head where he was thrown against the roof of his automobile on Sunday during the trip North. Very impatient with the slow progress of the deliberations. Says Clemenceau is the chief obstacle. He (C) has a kind of feminine mind: it works well on specific problems; but very poorly on general policies. The President told me that they would spend an hour getting Clemenceau around to a certain position & then find, the next time the subject was up, that his mind had reverted to its exact & obstinate former position. Lansbury who had breakfast with Lloyd-George the other morning told me that L.G. said that Clemenceau had failed much since the attack upon him in February.[1] I told the President this & he inclined to agree. Said Clemenceau had hard coughing fits. They are working on Reparations & neither Clemenceau nor L.G. can agree on figures & both are inclined to make the President an arbiter—leave it with him. More & more the real decisions are drifting into Wilson's hands— a kind of unity of diplomatic command.

In the meantime Lenin & Bolshevism loom ever higher. Bullitt is back from Russia & I have had a long talk with him: there is an increasing tendancy toward trying to deal with Lenin.

Without Col. House this peace commission work could not go on. He is the universal conciliator, smoother-over, connector! He is a kind of super-secretary—a glorified secretary. He is the only man who keeps closely in touch with the President—constantly informing & advising him, getting people together, helping along publicity by seeing the correspondents—a busy, useful, kindly, liberal little man. He can't make a speech, uses rather poor English, but is indefatigable in his service & so far as I can see is without personal ambition.

[1] About which see RL to WW, Feb. 19, 1919, Vol. 55.

From the Diary of Josephus Daniels

March Thursday 27 1919

Lunched with the President & Mrs. W. He took us all over the house, showing the wonderful bath-rooms.

"Now come let me show you the refrigerator where I sleep"—no heat at all in it. Also in Mrs. W's bath-room. Painted cherry blossoms on the walls.

"The only exercise I get is to my vocabulary," WW said

Lloyd George wished me to see Mr. Long, First Lord of the Admiralty, & Admiral Wemyss about naval building program, & President hoped we would talk it over and reach some right understanding.

Hw bound diary (J. Daniels Papers, DLC).

From Herbert Clark Hoover

My dear Mr. President: [Paris] 27 March 1919.

I have received the attached telegram[1] regarding Mr. Hurley's response to my request for 500,000 tons of food loaded in the month of April and in response to your direction to him and the War Department that he should find this tonnage. Mr. Hurley states that he will not find more than 300,000 tons.

In arriving at 500,000 tons, I took the theoretical necessity of the various peoples under relief, which amounted to 800,000 tons, I reduced each single item to the lowest point that I thought was possible, and arrived at 620,000 tons but knowing the acuteness of Mr. Hurley's position I reduced it en bloc to 500,000 tons. I wish to say that I simply cannot take the responsibility for this situation unless this tonnage is provided as we have requested. Every country that we have under relief is rumbling with social explosion. All the peoples in these countries are under drastic food regime and to cut their practical necessities to 60% can mean only a total collapse.

Faithfully yours,   Herbert Hoover

TLS (WP, DLC).
[1] Rickmarsh [E. Rickard and T. F. Whitmarsh] to HCH, March 26, 1919, T telegram (WP, DLC).

From William Phillips

Washington. March 27th, 1919

1334. Before Union League Club, Charles E. Hughes proposes following League amendments: Explicit provision regarding requirement unanimous decision, suitable limitation of field of League inquiries and action to make clear that internal concerns like immigration and tariff are not embraced, no foreign power hereafter acquire by consent, purchase or in any other way any possession on American continent or adjacent islands, settlement of purely American questions to be remitted primarily to American nations, European nations not intervene unless requested by American nations, omitting guarantee of article X, no member of League be constituted mandatory without its consent and no European or Asiatic power to be constituted mandatory of any American people, any member of League may withdraw at its pleasure on specified notice. Local papers say Taft co-operating with Paris in amendments to meet opposition. Poindexter tells Cincinnati business men League plan intolerable. Wadsworth in speech opposes League. McKellar defends it. Senator King says will ask President and Congress for 500,000 volunteers fight Bolshevism in Russia, Hungary,

Germany and elsewhere. Philadelphia LEDGER says Japan by abandoning straight out fight against racial discrimination playing adroit game of acting as great world power and conceding right United States, Canada, Australia to forbid Japanese labor immigration will in turn reciprocally exclude all American, British and Australian labor. [New York] AMERICAN says Commercial Telegraphers' Union has issued strike ballots to all telegraph and telephone employees proposing nation-wide tieup April 22nd, unless Union recognized and higher wages, reinstatement grievances adjusted both. House New York Legislature appropriate[s] for state Bolshevik investigation. Former German Ambassador Eckhardt[1] sails New York for Rotterdam. Daily official bulletin which compub[2] stopped March 31st to continue semi-weekly by Department Labor. Oswald Villard writing to NATION claims Germany punished enough and America should rush there food, milk, oils, grease and soap, and claims Germany hatred Allies increasing. Phillips, Acting.

T telegram (WP, DLC).
  [1] Heinrich von Eckardt, the German Minister to Mexico, 1914-1918, had been recalled in December 1918 at the instigation of the United States Government. See Friedrich Katz, *The Secret War in Mexico: Europe, the United States and the Mexican Revolution* (Chicago and London, 1981), pp. 540-42.
  [2] That is, the Committee on Public Information.

Three Telegrams from Joseph Patrick Tumulty

The White House, 27 March 1919.

Number 35. An acute situation is presented by the dispute between the telegraphers, organized and unorganized, and General Burleson. Representatives of the unions, men and women, have been here with pitiful appeals. They claim that rates of service have been largely increased since Government control and that millions have been added to the earnings of the holding corporations, and that practically nothing has been done for the men and women—the labor side of these vast institutions. They say they have sought redress by petition, by requests for interviews on behalf of their officials and through their officials, with General Burleson but without success. These people represent that many of the membership of their union are not able with their utmost endeavors and with all possible economies on present wages to live decently. A large majority of these workers have expressed by their votes to the union authorities their willingness to strike to remedy intolerable conditions. Their leaders realizing the inconvenience, almost calamity, which such action would bring upon the business of the country, are seeking every means of avoiding this unhappy conclusion, and are trying to suppress the bolsheviki elements in their own ranks.

These people are among the highly intelligent and well-educated class of labor and are willing to exhaust every reasonable expedient to save the situation. They have appealed in their respective areas of the country to leaders of thought and action to bring influence to bear on the Government in their cause.

I am personally aware of one prominent man on the Pacific Coast who has been instrumental in adjusting labor disputes who, on behalf of the Pacific Coast Telegraphers' Union, men and women, addressed a written appeal to the Postmaster General asking that he should meet the leaders on a broad American plan of discussion. His appeal was not even answered. This action is so out of harmony with your attitude that I feel it a duty to bring it to your attention as unless steps are taken by you to modify the action the Postmaster General takes towards these people, there can be to my mind but one ending,—that is a general telegraphers strike throughout the country that may spread to other forms of labor. These workers claim they have been denied the opportunity of using the machinery available for workers in private industry, namely, the National War Labor Board, and that no adequate machinery has been provided by the Post-Office Department for the adjustment of wage disputes, although other departments of the Government have organized machinery for this purpose.   Tumulty.

The White House, 27 March 1919.

#37 Republican opposition subsiding. Hope when you go to Belgium you will see Mercier. Statement from him on League of Nations would have fine effect. If he could visit this country and make addresses for it COMMA it would destroy Irish opposition which is being fanned into flame by professionals in this country.
                                        Tumulty.

The White House, March 27, 1919.

#38. Please do nothing in reference to dispute between railroad administration and Redfield's industrial board as to price of steel until you hear from me.   Tumulty.

T telegrams (WP, DLC).

From William Cox Redfield

Washington March 27, 1919

URGENT. For President from Redfield.

Success of Industrial Board, created by your authority, in reaching agreements for control of the price of steel, has been welcomed throughout country. Effect generally beneficial.

Have just returned from central west and northwest. Everywhere congratulations and new hopeful spirit. Other industries now acting similarly. Prospects would be bright for industries and labor except for unexpected refusal Railroad Administration to cooperate. Before my original cable asking authority appoint Industrial Board, important conference took place at office of Secretary Glass at which Director General Hines and myself present with Ritter[1] (for the president of Industrial Board), and many others. Ritter there explained necessity of government purchasing departments, including railroads, cooperating with Industrial Board, clearly stating that otherwise Board could not succeed. Hines and others agreed to buy current and reasonable requirements at reduced prices which Board might state, after careful study and discussion, were fair and reasonable. In conference with steel industry, Industrial Board found reasonable a price of $45 ton on Bessemer rails and $47 ton upon open hearth rails. This is a reduction of ten dollars ton below prices fixed by the former War Industries Board and Railroad Administration. Admit that three weeks ago the best quotation they could get was $52 ton on open hearth steel rails. At that time steel manufacturers stated they would close plants before accepting lower prices. Railroad Administration now refuse[s] to accept price found reasonable by Industrial Board, claiming it is two dollars too high. Coal industry now before Board. Seem willing to make reductions provided can be assured Railroad Administration will buy coal at prices decided upon. Railroad Administration refuses, preferring make prices independently of ultimate effect. This means using great purchasing power Railroad Administration as club to force price down from large operators, throwing upon individual consumers throughout country necessity paying higher prices, to provide working profit necessary because of low prices forced by Railroad Administration. Industrial Board carefully weighs all considerations having no objection to such prices as do not shift the burden to individual consumers. Failure Railroad Administration to cooperate threatens destruction work thus far done and if maintained will require Industrial Board suspend work and withdraw. Position is that industry has made marked concessions without reducing wages because Government has invited such action,

and now the Government itself through Railroad Administration
refuses to support the Board created with your approval and which
has carefully studied this matter, taking into account labor, capital
and interest of consumer generally throughout country. Respectfully urge that without delay instructions be cabled by you especially
to Railroad Administration and also to other government purchasing
departments to cooperate fully with Industrial Board. Difficult over-
state adverse effect on both business and social life of country by
stoppage of work Industrial Board now, but we cannot proceed
under existing conditions. Fullest consideration has been and will
be given to representations and evidence by buying departments,
respecting their needs and prices. No objection to governments
accepting lower prices than those reached by Industrial Board, if
such prices voluntarily offered, and if purchases thereunder are
not understood in too unreliable proportion so as throw burden on
private consumers. Railroad Administration, probably through sub-
ordinates, reflected on former railroad methods insists playing lone
hand. Essential this should be done, cooperate with Board. On
contrary they are endeavoring to break the market in behalf of the
Government itself and throw an unnecessary burden on everybody
else. Necessity getting business going, to provide employment, far
more important than any mere temporary difference. Several times
price on current government purchases affects private purchasers
disastrously, and may seriously affect coming victory loan. Believe
more important than anything else to pull together now, especially
when helpful spirit prevails in Board who desire to meet views
everyone fully as possible. It will be calamity to lose helpful spirit
industry and labor show; and this will certainly follow if purchasing
departments insist on going it alone.

Phillips   Acting

T telegram (WP, DLC).
  ¹ That is, William McClellan Ritter.

From Harry Augustus Garfield

Washington, March 27th, 1919.

For President Wilson.
  "Secretary Redfield has shown me his cable to you concerning
difficulties of Industrial Board. Please refer to my letter of March
4th to you concerning conference with Secretary Redfield, and to
its attached memorandum,¹ for my view of principle which should
be adopted by Government if Industrial situation is to be satisfactorily met. Without reference to my letter, both Secretary Redfield

and members of Industrial Board have expressed like opinions. I
have advised coal operators to meet Industrial board, and am myself
cooperating, but am satisfied that no progress will be made if railroads and purchasing departments of government do not cooperate
by placing normally a price found by Industrial Board to be fair. In
my judgement, in order to settle this cooperation, it is necessary
that Railroad Administration and departments of government receive strong statement, if not positive instructions from you. The
effort of the Industrial Board is not in conflict with plan to promote
public welfare by more effective cooperation between Government
of the U. S. and industry submitted at White House meeting February 26th as per memorandum which you have."[2] Garfield.

Phillips   Acting

T telegram (WP, DLC).
  [1] H. A. Garfield to WW, March 4, 1919, TLS (WP, DLC). Its significant portion reads
as follows: "The burden of what I had to say to Secretary Redfield was that in lowering
prices extreme care must be taken that the burden be equally borne, that the big
consumers of coal be not permitted to effect a reduction in their costs by throwing an
undue proportion of the reduction on coal or any other basic raw material. If the railroads,
for example, purchasing one-third of the entire output of bituminous coal, buy at substantially cost of production, and the steel companies and other great consumers follow
suit, it is clear that the domestic consumers and small manufacturers, constituting the
vast majority of the people, must pay disproportionately high prices, which is unfair."
The memorandum which Garfield enclosed is missing in WP, DLC.
  [2] That is, H. A. Garfield, "A PLAN TO PROMOTE THE PUBLIC WELFARE BY MORE EFFEC-
TIVE COOPERATION BETWEEN THE GOVERNMENT OF THE UNITED STATES AND INDUSTRY,"
Feb. 26, 1919, T MS (WP, DLC), which Garfield had enclosed in H. A. Garfield to WW,
March 3, 1919. The plan proposed the creation of a number of commissions, composed
of three representatives each of capital and labor and headed by a director appointed
by the President, to study the problems of the basic industries of the country and to
make appropriate recommendations to the President. The directors of the commissions
would form a so-called Industrial Cabinet, which would meet with the President at his
request to advise him with regard to industrial problems and policies.

Two Telegrams from Carter Glass

Washington March 27, 1919.

1335. For the President from Glass.

Redfield has shown me his cable to you concerning disagreement
between Industrial Board and Railroad Administration. Matter is a
very troublesome one, and I suggest that you suspend judgment
until you receive a further cable from me in which I shall give you
detailed statement of my views.   Phillips,   Acting.

T telegram (WP, DLC).

[Washington] March 27, 1919.

For the President from Glass.

The Industrial Board, appointed by Secretary Redfield, is proceeding along lines which I cannot approve and which I feel are fraught with danger to the country and to the Administration. At a conference of a number of Cabinet members including Redfield and others I had recommended an effort, under the guidance of the Department of Commerce, to bring about an agreement between the Railroad Administration and other Government agencies which had purchases to make on the one hand and industries of the country on the other as to fair prices at which the Government would buy. I felt that this would have a stimulating effect upon private enterprises and that, no doubt, prices which were acceptable to the Government would be accepted by private buyers. I made it very clear that nothing in the nature of an attempt to fix minimum prices should be made and that any such attempt would be contrary to the Sherman law and contrary to public policy. These views were concurred in by Daniels, Burleson, Hines and others. The Industrial Board of the Department of Commerce, however, has proceeded upon the other line and approved a scale of minimum prices below which it has announced the public should not expect to buy during the current year. These prices seem high to me and were declared by the Railroad Administration to be too high and unsatisfactory to it before the agreement was reached. In effect, therefore, the action of the Industrial Board, instead of fixing prices at which the Government would buy, is to fix prices for the general public above the level at which the Government is willing to buy. The newspapers have heralded the announcement of the action of the Industrial Board as carrying with it by implication the abandonment of the suit brought by the Government for the dissolution of the United States Steel Corporation as a monopoly under the Sherman law. I believe the action taken by the Industrial Board is thoroughly injurious and should be repudiated by you.

CC telegram (J. P. Tumulty Papers, DLC).

From Alexander Mitchell Palmer

Dear Mr. President: Washington, D. C. March 27, 1919.

I have your letter of the 12th instant, enclosing petition of Joseph F. Rutherford, et al., convicted under the Espionage Act and sentenced to twenty years at Atlanta.[1]

I have been much interested in this case because I think the

conduct of the defendants was bottomed on deep religious conviction, which is a situation that appeals to me strongly. Their chief
complaint, however, has been that they were not admitted to bail.
They were convicted nine months ago and before your letter was
received I had directed that if they would take immediate steps to
prosecute their appeal, the Department would withdraw objection
to their being released upon bail pending appeal.

This arrangement has now been carried out. The defendants have
agreed to file their briefs immediately, so that the case can be
disposed of in the appellate court in the very near future, and they
have been released on bail.[2]

Faithfully yours,   A Mitchell Palmer

TLS (WP, DLC).
    [1] About this case, see WW to A. M. Palmer, March 12, 1919, n. 1, Vol. 55.
    [2] Rutherford and his associates had applied again for bail in November 1918 and had
been released from the Atlanta penitentiary on March 26, 1919. As it turned out, the
United States Circuit Court of Appeals in New York, on May 15, 1919, annulled their
conviction on the ground that the original trial had not been fairly conducted and that
the attitude of the court had been "most prejudicial to the defendants." See the *New
York Times*, Nov. 10, 1918, March 27, 1919, and May 16, 1919.

From Josephus Daniels

My dear Mr. President: Paris, 27 March, 1919.

Just before leaving Washington, I called to see Mr. Bryan, who
has been quite ill but convalescent. A few days before I saw him,
the papers published that he was opposed to the League of Nations,
and he gave out a statement which was given wide publicity.

Mr. Bryan asked me to give you the enclosed,[1] which is a copy
of his statement published in the American papers and to say that
while he had suggested some amendments the importance of the
League was so transcendent and so necessary to the future of the
peace of the world that he was prepared to accept it without change
rather than to lose the benefits which can come in no other way
than through the united action of the free nations of the world.

He desires me to present his regards.

Faithfully yours,   Josephus Daniels

TLS (WP, DLC).
    [1] "Bryan Supports League of Nations. Suggests Amendments," T MS (WP, DLC). It
was published, e.g., in the *New York Times*, March 12, 1919. The League of Nations,
Bryan declared, was "the greatest step toward peace in a thousand years," and the idea
of substituting reason for force in the settlement of international disputes was "an epoch
making advance." To Bryan, the three most important points of the proposed Covenant
were the provisions for "deliberation before war," the reduction of armaments, and the
abolition of secret treaties. Even if the League did nothing more than put these three
provisions into effect, the American people would be justified in supporting it to the
utmost.
    However, Bryan continued, it would have been too much to expect that so great an

idea as the League of Nations could have been made perfect in such a short time. The Covenant contained certain defects which should be corrected, and the fullest discussion of proposed amendments should be invited. Although the President had achieved "the best he could," he would clearly benefit from "intelligent criticism" by supporters of the League. Bryan then went on to elaborate the amendments which, in his opinion, were necessary to make the League stronger and better.

From the Diary of Dr. Grayson

Friday, March 28, 1919.

The Council of Four, including the President, held two meetings again today, the morning conference, as usual, being held in the temporary White House, and the afternoon conference at the French War Ministry. In addition, a new organization was created, which was named the Council of Foreign Ministers, to which the Foreign Ministers of the four great powers were invited. They met with Pichon at the Quai d'Orsay and discussed the raising of the Austrian blockade and the revictualing of that country. They also discussed the German Schleswig frontier. Their function was not made very clear, but as a matter of fact they were simply expected to prepare data that could be passed on by the President and his colleagues when the time came. The situation in Hungary had made it necessary that something be done in order to combat the spread of Bolshevism there, and arrangements were made whereby foodstuffs would be diverted and sent directly into Austria to relieve distress there.

Clemenceau continued his excessive territorial demands, again urging that the Saar Basin should be turned over to France. The President asked him by what process of reasoning he arrived at this conclusion, inasmuch as the territory was essentially German. Clemenceau, however, insisted that a good many years ago this territory had belonged to France and that it simply would be turning it back in a proper way. Here Orlando interjected that it would be rather unfair to go back too many hundred years on a proposal of this kind, as it might embarrass his colleague, Lloyd-George, inasmuch as there was a time when England was a part of the Roman Empire. This amused the President very much and he laughed heartily, but Clemenceau failed to see any humor whatever in the statement.

Lloyd-George was late in arriving at the afternoon conference. On his arrival he addressed the President saying: "I apologize for being late." The President smilingly said: "I would hate to have to use the term the *late* Mr. Lloyd-George." The sally amused the pair of them very much.

The President was looking at map of Europe, which was hanging on the wall of his study, at the time Lloyd-George entered the room. Lloyd-George said: "I see you are studying your geography." The President said: "Yes, and I can't help but recall the feeling I had when as a boy I was studying geography. This seems as puzzling as it did when as a boy I studied all of the unknown country west of the Mississippi. The contrast is very striking to my mind. And in following out these maps it vividly recalls the study of geography in my boyhood days."

In the afternoon the Supreme War Council discussed the Polish situation again, without reaching a definite decision.

After dinner the President said: "I could not resist the opportunity to tell M. Tardieu just what I thought of him. It had come to my knowledge that he had been in communication with the leading Republicans in the United States in connection with the Peace Treaty, and also was confiding to them a great many of the difficult and complexing points that had arisen. I said to him with a smile on my face: 'M. Tardieu, I want to say to you that you are not helping France by communicating secrets to the leaders of the Republican party in America. You must remember that they are Nationalists and are selfish, and at this crucial time in the world's history sacrifices have to be made by all for the good of the peace of the world, and they (the Republicans) will not make any sacrifices for France. They will confine their interests solely to America. This is a time when everybody must give and take, not consider individual selves or individual countries. All should pull together for the good of the world and of mankind.' " Tardieu seemed extremely embarrassed and replied by saying that he was with the President, and in order to substantiate his position he said that he himself had written the speech delivered by M. de Billy, of the French High Commission, at Philadelphia, which had been commented upon so favorably by the American press two days ago.[1]

The President was completely fagged out this evening, after the last three days' continuous conferences. After dinner I amused him by repeating some of the stories told by the late Senator Ollie James of Kentucky. What seemed to amuse the President most was a speech which Ollie James made to me telling me that it was impossible for him to go to a horse-race the following day, much as he would like to go, because a friend had told him that if he were there he would give him a long-shot but could not do so until just before the horses went to the post. The Senator had said that he could not go because a bill would be up for final decision that would tax hundreds of children yet unborn. The Senator grew so eloquent in arguing in favor of his going that he converted himself. After telling the President a few other stories, he seemed greatly refreshed. He said to me: "These stories have had a real tonic effect upon me. My head feels rested. I appreciate Ollie James' arguments, because I have tried to write things and could not convince myself."

¹ Edouard de Billy, the Deputy French High Commissioner to the United States, had spoken on March 23 at the opening of an exhibition of French war pictures. Billy urged that Americans not be deceived by false rumors and reports about the position of France on certain vital issues. He stated that, despite reports to the contrary, France still greatly needed, and was very grateful for, American financial aid to relieve and restore her devastated areas. He quoted recent speeches of Tardieu himself on the relationship of the peace treaty and the League of Nations: "The treaty of peace and the League of Nations can only be one question, the League of Nations can be founded only on the treaty of peace, and on the other hand the very principles on which the League will be founded will give their lasting value to the clauses of the treaty." Billy also warned against rumors as to how the peace negotiations were progressing: "It is not possible that, on such important and numerous questions, on which depends, for many decades, the future of the world, the opinions of the whole delegations should be, at first unanimous. There must be differences at first. We must not allow ourselves to see in these differences anything else than the frank expressions of honest minds seeking the truth, all having come to the peace table with the utmost good-will." *New York Times*, March 24, 1919.

From the Diary of Colonel House

March 28, 1919.

Lloyd George asked me to come to lunch with him for the purpose of discussing the Russian question. However, when I got there, he had just returned from the President's house and showed signs of considerable excitement. It seems that the long expected row between either Clemenceau and the President, or Lloyd George and Clemenceau, had actually come. I am sorry it should have happened to be the President rather than Lloyd George. They came near calling one another names. The trouble arose over the question of the Western Boundaries and of the Sarre Valley. The President told Clemenceau that the French were bringing up territorial questions that had nothing to do with the war aims of anybody, and that no one had heard of their intention to annex the Sarre Valley until after the Armistice had been signed. Clemenceau grew angry at this and said that the President favored the Germans. The President replied that such a statement was untrue and that Clemenceau knew that it was.

Clemenceau then stated that if they did not receive the Sarre Valley, he would not sign the Treaty of Peace. To this the President replied, "Then if France does not get what she wishes, she will refuse to act with us. In that event do you wish me to return home?" Clemenceau answered, "I do not wish you to go home, but I intend to do so myself," and in a moment he left the house.

George said the President was very angry. It gave George a wholesome respect for the President which I augmented by telling him that he was the most difficult man I ever knew when aroused. That his anger was not like his, George's, or mine, quick to come and quick to go, but that it remained permanently and he would never get over this morning's scene.

I took this occasion to say that I had warned the Germans before they brought us into the war that they would forever regret arousing Wilson; that if we entered the war, he would use our last man and our last dollar to beat them. George was impressed by my talk and declared he had no intention of falling out with the President. He expressed a fervent relief that most of the questions between the United States and Great Britain had been settled.

We had a delightful lunch and did not talk "shop." I told him during lunch of my friend Captain Bill McDonald[1] and some of his exploits which seemed to amuse him greatly.

It was after lunch that we again took up the Peace Conference troubles. We got a map and went into the question of the Western Boundaries. He is in favor of giving France a part of the 1814 line but not all of it. He hoped I would go across the street and sooth[e] my distinguished friend, so that when they had their afternoon meeting he would be in a more amiable frame of mind.

We scarcely touched upon the Russian question except that I told him what I was doing and asked him to postpone any action on his part until I could get a more matured plan for our consideration. He is sympathetic toward a settlement with Russia and I think will meet me half way.

I found the President in conference with our financial experts, therefore, Mrs. Wilson and I talked for a half hour. At my suggestion, she invited Lady Northcliffe[2] to luncheon tomorrow. I suggested that she break it to the President gently that I wanted Melville Stone[3] invited to lunch within the next few days since he was leaving for home almost at once. When the President came in she broke the news to him by saying: "the Colonel has invited himself and Melville Stone for lunch on Monday." The President gave a whimsical sigh and replied, jestingly, "Oh dear, I shall be glad when I am out of office so I can eat with gentlemen."

The President told the same story about the trouble this morning that George did, so I shall not repeat. He is sending for Mezes, as we planned yesterday, and will ask him to do what I have already requested in regard to the boundaries. The President asking Mezes direct relieves me of embarrassment with my colleagues since Mezes can say he is doing the work by direction of the President.

I urged the President to bring the British into harmony with his position on the French boundary proposals. The British and ourselves are practically in agreement, therefore, I thought it would be a tactical mistake to have the United States take a stand in which she was not supported by Great Britain. I advised yielding a little in order to secure harmony so that the accusation could not be made that we were unreasonable. He promised to do this.

[1] William Jesse McDonald, about whom see the index references in Vol. 25 of this series.
[2] Mary Elizabeth Milner Harmsworth, Lady Northcliffe, wife of Alfred Charles William Harmsworth, Viscount Northcliffe.
[3] That is, Melville Elijah Stone, general manager of the Associated Press.

A Memorandum by Robert Lansing

INDICATIONS OF AN EXPLOSION.
(p.m.) March 28, 1919.

It looks as if the negotiations now being carried on by the President and the Premiers were reaching a very critical stage. Colonel House told me this evening that he had seen Lloyd George who described a meeting at the President's residence in the Place des Etats Unis this morning at which the President and Clemenceau quarreled bitterly, Clemenceau finally leaving the house.

The "Big Four" had been discussing the Saar Valley and neighboring territory. Clemenceau insisted that its cession and economic control by France of certain mining districts had been among the chief war aims of France. The President asked for an explanation asserting that France had never disclosed this purpose. The discussion continued and grew more heated until Clemenceau directly charged the President with being "the friend of Germany." To this the President replied that Clemenceau was deliberately stating what he knew to be untrue and that it was apparent that Clemenceau desired him to go home. "The Tiger" was furious and replied that he did not want the President to go but that he himself would. With that he got up and left the room.[1]

This is possibly not exact as it comes to me through two hands. However it is near enough to show the bitterness which exists.

Lloyd George further said that the President's great chin protruded and his jaws set in a most pugnacious manner, while he (Lloyd George) would not care to have the President look at him in the way he did at Clemenceau.

Knowing the President as I do, I am sure that he will not forgive, much less forget, this affair. From now on he will look upon Clemenceau as an antagonist. He will suspect his every suggestion and doubt his honesty. The President is a wonderful hater. Possibly Clemenceau is the same. It looks like a battle royal between them.

As to the episode itself, I am glad that it occurred, because it will show the President the Clemenceau policy, which has been to wear down Germany's power of resistence and then to insist on the most extravagant demands. France would never have dared make these demands while the German armies were intact, but now a weakened Germany is considered an easy prey, however dishonorable such procedure may be.

Clemenceau possesses an utterly ruthless spirit of revenge. He gloats over torturing Germany in every way and encourages Weygand and the rest to give another twist to the screws. His supreme desire seems to be to humiliate the Germans until they are so goaded to madness that they will resist their tormentors, when the armies of Foch will have excuse to march triumphantly into the heart of Germany.

Clemenceau's determination to grind Germany to powder and Marshal Foch's longing to complete the conquest of Germany now that she is powerless are today, in my opinion, serious obstacles to peace. The sooner the President realizes this the better for the world. I think that this disagreeable episode at his house will open his eyes to the truth.

"The Tiger" will find that in arousing the wrath of President Wilson he has set in motion a force which even his fierce and pitiless will cannot check. Possibly before long the President will be treading on a tiger-skin, or the jungle-beast will draw in his claws and begin to purr again. However it has come to "a showdown" and I am glad of it.

The report of this incident caused me to say to Colonel House that I heartily wished that the President had never come to Europe because it subjected him to such embarrassments, deprived him of the position of superior authority, and had caused him to lose steadily the exalted position which he held in the eyes of the people and to lose even more his influence with foreign statesmen.

The Colonel replied, "Yes, I quite agree with you. It was a mistake for him to come at all. However we must make the best of it."

This statement is extremely interesting because it was the Colonel, I am sure, who proposed and even urged the President's coming. It was a most serious blunder, and has worked badly here and still worse at home.

T MS (R. Lansing Papers, DLC).
[1] For another corroborative account of this episode, which it would be redundant to reprint, see the remarks by Isaiah Bowman printed in Edward M. House and Charles Seymour, eds., *What Really Happened at Paris: The Story of the Peace Conference, 1918-1919, by American Delegates* (New York, 1921), pp. 464-65.

From the Diary of Vance Criswell McCormick

March 28 (Friday) [1919]

Was called by the President to his house, with Davis and Lamont, to discuss a new proposal of Clemenceau and Klotz on Reparations.[1] Same old plan of leaving open in the treaty amount Germany is to pay, in other words, Germany is to give her signed check with the amount blank. We advised "Chief" it would not do, to which he assented. . . .

During the meeting at the President's house this afternoon the President told us of a spat he had at the morning meeting with Clemenceau. They were discussing the Saar Coal Basin and the President protested against it going to France and Clemenceau told the President he was pro-German; whereupon the Chief called him down and asked Clemenceau whether he wanted him to leave; whereupon Clemenceau cooled down and came off his high horse and everything was lovely again. I can see these final demands and decisions of peace negotiations getting on all the Chiefs' nerves and the President seems very tired.

[1] About which, see n. 1 to the Mantoux minutes printed at March 28, 1919, 11 a.m.

From the Diary of Ray Stannard Baker

March 28 1919

The difficulties deepen. I went down to the President's house at 11 place des Etats-Unis at 6:30 & had a talk with the President & found him impatient & somewhat discouraged. After a whole week devoted to conferences on Reparations, he said that the French had suddenly appeared with a wholly new plan. The weeks work had gone for nothing! A kind of silly optimism to the effect that "progress is being made" has generally prevailed—& this is the answer. There has been no progress at all. He said that at every point, the French objected & demanded. He said:

"We spend an hour reasoning with Clemenceau, getting him around to an agreement & find when we go back to the original question Clemenceau stands just where he did at the beginning."

It seems that they were near an open rupture. The French brought in their claim to the Saar valley & stated their historical rights, reaching back to 1814. The President said at once, & plainly, that he considered that the French claim to the territory & the people as contrary to the terms of the Armistice & to the fourteen points upon which they had all agreed. At this Clemenceau broke out: "Then I must resign." To this the President said he could make no comment, but suggested that if M. Clemenceau were not prepared to abide by the solemnly accepted terms of the Armistice that he (the President) might as well go home. To this Clemenceau responded hastily that he did not of course suggest any such action.

The "four" have had to consult their experts, and it is likely that the whole thing will now go over until next week.

I suggested to the President that I thought, it being near the close of the week, that the *Four* ought to issue some kind of a communique, at least giving the world some inkling of what was going on.

"How can we?" he asked, "we have nothing to report. We have actually accomplished nothing definite & if we were to tell the truth we should have to put the blame exactly where it belongs—upon the French."

"Isn't it time that this situation was known?" I asked. "Why shouldn't you come out squarely & tell what the trouble is?"

"The time has not come yet," he said.

"Then you should let some of our correspondents do it," I said.

"Well," he responded, "if some of them are indiscreet enough to tell the truth I shall have no objections."

I took this for a permission & told several of the correspondents— Grasty, Swope, Oulahan[1] & some of the press association men how the land lay & some, at least, of the situation is going across to America. As a matter of fact the Peace Conference is getting into deeper & deeper water—disagreeing about indemnities & reparations, both Clemenceau & Lloyd-George fearful of accepting too little lest they be turned out by their own governments. L.G. is now reaping the whirlwind of his election promises.

On the other hand if they make the terms of the treaty too stiff they fear that Germany will not sign. In the meantime Bolshevism creeps nearer daily: there is unrest all over the world.

[1] That is, Charles Henry Grasty, Herbert Bayard Swope, and Richard Victor Oulahan.

From the Diary of Edith Benham

March 28, 1919

I think I wrote you that Tardieu is playing a double game with the Republicans and is supposed to be the one responsible for the anti-Wilson attacks before we left, which have subsided now. He came here yesterday and the President said to some of the other conferees, "You know Mr. Tardieu is a very credulous person for he believes all the Republicans tell him." Then he continued to say that the Republicans were now representing the nationalists as against an international party and were in consequence the worst friends France could have. He says that Orlando is often amusing. Today the French were laying claim to certain territory because they had it 104 years ago. Orlando said, "If we go on back in this way, we will lay claim to all the territory of the Roman Empire."

The President is surely working at high pressure and I don't know how long he can stand it with conferences all day long and no fresh air. He looks very tired and today at luncheon seemed thoroughly down and out. One of the few times I have ever seen him so. Fortunately Mrs. Wilson keeps well.

Mantoux's Notes of Two Meetings of the Council of Four

March 28, 1919, 11 a.m.

Clemenceau. M. Klotz is going to explain to you the official view of the French government on the general matter of reparations to be asked of the German government.

Klotz. In the Armistice agreement we compelled the Germans to accept a clause worded as follows: "Reparation for damages." We must analyze this term and determine the amount of reparations due.

Today we do not know the price of materials and the price of labor, and it is very difficult for us to know what repairs will cost. The diversity of figures which have been submitted to us shows how imprudent it is to commit ourselves to estimates which will be considered by some as exaggerated, and which might, however, be lower in reality.

I have prepared a study analyzing and classifying the damages. If the list is too long or if there are omissions, we welcome all observations which may be offered. I did not attempt to give evaluations: I indicated qualities and not quantities. Who will fix the figures? If our governments do it today, they could be wrong either to the detriment of their own people or to the detriment of their associates. Regional commissions must be established, working according to fixed rules, as well as a central inter-Allied commission which will collect and evaluate the figures.

We want only our due. What is not subject to debate is that we are entitled to reparations; they will be estimated at their exact value. The document which I present to you only foresees a sum to be paid by the enemy, as an installment on his debt, for one or two years. Later, the commission will determine annual payments according to the debt decided upon and will fix the duration of payment.

M. Klotz explains the outline of his plan.[1]

Klotz. The advantage of this system is its absolute fairness among us and even toward the enemy himself. We cannot, at this time, fix the figures without a great element of doubt. If we state a total sum, the Germans might say to us that it is excessive. This system

[1] "DISPOSITIONS À IMPOSER À L'ALLEMAGNE CLAUSES FINANCIÈRES, 28 *mars 1919*, AVANT-PROJET PRÉSENTÉ PAR M. L. L. KLOTZ AU CONSEIL SUPRÊME," printed in Burnett, *Reparation at the Paris Peace Conference*, I, 726-54. It is abstracted by Burnett, I, 195-96, as follows:

"Section I: (1) Germany to compensate all damages; (2) to restore in 6 months all stolen movables and in 1 year equivalents of destroyed movables; (3) regional commissions to compile claims, supervised by central commission; (4) Germany also to return to Allies or nationals their property on German territory and reëstablish all rights of agreements formed before Nov. 11, 1918; no Allied property in enemy territory may be taxed for reparation.

"Section II: (5) annulment of pre-Armistice contracts between Allied and enemy nationals; (6) renunciation by Germany of all benefits of Treaties of Bucharest, Brest-Litovsk, etc.; (7) renunciation by Germany of all participation in foreign economic or financial bodies; (8) execution by Germany of all financial and economic engagements with nationals of her former allies; (9) surrender by Germany to Allies of all rights and property in her territory held by her former allies; (10) cost of Army of Occupation to be borne by Germany; (11) cost of repatriation of Allied and of maintenance of enemy prisoners to be borne by Germany; (12) all foregoing provisions applicable to Alsace-Lorraine; (13) right of Russia reserved for reparation.

"Section III: (14) restitution directly to each Allied government; (15) Germany to pay in gold dollars at rate of exchange for Dec., 1918—16 milliard marks in 3 months and 4 milliard marks in next 9 months, and annuities beginning with 8 milliard marks for second year and increasing each year by 2 percent over the preceding year, to be paid until all claims discharged; (16) reparation to be first charge, then claims to Allied nationals assumed before war; (17) Allies will assume fair proportion of public debt for ceded territories but France exempt for Alsace-Lorraine; (18) Allies will maintain occupation and complete control of German foreign trade until debt discharged, and special sanctions in case of default.

"Annex 1: (I) Reparation to each Allied Power by Germany and allies in proportion to military strength furnished by each Allied Power on each Allied front; (II) categories of property damage include various sorts of indirect damage, but do not appear to embrace war costs nor damage to military property; (III) categories of personal damage seem to include indirect damage, but pensions are not specifically mentioned.

"Annex 2: Technical provisions for restitution.

"Annex 3: Technical provisions for valuation of damage.

"Annex 4: Technical provisions for execution of Article 4.

"Annex 5: Technical provisions for execution of Article 5.

"Annex 6: Technical provisions for execution of Article 6.

"Annex 7: Provisions for Alsace-Lorraine.

"Annex 8: (Methods of Payment): Germany to file specified list of assets with Allies and figures of industrial production of certain commodities (coal, wood, potash, etc.). Immediate payments to be made in gold, silver, securities, bills of exchange, foreign bonds; also in specified quantities of oil, coal, wood, etc.; also cattle, boats, materials of transport, etc.—these in addition to restitution provisions; also German property held abroad. Inter-Allied Financial Commission of the German Debt: authorized to receive, evaluate, apportion, direct payments and to specify commodities in which payment to be made. Commission to control certain taxes and monopolies of Germany; has power to declare moratorium on payment, to take payments in marks and to claim new taxes as source of revenue; may propose sanctions of occupation or blockade in case of noncompliance.

"Table I: Schedule of annuities increasing 2 percent each year. Present value at 5 percent of these annuities for 35 years is about 162 milliard marks; for 50 years, about 194 milliard."

is more flexible; we only ask for a payment on account. We envisage a method to fix the amount of damages according to the definition given to them and to determine the number of annual payments.

If we can agree on this basis, the day when we find ourselves in the presence of the enemy negotiators, there will be no discussion about the figures. They have already accepted the principle in the text of the Armistice agreement; debate can only center on the nature of losses admitted to the list of damages and thus will be limited and facilitated.

M. Klotz reads the articles defining material damages and, at the request of Mr. Lloyd George, the article defining damages to persons.

Wilson. We must not enter here into an examination of details but decide on the principles. The idea is to determine the nature of damages for which reparations are due without fixing any figure, but while obliging the Germans to agree to pay our bill in proportion as it is presented to them. If I have clearly understood your general proposal, that is the question which we are going to discuss.

Lloyd George. I am also of the opinion that we should leave the examination of the details to the specialists. I consider the proposal presented to us as new and very important. To fix a principle and leave the determination of the figures to arbiters who will, moreover, hear the views of the Germans—that does not trouble me. I believe that one of our financial advisers, Mr. Keynes, has already made a proposal of this kind.

Mr. Keynes is introduced.

Keynes. Our uncertainty chiefly concerned Germany's capacity to pay. We proposed to tell the Germans: "Here is what you owe; but we have not yet determined how much you are able to pay." It is this second point that we will have to discuss with them.

Klotz. The system I present to you today is analogous to the judicial procedure in the case of a railroad accident: the victim immediately receives a sum which allows him to pay the doctor, and then damages and interest are fixed by expert opinion.

Wilson. My objection is that this system would be tantamount to asking Germany to extend us a blank check. Suppose that we went before one of our legislative assemblies and said: "We cannot determine the figure that such and such large public works will cost; we ask you for the authority to undertake them, and we will tell you afterward what they will have cost." The American Congress could never vote for a motion of this kind. Nothing is more difficult than to know the cost of projects for which there is no strictly limited appropriation. There will be large contracts for repairs, and it would be dangerous not to limit their cost. Germany will think it more severe to accept an unlimited obligation than to consent to pay even a very considerable sum.

This amounts to asking Germany to place at our disposal all that she possesses indefinitely. I understand that we should ask Germany to pay on account; but we must not forget that the first years will be the most difficult and those during which, as we have all recognized, it will be necessary to allow Germany the time and means to recover economically.

Mr. Keynes' proposal was very much different. He says: let us agree on what Germany owes us. No one of us knows what she is able to pay; that we are ready to discuss with the German representatives in order to discover how much and in what way Germany will pay. In a case of insufficient means, the burden of proof would be cast upon her. That is very different from what has been proposed to us.

Lloyd George. I recognize this difference; but there is no contradiction between the two proposals, and they can even be easily combined. I should say that my first impression is favorable to the plan presented by M. Klotz.

I accept the objection made by President Wilson against the procedure which would consist of presenting the bill of our expenses as they occur. We cannot each make our own reconstruction and then come and say: here is what this has cost us. But we can say to the Germans: "We know that you are not in a position to reimburse us for all that the war has cost us, as we would have the right to require. That is why we spoke in the Armistice agreement only of reparation for damages. We define damages by distinguishing between damages to property and damages to persons, and we give you precise details about the meaning of these terms; as for saying what this sum is, that is impossible for us at present. We are appointing a commission which will determine the figures; you will be given a hearing, and the approximate figure at which the commission arrives will be that which you will have to pay."

I see great advantages in not making known today the total figure of what Germany owes us. You may be sure that, whatever the figure is, many people in England as well as in France will exclaim at once: "It is too little!" M. Klotz's formula gives us a way to avoid discussions which might ensue in our respective parliaments. If our parliaments should disapprove because we have not asked enough, what will happen to the governments which succeed us in trying to do the impossible?

Another reason to welcome this project is that I do not much like discussion among us about the proportion of our claims; they are disagreeable, and they lead us to contest this or that figure. I prefer to have a commission which will study the facts. What is more important than the proportion of 1 to 2 or whatever other, as you please, is the maintenance of a good entente between France and England. We intend to continue our alliance with you, to come to your immediate aid in case of aggression—and you know that we generally do even better than we promise. We told you to expect the aid of six British divisions at the beginning of the war, and we sent you up to sixty. Our American cousins rather resemble us in this. I attach a supreme importance to good relations between us, and to all that can preserve them.

This does not contradict what Mr. Keynes has said. Let us suppose that the commission arrives at some total figure, five billion pounds sterling, for example; it remains to be seen how much the Germans can pay and how this sum should be divided into annual payments. At this point Mr. Keynes' system might be applied.

Orlando. As for the principle, I adhere completely to M. Klotz's plan. It offers the great advantage which Mr. Lloyd George has just indicated, that of avoiding discussions, very dangerous as well among us—for each will say that he is receiving too little—as with the Germans who will say that they are being asked for too much. The Germans will not be able to refuse to sign a clause which is only the detailed explanation of the obligation they have already taken in signing the Armistice.

President Wilson's objection regarding the danger of an unlimited obligation is serious. But it is better to wait until the Germans make it themselves; and there would be a way to overcome it, which would be to fix a maximum figure of payment. However, I do not think that we should do this at present. It is better to stand purely and simply upon the text accepted in the Armistice agreement.

The Germans will tell us: "Our means of payment are limited." Undoubtedly, but the moral advantage will be ours, for Germany, having agreed to repair damages which she caused, would be declaring herself incapable of paying what she should. On the other hand, if we fix a figure right now, Germany will say that the figure is excessive and that we seek to enrich ourselves by war. We thus place on our side not only the reality, but also the advantageous appearance of justice. If Germany says that she cannot pay, it will be up to her to prove it.

Lloyd George. We must plan for a means of reaching decisions if, in the commission, there are differences of view among our representatives. I should propose to accept as an arbiter a person who would be appointed by the President of the United States.

Wilson. I must reserve my judgment on the plan which has been presented to us. I see certain difficulties with it, and I have not yet been able to examine the details. I fear that this commission tha we will establish, like the one at Spa, will only report continually about the ingenious means used by the Germans to elude their obligations. Imagine the correspondence which we now receive from Spa continuing for thirty years!

Lloyd George. The estimate of damages and the payment are two different things. The commission envisaged by this plan would have as its task to determine the sums due. That does not mean that we would abandon the system mentioned earlier of having a commission fix, from year to year, the amount of annual payments and the sum of the total payments.

March 28, 1919, 4 p.m.

Tardieu. The region of the Saar and Landau have been French lands for a long, long time. Landau has been part of the kingdom of France since 1648. Saarlouis was built by Louis XIV. The two regions also took part in the Revolution, and their representatives were at the *fête de la Fédération* among those who swore in the name of all the French provinces to unite voluntarily to form but one single nation. In 1793, Landau suffered a famous siege and resisted heroically. The city was finally delivered, and the Convention declared by a solemn vote that Landau had merited well of the *Patrie*. It is at this time that Saarbrücken became French, amid the immense enthusiasm which has been described by Goethe,[2] and the petitions of the people preserved in our national archives provide enduring testimony to it.

M. Tardieu reads several of these documents.

Tardieu. If we had only isolated documents they would be of little value. But they express the unanimous sentiment of the entire population of every part of these territories. The following years give these countries a new reason to attach themselves to France, as a result of the excellent administration of Napoleon. It is then that the mines of the Saar were discovered and developed. Napoleon created an École des Mines and had maps of the coal basin drawn.

When Saarlouis and Saarbrücken were annexed by Prussia, it is an agent for the Westphalian mine owners, himself a native of the Saar region, who was the adviser to the Prussian state to prepare the annexation. One of the first clauses of the act of cession envisaged that the maps of the coal beds be handed over to the Prussian administration. In 1814, the allies deemed it impossible to take the Saar region from France; and to bring them to this decision

[2] Tardieu was in error here. There is no reference in any of the writings of Goethe to the reception of the French armies by the inhabitants of Saarbrücken in 1793.

Miss Benham, Dr. Grayson, Mrs. Wilson, and the President examining a German gun emplacement at Coincy on March 23, 1919

Sir Maurice Hankey

Lt. Paul Joseph Mantoux, with the cross of Knight of
the Legion of Honor

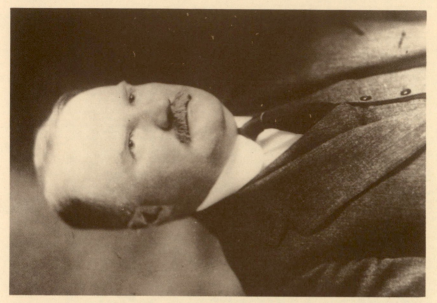

Charles Homer Haskins

James Wycliffe Headlam-Morley

Bernard Baruch, Norman H. Davis, Vance C. McCormick, Herbert C. Hoover

Jan Christiaan Smuts

Béla Kun

Louis Lucien Klotz

required the return from Elba, Waterloo, and the strong insistence of Prussia, which knew the value of this territory.

Here, then, are regions which became French voluntarily and which were separated from France by force, not in 1814 but in 1815. The opinion of the English plenipotentiaries, which has been preserved, is expressed in Castlereagh's phrase drawing attention to the danger of taking from France populations deeply attached to her. Metternich wrote: "Prussia has taken account neither of justice nor of decency."

Many inhabitants of the ceded territories emigrated during the following years; those who stayed called themselves "Prussians by force," *Musspreussen*. French sentiment manifested itself many times in both Saarlouis and Landau. At the time of the Crimean War, demonstrations in favor of France took place, as well as many enlistments in the French army. In 1865, William I, visiting the Saar basin, was received there very coldly. In 1866, Chlodwig von Hohenlohe,[3] the future Chancellor of the Empire, wrote about Landau: "These populations would not object if events should return them to France."

Finally, a still more precious piece of testimony is that of the great Prussian historian, Treitschke,[4] who, recognizing the age-old fidelity of these peoples to France, sees therein proof that they are true Germans—for fidelity, he says, is a Prussian virtue.

Wilson. I would like to know at what period the different parts of this territory were acquired by France. What is the proportion of those which belonged to her from the seventeenth century?

Tardieu. About two thirds. Saarbrücken became French only in 1793. I would remark, in addition, that the frontier of 1792 was more extensive than that of 1814.

The recent reception of French troops in Saarlouis and Landau has been the same as in Alsace, and the extreme reserve imposed upon the French authorities could not prevent them from stating the desire of the peoples to be reunited to France. The question poses itself in other parts of Europe which have been taken by conquest from their former possessors: we have here two little bits of French land united to France by their own will, separated from her against their will, and their desire to return to France has endured.

No doubt one finds there elements of the population who represent the conquerors of the last century. But must one sacrifice

[3] Chlodwig Karl Viktor, Prince of Hohenlohe-Schillingfürst and of Ratibor and Corvey, Bavarian Prime Minister and Minister of Foreign Affairs, 1866-1870; Chancellor of the German Empire, 1894-1900.
[4] That is, Heinrich von Treitschke.

the indigenous population out of consideration for them? These are territories which border France and that France considers her own. In other words, the systematic colonization of these regions by Prussia should not be invoked against the old inhabitants—the victims of this colonization—but should, on the contrary, be counted as an argument in their favor. This is the historical aspect.

From an economic point of view, France has three reasons to claim these territories: in the first place, the relations of Alsace-Lorraine with the Saar basin, which has always furnished to it the coal upon which its industrial life is based; in the second place, France's situation with regard to coal. Now, just after the war and after the reintegration of Alsace-Lorraine, our annual consumption had risen seventy-five million tons, while our production has fallen to twenty-four million. There will therefore be a deficit of fifty-one million tons, which is more than two thirds of our needs. If we are not to be abandoned to economic dependence upon foreign producers of coal, especially Germany, we must be able to exploit the Saar basin to our profit.

In the third place, it must be recalled that the destruction of our mines of the Nord was carried out by the Germans according to a systematic plan. Our basin in the departments of the Nord and of the Pas-de-Calais supplied industries which the Germans considered competitors. The documents we possess show that the destruction of our mines was part of a plan of economic warfare, and this destruction was complete: 220 pits, all surface installations, have disappeared—which represents a production of twenty million tons; a work force of 100,000 inhabitants was reduced to unemployment.

M. Loucheur is introduced.

Lloyd George. What is the annual production of the Saar basin?

Tardieu.   17,500,000 tons, including

4 million in Lorraine proper;

4.5 million beyond the frontier of 1814;

and 9.5 million in the territories ceded to Prussia in 1815.

This cession, if so well justified from the point of view of reparation, will not have the effect of depriving Germany of indispensable resources. In fact, in 1913 Germany produced 191 million tons of coal, without taking account of lignite. The Saar basin, if we subtract the part included in the former department of the Moselle, produced only about thirteen millions.

Loucheur. In addition, the basin's production, except two million tons, is consumed either on the spot or in Alsace-Lorraine.

Tardieu. As for the transfer of the mines to the French state, that is an easy thing, for before 1814 these mines were the property of the state; they passed into the hands of the Prussian state and even today, out of 116,000 hectares of mining land, 114,000 are owned by the state. Thus it is possible to accomplish the cession without violating private interests.

Under Prussian rule, the interests of the Saar basin were sacrificed to the interests of the Westphalian basin. Prussia opposed building a system of canals in the Saar and Moselle valleys, and the Canal des Houillères, which serves this region, only opens on to French territory. It is Germany herself which, in order to protect Westphalia, allowed the avenues of transport to be directed exclusively toward Nancy and Strasbourg.

In summary, our claims fall neatly into two categories. In the first place, we ask for our historical frontier, populations united to France by their own will, separated from her by force, and subsequently mingled with German poulations by systematic colonization. In the second place, we ask that Alsace-Lorraine be able to live, that France be not in a state of excessive dependence upon foreign countries for her coal needs, and that reparation be made to us for the systematic destruction of our mines of the Nord. To do that, this coal basin, first discovered and developed by French genius, must be returned to France.

Loucheur. From the industrial point of view, the Saar and Lorraine form a single entity. Half of the cast iron going to the Saar steel mills comes from Lorraine proper. All the iron ore used in this region comes from the mines of Lorraine. So true is this that, a few days ago, an important metallurgist from the Saar told one of my representatives: "Germany made war for ore; today we must go over to the side which has the ore." Without the Saar, the serious deficit of coal which France suffers would be considerably increased by the needs of the industries of Alsace and Lorraine.

Lloyd George. Let us suppose that France had a right to exploit these mines: could she increase their production?

Loucheur. Yes, at a rate of three or four million tons per year.

MM. Tardieu and Loucheur withdraw.

Lloyd George. Here is a new proposal which was handed to me this morning by a certain number of our English experts who reached agreement with some of your American experts.[5] Their conclusion is that the historical argument is dubious, and that the solid base of the French claim to the Saar basin is the principle of compensation. The solution they propose consists of placing all the mines in a small autonomous state, the mines themselves becoming the

[5] See the Enclosure printed with C. H. Haskins to WW, March 29, 1919.

property of France by way of reparation. The region would enjoy complete autonomy; it would have its own legislation, its schools, its police; it would be subject to the military law of neither France nor Germany. Above local authority, French sovereignty could be established, which would be comparable to British sovereignty over the Isle of Man and over the Anglo-Norman islands which are, in truth, perfectly independent small states, not even subject to conscription during the war.

Considering the systematic destruction of the French mines, those who drafted this report declare that it does not seem adequate to establish a purely temporary rule in the Saar region.

This proposal came to my knowledge this very day. If we are disposed toward accepting it in principle, it would be necessary that a definite plan be presented by France. It seems to me that that merits examination.

Clemenceau. I agree.

Lloyd George. I should say that concerning Landau our experts are opposed to the annexation of this territory. You must well understand the spirit of the British people: they fear doing anything which could repeat against the Germans the error committed by Germany herself when she annexed Alsace-Lorraine.

Wilson. I might observe that France never raised this question with us before the beginning of the present negotiations; it is thus a question which must be added to those for which we were prepared to seek solutions. In my mind, it is part of the entire economic problem raised by the war.

From an economic point of view, the Saar region must be treated as a unity, for this unity now extends beyond the small region located between the frontiers of 1814 and those of 1815.

It is a fact that the Germans have ruined the mines of northern France, depriving France for a certain number of years of the production of twenty million tons. It is a fact that this damage was caused systematically, and obviously some means of compensation must be found. Repairing the mines of the Nord will take a long time; however, the approximate number of years required can be calculated. We should find a compensation in kind, and, if possible, in the Saar region. Up to this point, no difficulty.

But it is desirable to preserve the unity of this industrial region; it is necessary not to carve it up in such a way that the coal it produces would be used only in a part of its area. The regions which use this coal must remain together. My principle accepted, France, if she has these mines at her disposal, will be obliged to allow the coal to be transported north as well as south, as previously. But if the owner of these mines, whoever it is, agrees to this, then the question of ownership becomes a mere question of sentiment.

I am ready to establish a plan: (1) to assure France compensation in kind during the period necessary to repair French mines; (2) to assure the integrity of this industrial unity which is the Saar region. Both can be done without annexation and without violation of our principles. We must not forget that these principles obligate us to Germany, to whom we made definite commitments at the time of the Armistice. If we do not wish to place ourselves in the wrong and break our word, we must not interpret our own principles too generously to our benefit. I say this solemnly: let us avoid acting in a manner which would risk creating sympathies for Germany; neither let us seek to interpret our promises with a lawyer's finesse.

Lloyd George. Please allow me to protest on behalf of lawyers.

Wilson. The question being asked here also applies to other parts of Europe, in the Danzig region, to Teschen, where the discussion between Czechs and Poles recalls in many ways this problem of the Saar. Mr. Lloyd George said the other day: if you try to establish frontiers according to historical or strategic considerations—and I will add, economic—there will be no limit to the claims. We must hold to the principles we have enunciated, and, in that way, we will not be wronging France.

Clemenceau. Maybe, provided France agrees.

Wilson. There is no nation more intelligent than the French nation. If you permit me to explain my point of view frankly to her, I have no fear of her judgment. Undoubtedly, if they saw that we were not applying the same principle everywhere, the French would not accept a solution which appeared unfavorable to them; but if we show them that we are doing our best to act justly everywhere in all analogous problems, the sense of justice which is in the heart of the French people will rise up to answer to me: "You are right." I have such an exalted idea of the spirit of the French nation that I believe she will always accept a principle founded on justice and applied with equity.

The annexation of these regions to France does not have a sufficient historical basis. One part of these territories was French only for twenty-two years; the remainder has been separated from France for over one hundred years. I realize that the map of Europe is covered with ancient injustices which cannot all be redressed. What is just is to assure France the compensation which is due her for the loss of her coal mines, and to give the entire Saar region the guarantees which it needs for the utilization of its own coal. If we do that, we will do all that could reasonably be asked of us.

Clemenceau. I will keep in mind the words and excellent intentions of President Wilson. He eliminates sentiment and memory: it is there that I have a reservation about what has just been said. The President of the United States disregards the depths of human nature. The fact of the war cannot be forgotten. America did not see this war at a close distance for its first three years; during this time, we lost a million and a half men. We have no more labor. Our English friends, who lost less than we, but still enough to have suffered much, will understand me.

Our trials have created in this country a profound feeling about the reparations which are due us; and it is not only a matter of material repairs: the need for moral redress is no less great. The doctrines just invoked, if they were interpreted in all their rigor, would allow refusing us even Alsace-Lorraine. In reality, the Saar and Landau are part of Lorraine and Alsace.

Our great enemies of 1815, against whom we fought for so many centuries, the English, insisted after the fall of Napoleon that Prussia should not take the Saar basin. A generous gesture toward a people who suffered so much would not be in vain. It is an error to believe that the world is governed by abstract principles. These are accepted by certain parties, rejected by others—I do not speak of supernatural doctrines, about which I have nothing to say. But I believe that human dogmas do not exist; there are only rules of justice and of good sense.

You seek to do justice to the Germans. Do not believe that they will ever forgive us; they only seek the opportunity for revenge. Nothing will destroy the rage of those who wanted to establish their domination over the world and who believed themselves so close to succeeding.

I will never forget that our American friends, like our English friends, came here to assist us in a moment of supreme danger; and I will tell you the argument I hold in reserve for the French, if I cannot manage to convince you. I will say to them: "Suppose that the English and the Americans had offered conditions before coming to our help; would you have accepted them or not?"

I hand over my argument to you, I place myself in your hands, to prove to you how much I appreciate all that we owe you. But you will do justice to humanity in recognizing a sentiment which is something other than your principles, but is no less profound.

Likewise, when those young men, Lafayette and Rochambeau, went to help the Americans fighting for their independence, it was not cold reason, it was not deeds of war, after all ordinary, which created the memory of their intervention; it is an impression, a profound sentiment which has always bound our two nations. The world is not led by pure principles.

I am old. In a few months, I will leave political life foreover. My disinterestedness is absolute. As Mr. Lloyd George said the other day, there is no finer role than to succumb in defending a just cause. I do not wish a finer end; I do not wish anyone a finer end. I will support before Parliament whatever conclusions we arrive at together. But here, among us, permit me to tell you that you will miss an opportunity to forge one more link in the chain of affection which attaches France to America.

I will not change your opinion, I fear; you consider yourself bound by your word. I would observe nevertheless that these 350,000 men, of whom at least 150,000 are French, do not constitute a nation. You do not want to make an exception to the principle? You will certainly be forced to do so by the facts. How will you tear the Germans of Carlsbad away from Bohemia without destroying Bohemia itself? Peoples who fought against each other for centuries have remained as mingled as in battle. In the Balkans, you will not be able to create a Greece which does not contain Bulgarians, a Serbia which does not contain Albanians.

I respect your sentiment, which is very honorable. Your role is grand. But you are moving away from your own goal. You will not sow hatred; but you will encounter bitterness and regrets. This is the reason why we must arrive, not at a mathematical justice, but at a justice which takes sentiment into account.

You are ready to render us justice from an economic point of view; I thank you for it. But economic necessities are not everything. The history of the United States is a glorious history, but short. A century for you is a very long period; for us it is a little thing. I have known men who saw Napoleon with their own eyes. We have our own conception of history which cannot be quite the same as yours.

I simply ask you to think about what I have just said when you are alone and to ask yourself in conscience if that does not contain a part of the truth.

Wilson. I thank you for the very beautiful words which you have spoken; I am conscious of all their gravity. I do not have excessive confidence in my personal judgment. But before terminating this discussion, I would like to return to a single point.

I believe as you do that sentiment is the most powerful force which exists in the world. Someone once told me: "Intelligence is the sovereign of the world." I replied to him: "If that is so, it is a sovereign who reigns but who does not govern."

Today there is throughout the entire world a passion for justice. Even some errors and crimes which have been committed came from a false view of what is just. The sentiment which brought together into combat peoples come from all points of the earth is the sentiment that they were fighting together for justice. That is why I sometimes have said here that we represent less states than the opinion of the world. This enthusiastic aspiration for solutions of justice will change into cynical skepticism if we give the impression that we have fallen short of the rules of justice which we have proclaimed.

You have said that, in pushing logic to the extreme, one could say of Alsace and Lorraine what I said of the Saar. I do not believe that this would be possible except by abusing pure logic. The world had its eyes turned toward Alsace-Lorraine for a half-century; during a half-century, the world never thought of Alsace-Lorraine as German land. Of all the questions which we have to resolve today, this is perhaps the only one whose solution has never seemed doubtful.

I greatly fear the transformation of the enthusiasm into a despair as violent as Bolshevism, which says: "There is no justice in the world; all that can be done is to take revenge by force for injustices previously committed by force." What I seek is not to deviate from the path being followed by this great world movement toward justice. I wish to do nothing which would allow it to be said of us: "They profess great principles, but they admitted exceptions everywhere, wherever sentiment or national interest made them wish to deviate from the rule."

I apologize for having spoken thus. It is painful for me to oppose you; I could not do otherwise without shirking my duty.

Clemenceau. My response when Luxembourg was discussed shows that I do not seek territorial acquisitions. Nor did I ask for the frontier of 1792. You speak of justice; but the people of Landau who sent their petitions to President Poincaré are also men who have a right to justice. One cannot satisfy everyone. By seeking general satisfaction, you run the risk of sowing the seed of general discontent.

Lloyd George. I agree with the declaration of principle so forcefully presented by President Wilson, and the country which I represent is bound in honor not to stray from these principles. The Armistice agreement established the foundations of the peace, differing in that regard from the usual armistice agreements. Nothing would do more harm to a great country than not to keep the word which it has given, even to an enemy. Great Britain declared war on Germany in 1914 in order to honor its signature to a treaty which guaranteed the neutrality of Belgium. If we violate a promise given to the Germans several months ago, how can France, when we promise her support in case of aggression, depend upon our word?

The question is to know whether territorial annexations constitute a violation of our commitments. I think they do, and this applies to questions other than that of the Saar. I adopted this attitude first on questions not concerning France, for example, when, the other day, it was a question of the frontiers of Poland. We cannot, when we are face to face with the Germans, expose ourselves to those who have the right to say to us: "You have gone back on your word."

I remind you of the enthusiasm from all sides which greeted the signature of the Armistice. After that we saw the birth and growth of appetites. I do not believe that one can substitute appetites for principles, and this applies to small as well as to great nations. At the time of the Armistice, there were no murmurs of protest against the clauses we signed; I saw everywhere only great rejoicing.

Clemenceau. People everywhere had suffered for a long time.

Lloyd George. Almost at the same time as President Wilson did so, in January 1917 [1918][6], I, in the name of the British government, made a declaration of our war aims. I said then that the wrong done to France in 1871 had to be redressed, not a word about the Saar valley. And yet I received a congratulatory telegram from M. Clemenceau the next day.

Now I hear talk for the first time about this question of the mines, after the signing of the Armistice.

I do not believe that one can accuse us of lacking generosity toward France. We did our best to support her. Hundreds of thousands of our young men died on French soil. Our personal feeling for France became a passion.

You wish to repair the injustice of 1815? Recall that, when the Germans took Alsace in 1871, they said that it had been taken from them in 1648. But the resentment that the annexation of Alsace created was justified by the fact that, since 1648, the Alsatians had become French at heart. This error must not be repeated. The English people are haunted by the fear of making new Alsace-Lorraines.

The proposal contained in the report of which I just spoke gives France nearly everything she wants. France does not want to absorb populations against their will. On the other hand, she has the right

[6] See British embassy to WW, Jan. 5, 1918, n. 2, Vol. 45.

to compensation. The system suggested would not place these populations under French domination. They are obviously Germans; a few manifestations in honor of President Poincaré do not prove the contrary. But we can give them an autonomous government, the mines going to France; I believe she has a right to them.

Wilson. She has a right to the use of the mines.

Lloyd George. I would go as far as ownership. My opinion is that we must have a consultation with the experts who drafted this document.

Wilson. I wish that also. We must see them separately and ask them to explain their report to us. But I believe that we violate the principle of the right of peoples to self-determination as much by giving one people an independence it does not request, as by making it pass under the sovereignty of another. The sole principle which I recognize is the one of the consent of the governed, and that is why the conclusions of the report you have just spoken of seem to me debatable.

Lloyd George. There are cases in which equally respectable principles are in conflict. We, too, recognize the right of peoples to self-determination. To reconcile them, each side must consent to some sacrifice.

Orlando. Permit me to make a declaration. When the representatives of the Yugoslavs addressed a protest to France which noted that Italy, being a party to the case, should not at the same time be a judge, they thought that every gentleman and every man who represents a highly civilized country would understand immediately that it was impossible to be judge and party at the same time. I sense this limitation so much that I hesitate to intervene in a discussion where principles affecting our own interests might be involved. I am not sure I am free enough to judge.

This reservation made, I would like to say that economic reasons should be excluded as principles determining sovereignty. Likewise, the historical argument in and of itself must be excluded; otherwise, Italy could, if she wished, claim all the former territories of the Roman Empire.

M. Tardieu has made the most of the sentiment of these populations, their desire to be reunited to France; this falls within the principles of justice proclaimed by President Wilson. We agree on the Fourteen Points; but just as the principles which they proclaim will not prevent considerable territories being taken from Germany in order to resolve several great problems, so they should not prevent us from finding a solution to this relatively restricted problem.

About the sentiment of the populations, naturally I have nothing to say. But Mr. Lloyd George proposed a compromise solution which would permit this sentiment to be expressed. We should, in my opinion, meanwhile question the specialists who have studied the question closely.

Mantoux, I, 58-75.

A Memorandum[1]

28 mars 1919

Proposition initiale du President Wilson
PROPOSAL
STIPULATIONS TO BE EMBODIED IN THE TREATY

1) No fortifications west of a line drawn fifty kilometers east of the Rhine (as in the military terms already provisionally agreed upon).

2) The maintenance or assembling of armed forces, either permanently or temporarily, forbidden within that area, as well as all manoeuvres and the maintenance of physical facilities for mobilization.

3) Violations of these conditions to be regarded as hostile acts against the signatories to the treaty and as calculated to disturb the peace of the world.
In a separate treaty with the United States:

4) A pledge by the United States, subject to the approval of the executive Council of the League of Nations, to come immediately to the assistance of France so soon as any unprovoked movement of aggression against her is made by Germany,—the pledge to continue until it is agreed by the contracting powers that the League itself affords sufficient protection.

CC MS (WP, DLC).
[1] Wilson undoubtedly sent this as a WWT MS to Clemenceau or Tardieu. The text printed below was typed in the French Foreign Office or secretariat and returned to Wilson. There is a WWT and WWsh draft of this document in WP, DLC.

To Robert Lansing

My dear Mr. Secretary: Paris, 28 March, 1919.

Referring to our correspondence about the directions which should be given to General Graves in Siberia, I would be very much obliged if you would send a message to the Secretary of War embodying the suggestions you made to me,[1] and saying that the course of action suggested has my approval if it meets with his approval.

He is nearer to the situation than we are, and I should not like to give him directions without his own concurrence.

Faithfully yours,   Woodrow Wilson

TLS (SDR, RG 256, 861.00/392 1/2, DNA).
   [1] In RL to WW, March 21, 1919. For the instructions to Graves which Wilson and Lansing agreed upon, see RL to FLP, April 1, 1919.

To Herbert Clark Hoover

My dear Hoover: Paris, 28 March, 1919.

If ever a man has earned the right to retire from great responsibilities, you have earned it by the admirable way in which you have done the work, the very burdensome and difficult work, which has fallen to you in this great war, and yet I experience a pang in thinking of your retirement.[1]

I won't discuss that right now. I will instead turn to the suggestion you make about the handling of the 1919 wheat crop.[2] I am quite ready to subscribe to your judgment of Mr. Julius Barnes and to concur in your plan for putting him at the head of the work which lies before us, and if you will be kind enough to make me a brief memorandum of just what steps are necessary and when they should be taken, I would be very much obliged to you indeed.

With warmest regards,

Faithfully yours,   Woodrow Wilson

TLS (Hoover Archives, CSt-H).
   [1] Wilson was responding to HCH to WW, March 25, 1919.
   [2] In the letter cited in n. 1.

To Vance Criswell McCormick, with Enclosure

My dear McCormick: Paris, 28 March, 1919.

I am very eager to remove this censorship on the cables which is becoming so annoying to our business men and would very much like to act upon the suggestions of the enclosed cable. I would like to know, first whether you think we can honorably act before the 4th of April and second, whether the way will be entirely clear after that date.

Cordially and faithfully yours,   [Woodrow Wilson]

CCL (WP, DLC).

ENCLOSURE

The White House, 25 March 1919.

[#34] I have referred your cable[1] to the Postmaster General to the War Trade Board and the Chief Cable Censor also.

The War Trade Board points out:

First. The censorship is maintained solely for the purpose of blockading enemy trade in all parts of the world.

Second. It would be unfortunate for Great Britain and France to continue the censorship of messages to and from the United States after we had abolished our censorship.

Third. The British do not now censor messages between the United States and the northern neutrals, but would again begin to censor them if we did not.

Fourth. That McCormick has agreed with Lord Robert Cecil not to abolish our censorship prior to April 4th.

The Chief Cable Censor states:

First. There is a great and increasing public impatience at the continuance of censorship.

Second. Since cablegrams have to be in plain language or public code they are materially longer than they would be if private code were permissible.

Third. Shorter cablegrams would not only help to relieve the great congestion on the cables but would save the American business man the millions of dollars annually which he has to pay as a result of not being allowed to abbreviate his cablegrams.

Fourth. Permission to use undecipherable private codes would be tantamount to the abolition of cable censorship.

Our merchants and citizens generally confidently expected our censorship to come to an end shortly after the Armistice and they now look for its discontinuance daily. In fact, I am sure many would be shocked to learn that it is still in operation. There has been no censorship of press matter by the United States since shortly after the Armistice, but the censorship of trade communications.

I strongly urge that we discontinue both cable and postal censorship on April 4th.

I do not understand that we are, after April 4th, under any obligation to continue a burdensome war time measure which is at once repugnant to our people and not essential to our welfare. We can stop the censorship and by so doing we will save the government the very heavy expense incident to its maintenance; save the business man from the present increased cable tolls resulting from the longer messages and save the Administration from its attacks to which it will be subjected because of its continuance.

We could hardly justify its continuance before an investigating committee.

Aggressive action on your part will be necessary to end this business. The Postmaster General, with whom I have conferred, agrees with me in this vital matter.   Tumulty.

T telegram (J. P. Tumulty Papers, DLC).
    [1] WW to ASB, March 24, 1919.

To Edward Nash Hurley

[Paris] March 28th, 1919.

No. 1355. For Hurley from the President. It is essential that at least 500,000 tons of shipping for April loading in addition to Hoover's March programme be found for the relief situation and I hope that you will without delay make this amount available even if ships have to be taken from trades.   Woodrow Wilson.

TC telegram in the Diary of Gordon Auchincloss, T MS (G. Auchincloss Papers, CtY).

To Marguerite de Witt Schlumberger

My dear Madame Schlumberger: Paris, 28 March, 1919.

I some days ago received a letter from Lady Aberdeen requesting on behalf of the International Council of Women and of the Interallied Suffrage Conference an interview with the Commission on the League of Nations.[1] Am I wrong in supposing that the Conference on behalf of which you were kind enough to write me your letter of March 25th[2] was not represented among the ladies for whom Lady Aberdeen wrote?

It would be very difficult with the amount of work which lies before the Commission and must be done in a very brief time to arrange for more than one such hearing, and that must be my excuse for this question.

Sincerely yours,   [Woodrow Wilson]

CCL (WP, DLC).
    [1] See n. 1 to the minutes of the League of Nations Commission printed at March 24, 1919.
    [2] Marguerite de W. Schlumberger and Cécile Kahn Brunschvicg to WW, March 25, 1919, ALS (WP, DLC).

From Herbert Clark Hoover

Dear Mr. President: [Paris] 28 March 1919.

As a result of Bolshevik economic conceptions, the people of Russia are dying of hunger and disease at the rate of some hundreds of thousands monthly in a country that formerly supplied food to a large part of the world.

I feel it is my duty to lay before you in just as few words as possible my views as to the American relation to Bolshevism and its manifestations. These views at least have the merit of being an analysis of information and thought gleaned from my own experience and the independent sources which I now have over the whole of Europe, through our widespread relief organization.

It simply cannot be denied that this swinging of the social pendulum from the tyranny of the extreme right to the tyranny of the extreme left is based on a foundation of real social grievance. The tyranny of the reactionaries in Eastern and Central Europe for generations before the war, and the suffering of their common people is but a commonplace to every social student. This situation was thrown into bold relief by the war and the breakdown of these reactionary tyrannies. After fighting actually stopped on the various fronts the famine which followed has further emphasized the gulf between the lower and upper classes. The poor were starved and driven mad in the presence of extravagance and waste.

It is to be noticed that the Bolshevik ascendency or even their strong attempts so far are confined to areas of former reactionary tyranny. Their courses represent the not unnatural violence of a mass of ignorant humanity, who themselves have learned in grief of tyranny and violence over generations. Our people, who enjoy so great liberty and general comfort, cannot fail to sympathize to some degree with these blind gropings for better social condition. If former revolutions in ignorant masses are any guide, the pendulum will yet swing back to some moderate position when bitter experience has taught the economic and social follies of present obsessions. No greater fortune can come to the world than that these foolish ideas should have an opportunity somewhere of bankrupting themselves.

It is not necessary for any American to debate the utter foolishness of these economic tenets. We must all agree that our processes of production and distribution, the outgrowth of a hundred generations, in the stimulation to individual initiative, the large equality of opportunity and infinite development of mind and body, while not perfect, come about as near perfection as is possible from the mixture of avarice, ambition, altruism, intelligence, ignorance and education, of which the human animal is today composed. The Bolshevik's land of illusion is that he can perfect these human qualities by destroying the basic processes of production and distribution instead of devoting himself to securing a better application of the collective surplus.

Politically, the Bolsheviki most certainly represent a minority in every country where they are in control, and as such they constitute a tyranny that is the negation of democracy, for democracy as I see it must rest on the execution of the will of the majority expressed by free and unterrified suffrage. As a tyranny, the Bolshevik has resorted to terror, bloodshed and murder to a degree long since abandoned even amongst reactionary tyrannies. He has even to a greater degree relied upon criminal instinct to support his doctrines than ever autocracy did. By enveloping into his doctrines the cry of the helpless and the downtrodden, he has embraced a large degree of emotionalism and has thereby given an impulse to his propaganda comparable only to the impulse of large spiritual movements. This propaganda, however, in my view will stir other populations only in ratio to their proportions of the suffering and ignorant and criminal. I feel myself, therefore, that the political danger of spread of Bolshevism by propaganda is a direct factor of the social and political development of the population which they attempt to impregnate. Where the gulf between the middle classes and the lower classes is large, and where the lower classes have been kept in ignorance and distress, this propaganda will be fatal and do violence to normal democratic development. For these reasons, I have no fear of it in the United States, and my fears as to other countries would be gauged by the above criterion. It is possible that the Soviet type of government might take hold in some other countries as a primitive form of democracy, but its virulence will be tempered by their previous degree of political subversion.

There remains in my mind one more point to be examined, that is as to whether the Bolshevik centers now stirred by great emotional hopes will not undertake large military crusades in an attempt to impose their doctrines on other defenseless people. This is a point on which my mind is divided with the evidence at hand, and it seems to me that the whole treatment of the problem must revolve on the determination of this one question. If this spirit is inherent in their doctrine, it appears to me that we must disregard all other questions and be prepared to fight, for exactly the same reasons that we entered the European War against Germany. If this is not the case, then it appears to me that from an American point of view we should not involve ourselves in what may be a ten year military entanglement in Europe. The American people cannot say that we are going to insist that any given population must work out its internal social problems according to our particular conception of democracy. In the event, I have the most serious doubt that outside forces entering upon such an enterprise can do other than infinite harm, for any great wave of emotion must ferment and spread under repression. In the swing of the social pendulum from the extreme left back toward the right, it will find the point of stabilization based on racial instincts that could never be established by outside intervention.

I think we also have to contemplate what would actually happen if we undertook military intervention in, say, a case like Hungary. We should probably be involved in years of police duty, and our first act would probably in the nature of things make us a party to reestablishing the reactionary classes in their economic domination over the lower classes. This is against our fundamental national spirit, and I doubt whether our soldiers under these circumstances could resist infection with Bolshevik ideas. It also requires consideration as to whether or not our people at home, on gradual enlightenment as to the social wrongs of the lower classes in these countries, would stand for our providing power by which such reactionaries held their position, and we would perchance be thrown into an attempt as governors to work out some social reorganization of these countries. We thus become a mandatory with a vengeance. We become, in fact, one of four mandatories, each with a different political and social outlook, for it would necessarily be a joint Allied undertaking. Furthermore, in our present engagements with France, England and Italy, we become a junior in this partnership of four. It is therefore inevitable that in these matters where our views and principles are at variance with the European Allies we would find ourselves subordinated and even committed to policies against our convictions.

In all these lights, I have the following three suggestions:

First: We cannot even remotely recognize this murderous tyranny without stimulating actionist radicalism in every country in Europe and without transgressing on every National ideal of our own.

Second: That some Neutral of international reputation for probity and ability should be allowed to create a second Belgian Relief Commission for Russia. He should ask the Northern Neutrals who are especially interested both politically and financially in the restoration of better conditions in Russia, to give to him diplomatic, financial and transportation support; that he should open negotiations with the Allied governments on the ground of desire to enter upon the humane work of saving life, and ask the conditions upon which ships carrying food and other necessaries will be allowed to pass. He should be told that we will raise no obstructions and would even help in his humanitarian task if he gets assurances that the Bolsheviki will cease all militant action across certain defined boundaries and cease their subsidizing of disturbances abroad; under these conditions that he could raise money, ships and food, either from inside or outside Russia; that he must secure an agreement covering equitable distribution, and he might even demand that Germany help pay for this. This plan does not involve any recognition or relationship by the Allies of the Bolshevik murderers now in control any more than England recognized Germany in its deals with the Belgian Relief. It would appear to me that such a proposal would at least test out whether this is a militant force engrossed upon world domination. If such an arrangement could be accomplished it might at least give a period of rest along the frontiers of Europe and would give some hope of stabilization. Time can thus be taken to determine whether or not this whole system is a world danger, and whether the Russian people will not themselves swing back to moderation and themselves bankrupt these ideas. This plan, if successful, would save an immensity of helpless human life and would save our country from further entanglements which today threaten to pull us from our National ideals.

Third: I feel strongly the time has arrived for you again to reassert your spiritual leadership of democracy in the world as opposed to tyrannies of all kinds. Could you not take an early opportunity to analyze, as only you can, Bolshevism from its political, economic, humane and its criminal points of view, and, while yielding its aspirations, sympathetically to show its utter foolishness as a basis of economic development; show its true social ends; rap our own reactionaries for their destruction of social betterment and thereby their stimulation of Bolshevism; point, however, to the steady progress of real democracy in these roads of social betterment. I believe you would again align the hearts of the suffering for orderly progress against anarchy, not alone in Russia but in every Allied country.

If the militant features of Bolshevism were drawn in colors with their true parallel with Prussianism as an attempt at world domination that we do not stand for, it would check the fears that today haunt all men's minds.

Faithfully yours,   Herbert Hoover

TLS (WP, DLC).

From Tasker Howard Bliss, with Enclosure

My dear Mr. President: Paris, March 28, 1919.

The plan which was presented yesterday afternoon in Mr. Clemenceau's office to you and your colleagues,[1] was unknown to me thirty minutes before that. I was told that it was made "in execution of the decision taken by the Associated Governments." I therefore could not express my real opinion about it without instructions from you. I think that it brings you face to face with the gravest decision yet called for at the Peace Conference. If carried into execution it means the resumption of general war and the probable dissolution of the Peace Conference. I believe that this is the deliberate intention of those who have proposed it. Various facts and, I think, justifiable inferences from facts, have come to my knowledge which I hesitate to commit to writing. I beg you to take no action either in respect to the plan proposed yesterday or the previous plan of providing supplies to the Roumanian Army, until you can give me a very short time in which to state the case to you.

I have this moment had a conference with Mr. House on the subject and it is on his recommendation that I write this letter.[2]

Very sincerely,   Tasker H. Bliss.

P.S. I invite attention to the marked paragraphs[3] of my attached memorandum prepared last night.   T.H.B.

TLS (WP, DLC).
[1] See the memorandum by Marshal Foch printed at March 27, 1919, and the discussion of it by the Council of Four in the meeting beginning at 3:30 p.m. on that date.
[2] On his TC of this letter, Bliss wrote: "Mr. House informs me that he was present in the President's house when he received this letter. He sent me word by Mr. H. that under no circumstances would he send a man to South Eastern Europe but that he might have to send the Roumanians some military supplies. THB."
[3] Pars. 6, 7, and 8.

E N C L O S U R E

Paris, March 27, 1919.

MEMORANDUM

1. The armistice with Hungary, signed on November 13th by Gen. Franchet d'Esperay and Count Karolyi, fixed the line of demarcation between the Hungarian and Roumanian troops as the river SZAMOS-BISTRITZ, river MAROS. Gen. Charpy,[1] Chief of Staff of Gen. Franchet d'Esperay, reported on Feb. 25, 1919, that the Hungarians had carried out all the conditions of the armistice but that the Roumanians had not, as without informing General Franchet d'Esperay, they had crossed the demarcation line and had commenced an advance which on that date had reached the line MA-

RAMAROSSZIGET-CSURSA. General Charpy expressed the opinion that the Roumanians should remain on their present line (see copy herewith of statement of General Charpy).

2. On February 26th, 1919, the Supreme Council aproved a recommendation of the Military Representatives for the establishment of a neutral zone about 50 kilometers in width, the Western or Hungarian limit of which is the line VASAROS NAMENY-SZEGED, that is the treaty line of 1916,[2] and the Eastern or Roumanian limit the line SZATMAR NEMETI-ARAD. The creation of this zone permitted a further advance of the Roumanian forces of about 70 kilometers and imposed a corresponding retirement on the Hungarian forces.

3. The Neutral Zone approved by the Supreme Council is open to the objections: a) That the entire zone lies within the limits of territory that is ethnically Hungarian; b) That through sanctioning a further and extended advance of the Roumanians beyond the demarcation line of the armistice, it subjects the Associated Powers to a charge of breach of faith; c) That it has been interpreted by the Hungarians as a recognition by the Supreme Council, of the Treaty of 1916.

4. A more equitable neutral zone would have been one whose median line corresponded with the line of ethnic cleavage, that is the line SZATMAR NEMETI-ARAD, or the Eastern limit of the zone established by the Supreme Council. Such a zone would be made up of about equal parts of Hungarian and Roumanian ethnic territory, and would not raise the question of the Treaty of 1916.

5. On March 22, 1919, General Franchet d'Esperay telegraphed that when on March 19th he notified the Hungarian Government of the decision of the Supreme Council, that Government resigned, declaring itself unable either to receive the decision or to prescribe measures for its execution. The Karolyi Government has been replaced by a government of Bolshevik tendencies which is reported to be seeking an alliance with the Bolshevik Government in Russia.

6. The question now confronting the United States is one of fundamental and far-reaching importance. If we join the other Associated Powers in attempting the coercion by armed force of Hungary aided by Russia, we shall be committing ourselves to a war of enormous magnitude, and of indefinite duration; one which will have to be financed entirely by us; and one in which, because of the war-weariness of the peoples of our Allies, we may find ourselves standing alone.

7. The present conditions in Hungary are the direct result of the action of the Supreme Council on February 26, 1919. That act, therefore, was politically unwise. It cannot be justified morally before the people of the United States.

8. It is believed that the United States should decline categorically to participate in armed intervention in this theatre through the contribution of men or money or supplies. It is believed also that if the United States is to continue to act with the Associated Powers in the determination of territorial and economic questions relating to the former Austrian-Hungarian Empire, it insist upon the immediate reversal of the action of the Supreme Council of February 26, 1919; upon the issuance of orders to the Commanding General of the Army of the Orient[3] and all other representatives of the Associated Powers in the countries bordering on Hungary, that no action will be taken by them with respect to the Hungarian people or territory that is not clearly within the scope of the terms of the armistice concluded with Hungary; and that meanwhile every effort be made by the Supreme Council to reopen communication with the Hungarian people and to assure them that it is the purpose of the Associated Powers to conclude a peace with Hungary on a basis of the declarations of President Wilson contained in his address of January 8, 1918 and subsequent addresses.   T.H.B.

TI MS (WP, DLC).
    [1] Gen. Charles Antoine Charpy.
    [2] That is, the Treaty of Bucharest of August 17, 1916, by which the Allies recognized Rumania's right to annex territories, including the Banat and Transylvania, long held by Hungary, in return for Rumania's entry into the war on the Allied side. For the text of this treaty, see Harold William Vazeille Temperley, ed., A History of the Peace Conference of Paris (6 vols., London, 1920-24), IV, 516-17.
    [3] That is, Gen. Franchet d'Espérey.

From Tasker Howard Bliss, with Enclosures

My dear Mr. President: Paris, March 28th, 1919.

    I enclose, herewith, telegram N.D.B. 10 received by me for you from Mr. Secretary Baker.[1] Should you so desire, I will transmit to him any reply you desire to make.

    I also enclose memorandum which was intended to complete the one attached to my letter handed to Mr. Hoover about 1:50 p.m. today and which I omitted to enclose.

                    Sincerely yours,   Tasker H. Bliss

TLS (WP, DLC).
    [1] The Enclosure with T. H. Bliss to WW, March 27, 1919.

E N C L O S U R E   I

STATEMENT OF GENERAL CHARPY, CHIEF OF STAFF
OF GENERAL FRANCHET D'ESPEREY TO THE
MILITARY REPRESENTATIVES AT VERSAILLES, ON
FEBRUARY 25, 1919.

GENERAL CHARPY said that on November 7th, 1918, General Franchet d'Esperey and Count Karolyi had met at Belgrade to sign a supplementary armistice with Hungary on the same lines as General Diaz had signed with Austria. At that time Roumania was still under German domination and therefore only French, Serbian and Hungarian representatives were present at Belgrade. They all knew the terms of the Hungarian armistice. A certain zone was to be definitely occupied and further zones could be occupied for strategic reasons. The armistice was signed on November 13th and the Hungarians had made no difficulties and had carried out all the conditions. The French and Serbians advanced as agreed. The only difficulties occurred with Roumania.

Without informing General Franchet d'Esperey, the Roumanians had advanced, especially in the region of Klausenburg. The Hungarians at once protested that this was a breach of the armistice conditions. The Roumanians replied that they were in agreement with the Hungarians. This was not correct, but eventually an agreement was reached. The Roumanians were allowed to advance up to a line well in advance of the armistice line. This was reported to the Allied Governments.

Unfortunately, the Roumanians advanced still further with the result that certain incidents took place; the Roumanians oppressed the local population and the Hungarians became incensed. Up to that time the position had not become serious, however.

The Roumanians stated that they feared an attack by Hungarian armies; that was absolutely impossible. Hungary had no organized troops, whereas the Roumanian Army was well organized. Naturally, there was much unrest in Hungary and some Bolshevism, but nothing important, and Bolshevism in Transylvania was not apparent. The Roumanians had for some time tried to advance to the Treaty Line, but General Franchet d'Esperey had refused so far, though he had sent a mission to make enquiries into alleged atrocities. The information received was that the local situation was quite quiet.

Taking these facts into consideration the Roumanians should remain on their present line as all the trouble had been caused by their advance. It was not for him to give advice on a political question, but the Roumanians should not be allowed to cross the line

Arad-Grosswardein Szatmar-Nemeti, and it would be preferable to send Allied Troops there; a neutral zone would be of no advantage as there were not sufficient troops to guard it.

To maintain order it would be sufficient to garrison Grosswardein and Stulimar with Allied troops which were already at Arad.

CC MS (T. H. Bliss Papers, DLC).

ENCLOSURE II

March 28, 1919.

MEMORANDUM

Showing the sequence of events connected with the establishment of the Neutral Zone in Hungary, and of events subsequent to the establishment of that Zone.

NOTE: From February 13th until some time after the President's return from Washington, I was entirely occupied with work on the Committee drafting the final military, naval and air peace terms with Germany, and became acquainted with the following sequence of events only in connection with the preparation of my memorandum to Mr. Lansing dated March 8th, 1919.[1]

1. On the signature of the Armistice between the Hungarians and the French Army of the East, General Franchet d'Esperey fixed a fair armistice line beyond which neither the Roumanians nor the Hungarians were to advance. Continued violation of this agreement on the part of the Hungarians [Rumanians] resulted in serious trouble.

2. February 19. On this date the Committee on Roumanian Affairs had under consideration a proposed Neutral Zone in Hungary to avoid further conflict between the Hungarians and the Roumanians. General Alby, representing the French War Ministry, read a Note to the Committee in which he said, *inter-alia*, that *"General Berthelot's Army must be kept ready for disposal and eventual employment in South Russia."* This matter was brought before the Committee on Roumanian Affairs by the French Foreign Office, as a matter of urgency.

I understand that the French F.O. submitted the boundaries of the proposed Neutral Zone.

NOTE: The underscored lines refer to some unknown plan of operations against Russia.

3. February 25, Marshal Foch outlined to the Council of Ten a plan which he had prepared for forming, immediately after sig-

[1] T. H. Bliss to RL, March 8, 1919, CC MS (T. H. Bliss Papers, DLC).

nature of peace with Germany, an army of Greeks, Serbs, Roumanians, Poles, Czecho-Slovaks, Esthonians, etc., under French direction, to fight Bolshevism. Mr. Balfour's remarks on this subject, in the minutes of that session, are interesting.

NOTE: The vaguely expressed plan of Marshal Foch indicates the motive for the dispatch of three Greek divisions to Odessa.

4. The final recommendation of the Committee on Roumanian Affairs was submitted to the Council of Ten and by it referred to the Military Representatives on the Supreme War Council at Versailles.

5. February 25. The Military Representatives concurred in a recommendation as to the Neutral Zone. The officer of the American Section who was present made the reservation that this was not in any way to commit the United States to military action, as we were not represented in Southeast Europe.

6. February 26. The Council of Ten approved the Neutral Zone.

7. March 8. Mr. C. M. Storey,[2] who had just previously returned from Hungary, sent me a memorandum, through Mr. Lansing who asked for any comments I might desire to make, on the subject of the proposed Neutral Zone. I returned it to Mr. Lansing on March 8th with my comments. It is the study which I then made that acquainted me with the facts set forth above.

8. In the sessions of the Council of Ten where was discussed the transportation of the Polish divisions to Dantzig, Marshal Foch brought up in various ways his intention to unite these with the Roumanians in order to fight the Ukrainians at Lemberg. On March 17th he urged that he be authorized to study the question of the transportation of these divisions or a part of them by rail via Vienna. The Council, as I remember it, refused to give him this authorization.

9. March 19th. *On this day, two days after disapproval of the idea of transporting the Polish divisions by rail, the official note establishing the Neutral Zone was delivered to Karolyi's Government in Budapeste and that Government fell and was succeeded by a so-called Bolshevik Government. What is the connection between these two dates?*

10. March 25th. On this day the Council of Four had before them telegrams from General Berthelot relating to the situation in Odessa. Sending for Marshal Foch, they learned from him that he did not consider it worth while to hold Odessa, but that the forces of Roumania and Poland should be strengthened. This led to the question

---

[2] Charles Moorfield Storey, recently an agent of the Coolidge Mission in Budapest.

of participation by the Four Governments in the equipment and maintenance of the Roumanian Army.

11. March 27. Marshal Foch presented his plan to the Council of Four for the organization of an army of French, British, Americans, Greeks, Serbs and Roumanians, to extend from Odessa on the Black Sea around Hungary, and to occupy Vienna. This army is to extinguish Bolshevism in Hungary and unite to close the "Lemberg Gap."

Thus, after many variations and deviations, we come to the original plan of the great army to be formed to fight Bolshevism.

12. There is reason to believe that General Franchet d'Esperey and his officers on the spot do not favor the plan of military intervention. His chief-of-staff, on February 25th, opposed the proposed Neutral Zone. It is said that General Franchet d'Esperey made a report opposing intervention.

On the other hand, General Berthelot has been in Roumania as the immediate agent of the French Ministry of War. He has favored the Roumanians and the French Government appears to be guided by his advice.

13. There appears to be no doubt from what Mr. Norman Davis has told me, that some days prior to March 25th (when the evacuation of Odessa and provision for the maintenance of the Roumanian Army were discussed by the Council of Four), the British and French Governments agreed with the Roumanian Government to provide for the entire maintenance of the latter's army.

From General Browning's reports to me of the proceedings of Marshal Foch's Committee, there seems to be no doubt that the European Allies expect that the United States will not merely provide certain food, clothing, &c., for the Roumanian Army, but will also share in all of the other expenses of its maintenance. *There is no law under which this can be done.*

14. Another grave fact to notice is that the negotiations by the French with the Germans for authority to move the Polish divisions through the port of Dantzig will in all probability, in view of the manner in which the matter has been presented heretofore to the German Government, result in the refusal of the Germans to permit it.

It looks as though, either through the action taken in Hungary or the proposed action in respect to the port of Dantzig, or through both of those means, it was determined to break off the general armistice, both with Germany and with the Austro-Hungarian States. The United States is being dragged into a resumption of the war through the fact that all negotiations or dealings with the enemy are in the hands of the French. They can do nothing except with the hope that the United States will see them through. Nothing but the most complete understanding with them as to the general attitude of the United States will alter the present tendency of events. I believe that the issue must be met within a very few days.

                                                        T.H.B.

TI MS (WP, DLC).

From the American Commissioners, with Enclosure

                                        Paris, March 28th, 1919.

The American Commissioners to Negotiate Peace have the honor to transmit herewith to the President of the United States a memorandum containing a statement made to a member of the Commission by M. Cachin,[1] the Editor of l'Humanité and the leader of the Moderate Socialists in the Chambre des Députés.   RL.

TI MS (WP, DLC).
  [1] That is, Marcel Cachin.

E N C L O S U R E

MEMORANDUM
INTERVIEW WITH M. CACHIN.

In a rather remarkable interview Mr. Cachin made an eloquent expose of the present popular tendencies, as he sees them.

He says the remarkable fact during the past two weeks has been the change in popular feeling towards Mr. Wilson. In the early days of the Conference Mr. Wilson was the personification of popular idealism. The hopes of the people were in him for the realization of a liberal democratic peace. Now, after nearly five months, no real accomplishment can be credited to the Conference. Though Mr. Wilson is not directly blamed, it is being realized that he is becoming more and more impotent, in the midst of imperialistic diplomacy. To all appearances, Mr. Wilson has compromised himself with, and is following the persons whom he stigmatized in his New York Speech.

The fact now is that the futility of the Paris Conference is being more and more realized, and popular interest has shifted from it, and is being drawn to the East of Europe where the peoples themselves are finding their own salvation.

The People are rapidly perceiving that what the Conference does WILL NOT MATTER, for if it ignores the wishes of the mass of the populations, the work will be either ignored or soon undone.

Mr. Cachin says he hopes it is not yet too late, and believes that

Mr. Wilson can, through a strong decisive stand, save the day, so that liberalism may come through well-ordered channels rather than through class upheavals.

First and foremost, says Mr. Cachin, is a liberal Russian policy:— that is, (1) Recognition of the Soviets, (2) Raising of the blockade, (3) Recall of troops from Russia; and then a liberal non-imperialistic peace with Germany.

T MS (WP, DLC).

A Memorandum by William Christian Bullitt

[c. March 28, 1919]

MEMORANDUM FOR THE PRESIDENT AND THE COMMISSIONERS PLENIPOTENTIARY TO NEGOTIATE PEACE.

Subject: RUSSIA

Economic Situation   Page 1.
(Summary: The economic situation of Russia is extremely bad because of lack of the essentials of transportation which is sapping the life of industry and causing the slow starvation of the people of the cities.)

Social Conditions   Page 3.
(Summary: Good order has been established and the Government has done much constructive work on educational and social lines.)

Political Situation   Page 4.
(Summary: The Soviet Government is firmly established. The Communist Party is very strong, the only ponderable opposition coming from parties more radical than the Communists. Lenin is ready to compromise at many points in order to obtain peace.)

Peace Proposals   Page 7.
(Summary: The Peace statement of the Soviet Government is not an irreducible minimum, but would be acceptable in a modified form.)

Conclusions   Page 9.
(Summary: It seems most essential as soon as possible to make a proposal following the general line suggested by the Soviet Government.)

Appendices   Page 10.
Text of Peace Proposals   Page 22.

ECONOMIC SITUATION

Russia today is in a condition of acute economic distress. The blockade by land and sea is the cause of this distress and lack of the essentials of transportation is its gravest symptom. Only one fourth of the locomotives which ran on Russian lines before the war are now available for use. Furthermore, Soviet Russia is cut off entirely from all supplies of coal and gasoline. In consequence, transportation by all steam and electric vehicles is greatly hampered; and transportation by automobile and by the fleet of gasoline-using Volga steamers and canal boats is impossible. (Appendix Page 10)[1]

As a result of these hindrances to transportation it is possible to bring from the grain centres to Moscow only twenty-five carloads of food a day, instead of the hundred carloads which are essential, and to Petrograd only fifteen carloads, instead of the essential fifty. In consequence, every man, woman and child in Moscow and Petrograd is suffering from slow starvation. (App. P. 11)

Mortality is particularly high among new-born children, whose mothers cannot suckle them, among newly-delivered mothers, and among the aged. The entire population, in addition, is exceptionally susceptible to disease; and a slight illness is apt to result fatally because of the total lack of medicines. Typhoid, typhus and small-pox are epidemic in both Petrograd and Moscow.

Industry, except the production of munitions of war, is largely at a standstill. Nearly all means of transport which are not employed in carrying food are used to supply the army, and there is scarcely any surplus transport to carry materials essential to normal industry. Furthermore, the army has absorbed the best executive brains and physical vigor of the nation. In addition, Soviet Russia is cut off from most of its sources of iron and of cotton. Only the flax, hemp, wood and lumber industries have an adequate supply of raw material.

On the other hand, such essentials of economic life as are available are being utilized to the utmost by the Soviet Government. Such trains as there are, run on time. The distribution of food is well-controlled. Many industrial experts of the old regime are again managing their plants and sabotage by such managers has ceased. Loafing by the workmen during work-hours has been overcome. (App. P. 12)

SOCIAL CONDITIONS

The destructive phase of the revolution is over and all the energy of the Government is turned to constructive work. The terror has ceased. All power of judgment has been taken away from the Extraordinary Commission for Suppression of the Counter-Revolution, which now merely accuses suspected counter-revolutionaries who are tried by the regular, established, legal tribunals. Executions are

[1] Appendices not printed herein. They are printed in *FR Russia, 1919*, pp. 89-95. The version of the main report in *ibid.*, pp. 85-89, is incomplete.

extremely rare. Good order has been established. The streets are safe. Shooting has ceased. There are few robberies. Prostitution has disappeared from sight. Family life has been unchanged by the revolution—the canard in regard to "nationalization of women" notwithstanding. (App. P. 13)

The theatres, opera and ballet are performing as in peace. Thousands of new schools have been opened in all parts of Russia and the Soviet Government seems to have done more for the education of the Russian people in a year and a half than Czardom did in fifty years. (App. P. 14)

POLITICAL SITUATION

The Soviet form of Government is firmly established. Perhaps the most striking fact in Russia today is the general support which is given the Government by the people in spite of their starvation. Indeed, the people lay the blame for their distress wholly on the blockade and on the Governments which maintain it. The Soviet form of government seems to have become to the Russian people the symbol of their revolution. Unquestionably it is a form of Government which lends itself to gross abuse and tyranny but it meets the demand of the moment in Russia and it has acquired so great a hold on the imagination of the common people that the women are ready to starve and the young men die for it. (App. P. 15)

The position of the Communist Party, (formerly Bolsheviki) is also very strong. Blockade and intervention have caused the chief opposition parties, the Right Social Revolutionaries and the Menshiviki, to give temporary support to the Communists. These opposition parties have both made formal statements against the blockade, intervention and the support of Anti-Soviet Governments by the Allied and Associated Governments. Their leaders, Volsky and Martov,[2] are most vigorous in their demands for the immediate raising of the blockade and peace. (App. P. 16)

Indeed, the only ponderable opposition to the Communists today comes from *more radical* parties—The Left Social Revolutionaries and the Anarchists. These parties, in published statements, call the Communists, and particularly Lenin and Tchitcherin, "the paid bourgeois gendarmes of the Entente"! They attack the Communists because the Communists have encouraged scientists, engineers and industrial experts of the bourgeois class to take important posts under the Soviet Government at high pay. They rage against the employment of bourgeois officers in the army and against the efforts of the Communists to obtain peace. They demand the immediate massacre of all the bourgeoisie and an immediate declaration of

---

[2] V. K. Volskii, a leader of the Socialist Revolutionary party and L. Martov (pseudonym of Yulii Osipovich Tsederbaum), leader of the Menshevik party.

war on all non-revolutionary governments. They argue that the Entente Governments should be forced to intervene more deeply in Russia, asserting that such action would surely provoke the proletariat of all European countries to immediate revolution.

Within the Communist Party itself, there is a distinct division of opinion in regard to foreign policy; but this disagreement has not developed personal hostility or open breach in the ranks of the Party. Trotsky, the Generals and many theorists believe the Red Army should go forward everywhere until more vigorous intervention by the Entente is provoked, which they, too, count upon to bring revolution in France and England. Their attitude is not a little colored by pride in the spirited young army. (App. P. 18) Lenin, Tchitcherin and the bulk of the Communist Party, on the other hand, insist that the essential problem at present is to save the proletariat of Russia, in particular, and the proletariat of Europe, in general, from starvation, and assert that it will benefit the revolution but little to conquer all Europe if the Government of the United States replies by starving all Europe. They advocate, therefore, the conciliation of the United States even at the cost of compromising with many of the principles they hold most dear. And Lenin's prestige in Russia at present is so overwhelming that the Trotsky group is forced reluctantly to follow him. (App. P. 19)

Lenin, indeed, as a practical matter, stands well to the right in the existing political life of Russia. He recognizes the undesirability, from the Socialist viewpoint, of the compromises he feels compelled to make; but he is ready to make the compromises. Among the more notable concessions he has already made are: the abandonment of his plan to nationalize the land and the adoption of the policy of dividing it among the peasants, the establishment of savings banks paying three percent interest, the decision to pay all foreign debts, and the decision to give concessions if that shall prove to be necessary to obtain credit abroad. (App. P. 20)

In a word, Lenin feels compelled to retreat from his theoretical position all along the line. He is ready to meet the western Governments half-way.

PEACE PROPOSAL

Lenin seized upon the opportunity presented by my trip of investigation to make a definite statement of the position of the Soviet Government. He was opposed by Trotsky and the Generals, but without much difficulty got the support of the majority of the Executive Council and the statement of the position of the Soviet Government which was handed to me was finally adopted unanimously. (App. P. 22)[3]

[3] This Appendix is missing both in manuscript and in the printed version cited above. However, it is embodied in W. C. Bullitt to WW, March 16, 1919, Vol. 55.

My discussion of this proposal with the leaders of the Soviet Government was so detailed that I feel sure of my ground in saying that it does not represent the minimum terms of the Soviet Government and that I can point out in detail wherein it may be modified without making it unacceptable to the Soviet Government. For example, the clause under Article 5—"and to their own nationals who have been or may be prosecuted for giving help to Soviet Russia"—is certainly not of vital importance. And the clause under Article 4, in regard to admission of citizens of the Soviet Republics of Russia into the Allied and Associated countries, may certainly be changed in such a way as to reserve all necessary rights to control such immigration to the Allied and Associated Countries, and to confine it to persons who come on legitimate and necessary business, and to exclude definitely all possibility of an influx of propagandists.

CONCLUSIONS

The following conclusions are respectfully submitted:

1. No Government save a Socialist Government can be set up in Russia today except by foreign bayonets and any government so set up will fall the moment such support is withdrawn. The Lenin wing of the Communist Party is today as moderate as any Socialist Government which can control Russia.

2. No real peace can be established in Europe or the world until peace is made with the revolution. This proposal of the Soviet Government presents an opportunity to make peace with the revolution on a just and reasonable basis—perhaps a unique opportunity.

3. If the Blockade is lifted and supplies begin to be delivered regularly to Soviet Russia, a more powerful hold over the Russian people will be established than that given by the blockade itself—the hold given by fear that this delivery of supplies may be stopped. Furthermore, the parties which oppose the Communists in principle but are supporting them at present will be able to begin to fight against them.

4. It is, therefore, respectfully recommended that a proposal following the general lines of the suggestion of the Soviet Government should be made at the earliest possible moment, such changes being made, particularly in Article 4 and Article 5, as will make the proposal acceptable to conservative opinion in the Allied and Associated Countries.

Very respectfully submitted,   William C. Bullitt.

TS MS (WP, DLC).

Joseph Edward Willard to the American Commissioners

Madrid, March 28, 1919.

100. IMPORTANT. CONFIDENTIAL.

In personal interview yesterday evening, King[1] asked that President Wilson be requested to hasten Peace as he, the King, believed that law and order in Europe was vitally dependant upon its conclusion and that in the meantime civilization was trembling in the balance. Reply was ventured that President Wilson was thoroughly aware of the gravity of the situation. His Majesty was optimistic concerning immediate situation in Spain although he recognized that existing disturbances were not simply contests between labor and capital but were evidences of incipient revolution. He stated that German influence, encouraged by delays in conclusion of peace, had again become active in Spain as elsewhere in Europe. (Englehardt,[2] German Vice-Consul at Seville, has been arrested charged with inciting disturbances.) His Majesty expressed the hope that present ministry would be able to tide over situation in Spain without serious trouble, but stated on the other hand that if conditions became graver and demanded a firmer hand, a military ministry would be created for the temporary purpose of restoring law and order. He admitted probability of political crisis immediately after adjustment of existing conditions, when he would endeavor to form a ministerial combination able to pass the annual appropriation bill through this *Cortes*. He desires to avoid a dissolution of this Cortes and feels that it is an inopportune time to hold general elections. He expressed relief and appreciation that United States was willing to license export of needed wheat for Spain in return for lease of Spanish tonnage for transport purposes. He said that the generous attitude of the United States toward Spain was great influence towards maintenance of law and order in this country.

Apparently general situation throughout Spain improved this week. Department is informed. Number 2521, March 28, 11 a.m.

Willard.

T telegram (WP, DLC).
 [1] That is, Alfonso XIII.
 [2] Actually, O. Engelhardt. The Editors have been unable to learn his given name.

Thomas Nelson Page to the American Commissioners

Rome March 28, 1919.

210. Italian Press apparently more and more confused as to general policy. Its salient note remaining continued criticism on one reason or another of (?) attitude, and action of Peace Conference,

with special criticism of League of Nations as means of securing peace. Press it is felt, that Italy has established her position touching Adriatic problems and press now pushing for the securing Italy's interests beyond Adriatic, which it considers endangered by suggested Danubian confederation.[1] This latter considered by some as fruit of Franco-British understanding. CORRIERE DELLA SERRA alleges, with a series of facts and circumstances supporting contention, that Italian delegates Paris not sufficiently alert against active movement aimed at perpetuating Austria Hungary under form of Danubian Confederation, hinting that to such movement certain of Allies are not strangers. Same paper charges that leading British shipping interests behind British opposition to cession Fiume to Italy, and alleges these British interests have secured an agreement with Jugo-Slav leaders granting British practically the trade monopoly of Fiume. Other papers reproduce this despatch with headlines, declaring it British plot against Italy. Meantime, some papers attack alleged British-American entente. These criticisms apparently have as their source Paris.

Paris correspondent Rome TRIBUNA, who is its editor in chief[2] and has large following, criticises those critics who openly or secretly seek to fasten responsibility for present situation on President Wilson and his League of Nations, but criticises only the grounds on which their attacks based, he himself alleging deeper and truer reasons for situation.

The recent Hungarian crisis has brought Conference face to face with the fact that after five months since the Armistice, its entire program and the principles upon which it was based are being challenged. Conference has made, he says, a grave mistake from the beginning of forgetting that it was not merely a deliberative party, but an executive body.

A singular movement is reproducing itself with greater frequency near Rome, in the region Italy's biggest towns of Albano and Arriccia and some other regions, also where the people who work the fields are "circulated into uncultivated land" for the purpose of farming. This trespass is thereafter legalized by a proceeding before a special agrarian court which establishes that such trespass may continue on condition that trespasser pay half the proceeds from farm to landlord. Deputy Cabrini[3] on Italian Labor Commission, Paris Conference, can give interesting information on such legalized trespasses.

Paris correspondent Rome MESSAGGERO, examining Italy's economic problems, urges Italian technical delegates at Peace Conference insist on assuring this country sufficient coal for its needs on the principle of Allied solidarity, securing it if necessary from enemy countries or by Colonial assignment as part of the war indemnity due Italy.

The press is preparing public opinion to face the sharp rise in exchange which has already begun, by explaining the necessity of allowing freedom of trade, and suppressing national institute of exchange.   Nelson Page

T telegram (WP, DLC).
¹ About early discussions concerning this subject, see D. Perman, *The Shaping of the Czechoslovak State* (Leiden, 1962), pp. 188-91. In addition, a committee of American experts headed by Charles Seymour, on March 18, 1919, had submitted a memorandum concerning Dalmatia and Fiume to the American commissioners. The experts recommended the award of Dalmatia and Fiume to Yugoslavia. As for the latter, they argued that central European interests should be a primary consideration in determining the disposition of Fiume and that these interests would be better safeguarded by the competition that would result from the assignment of Trieste to Italy and of Fiume to Yugoslavia. This report, which the Editors have been unable to find in any collection, is printed in Ray Stannard Baker, *Woodrow Wilson and World Settlement* (3 vols., Garden City, N. Y., 1922-23), III, 263-65. Perhaps news of this report had leaked to the Italians in Paris.
² Olindo Malagodi.
³ Angiolo Cabrini, a founder of the Italian Socialist party and member of the Chamber of Deputies.

Arthur James Balfour to Edward Mandell House

Dear Colonel House,   Paris March 28th, 1919.

I wish to approach you in regard to the present situation in Montenegro.

You will remember that so soon as it became evident that a state of civil war had broken out in Montenegro an endeavour was made by the French and British Governments to induce the United States Government to send American forces to occupy the country. The United States Government, were, however, unwilling to do so and suggested that the best course to pursue would be merely to insist on the withdrawal of the Serbian forces operating in Montenegro.

The British and French Governments, however, were of the opinion that this would merely lead to renewed disorders and civil war, and they were prepared in principle to consider a joint Franco-British occupation. On examining the question however the British Military authorities decided it would be impossible for them to send British troops to Montenegro and further representations were therefore made to the United States Government, in the hope that they would reconsider their decision.

The United States Government replied on March 2nd that they were quite unable to modify their refusal to send American troops to Montenegro, and General Franchet d'Esperey has therefore given instructions that all Allied troops should be withdrawn from the country. These instructions apply not only to the French, British and American detachments but also to the Serbian and Italian detachments, and the result will be that the Montenegrins will be left to fight out their dispute alone.

So far as can be ascertained the majority of the Montenegrin people really desire to enter the Jugo-Slav State and the conflict which has arisen centres rather on the question as to whether this union should or should not be in the nature of complete fusion or whether, alternatively, some federal arrangement should be agreed on such as would reserve to Montenegro its autonomous rights. So far as our information goes we have no ground for supposing that there is any important movement in Montenegro either for complete independence or for the return of the Petrovich dynasty and we are ourselves inclined to feel that any statements which represent such a movement as being in existence emanate from Italian or other anti-Serbian sources.

It is fair to add that M. Radovich,[1] the leader of the party of complete fusion, who has just arrived in Paris, has assured us in the most categorical manner that all reports which have reached us as to internal dissension in Montenegro have been wilfully exaggerated for the purposes of Italian propaganda.

The main conclusion which may be drawn from the above is that we do not actually know the real wishes of the Montenegrin people. In order that these wishes should be ascertained I would suggest that an Anglo-American Commission should proceed to the spot and I should be glad to learn whether the American Government will agree to this proposal and will nominate a representative accordingly. It is suggested that our own representative should be Count Salis,[2] formerly His Majesty's Minister at Cettinje.

A. J. Balfour.

If you agree to Balfour's suggestion I would be glad to give you some names for your consideration.					E.M.H.[3]

TCL (WP, DLC).
 [1] Andrija Radović, head of the Montenegrin Council for National Union and a technical adviser in the Serbian delegation to the peace conference.
 [2] John Francis Charles de Salis, Count de Salis.
 [3] EMHhw.

From the Diary of David Hunter Miller

Friday, March 28th [1919]

Doctor Mezes came in in the afternoon and told me of the situation about the Polish report.[1] Mezes had seen the President and it appears that Lloyd George was opposed to giving Danzig to the Poles, and the President agreed to this because he did not want

Fiume to go to the Italians, and if Danzig went to the Poles he would have to consent to Fiume being Italian. So in his talk with Mezes he said that Danzig and the area around it was to be either free or international or independent. Mezes said all three words had been used, and when I asked Mezes specifically if it was to be connected with East Prussia, he said "no."

We discussed the matter with a map and Mezes said the other difficulty was the railroad which runs to some extent through the German part of the country and it had been proposed to put the frontier east of the railroad. The President had said that the line was to be an ethnic line so as not to have so many Germans in Poland. I told Mezes that the railroad presented a great difficulty but that so far as the independent Danzig was concerned the map could be drawn so that it would never be of much use to Germany.

I went to Mr. Lansing's dinner to Mr. Sharp. There were about twenty-five present, including Secretary Daniels, General Bliss, Admiral Benson, Mr. White, Mr. Baruch, Norman Davis, Mezes, Dr. Scott, Laughlin,[2] who used to be Counsellor of our Embassy at London, Mr. Gregory[3] and Mr. Bliss of the Embassy here. It was a wholly American dinner and I sat between Butler Wright,[4] who is now Counsellor of our Embassy at London, and Colonel Wallace[5] of General Bliss's staff.

Mezes asked me up to his room after dinner and he talked over the Polish question again and got Bowman in. It appeared that Lloyd George has named Sir Eyre Crowe for the British and the President has named Mezes for the Americans to agree on the Polish question. Mezes asked me to go with him whenever he went with Crowe and I promised to do so.

As there was some doubt as to just what the President said to Lloyd George and how far the agreement went into detail, I suggested to Bowman that he get up a map, and showed him how it should be made, which would preserve as much of the Policy Committee's report as possible consistent with our understanding of what the President had said. Mezes is very anxious to go as far for the Poles as he can consistently with the President's understanding.

I came back to the office and discussed some questions of the text of the covenant with Warrin[6] and also informed him of the Polish situation so that if necessary he could go with Mezes in my place.

I went home at one o'clock.

Miller, *My Diary at the Conference of Paris*, I, 208-209,

[1] That is, Report No. 1 of the Commission on Polish Affairs, cited in n. 3 to the minutes of the Council of Ten printed at March 19, 1919. Wilson and Lloyd George had asked Mezes and James Wycliffe Headlam-Morley (not Sir Eyre Crowe), Assistant Director of the Political Intelligence Department of the Foreign Office and a technical adviser on

political and diplomatic questions in the British delegation to the peace conference, to work out a unified British-American position on proposed modifications of this report. See Lundgreen-Nielsen, *Polish Problem*, pp. 240-41.
  [2] That is, Irwin Boyle Laughlin.
  [3] That is, Thomas Watt Gregory.
  [4] That is, Joshua Butler Wright.
  [5] Lt. Col. William B. Wallace.
  [6] That is, Frank Lord Warrin, Jr.

To Carter Glass

Paris. March 28, 1919

In view of the amounts returned to the fund for National Security and Defense as reported by your cable of the 25th,[1] I am quite willing that five hundred thousand dollars should be allotted to carry the pay rolls and incidentals of the War Risk Bureau until May 15th and that one hundred thousand dollars should be allotted to the Treasury for stationery.   Woodrow Wilson.

T telegram (J. P. Tumulty Papers, DLC).
  [1] Wilson was responding to C. Glass to WW, March 25, 1919, T telegram (WP, DLC).

From Peter Goelet Gerry and Others

Mr. President: [Washington] March 28, 1919.

It has occurred to a number of your friends who send this letter that they ought, in justice to you and in the fulfillment of their public duties, to call your attention to the necessity of seeing that some progress is made before the Peace Conference adjourns toward a solution of the vexing question of self-government for Ireland.

It is difficult at your distance from our shores to appreciate, and your brief stay on this side, on your return at the close of the late session, could not give you much opportunity to become fully cognizant of the intensity of the feeling that now prevails throughout our country on the subject referred to. We assure you that it has become a very serious matter. It may be that the subject is more prominently in the public mind because of the efforts of those who are endeavoring to arouse sentiment against the plan of a League of Nations to excite the prejudices of those of your citizens of Irish birth or descent, or it may be that Ireland is generally regarded as pre-eminently entitled to the right of self-determination in respect to her government. Doubtless both considerations have contributed to give to the question the serious aspect it has attained.

It is not alone that the future of our party imperatively demands that something be done before the work of the Peace Conference comes to an end to meet the reasonable expectations of the Irish people, but we all concur in the view that the prospect of the early ratification of the treaty by the Senate will be jeopardized otherwise.

It is quite generally believed here that Great Britain is most desirous of launching the League. Indeed, it is persistently offered by its opponents here that we pay a heavy price for the privilege of aiding her in keeping the peace of the world, indeed that we get practically nothing in return for very considerable sacrifices. Anyway she is asking much more from the Conference than we are. If these views are even measurably true, she ought to be quite willing to give assurances in some form that Ireland should at least be accorded the same measure of self-government as is enjoyed by the favored colonies.

It may be that nothing can be accomplished before the Conference, that none of the representatives from the countries whose voice is potent therein other than yourself and your American associates care to concern themselves with the claims of Ireland, but we are agreed that, in view of the considerations adverted to and your attitude so frequently and forcibly stated as to the rights of submerged nationalities, it would be a happy thing if you could, in some way, ask some action along the line suggested.

In the confident belief that your well matured plans will have the approval of the Conference, and with the assurance that in any case we shall gladly render all possible aid to secure for them the approbation of the American people and the American Senate, we are,

                    Cordially yours,   Peter G. Gerry
                                       David I Walsh
                                       Key Pittman
                                       John B Kendrick
                                       T. J. Walsh

TLS (WP, DLC).

From William Howard Taft

[The White House] March 28 [1919]

No. 41 Following just received from Mr. Taft:

"Venture to suggest to the President that failure to reserve Monroe Doctrine [more] specifically in face of opposition in conference will give great weight to objection that League as first reported is dangerous to Doctrine. It will seriously embarrass advocates of League, and it will certainly lead to Senate amendments embodying Doctrine and other provisions in form less likely to secure subsequent acquiescence of other nations than proper reservation now. Deem some kind of advisory[1] Monroe Doctrine amendment now to Article X vital to acceptance of League in this country. I say this with full realization that complications in conference are many and not clearly understood here. A strong and successful stand now will carry the League."   Tumulty.

T telegram (WP, DLC).
   [1] "advisory" not in the copy in the Tumulty Papers.

From Walker Downer Hines

[The White House] March 28, 1919.

#43 Director Genl Hines requests me to send you the following Quote: I have just seen copy of Secretary Redfield's cable of last night to you.[1] This was sent without any consultation with me in order to ascertain the position of the Railroad Administration or the reasons therefor, and therefore is fil[l]ed with erroneous statements. First as the steel prices. The Industrial Committee formed by Redfield with your approval made in my opinion a grave mistake in departing from the principle on which you authorized it to act. That principle was expressed in Secretary Redfields cable of February sixth to you[2] and was that the committee should endeavor to secure by voluntary action the establishment of a reduced level of prices at which the Railroad Administration and other Government Agencies would be justified in buying freely. The Railroad Administrations representative on the Committee insisted that the prices proposed by the Steel Interests were too high and stated specifically to the Committee that the Railroad Administration would not be justified in buying at those prices. The Committee in spite of attitude of Railroad Administration and without taking the time to make any effort to bring about voluntary action looking to purchase by the Railroad Administration at a reduced level of prices proceeded at once to announce the prices which were agreeable to the steel interests but objectionable to the Railroad Administration and now Secretary Redfield takes the position that by reason of that fact the Railroad Administration is under compulsion to buy at prices thus fixed against its protest and without any serious effort to bring about a voluntary adoption of a price level mutually agreeable. The Railroad Administration must either regard itself as without responsibility and compelled against its judgment to buy freely at any price which a majority of the committee may fix over the Railroad Administrations protest, or it must exercise its judgement in considering the merits of prices so fixed. Believing that the Railroad Administration had not been absolved from responsibility in this direction I began immediately upon the announcement of the committees steel prices to secure advice as to the appropriate position to take. The unanimous opinion of such advisers as I have so far been able to consult is that the prices announced by the committee are unreasonably high and that the Railroad Administration ought not to buy at those prices. These advisers include Judge Lovett[3] and Mr. Henry Walters. Today in Chicago I have explained to Messrs. Peek and Ritter[4] who are here on other business, the conditions as above stated and have indicated to them that I am still giving careful consideration to the question as to what position the Railroad Administration ought to take. It is not true that the Railroad Administration has refused to cooperate. It has merely insisted that it must take time to act with intelligence upon prices which appear to have been fixed without due regard to the principle upon which the committee was appointed. I am compelled on account of some labor matters of the most pressing and critical importance to be in Chicago and Atlanta and cannot be in Washington until next Wednesday at which time I hope to have final reports upon this subject. In the event I feel that the Railroad Administration cannot properly buy at the prices fixed by the Committee I will, of course, submit the matter to you with my recommendation. The fact that I have taken time to consider this matter deliberately has been on my own motion and not the result of any advice from prejudiced sources.

Second, as to the coal situation. There is no basis whatever for Secretary Redfields statements because the matter of the Railroad Administrations attitude towards the prices to be fixed by the Industrial Committee was never presented to me until after Secretary Redfields message was sent to you, having been presented for the first time in Chicago this morning by Messrs. Peek and Ritter as a result of a preliminary conference which they had a day or two ago with the coal interests. The Railroad Administration has not refused to accept coal prices which may be fixed by the Industrial Board and has not even had an opportunity to consider the matter. I can say now, however, that I shall be greatly pleased to co-operate with the Industrial Committee along the lines which I understand were sanctioned by you for its action which contemplates, as I understand it, that it will aid the coal interests and the Railroad Administration in adopting voluntary action creating reduced price levels at which the Railroad Administration will be justified in buying freely. I do not understand you have ruled that the Railroad Administration should wash its hands of responsibility in this matter and I believe its doing so would be injurious to the interests of the public. The statements of Secretary Redfield relative to the attitude of the Railroad Administration toward the coal operators are merely a restatement of the incorrect assertions which the coal operators themselves have made in what I am compelled to believe is a deliberate propaganda to force the Railroad Administration to subsidize them so they can retain a large part of the extravagant profits which many of them enjoyed during the war. A newspaper attack, apparently authorized by the Coal operators, was sent out from Washington last night assailing the Railroad Administration and charging it wholly contrary to my known policy with adopting unfair practices to drive the price of railroad fuel below the cost of production and to put a loss on the general public. The only purpose of such misleading statements is to try to coerce the Railroad Administration into a course which will unduly swell the profits of the coal operators. The Railroad Administration weeks ago established a policy of having each railroads purchasing agent make its coal purchases so as to avoid unduly combining the purchasing power of the railroads in a way to break prices to the detriment either of labor or the public. The Railroad Administration also instructed the purchasing agents not to accept any bid for coal which was not based on the existing wage level and has been endeavoring to bring about a reasonable distribution of coal to protect coal mining labor and the general situation. It has also at the request of mine labor instructed that the prices which are paid for coal be made available both to mine operators and mine labor, so as to allay any suspicion that the Railroad Administration is taking advantage of prices so low as would endanger existing wage levels. I have explained this matter to representatives of mine labor and have understood that they were pleased with our attitude in the premises. The matter has also been explained weeks ago to the coal operators and we have asked that wherever mine operators believe my instructions are not being carried out or Railroad Administration policy is having injurious effect they call our attention to specific cases. Have had few such specific complaints and all have been settled in way understood to be satisfactory. The efforts we have made to protect this situation have probably resulted in many instances in giving coal operators more profits than they ought to have, but I have felt the existing critical situation justified an extremely liberal and considerate policy for the sake of mine labor.

Third, as to the general situation. I am convinced that no agency, public or private, has a greater interest in protecting the labor situation and in promoting general business than the Railroad Administration has because its operating revenues are dependent upon business prosperity which in turn is largely dependent upon labor tranquility. I have felt, however, that I have an independent responsibility in this matter which would not permit me to be driven blindly and without independent consideration into committing the government to prices which have not been fixed according to your policy as I understand it.   unquote   Tumulty

T telegram (WP, DLC).
    [1] WCR to WW, March 27, 1919.
    [2] WCR to WW, Feb. 6, 1919, Vol. 54.
    [3] That is, Robert Scott Lovett.
    [4] That is, George Nelson Peek, chairman, and William McClellan Ritter, chairman of the Price Conference Committee of the Industrial Board of the Department of Commerce.

Two Telegrams from Franklin Knight Lane

Washington, March 28, 1919.

1342. CONFIDENTIAL. For the President from the Secretary of the Interior.

In order to provide opportunity for the people to discuss intelligently and to express their opinion in regard to the constitution of the League of Nations, I suggest that the Commissioner of Education[1] prepare and distribute to all school districts of the United States a bulletin containing the Constitution of the Leag[u]e as finally adopted in Paris, together with your New York and Boston speeches, and appropriate introductory material on the value of oratorical nonpartisan discussion, and that through this bulletin the public press and particularly the people be requested to come together in community meetings for this purpose. This will stimulate intelligent practice of citizenship in the future, a question of paramount national importance.   Phillips,   Acting.

    [1] Philander Priestly Claxton.

Washington, March 28, 1919.

1343. For the President from the Secretary of the Interior.

Referring to our number 1342. If you approve the above suggestion, please send an answer which we can publish in the bulletin with this message, and allocate from your funds enough to cover necessary expense not to exceed the sum of $10,000.

Phillips,   Acting.

T telegrams (WP, DLC).

A Telegram and a Letter from Albert Sidney Burleson

Washington D C Mar 28 1919

Taking advantage of your absence comma and counting on the fact that you may not be able to have before you full information comma cablegrams may be sent you by labor leaders alleging disturbance of labor situation in connection with wire administration period[1] In my judgment comma with a full knowledge of all the facts comma there is none comma and no danger of any occurring period Every complaint about wages has been fully considered and fairly met and every opportunity for consultations and bargaining comma either by individuals or organizations of employees comma has been accorded comma and will continue to period In dealing with the employees of the wire systems comma the wire administration has followed the policy laid down by the War Labor Board in the Western Union case prior to government control period[2] The few would-be disturbers comma outside the wire employment comma representing less than one percent of the employees comma headed by the agitator Konenkamp[3] comma who has repeatedly threatened strikes and always failed to bring same about comma are constantly making false representations of the facts comma but judging the future by the past he will be unable to secure any following among the faithful and efficient employees period The Postal Telegraph Cable Company refused to put into effect the increased wages authorized by me comma also to reduce the working hours of their men to eight a day comma and it became necessary for me to remove the officers of that company from the operation of the service period This action will greatly reduce complaints on the part of telegraph employees period More than fifteen millions of the revenues of the Bell Company alone have been absorbed by wage increases ordered by me since August one and more than ten millions of wage increases have been granted Western Union employees during the past year comma an amount equivalent to the approximate net revenue of the Western Union Company comma thus making a substantial increase in telegraph rates necessary to enable us to pay the compensation for use of the properties without incurring a deficit period Up to the present time there has been no increase in telegraph rates whatsoever comma and the wage increase in the telephone service far more than absorbs the rate increases made since August one period Am writing you fully.   Burleson

T telegram (WP, DLC).
    [1] See J. P. Noonan and Julia S. O'Connor to JPT, March 26, 1919, and JPT to WW, March 27, 1919 (first telegram of that date).
    [2] See the index references under "telegraph system" in Vol. 48 of this series.
    [3] That is, S. J. Konenkamp.

My dear Mr. President: Washington, D. C. March 28, 1919.

I fully realize the stress of mind you are laboring under at this time in dealing with the tremendous problems confronting you at the Peace Council, and I hesitate to bring before you the minor troubles of the Postal Establishment in dealing with the wire system. I have information from Mr. Tumulty that certain cables have been sent you by representatives of the International Brotherhood of Electrical Workers. Of course I have no means of knowing what they have said, but in order that you may have before you a full statement of the facts, showing just what policy has been pursued by the Wire Administration in dealing with the telegraph and telephone employees, I am attaching hereto a letter dealing with this subject addressed to the Secretary of Labor in reference to a memorandum submitted to the Secretary by Mr. Felix Frankfurter.[1] The memorandum and my letter to Secretary Wilson places you in full possession of the facts, disclosing that in every particular the Wire Administration has strictly conformed to the principles laid down by the War Labor Board to be followed in dealing with laborers and labor problems.

After my talk with Mr. Tumulty and receiving the information that cables had been forwarded to you, I sent you the cable a copy of which is also attached hereto. I am also enclosing copy of letter furnished me by Mr. Tumulty from officers of an organization setting forth certain complaints.[2] Miss Julia S. O'Connor, who signs this letter as President of the Telephone Operators' Department, is a former telephone employee. She was appointed by me as a member of the commission to standardize wages and deal with the working conditions of employees. Immediately upon her appointment she abandoned her post with the telephone company and attempted to capitalize her position and unionize the telephone employees of the country. In addition she greatly misrepresented the position of the Post Office Department. Because of her abandonment of her post of duty and her other actions, it was necessary for the telephone companies to drop her from their employment. This fact, no doubt, accounts for her hostility toward the Wire Administration and her gross misrepresentations of the facts and other subsequent acts.

The letter to Secretary Wilson answers every complaint set forth in her communication.

I apologize for worrying you about this matter, but I feel that you would desire a full knowledge of the facts as they exist.

                              Faithfully,   A. S. Burleson

TLS (WP, DLC).
    [1] F. Frankfurter to WBW, Feb. 4, 1919, TCL, and ASB to WBW, March 15, 1919, TLS, both in WP, DLC. In response to a request from W. B. Wilson, Frankfurter had

investigated the growing unrest among telephone and telegraph workers in all parts of the country. He had found that strikes or threatened strikes at Norfolk, Wichita, Salt Lake City, and San Francisco were caused by the refusal of the Telephone and Telegraph Administration of the Post Office Department to allow telephone companies under its control to deal with the labor organizations of their workers and by the failure to enforce the government's stated policy against discrimination because of labor union affiliation, as well as by specific grievances in regard to wages and working conditions. However, Frankfurter concluded that the deepest source of the discontent lay "in the feeling and fear on the part of the ·workers that there is no process for adjusting difficulties, that there is no opportunity afforded them to have 'their day in court,' and that they are entirely at the mercy of the good will of those in authority." He stated that the subcommittee appointed by Burleson to look into labor matters had "not fulfilled the hopes of its creation," and he declared that the resignation from that subcommittee of Julia S. O'Connor, "one of the most conservative and influential members of the Brotherhood of the Electrical Workers," was a "cause for the gravest concern." He recommended that either the Post Office Department should formally announce that all matters of industrial relations in the telephone and telegraph companies would be dealt with in accordance with the principles set forth by the War Labor Conference Board (about which, see the index references in Vols. 46 and 47) and ratified by President Wilson or that the department should draw up a new code or set of principles to apply to the telephone and telegraph companies. In either case, or even if the department did not see fit to announce any guiding principles, an effective wage adjustment board should be established to deal with local grievances as they arose.

Burleson's letter was a lengthy, point-by-point refutation of Frankfurter's report. He asserted that Frankfurter had consulted with no one in his department and that all reasonable grievances of the telephone and telegraph workers were being adequately dealt with through existing organizations and procedures. He revealed his own point of view in the following comment: "In presenting his arguments Mr. Frankfurter has looked on this matter solely from the standpoint of union labor and organized employees. He has failed to give any consideration to the employees who are not members of any union or members of associations not affiliated with organized labor. The latter employees represent not only an overwhelming majority but the older and more efficient employees. They are certainly entitled to the same consideration from the Government as the small minority who are members of labor organizations."

[2] That is, J. P. Noonan and Julia S. O'Connor to WW, March 26, 1919, summarized in n. 1 to J. P. Noonan and Julia S. O'Connor to JPT, March 26, 1919.

Gilbert Fairchild Close to Eugene Francis Kinkead

My dear Mr. Kinkead: Paris, 28 March, 1919.

The President requests me to acknowledge for him the receipt of your letter of March 8th[1] and to say that of course it will receive his friendly attention. His days are so filled with engagements that he finds it practically impossible to make personal replies to any part of his personal correspondence except that which strictly bears upon the work of the day.

Sincerely yours,   [Gilbert F. Close]

CCL (WP, DLC).
[1] E. F. Kinkead to WW, March 8, 1919, Vol. 55.

From the Diary of Dr. Grayson

Saturday, March 29, 1919.

There was no session of the Big Four in the morning, because Lloyd-George had asked that the session be deferred in order that he could compile the figures dealing with the British position on the indemnities and claims for reparation. In the afternoon, however, the Council of Four sat for two hours.

Lady Northcliffe was a luncheon guest, her husband, Lord Northcliffe, the publisher of the London TIMES and the London DAILY MAIL, being unable to come to Paris as he is under treatment in the south of France for a severe throat infection. Lady Northcliffe started the conversation by asking the President a number of very pointed questions dealing with the Peace Conference. She particularly wanted to know whether the British and French attitude was one of complete cooperation in the great crisis or whether they were not hindering progress, which she realized was so urgent. However, the President very diplomatically side-stepped direct reply, explaining to her that there were very many difficult and complex details which both the French and the British governments were trying to work out, and he said that these difficulties were very hard to explain without going into the subject far more fully than would be possible at a luncheon engagement. He also told her that were he to give her details without dealing fully with every subject he might create in her mind an impression that he did not intend. As a matter of fact, the President was suffering from a slight cold, which I was treating, and he explained to Lady Northcliffe that I was in a great sense his guardian and that I would not allow him to dwell too much on business matters during his meals or during such short periods of relaxation as it was possible to secure.

In connection with his slight cold, I had told him when I began treating him for it that he must be very careful; that we had no time to permit a cold to gain a foothold in his system. I told him that it was a ground-hog case. He explained to me the origin of the phrase "ground-hog case," as follows: A man was driving along a country road near a small stream, and he saw another man with a spade digging in the ground. He hailed him and asked him what he was doing. The reply was that he was digging for a ground hog and he had to have one. The man said: "Do you think you are going to get him?" The man with the spade replied: "I've got to get him; there aint any meat at home."

After we left the luncheon table the President said to Lady Northcliffe: "You must pardon me for seeming to have failed to answer some of your questions, but you know our servants are French and we have discovered that one of them speaks English perfectly, although he only speaks to us in French; therefore, we have made it a rule not to discuss official matters at the table."

The President said to Lady Northcliffe: "You have asked me questions of various individuals and my impressions of them, and perhaps the following story will convey to you an impression of a sense of humor in some of the men in whom you are interested." The President then related my Haig and Haig experience at Buckingham Palace.[1] He said: "I tried the story first on Mr. Balfour, and he grasped the point at once; then I told it to Lloyd-George, but he took some seconds before he understood just what it meant." Here Lady Northcliffe broke in and said: "Doesn't that show the difference between the two men? Isn't it typical of the differences between them?" Incidentally, Lady Northcliffe is far from being an admirer of Lloyd-George. The President, continuing, said: "I then told the story to Marshal Haig, but it took some minutes before he grasped what it was all about, because he seemed to think that the story had some connection with himself, and he was trying to figure out just what that was."

After luncheon Lady Northcliffe said to the President: "Mr. President, we feel that you are the hope of the world. This is such a terrible crisis that I think that but for you we would hardly know what the outcome would be. Do you think, speaking of us, that there is a remedy for Bolshevism? We in England feel that it is an ever-present danger, and we do not think our leaders realize the remedy, if there is one." The President said that the cure was not force but to redress their grievances. He said he had no desire to preach a sermon but that it must be remembered that after all the spread of Bolshevism has been coincident with a scarcity of food. "A hungry man is not a normal individual," the President said, and added, "You must remember the Bible supplication: 'Give us this day our daily bread.'"

The conversation then drifted to the question of the freedom of the seas, which had promised to be one of the big problems when the Peace Conference first started. Lady Northcliffe said: "We do not hear anything about that these days"; and the President replied: "It is true that the whole problem has disappeared, because originally it was suggested that neutral nations be granted the right of free commerce during all wars. However, the League of Nations makes a neutral nation in wartime an impossibility, and therefore, the problem has solved itself." He then related a story to illustrate the point of view of the British on this very question. It was that of some captured German officers, who were being interrogated on board a British warship. When asked what they thought of the British Empire, one of the officers spat to illustrate his contempt. Asked what he thought of the High Seas [Grand] Fleet, he did the same thing. Asked what he thought of Admiral Beatty, he did the same thing. Then the British officer, who was addressing him, rather angered over the episode, told him that he could spit as much as he pleased so far as the British Empire or the Admiral of the Fleet was concerned, but he would have to be very careful whose ocean he was spitting into.

After luncheon the President went to the Council of Four meeting at the French War Office. Before he left he told me that he was going down there to talk in very plain language to Clemenceau and Lloyd-George and to tell them that temporizing must cease. He said that a week had practically been wasted and that he could no longer permit such a situation to continue. The President declared that in a crisis such as now existed it was a time for courage and audacity and that was going to be his position at the afternoon meeting. He said: "I want Mr. Lloyd-George to understand that he is to stay put when he agrees with me on a subject and that he is not going to be permitted to agree with me when he is with me and then to change his position after he leaves me and joins the opposition. And I want Mr. Clemenceau to know also where he gets off. I intend telling both Mr. Clemenceau and Mr. Lloyd-George that this constant shifting of position is entirely without warrant and that so far as I am concerned if they will not deal with the problems as they should, I will reveal the facts and show where I stand, and the world will judge as to the right behind the matter and will place the responsibility where it belongs."

The President in order to relax himself played Canfield during the evening, while Mrs. Wilson sat by knitting. I sat and talked with the President making every possible effort to divert his mind from the difficult task which had confronted him during the day. I also treated his cold before going to bed. I asked him whether he would stay in bed in the morning and sleep and rest and not go to church. He said: "You are a good physician for the body but not a good one for the soul."

¹ See the extract from the Grayson Diary printed at Dec. 27, 1918, Vol. 53.

Hankey's and Mantoux's Notes of a Meeting of the Council of Four¹

I.C.169C   Clemenceau's Room at the Ministry of War,
                            14 Rue Dominique,
                            March 30 [29], 1919, 3 p.m.

(1) The attached telegram from General Nudant, notifying the attitude of the German Government towards the demand for the passage of General Haller's army to Poland through Danzig was discussed. (*Appendix I.*)²

¹ The complete text of Hankey's minutes is printed in *PPC*, V, 15-20.
² Nudant's telegram No. 806 read as follows: "Secret. Extremely urgent. German answer received at 20 hours.

§ Mantoux's notes:[3]

Marshal Foch and Generals Weygand, Sir Henry Wilson, Bliss, and Diaz are heard about the question of transporting Polish troops by way of Danzig.

President Wilson. We must take care to show that we are not departing from the terms of the Armistice. The Armistice authorizes us to send troops to Poland to maintain order. The Germans must be informed that it is for this reason, and to protect Poland from the Russian Bolsheviks, that General Haller's troops are sent to Warsaw. I believe we will avoid difficulties by leaving no doubt on this point.

Lloyd George. It is not in the interest of the German government to prevent us from forming a barrier against Bolshevism.

Wilson. I could not speak with such certainty on this last point.

Lloyd George. In any case, the German military leaders, from whom surely come most of the difficulties we face right now, greatly desire to protect themselves against Bolshevism.

Clemenceau. How shall we respond to the Germans about the ports of debarkation they suggest to us?

Foch. They have added Stettin to the list, which is much further west. They offer all the ports that one could want, except Danzig.

Clemenceau. Let us be clear: we must not renounce Danzig.

Lloyd George. We must stand fast about Danzig, even if we only have to have a small portion of the Polish troops pass through there. But we can use other ports; that will only speed up the transport.

Foch. Then I will accept Königsberg and Stettin.

Clemenceau. With Danzig.

Foch. The last German telegram sent to Spa says: "We cannot take the responsibility for measures which, if they were not covered by adequate guarantees, would provoke civil war in our own country."

Wilson. What they are asking for, then, are guarantees.

Lloyd George. The truth is that the maps of the western frontier

---

"In concluding Armistice Germans certainly had in view only passage of Allies through Danzig and not of Poles whom the German Government do not regard as forming part of Allies. Second, textually. After close examination the German Government cannot take responsibility of a measure which failing sufficient guarantee would bring about civil war in its own country.

"On the other hand it is ready to facilitate by all means disembarkation of Haller's Army at Stettin, Koenigsburg, Memel, or Libau and thus, with all its power, assist Allied intention of maintaining order in Poland. Third. Finally, in reply to your telegram 1704 of 27th March, German Government with a view to preparing execution requires information regarding composition, effectives, date of first disembarkation, subsequent relays, transport, and what guarantees would be furnished to prevent all or part of Haller's Army from participating in political manifestations or eventual rioting by Polish minority."

[3] Selected portions of Mantoux's notes of this conversation and many subsequent conversations are printed in this and subsequent volumes at appropriate places in the texts of Hankey's more formal notes. In these instances, Mantoux's notes are printed between section signs, to wit: §.

of Poland published prematurely have done the greatest harm. Sir Henry Wilson just received a telegram from General Franchet d'Espérey asking him to ask us to do everything possible to avoid the publication of maps showing modifications of the Bulgarian frontier. "Otherwise," he writes, "it will not be possible to maintain order in this country." Publishing those maps was madness; coming so long before the final decision, they could only provoke a very dangerous agitation.

Foch. The German government will tell us: "Disembark at Danzig at your own risk."

Clemenceau. We can study the question of guarantees to give the German government for the behavior of the Poles during their passage across German territory.

Lloyd George. We must tell the Germans: "This has nothing to do with the problem of Danzig's future, for which we are still studying the solution. We are only invoking Article 16 of the Armistice to allow Allied troops to pass through Danzig without stopping there. Our only goal is to send these troops to Poland against Bolshevism."

Wilson. The Germans have the right to a clear explanation of this.

Lloyd George. We must add: "These troops are Allied troops, in conformity with Article 16 of the Armistice; they fought in Allied armies on the western front." I insist upon that because it has not been sufficiently emphasized.

Foch. Other guarantees are possible. We can have the trains accompanied by Allied officers and have Allied *commissaires* placed in the train stations to prevent political demonstrations and disorder during the passage. Otherwise, in the event that some incident takes place, it will be impossible to know whether it was Germans or Poles who started it.

Clemenceau. If we agree on all these points, the text of instructions can be drafted which will be dispatched to the Polish troops. There will be delegates on the spot to guarantee order, as the Marshal proposes, and I am asking the Marshal to inform the German government of our intentions without delay.

Lloyd George. Do you mean that the Marshal will communicate with the Germans without meeting with them personally?

Foch. I await their plenipotentiary.

Wilson. It is better to wait for him and to speak with him directly.

Clemenceau (to Marshal Foch). You will therefore telegraph to the Germans: "We shall give all explanations to your plenipotentiary."

Foch. We must also ask that this be a true plenipotentiary, which is to say that he have full powers.

Lloyd George. If they send Hindenburg, that would be an interesting interview.

Foch. He would not eat me.

Wilson. The date for the meeting must be fixed.

Foch. I propose the fifth or the sixth. The Germans must not be given a pretext to complain that we have not allowed them enough time to have their experts come from Königsberg or elsewhere.

Clemenceau. That is late.

Wilson. We must choose the earliest possible date.

Lloyd George. Things will deteriorate if this affair drags on; they are deteriorating both in Germany and in our press. The sooner the better.

Foch. Then we will fix the date for the third.

Mr. Lloyd George reads the *procès verbal* of the decisions just taken, drafted by Colonel Hankey.§

After some discussion, the following decisions were reached:

(1) That Marshal Foch shall invite the Germans to send a plenipotentiary to meet him at Spa on April 3rd, and shall notify them that he will give them all the explanations and guarantees referred to in General Nudant's telegram No. 808 [806].

(2) That Marshal Foch, in making the demand for the passage of General Haller's army through Danzig, shall state that the Allied and Associated Governments think it right to explain to the German Plenipotentiaries that General Haller's army consists of allied troops, who have long been fighting on the western front; that this detachment of allied troops is sent to Poland for the preservation of order under the terms of Article 16 of the Armistice of Nov. 11th, 1918, and they have been selected for this purpose on account of their Polish nationality; that these troops are not intended for the occupation of the town of Danzig, and will only require temporary accommodation during their passage through the port; finally, that the present decision has no connection with the final disposition of Danzig in the treaty of peace. This question is not decided, and will not be finally decided until the signature of the treaty of peace.

(3) That Marshal Foch shall further be authorized, if he thinks it desirable, to arrange for the use of Stettin and other ports to supplement Danzig, where a portion of the troops will have to be disembarked.

(4) That any refusal on the part of the Germans to accede to this demand will be interpreted as a breach of the armistice by Germany. In this event Marshal Foch shall confer with the Supreme War Council as to the action to be taken.

Note: The text of the telegram sent by Marshal Foch to General Nudant in execution of conclusion (1) is as follows:

"Toutes les explications et garantis demandés seront données par moi a Spa au Plenipotentiaire demandé par moi (télégramme, March 27). Il est sans dire que celui-ci sera fourni des pleins pouvoirs necessaires pour décider dans les 48 heures. La réunion aura lieu le 2 Avril à moins d'empêchement (?) absolu."[4]

§ Mantoux's notes:

Foch. And if the Germans respond that they accept none of all that?

Lloyd George. We will not tolerate it.

Foch. Should I then threaten them with a rupture of the Armistice?

Lloyd George. It seems to me that there is nothing else to do.

Foch. Then I would like to be told what I can threaten them with.

Lloyd George. Tell them: "Your refusal ruptures the Armistice, and the Allied governments will immediately consider what measures to take." We have already reached a decision in this sense. As for the measures to be considered, it might be the occupation of Danzig, which would be both a naval and military operation, the occupation of Westphalia, or tightening of the blockade. The governments will have to choose.

Foch. Must it be told them, as in the text just read, that the question of Danzig will not receive its definitive solution before their plenipotentiaries are at Versailles?

Lloyd George. I think it is important to say this because of the distressing coincidence which has occurred between the indiscretions of the press concerning the western frontier of Poland and our discussion about sending troops into Poland to maintain order. It absolutely must be shown that these two questions are distinct.

Wilson. I understand Marshal Foch's difficulty. He wonders whether we should use a phrase which will lead the Germans to believe that they will be able to discuss our conditions at Versailles, or if we intend to present them with a solution which they must accept without modification.

Lloyd George. My text states simply that the question will not have received its final solution so long as the representatives of the Allies and the Germans have not met at Versailles.

Orlando. In that case, it would be more simple and brief to say: "The question will not be decided before the signature of the peace treaty."

Clemenceau. I prefer this text.

Lloyd George. I think it is indeed clearer.

---

[4] Translation supplied in *PPC*, V, 16: "All the information and guarantees requested will be furnished by me at Spa to the Plenipotentiary I have asked for (telegram, March 27). It is understood that he is to be given the full powers necessary to make a decision within 48 hours. The meeting will take place April 2 unless unavoidably prevented."

Foch. Then I must not give them guarantees about the future of Danzig. But the mere fact that I will not offer them these guarantees will make the Germans say: "You wish to stay there."

Clemenceau. You have only one response to make: "This question does not concern me."

Lloyd George. Or rather: "It is a question which is still under discussion."

Foch. I am leaving for Spa. The German plenipotentiary might try to prolong things. A time limit must be set for the conversation, for example, forty-eight hours.

Lloyd George. That seems to me sufficient.

(The time limit is adopted.)

Lloyd George. A parenthetical note: the Germans have troops at Libau,[5] where they are fighting the Bolsheviks, and with success. They report to us that if we give them locomotives, they will drive the Bolsheviks out of Riga. What do you think of that?

Wilson. We cannot give them to them. By doing that we would become allies of the Germans against our former allies, who have not attacked us.

Lloyd George. One word, before the Marshal's departure. I hope that he will succeed in this negotiation. If the Germans give him a refusal, we absolutely must carry out the Armistice; but we do not wish to break over a decision which is small in comparison with more serious ones which we have to impose on the Germans. We must do all that we can to succeed without using force, all the while reserving the right to use it if the Germans prove intractable.

Wilson. We cordially invite Marshal Foch to be a diplomat rather than a solider, as far as possible.

Weygand. A telegram has just been transmitted to us from Kowno,[6] where we have an officer, Colonel Reboul.[7] It asks us whether, in conformity with the Armistice, the Allied governments will not prevent the Germans from withdrawing from Lithuania. At present, the Germans are fighting the Bolsheviks in Lithuania, side by side with the Poles. If they withdraw, as they seem disposed to do, the Bolsheviks will gain ground, and the Armistice compels them to stay where they are.

Clemenceau. Answer that the Armistice must be respected.

Marshal Foch and the generals withdraw.§

(2) M. Orlando communicated the attached *aide-memoire*, handed to Prince Borghese, the Italian Minister in Belgrade, by the new Hungarian Government. (*Appendix II*).[8]

---

[5] Now known by its Lettish name, Liepaja, a Latvian port on the Baltic Sea.
[6] The Polish name for the Lithuanian city of Kaunas.
[7] He cannot be further identified.
[8] See the memorandum by Béla Kun printed at March 24, 1919.

§ Mantoux's notes:

Orlando: An Italian officer has just arrived from Budapest carrying a letter from Prince Borghese.[9] The latter, appointed minister plenipotentiary at Belgrade, left that city after the incident which you know about concerning his letters of credence, and he is returning to Italy by way of Budapest and Vienna. Having stopped at Budapest, where one of his sisters lives, he found himself there during the so-called revolution, and he sends us a very interesting letter, which I can have translated if you wish.

The important point is that the new government approached Prince Borghese, stating to him that the revolutionary movement had been provoked by political more than by social causes, that this movement was socialist, but not Bolshevik, and that it desired to have friendly relations with the Entente. They asked Prince Borghese to deliver to us a sort of declaration or memorandum. Prince Borghese responded that he was in Budapest in a purely private capacity. But he could not refuse to transmit the memorandum by way of this officer whom I mentioned to you.

I had the same hesitation as Prince Borghese before communicating this document to you. But I thought it preferable to show it to you. I add that we have not assumed any kind of obligation toward the Hungarians.

Wilson (after reading). This is a very interesting document, and I believe what it says. Can we not immediately discuss the question of sending an inter-Allied mission to Budapest, as requested by the signer of this memorandum?

Lloyd George. After all, I do not see why we should treat the Magyars differently from the Croats. The Croats, like the Magyars, fought us until the very end and very vigorously. The Magyars have never been the enemies of France or England. Undoubtedly they have had statesmen like Tisza, who bears great responsibility, but they were only supported by a very limited electorate. We maintain relations with the Croats and the Slovenes, who have on their consciences the death of a very great number of Allied soldiers. Why not enter into conversation with the Magyars as well?

Clemenceau. We could however await the return of the representatives whom we had in Budapest. They tell us that the Hungarian revolutionaries have imprisoned Colonel Vix.[10]

Orlando. A curious thing, which makes one believe in telepathy,

[9] See the memorandum by V. E. Orlando printed at March 25, 1919.

[10] Actually, Lt. Col. Ferdinand Vix and other members of the French military mission had departed from Hungary on March 26. Clemenceau undoubtedly here refers to the efforts of the Kun regime to delay their departure. Although Vix and his colleagues were subjected to verbal abuse, there is no evidence that any of them was imprisoned even temporarily. See PPC, XII, 422-24.

is that Mr. Lloyd George has just said precisely what the Hungarians said to Prince Borghese: the Croats and the Poles are accepted as friends of the Allies; why not the Hungarians?

Lloyd George. Some Poles fought against us in France up until the final days.

Clemenceau. It would be better not to take a decision before having had an opportunity to consult our Foreign Ministers.

Wilson. I do not know if they are not a bit bound by the particular point of view of the chancelleries, the idea of precedents, etc.

Lloyd George. Let us take a decision; let us not deal with Hungary as with Russia. One Russia is enough for us.

Clemenceau. Take note that this Hungarian government has made an offer of alliance to the Bolsheviks.

Wilson. By taking it at its word, we can do something useful for peace. §

A proposal was made, without sending a formal diplomatic mission, some discreet and confidential person should be sent to ascertain the real position.

No final decision was taken, but it was agreed:

(1) That each Prime Minister should consult his Foreign Minister on the question:

(2) That the question should be considered again on Monday:

(3) That President Wilson should consider the name of some discreet and trustworthy American subject, who might, subject to agreement on Monday, be sent on behalf of the Allied and Associated Powers, to Budapest, with a view to making a report. It was suggested that he might perhaps be associated with Prince Borghese in these inquiries. The Prime Minister suggested the name of General Smuts, which did not altogether commend itself to M. Clemenceau.

§ Mantoux's notes:

Clemenceau. First I would send some men there to look at the situation. To send a regular mission right away to extend a hand to the Hungarians—I do not know if we can do that.

Wilson. After all, have we not sent missions of inquiry far and wide?

Lloyd George. We even have missions in an enemy country, in Vienna, for example.

Clemenceau. I remind you that our representative in Budapest, Colonel Vix, was arrested by the new Hungarian government.

Orlando. Our officer says that they have released him, and that he has left for Belgrade.

Clemenceau. In any case, I would prefer to wait for news about this matter before sending another representative there.

Lloyd George. I would be glad to send a man like Smuts. (*To M. Clemenceau*:) I know that you do not like him after the letter I read you.[11]

Clemenceau. I respect him; but I would prefer that you send someone else there.

Wilson. I have a comment to make on the subject of our meetings. We must explain to the representatives of Japan why we have been meeting without them. I fear offending them.

Clemenceau. The truth is that we are meeting in order to study a small number of given questions in which, precisely, Japan is not interested.

Wilson. Undoubtedly; but should we not say this, to avoid offending them?

Clemenceau. I agree with you. On the other hand, I truly believe that there are questions which it would be better to discuss among ourselves. Nothing is easier than to inform them of the nature of these questions, and it would be good to add that we will invite them here at the first opportunity.

Lloyd George. Their presence will be necessary when we discuss the future of the German colonies.

Clemenceau. When can we resume study of the Klotz plan for reparations?[12]

Lloyd George. I am ready.

Wilson. So am I.§

(3) Mr. Lloyd George read the attached memorandum, and handed copies round. (*Appendix III.*)

---

[11] J. C. Smuts to D. Lloyd George, March 26, 1919, printed in William Keith Hancock and Jean van der Poel, eds., *Selections from the Smuts Papers* (7 vols., Cambridge, 1966-73), IV, 83-87. Smuts' severe criticisms of the proceedings of the peace conference to date are well conveyed by the following extract from his letter:

"I am seriously afraid that the peace to which we are working is an impossible peace, conceived on a wrong basis; that it will not be accepted by Germany, and, even if accepted, that it will prove utterly unstable, and only serve to promote the anarchy which is rapidly overtaking Europe. I say nothing about the long delays of our Conference work, and the rapid growth of dissatisfaction in all the Allied countries. Our daily communiqués with their record of small details which appear to the world to be trivialities and futilities, are enough to raise great discontent. But it is about the sort of peace we are preparing that I am alarmed.

"To my mind certain points seem quite clear and elementary: 1. We cannot destroy Germany without destroying Europe; 2. We cannot save Europe without the co-operation of Germany. Yet we are now preparing a peace which must destroy Germany, and yet we think we shall save Europe by so doing! The fact is, the Germans are, have been, and will continue to be, the *dominant factor* on the Continent of Europe, and no permanent peace is possible which is not based on that fact. . . . My fear is that the Paris Conference may prove one of the historic failures of the world; that the statesmen connected with it will return to their countries broken, discredited men, and that the Bolshevists will reap where they have sown."

The balance of the letter consisted of a selection of specific examples, laced with heavy sarcasm, of the policies laid down by the peace conference thus far which Smuts believed could only lead to the destruction of Germany and, hence, of all Europe.

[12] About which, see n. 1 to Mantoux's minutes of the Council of Four printed at March 28, 1919.

§ Mantoux's notes:

Lloyd George. I asked my experts to sift out the principles of the Klotz proposal. I believe they have seen the American experts before drafting the document which I will show you.

I call attention to the importance, from the point of view of British domestic politics, of not abandoning our claim to the total of war expenses, while admitting the obligation imposed upon us by the practical necessity to limit ourselves to a more modest demand. We would begin by indicating the immensity of the charges of every kind which have been imposed upon us by the war. They amount, for all Allied and Associated governments, to more than 750 billion marks.

Wilson. This includes our war debts, for which we do not have a right to ask reimbursement, according to our commitments preceding the Armistice.

Lloyd George. Neither do I intend to ask for this reimbursement; I restrict myself to stating the fact. In Article 3 of the document which you have before you, it is indicated that damages caused to persons include damages suffered by dependents of a combatant by reason of his death or mutilation.

Wilson. That is a point which the Germans could argue and about which jurists might differ.

Lloyd George. Let us be clear about this: we cannot leave the interpretation of such clauses to lawyers.

Wilson. I will reread you the letter sent by the Allied governments to the government of the United States explaining the nature of reparations demanded: "All damages caused to the civilian populations of the Allied and Associated States and to their property."

Lloyd George. That formula would permit us to ask more than I will ask.

Wilson. I do not deny that; but it is better to repeat in your document the terms of our correspondence of the month of November.

Lloyd George. Article 4 specifies our definition of damages caused to persons. You will notice that we ask no reparations for the failure to earn and all other indirect damages.

Clemenceau. I believe that we must indicate some priorities in Article 8.

Lloyd George. We think that this priority will take the form of a proportion to be determined.

Clemenceau. I reserve my judgment on that.

Wilson. May I observe that Article 4, on damages caused to persons, appears to extend the definition given in Article 3, and I renew my objection to Article 1, which states the total of Allied expenses.

Is it truly an advantage to say: "You owe us all that, although we would not claim it from you?"

Why not simply say, without giving figures, that the losses are so colossal that Germany could not pay them all?

Lloyd George. Undoubtedly, on the condition that we do not renounce our right to total reparation, limited only by material possibilities, which we have recognized by claiming only reparations for damage done to civilians and their property.§

Article 1. President Wilson did not like the mention of the sum of £30,000,000,000. He suggested that the first few articles should be re-drafted so as to commence as follows:

"Recognizing the central fact that the loss and damage to which the Allied and Associated Governments and their nations have been subjected as a direct and necessary consequence of the War is so colossal, that it would be impracticable for the enemy States to make complete reparation," &c., &c.

Article 3. President Wilson proposed, and Mr. Lloyd George agreed, that Article 3 should be so altered as to introduce the words mentioned in the last paragraph of the observations by the Allied Governments forwarded by the United States Government with their Note to Germany of November 5, 1918, namely:

"By it they understand that compensation will be paid by Germany for all damage done to the civilian population of the Allies and their property by the aggression of Germany by land, by sea, and from the air."

Article 4. President Wilson expressed doubts as to whether Article 4 could be included within the terms of the observations of the Allies forwarded with the Note of November 5.

Article 8. M. Clemenceau was anxious, if possible, to insert the word "priority."

The question was adjourned for independent consultation with experts.

(4) It was agreed that the next meeting should take place on Monday, April 1, at President Wilson's House at 11 a.m. when the following subjects would be discussed:

1. The despatch of a Representative to Hungary:
2. Reparation:
3. The Saar Valley.

APPENDIX III.

1. The loss and damage to which the Allied and Associated Governments and their nationals have been subjected as a direct and necessary consequence of the war, imposed upon them by the aggression of the enemy states by land, air and sea, is upwards of £30,000,000,000.

2. Notwithstanding the indisputable claim of the Allied and Associated Governments to full compensation, they recognize that the financial and economic resources of the enemy states are not unlimited and that it will therefore, so far as they can judge, be impracticable for the enemy states to make complete reparation.

3. The Allied and Associated Governments, however, require that the enemy states should at least make good, at whatever cost to themselves, the value of the material damage done and of the personal losses and injuries, including those to the civilian dependents of combatants which the enemy states have caused.

4. Each of the Allied and Associated Powers ought to receive from Germany a just reparation in respect of the death and disablement or permanent injury to health directly caused to any of its subjects by hostilities or by operations of war, whether on sea or land or in the air, or by the acts of enemy forces, populations or authorities in occupied, invaded or enemy territory. For each Power interested this reparation may always be measured by the rate of pensions or allowances now established in its territories.

5. Each of the Allied and Associated Powers ought to receive from Germany a just reparation in respect of all property belonging to the State or to any of its subjects with the exception of military works or material, which has been carried off, seized or destroyed by the enemy, or damaged directly in consequence of hostilities or of any operations of war:

(a) by immediate restoration of property carried off which can be identified in specie, with just compensation if it has been damaged;

(b) by payment of the full cost of replacing, repairing or reconstructing such property carried off, seized, damaged or destroyed, as cannot be identified in specie, or by payment of its value.

6. The amounts to be paid, the time and mode of payments and the securities to be given therefor shall be determined by an Inter-Ally Commission after examining into the claims and giving to Germany just opportunity of being heard.

7. Compensation may be required, either in the form of payment in gold or securities or in the form of mineral deposits, delivery of commodities and chattels and other reparation in kind, to be credited by the recipient power at a fair value at the time of delivery. The "ton for ton" and other analogous principles being adopted.

8. Each of the Allied Powers interested will receive out of each payment as and when it is made by the enemy a rateable share in proportion to its losses above mentioned.

9. In order to enable the Allied and Associated Powers to proceed

at once to the restoration of their industries and economic life pending the full determination of their claims, Germany shall pay in such instalments and in such manner (whether in gold, securities, commodities or ships as they may fix) in 1919 and 1920 the equivalent of £1,000,000,000 sterling to include a due provision for the maintenance of the Armies of Occupation and for indispensable supplies of food.

10. This scheme will be developed along the above lines in further discussion.[13]

(29.3.19)

T MS (SDR, RG 256, 180.03401/102, DNA); Mantoux, I, 76-84.
[13] There is a T MS of this memorandum in WP, DLC.

From Charles Homer Haskins, with Enclosure

Dear President Wilson,   [Paris, c. March 29, 1919]

Herewith I leave you the result of our conversation with the British expert, Mr. Headlam Morley. I trust it furnishes an acceptable basis of preliminary agreement in the direction discussed this morning.   Sincerely yours,   Charles H. Haskins

ALS (WP, DLC).

E N C L O S U R E

It is agreed in principle

1. That full ownership of the coal-mines of the Saar Basin should pass to France to be credited on her claims against Germany for reparation.

2. That for the exploitation of these mines the fullest economic facilities shall be accorded to France, including particularly—

  (a) Exemption from taxation on the part of Germany, including import and export dues.
  (b) Full mobility of labour, foreign and native.
  (c) Freedom for the development of adequate means of communication by rail and water.

3. That the political and administrative arrangements necessary to secure the foregoing results be enquired into.

T MS (WP, DLC).

David Lloyd George to Edith Bolling Galt Wilson

Dear Mrs Woodrow Wilson   Paris. March 29th 1919

I shall be very happy to lunch with you & the President Monday next   Ever sincerely   D Lloyd George

ALS (WP, DLC).

From Bernard Mannes Baruch

My dear Mr. President: Paris March 29, 1919

Already overburdened as you are, it is with regret that I am inflicting this long letter upon you, but if you are not already aware of these facts, its contents may save some embarrassment later on.

The reparational, economic and financial questions are so intermingled that it appears impossible to come to a judgment regarding one without considering the others. The Conference has divided them as follows:

1. Reparation,
2. Transitory measures,
3. Economic measures, permanent,
4. Financial measures.

Germany has been deprived of the greater part of the commercial advantages which she possessed before the war. There will have been taken from her the merchant marine, the various advantageous contracts for raw materials which her citizens had obtained, such as phosphate from Algiers, beauxite from France, zinc concentrates from Australia, and alloy metals from all parts of the world. She has also lost the larger part of her great commercial trading houses scattered all over the world for the purchase of raw materials and the distribution of products manufactured in Germany. She will also have lost in the Allied countries the revenue derived from patents, trade-marks, etc. She has also lost the territory of Alsace-Lorraine, with its iron and steel and textile capacity, and its potash. Prior to the war this potash was a considerable source of income, as the cartel handling potash constituted an absolute monopoly. With Alsace, which contains immense deposits of potash, in the hands of the French, the value of the German monopoly is gone. If she also loses the coal in the valley of the Saar and part of the coal in the Silesian fields, the revenue from this source will be greatly reduced, and her self-supporting manufacturing facilities greatly curtailed.

The dye-stuffs and allied chemcial [chemical] industries were formerly large revenue producers in Germany, practically one-half of which came from the west bank of thw [the] Rhine, which is now being discussed as a neutral or buffer State.

We must therefore realize that we are dealing today with a much weaker Germany than the one we knew before the war, and we must recognize that any indemnities based on pre-war conditions would be impossible. To talk of these indemnities in exaggerated terms would result in raising false hopes in the minds of the peoples of the Allied nations that would react in a serious manner.

The amount to be collected and the ability of Germany to pay are also limited by the method of collection or control and guarantee of payment. If any action along these lines is taken, it must be taken with the least possible interference with the life of the nation or its ability to pay will be seriously affected.

Before a conclusion is reached regarding reparation, an understanding should be arrived at on the economic terms to be imposed. One might easily contradict or destroy the other; one supplements and is dependent upon the other. In this connection it will of course be obvious to you that the territorial terms to be imposed upon Germany are factors of vital importance in establishing the final economic and reparational conditions.

In connection with the transitory measures, involving the question of the priority of the needs of the devastated regions—which priority has been virtually promised—there must now be given to the devastated countries sufficient credit upon which to base their orders, or some economic relations must be established whereby the districts involved, including the destroyed industries, shall be restored under a rule of priority for a limited period through the delivery of raw materials and finished products; particularly machinery from Germany, which should be delivered to the affected sections in preference to the other markets which Germany might find for this portion of her products. This question, affecting both the reparational and economic measures, should be decided at once.

As regards permanent economic conditions, the discussions of the Commission have brought us to the point where we must have a decision as to policy. The necessity of the work of the Commission grows out of the following facts:

1. All of the commercial treaties with enemy states are automatically abrogated by the war. These treaties cover such matters as tariffs, port and harbor dues, consular relations, etc.

2. Practically all of the belligerent states, including the United States, have taken action with respect to enemy patents, copyrights and other property that will give rise to an enormous crop of litigation after the war unless the situation is cleared up in the treaty.

3. Something must be done to determine the status of contracts

between the citizens of belligerent states entered into before the war, suspended during the war, and remaining enforceable, unless provision to the contrary be made in the treaty.

It is essential that when the Treaty of Peace is signed some tariff system shall immediately go into effect, in order that Germany may start with something by which she can raise revenue. It is proposed for this purpose that immediately upon the signing of the Peace Germany shall start with the lowest duties in effect on August 1, 1914. This provisional or transitional arrangement is to last but a short time, say one year, leaving Germany free at the end of that period to make such changes in her tariffs as she may desire; provided that she shall always grant to the Associated Governments treatment not less favorable than that accorded any other state.

The simplest and easiest way of dealing with the treaties defining Germany's general commercial relations (other than tariff duties) which have been abrogated by the war is to provide that, in principle and substantially, these treaties shall be revived, and that Germany shall start as she was in pre-war times. It should be provided, however, that any special favors which Germany granted to other countries before the war shall inure to the benefit of the Allies, and that any special favors which she granted to her own Allies *during* the war shall be abrogated.

All the governments save our own are insisting upon various measures which will be serious handicaps, if not actual restrictions, upon the resumption of trade by Germany. This of course will affect not alone the ability of Germany to pay, but the future peace of the world.

All of Europe is facing serious financial difficulties, which in time may find their reflex in America. This involves: (1) The questions of the adjustment of the present terms of our loans to the Allies; and (2) the advancing of a further limited amount of money to France, Italy, Belgium and the new governments. Restoration work in the devastated areas cannot be started unless credit is obtained somewhere, and the promised priorities can be granted by placing the orders now for the needed materials. Unless railroad facilities are improved, and the coal production in Europe increased, there will be more suffering during the coming year than in any year of the war. To me it seems that there is an obligation upon us to help these countries—especially the new ones, which will fall if help is denied them—by limited advances for the partial equipping of their railroads and for the purchase of raw materials to start their industries going.

Some financial and economic questions can be referred to commissions under the League of Nations, but matters affecting rep-

aration, and the establishment of economic relations with the enemy countries, the needs of the devastated areas, the finding of the
necessary money to help the newly founded governments must be
settled in order to set the world at work again, and the Treaty of
Peace cannot be signed until these questions are settled.

It is very important that a decision be reached upon the economic
questions, and I am asking if you cannot make an early appointment.   Very sincerely yours,   Bernard M Baruch

TLS (WP, DLC).

From the Diary of Colonel House

March 29, 1919.

My list of callers today is a formidable one. Tardieu arrived early
with Aubert to bring a message from Clemenceau and to talk of
the Sarre Valley difficulty. I promised to immediately call in our
Experts and see what could be done to straighten out the situation
between the President and Clemenceau.

I sent for Haskins and Mezes. Haskins believes the President is
too severe and that the economic reasons for letting France have
the Sarre Valley are fairly reasonable. I saw Haskins several times
during the day and also Mezes and Bowman. They had conferences
with Tardieu, with the British and with the President, and each time
reported back to me for my information and instructions. Haskins
and Tardieu have tentatively thought that if France could get a ten
or fifteen year total occupation of the Sarre Valley and then have
a plebecite held, it would perhaps be the best solution. I am inclined
to think so myself. I do not like the latest proposals to let France
have the ownership of the mines and work them while the territory
remains in German hands. It would certainly lead to trouble.

From the Diary of Vance Criswell McCormick

March 29 (Saturday) [1919]

President sent for Davis, Lamont and me to meet him at Clemenceau's office for reparation discussion. After sitting for some
time in ante-room at Clemenceau's office, I sent in note and the
President came out and advised us that we could not take up matter
now as they had already discussed it and he would come to Crillon
to tell us of Lloyd George's new plan.[1] This he did, meeting Davis
and Lamont, but I happened to be out when he called. I am convinced plan will not work. Lloyd George and Clemenceau trying to

duck responsibility of telling people they cannot get what they had promised them before the election and this plan is simply putting off the evil day.

[1] That is, Appendix III to the minutes of the Council of Four printed at March 29, 1919.

From the Diary of Ray Stannard Baker

Saturday [March 29, 1919]

Still pessimistic—everyone pessimistic. I took a walk with Colonel House this morning. He is usually the most cheerful & hopeful of men, but he now begins to be worried; blames the "Four" for not getting down to answers, recalls the fact that he wanted the Conference at Geneva away from French influence but was overruled by the President. I urged the necessity of a plain statement of fact from the President & an appeal to the people of the world on broad grounds.

We discussed Bullitt's report[1] from Russia which I got this morning, but could get no authority to put it out. The Colonel advised me to take it down to the President & see if he would release it for publication, which I did this evening, without result. It is dangerous, unless we have taken up the policy of dealing with the Bolsheviks.

No progress of any consequence to-day.

Lenin looms always on the horizon to the East.

[1] Printed at March 28, 1919.

To Tasker Howard Bliss

My dear General Bliss: Paris, 29 March, 1919.

Thank you for the message from Mr. Baker about the method he is adopting to meet the criticism on Court Martial decisions.[1] Please tell him that I warmly approve of what he has done, and that I shall be delighted to see him here in France.

Cordially and faithfully yours,   [Woodrow Wilson]

CCL (WP, DLC).
[1] See T. H. Bliss to WW, March 27, 1919, and the Enclosure thereto.

To Herbert Clark Hoover, with Enclosure

My dear Hoover: Paris, 29 March, 1919.

When I wrote you yesterday, I had not seen this telegram from Houston. There was some mixup about it, and it had not come under my eye. Do the suggestions contained in your letter of the other day,[1] which I answered yesterday, in your judgment take care of the exigencies mentioned by Houston?

You see I have not been able to study the matter at all.

Cordially and faithfully yours,   Woodrow Wilson

TLS (Hoover Archives, CSt-H).
[1] HCH to WW, March 25, 1919.

ENCLOSURE

Washington, D. C., March 19, 1919.

Conference with Rickard yesterday made it plain that neither food administration nor grain corporation has developed any plans or taken any of numerous important preparatory steps required to enable Government effectively to execute wheat price guarantee for 1919. Strong doubt was expressed as to the intention and willingness of the grain corporation to continue to function till the guaranty of the 1919 wheat is made good and closed out. I think it would be highly unfortunate for the existing corporation not to continue till the work is completed. It would be difficult now to devise effective new machinery and if it were done, embarrassment would result over part of period because the old corporation would be handling 1918 wheat after the 1919 crop comes into the market. It seems that Congress contemplated continuance of Food Administration grain corporation. Section two of the Act, among other things, authorizes the President to use any existing agency or agencies and to utilize any Department of the Government, including the Food Administration Grain Corporation. Only other existing agency is Department of Agriculture and it would have to create new machinery. Believe it imperative that Grain Corporation continue. Hope you will request and secure continuance of services, through Hoover, of Barnes and his aides. Very prompt action necessary. Task is one of great magnitude and only ten weeks remain till crop movement starts. Necessary that general policies and plans be outlined. Immediate decision all the more necessary if Grain Corporation will not continue.   D. F. Houston.

TS telegram (WP, DLC).

To Herbert Clark Hoover

My dear Hoover: Paris, 29 March, 1919.

Here is a telegram which you ought to "read, ponder, and inwardly digest."[1] It certainly is a high tribute to you and one to which I entirely subscribe.

Cordially and faithfully yours,   [Woodrow Wilson]

CCL (WP, DLC).
    [1] A. A. Elmore to WW, March 27, 1919, T telegram (WP, DLC). Alfred A. Elmore, president of the Joint Organization of the Farmers' Union and State Granges of the States of Washington, Oregon, and Idaho, begged Wilson to urge Hoover not to resign as United States Food Administrator on the grounds that he was absolutely indispensable to the American farm economy and the starving peoples of the world.

From William Harrison Short

Dear Mr. President: New York, March 29, 1919.

The League to Enforce Peace sends you herewith a list of 204 organizations from which we have received, during the first three weeks of March, copies of resolutions endorsing the establishment of a League of Nations.[1]

The significance of this list lies not in its size—we have reason to believe that these 204 organizations are only a small portion of all that have adopted such resolutions during this period—but in its variety and wide geographical distribution. It represents twenty-six states and almost every kind of group in which our people are associated.

None of these resolutions calls for changes in the Paris Covenant. A large proportion of them specifically favor the Paris plan. The rest support the general principles of a League.

Similar resolutions are reaching this office every day in increasing numbers. More than 400 have been received since the publication of the Paris Covenant. They come from national, state and local organizations and include such important groups as the National Grange, the American Economic Association, the Farmers National Council, the Farmers Educational Co-operative Union of America, the American Society of Equity and others of equal size and influence.

Yours very respectfully,   LEAGUE TO ENFORCE PEACE,
W. H. Short Secretary.

TLS (WP, DLC).
    [1] "Organizations That Have Endorsed League of Nations (From March 1 to March 20, 1919)," printed list (WP, DLC).

From the Diary of Dr. Grayson

Sunday, March 30, 1919.

The President and Mrs. Wilson attended church services at the Rue de Berri at 11:00 o'clock, and went for a short walk after church.

At 10:00 o'clock, before going to church, I treated the President for his cold and told him that Mr. B. M. Baruch had just telephoned me that he had received encouraging news concerning his father,[1] who has been ill with double pneumonia. The President has shown a genuine affection for Mr. Baruch and greatly admires him for his ability. He said: "The father has certainly a smart son." He also said: "I hate to think of Baruch over here without his family, feeling lonesome and distressed and worried about his father's condition. I wish you would see if you can get hold of him and ask him if he will not have a family lunch with us alone." I extended the invitation to Mr. Baruch and he had lunch with the President and Mrs. Wilson at the temporary White House. Both the President and Mrs. Wilson seemed to make him feel thoroughly at home, and it was apparent that the interest they manifested towards him did him a lot of good.

At 2:30 o'clock the President posed for the artist, M. Deschamps,[2] for the medal which the French Academy of Science wished to bestow upon him.

At 3:00 o'clock the President had a conference with twelve Congressmen—six Democrats and six Republicans[3]—who were over here for the purpose of studying conditions and visiting the battlefields. The President had a very frank and candid talk with them. They explained to him the exact condition of public opinion in the United States from their viewpoint, and naturally that viewpoint differed according to the political faith of the Representative. They asked the President a number of questions regarding the progress that was being made in connection with the Peace Conference itself. The President was extremely frank in his dealings with the Congressmen, and when they left him they expressed the belief that he was doing a good job in a good American way. Talking to the newspaper correspondents later on at the Hotel Wagram, the Congressmen said that they believed it would be a very excellent thing if the President were in a position to tell the people of the United States all that he had told them. Naturally, much of it was in confidence but it was admitted that the President had explained the great obstacles which had arisen in connection with his meetings here in such a way that the sympathies even of the Republicans, who naturally were in opposition, was aroused.

After this conference the President and Mrs. Wilson and myself went for a motor ride for two hours and twenty minutes. The President slept for nearly an hour in the car as the result of fatigue. As usual, scarcely any one recognized him along the road except little children. They would call out: "M. Le Président Wilson."

At 6:30 former Ambassador Henry White, a member of the Peace Commission, called for a conference with the President, which lasted until dinner time.

After dinner the President and Mrs. Wilson and I sat down by the open fire in the President's study and talked about various matters pertaining to the present day. The President gave us the happenings of the week and his opinions about the various members of the Peace Commission, especially Lloyd-George, Clemenceau, Orlando, Balfour, Bourgeois, Pichon, Marshal Foch and Venezelos. The conversation lasted until about 10:30, when I gave the President his night treatment for his cold and bid him good night.

It developed tonight that for the first time the British and American newspaper correspondents who are here are realizing what a tremendous task the President is facing in endeavoring to reconcile the extravagant views of the French politicians who desire a peace based upon might rather than right. I learn that a number of correspondents sent stories along that line tonight, and also emphasizing that it was unfair to blame the President for this delay. What effect these stories will have on the final negotiation is hard to say but they are all drawn to the attention of the French officials by the Censor's Office after they have been passed through the cables.

[1] Simon Baruch, M.D., physician of New York, former surgeon in the Confederate Army, a pioneer in hydrotherapy.

[2] We have been unable to identify Deschamps further. Wilson spoke to the French Academy of Moral and Political Sciences on May 10, 1919, which presented him with a gold medal. However, it bore the image of Minerva. Paris *Le Temps* and the *New York Times*, both May 11, 1919.

[3] Actually according to the report of the Associated Press, printed, e.g., in the *New York Times*, March 31, 1919, eleven congressmen were present at this conference. The Democrats were Tom (Thomas Terry) Connally and Hatton William Sumners of Texas, William Albert Ashbrook of Ohio, John Edward Raker of California, Ladislas Lazaro of Louisiana, and William Wirt Hastings of Oklahoma. The Republicans were Addison Taylor Smith and Burton Lee French of Idaho, William Raymond Green and Christian William Ramseyer of Iowa, and James Peter Glynn of Connecticut.

To Henry Mauris Robinson

My dear Mr. Robinson: Paris, 30 March, 1919.

It is so difficult to find a time for a conference, simply because I never know what time is going to be my own, that I write you the following lines in answer to your note[1] herewith returned.

It is clear to me that you should protect the title of the United States in the seized German ships and also, of course, the title of all other governments which have acted in the same way, by some specific provision.

I take it for granted that the German merchant ships are not being merely taken, but will be regarded as part of the payment of indemnity.

If this does not fully answer your question, I would be very much obliged if you would call Mr. Close up and let him know.

Cordially and sincerely yours,   Woodrow Wilson

TLS (WP, DLC).
    [1] H. M. Robinson to WW, March 29, 1919, TLS (WP, DLC). Robinson requested Wilson's opinion as to whether the American negotiators should protect the title of the United States to German ships seized during the war by a specific provision in the treaty of peace or should simply assume that that title would utlimately be held valid under international law.

From Josephus Daniels

My dear Mr. President: Paris, 30 March, 1919.

Admiral Weymss [Wemyss] came over from London and Admiral Benson and I had a conference with him on Saturday, and Mr. Long,[1] First Lord of the Admiralty, will be over tomorrow to have a conference at 11 o'clock in accordance with your suggestion. After we have talked the matter over, I would like to see you sometime Monday afternoon to give you the result of the interview and to get your point of view.

Will you be good enough to have a message sent to me at the Ritz at what hour Monday afternoon would suit you for me to call?

I found Admiral Weymss in hearty accord with Admiral Benson's feeling that the German fleet should be sunk. The more I think about it, the more I am impressed by the conviction that it would be a mistake to divide the ships between the nations and for Great Britain to sink the portion that comes to her and for other nations to keep their portions. If a portion of them is sunk, they should be sunk as the result of action of all the nations and not upon independent action of any of them. The most tangible evidence of faith in reduction of armament would be the impressive act of eliminating this great fleet as one whole. This impression would be lost if one nation should sink them and the others fail to do so. Moreover, if they are divided, there will be debate in the country whether they should be sunk or not and there is no certainty that the major portion of the fleet would be sunk. If it is the best policy to sink any of them, it is best that all of them should be sunk by action of the Council and not by independent action of any nation.

I confess that at first the idea of sinking them did not appeal to me, but when I reflect that it is not sinking many millions of dollars that would be useful and they could not be used by any nation without large investment of money to put in munition works to supply the ammunition to fit the German ships, it would really constitute a liability rather than an asset. It is a great question—whether the Council ought to favor permitting this liability to rest upon the nations which are already greatly burdened with debt.

Faithfully yours,   Josephus Daniels

TLS (WP, DLC).
¹ That is, Walter Hume Long.

From Charles Homer Haskins

Dear President Wilson,   [Paris] 30 March 1919.

A word may be useful to supplement our conversation of yesterday on the matter of the Saar basin. I am sorry I did not succeed in my efforts to confer with you on this subject before your departure in February.

Among the results of the conversations with the British experts on 21 February, which I assumed had been communicated to you, the only element which might be considered at all new as compared with previous memoranda was the suggestion of "some special form of political régime ∗ ∗ ∗ devised with the object of avoiding the subjection of considerable German population to French institutions." This was made for the purpose of limiting rather than extending French control, and in our minds certainly did not involve the creation of an autonomous state, as Mr. Lloyd George seems to have supposed.

In my original memorandum on the Saar frontier,¹ which I understood was shown to you shortly after our arrival in Paris in December, the frontier of 1814 was recommended in the Saar valley (but *not* on the Rhine), with the addition of the adjacent mining area. This, it should be noted, was drawn up before the armistice, at a time when your Fourteen Points, while expressing the fundamental principles of American policy, had not become the definitely agreed basis of negotiations. It seemed to me then, as it still seems, that the frontier of 1814 represented the peace of justice, and the frontier of 1815 the peace of violence. The frontier of 1814 was fixed as a just equivalent for the frontiers of France as they stood before the Revolutionary wars of conquest; the frontier of 1815 was imposed partly as a punishment for the Hundred Days of Napoleon, partly in order to give Prussia the coveted coal of the Saar.

Whether the frontier of 1814, however desirable on general grounds, can be reconciled with the agreed basis of the peace negotiations, it rests of course with you to determine. The larger part, however, of the territory involved lies within the coal basin, and for its transfer ample justification exists within the accepted limits of reparation to France for the systematic destruction of her coal fields and for other acts of devastation. Accepting the economic right of France to whatever reparation this coal basin can give her, the question then becomes one of the degree of political authority which should go with it. One can imagine either full economic ownership and control of the mines and their accessories, with a minimum of French political authority; or exploitation of the mines for a term of years under French occupation, with a plebiscite at the end, held under the auspices of the League of Nations, to determine the ultimate political disposal of the district. These are matters for more specific consideration.

Sincerely yours,   Charles H. Haskins

TLS (WP, DLC).
[1] "Alsace-Lorraine—Report on the Problems of Alsace-Lorraine," Nov. 14, 1918, T MS (SDR, RG 256, 185.1135/1, DNA).

From David Carb[1]

Dear Mr. President,   [Paris] March 30, 1919

I am the American in the French Army whom Mr. Baruch brought in to lunch at the Croix d'Or at Soissons last Sunday. I have no other introduction to you. But what I have to say begins and ends with this letter and therefore needs no formalities. It is just to tell you, as you have doubtless been told many times, of the faith the poilu has in your faith. His attitude is not complicated; he doesn't see how you are going to do it but he stands ready to be used by you when you desire him. Two things I have heard innumerable poilus say: "But, monsieur, every generation in France has had to fight its war," and "I didn't believe Maréchal Joffre could do it at the Marne. And he did it. Maybe President Wilson can do the impossible too" In other words all his tradition has taught him that wars go on and on, and each generation must face its wars bravely. I think that accounts for his tragic shrug when he says "C'est la Guerre," and for his silent courage. On the other hand he has learned to believe in miracles these last four years, especially miracles that emanate across the Atlantic. So, although his tradition and his experience make him skeptical, his faith is solidly behind you.

His government embarrasses the poilu. He feels that it is more political than governmental. He is not interested in empire and power—he loves his land with paternal intensity; he wants to live on it uninterrupted. He never talks of his achievements in the war (as he has a good right to talk); his conversation is all of the demobilization and his home. And with that hope ahead he continues to subsist on the coarse, never changing food that has been his fare for nearly five years, and to do the work cheerfully that is even more routine now that the adventure has departed.

I have served about two years of the war with the poilu—as an American Ambulance driver in 1915, later in the American Red Cross, and finally in his army. So what I have written you is based on long and varied contacts and observations.

I am sending you this letter, Sir, merely to amplify the number of such testimonies as mine that must come to you daily in the hope that their very number will lighten your hours of discouragement, and to be one more witness to the fact that a Foreign Office does not always express a people, nor a Parliament its desires and its ideals.

   I am, Sir,   Respectfuly yours   David Carb

ALS (WP, DLC).

[1] Former Instructor in English at the Massachusetts Institute of Technology and ambulance driver for the American Field Service in France. At this time a sous-lieutenant in the Foreign Legion of the French Army, who had been awarded the Croix de Guerre.

A Translation of a Letter from Louis Lucien Klotz

Mr. President,   Paris, March 30, 1919.

I had the honor of handing to Your Excellency, at the meeting of the Committee of Four, held on the 28th of March, a preliminary plan of the financial conditions to be imposed on Germany.[1]

This text has been the subject of a certain number of modifications, intended both for the purpose of making a better wording and that of bringing the preliminary plan into agreement with the decisions adopted by the sub-committees having to do with Financial Matters and those for Reparations and Damages.

I have the honor to send you a copy of this new text,[2] begging Your Excellency to substitute it for the text which I handed him at the meeting of yesterday[3] and which should be considered as null and void.

I beg Your Excellency will agree to the expressions of my high consideration.   L. L. Klotz

T MS (WP, DLC).

[1] About which, see Mantoux's minutes of the Council of Four, March 28, 1919, 11 a.m., n. 1.

[2] This is probably the document printed in Burnett, I, 786-87, and was, in contrast to the document just cited, a statement of general principles to govern the reparations settlement. It stated (1) the right in principle of the Allied and Associated governments to demand complete restitution from the enemy for *all* losses caused by his aggression, but that the Allied and Associated governments recognized that, for various reasons, such restitution was not possible; (2) the Allied and Associated governments demanded that the enemy states, regardless of the consequences to themselves, pay for all damages caused to the civilian populations of the Entente powers, by land and by sea, also all damages causing permanent disablement to each one of their nationals, and all damages resulting from enemy violations of treaties and international law; (3) that the sum of the damages should be determined by an inter-Allied commission, which should present a bill to the enemy states on about May 1, 1921, with provision for payment of the total sum over a period not to exceed forty years; (4) that the commission be empowered to make arrangement for these payments in various ways; (5) and that, in order to help the Entente countries to begin reconstruction, the enemy states should pay, in money or in kind, in 1919 and 1920 the equivalent of 5 billion United States dollars in gold. In addition, the Entente powers would decide upon a fair formula for distribution among themselves; goods, etc., seized or sequestered from Germany would not be counted as reparations until six months after the ratification of the present treaty; and, finally, that all these arrangements should be formalized by special treaties among the Allied and Associated powers.

[3] He meant the meeting of March 28, 1919.

From the Peace Conference Diary of George Louis Beer

March 30th, 1919.

Lord came up and asked me some questions about possibilities of an agreement of an international port at Danzig. I explained then fully my views as to the report of the Commission on the Polish situation.[1] He told me that Lloyd George was holding out on this question against all. According to Lord, W.W. had a serious row with Clemenceau about the Saar Basin on Friday night, March 28. Clemenceau called W.W. pro-German and left meeting in anger. Plan now is to give France all the coal and to leave people and territory to Germany politically. Yesterday President had Haskins, Bowman and Johnson[2] in to discuss this question and said that Lloyd George was able to quote the opinions of the American experts to him while he, W.W., was in the dark. I wonder if he quoted what I said to Kerr.[3] W.W. complained to Bowman that he did not know what the American experts thought! In view of his inaccessibility, this is delightful!

T MS (G. L. Beer Papers, NNC).
    [1] About which, see n. 3 to the minutes of the Council of Ten printed at March 19, 1919.
    [2] Douglas Wilson Johnson, Chief of the Division of Boundary Geography in the A.C.N.P.
    [3] That is, Philip Henry Kerr.

From the Diary of Lord Robert Cecil

March 30 [1919]

Dinner with the Cranbornes,[1] Harry White, and Baruch. We dined in what I called the "beer garden," which is the restaurant of the Majestic! Afterwards went up to my room for coffee, which is a good plan. Harry White is extraordinarily unchanged, except that he is a good deal older, and much lamer. Bobbity and Betty[2] seemed to like him, which is a good thing. Baruch talked to me about his financial schemes, which seem to be progressing, though a good deal hampered by what Bob Brand[3] calls the Byzantine system of the government of the United States. He has to keep it a profound secret from his American colleagues whenever he sees the President for fear of exciting their jealousy, and he is intriguing to get the control of the financial policy, and to do so glosses over the fact that the main question is financial, laying stress on the commercial aspects of the problem, so that the President shall not call in the financial experts.

[1] Robert Arthur James Gascoyne-Cecil, Viscount Cranborne, and Elizabeth Vere Cavendish, Viscountess Cranborne. Cranborne was the eldest son and heir of James Edward Hubert Gascoyne-Cecil, the 4th Marquess of Salisbury, and a nephew of Lord Robert Cecil.

[2] That is, Viscount and Viscountess Cranborne.

[3] Robert Henry Brand, a partner in Messrs. Lazard Brothers and Co., merchant bankers of London, at this time a financial adviser to Lord Robert Cecil in the latter's capacity as a British member of the Supreme Economic Council. He had spent nine months in Washington in 1917-1918 as deputy chairman of the British Mission to the United States.

Two Telegrams from Joseph Patrick Tumulty

[The White House] March 30, 1919.

No. 44. In an editorial entitled "Treat or Fight" Springfield Republican says: "It is plain the Allies dare not commit themselves to an avowed war on the Soviets and that it is not possible for the Allies with the world in its present temper to take the position that the existence of the Soviet form of gover[n]ment in any country constitutes a casus belli; that the world would recoil from the proposal to begin a new series of wars with so dubious an object; that Russia should be left to manage its own domestic affairs."

Editorial disagrees with policy of French Gover[n]ment toward Russia and Soviets. Calls attention to disastrous result of foreign intervention during French Revolution. Editorial further says "Impossible to fight Revolution in one place and be at peace elsewhere. If Allies mean to fight Hung[a]ry because it has set up a Soviet form of government and allied itself to Russia they will have to fight Russia. If they fight Russia they will have to fight the Ukraine. Such a war would mean the end of the League of Nations. It is plain that the Allies dare not commit themselves to an avowed war on the Soviets."   Tumulty

Hw telegram (WP, DLC).

[The White House] March 30 [1919]

No. 45. Dispatches from Simonds[1] and others whose stories of weeks ago were most optimistic now touched with deep pessimism. Stories [Simonds][2] in article of Saturday says, "No common objective in Council; no dominating influence; drifting, etc."[3] I fear your real position in Council not understood here and that lack of publicity strengthening many false impressions. The responsibility attaching to those associated with you, including France and England, when they accepted Fourteen Points evidently lost sight of by them. Do not know what your real situation is, but it appears to me that Germany is not prepared to accept the kind of peace which is about to be offered, or if she does accept it with its burdensome conditions, it will encourage the spread of Bolshevism throughout Germany and Central Europe. It seems to me you ought in some way to reassert your leadership publicly. I know the danger, but you cannot escape responsibility unless you do so. Now is the moment in my opinion to strike for a settlement permanent and fair.

                                                        Tumulty.

T telegram (WP, DLC).
    [1] Frank Herbert Simonds, a former editor of the New York *Sun* and former associate editor of the *New York Tribune*. At this time he was writing syndicated feature articles from the peace conference and was in the process of writing a *History of the World War* (5 vols., Garden City, N. Y., 1917-20).
    [2] Correction from the copy in the J. P. Tumulty Papers, DLC.
    [3] Frank H. Simonds, "Peace Parley Within 'Two Steps' of Failure; Leaders Lose Prestige," *New York Tribune*, March 29, 1919.

From the Diary of Dr. Grayson

Monday, March 31, 1919.

The Council of Four met this morning at 11:00 o'clock. Lloyd-George came in about a half hour before Clemenceau and Orlando arrived. After they were all here, the President said that he was glad to see that the teaching profession had at least been recognized; that in the gathering here of the representatives (four) of the four leading powers, the teachers were in a majority of three to one. Clemenceau taught school at Stamford, Connecticut; Orlando is a professor of law in Rome; and the President was at the head of Princeton University. Lloyd-George was the only one who could not qualify.

The President had a second conference this morning in an adjoining room with the Finance Committee, consisting of Mr. Baruch, Mr. McCormick, Mr. Norman Davis and Mr. Lamont.

He invited Mr. Lloyd-George, and Mr. Melville Stone, General Manager of the Associated Press, and Colonel House to lunch. The President followed his customary rule by not talking business at lunch. The others started but he turned the subject to other channels. Finally, Mr. Lloyd-George said: "Did you ever discover whether the MAINE was sunk by the Spaniards." The President said that there were some special examining boards that had put in reports. But he added: "I think Mr. Tom Reed, who was Speaker of the House of Representatives, and a very able man from the State of Maine, expressed it pretty well on one occasion when there was heated discussion on all sides as to whether we should declare war against Spain. Mr. Reed was opposed to America making such a declaration. One afternoon while going home from the Capitol, he boarded a street car and sat down by the side of a fellow-Congressman, named Handy,[1] who had just made an impassioned speech that day emphasizing why we should go to war. Mr. Reed said: 'Handy, why did you make that speech today with such blood and desire to fight with Spain.' Handy replied: 'Well, didn't she sink the MAINE and isn't that cause enough to go to war.' Reed said: 'Now, Handy, your argument reminds me very much of a man I knew in Maine who went out shooting with a double-barreled shotgun and a setter dog; while going through the woods the dog treed a bear, and the huntsman fired both barrels at the bear. Seeing that the bear had a lot of fight in him, the huntsman ran; but the bear came down the tree and practically did away with the dog. But that dog never could convince the bear that he didn't do the shooting.' "

Among other subjects discussed were Abraham Lincoln and Slavery. During the lunch the President said: "A Southern gentleman was once asked the question who, in his opinion, was the most remarkable man in America, and he replied: 'Booker T. Washington.' The inquirer asked: 'How about Theodore Roosevelt?' The Southern gentleman answered: 'I did think Roosevelt was until he invited Washington to dine with him; now I would not dine with Roosevelt.' "

The President paid beautiful tributes to Abraham Lincoln. He spoke of the debates between Lincoln and Douglas, and of the deep friendship which existed between these two men notwithstanding their differences of opinion on slavery. The President said that

Douglas accused Lincoln of believing in social equality between the whites and the blacks. Lincoln replied to this accusation:

"My friend has misrepresented me when he said that I believe in social equality. I know him so well and I can say this to his face—I would not say it if he were not present. What I said was that every man was created equal and that every one was entitled to an equal start. That does not mean that I believe in social intercourse between the whites and the blacks. I did not refer to that, and my friend knows I would not favor that. But the thing that I would not say if my friend were not present is that this morning I saw his wife driving in a carriage with a black negro." Here Lincoln paused (it was at one of their joint debates), and the audience sat aghast; then Lincoln smilingly resuming said: "But I must finish the recital, Mrs. Douglas was in the rear seat of the carriage while the negro was on the box driving."

Lloyd-George said to Mrs. Wilson: "We think your husband is the most wonderful man in every respect of them all. And I don't know what would become of our meetings in the moment of terrible tension, in this terrible crisis, when many of us feel that the future of the world is hanging by a thread—if it were not for his wonderful sense of humor that never fails to come to the rescue in the most trying time and in the most appropriate way. It gives a new breath of life to us all."

Lloyd-George said that the President had given them great delight in England over the way in which he handled Judge Cohalan and the Irish on the night previous to his departure from New York for Paris.[2] He said that the Irish question was absolutely impossible; that the Crown of England had allowed them to appoint their own delegates to come and state their desires and their wishes and how they wanted them carried out. They sent so many committees that they fought among themselves and were unable to reach any conclusion at all. The President interjected and said: "I gave you the solution of that question if you had only followed it out, namely, give them Home Rule and reserve the moving-picture rights."

The subject turned to birds, particularly the English sparrow. The President said that the English sparrow in America was a menace, because it whipped away the thrush, the robin and other song birds. Lloyd-George was surprised to hear that, because, he said, "it was such a *quiet* bird at home in England." The President said: "How do you account for the fact that it is so peaceful at home and such a fighter with us?" Lloyd-George said: "I think it is due to the fact that your climate is more energetic; that you have more champagne in the atmosphere." The President said: "That might have held good in the past but it will not hold good now, because we are dry (prohibition)."

The President said that he knew of a case where the English sparrow had had a bad political effect. And he recited the story which Mrs. Wilson told him of a Congressman in the Ninth Virginia Congressional District, who had brought some English sparrows to his district with the object of killing out a certain species of moth. However, the birds multiplied so rapidly and were so destructive to the other birds, that they became very unpopular, and when this man came up for re-election, his opponent used the argument against him that he had brought the sparrows into the community and that they had proven such a pest—and he defeated him on that platform.

The President quizzed Lloyd-George as to how well informed he was on the cootie, telling him the story of the experiments of Miss [blank] with cooties. She kept them in a glass tube, and they could not live on anything but human beings. So she had a drunken French soldier come in to feed the cooties. She turned them loose on his bare arms, put them back in the glass tube after they had partaken of a meal from the arm of this drunken French soldier, and they all showed evidence of intoxication; the large cooties fought the small cooties, and then ate them up, proving that they were cannibals. She further experimented with them and said that if you gave a patient fifteen grains of quinine a day the cooties could not live; that it had a deleterious effect on them and would kill them if you continued administering the quinine long enough.

Lloyd-George quizzed me on the subject of the dosage of quinine and the amount that could be taken in cold climates and in tropical climates. He wanted to know whether there was any difference in the dosage of quinine administered in cold or tropical climates.

Lloyd-George said that Earl Grey[3] was very fond of squirrels; that he (Lloyd-George) had been at his house, and that while Earl Grey was seated at a table, the squirrels would come in through the open window, jump up over the back of his chair and walk over the sheet of paper on his desk while he was writing, showing no signs of fear whatever. Lloyd-George would be seated at another desk in the same room and the squirrels would not come near him.

The President while speaking of atmospheric and climatic conditions said that it was a curious fact that one can put in more hours at study in this climate with less fatigue than in the American climate. He said that this explains why the Germans could devote so many hours of study but that they could not do the same kind of work in the American climate.

Just as he was leaving, Lloyd-George challenged the President and myself to a game of golf at the very first available opportunity. Lloyd-George said to me: "I have followed you with much interest, and I feel I know a good deal about you. I wish you would come to my apartment some evening for a visit. Incidentally, I would like for you to bring with you the secret as to how you have taken such care of the President through the trying times of these past years." He turned to me and whispered to me: "What is the President's best score and what is your best?" I replied that I did not care to commit myself as our contest was so near at hand.

After the luncheon party left the President conferred with Mr. Stone.

I left the house with the President at 3:15 for the Chamber of Deputies where the Supreme War Council held a meeting. Clemenceau killed over an hour reading a paper, which had also been translated into English, to be turned over to the various members of the War Council. Lloyd-George and one of the Belgian representatives had a clash on the subject of Belgian reparations. Bourgeois also killed nearly an hour in talk. The President arose and insisted on less discussion and more decision; and for the next hour they really made progress.

The President returned home a half-hour late for dinner, and immediately, before entering the dining room, conferred with Secretary of the Navy Daniels concerning the shipbuilding program. He then had a talk with Ray Stannard Baker.

The President and Mrs. Wilson and I had dinner alone. No reference whatever was made to the business of the day at the table. After dinner we had a small cup of coffee in the sitting-room. The President repeated a number of limericks, saying that some medals had been sent to him from which to select one for the French Academy. One copy is to be presented to the President and the other deposited in the archives of the Academy as a memorial of the conferring of the Academy degree upon the President. He then repeated the limerick:

> For beauty I am not a star,
> There are others more perfect by far,
> But my face I don't mind it,
> For I am behind it,
> It is those in front that I jar.

The President retired to his study to look over some important papers, saying: "My dear doctor, I report to you. I feel as if my cold is cured. And I hope you will not give me any medicine tonight."

This is a sample day in detail of what he has been going through practically every day since he has been in France.

[1] Levin Irving Handy, Democratic congressman from Delaware, 1897-1899.
[2] See the news report printed at March 4, 1919, Vol. 55.
[3] That is, Viscount Grey of Fallodon.

From the Diary of Ray Stannard Baker

Monday March 31 [1919]

Another day of talk without much of anything being done. The Big Four met at the President's house in the forenoon & with Clemenceau at the War office this afternoon. I went over to the Presidents house about 6:30. Secretary Daniels & Admiral Grayson were there & I had an interesting talk with the Secretary, who is as smiling & even-tempered as ever. He is going to Italy in a day or two. When the President came in from his meeting he had a short conference with Daniels & then talked with me about the day's doings. He said Klotz had talked interminably upon obvious matters most of the forenoon urging the new French plan of reparations: & in the afternoon Foch had talked with equal length & equal obviousness on the French claims to the west bank of the Rhine. Belgium presented its claim and the now serious Hungarian situation was considered. No decisions & very little real progress, the President said.

He is working fearfully hard. Had breakfast at 8 this morning & his schedule for the day was about as follows

8:30-10:30 with Close on his correspondence

10:30 Lloyd-George came in for a short conference

11. The Big Four met—with a meeting in another room between the financial experts of the various governments. The President went back & forth between the two

1:20 luncheon with Lloyd-George Col. House & M. E. Stone present

3. Meeting at French War office with Clemenceau lasting until 7 o'clock.

7:15 met Secretary Daniels

7:25 met me

8: Dinner

9: Studying maps & reports of experts &c &c.

I had a long talk with Col. House this afternoon. He is much discouraged, says he could make peace in a week (and I believe he could) says the situation is growing more & more serious & unless something can be done soon, there will be a break. I forgot to say that I talked with the President about the feeling that I everywhere met of the danger of the situation. "I know it," he said.

I told him also that he was being blamed on all sides for the delay.
"I know that, too," he said. I then suggested cautiously that sooner
or later he would have to show what the reasons really were for
the delay.

"If I were to do that," he said, "it would immediately break up
the Peace Conference—and we cannot risk it yet."

He is determined to be patient & try to work it through. . . .

President King was in & asking about the Syrian Mission.[1] He
said there were rumors that it would not go. I spoke to the President
about it & he apparently had clean forgotten it. Said King & Crane
were appointed. They resolute commissions into existence, but there
is no agency to work out the plans or get them off. The President
himself has no real secretary to catch up the loose ends. Such a
picture as I could draw of his household! No one there with any
authority & all afraid of the President.

I came into my office & found it smelling like a sheep-pen—two
peasants from northern Czecho-Slovakia in their home-spun natural wool peasants' clothing—a Polish chaplain was there to interpret. Here is the account—

A quaint petition in boots reached Paris today in the form of a
party of Polish peasants from the Orowa and Spisz districts of Northern Hungary. They object to the proposed plan of annexing them
to Czecho-Slovakia and are seeking an audience with President
Wilson in the hope of having one hundred and twenty thousand
isolated Poles incorporated in the New Poland. The Delegation,
wearing suits of thick, white wool felt, gayly decorated with red
embroidery, and high cossack caps of black shaggy fur, attracted
much attention when they arrived at the Crillon and sought an
audience with the President. Two members of the party, Pierre
Borowy and Adelbert Haboczyn, lived in the United States years
ago, and remember enough English to make their desires known.
Borowy, who lived in Pittsburg twenty-five years ago said: "I read
Wilson's speeches and told my friends we are sure of help. He will
not allow us to be annexed to Czecho-Slovakia if we tell him how
loyal our Polish colonies are to Poland. We have the same religion
as Poland and our priest came with us to help save us from being
swallowed up by a people of different blood and religion." Haboczyn,
who once lived in Ironton, Michigan, and has forgotten most of his
English said: "We go feet two days, then two weeks train to see
your President. Tell him I got boy thirty years old in United States.
I like America. I think she help us if she only know." The peasants
say they have only small mountain farms and their districts have
no big factories or wealth which can attract the Czechs. Some
members of the party visited the Allied Commission when it was

at Lemberg and presented their claims, but got no definite answer, so they are now anxious to make Wilson their referee.

Sooner or later everyone gets to our office. We are on the ground floor at the corner—& the PRESS is supposed to know ALL. In the course of a day we have Italians (who are the most energetic of all propagandists) Russians, Poles, Serbs &c &c. The other day the President of the Armenian republic[2] appeared with a sad story of the terrible sufferings of his people—trying to get to the President. They all try that! We also have labor delegations & woman suffrage leaders, & home-sick soldiers.

[1] About which, see the minutes of the Council of Four printed at March 20, 1919, the memorandum printed at March 25, 1919, and the notes to both documents.

[2] He almost certainly referred to Avetis Aharonian (about whom see B. Nubar to WW, Feb. 6, 1919, n. 2, Vol. 54), who held the title of "President" or chairman, of the delegation of the Republic of Armenia in Paris. There was no "President of the Armenian republic." The "Minister-President," or Premier, of the Republic, Hovhannes Kachaznuni, had in fact set out from Erevan in February 1919 at the head of a mission to Europe and the United States to negotiate for the importation into Armenia of food and other vital goods. However, detained by British officials in Tiflis, he returned to Erevan on April 2 and did not recommence his journey westward until mid-April. See Richard G. Hovannisian, *The Republic of Armenia* (2 vols. to date, Berkeley and Los Angeles, 1971-82), I, 151-52.

From the Diary of Edith Benham

March 31, 1919

All today I have been thinking of something Mr. Baruch said yesterday about Russia: that the civilized world has been letting this monstrous oppression of one hundred and eighty million people go on for years, and has never raised a finger to prevent it and now Bolshevism is spreading over and tainting all the world.

Mr. Lloyd George, Mr. Melville Stone of the Associated Press and Colonel House came to luncheon today. Mr. L.G. has one of the loveliest pink and white skins I have ever seen and a mane of fine white hair. His face is so clean and nice but he is rather untidy in his dress. He is a person of a great deal of charm and very amusing. He held forth on the Irish question and said he had had the various leaders before him and could never get from them what they wanted. The President said he would simply turn the whole question over to the Irish people, if he were the British Government, and reserve the motion picture rights! Mr. Lloyd George spoke of T. P. O'Connor[1] and said he might have been one of the foremost statesmen in the United Kingdom, for he has a statesman's mind, if he hadn't devoted himself to Ireland and all he gets now is the dislike and suspicion of his fellow countrymen. Lloyd George spoke of the President's remarkable patience with Clemenceau and said often he had marvelled how he could keep his temper as he did. . . .

This morning a body blow came. The French government sent to the Peace Commission a bill which they sent here to be okayed for the President's travelling expenses. Mind you, the Government sent the trains for him at different times and now they have sent a bill of 32,000 francs ($6,400)! Can you beat that? They are running mad. H.S.K.[2] told me that Evans[3] told him our government had given to the French government owned railroads some materials for which they had asked and were very eager to have. Then they sent a bill for hauling it from the naval base at Pouillias where it was, to the place the government wanted it dumped!

[1] That is, Thomas Power O'Connor.
[2] That is, Rear Adm. Harry Shepard Knapp.
[3] Capt. Frank Taylor Evans, U.S.N., commander of the United States Naval Air Station at *Pauillac*, France.

From the Diary of Vance Criswell McCormick

March 31 (Monday) [1919]

Met with Lamont and Davis on Reparations before going to President's house. Found the President, Lloyd George, Clemenceau, and Orlando closeted. President came out for a few minutes and gave us an opportunity to explain to him that under Lloyd George's plan we would still have to face the question of principle. We showed him the difficulties to be encountered. He told us to try to overcome them that we should try to meet Lloyd George's and Clemenceau's suggestions as otherwise, he was told by them, their ministries might fall and we would have no governments to make peace with for some time to come. Their plan is to postpone the fixing of the amount Germany is to pay and leaving determination of claims to commission to report upon later. The Prime Ministers sent for their experts to meet with Davis, Lamont, Baruch and me, so Montague and Keynes for Great Britain, Klotz and Loucheur for France, and Crespi and Chesa[1] for Italy, appeared at the President's house and we went at it. Nothing accomplished but hot air and we adjourned until tomorrow at 2.30. We were surprised at the appearance of Montague and Keynes, being back again in the conferences as they had been supplanted by Cunliffe and Sumner.

[1] Eugenio Chiesa, not Chesa, member of the Italian Chamber of Deputies and a technical adviser on reparations in the Italian delegation to the peace conference.

A Memorandum by Ferdinand Foch

March 31st, 1919.

NOTE.

In the note of January 10th,[1] the necessity was demonstrated for the Western Powers to have for military frontier a natural barrier (and there is only one—the RHINE), in order to stem the invasion of a Germanic mass of about 70,000,000 of subjects, which could, moreover, be re-inforced by a Slav mass more numerous yet.

As will be shown in the present Note, all other combination appears as insufficient, either on account of its being inefficient, or on account of the time it would need to work.

Such would be the case if the Rhenish Provinces were simply neutralised, this neutrality being consolidated by a powerful alliance.

Let us, for instance, suppose the existence of a neutral zone, 50 kilometres wide on the left and right bank of the RHINE, which would thus be free of any garrison: it is certain that whenever a German Command would decide on renewing the attack, he could, without any outward evidence thereof, take such measures as would enable him to seize the passages of the RHINE without striking a single blow, and to occupy a sufficiently broad area on the left bank to serve as a basis for an attacking force, which would have been assembled elsewhere,—thus putting us face to face with an accomplished fact, about which it would be too late, and anyhow vain to argue. It is also evident that this Command would have thereafter in hand the advantage of being over the barrier, and could, therefore, not only make a successful use of it for defence, but also advantageously bring his masses across it.

Given this unfavourable situation, which would amount to the loss of a great battle, what would then be left for us to do? To concentrate as soon as possible the Allied Armies on the frontier of our States. Unfortunately we find no natural obstacle there sufficient to cover an operation which must always be lengthy and full of peril for the Nations who will be the first engaged in battle, namely FRANCE and BELGIUM, and more so still in view of enabling them to await the arrival of the Armies of our Allies, ENGLAND and AMERICA, which must necessarily be delayed. Even if this first operation be successful, FRANCE and BELGIUM will yet only bring forward an inferior total strength, since their joint population amounts to less than 50,000,000 inhabitants against the German population unquestionably more numerous. This must, therefore, be a lost battle if these two Nations are to engage upon it alone. There is but one way of preventing such an emergency, which would have the above mentioned consequences, and which does not suppose in our enemy Army extraordinary capacity: it is for us to remain on the RHINE ourselves.

The help of an alliance cannot make up in sufficient time for the disadvantageousness of such a situation for it is doubtful whether ENGLAND could bring forth, as first help in a European War, a greater strength than she did in 1914, since she has a vast Empire to hold, and since she does not have compulsory service. But, moreover, this insufficient help can only be a late one, on account of distance, on account of the crossing of the Channel, and because, even if there is a submarine tunnel—anyhow subject to possible destruction—a single line (even be it double railed) cannot give a greater rapidity of transportation than that which we knew in 1914.

As to the American help it is not weeks but months that it will require.

Under these conditions, therefore, the battle which we will have to face in the Plains of BELGIUM will be one in which we shall suffer from a notable numerical inferiority, and where we shall have no natural obstacle to help us. Once more, BELGIUM and Northern FRANCE will be made a battlefield of, a field of defeat; soon after the enemy will reach the coast of OSTEND and CALAIS and once again those same countries will fall a prey to havoc and devastation.

If in 1914, we succeeded in holding out long enough for ENGLAND to create her big Armies, if we managed to hold on at the MARNE, at ARRAS and finally on the YSER, it is because RUSSIA was keeping on her side a notable portion of German forces, it was because she was invading SILESIA and threatening BERLIN.

This counterpoise exists no more for many a long day probably. It may even perhaps go to reinforce the hostile mass. Thereby is demonstrated the danger, on the Western Frontier of GERMANY, of a situation more serious for us than that of 1914. It is a consequence of the political changes in Nations and in alliances. This new situation cannot be overlooked: the only remedy there is to it consists in utilising, so as to reinforce it, the only frontier which Nature has created in North-Western EUROPE: the barrier of the RHINE.

After all, if we do not permanently hold the RHINE, there is no neutrality, no disarmament, no written clause of any kind whatsoever that can prevent GERMANY from seizing the RHINE and successfully debouching across it. There is no English or American help which can be strong enough, and which can arrive in sufficient time, to prevent the disaster in the Plains of the North, to preserve FRANCE from a complete defeat, or if she wants to guard her Armies therefrom, to save her from the necessity of drawing them back behind the SOMME, or the SEINE, or the LOIRE, in order to await the help of her Allies.

The RHINE remains, therefore, to-day the barrier which is indispensable to the safety of the Nations of Western EUROPE, and thereby to the safety of civilisation. There is, on the other hand, no superior principle which can force a victorious Nation to hand back to her enemy its own indispensable means of safety, which it has reconquered in a defensive war. There is no principle which can force a free Nation to live under a perpetual threat, and to count only on its Allies to be saved from disaster, when that Nation has just paid for its independance a ransom of 1,500,000 lives, and of an unprecedented devastation of its land. There is no principle which can prevail over the right of Nations to exist, against the absolute right of FRANCE and BELGIUM to ensure their independance.

Under these conditions it seems difficult to refuse to give FRANCE and BELGIUM, those Nations who are in the foremost ranks of the battle, the protection they deem indispensable to enable them to live and fight on until the arrival of their Allies, and to deprive them of the shield which will enable them to defend themselves, but not to attack: the RHINE.

Our Peace must be a just one, but also a lasting one. Whether the people of the left bank of the RHINE remain German or not the political frontier of the Nations of Western EUROPE is on the RHINE.

It will be the duty of the Conference to settle the political condition of the States on the left bank of the RHINE, and to endow them with such a constitution as will be compatible with the principle of the freedom of Nations. As a matter of fact these countries have never been anything but independant States, or odd-parts of States of Central GERMANY.

To give up the barrier of the RHINE, is to admit the following unthinkable monstrosity: that, although she be beaten, GERMANY, all covered with blood and crime, GERMANY, who is responsible for the death of millions of human beings, GERMANY, who wanted to destroy our country and turn it into a heap of ruins, GERMANY, who has undertaken to dominate the World by sheer force, would be, by our voluntary withdrawal from the RHINE, maintained in such a position that she could renew her undertakings just as if she had been victorious.

I instantly [insistently] beg the Allied and Associated Governments, who, in the most critical hours of the War entrusted me with the leadership of their Armies and the welfare of the common cause, to consider that, to-morrow just as to-day, that welfare can only be ensured in any lasting manner, by making the RHINE our military frontier, and by holding it with Allied forces. We must, therefore, maintain our present indispensable position.

T MS (WP, DLC).
    [1] It is printed as an Enclosure with F. Foch to WW, March 14, 1919, Vol. 55.

Mantoux's Notes of Two Meetings of the Council of Four

March 31, 1919, 11 a.m.

Clemenceau. M. Klotz has asked to be heard concerning Mr. Lloyd George's memorandum about reparation for damages.[1]

Klotz. The memorandum drafted by Mr. Lloyd George appears satisfactory to the French government in its general lines. We are grateful to him for having made this useful contribution to our discussion. The last article indicates in effect that it will be necessary to extend the aforesaid plan; we must arrive at formulas which can be written into the peace treaty.

Do you not believe that Articles 1 and 2 are rather for ourselves than for the enemy? It seems to me that there would be a serious disadvantage to having this kind of formula discussed by the enemy. But we can notify him of them in the form of a declaration, without including them in the preliminary articles.

Clemenceau. It is a question of form and of wording. But I believe that it is important to state that our right to compensation is not limited, and that it is we ourselves who have set a limit in view of the possibilities.

Lloyd George. We must remember that the formula used at the time of the Armistice was already written in that sense and with that intention. From the political point of view, in France and in Italy as well as in England, it is very important to indicate that our right is unlimited, and that the formula that we have adopted represents a voluntary limitation on our part.

Wilson. The document presented by M. Klotz has changed the entire status of the problem of reparations. Let us be careful of adopting a text which, by its imprecision, could lead to infinite discussions with the Germans in the future. I asked Messrs. Baruch, Davis, and Lamont to study this text, and they should get together with your specialists. I would like them to study together the difficulties to which this system, which is submitted to us, could expose us.

Lloyd George. I will put them in touch with Mr. Montagu, who

    [1] That is, the so-called Lloyd George draft printed as Appendix III to the minutes of the Council of Four printed at March 29, 1919.

has a more flexible mind than Lord Sumner and who is above all accustomed to looking at problems from the political angle.

Wilson. I wish to make my intention clear: I wish to avoid, in escaping certain difficulties by the adoption of a new system, to throw ourselves into other difficulties. We must examine this closely and be careful to avoid acting rashly.

Clemenceau. We also will send you our specialists.

Lloyd George. M. Klotz must be present, all the more since he has a personal interest in this plan, having presented it himself.

Klotz. I am going to ask you questions according to the order of the articles. And my comments will be of unequal importance.

Article 3, concerning damages caused to persons, contains these words: "including those which affect civilians dependent upon combatants." Does this include indemnities and family benefits?

Lloyd George. Certainly.

Klotz. I notice one omission: there is no provision to reimburse expenses that we have incurred in order to feed and evacuate people from invaded regions and to succor refugees. Without any possible doubt, that is a matter of damages inflicted upon civilians because of the war.

Clemenceau. Would not England, which has contributed to the revictualing of Belgium, have something additional to claim under this article?

Lloyd George. We did in fact participate in the revictualing of Belgium. I should like to know President Wilson's opinion.

Klotz. I would also include under this heading damages caused to the populations of invaded regions because of deprivation of the free use of their property rights. I ask President Wilson if he does not consider that this constitutes damage to the civilian population.

Concerning the expenses for revictualing, we know about the part America has taken. Without the aid of the Allies and of America, the populations which we have aided would be dead from hunger. The nature of the damage is not contestable.

Wilson. I am of the opinion that we should not take the trouble to make such complete catalogues of our claims. We know very well that what we will receive can only pay for that which we can formulate according to the most limited definition.

Klotz. I observe that these classifications retain their importance as far as distribution is concerned. We must take account of certain damages suffered exclusively in the invaded countries.

About Article 5, I have to present a rather important observation. Should it not be said here that the estimate of damages will be made by an inter-Allied commission, as we have agreed? In the memorandum that I have given you, I suggested this procedure.

This question concerns the Germans, who could rightly say: "Will it suffice for each of you to give figures without comparison and without guarantee?"

Lloyd George. I am entirely in agreement with you; but if you read Article 6, you will see that the commission is mentioned there and that it is said that it will examine the claims beforehand. Thus it is unnecessary to insert this clause into another part of the text.

We spoke the other day of an arbiter who could be designated by the President of the United States; it seems that there are difficulties with this manner of proceeding, and that the arbiter would have to be designated by the Chief Justice of the United States.

Klotz. I find further down the words "guarantees of payment." If this concerns economic and territorial guarantees, the governments must indicate it now; this task cannot be left to a commission.

Lloyd George. The word which has been translated as "guarantees" is "securities," which means rather *"cautions"* in French, in the financial sense of the word. It goes without saying that guarantees for execution of the financial clauses can only be stipulated by the governments.

Klotz. Furthermore, Germany must commit herself in advance to accept the decisions of the inter-Allied commission.

Clemenceau. Germany will have signed the treaty.

Klotz. Yes, but the subsequent decisions of the commission will come long after the signature of the treaty, and the commission will be invested only indirectly with the authority of the governments. I would prefer that it be written here that the decisions of the commission will have self-executing force.

As to Article 8, I must point out that thefts were committed by the enemy, restitution of which has been provided for. Is it not necessary, if there is a distribution among us, that what has been stolen and can be restored in kind be left outside of the distribution? Otherwise, we would be allowing all concerned to receive a proportional part of what has been stolen from only one of us.

Lloyd George. I have no objection to that amendment.

Klotz. Article 9 provides that the Germans make a down payment of one billion pounds sterling. In my opinion, we could say 1.2 billion pounds sterling, which is 6 billion dollars, or 30 billion francs. But I would withdraw from this article the charge on this credit for German revictualing, except for the sums already pledged. In fact, we can predict exactly neither the amount, nor the duration of payments necessary under this rubric, and it seems to me inopportune to inflate our figures of sums intended to meet Germany's needs. In my opinion, we must separate and not link these two questions.

Lloyd George. There is much to be said in favor of this, and I accept this point of view, which does not prejudice our discussions with the Germans about their needs and about the means to meet them.

Klotz. I note an omission in Article 6. There is mention of a payment which will take place at certain periods. I would prefer to reword it as "by annual payments."

Lloyd George. Of course; the payment could not be made otherwise. That is a matter of wording.

Klotz. The document which I have just examined treats only reparation for damages. But there will be other financial clauses in the preliminaries; these are the ones which have been studied by the financial commission, under the chairmanship of Mr. Montagu. Such are the questions of debts and contracts, the cession of German properties abroad, such as the Baghdad railway; the exclusion of Germans from international financial commissions, for example that concerning the Ottoman debt; the expenses of prisoners of war; the order in which Germany will have to meet her debts— taking account of her prewar debts; Germany's confirmation of her renunciation of the financial clauses of treaties she has concluded since 1914. It is only a mattter of authorizing the financial commission to prepare the text of the articles which will have to be included in the treaty.

Clemenceau. I think everyone is in agreement about that.

Orlando. Under the heading of reparations, we must not forget the compensation owed for putting into circulation paper money which was counterfeited or issued arbitrarily.

M. Klotz withdraws.

Wilson. On the question of the Saar, I have a proposal to make in the sense of what was said the other day. It is crucial to do nothing which alters a principle to which we are committed. Here is a draft[2] which has been made taking into account the particular importance and the difficulty of the case.

1) Complete ownership of the coal mines in the entire Saar basin would be awarded to France.

2) For the exploitation of these mines, all economic facilities would be guaranteed: no tax, no duty, including customs duties, could be made an obstacle. The mobility of labor will have to be assured in the entire region and in the neighboring regions. Freedom to develop avenues of land and river communication will be complete. We must seek the political and administrative means to permit the establishment of this state of things with all the desirable guarantees.

I continue to see great difficulties in the establishment of a sep-

[2] See the Enclosure printed with C. H. Haskins to WW, March 29, 1919.

arate state. The above-mentioned guarantees are necessary in order to give France full use of the mines, which will give her the compensation to which she has a right for the destruction of her coal mines in the Nord. But we cannot say to these peoples: "You must accept the form of government which we will impose upon you." That is what must be avoided as far as possible, although it must be admitted that it is inevitable, especially in countries where different populations are mixed, that some elements will find themselves detached from their national group and joined to the neighboring group.

Clemenceau. Leave me your document; we shall study it.

Lloyd George. I agree in principle with what President Wilson has just proposed.

Clemenceau. I would have much to say about President Wilson's document. I want very much for France to have ownership of the mines but not under conditions which would lead us into perpetual conflicts with the Germans in the future.

We will have to examine another question, that of the occupation of German territories as a guarantee for payment of indemnities.

Lloyd George. I am not much in favor of occupation. Since the Germans have almost no more merchant fleet and only an insignificant navy, we still have the weapon of the blockade to compel them to execute the treaty.

Clemenceau. We could not be satisfied with that; we are not so sure of its effectiveness, and public sentiment in France would not forgive us for not having imposed upon the Germans the same efficacious guarantees that they themselves imposed upon us in 1871.

Wilson. Would you think of occupying German territories until complete payment of all that Germany owes?

Clemenceau. No, but for a certain period of time, which could be divided into several parts, with gradual reduction of the occupation.

Wilson. You conceive of this occupation as an occupation by the Allies?

Clemenceau. That is what I would wish. But if we cannot obtain it, we will ask you to give France a mandate.

Lloyd George. We cannot dream of maintaining conscription in England in order to occupy German territories; British public opinion would never tolerate it.

Wilson. On the question of reparations, the text which we have discussed a short time ago avoids stating a total figure for our claims and the total figure for what Germany can pay. What troubles me is this:

When the Germans arrive at Versailles, the first thing which they will do will be to ask these two questions. If we cannot answer them, they will say: "You want to impose an indefinite obligation upon us. We wish to know today the amount Germany is commiting itself to pay." The very least that they have the right to ask is a very precise definition of the basis for compensation. Do we agree on these definitions? We must be able to respond to the Germans, or else we will appear divided among ourselves in their presence, and those among us having the most limited definitions will appear to side with the Germans.

M. Klotz wishes to avoid figures. Mr. Keynes says correctly that we can only guess somewhat randomly about what these figures will be. In any case, it is essential to agree completely about the basis of compensation and to be able to tell the Germans: "Here is our common and single interpretation."

President Wilson reads a letter from Mr. Baruch[3] laying out all the resources for payment which Germany will be deprived of due to her territorial losses.

March 31, 1919, 3 p.m.

Marshal Foch reads a report on the Rhine considered as the necessary military frontier of the western powers.[4]

Foch (commenting on the map). This map shows you that no strategic frontier exists between the Rhine and the Meuse; neither mountain nor river; nature has offered no obstacle other than the Rhine. In all his reports written before the war of 1870, Marshal von Moltke considers the line of the Rhine as Germany's frontier, for defense as well as for attack. If we gave up the Rhine, not only would we lose the trump card in our hands, but we would place it in the enemy's hands.

I ask permission to respond in advance to an argument which I foresee. One would like to avoid creating, in an inverse sense, a new Alsace-Lorraine. I beg you to reread the treaty of 1871 to see the difference between the treatment of Alsace-Lorraine by the Germans and the regime that one can envisage for the left bank of the Rhine.

By the Treaty of Frankfurt, France renounces in favor of the German Empire all her claims to Alsace-Lorraine. Germany was to possess those territories in perpetuity, with all sovereignty and ownership. When I ask for the yielding of the left bank of the Rhine, I conceive the possibility of leaving the territories to the west of the river masters of their own administration.

---

[3] See B. M. Baruch to WW, March 29, 1919.
[4] That is, the memorandum cited in n. 1 to the preceding document.

In order to understand better the importance of a strategic frontier for the western powers, I simply remind you that, without Russia, the assistance of the maritime powers in 1914 would have been to no avail.

Clemenceau. Have you anything to add?

Foch. Militarily, the results which we have obtained are guaranteed only by our occupation of the line of the Rhine. If we give it up, the situation could be reversed, and we will have only an unstable peace.

Lloyd George. Let us suppose that Germany, in 1914, had had the least idea that not only Great Britain but also America would come to the aid of France and Belgium. Would there have been a German general in his right mind who would have advised his government to go to war?

Then again, do you believe that the German generals would give similar advice to Germany at a time when her army will have been reduced to such a proportion that it will be no stronger than the British army?

Foch. To the first question, I answer: if we go back to 1914, but supposing that Russia did not exist, an officer of the German general staff could have made the following calculation: "We have enough forces to throw the French back from the Meuse, beyond the Seine, beyond the Loire, before the English would have the time to intervene effectively; all the more reason for us to have time to defeat the English and what remains of the French before the Americans make their appearance."

As for the reduction of German forces, we will pursue it, but we will never be certain of it. We cannot build upon something which is not in our hands. The Germans can elude the stipulations which will be imposed upon them in all sorts of ways.

I conclude therefore that a German general, counting on the effectives known to him but not to us, may think himself in a position to put the French army out of action before the English could appear, and the English army before the arrival of the Americans.

Lloyd George. But do you think that Germany could reconstruct an army comparable to that of 1914 without anyone knowing about it?

Foch. I can say neither yes nor no. It is not impossible. "Comparable to the army of 1914," perhaps not; but we do not know what resources the Germans may find in Russia.

Lloyd George. Before the war, we had serious reasons to watch all that Germany did from the naval point of view. For we were always informed about all her construction, and we even knew with what types of cannons she equipped her warships. If there was an error in our information, it was in excess of realities.

Wilson. Likewise, the American War College was completely informed about all changes in the German army.

Foch. We know what we know. In war, you cannot depend upon what you think you know about the enemy, but only upon your own means. I repeat what I have already told you: my enemies, I have never numbered them.

Wilson. How long would the occupation which you envisage last?

Foch. The peace can only be guaranteed by the possession of the left bank of the Rhine until further notice, that is to say, as long as Germany has not had a change of heart.

Wilson. What contingents do you foresee for the occupation?

Foch. As the disarmament of Germany is gradually completed, one could reduce the army of occupation, beginning with twenty divisions and ending with ten or twelve.

Clemenceau. What is the present strength of Allied forces on the left bank of the Rhine?

Foch. Forty-five divisions, of which three are cavalry.

Lloyd George. And that, at the moment when the military power of Germany is at its lowest!

Clemenceau. How many men does that represent?

Weygand. Nine hundred thousand combatants.

Lloyd George. I learn from an American source[5] that at this time the Germans can only assemble, for all practical purposes, around 100,000 men.

Wilson. What is the strength of a division in your calculations?

Foch. The French division in full force, a total of 17,000 men.

Weygand. Which makes 20,000 men with the services of supply.

Clemenceau. How many classes must be kept under arms in order to maintain this army of occupation?

Foch. One can maintain it with three classes. In the memorandum which I have read you, I showed the reasons we have for occupying the Rhine. In a second memorandum,[6] which I ask permission to read you, I show that any other solution is not only less certain, but more costly.

Reading of the second memorandum.

Wilson. I thank Marshal Foch for the strong and luminous manner in which he has presented his views.

Lloyd George. I would like to ask General Wilson a question. Marshal Foch seems to believe that the Channel tunnel would not assure us of more rapid transportation than in 1914.

[5] See WW to D. Lloyd George, Jan. 27, 1919, Vol. 54.
[6] That is, the memorandum printed as the preceding document.

Sir Henry Wilson. I believe that Marshal Foch sees the tunnel as an alternative to transport by sea. Obviously everything would be changed if one were added to the other.

Lloyd George. It seems to me that in that case you could double the speed of the transports?

Sir Henry Wilson. That depends upon the state of the French railroads and their congestion at the time of a mobilization.

Marshal Foch, Generals Weygand, Sir Henry Wilson, Bliss, and Diaz withdraw.

Audience of M. Paul Hymans, Foreign Minister of Belgium.

Clemenceau. We will ask M. Paul Hymans to inform us of what he desires to say to us.

Hymans. I was summoned a short time ago by M. Tardieu, who told me that you expected to hear me speak about the question of the frontier between Belgium and Germany. But I am not prepared.

Clemenceau. Did not you yourself ask to be heard?

Hymans. Indeed I asked to be heard by the "Four"; but that was because I had to speak to you about general questions relating to the future of Belgium. It would not be just if we were not present here during the discussion of the distribution of indemnities. The same observation applies to the question of the Rhine, which concerns Belgium as much as any other power. If there is an occupation of the left bank of the Rhine, Belgium will be obliged to take part in it. We would not wish to hear it said one fine day that the great powers took such and such a decision without consulting us.

My position is delicate: I never see you. During the last two months, I have asked twice to see Mr. Lloyd George; I have not met him.

Lloyd George. I apologize if that is the case; I was never informed of it.

Hymans. I believe that I have been very discreet. It would only be fair to allow me to discuss with you questions affecting the future of my country.

Wilson. I believe that there has been a misunderstanding here; M. Hymans must well understand that, if we are met as four, it is only to move more quickly and at the same time to avoid those indiscretions which have several times caused difficulties, for example the case of the Polish frontiers. We seek a settlement among ourselves of some difficult questions.

Hymans. On the question of indemnities, you heard M. Loucheur, and we have the right to be heard also. My country will find itself in a terrible situation if it is not assisted immediately.

Lloyd George. England is also in a very unsatisfactory state.

Hymans. Excuse me! You have raw materials, you have machines, your industries are working, you can sell and buy.

Lloyd George. We have a million unemployed.

Hymans. Everything is relative. In our country, it is not hardship, but complete paralysis and misery, in a country which was one of the richest in the world. You must hear me as you have heard M. Loucheur and M. Lebrun.[7]

Wilson. So far we have only studied the means for making Germany pay. Thus, you have not been excluded from a discussion concerning what Belgium should receive. Until now the question of distribution has only been discussed by a commission in which you are represented.

Hymans. That commission will come up with nothing; it is you who will decide, and it is you who must hear us.

Another question: we asked for a revision of the treaty of 1839.[8] For three years, we have discussed this question with the French and English governments. We have talked with Sir Edward Grey, with Mr. Balfour, with the French Ministers of Foreign Affairs. Six months ago, we informed the Allied governments of our intentions; at no moment did they make any objection or any suggestion. At the conference, I came to explain the views of Belgium. You listened to me; but I did not receive any advice from you; I do not know your opinion. We need to know what you think; we need your advice. This silence and the manner in which we are treated are creating a distressing impression in Belgium, which could turn against the Allies.

Lloyd George. You do not have any right to speak thus of France and Great Britain. English soldiers died by the hundreds of thousands for the liberation of Belgium. Australia sent you men all the way from the other end of the world, and she lost four times as many as you did.

Hymans. If we did not have more soldiers, that was because our country was occupied. You do not know what an invasion is. You have not seen your country under the boot of a conqueror for several years. We are waiting for the support which you promised us.

Lloyd George. It seems to me that we have given Belgium a promise which has cost us the lives of 900,000 men. If you speak to us in this way, we will not listen to you any longer.

Hymans. I simply ask you to listen to me when it is a matter of my country's interests.

Wilson. Regarding the treaty of 1839, I will say to you that we

[7] Albert François Lebrun, French Minister for the Liberated Areas and a technical adviser on economic questions in the French delegation.

[8] That is, the three interrelated treaties signed on April 19, 1839, which had established the boundaries and the neutrality of Belgium. For a summary of their contents, see Sally Marks, *Innocent Abroad: Belgium at the Paris Peace Conference of 1919* (Chapel Hill, N. C., 1981), pp. 7-10. See also C. H. Haskins to WW, Feb. 11, 1919, Vol. 55, and the minutes of the meeting of the Council of Ten printed at Feb. 11, 1919, *PPC*, III, 957-69.

do not know how to act, inasmuch as Holland has not been approached. I learned before my recent voyage to America that the Dutch were ready to discuss it; but they were wounded by the idea that one could treat them summarily and forget their neutral status. I have the impression that to plead first your cause before the "Ten" was to approach the matter from the wrong side. If you had come to me first, I would have told you: "I want to listen to you only in debate with Holland."

Hymans. The conference declared, by approving the commission's report, that there was ground for revising the treaty of 1839; it declared that France and England would invite Holland to discuss the question with them and with us. What I ask today is that you do not leave us without response and without advice, after having heard our declarations.

Wilson. You suggested an exchange between Dutch Flanders and German territories west of the Ems. I do not understand how these German territories could be given to a state which did not take part in the war. This case cannot be compared to that of Schleswig, which was once taken away from Denmark.

Hymans. I only ask you to hear me when you discuss the distribution of indemnities and the question of the left bank of the Rhine.

M. Hymans withdraws.

Messrs. Pichon, Balfour, Sonnino, and Lansing are introduced.

Orlando. I repeat what I have already said last Saturday in our Council of Four. An Italian officer arrived from Budapest carrying a letter from Prince Borghese who, as you know, was appointed Minister to Belgrade but was obliged to leave because his letters of credence were not accepted. On his return, he stopped in Budapest, where one of his sisters is married, and he was there when the revolution took place.

A member of the new government asked to see him and explained to him that this government did not wish to break with the Entente. Prince Borghese responded that he was not qualified to receive overtures, but that he could not refuse to transmit a written declaration, if it was signed by all the members of the provisional government. It is this declaration which was brought to us by the officer whom I just mentioned. This document expresses the desire for good relations with the Entente and asks that an inter-Allied mission be sent to Budapest.

Wilson. In sum, the Hungarians appeal to us so as not to be rejected from the League of Nations.

Pichon. I consider it absolutely impossible to respond to this overture of the provisional government of Hungary. That would be the worst of mistakes. What are the circumstances? Following bloody conflicts between Rumanians and Hungarians in Transylvania—a country which, we recognize, should belong to Rumania—we decided to interpose a neutral line between the combatants. We informed Budapest that the drawing of this line did not prejudice our final decision about the Rumanian-Hungarian frontier.

What happened? That still remains obscure, although the departure of Count Károlyi and the change which followed lead us to suspect that the fall of the preceding government was not involuntary. A republic of soviets was proclaimed. Our missions were expelled, and the first act of the new government was to address Lenin and to tell him that it was ready to march with him. Today, the provisional government of Hungary writes us that there is no alliance between it and the Soviet Republic. That is not very clear.

It goes without saying that I do not desire to intervene in the internal affairs of Hungary. But we are asked, in the document we have just read, to enter into conversation about territorial questions. The territorial questions concern peoples oppressed by the former Hungarian government—the Slovaks, the Transylvanians, the people of the Banat, of Croatia and of Bosnia, to whom we have promised freedom.

We cannot forget that the Hungarians are among our most bitter enemies. The responsibility of the Hungarian government in the origins of the war is terrible. It is enough to recall the role of a man like Tisza. Hungarian policy guided that of the monarchy, and the Hungarians fought to support it. This is an enemy who is offering to negotiate with us, and to negotiate about the interests of nationalities which we have promised to liberate. If we accept this offer, we will alienate ourselves from those nationalities who are or will be our allies; they would not understand it if we discussed the matter with the Hungarians when we set about here to draw their frontiers. As for Rumania in particular, we are bound more than ever to support her now that we consider her a barrier against Bolshevism.

I cannot agree to enter into negotiations with Hungary on territorial questions. When this government protests that it does not have an alliance with Russia, I cannot forget that its leader, Béla Kun, was Lenin's friend and accomplice. Are we to enter, against our allies, into relations with a government of soviets? Would that be the preface to negotiations with Russia? In that case we would be embarking on a new route, which, as far as I am concerned, I cannot accept.

Lansing. It seems to me that we have a certain responsibility for what has happened in Hungary. We tried to be just in establishing a line of demarcation between Rumanians and Hungarians. It is a question of knowing if the line itself is just.

It is the Rumanians who first crossed the line fixed by the Armistice. When it came to stopping hostilities, our experts drew a line following rather exactly the ethnographic indications; but we asked Hungary to withdraw one hundred kilometers to the west of that line. The effect of that decision was to lead them to believe that their frontier would be that of the Rumanian treaty of 1916.[9] There is no government in Hungary which could accept that, and it is that which has thrown the country into Bolshevism.

Pichon. I recall that this involves a decision by the conference. The question has been studied in depth. Generals have come to report the results of that study to you. We have acted with full knowledge of the case. What we have done displeased Hungary. But if the conference is incapable today of imposing its decision upon an enemy state, we cannot hope to make peace anywhere.

Hungary answers us with revolution, with the expulsion of our missions. We are bound to Rumania, whom we have promised to liberate the Transylvanian peoples. We have traced a line that we believe just. Are we going to repudiate Rumania? That would be an unpardonable error.

Lloyd George. Can we not separate the question of the neutral zone from the decision to take today? M. Pichon has said that we have tried to be just, and that is true. But the determination of a neutral zone can always cause misunderstandings. We had said that the Hungarians would be informed that the decision taken would not prejudice the definitive tracing of the frontier. I do not know if this has been told them clearly enough.

Balfour. It was a mistake if we neglected to do that. Besides, I do not know if we ought to look there for the cause of the events in Budapest. What I read in the newspapers shows me that the Bolshevik government has a nationalistic side, which would seem rather contradictory. The message from the Hungarians does not say much about territorial questions.

Pichon. I beg your pardon.

M. Pichon rereads the text of the message.

Balfour. Either this is only a commonplace, or we cannot accept it. I see nothing in these proposals which would place Hungary in a different situation from that of other enemy countries. It could be an advantage for us to send a mission to Budapest, and we .certainly have an interest in knowing what is truly behind all that. One suspected Count Károlyi of having used Bolshevism for his

---

[9] About which, see n. 2 to the Enclosure printed with THB to WW, March 28, 1919 (first letter of that date).

own ends. To discover what truth is in that, the best thing to do is to send men there who will look around.

Sonnino. My impression is that Colonel Vix did not say clearly enough that the determination of the neutral zone did not settle the question of the frontier. What would tend to prove this is that the declaration published at that time by Károlyi says the contrary. I read afterwards a second declaration from Vix saying to Károlyi: "That is not correct, we are not fixing the frontier at this time." But it is possible that he said it too late. We must do everything possible to clarify the situation.

With M. Pichon, I think that we cannot use a procedure with Hungary different from that which we are using with Germany or Bulgaria. Bolshevist blackmail must not procure an advantage for the Hungarians; that would be a very dangerous precedent. But no doubt must be left about our intentions; we must repeat that the line of demarcation has no other object than to avoid a collision.

Pichon. I accept this.

Wilson. We are talking as if we intended to enter into diplomatic relations with Hungary in order to fix the frontiers. That is not what we wish to do. But we can send a mission to Hungary to find out what the Hungarians think. It is impossible, I agree with M. Pichon, to enter into normal relations with them without having the other enemy states be able to ask for the same privilege. But we must avoid, by having too harsh an attitude, driving one country after another into Bolshevism.

The same danger exists in Vienna. If we had to trace a line of demarcation there, Vienna might plunge into Bolshevism the next day. If similar events repeat themselves, we will not have peace, because we will not find anyone with whom to conclude it.

Concerning Hungary, we want to separate her from Austria. It will not serve any purpose to tell her: "We wish to have nothing to do with you; we are pure and white as the snow, none of us has ever had anything to do, neither the one nor the other, with revolutionary governments." As for myself, I am ready to enter into conversation with any rascal whatever, if what he proposes to me is acceptable and my honor remains intact.

We cannot consider sending diplomatic agents to Budapest, but rather a confidential agent, having the requisite experience and authority, who would go to tell the Hungarians: "I have no powers from the associated governments, except on one point. You tell us that you wish to explain your position: do it; we do not understand what is happening among you. You say that you do not have an alliance with Bolshevism; explain to us what you have done."

It is possible, as Mr. Lansing and Baron Sonnino have said, that we are not without responsibility for the events in Budapest. Above all, the situation must be clarified. The government of Budapest is not charged with the crimes with which we reproach the Russian Bolsheviks. It is probably nationalistic. It is a government of soviets, because that is the fashionable form of revolution, and there may be many types of soviets. We have only to say to the provisional government of Hungary: "We have read your aide-mémoire, and we come to ask you what you have to say."

Lloyd George. May I observe that, according to the terms of the Armistice, nothing obliges the Hungarians to withdraw from the territories into which the Rumanians have advanced? One article authorized us to take possession of them; it is the one enabling us to occupy strategic points to maintain order. In the armistice with Hungary signed by Generals Henrys and Michitch,[10] an article stipulates that a representative of the Allies will be attached to the Hungarian ministry of revictualing. If we send someone there under that title, we are only doing what conforms with the Armistice.

Clemenceau. I would not be surprised if Colonel Vix had that very role.

Lloyd George. We are not considering sending someone there to negotiate questions of frontiers; that belongs only to the conference. But there is a misunderstanding to clear up which is very similar to that over Danzig. The Germans believed that sending Polish troops by way of Danzig meant that Danzig was going to be taken from them immediately. Likewise, the Hungarians think that we want to take from them all the territory bounded by the line of demarcation.

The King of England received from Archduke Joseph, who is not a Bolshevik, a letter expressing the fear of the Hungarians of seeing their territory divided among the Rumanians, the Czechs, and the Serbo-Croats.[11] It is a rather moving document, which conveys the idea of a current of national despair. Count Károlyi is a tired man, who threw the helve after the hatchet, and Bolshevism was only filling a void.

[10] Gen. Paul Prosper Henrys, commander of the French Army of the Orient, and Field Marshal Živojin Mišić, chief of staff of the Serbian army. See Bogdan Krizman, "The Belgrade Armistice of 13 November 1918," The Slavonic and East European Review, XLVIII (Jan. 1970), 67-87.

[11] Archduke Joseph of Habsburg to George V, Dec. 21, 1918, summarized briefly in Thomas L. Sakmyster, "Great Britain and the Making of the Treaty of Trianon," in Béla K. Király, Peter Pastor, and Ivan Sanders, eds., War and Society in East Central Europe, Vol. VI, Essays on World War I: Total War and Peacemaking, A Case Study on Trianon (Brooklyn, N. Y., 1982), p. 120. Joseph asked George to demand that the invaders of Hungary leave that country and suggested a political and economic alliance between Hungary and Great Britain.

Archduke Joseph was Joseph August Viktor Klemens, Prince and Archduke of Austria, Prince of Hungary, etc. He was the grandson of Joseph (1776-1847), who was in turn the son of Leopold II (1747-1792) and Maria Luisa.

The Austro-Hungarian Armistice was drawn up a bit hastily; it does not contain the equivalent of Article 24 [34] of the German Armistice.[12] We might try to fill that gap by designating someone to speak in our name to the Hungarians, just as Marshal Foch speaks in our name to the Germans.

I do not fault the decision taken about the neutral zone; I consider it reasonable. But I strongly support what was said by President Wilson. It would be pointless to send a subordinate man there; it must be a man who has authority.

Do not forget that these peoples are terribly afraid of us. They know that we have destroyed two great empires, and that we can do them much harm. We must speak to them firmly and send not some colonel, but a man of weight capable of representing us and of putting things back into order.

Balfour. Could he not visit other centers than Budapest?

Clemenceau. Do we not have two different proposals before us? President Wilson wishes to send someone to Budapest to conduct an inquiry. Mr. Lloyd George wishes to send a military leader to impose our will.

Wilson. To avoid the appearance of a diplomatic negotiation, it might be better to send a soldier of high rank there, who also has the personal qualities of a diplomat.

Lloyd George. I would be inclined to send General Smuts, who is a statesman as well as a military leader.

Pichon. What I have resisted is the idea of establishing diplomatic relations with Hungary. But is it possible to send someone to Budapest without first demanding satisfaction for the arbitrary measures taken against the missions which we have already sent there following what Mr. Lloyd George himself has just described as a reasonable measure?

Sonnino. The first thing to do is to impose respect for the neutral zone.

Wilson. If it seems, after an inquiry on the spot, that there are grounds for modifying the neutral zone, our representative could make such recommendations as he deems advisable on this subject.

Sonnino. That is a dangerous procedure. If, after a violent refusal, we appear to give in, there is no reason that the same thing might not happen everywhere, at Teschen, for example.

Wilson. Personally, I am not sure that the determination of that

[12] In addition to specifying the duration of the original Armistice with Germany, it included the following paragraph: "To assure the execution of the present convention under the most favorable conditions, the principle of a permanent International Armistice Commission is recognized. This Commission shall act under the supreme authority of the High Command, military and naval, of the Allied Armies." See Harry R. Rudin, *Armistice, 1918* (New Haven, Conn., 1944), pp. 431-32.

neutral zone was wise. It is possible that the tracing was not exactly what it should have been. As for the treatment of Allied missions in Budapest, we would have to know exactly what happened.

Lansing. We are told that the provisional government of Hungary only had them arrested in order to insure their safety.

Lloyd George. First we must obtain information.

Orlando. I will observe that the Hungarian document opens with a helpful statement: "The new Hungarian government recognizes the treaty of Armistice." It would be odd on our part if we did not take formal notice of this declaration. As for the treatment of the missions, the Italian mission at Laibach was expelled by the Croats. I do not see why we should make such a distinction among the different peoples of Austria-Hungary; except for the Czechs, whom I respect, all the others were our enemies. One of the reasons for the revolt of the Hungarians is the feeling that other nationalities only had to make some demonstrations in order to be treated as allies by us.

They also say that they do not believe that their refusal to accept the note presented by Colonel Vix constitutes a violation of the treaty of Armistice. I compare this attitude to that of the Germans refusing to discuss at Posen the question of the transit of Polish troops, and demanding to discuss it at Spa, invoking the text of the Armistice. We admitted, in this case, that the German observation was justified.

I accept the proposal of Messrs. Lloyd George and Wilson to send an important person to Budapest to clear up the ambiguity. General Smuts seems to me to have the desired authority. We must first demand the reestablishment of our missions, with all necessary reparations.

Sonnino. Mr. Balfour proposed that General Smuts could also visit Vienna. I would oppose that. It is better to treat the Hungarian question as a particular question, all the more so because we already have agents who inform us in the most important places of the former Austro-Hungarian monarchy.

Clemenceau. Then we agree to send to Hungary General Smuts, who will conduct an inquiry about the treatment of our missions and examine the question of the neutral zone.

Lloyd George. If Baron Sonnino has an objection to General Smuts going to Vienna, I would like that he at least be permitted to go to Bucharest, if he believes he has some chance of facilitating by that the settlement of the questions between Rumanians and Hungarians.

Mantoux, I, 85-104.

Resolutions by the Council of Four

SECRET.   Villa Majestic, Paris, April 1, 1919.[1]

RESOLUTIONS IN REGARD TO THE SITUATION IN HUNGARY.

The following action is agreed to:

(1) That General Smuts should be invited to undertake, on behalf of the Allied and Associated Powers, the following Special Mission:

To proceed to Hungary in order to examine the general working of the armistice concluded at Villa Giusti on November 3, 1918, and in particular the arrangement made by the Supreme Council for providing a neutral zone between Roumania and Hungarian troops in Transylvania. In this connection it will be the duty of General Smuts to explain to the Hungarian Government the reasons for which the zone was established, and to make it clear that the policy was adopted solely to stop bloodshed and without any intention of prejudicing the eventual settlement of the boundaries between Hungary and Roumania. This subject has not yet been adequately considered, and will not be finally settled till the signature of the Treaty of Peace.

General Smuts may make any ⟨alteration⟩ *adjustment*[2] in the boundaries of the neutral zone or the method of its occupation by allied troops which he thinks will further the objects of the allied and associated governments.

It will further be the duty of General Smuts to investigate the treatment of the Allied Missions in Budapest since the recent change of Government.

General Smuts has full discretion to proceed to any place, whether in Hungary or elsewhere, and to take any steps which may enable him to carry out these objects or others closely connected with them.

He will report fully to the Supreme Council.

(2) That M. Clemenceau shall write a letter, on behalf of the Allied and Associated Powers, authorising General Smuts to undertake this Mission.

(3) That M. Clemenceau shall notify the scope of General Smuts' Mission to the General Officers Commanding the Allied troops in South Eastern Europe, and shall instruct them to comply with such directions as he may give for ⟨alterations⟩ *adjustments* in the boundaries of the neutral zone, or the method of its occupation by Allied troops, and generally to give him every facility for carrying out his Mission.

(4) That M. Orlando shall instruct Prince Borghese to inform the Hungarian Government of General Smuts' Mission.

T MS (WP, DLC).
    ¹ This memorandum is printed here, because, although typed on April 1, 1919, it embodied resolutions adopted on March 31, 1919. The Majestic Hotel was the headquarters of the British delegation in Paris.
    ² Words in angle brackets deleted by Wilson; words in italics added by him.

From the American Commissioners, with Enclosure

Paris, March 31st, 1919

The American Commissioners to Negotiate Peace have the honor to transmit herewith to the President of the United States a copy of a Memorandum prepared by the Russian Section of the Commission,¹ containing suggestions regarding a Russian policy.

RL

TI MS (WP, DLC).
    ¹ The members were Robert H. Lord, chairman, William C. Bullitt, and Walter W. Pettit. Pettit was in Helsinki at this time.

E N C L O S U R E

MEMORANDUM FROM THE RUSSIAN SECTION
THE RUSSIAN POLICY.

Under date of March 27th, the Russian Section recommended a declaration in regard to Russia, similar to those which led to the German Armistice.¹

Aside from the general proposition (the truth of which is now obvious) that failure to deal frankly with the Russian problem has already had disastrous effects endangering the success of the whole Peace Conference, the following considerations are submitted in favor of the action recommended.

FIRST There is strong reason to take action, even before the German treaty is presented. Observers in Germany, including Mr. Franklin Day,² of the American Mission to Berlin, Mr. O. G. Villard³ and various British officers, report the entire probability of the Present German Government's turning the country over to the Spartacist-Bolshevist bloc, just as the Karolyi government has done in Hungary, if the peace terms prove severe. This is confirmed by statements of German official newspapers, government officials, and by the recent German attempt to open relations with Moscow.

SECOND No military barrier separates Germany from the Red Armies. In Lithuania, German and Bolshevist troops are in direct contact, as the so-called "Lithuanian" forces are dominated by the German units which form the real fighting nucleus. In the event of Spartacist uprising, this front would change to a line of communication, with an easy avenue through East Prussia into Germany.

Hungary is separated from Russia only by the weak Ukrainian troops under Petliura.[4] These are of bad quality, hard pressed, tend to be anti-Entente, and are reported to be at present in negotiation with the Moscow Government. Their elimination by defeat or defection would open several entrances, with adequate railway lines, into the Hungarian plain.

Isolation of the Russian revolution from the German and Hungarian problem would seem to be of obvious military advantage. An armistice under suitable conditions would accomplish this result.

Failure to isolate the Russian Revolution may involve us in the disastrous policy of having to fight the European Revolution (a thing we neither can nor should do), through inability to dissociate the German and Hungarian revolutions, of whose sincerity there is doubt, from the terribly genuine radical movement in Russia.

THIRD The Bolshevist Government sincerely desires an armistice. This government has made repeated offers the last of which has only just been received.[5] Our own offer, included in the Prinkipo proposal,[6] was accepted without reserve; it is believed that armistice would then have been consummated had the Allied governments sent suitable officers to meet the Bolshevist representatives under flag of truce to arrange details. Russian economic disarrangement demands peace to permit reconstruction; every report demonstrates the effectiveness of the blockade. However, insolently expressed, the Bolshevist offers have been dictated by a real desire for peace.

FOURTH A declaration by the President, like that leading to the German armistice, and backed by action, would go far toward securing an armistice. Such a statement could include:

(1) A repudiation of the bribe implied in offers to buy peace with commercial concessions.

(2) A condemnation of the excesses of the Revolution: the Terror, atrocities, violation of the embassies, violence and incitement to violence against and within neighboring nations, suppression of free speech and free political action; coupled with a declaration of intention to defend by all means ourselves and the states whose autonomous existence is contemplated by the Fourteen Points.

(3) A declaration of friendship for the ideals of the Revolution along the lines of the statement in the President's speech of April 2, 1917 (urging the declaration of war) and renewing the assertions of friendship made in the Prinkipo proposal.

(4) A declaration of readiness to cease operations and (except as to military supplies) to lift the blockade, provided armistice is made,

with guarantees by the Bolshevist governments of peaceful intention and cessation of the excesses condemned.

(5) A declaration of willingness to extend formal recognition and
positive aid only to a government which, seeking to realize the ideals
of the Russian Revolution, has a plain mandate from the people.

(6) A statement of the policy of relief for Russia so far as possible,
not as a bargain, but as simple humanity.

FIFTH Independently of our Russian policy, but preferably coordinated with it, the Russian Section believes the independence
of Esthonia, Latvia and Lithuania ought to be recognized in principle, and that so long as their struggle with Bolshevism continues,
they ought to be supported. Recognition should be limited by the
reservation that questions of frontiers, free ports and transit to Russia must be regulated by the Peace Conference or the League of
Nations, at such time as Russia is able to present her case.

The door to eventual federal union with Russia should not be
closed.

T MS (WP, DLC).
   [1] This memorandum of March 27, 1919, prepared by William C. Bullitt with the
assistance of Whitney Shephardson, one of Colonel House's aides, is printed in [William
C. Bullitt] *The Bullitt Mission to Russia* (New York, 1919), pp. 69-73. It repeated the
arguments and recommendations embodied in the memorandum printed herein. Bullitt
later implied that he did not think that Wilson ever saw the memorandum of March
27, 1919. John M. Thompson, *Russia, Bolshevism, and the Versailles Peace* (Princeton,
N. J., 1966), pp. 242-43, says that House buried the memorandum. For conjecture as
to whether Wilson read the memorandum printed herein, see WW to RL, April 1, 1919
(first letter of that date), n. 1.
   [2] He cannot be further identified.
   [3] He had accompanied Ellis Loring Dresel when he went to Berlin in late December
1918.
   [4] That is, Symon Vasyl'ovych Petliura.
   [5] See W. C. Bullitt to WW, March 16, 1919, Vol. 55.
   [6] Embodied in the minutes of the Council of Ten printed at Jan. 22, 1919, Vol. 54.

From Tasker Howard Bliss

My dear Mr. President: Paris, March 31, 1919.

Last night the telegram of which a copy is attached was received
by me from General Kernan.[1] It appears that he has successfully
arranged a temporary truce between the Poles and Ukrainians fighting about Lemberg. I at once took the matter up with Mr. Lansing
and at his request conferred with Dr. Lord, the expert on Polish
affairs, who prepared the attached memorandum dated April 1 with
its final recommendation.[2] Mr. Lansing requests that I send it at
once to you with the suggestion that you secure the approval and
the signature of Mr. Clemenceau, Mr. Lloyd George and Mr. Orlando to the draft of a telegram which he proposes on pp 2 and 3
of his memorandum. I think that the telegram when approved

should be signed by the Secretary General and sent. It would seem that the matter is urgent because with those "cranky" people fighting may be resumed at any moment unless we clinch the nail while it is hot. To make assurance doubly sure, I can transmit, unofficially, a copy of the telegram to General Kernan as I did with the previous one.   Sincerely yours,   Tasker H. Bliss

CCL (T. H. Bliss Papers, DLC).
    [1] F. J. Kernan to T. H. Bliss, March 28, 1919, T telegram (WP, DLC). The significant portion reads as follows: "Have seen Polish and Ukrainian Commanders in East Galatia [Galicia] and delivered into their hands your messages. Both have telegraphed to Paris accepting in principle of an immediate suspension of arms."
    [2] It is missing, but see the following document.

Tasker Howard Bliss to Francis Joseph Kernan

[Paris] 31st March 1919.

29. For General Kernan.

The Allied and Associated governments have considered your telegram of March 28th. They thank you for the efforts you have already made to bring about a truce and convey to you the following instructions:

1. If a convention for a suspension of arms has not already been concluded you are requested to make every effort to bring one about.

2. An Inter-Allied Military Mission will be sent to Lemberg as quickly as possible for the purpose of supervising the execution of the suspension of arms and ultimately the Armistice.

3. You are requested to remain in Lemberg until this Mission arrives and then to give it what instructions you may deem essential.

4. As soon as the suspension of arms has been signed you should approach the Polish and Ukrainian Commanders in Eastern Galicia with a request in the name of the Allied and Associated Governments that plenipotentiaries of both sides should at once be appointed to conduct a negotiation for an armistice. This negotiation is to be carried on in Paris under the supervision of the Conference. Signed by Woodrow Wilson, Lloyd George, Orlando, Clemenceau. Bliss 29

T telegram (WP, DLC).

Two Letters from Herbert Clark Hoover

My dear Mr. President: Paris 31 March 1919.

Our food trains for Hungary from Trieste and our other arrangements, which were proceeding for the supply of foodstuffs from certain surplus districts in Jugo-Slavia, have been stopped by various authorities in that region. I have the following telegram this morning:

"Food train for Hungary still held at Zagrab by order of Commanding General French Army, Belgrade.[1] Serbians released this train last night so far as they were concerned. Demand was made on the French to release this train this morning. No reply has been received. Direct telephone communication Trieste to Budapest this afternoon reports everything quiet, and urgent request made for delivery of food which has been purchased from American Relief Administration. Can you bring pressure to bear on French to release food train now held at Zagrab? Gausey."[2]

This food and more has been paid for by the Hungarians and is their property. This raises the whole question as to whether or not in the present situation the provisioning of Hungary should proceed, and it involves political issues which are beyond myself and my colleagues to determine. My own view is that this provisioning of Hungary should go on, so long as no excesses are committed by the Government of the day, and it is my belief that if the feeding of Hungary were put on this basis and dissociated from all political interest except this one requirement, it would do more than anything else to hold this situation in check.

We have a clear proof of the value of feeding in the maintenance of order in the case of German-Austria where any action of the Bolshevik element is, on statement of their own leaders, being withheld until harvest, because of their dependence upon us for their daily supply of food. I am confident that the only thing today that prevents German-Austria from falling into a complete state of anarchy is this daily arrival of 1000 to 1500 tons of food, together with the steady arrival of coal which our staff have arranged from Czecho-Slovakia and Germany.

I regret to have to add to your burdens, but this is a problem that can be determined by no one short of the four heads of government.

Yours faithfully,   Herbert Hoover

[1] That is, Gen. Paul Joseph Jean Hector de Lobit.
[2] Lt. Col. William Bowdoin Causey (not Gausey) U.S.A., president of the Allied Railway Commission, with headquarters in Trieste.

Dear Mr. President: Paris, 31 March 1919.

Mr. Houston's telegram[1] is exactly in line with my own recommendations which you approved, i.e. that Mr. Barnes and the present organization be continued.

My minor amendment is that the Grain Corporation needs some simple legal reorganization to bring it in line with the new act, and in these matters we are preparing the necessary executive order to make the arrangements effective.

I am obliged for the copy of the complimentary telegram you received from the combined farmers associations of the Northwest.[2]

I enclose draft telegrams to Mr. Houston and to the Farmers Associations which I suggest would be in order for you to dispatch.[3]

Faithfully yours,   Herbert Hoover

TLS (WP, DLC).
[1] The Enclosure printed with WW to HCH, March 29, 1919 (first letter of that date).
[2] See WW to HCH, March 29, 1919 (second letter of that date), n. 1.
[3] See WW to DFH and WW to A. A. Elmore, both March 31, 1919.

A Memorandum by Sidney Edward Mezes

Memorandum

To: The President   March 31, 1919.
From: Dr. Mezes
Re: Danzig Region: Map attached.[1]
         (The red shading on the map covers the regions where Germans predominate, their numbers being indicated in thousands. The density of settlement, of course, varies greatly, being highest about cities and towns.)

PLAN I

This plan (see map) would establish an independent state, with a constitution insuring, as far as possible, internal freedom and internal and external impartiality. Its chief executive might well be a High Commissioner selected by the Executive Council of the League.

The territory involved would stretch from a line five miles distant from the railway west and south of Danzig to the line of the East branch of the Vistula, and so bounded would include 140,000 rural Germans and 170,000 Germans in Danzig, or 310,000 Germans all told.

If to this territory is added the region east of the Vistula, as far south as the broken red line (the East Prussian boundary prior to 1770), 73,000 Germans and about half as many Poles would be added. We think this addition would damage the 25,000,000 Poles so much more than it could help the 73,000 Germans as to be unjustified.

Plan I would accord well with the present distribution of population, and might, for the present, give Poland a good chance of access to the Baltic.

Its outstanding disadvantage is that it leaves to Germany a weapon of great power in the peaceful war she will have to wage for the economic subjugation (and consequently the political vassalage) of Poland, as a handy field of exploitation, and a waystation to the rich opportunities of Russia and the East. It would be difficult to overestimate the aid German agents in Poland would receive from 300,000 independent Germans in and about Poland's only port.

It also seems more likely than not that the "independence" of the area in question would be short lived. No doubt this solid block of Germans would press steadily for union with East Prussia, and would not, and could not in fact, be long denied.

In sum, therefore, we think that, while Plan I is attractive for the present, the verdict of history would probably be that Poland, when reborn, was denied an essential port and foredoomed to vassalage.

PLAN II.

This is the proposal of the Polish Committee,[2] and is shown on the map by the unbroken red lines. With it you are familiar.

All our specialists think it the best.

All the British specialists agree with them; at times the latter made reserves, but evidently under instructions and without connection. When the Council of Ten re-committed the Polish report, it was the British specialists who appeared at the Committee meeting with a draft of a report adhering to the original recommendations.

Plan II (Plan III also) has the advantage of giving a free hand in dealing with Fiume, since according Danzig to Poland has as a parallel, in fact and in reason, according Fiume to the Jugo-Slavs; and anything else for Fiume is, relatively, a favor to Italy.[3]

Our specialists believe that Danzig, as the port of 25,000,000 ardent and patriotic Poles, would before long become a Polish city; and that history would approve Plan II as a brave and sound solution of a distressingly knotty problem.

PLAN III.

This Plan (see map) would leave to Germany the territory east of the main Vistula (strengthened blue line) as far south as the broken red line, including some 130,000 Germans and, say, 40,000 Poles; but would give Danzig and its environs west of the main Vistula to Poland.

This is a compromise, the fairest we can suggest if it be decided that the settlement must recognize, in some measure, the presence of Germans towards the mouth of the Vistula.

The Poles lose some thousands of their number, the unhampered control of their great artery, the Vistula, and the shortest and best railway connecting their capital and their only port.

The Germans lose a German city and its environs. What significance should be accorded the fact that city and environs were made German by German political devices and at infinite pains, I confess I don't know. But no doubt many German functionaries, their families and dependents, would leave.   S.E.M.

TI MS (WP, DLC).
   [1] Not reproduced.
   [2] That is, the "Report No. 1 of the Commission on Polish Affairs," cited in n. 3 to the minutes of the Council of Ten printed at March 19, 1919.
   [3] Wilson drew a line along the side of this paragraph.

From John William Davis

London, March 31, 1919.

103. The HERALD, new labor daily, publishes today article on Russian situation by the Editor George Lansbury, in which following passages occur:

"Less than three weeks ago two representative Americans were allowed to go to Russia, via Great Britain. These two men, William Bullitt and Lincoln Steffens, are both well known in America, one as a leading official in the Peace Delegation, the other is an eminent writer on social and industrial affairs. Consequently their report cannot be brushed aside as of no importance or as unworthy of credence. So far their report has not been published. I have the highest authority for saying that these men have informed their Governments of the true facts in regard to the present position and I here and now challenge the British Government at once to take the British people into their confidence and tell us all there is to tell. I know and our Government and the American Government knows peace on honorable, just conditions can be secured now and British labour must insist on this. The first thing to call for is the immediate publication of every communication received from Messrs. Bullitt and Steffens while in Russia and the immediate publication of their verbal or printed reports. There is no time to be lost, it is now or never." Repeated to Department as 1590, March 31st.

Davis.

T telegram (WP, DLC).

From George Davis Herron

Dear Mr. President,   Geneva, Switzerland March 31st, 1919.

I am sending you herewith a memorandum which Count Sigray,[1] one of the principal Hungarian magnates, has prepared especially for your eyes. I know you will have no time to read it, but perhaps one of your secretaries can provide you with the substance of it. I only send it because of the urgent request of Count Sigray, who says that you will remember him. He is related by marriage, I believe, to Mr. Gerard.

Most faithfully yours,   George D. Herron

TLS (WP, DLC).
  ¹ That is, Antal, Count Sigray, "The present situation in Hungary," T MS (WP, DLC). The digest of this memorandum, which Wilson read, is printed as the next document.

A Digest of a Memorandum by Count Sigray

[c. March 31, 1919]

After the October Revolution Karolyi took over the running of the country with unusually great power, due largely to his enormous popularity. As, during the whole war his attitude had been anti-German and always friendly toward the Allies, especially toward France, the whole country saw in Karolyi the one man who could get the most favorable conditions of peace for Hungary. An idealist, his entire party took the idea that not might but justice would decide the fate of all nations. Following this point of view, the Hungarian Army was ordered to lay down its arms before knowing the conditions of the armistice.

The attitude of hope for the future suffered a severe shock by the interview in Belgrade with the French Commander (Colonel Vix), who was the sole medium through whom the Hungarian Government could communicate with the Allies, while other nations were given an opportunity to send their delegates to the Paris Conference. Hungarians have suffered many wrongs for the lack of direct communication with the leading men in Paris.

People began to see their territories encroached upon by their neighbors, and began to give up hope that the Hungarian cause should be considered and judged by the Peace Conference. The condition became more critical.

Unable to get the support of the Entente, Karolyi was forced to yield more and more to the Socialists. Finally, under the pressure of great discontent and dispair, the Government resigned and the power was taken over by the Socialists, who proclaimed an alliance with the Bolshevik Government in Russia.

Bolshevism has very little real basis for success in Hungary. Its chances are mainly due to two causes, first, that the City of Budapest, with 1,800,000 inhabitants, represents too large a proportion of the population of the country still under Hungarian control, which numbers only some 10,000,000; and, second, and most important, is that the Bolshevists, making use of the national feeling, have attached the patriotic population to their cause by proclaiming that they are fighting against the dismemberment of Hungary. It is a matter, therefore, of vital importance to separate immediately all national motives from Bolshevist motives, and to prevent a war declared by the Bolshevists from being carried on under the national flag.

For this reason it is of the utmost importance to declare immediately that the troops of the Allies advancing into the country are coming only as the enemies of Bolshevism and not as the enemies of the Hungarian nation.

The Hungarian people must be assured by the Allies and their Commander empowered to declare, that their national and economic existence will be made possible in future as soon as they rid themselves of Bolshevist rule, that they will be able to put the cause of their country freely, like all other nations, before the Peace Conference, and that their cause will be judged according to the principles of impartial justice that knows no standard but the equal rights of the several peoples concerned.

Furthermore, to regain their lost confidence the people of Hungary must be assured by the Allies that armed intervention does not wish to force any form of government or the rule of any political party on the country, and guarantees of a substantial character must be given that can leave no doubt as to the practical results to the people of Hungary, who will be ready to support them in crushing Bolshevism.

As no final decision has been made by the Paris Conference in regard to territorial questions, the Allies can take the position outlined above without the question being raised or the appearance being given that they are yielding from any previously taken decision from fear of Bolshevism.

The Allies must use all their influence to moderate the claims of our Czech, Roumanian and Serbian neighbors, who must give up their extravagant ideas of imperialism, fatal to themselves and to the peace of the world, and whose only results so far have been to make themselves disliked and hated by the nationalities they profess to deliver.

The Hungarian people are ready to give all nations in Hungary the same political rights they enjoy themselves, willingly submitting territorial and other questions which may come into dispute to decisions according to the principles laid down by President Wilson, and it should be declared over again that no claims to any territories occupied under the armistice can be considered final unless they will prove to be in harmony with those principles of justice and the express desire of all people concerned.

The condition of the population and especially the Hungarian speaking population of the occupied territories who have had to suffer undeservedly should be relieved at once by giving all higher commands to officers of the great powers, who would be more impartial than the officers of the neighboring nationalities have proved themselves to be.

If the action outlined above be taken immediately and energetically, and in a conciliatory spirit, the situation in Hungary can be solved without enormous difficulty.

Count Sigray is a territorial magnate of Hungary, married to Miss Daly,[1] daughter of the late Marcus Daly[2] and a sister of Mrs. Gerard,[3] wife of the former American Ambassador to Germany. He has been a good deal in America and his point of view, therefore, may be considered as being broader than that of many of his countrymen of the same class.

His views as outlined are very interesting when compared with the memorandum of conditions in Hungary sent by Prince Borghese to Premier Orlando. In the main, not only the reasons for the overthrow of the Karolyi Government coincide, but also the remedies suggested in each case are practically the same.

The great point of difference between the two is that Prince Borghese, suggesting almost identical action with that suggested by Count Sigray, contemplates recognition of the present existing form of Republican-Socialist Government in Hungary, which government, according to statements of its leaders as quoted by him, is prepared, if recognized by the Allies, to sever connections with the Russian Bolsheviks and maintain a stable government; while Count Sigray nowhere suggests that the Allies recognize the present existing government in Hungary, but merely gives the reasons which put it in power and asks the Allies to treat directly with the Hungarian people, the inference being that once Bolshevism is overthrown he himself and the class to which he belongs do not contemplate the continuance of the present government, probably hoping for a return to power of a government of the Karolyi type which might be more easily influenced by the old aristocratic elements.

T MS (WP, DLC).
[1] Harriot Daly Sigray.
[2] Of Montana, founder of the Anaconda Copper Mining Co. and the Amalgamated Copper Co.
[3] Mary Daly (Mrs. James Watson) Gerard.

A Translation of a Letter from Georges Clemenceau, with Enclosure

Mr. President: Paris, March 31, 1919.

You will find, herewith enclosed, a note in reply to the note of Mr. Lloyd George, of March 26, 1919.

Please accept, Mr. President, the assurance of my high consideration.   Georges Clemenceau.[1]

T MS (WP, DLC).
[1] The TLS is in WP, DLC.

ENCLOSURE

GENERAL OBSERVATIONS ON MR. LLOYD GEORGE'S NOTE OF MARCH 26TH.

28th of March, 1919.

1. The French Government is in complete accord with the general purpose of Mr. Lloyd George's note: that is to say, to make a durable and consequently a just peace.

It does not believe, on the other hand, that the principle, which it shares, really leads to the conclusions drawn by the note in question.

2. The note suggests that moderate territorial conditions should be imposed upon Germany in Europe in order not to leave a profound feeling of resentment after peace.

This method might have value, if the late war had been for Germany a European war. This, however, was not the case. Before the war Germany was a great naval power whose future lay upon the water. This world power was Germany's pride; she will not console herself for having lost it.

But, without being deterred by the fear of such resentment, all of her colonies, her entire navy, a great part of her commercial fleet, (as a form of reparation), and her foreign markets over which she held sway, have been taken from her, or will be taken from her. Thus the blow which she will feel the most is dealt her, and people think that she can be appeased by a certain amelioration of territorial conditions. This is a pure illusion and the remedy is not proportionate to the evil. If a means of satisfying Germany is sought, it should not be sought in Germany. This kind of conciliation will be idle, in case Germany is severed from her world policy. If it is necessary to appease her she should be offered colonial satisfaction, naval satisfaction or satisfaction with regard to her colonial expansion. The note of the 26th of March, however, only takes into account European territorial satisfaction.

3. The note of Mr. Lloyd George fears that too severe territorial conditions will be playing the game of Bolshevism in Germany. Is it not to be feared that the method suggested will have precisely this result?

The conference has decided to call to life a certain number of new states. Can the Conference, without committing an injustice sacrifice them, out of consideration for Germany, by imposing upon them, inacceptable frontiers?

If these peoples, especially Poland and Bohemia, have been able to resist Bolshevism up to now, it is because of a sense of nationality. If violence is done to this sentiment, Bolshevism will find these two peoples an easy prey and the only barrier, which at the present moment exists between Russian Bolshevism and German Bolshevism will be shattered.

The result will be either a confederation of Eastern and Central Europe under the domination of a Bolshevist Germany, or the enslavement of the same countries by a reactionary Germany, thanks to the general anarchy. In both cases, the Allies will have lost the war. On the contrary, the policy of the French Government is resolutely to aid these young peoples with the support of the liberal elements in Europe, and not to seek at their expense, ineffectual attenuations of the colonial naval and commercial disaster inflicted upon Germany by the Peace. If one is obliged, in giving to these young peoples frontiers without which they cannot live, to transfer to their sovereignty the sons of very Germans who have enslaved them, it is to be regretted and it must be done with moderation, but it cannot be avoided.

Moreover, while one deprives Germany totally and definitively of her colonies, because she maltreated the indigenous population, by what right can one refuse to give Poland and Bohemia normal frontiers because the Germans have installed themselves upon Polish and Bohemian soil as guarrantors of oppressive pan-Germanism.

4. Mr. Lloyd George's note insists—and the French Government is in agreement—upon the necessity of making a peace which shall seem to Germany to be a just peace. But, in view of German mentality it is not sure that justice is conceived by the Germans as it is conceived by the Allies.

Furthermore, it should not be forgotten that this impression of justice must be obvious not only to the enemy, but also and principally to the Allies. The Allies who have fought side by side must terminate the war with an equitable peace. But, what would be the results of following the method suggested by the note of March

26th? A certain number of total and definitive guarantees will be acquired by maritime nations which have not known an invasion. The surrender of the German colonies would be total and definitive. The surrender of the German navy would be total and definitive. The surrender of a large portion of the German merchant fleet would be total and definite. The exclusion of Germany from foreign markets would be total and would last for some time. On the other hand, partial and temporary solutions would be reserved for the continental countries, that is to say those which have suffered most from the war. The reduced frontiers suggested for Poland and Bohemia would be partial solutions. The defensive agreement offered to France for the protection of her territory would be a temporary solution. The proposed regime for the coal fields of the Sarre would be temporary. Here we have a condition of inequality which might risk leaving a bad impression upon the after war relations between the Allies, more important than the after war relations between Germany and the Allies.

In paragraph I. it has been demonstrated that it is vain to hope by territorial concessions to find sufficient compensation for Germany for the world disaster which she has undergone. It may be permitted to add that it would be an injustice to impose the burden of these compensations upon those of the allies who have felt the weight of the war most heavily.

These countries, after the expenses of war, cannot incur the expenses of peace. It is essential that they also should have the sensation of a just and equitable peace. In default of this, it is not alone in Central Europe that Bolshevism is to be feared, for no field can be more favorable to its propagation, it has been well noted, than the field of national disappointment.

5. For the moment the French Government desires to limit itself to observations of a general nature.

It renders full credit to the intentions which have inspired Mr. Lloyd George his memorandum. But it believes that the deductions made in the present note are in harmony with justice and with the general interest of all.

The French Government will be inspired by these considerations in the forthcoming meetings when the terms suggested by the British Prime Minister are discussed.[1]

T MS (WP, DLC).
[1] The T MS in French is also in WP, DLC.

A Memorandum by Jan Christiaan Smuts

Paris. 31st March, 1919

NOTE ON REPARATION.

The extent to which reparation can be claimed from Germany depends in the main on the meaning of the last reservation made by the Allies in their Note to President Wilson of __ [4] November, 1918.[1] That reservation was agreed to by President Wilson and accepted by the German Government in the Armistice negotiations, and was in the following terms:

"Further, in the conditions of peace laid down in his address to Congress on January 8th, 1918, the President declared that invaded territories must be restored, as well as evacuated and made free. The Allied Governments feel that no doubt ought to be allowed to exist as to what this provision implies. By it they understand that compensation will be made by Germany for all damage done to the civilian population of the Allies and to their property by the aggression of Germany by land, by sea, and from the air."

In this reservation a careful distinction must be made between the quotation from the President, which refers to the evacuation and restoration of the invaded territories, and the implication which the Allies find in that quotation and which they proceed to enunciate as a principle of general applicability. The Allies found in the President's provision for restoration of the invaded territories a general principle implied of far-reaching scope. This principle is that of compensation for all damage to the civilian population of the Allies in their persons or property, which resulted from the German aggression, and whether done on land or sea or from the air. By accepting this comprehensive principle (as the German Government did) they acknowledged their liability to compensation for all damage to the civilian population or their property wherever and however arising, so long as it was the result of German aggression. The President's limitation to restoration of the invaded territories only of some of the Allies was clearly abandoned.

The next question is how to understand the phrase "civilian population" in the above reservation, and it can be most conveniently answered by an illustration. A shop keeper in a village in northern France lost his shop through enemy bombardment, and was himself badly wounded. He would be entitled as one of the civilian population to compensation for the loss of his property and for his personal disablement. He subsequently recovered completely, was called up for military service, and after being badly wounded and spending some time in the hospital was discharged as permanently unfit. The expense he was to the French Government during this period as a soldier (his pay and maintenance, his uniform, rifle, ammunition, his keep in hospital, etc.) was not damage to a civilian, but military loss to his Government, and it is therefore arguable that the French Government cannot recover compensation for such expense under the above reservation. His wife, however, was during this period deprived of her bread-winner, and she therefore suffered damage as a member of the civilian population, for which she would be entitled to compensation. In other words the separation allowances paid to her and her children during this period by the French Government would have to be made good by the German Government, as the compensation which the allowances represent was their liability. After the soldier's discharge as unfit, he rejoins the civilian population, and as for the future he cannot (in whole or in part) earn his own livelihood, he is suffering damage as a member of the civilian population, for which the German Government are again liable to make compensation. In other words the pension for disablement which he draws from the French Government is really a liability of the German Government, which they must under the above reservation make good to the French Government. It could not be argued that as he was disabled while a soldier he does not suffer damage as a civilian after his discharge if he is unfit to do his ordinary work. He does literally suffer as civilian after his discharge, and his pension is intended to make good this damage, and is therefore a liability of the German Government. If he had been killed on active service, his wife as a civilian would have been totally deprived of her bread-winner, and would be entitled to compensation. In other words the pension she would draw from the French Government would really be a liability of the German Government under the above reservation, and would have to be made good by them to the French Government.

The plain, commonsense construction of the reservation therefore, leads to the conclusion that, while direct war expenditure (such as the pay and equipment of soldiers, the cost of rifles, guns and ordnance and all similar expenditure) could perhaps not be recovered from the Germans, yet disablement pensions to discharged soldiers, or pension to widows and orphans or separation allowances paid to their wives and children during the period of their military service are all items representing compensation to members of the civilian population for damage sustained by them, for which the German Government are liable. What was spent by the Allied Governments on the soldier himself, or on the mechanical appliances of war, might perhaps not be recoverable from the German Government under the reservation, as not being in any plain and direct sense damage to the civilian population. But what was or is spent on the citizen before he became a soldier, or after he has ceased to be a soldier, or at any time on his family, represents compensation for damage done to civilians and must be made good by the German Government under any fair interpretation of the above reservation. This includes all war pensions and separation allowances; which the German Government are liable to make good, in addition to reparation or compensation for all damage done to property of the Allied peoples.   J. C. Smuts.[2]

T MS (WP, DLC).
    [1] EMH to WW, Nov. 4, 1918 (first telegram of that date), Vol. 51.
    [2] For an insightful commentary on Lloyd George's success in using Smuts to impress this argument on Wilson, see Lentin, *Lloyd George, Woodrow Wilson and the Guilt of Germany*, pp. 128-30.

From the Diary of Josephus Daniels

March Monday 31 1919

Had a conference with Mr. Long (GB). He had been sent for by Lloyd George to come over after LG had asked WW to see if we could not reach an agreement as to size of Navy. I explained that so far as programme already authorized, could do nothing but build those ships. The larger program (for 3 years) that passed the House was dependent upon League of Nations & would not be necessary if League was firmly established and all nations agreed to reduction of armament. He said LG could not support League of Nations if U. S. accompanied it by big building program, for GB could not consent to any other nation having the supremacy of the sea. I pointed out that G. B. would still have more ships than America. Long said it would not be difficult for us to agree but public sentiment in Great Britain was very much alarmed by our building program. He said he was not fully informed as to Prime Minister's desire, but would see him and have later conference. Later I sent word to L. G. that I must go to Rome Tuesday & would like to see him (the President wished it) before going. He asked me to come to breakfast the next morning.

Saw President at 6 pm.

To Edward Mandell House, with Enclosure

Confidential.

My dear House: Paris, 31 March, 1919.

Here is a despatch somewhat belated in transmission stating Mr. Root's ideas as to amendments which should be made to the Covenant. I think you will find some of these very interesting. Perhaps you have already seen it.

In haste, Affectionately yours, Woodrow Wilson

TLS (E. M. House Papers, CtY).

ENCLOSURE

Washington, March 27, 1919.

1312. For Secretary Lansing from Polk:

Following are proposed amendments to the Constitution of the League of Nations which have been drafted by Mr. Root:

"First amendment. Strike out article thirteen and insert the following: The high contracting Powers agree to refer to the existing permanent Court of Arbitration at The Hague or to the Court of Arbitral justice proposed at the second Hague tribunal, when established, or to some other arbitral tribunal, all disputes between them, including those affecting honor and vital interests (?) which are of a justiciable character and which the Powers concerned have failed to settle by diplomatic methods. The Powers so referring to (?) agreement signed and give effect to the award of the tribunal.

Disputes of justiciable character are defined as disputes as to the interpretation of a treaty, as to any question of international law, as to the existence of any fact which, if established, would constitute a breach of any international obligation, or as to the nature and extent of the reparation to be made for any such breach.

Any question which may arise as to whether a dispute is of a justiciable character is to be referred for decision to the Court of Arbitral Justice when constituted or until it is constituted to the existing permanent Court of Arbitration at the Hague.

Second amendment. Add to article fourteen the following: The Executive Council shall call a general conference of the Powers to meet not less than two years or more than five years after the signing of this convention for the purpose of reviewing the condition of international law and of agreeing upon and stating in authoritative form the principles and rules thereof.

Thereafter regular conferences for the purpose shall be called and held at stated times.

Third amendment. Immediately before the signature of the American delegates, insert the following reservation: Inasmuch as in becoming a member of the League the United States of America is moved by no interest or wish to intrude upon or interfere with the political policy or internal administration of any foreign state, and by no existing or anticipated dangers in the affairs of the American continents but accedes to the representations of the European states that it shall join its power to theirs for the preservation of general peace, the representatives of the United States of America sign this convention with the understanding that nothing therein contained shall be construed to imply a relinquishment by the United States of America of its traditional attitude towards purely American questions, or to require the submission of its policy regarding such questions, (including therein the admission of immigrants), to the decision or recommendation of other powers.

Fourth amendment. Add to article ten the following: After the expiration of five years from the signing of this convention any party may terminate *itself* obligation under this article by giving the President's notice in writing to the Secretary General of the League.

Fifth amendment. Add to article nine the following: Such Commission shall have full power of inspection and verification personally and by authorized agents as to all armies, equipment, munitions, and industries referred to in article eight.

Sixth amendment. Add to article twenty-four the following: The executive council shall call a general conference of members of the League to meet not less than five or more than ten years after the signing of this convention for the revision thereof, and at that time, or at any time thereafter upon one year's notice, any member may withdraw from *take* League."   Phillips,   Acting.

N.B. Message badly garbled, accounting for delay in delivery. Have asked State Department for verification.

T telegram (E. M. House Papers, CtY).

From Oscar Solomon Straus

[Paris, March 31, 1919]

On March 23rd I sent the following cable to the League to Enforce Peace:

"Have Taft promptly telegraph me amendments essential for Senate Confirmation. STRAUS"

The answer follows:

"New York March 29, 6 p.m.
Rec'd March 31st, 9:45 AM.

Oscar Straus,
  Redstar, Paris.
    Mr. Taft answers as follows: 'More specific reservation of Monroe Doctrine. Fix a term for duration of League and limit of armament. Require expressly unanimity of action in Executive Council and Body of Delegates. Add to Article XV a provision: That where the executive Council or Body of Delegates finds the difference to grow out of an exclusively domestic policy it shall recommend no settlement. Reservation of Monroe Doctrine as follows: "Any American State or States may protect the integrity of American territory and the independence of the government whose territory it is, whether a member of the League or not, and may in the interest of American peace object to and prevent the further transfer of American territory or sovereignty to any European or non-American Power. The unanimity of Executive Council, the American representative on it, will secure reasonable distribution of burdens for the United States in enforcement of Article X and Article XVI.' SHORT."

T MS (WP, DLC).

To David Franklin Houston

Paris, 31 March, 1919.
    Hoover has secured Barnes' consent to continue as head of the Grain Corporation in execution of 1919 wheat guaranty. It appears that Grain Corporation will require some legal and financial reorganization in order to bring it into more effective alignment with the new Act and the new task. Hoover will continue as Chairman of the Grain Corporation until July first. Barnes will thereafter act directly under myself.   Woodrow Wilson

T telegram (WP, DLC).

To Alfred A. Elmore

Paris, 31 March, 1919.
    I am indeed obliged for your kind telegram of recent date. Mr. Hoover will continue to head the administration of our food problems both here and in the United States until the next harvest, by which time it is confidently expected that the critical period in the

world's food supply will have passed and he can rightly retire with our national task in this particular completed. I have approved Mr. Hoover's recommendation that Mr. Barnes, who you know has been Mr. Hoover's assistant during the past two years, shall succeed Mr. Hoover in charge of the organization to be set up for the execution of the 1919 wheat guaranty. I am sure these arrangements will meet with your approval.   Woodrow Wilson.

T telegram (WP, DLC).

To Franklin Knight Lane

[Paris, March 31, 1919]

1408. For Secretary of Interior in reply to his Nos. 1342 and 1343 March 28th:[1]

"Your plan has my approval but I doubt whether I am at liberty to assign funds for the purpose out of the appropriation at my disposal because it would involve circulating my own speeches and I am afraid that would be a matter of legitimate criticism. Woodrow Wilson."

T telegram (WP, DLC).
[1] FKL to WW, March 28, 1919 (two telegrams of that date).

From George Creel

My dear Mr. President: New York March 31st, 1919.

Please let me urge that you give Frank Walsh an informal, unofficial and confidential interview at the earliest possible moment.[1] You can talk with him frankly in the absolute faith that whatever you say will be respected in every sense of the word. You have no truer friend or more loyal supporter, and he desires to conduct himself in such manner as to cause you no embarrassment.

The importance of this Irish question cannot be exaggerated. Nothing can stop the movement, and I think it is a matter of congratulations that Walsh and Dunne have been selected rather than enemy voices.[1] Please feel that you can talk to Frank Walsh in entire openness and complete confidence.

                    Respectfully,   George Creel

TLS (WP, DLC).
[1] The Third Irish Race Convention, which had met in Philadelphia on February 22-23, 1919, had chosen an American Commission for Irish Independence, composed of Francis Patrick Walsh, Edward Fitzsimons Dunne, and Michael J. Ryan, lawyer and former city solicitor of Philadelphia. The commission was instructed to go to Paris to present to the peace conference the case for Irish independence. See Charles Callan

Tansill, *America and the Fight for Irish Freedom, 1866-1922* (New York, 1967), pp. 296-302, 312-22. See also F. P. Walsh *et al.* to WW, April 16, 1919.
    It had been announced on March 28 that the commission would sail for France on April 2. *New York Times*, March 29, 1919.

A Memorandum by Robert Lansing

FRENCH SPIRIT OF MILITARISM
AND ITS CONSEQUENCES.

APRIL 1, 1919.

Yesterday I received a telephone message saying that the President wished me to be at the Ministry of War at 5:30 p.m. The subject to be discussed was not stated. I found on arriving at M. Clemenceau's office the President, M. Clemenceau, Mr. Lloyd George, Signor Orlando, Mr. Balfour, M. Pichon and Baron Sonnino. No military men were present.

The subject for discussion was an *aide memoire* received through Italian sources from the new Hungarian Government affirming a desire to be at peace with everybody and asking us to consider negotiating territorial questions and the arrangement of other matters through an inter-allied commission.

Pichon opened the discussion by a rather violent attack on the new Government asserting that we must not deal with it, that it was arranging an alliance with the Russian Bolsheviks, and that the thing to do was to send troops into Hungary, to crush Bolshevism and to enforce the demand made by the French Colonel Vix who had presented the demand as to the neutral zone in Transylvania.

I followed Pichon and said that it seemed to me that we ought to face the facts frankly, that I believed that the overthrow of the Karolyi Government was due chiefly to the fact that we had been unintentionally unjust in laying down the neutral zone in Transylvania and that the facts were as follows: The Roumanians, *not* the Hungarians, had crossed the armistice line fixed by the French commander; instead of making the Roumanians retire we had referred the matter to the territorial commission which had established an "ethnic line" much further west than the Roumanian advance and recommended that the Roumanians be permitted to continue to that line and that the Hungarians be required to retire 100 kilometers west of it; the new Hungarian line being practically the line agreed upon in 1916 by the Allies and Roumania;[1] and that naturally the Hungarians considered that Roumania's extreme claims were to be allowed, the result being a nationalistic movement against a government too weak to resist the demand and a turning to Russia as the only hope since the Allies supported the Roumanian claims.

I said then with some emphasis: "The responsibility for the Hungarian revolution rests here in this room. We should endeavor to repair the injustice we have done. It cannot lessen our prestige to admit an error. It will show we wish to be just and so strengthen us with those people."

Clemenceau interrupted to say that, as he had made a demand, we must insist upon it or we would lose the respect of the enemy; that they would be always threatening us with a Bolshevik revolution if we did not change our orders; and that this new government being Bolshevik ought not to be dealt with except with weapons.

I replied that in this case it might be too late to effect a change in the government by doing justice, but that I thought the time had come to change our policy in dealing with the enemy. I continued: "We have been making demands on the enemy in the most peremptory and offensive way. The generals (I meant Foch of course) charged with the duty of presenting demands have not been allowed to explain them to, much less discuss them with, the enemy. That was our course in the case of the German merchant ships and of Dantzig. The result is we are turning all these people into Bolsheviks. Today we are the best friends that Bolshevism has. In my opinion the hard brutal military way is the wrong way, unless we wish to see all Central Europe turn Bolshevik."

The President followed more mildly agreeing with what I had said but adding some caustic remarks about "military envoys." Orlando and Lloyd George showed by their remarks that they agreed as to the policy in regard to Budapest. Pichon said nothing. Clemenceau shrugged his shoulders, raised his eyebrows and gazed up at the ceiling. Balfour assented but made no remarks.

The President said that it might be well to send a diplomat to Hungary to deal with the situation. To this Clemenceau objected saying that it must be a military man because it was a question of armistice. The President agreed that Clemenceau was right. I then said that we might find a general who was also a diplomat, and turning to Lloyd George asked, "Have you no one in mind who would fill the bill?"

He thought for a moment and then said "I was thinking of General Smuts." The President, who admires Smuts extravagantly on account of his plan for a League of Nations,[2] nodded vigorously and said that he was "just the man."

I whispered to the President that to complete the job of keeping this matter out of French control Lloyd George ought to draw the instructions. This he did, and it was agreed to.

The record of this meeting is made because of the conviction, upon which my remarks were made. I have come to it very reluctantly. It is that French foreign policy is today dominated and directed by a military clique and that it is militaristic in character.

This is apparent by a review of events since the armistice of November 11th, 1918, was signed that the French generals desire to humiliate and exasperate the defeated peoples until they resist so that an excuse may be found to use troops against them. They seem to have the purpose of keeping the French armies mobilized in order that they may continue to practice their trade and to dominate the situation. Whether this is done because of personal vanity or because of a spirit of military imperialism or because of a desire to intimidate Italy, whom they suspect of secret hostility, I do not know. It may be one or all of these reasons.

Marshal Foch, when the suggestion was made that he should, with the demand for the use of the German merchant ships, tell the German envoy that they would be furnished with a certain amount of food monthly, flatly refused. He said that he would make the demand with a time limit, and then, if they complied, he would tell them about the food, but he would not do so until the Germans had unconditionally agreed to give up the ships.

Fortunately Lloyd George saved the situation by pointing out that the surrender of the ships had to do with the naval terms of the armistice and that those matters were in the hands of a British admiral. Even then Clemenceau attempted to inject the same harshness into the demand by insisting that it should be without condition or explanation. While this was agreed to I am sure Lloyd George had a twinkle in his eye, because the Germans at Brussels *were* secretly told the advantage of promptly agreeing to surrender the ships, which they did without demur when Admiral Wemyss made the formal demand.

The same temper has been shown by the French militarists in the matter of demanding of the Germans the use of Dantzig in sending General Haller's Polish army to Poland. Foch declared to the Supreme War Council that he would only make an unconditional demand on the German plenipotentiary. The Germans had proposed the use of Koenigsberg, Libau or some other port, whose final disposition was not in question, rather than Dantzig, since the German population would be incensed at Polish troops coming there because they would interpret it to mean permanent occupation. The German proposal was intended to avoid bloodshed and disorders. It seemed reasonable and expedient but Foch said he would not go to Spa and discuss the question, that he would demand Dantzig firmly and make the Germans accede. He was, however, intructed to do so *after* the Germans consented. The matter is still unsettled.

The whole attitude of Foch has become that of a military dictator. His supreme desire seems to be to lash the vanquished into a fury. "You are conquered. You have no right to think. You must obey because *I*, Foch, command you." That is his way, and the "I" is underscored many times. He is literally drunk with power. He is not firm alone; he is more—he is insolent.

Foch, or more probably Weygand, is driving the moderate elements of the Central Powers to turn to the Russian Bolsehviks as the only hope of avoiding complete disruption and the tyranny of a new militarism more arbitrary even than that of the Prussians.

T MS (R. Lansing Papers, DLC).
  [1] That is, in the Treaty of Bucharest.
  [2] About which, see the memorandum printed at Dec. 26, 1918, Vol. 53.

From the Diary of Dr. Grayson

Tuesday, April 1st, 1919.

The Council of Four met both morning and afternoon, with the President, while at the same time the Council of Foreign Ministers assembled at the Quai d'Orsay and dealt with questions of procedure for dealing with the German delegates should they ever be summoned to sit at Versailles. The Council of Four made slightly more progress today than yesterday, the President having again read the riot act, declaring that unless something was done to shorten the killing of time, he would be forced to take action along other lines. The Saar Valley proposal, the Polish situation, and the Rhine Barrier were again the topics of discussion. Whenever Clemenceau would seem to start off on one of his interminable arguments, the President would check it and change the situation and keep them buckling down to business. The result of today was a little better, and the outlook was a little brighter when the final meeting was held tonight, although the progress that had been made was far less than should have been. It was very plain that the constant strain of trying to make men work, who had no desire to work, along the lines necessary was having its effect on the President.

The Bishop of Saloniki[1] visited the President to discuss the Czecho-Slovak situation. He was a big, fine-looking man and wore a gold chain of office which was at least the equal of that which the Lord Mayor of Manchester wore at the time of our memorable visit to that northern British city. The Bishop talked some English but could not trust himself in the language and so he wrote out what he was going to say and read it to the President.

After dinner the President worked in his study and retired about 11:00 o'clock.

[1] Grayson apparently was confused here. The Associated Press reported, e.g., in the *New York Times, New York Tribune,* and New York *World,* all of April 2, 1919, that Wilson had received the Bishop of Spalato (the Italian name for Split), who represented the Yugoslavian position on the controversy over the Dalmatian coast. The Roman Catholic Bishop of Spalato and Macarska in 1919 was the Most Rev. Msgr. Georges Caric.

From Tasker Howard Bliss, with Enclosures

Dear Mr. President: Paris, April 1, 1919.

I inclose you herewith the two memoranda received by me last night from General Nolan,[1] Chief of the Intelligence Department, Headquarters of the American Expeditionary Forces.

I do not know in what way Germany can be approached in order to elicit from her an official statement. But if the spirit of her government is anything like that which is indicated in these memoranda it seems a pity that she cannot in any way be heard while the peace terms are being discussed. As it is, I am afraid that after all our work is done we may be confronted by a counter-proposal which in this or that respect may appeal so strongly to the sense of fairness of the world that we may be obliged to undo some of our work and accept their suggestions after all.

Sincerely yours,   Tasker H Bliss

P.S. In regard to the transportation of Haller's Division by rail through Germany, it seems to me that this matter is so important that the Supreme Council should direct Marshal Foch to take this matter up with the German Plenipotentiary when he meets him to-morrow, whether the latter broaches the subject first or not.

I believe that the present German Government is fighting for its life. It may be overwhelmed if it consents to the use of Dantzig. What possible interest have we in overwhelming that government if, without doing so, we can get all we want and save our pride at the same time?   T.H.B.

TLS (WP, DLC)
[1] That is, Dennis Edward Nolan.

E N C L O S U R E   I

[Chaumont] March 31, 1919.

MEMORANDUM FOR GENERAL BLISS (GERMANY)

NO. 5 POLITICAL

From an authoritative and confidential source the following has been received with regard to the peace terms acceptable to Germany:

"Peace conditions Acceptable to Germany.

Generally, Germany will accept any peace which is based on the 14 points of President Wilson, as it agreed in its note to Secretary of State Lansing on the opening of the Armistice negotiations.

1. Regarding Point 4, it is impossible for Germany to exist without an army and navy, unless neighboring nations in Europe are similarly disarmed.

2. If the League of Nations is formed, Germany must become a member, with equal rights.

3. As far as the territorial questions are concerned, German claims are based on Points 1 and 2 of the speech to Congress February 11, 1918. On this basis Germany cannot agree to hand over any part of the Left Rhine bank, the Palatinate or the Saar territory to the enemy. As regards Poland, Germany will abide loyally by the self-determination of the people of the province of Posen. So far as Upper Silesia and West Prussia are concerned, Points 1 and 2 of address to Congress mentioned above states clearly that this is purely German territory, and the percentage of Poles is so small that the vote is unnecessary and the question of self-determination does not there enter. If these two provinces should be taken from Germany, everybody who knows Germany and its condition can clearly see that Germany will be ruined economically.

4. In regard to Alsace-Lorraine, the German Government urges the rule of self-determination be applied to this province, but if this be the only obstacle to peace it will not be insisted upon.

Since Alsace Lorraine has been the cause of wars in Europe for the past 400 years, it would be naturally better for the freedom of the world if self determination would decide the question. Otherwise there will always be a chance for the Nationalists in Germany to build up in later times a demand for a War of Revenge.

As to Points 3 and 4, Germany will guarantee to be absolutely loyal.

Point 5. In view of the overpopulation of Germany, the German government desires to get back at least some of its colonies. But if this again be the only obstacle to peace, Germany will be willing to accept that they be handed over to the League of Nations and administered for the common benefit of all the members of the League, provided that some of them be given to Germany to administer for the League. This will be in accordance with the 5th of President Wilson's 14 points.

Point 6. According to Point 3 of the 14 points, Germany will not accept any economic barriers and asks for the establishment of an equality of trade conditions among the nations "consenting to the peace and associating themselves for its maintenance."

Point 7. War Indemnities: The German Government will fulfill loyally point 7 of the 14 points including the last paragraph of the note of Secretary of State Lansing to the German Government Nov. 5, 1918 saying that compensation will be made by Germany for damage done to the civilian populations of the Allies and their property by the aggression of Germany by land, by sea, and from the air, but the German Government understands that under this point is not included the damage which is caused by officially declared submarine war, since, according to international War, Cruiser Warfare is permissible.

Regarding the reconstruction of Belgium and Northern France, Germany makes the following proposal:

Germany will build up Belgium and Northern France with her own workmen, her own material, as may be arranged in conjunction with the French and Belgium Governments.

To carry out this proposal the Cabinet has handed over the preparatory work to Mr. Erzberger.

Germany will build new towns and villages, wherever France and Belgium wants them, equal to those there before and situated at any place either Government desires. By this only civil damages are meant. This will be loyally carried out.

Point 8. To carry this out it is naturally necessary to give Germany raw materials.

Point 9. The Blockade and Blacklist will have to be suspended to enable this to be carried out.

The Prisoners of War must be returned.

Germany wishes, for the purpose of carrying out the food contract, the contract for the rebuilding of the destroyed provinces and also to pay for the raw material necessary, a credit from the United States on the basis that the interest for the first 10 years should be taken up in advance.

In the peace treaty it should be provided that occupation be immediately released, and also that no colored troops are to be left in the occupied territories."   D. E. NOLAN,
                                                  Brigadier General, G.S.,
                                                  Ass't. Chief of Staff, G-2.

E N C L O S U R E   I I

SECRET: [Chaumont] March 31, 1919.
MEMORANDUM TO: General Tasker H. Bliss:

In our memorandum No. 5, transmitted this date, giving the political situation in Germany, the portions included in quotation marks, under the heading "Peace Conditions Acceptable to Germany," are known to have been discussed by the president[1] and principal members of the German cabinet and may be taken as a first-hand indication of the point of view of the present German government. I think it is important that you understand this, so I am calling your attention to it in this separate and secret memorandum.

Of course, it is understood that the German government does not bind itself by the quoted statement, but it does give a clear idea of what the German government thinks of the peace terms, as stated in the press news received in Germany.

In connection with the statement quoted in Memorandum No. 5, it has come to our attention that the German government would like to suggest, in order to clear up the question of the entry of the Polish Army thru Dantzig to the satisfaction of every one concerned, that President Wilson propose to let the army of General Haller go straight thru Germany and that Germany will undertake its transportation over its own railroads. If the number 25,000 is correct, the German government claims that the whole movement can be accomplished in ten days time. The Associated and Allied governments need only designate one of the bridge-heads thru which the troops may be sent and Germany will send them straight thru to Posen, or any other point in Poland. The suggestion is made that the payment for this transportation can be charged to the account of the food contract. In this way, the suggestion is also made by the German Government, that the army of Haller will arrive at Posen much more quickly than by any sea route and no ships will have to be used for this transportation.

It is increasingly clear that the leaders of all different parties in Germany are agreed on the point that the German government could not accept the proposal that Polish troops be landed at Dantzig. The main argument put forth is that "Germany now has peace in west Prussia and has a right to maintain that peace."

I am enclosing, in case it may not have been called to your personal attention in this connection, a copy of the German reply, dated March 28th, to the Allied note on the question of the landing of troops in Dantzig.[2]   D. E. NOLAN,
                                                 Brig. General, G.S.
                                                 A. C. of S. G-2

T MSS (WP, DLC).
  [1] That is, Friedrich Ebert.
  [2] See n. 2 to the minutes of the Council of Four printed at March 29, 1919.

Mantoux's Notes of a Meeting of the Council of Four

April 1, 1919, 11 a.m.

Wilson. I have received information from a confidential source about the present state of mind of the German government. There is there a sincere fear of seeing the passage of Polish troops through Danzig provoking a violent conflict in the region. The passage of Paderewski has already given rise to some tumultuous demonstrations. To avert this danger, the German government would go so far as to accept the transport of Polish troops by German rail, starting from the Rhine bridgeheads. If the Germans admit in writing our right to have Polish troops pass through Danzig, it would be possible to send there only a small contingent, in order to well establish this right. Could we not instruct Marshal Foch in the sense which I have just indicated?

Lloyd George. Sir Joseph Maclay has always said that this is the true way to solve this problem; in fact it is very difficult to find the necessary tonnage, at a time when Italy lacks coal and Australian troops are complaining about not having been repatriated quickly enough, to the point that there was a mutiny among them in which thirty soldiers were shot dead.

Clemenceau. We will have a certain number of Poles pass through Danzig, to establish our right. That is acceptable; but we must confront the question of tracing Poland's western frontier.

Lloyd George. Is it necessary to decide immediately the fate of Danzig?

Clemenceau. Without that, I do not see how you can trace the frontiers of Germany.

Wilson. The opinion of most of the experts is that the Poles should be able to have the use of Danzig. Bismarck one day said to Crispi:[1] "The resurrection of Poland is impossible unless Thorn and Danzig are taken from Prussia, and unless the German Empire is dismembered." It is better not to raise this formidable question in connection with the transport of the troops.

Lloyd George. I would be inclined to accept the German proposal to transport the troops by land.

Wilson. While making the Germans recognize their obligation to permit troops to pass through Danzig.

Clemenceau. I can accept this.

  [1] Francesco Crispi, Premier of Italy, 1887-1891, 1893-1896.

Wilson. I have other information about the German attitude; this concerns reparation for damages. In fulfillment of the commitment they have already made in the Armistice agreement, they would agree to reconstruct all the buildings destroyed in France and in Belgium, at their own expense and furnishing the labor.

Lloyd George. There is something to be said in favor of this proposal. I believe that there will be a shortage of labor. In England, we cannot construct the workers' housing we need because of it. The proposal seems practical to me.

Wilson (after reading the note which had been communicated to him). I do not know what use we can make of this document, which is not an official document.

Clemenceau. We can propose this to the German government ourselves, adding that the same requirement would apply to other reparations, such as those for agriculture and railways.

President Wilson reads the draft of a resolution on the transport of the Polish troops by German railways.[2]

Clemenceau. If we adopt this document, it is we who are proposing to the Germans passage by land; I would prefer that it were done by the Germans.

Wilson. The wording can be modified along those lines by authorizing Marshal Foch simply to examine, if it is presented to him, a proposal to transport General Haller's troops by rail starting from the Rhine bridgeheads.

Marshal Foch and General Weygand are introduced.

Clemenceau. President Wilson has received information indicating that the Germans are ready to furnish General Haller's troops facilities for passage by their railways to leave from the line of the Rhine. That seems acceptable to me, on the condition that we obtain written recognition from the Germans of our right to have Polish troops pass through Danzig.

That would have some advantages. The first is that we could transport troops in ten days instead of two months; the second is that we would have the Polish troops there when our decision on the subject of the future of Danzig, which might provoke disorders, will be definitively known.

Foch. You think that this combination is advantageous; I think that it places the Poles in the jaws of the wolf. The trip all the way across Germany is long. All along the route, the Poles will be at the mercy of the Boches. If the Germans want to let them pass, they

---

[2] "In case the German authorities will say in writing that they fully admit their obligation under the terms of the Armistice to permit the transportation of General Haller's forces through Dantzig and Thorn, Marshall Foch is instructed to entertain a proposal for the direct and immediate transportation of those troops by rail to Poland from one of the points under allied control on the Rhine." WWhw MS (WP, DLC).

will pass; but the Germans can stop them. They can also say that such and such a local soviet is stopping them, and that they themselves can do nothing.

Nevertheless, one can examine the proposal.

Clemenceau. The difficulty is that, if we take our decision about the fate of Danzig before the Polish troops should arrive in Poland, we run the risk of grave disturbances. When we have sent Polish regiments to Warsaw, then we can say to the Germans: "Danzig is no longer yours."

Wilson. It is not very easy for soviets to stop troops who wish to pass. The Russian soviets tried to do it with the Czechoslovaks; they did not succeed.

M. Clemenceau rereads the text of the resolution proposed by President Wilson.

Weygand. The transport of the Haller troops would require at least 400 trains.

Wilson. What! for 25,000 men?

Weygand. Altogether, there will be up to 80,000 men. At a rate of fifteen trains per day, the transport would require one month. Moreover, a part of the divisions will only be ready by May 1st. This is the observation that I would like to make.

Wilson. I am surprised by the figure you give me. We had understood that it would be a matter of sending 25,000 men to Poland.

Weygand. General Haller's army is composed of six divisions, with non-divisional elements equivalent to a seventh division. At fifty trains per division, that makes 350 trains, and fifty more must be provided for supplementary equipment.

Lloyd George. How many divisions will be ready before May 1st?

Weygand. Two or three.

Lloyd George. Between now and May 1st, we will have taken our decision on the fate of Danzig. What is important is to act immediately. Two or three divisions must be sent to Poland as soon as possible.

Orlando. When French and English divisions were transported to Italy, one division per week was sent, and communications were difficult.

Clemenceau. Yes, we only had two rail lines between France and Italy, which really amounted to one and a half.

Foch. Undoubtedly the Germans will ask us for cars and locomotives. I am not leaving for Spa until tomorrow evening. We are going to study the question in its quantitative aspects; I can inform you about the result of this study before my departure.

Marshal Foch and General Weygand withdraw.

Wilson. I wish to say a word about the subject of the revictualing

of Bavaria, which I have already discussed with M. Clemenceau.
Mr. Lansing, who has been said to oppose the plan, does not have
a political objection; but M. Pichon did not inform him sufficiently
about the political aspect of the project, which has as its goal above
all assisting Dr. Muehlon[3] and his party. The objection comes from
Mr. Hoover, who has recalled the commitments that we have undertaken toward Germany,[4] and who thinks that we cannot furnish
Bavaria what is proposed without violating our obligations.

Clemenceau. What we ask is not that Bavaria receive more, but
that she be revictualed through Switzerland; which will give her a
feeling of independence.

Wilson. This is something which might disrupt Mr. Hoover's
system of distribution.

Clemenceau. Can nothing be done to overcome this difficulty?

Wilson. I will explain the situation to Mr. Hoover and ask him
to take account of the political reasons.

Brief exchange of views on the question of the left bank of the
Rhine. President Wilson states that, according to the last deliberations of the League of Nations Commission, the Executive Council
of this organization will be assisted by a military and naval general
staff. It will be the task of the Executive Council to give this general
staff all the necessary instructions to prepare plans of action in case
of aggression. The British and American guarantee which has been
envisaged could be in operation until the security provided by the
League of Nations was considered sufficient.

Mantoux, I, 105-108.
    [3] That is, Dr. Wilhelm von Muehlon, the German pacifist.
    [4] That is, the so-called Brussels Agreement, about which see EMH to WW, March 7,
1919, n. 1, vol. 55.

A Memorandum by John Foster Dulles

Memorandum of conference had at President Wilson's hotel, Paris,
    April 1, 1919, at 2 p.m.

There were present President Wilson, and Messrs Baruch, Davis,
Lamont McCormick & Dulles. The President was first shown the
reparation plan which had been agreed to the previous day with
Messrs Montague and Keynes[1] and which provided for a determination by a com[m]ission of the amount of damage for which
the enemy should make reparation and which further provided for
a reference to arbitral decision of the question of the inclusion of
any category of damage as to which any member of the commission
entertained doubt and provided the capacity of the enemy to pay
was not exhausted without the inclusion of such item. It was ex-

plained to the President that this was a scheme to avoid a present decision by the American Commissioners on the propriety of including pensions and separation allowances. It was further stated to tje [the] President that Mr. Lloyd George had refused to accept this plan and had insisted unqualifiedly for the inclusion of the items mentioned. This compelled a decision by the U. S. The President stated that he had been very much impressed by a memorandum by Smuts in favor of pensions and separation allowances and was clearly disposed to feel that the deprivation of the civilian population of the services and earning capacity of persons who were called to the colors and then perhaps killed or wounded was "damage to the civilian population" in the sense of the Allied declaration of Nov. 4th.[2] Mr. McCormich [McCormick] pointed out that the legal advisors of the Commission, and including Mr. John W. Davis felt that such damage was not within the meaning of such Allied declaration when this declaration was subjected to construction and in the light of the surrounding circumstances. The President stated in substance that he did not regard this as a matter for decision in accordance with strict legal principles; that it was probable that the question of pensions was not specifically considered in November and that the statement then made was in a very general a loose terminology. He was, however, continuously finding new meanings and the necessity of broad application of principles previously enunciated even though imperfectly, and that he felt that justice would be done by compelling the enemy to make good, if they were able, damage of this category. Mr. Dulles pointed out that it was very difficult to draw any logical distinction between a family which had been damaged by having their bread-winner drafted and another family which had been damaged to an equivalent extent by having to pay for the equipment of that soldier and that there was danger that to accept pensions would involve admitting against the enemy all war costs, including the cost of maintaining military organizations. The President stated that he did not feel bound by considerations of logic and that where in fact the state had made payments to the civilian population to save them from loss to which they would otherwise have been subjected it was a proper subject of reparation under the agreed terms of peace. It was thereupon agreed that pensions, including those in the form of separation allowances would be allowed. The President proposed that the French scale should be adopted.[3]

John Foster Dulles

April 1. 1919. 11 p.m.

Duplicate to Mr McCormick who signed.

TS MS (J. F. Dulles Papers, NjP).

¹ This draft, printed in Burnett, I, 764-65, was the American revision of the so-called Lloyd George plan, for which see Appendix III to the minutes of the Council of Four printed at March 29, 1919, 3 p.m.

² See EMH to WW, No. 42, Nov. 4, 1918, Vol. 51.

³ It might be pointed out that neither Wilson nor the American financial experts regarded this as a crucial concession. They all assumed that the United States would be represented on the proposed Permanent Reparations Commission. That commission would, by May 1, 1921, fix the sum that Germany was to pay and would also determine the time and mode of payments. In addition, Germany would have the right to be heard on all matters, and, if a minority of the Permanent Commission had any doubt as to the propriety of the inclusion of any item of damage or of the application of any method of evaluation, the commission should submit the matter in dispute to the Permanent Court of International Justice. To reiterate, the Americans assumed that Germany's reparations liability would be determined according to her capacity to pay, and that Germany would pay a fixed sum over a definite period. So long as the reparations bill was reasonable and had a time limit, it mattered little to the Americans how the Allies divided up the proceeds from reparations. See, in particular, Norman H. Davis' explanation of Wilson's understanding, printed in the minutes of the Council of Four, April 5, 1919, 11 a.m. Moreover, the Americans were well aware of the fact that, if reparations were to be paid only on a basis of *direct* damage to civilians and civilian property, Great Britain and the Dominions would never receive the 30 per cent of the reparations that Lloyd George had insisted upon. Indeed, the Dominions would have virtually no claim at all to reparation.

We think that the most sensible commentary on this subject is in Paul Birdsall, *Versailles Twenty Years After* (New York, 1941), and in Seth P. Tillman, *Anglo-American Relations at the Paris Peace Conference of 1919* (Princeton, N. J., 1961), and we quote from them as follows:

Birdsall (pp. 251-53): "Although many of the American experts were bitterly disappointed because they felt that the President had laid himself open to criticism for abandoning his principles, most of them did not take this surrender tragically. It was certainly a violation of the letter of the Pre-Armistice Agreement, but both President Wilson and the experts were sure that they still had adequate means of enforcing the spirit of the agreement. If a Reparation Commission were to calculate the total bill of damages on the basis of their estimate of what Germany could afford to pay in thirty years, if it then lay within their discretion as to what Germany must pay in any single year, and finally, if they had authority to conclude Germany's payments at the end of thirty years, or thirty-five at most, no matter how much or little Germany had actually paid in that time, then categories of damage meant very little. Total German payments would have been kept within the limits of German financial capacity, and the legal categories of damage written in the treaty would merely have affected the distribution of the money among Germany's creditors.

"It could even be argued that conceding pensions and separation allowances might be the most effective way of tying Lloyd George to the American program. It increased the British percentage of German payments, and thereby increased the British stake in German solvency—a stake already sufficiently large to argue the wisdom of that course. The French, to their own financial disadvantage, had supported the pensions proposal since early March, either because of its humanitarian appeal to their own electorate, or because they approved of the biggest possible German debt in order to weaken Germany politically and to justify continued military occupation of the Rhineland. At a time of complete French recklessness and irresponsibility, vital British interests dictated the closest collaboration with the American Delegation. While the concession on pensions might purchase British Support, it made that support more than ever essential to the American Delegation, since the concession itself had exactly doubled the American stake in the outcome. If the French conception of the Reparation Commission were to prevail, pensions would double the bill and the Commission would be under mandate to collect it, no matter how long it might take.

"Just as the American victory in excluding war costs was largely verbal, so the defeat on pensions would be a simple matter of words, if the American conception of a Reparation Commission could be made to prevail. The major battle was still to be joined."

Tillman (pp. 245-46): "Wilson's decision of April 1 was widely condemned as an unwarrantable surrender. Keynes, for instance, thought it 'perhaps the most decisive moment in the disintegration of the President's moral position and the clouding of his mind. . . .' The American experts, on the other hand, although greatly disappointed, believed that the inclusion of pensions, in view of the limited capacity of Germany to pay, would only alter the apportionment and not the sum of reparations.

"Whatever the responsibility of President Wilson for the inclusion of pensions, General Smuts was certainly no less responsible. It was undoubtedly the influence and prestige of Smuts, with whom Wilson shared so deep a community of thought regarding the League of

Nations, that persuaded the President to overrule his experts in the decision of April 1. Long afterwards, Smuts said that if he had known that so much would hang on his opinion, he would not so readily have given it. Both Wilson and Smuts, however, were almost certainly convinced at the time that they were making a decision as to the distribution of a fixed sum and not as to the size of that sum."

In any event, Wilson's decision to include pensions in the total reparation bill assumed great significance only after Colonel House, in a meeting of the Council of Four on April 5, agreed to jettison the stipulation of a time limit. But more about this later in the next volume.

From the Diary of Vance Criswell McCormick

April 1 (Tuesday)

Was called into conference in Lamont's room to meet with Davis, Baruch and Dulles to consider Lloyd George ultimatum that Great Britain would insist upon putting in pensions as category of claims and would not leave question open for a future determination and arbitration. This made it necessary to get from President, after explaining to him the line upon which we had been arguing, principles of claims under 14 points and armistice terms, a definite statement as to whether or not he could accept pensions. We called upon him at his house at 2.00 P.M. There were present Davis, Lamont, Baruch, Dulles and myself. We explained to him the limitations of the 14 points and armistice terms as the basis of peace in regard to its interpretations covering categories like pensions. He was very clear in his mind that there was no intention of including pensions when the peace and armistice terms were discussed and that particular categories of that character were not considered by themselves and that he felt that as pensions were such a just and equitable basis of claim, he would support them upon the French basis of valuations and it was particularly important to do this, otherwise England would not get what she was entitled to in proportion to the other countries. We all agreed to the Lloyd George proposal[1] which established a commission to determine the amount Germany can pay and the amount of the claims before 1921 which will relieve Great Britain and France from their troubles of making public the small amount they are to get from reparations because both Prime Ministers believe their government will be overthrown if the facts are known. I am afraid this camouflage will not work but it may, as the people forget so easily. As far as the United States is concerned, it does not affect us as our claims are small and we do not violate any principles, as the claims are just.

We went to our office after our talk with the President to meet Montague and Keynes of the British Delegation. We told them of our agreeing to pensions and we prepared a report for the Prime Ministers to be submitted at 4.00 o'clock.

We went to the President's house again to meet the Big Four and Klotz, Loucheur, Montague, Keynes, Crespi and Cheasa[2] and the United States advisers, Davis, Lamont, Baruch, Dulles and self, and discussed Lloyd George's plan after telling French and Italian delegates President had agreed to pensions. Klotz, of course, had many modifications and new schemes. Loucheur had a few minutes to talk with Clemenceau in the hall and when he came back took Baruch aside and told him Clemenceau was with the British and ourselves on the Lloyd George plan but to let Finance Minister Klotz have his talk and get through with it and they would make it all right later. We adjourned to meet tomorrow morning for final action; United States to submit categories of claims they can agree upon to be presented to Germany.

[1] Again, see Appendix III to the minutes of the Council of Four printed at March 29, 1919, 3 p.m.
[2] That is, Eugenio Chiesa.

From the Peace Conference Diary of Thomas William Lamont

Tuesday 1st [April 1, 1919]
Conf. w. BMB re Economic Comn. work. Then w. Montague & Keynes re reparation. They announced that L-G insisted on including pensions. Our crowd conferred & advised w. Col. EMH who tho't we ought to stand on our memo.[1] & against pensions. Lunched Crillon w. McC., NHD, Dulles & BMB. At 2 p.m. Pres't who announced he had agreed include pensions in French system of payments. We presented facts in matter & pointed out that including pensions wd lead logically to inclusion of all war costs. He retorted: "I don't give a damn for logic." . . . We sat in the Prest's library in a circle about him. He seemed fresh, a trifle impatient of prolonged discussion. But he had evidently given careful thought to subject.

Hw bound diary (T. W. Lamont Papers, MH-BA).
[1] See the declaration, "Principles of Reparation," printed at Feb. 8, 1919, Vol. 55.

A Memorandum of Anglo-American Progress on Reparations

April 1, 1919
British, United States, French and Italian financial representatives met yesterday morning.

After preliminary discussion, the conference was adjourned, to enable Mr. Klotz to submit amendments to Mr. Lloyd-George's proposals.[1] Since then, the United States representatives and the British representatives have been in almost continuous session.

It has been agreed between them that Mr. Lloyd-George's plan shall be in substance adopted, that is to say:

1. That Germany shall be compelled to admit her financial liability for all damage done to the civilian population of the Allied and Associated powers and their property by the aggression of the Enemy States by land, by sea and from the air, and also, for damage resulting from their acts in violation of formal engagements and of the Law of Nations.
2. That a commission should be established to decide:
    (1) The value of the claims in the categories agreed by the Allies as falling within Germany's liabilities as above.
    (2) The total amount which Germany was capable of paying to satisfy these claims.
3. That the commission should report by the end of 1921, but should have power to modify, from time to time, the time and mode of Germany's payments subsequent to 1921.
4. That payments should be made by an initial sum and annual instalments over a period of not more than thirty years.

It was further agreed that an interpretation document should be prepared, to be handed to the Germans as an explanation of what the Allied and Associated Powers regarded as the liabilities payment for which they were in a position to enforce under the above clause, subject to Germany's capacity to pay as determined by the commission. The United States and British representatives agreed that among the categories to be included should be the cost of pensions and the cost of damage to property.

It was understood that Mr. Lloyd-George and Mr. Clemenceau have agreed that pensions shall be calculated on the French basis of payments.

In order to avoid the challenging and putting forward of doubtful claims, we think it would be expedient to agree at once between the Allies a proportionate distribution of all payments received from Germany.

We propose to meet further in order

1. To draft the interpretation clause and to consider Mr. Klotz' amendments which are directed towards this end, and
2. To make proposals as to the proportionate distribution of receipts between the Allies.

CC MS (WP, DLC).
[1] Again, see Appendix III to the minutes of the Council of Four, March 29, 1919, 3 p.m.

First Draft of an Anglo-American Accord on Reparations

April 1, 1919.

1. The Allied and Associated Governments recognize that the financial resources of the enemy States are not unlimited, and, after taking into account permanent diminutions of such resources, which will result from other treaty clauses, they judge that it will be impracticable for the enemy states to make complete reparation for all loss and damage to which the Allied and Associated Governments, and their nationals, have been subjected as a direct and necessary consequence of the war imposed upon them by the aggression of the enemy states.

2. The Allied and Associated Governments, however, require that the enemy states, at whatever cost to themselves, make compensation for all damages done to the civilian population of the Allied and Associated Powers and to their property by the aggression of the enemy states by land, by sea, and from the air, and also from damage resulting from their acts in violation of formal engagements and of the law of nations.

3. The amount of such damage for which compensation is to be made shall be determined by an Inter-Allied Commission, to be constituted in such form as the Allied and Associated Governments shall forthwith determine. This Commission shall examine into the claims and give to the enemy states a just opportunity to be heard. The findings of the Commission as to the amount of damage shall be concluded and communicated to the enemy states on or before May 1, 1921; and a schedule of payments to be made by the enemy states shall be set forth covering a series of years not to exceed 30, and in general to be based upon the reasonable capacity of the enemy states to pay.

4. The Inter-Ally Commission shall further determine from time to time any necessary modifications in the time and mode of payments to be made by the enemy states, after giving them a just opportunity to be heard. Payment may be required and, with the approval of the Commission, accepted in the form of properties, chattels, businesses, rights, and concessions in ceded territory or in territory outside the enemy state, ships, gold and silver, bonds, shares and securities of all kinds, foreign currencies or the currency of the enemy state, or in German Government bonds.

5. In order to enable the Allied and Associated Powers to proceed at once to the restoration of their industries and economic life, pending the full determination of their claim, the enemy states shall pay in such installments and in such manner (whether in gold, commodities, ships, securities or otherwise) as the Inter-Allied Commission may fix, in 1919 and 1920, the equivalent of

£1,000,000,000 sterling. Out of such payment provision shall be made for the maintenance of the Allied Armies of Occupation, and for indispensable supplies of food and raw materials for the enemy states. The balance shall be credited on account of the sum that may be determined to be due as compensation for damages.

6. The successive instalments paid over by the enemy states in satisfaction of the above claims shall be divided by the Allied and Associated Governments in proportions which have been determined upon by them in advance, on a basis of general equity, having regard to all relevant circumstances.

CC MS (J. F. Dulles Papers, NjP).

A Memorandum by Sidney Edward Mezes

[Paris] April 1st, 1919.

Re: Danzig Region.

Mr. Headlam-Merley,[1] designated by Mr. Lloyd George for our conference, made a proposal which we worked up into the form given below. He is to submit it to his chief.

The proposal is that the treaty with Germany shall include articles providing,

I. Ceding (not to Poland but) to the League of Nations, Danzig and adjacent territory West of the main branch of the Vistula, this territory to be ceded in turn to Poland as a free port area with guarantee by the League of Nations of generous autonomy.

II. Ceding, also to the League, the territory east of the main Vistula to the line proposed by the Polish Committee on the East, and to the former line of East Prussia on the South, it being left to the Executive Council of the League to draw the boundary between East Prussia and Poland within this area, after examining conditions on the spot.

III. Granting both Germany and Poland special and secure rights on railways as needed by them respectively.

If this moves in the wrong direction won't you be good enough to let me know, against my next conference with Mr. Headlam-Merley.

Advantages: (1) Gives time to consult the people concerned.

(2) Ties the League of Nations into the treaty.

(3) Avoids delay in drafting treaty by postponing difficult questions for the further examination they need.　　　　　　　　　　S F M

TI MS (WP, DLC).
[1] Sic.

Mantoux's Notes of a Meeting of the Council of Four

April 1, 1919, 4 p.m.

Wilson. I saw the American financial experts at two o'clock, and I told them, remembering the exchange we had here: "If, when we are in the presence of the Germans, we tell them that it is impossible for us to indicate the figure of what they owe and what we believe them capable of paying, they will certainly reply: 'At least tell us what the purpose of the reparations will be.' " To respond to this question, we must together draw up a classification by categories, while not losing sight of the formula we have adopted: "Reparation for damages to property and persons of the civilian populations." It is understood that this formula should include pensions.

It is a matter of establishing a list which we will sign in common. From that time on, we will be in a position to respond to the question that the Germans certainly will ask us. We agree to exclude everything that is not direct damage, such as the failure of business to make profits.

Lloyd George. We can tell the Germans that if they refuse to accept one of our categories, for example pensions, we will resume our unlimited right to claim for all damages suffered, whatever they may be.

Wilson. Our definitions must include compensation due for the deportations of workers.

Lloyd George. Undoubtedly, and for the outrages against the crews of the merchant fleet.

Wilson. I have reviewed the proposals made about Danzig. They are four in number.[1]

The first would make Danzig a free city, somewhat like the Hanseatic cities of the Middle Ages, with sufficient territory surrounding her, but limited so as to include an almost exclusively German population. On the other hand, the frontier of East Prussia would be extended toward the west, in order to include in that province the Germans of the lower Vistula. The Poles would keep the left bank of the river and would have on the right bank a small territory shaped like a balloon, between East Prussia and the Republic of Danzig.

The second plan gives Danzig to the Poles, while extending the territory of East Prussia as above.

The third is the commission's plan, which you know.

The fourth has just been presented by an expert of the British

[1] See the memorandum by S. E. Mezes printed at March 31, 1919, and the one just printed.

delegation, Mr. Headlam-Morley. Germany would cede Danzig along with its territory to the League of Nations, and the League of Nations would give it to Poland on the condition that it be assured relative autonomy. The Executive Council of the League of Nations would fix the definitive frontiers of this little state, as well as those of East Prussia.

This exhausts all the hypotheses, it seems to me.

The danger of the first plan is that it would give the Germans of Danzig the temptation to reunite with Germany. The second, with its concession to East Prussia and the cession of Danzig to the Poles, is a compromise. The last has the same character, and has the advantage of having the League of Nations intervene as a guarantor of the proposed system; but it has the disadvantage of leaving in suspense part of the decisions to be taken.

Lloyd George. I would prefer rather a combination of the first and fourth systems. I do not dislike the idea of reviving the free cities. They flourished in a time when, it seems, international law was more respected than today.

Wilson. It is above all military means that have changed.

Lloyd George. I would conceive of a city of Danzig independent, with a large enough territory to give it breathing space. I would place this small state within the customs frontiers of Poland, which would make it impossible for Germany to use it to strangle Poland from the economic point of view.

The inhabitants of Danzig would know that their future is bound to the economic future of Poland. Moreover, all their opportunities for commerce lie on this side. By making them independent you will interest them in the prosperity of the Polish state, to which we would gradually attach them by the economic bond. I am persuaded that the same thing will happen in the Saar basin, when the latter is united to France by its interests, without political bonds. I would see to it that all the interests of Danzig's inhabitants be turned toward the side of Poland, while leaving to them, if they wish to maintain them, all the German laws and institutions that will please them.

My great concern is to avoid putting too many Germans in Poland. According to the commission's report, the province of Marienwerder alone would include 420,000. I would leave this province to East Prussia, while giving Poland absolute right to the railways.

Wilson. Could not the fate of these German-speaking regions be decided by means of a plebiscite?

Lloyd George. If there is a plebiscite, I would accept the decision of the population.

Wilson. The question is to know how the Poles will welcome this plan. When I earlier mentioned to M. Dmowski the hypothesis of Danzig as a free city, he hit the ceiling. In this case we must give the Poles sovereignty over the river whose western bank they will occupy. Only a small part of the Vistula would flow along German territory of East Prussia.

Lloyd George. The railroad from Danzig to Thorn would remain in Polish territory.

Orlando. Would the territory of Danzig be in direct contact with Polish territory?

Lloyd George. Certainly. (Mr. Lloyd George shows the map.)

Clemenceau. We cannot take a definite decision on this subject without the presence of the Poles.

Wilson. No, but we can agree among ourselves beforehand.

Lloyd George. I believe that it would be vain to hope to satisfy the Poles.

Wilson. They must accept the solution that we judge reasonable.

Clemenceau. They will not accept it without difficulty.

Lloyd George. If they do not accept it, let them do better on their own. My advice is to decide upon a plan and then to summon the Poles.

Wilson. Do we agree to form a free state around Danzig?

Lloyd George. Yes, but under the authority of the League of Nations.

Wilson. In what form do you conceive this authority?

Lloyd George. I would prefer to see the League of Nations represented in Danzig by a high commissioner. That would prevent the Germans from intriguing in this little state. This high commissioner could have a role analogous to that of our Governor-General in Canada and Australia, whose presence does not prevent the inhabitants from governing themselves freely.

Wilson. The union of the province of Marienwerder to East Prussia must be added, with freedom of transit guaranteed to the Poles; this could be settled by plebiscite. I would remark that this solution is, for the most part, the one which I have always preferred.

Lloyd George. Our Foreign Office has always advised us in this sense. After all, we do not owe much to the Poles, who fought as much against us as for us. We must avoid whatever would make it difficult for the Germans to sign the treaty.

Wilson (to M. Clemenceau). What are your thoughts on this last point?

Clemenceau. I am not entirely sure that you would succeed in coaxing the Germans in this way.

Wilson. We must not allow ourselves to be influenced too much by the Polish state of mind. I saw M. Dmowski and M. Paderewski in Washington, and I asked them to define for me Poland as they understood it, and they presented me with a map in which they claimed a large part of the earth.

Lloyd George. What I ask is that we do not put in the treaty articles for which we are not prepared to go to war in the future. France would make war tomorrow for Alsace, if it was contested. But would we make war for Danzig?

Wilson. Furthermore, we should not violate the principles that we ourselves have set forth as the basis of the peace. All that we have promised to Poland is access to the sea; and at the same time, we have always declared that we would respect ethnographic frontiers as much as possible.

If you really wish it, I will have Professor Haskins study this question anew.

Here is a document which has been sent to me by Mr. Norman Davis.[2] There is agreement among our financial representatives to accept, in its general outlines, the plan which Mr. Lloyd George submitted to us: the Germans recognize their debt according to our formula, a permanent commission being established to examine claims and to determine Germany's capacity to pay, with the right to fix annual payments, etc.

It proposes a date for the announcement of figures: it would be May 1, 1921.

Lloyd George. I am told that the experts do not agree, because M. Klotz would wish, on the contrary, that the annual payments should be stipulated in the peace treaty.

Mr. Loucheur is introduced.

Loucheur. Your financial delegates are examining the question of reparations. The English and the Americans are in accord, and we will arrive at a general agreement. I hope that we will be able to bring you our conclusions at noon tomorrow.

However, we would need precise instructions about the categories of damages admitted for reparation. Since we accept the principle offered by the American delegation, agreement should be easy.

Wilson. I believe that the question of Polish frontiers is nearly settled.

Clemenceau. I was not very favorably disposed toward adopting this type of solution. But after having listened to you, I am inclined to go along with you, although thinking that the greatest precautions must be taken if we wish to avoid throwing the Poles into disorder.

[2] That is, the memorandum of Anglo-American progress, just printed.

Wilson. We must consider the agenda for the coming days. Peace with Germany will not remove all the causes of possible difficulties. I greatly fear those which could arise from the situation of all these nationalities in formation in Central Europe. There is there an inexhaustible source of disorders and of war, if we are not very careful.

I propose to ask our territorial commissions to review their reports, modifying them as may be in the sense indicated by our fundamental principles. Then we can conclude rapidly.

Lloyd George. We can, I hope, be ready on all the great questions in a week. During the time necessary for the work of the drafting commission, we could tackle among ourselves the questions of the nationalities of Austria-Hungary, as well as the Bulgarian and Turkish questions.

Orlando. It is necessary, from the Italian point of view, that our decision on the eastern frontier of Italy not be delayed. For the Italian people, this is a question of self-respect, in addition to our concern for national security. If the Italian people learn that the German questions are completely settled, and that the Austrian questions are postponed, that would produce a bad impression.

Lloyd George. I am completely ready to discuss this question next week, during the final drafting of our decisions on the German treaty. We have also the report on the question of responsibilities that we could consider here.

Wilson. I have a word to say on this subject. Charles I was a contemptible character and the greatest liar in history; he was celebrated by poetry and transformed into a martyr by his execution. The same for Mary Stuart, whose career was not in the least estimable.

Lloyd George. Concerning Mary Stuart, the poetry could be explained otherwise: she was a very seductive woman.

Wilson. Napoleon who—by different methods, I concede,—tried, exactly like the German Emperor, to impose his domination upon the world, was surrounded by legend because of his captivity at Saint Helena.

Lloyd George. It was not only Saint Helena which created the Napoleonic legend.

I would like to see the man responsible for the greatest crime in history undergo punishment for it.

Wilson. He has drawn universal contempt upon himself; is that not the worst punishment for a man like him?

An exchange of views takes place about the Turkish questions. It is agreed to say that Turkey need only be informed of her territorial limits on the Armenian side. On the Greek side, they can be extended beyond strictly ethnographic limits, in such a way as to give the ports on the western coast some breathing space. Constantinople and the region of the Straits would be placed under a separate mandate of the League of Nations. It remains to be decided if Turkey would be independent or itself placed under a mandatory different from that for Constantinople.

Mantoux, I, 109-14.

From the American Commissioners, with Enclosure

PARIS, April 1st, 1919.

The American Commissioners to Negotiate Peace have the honor to transmit herewith to the President of the United States a copy of a memorandum which has been prepared by Professor Coolidge, regarding the rights of national minorities.   RL

TI MS (WP, DLC).

E N C L O S U R E

MEMORANDUM
RIGHTS OF NATIONAL MINORITIES

The rights of nationalities include those of minorities as well as of majorities.

All the assignments recommended to the Commission of disputed territories are doubtless based on the presupposition that proper treatment will be accorded to the dissentient minorities who are handed over to alien rule. But such mere assumption is not sufficient. On the contrary, it is urgent that some understanding should be reached and proclaimed by the Conference as to what constitutes at least the minimum of these rights, political, linguistic, religious. No authoritative statement on the subject has been issued. So far we have nothing to rely on but vaguely benevolent assurances on the part of the governments interested. The question, however, is of vital interest to the people concerned and on its answer depends not only their own happiness but in great measure the prospect that the settlement arrived at will in the end prove satisfactory and permanent. Even the actual fixing of boundaries should be affected by this consideration. Take for instance the case of the German parts of Bohemia where the principles of historic, geographic and economic unity on the one side have to be weighed against that of self-determination on the other. It should make a difference in the weighing of the respective value of these claims whether the Bohemian Germans are to be subjected to a systematic process of Czechisation, official language, courts, schools, street signs, etc., or whether they are to be allowed to remain in their community with one of the great cultural languages of the world. Mere general declarations on the part of the Czecho-Slovak government are not sufficient, however benignant and however sincere. Something more is required to tranquillize the populations whose destiny is being decided presumably for all time. It would be easy to multiply instances of this kind. There are today many millions of people who are about to be handed over to or left under the rule of others with whom they are at present in deep enmity and from whom they can see no reason to expect generous treatment in the future. Naturally the statesmen of the countries to be benefited are prodigal in their declarations of the most liberal intentions and will continue to be, at least until the question of frontiers is definitely settled. But however honestly made, such declarations are not enough to reassure the excited populations now looking forward to a prospect of foreign domination, especially as the conduct of the officials and the soldiery in the occupied districts has not been such as to inspire confidence. What is needed is some binding declaration on the part of the Allied powers which will tranquillize apprehensions and will serve as some sort of guarantee for the future. It need not enter into details which can be settled by the League of Nations at a future date. All that is practicable for the moment and that is urgently needed is a statement of the broad principles of human rights which should and must prevail in assuring the new national minorities the life, liberty and pursuit of happiness to which they are entitled and which now seem so gravely menaced.

T MS (WP, DLC).

Two Letters to Robert Lansing

My dear Lansing: Paris, 1 April, 1919.

I think the settlement suggested by you and our colleagues in this matter[1] is the right and necessary one.

Cordially and sincerely yours,   [Woodrow Wilson]

[1] Was Wilson referring to the Russian Section's memorandum printed as an Enclosure with the American Commissioners to WW, March 31, 1919? It is impossible to answer this question with any degree of confidence. Pointing toward a positive answer, Lansing did initial the covering letter, and Wilson might have thought that the Russian Section's memorandum came to him with the commissioners' endorsement. Moreover, the document, unlike Bullitt's memorandum of March 27, 1919, *is* in the Wilson Papers. In addition, the Editors have been unable to find *any* other communication to which Wilson's letter might have been a reply. Finally, as the reader will remember, Robert H. Lord, for whom Wilson had great respect, was head of the Russian Section. Pointing

toward a negative answer, the memorandum sent to Wilson by the American Commissioners on March 31, bears no evidence that Wilson read it, that is, it has no marginal markings, underlinings, question marks, etc., such as Wilson often made on important documents. In the second place, Wilson obviously did not implement the Russian Section's recommendations. However, these observations are not necessarily conclusive. Wilson did not always mark up important documents; moreover, as the documents in this series will disclose, developments in Paris, abroad, and in the United States soon took control of Russian policy out of Wilson's hands. However, it is interesting that, as late as April 21, 1919, Wilson wrote: "I find my mind going along with yours in your comments upon the Russian situation" in reply to a letter from William G. Sharp, in which Sharp strongly urged Wilson to extend some form of recognition to the Bolshevik regime. See W. G. Sharp to WW, April 18, 1919, and WW to W. G. Sharp, April 21, 1919.

My dear Mr. Secretary: Paris, 1 April, 1919.

I am myself surprised by this bill,[1] but of course we must pay it, and I am very much obliged to you for bringing it to my attention.
Sincerely yours,   [Woodrow Wilson]

CCL (WP, DLC).
  [1] It is missing; however, see the extract from the Benham Diary printed at March 31, 1919, and RL to WW, April 2, 1919 (first letter of that date).

From Charles Homer Haskins, with Enclosure

Dear President Wilson,   [Paris] 1 April 1919

I enclose herewith certain heads of proposals based on my conference with the British and French experts. The formulation is my own but I believe they could be made the basis of agreement.

The strongest French point seems to me to be the possibility of consulting the people after a reasonable time has been given to offset a hundred years of Prussification. I understand they feel that such a consultation might take place comparatively soon in rural districts, but would be obviously unfair now in the great industrial centres largely filled with people from other parts of Germany.

From the point of view of general interests I see more possibility of friction in French exploitation of the mines under Prussian administration than in a temporary administration by France under a definite mandate with ample guarantee of all local liberties, especially in view of the obvious French interest to conciliate the population in view of an ultimate plebiscite.
Sincerely yours,   Charles H. Haskins

TLS (WP, DLC).

ENCLOSURE

SAAR BASIN

1. France to have permanent ownership of the mines, with full facilities for their exploitation.

2. The mining area to be held for a period of 15 years by the League of Nations, which will hold a plebiscite at the end of this period, either *en bloc* or by communes, and will thereupon hand over the area, or the respective parts, to Germany or France according as the vote shall determine.

3. During this interval France to administer the territory under a mandate from the League of Nations.

By the terms of the mandate France shall be charged with the maintenance of order, including the appointment of such officers as are now named by the Prussian or Bavarian governments. There shall be no fortification or military establishment within the territory.

The inhabitants shall retain their German citizenship (except that any individuals so desiring may be free to acquire French citizenship), their local representative assemblies, religious arrangements, law, language, and schools, and shall be exempt from military service. They shall not be entitled to vote for representatives in either the German Reichstag or the French Chambers. Any who desire to leave the district shall have full opportunity to dispose of their property on equitable terms.

T MS (WP, DLC).

From Vance Criswell McCormick

My dear Mr. President: Paris. April 1, 1919.

I have received your letter of March 28th, enclosing a copy of a message from Tumulty,[1] concerning the censorship on cables.

I appreciate the importance of this matter, and have been urging upon the Allies the complete removal of the censorship unless it is necessary for military purposes, because, in my opinion, it is no longer needed for Blockade purposes, except insofar as Germany and Bolshevik Russia are concerned. While we have succeeded in bringing about a considerable relaxation, yet I am convinced that the existing system is not only most irritating to legitimate trade interests, but is preventing the resumption of the normal economic life of the world, and is thereby proving exceedingly harmful.

I feel that on account of our close co-operation with the Allies in the past, and on account of the recent relaxations made only upon the strong representations of Lord Robert Cecil to his government, that we should not peremptorily withdraw our censorship, but notify Lord Robert Cecil at once that on a certain date, in the very near future, the United States will be compelled to abolish all telegraph and cable censorship on messages passing between the United States, and Great Britain, France, and Italy, and also upon all cables between any of the above mentioned associated countries and Central and South America and Cuba, and we will further insist that all cables to and from certain countries in which it has been determined censorship is necessary, shall only be censored by the associated Government in whose jurisdiction the message shall originate or terminate.

I expect to take this matter up at once with Lord Robert Cecil, and would appreciate your withholding action until I can remove any possible obligation which may exist, so that we can act honorably, if it is necessary to take action independently, which I am afraid we will have to do.

Very Sincerely Yours,   Vance C. McCormick

TLS (WP, DLC).
  [1] The Enclosure printed with WW to V. C. McCormick, March 28, 1919.

Henry Wickham Steed to Edward Mandell House, with Enclosure

Dear Colonel House: Paris, April 1st, 1919.

I had a short conversation this afternoon with M. Clemenceau. I found him under considerable misapprehension as to what I believe to be the real attitude and intentions of President Wilson. I discussed with him various suggestions for a solution of the issues concerning the Sarre Basin and the organization of the zone protective of the eastern frontiers of France.

M. Clemenceau asked me to bring him tomorrow, Wednesday, afternoon at two-thirty, a short written formula, which as far as I could judge, President Wilson might be inclined to accept. I therefore drafted the enclosed formula as being one which I think M. Clemenceau would be disposed to accept.

M. Clemenceau added that if such a formula could be found he, for his part, would be willing to cooperate most heartily with President Wilson in securing its acceptance by the Peace Conference.

Yours very sincerely,   Wickham Steed

Steed is a very old friend of Clemenceau's and it may be well to let him try his hand on this if you consider this reasonable.

EMH

TLS (WP, DLC).

ENCLOSURE

The Sarre Basin

The Sarre Basin shall be occupied and administered by France on a mandatory basis for a period of fifteen years.

At the end of this period the allegiance of the inhabitants shall be decided by a plebiscite organized under the authority and control of the League of Nations, the plebiscite to be taken either *en bloc* or by communes and the ultimate allegiance of the whole area or of the respective parts to be determined by the vote.

The mines shall be exploited by France during the mandatory period as partial reparation for the damage done by Germany to French coal mines. Should it appear that French coal mines have been permanently damaged or rendered entirely useless by the Germans, the coal mines of the Sarre Basin shall, at the end of the period of fifteen years, remain permanently the property of France irrespective of the result of the plebiscite.

There shall be no fortifications or military establishments in the Sarre basin other than a police force or gendarmarie for the maintenance of public order.

Under the French administration the citizenship of the inhabitants shall be unchanged except in so far as individuals may be allowed to acquire French citizenship; their local representative assemblies, their religious institutions, language and schools shall be maintained and the inhabitants shall be exempt from military service. They shall not be entitled to representation either in the German or French parliaments. Any who may desire to leave the district shall have full opportunity to dispose of their property on equitable terms.

Protection of Eastern France.

Upon the signature of peace all fortified works, fortresses and field works situated on German territory to the west of a line drawn fifty kilometers to the east of the Rhine shall be disarmed and dismantled. No new fortifications of any kind shall be constructed there nor shall there be any armed or military organization nor any manufacture of materials of war within that zone save such as may be requisite under the terms of Allied occupation during the period of reparation.

Any Allied occupation that may be requisite during the period of reparation shall be undertaken by French or other Allied detachments as mandataries on behalf of the League of Nations. Officers of the Allied and Associated armies shall be attached to any forces of occupation.

Any violation of these provisions shall be an hostile act directed against the signatories of the present treaty and in particular any attempt on the part of Germany to evade or infringe them shall involve *ipso facto* immediate action by the League of Nations or mandataries that it may appoint *ad hoc*.[1]

T MS (WP, DLC).
[1] Hugh Arthur Frazier delivered Steed's letter and its enclosure to Wilson on April 1. According to Steed, he had the following conversation with Frazier on the next day:
"'He turned me out,' said Frazier.
"'Who?' I asked.
"'The President,' he answered. 'I took your letter and formulas up to him last night. He had hardly glanced through them when he flew into a terrible rage. He threw them on to the table and shouted, "I will not have it. I will not have it. Unless my principles are accepted integrally I will order the *George Washington* at once and go home. What do you mean by bringing me things which are in flagrant contradiction with my principles?"—and, literally, he turned me out of his room.'
"'Then Clemenceau is quite right,' I replied. 'Your President is an utterly impossible fellow. How do my formulas violate his principles?'
"'I cannot guess, and he did not say,' answered Frazier. 'He explained nothing, but just bundled me out.'" Henry Wickham Steed, *Through Thirty Years, 1892-1922, A Personal Narrative* (2 vols., Garden City, N. Y., 1924), II, 313.

From the Diary of Colonel House

April 1. 1919.

The President and I confer quite frequently over our private telephone. This morning I arranged with him to send Col. Sherman Miles to Montenegro in response to Mr. Balfour's letter of last night,[1] which is a part of the record. I submitted three of four names to the President and he chose Miles. I have arranged to have him notified.

Yesterday the Council of Four decided to ask General Smuts to go to Roumania and Hungary to look into the situations there. It was understood that he should go alone, but Smuts sent me word this morning by Wiseman that he would like very much if I would pick out an American to go with him, and we would keep the fact of his going confidential in order that there might be no hurt feelings with the French and Italians. I selected Major Stephen Bonsal.[2] . . .

Lloyd George is a mischief maker who changes his mind like a weather-vane. He has no profound knowledge of any of the questions with which he is dealing. Orlando is level-headed, but he is handicapped by not speaking English, and by the fact that they are not taking up the questions in which he is interested. Clemenceau is of the old regime. He told Steed yesterday that the President thought himself another Jesus Christ come upon the earth to reform men. He is the ablest reactionary in the Conference, but it is almost hopeless to try to deal with him except in ways that the world will no longer consider, and which we hope to make forever obsolete.

The President is becoming stubborn and angry, and he never

was a good negotiator. So there you are. I think the President is becoming unreasonable, which does not make for solutions. Nothing is being run in an orderly way. The Commission to Syria has been appointed and they are still awaiting instructions. There is no one to give the word, and so it is with innumerable other matters. It could be done so easily that it is maddening to see the days go by and nothing decided.

[1] A. J. Balfour to EMH, March 28 (not March 31), 1919.
[2] Foreign and war correspondent for many years, first with the *New York Herald* and later with the *New York Times*. He had also spent several years in the United States diplomatic service and as a colonial official in the Philippines. He had more recently served with the A.E.F. in France and was assigned as an aide to Colonel House in Paris in October 1918. He later published two books which consisted largely of extracts from his diary of the peace conference: *Unfinished Business* (New York, 1944), and *Suitors and Suppliants: The Little Nations at Versailles* (New York, 1946).

From the Diary of Ray Stannard Baker

Tuesday the 1st [April 1919]

A better barometer to-day & a more hopeful feeling. When I went up to the place des Etats-Unis this afternoon I found the President much more cheerful, said that progress was really being made & that decisions would probably be reached on several matters soon. Said that they had apparently got Clemenceau "down." "He is like an old dog trying to find a place to rest," said the President, "he turns slowly around & around, following his tail, before he gets down to it."

He said that they hoped to finish with the German problems this week & go on with the Austria[n] Hungarian & Turkish problems next week. This was his *hope*, not his prediction. The report that a draft of the actual treaty, made by Lloyd-George, was [undecipherable word] them was false. He had seen Orlando separately, & there had been much discussion of Italian claims.

The President looks well, but is working too hard. He had all the financial experts meeting in another room to-day & saw them frequently.

From the Diary of Josephus Daniels

1919 Tuesday 1 April

Up early & breakfasted with Lloyd George and Long and discussed League of Nations. L. G. said L of N would be worth nothing if we continue to build—he would ostentatiously throw into the sea & sink all German ships awarded to GB. They had stopped work on their cruisers, & we ought to stop work if we really trusted the

League Wilson wanted. I asked him if such an agreement was a condition precedent. Of course not, but L of N would be a mere piece of rhetoric if we continued to build. If America has no confidence in it, who could have. I told him I could not make such agreement or understanding, for anything done must be published & printed in all papers. He said he never meant any agreement that could not be submitted to Parliament & Congress. We parted to go see President at 11. Saw him. LG rather insisted I should not go to Rome but go at some later date. I convinced President it would be unwise after all arrangements had been made to postpone, but would cut my trip short & return Monday. Acquiesced. I called to see Long & told him.

Robert Lansing to Frank Lyon Polk

[Paris, April 1, 1919]

1421.

Your cipher telegram 1346, March 28, 6 P.M.[1]

Our records do not show telegrams from General Graves numbered 214, March 17, and 229, March 26, nor any telegram from Admiral Rogers, No. 216, March 16.

The President authorizes instruction to General Graves as below, provided the Secretary of War concurs. Please consult with him accordingly. General Graves should be instructed that the United States favors economic rehabilitation of the country and feels strongly that a policy of political moderation among the several Russian factions is a necessary condition. In particular General Graves should be told that his mission is to insure in cooperation with his Allies uninterrupted operation of the Trans-Siberian and Chinese Eastern Railways and it is suggested that the movements of his forces be limited to a zone of say three miles on either side of the railways. Within zone he should exercise definite police power and prevent any disturbances that might interfere with the operation of the railways. It is suggested further that the Department might say to the governments having forces in Siberia and that in the view of the American Government the inter-Allied forces in Siberia have been retained there for the purpose of protecting the railways and the men operating them under the direction of the Inter-Allied committee, that the American Government suggests the establishment of a zone as proposed above and that the inter-Allied committee might issue a statement to this effect and add that they will not permit any disorder within the railway zone and will use the forces at their disposal to preserve the peace within that zone.

Ammission.

T telegram (WP, DLC).
¹ W. Phillips to Ammission, No. 1346, March 28, 1919, T telegram (SDR, RG 256, 861.00/4301, DNA). Phillips said that Graves and Rodgers had reported on conditions in eastern Siberia. They pointed to the aggressive attitude of the Japanese military authorities and the ruthless methods of troops under Ivanov-Rinov in suppressing Bolshevik tendencies.

To Bernard Mannes Baruch

My dear Baruch: Paris, 1 April, 1919.

May I trouble you to read the enclosed cables¹ and give me your advice as to what I should do? The position of the Railway Administration seems to me entirely reasonable, and yet I do not want to do anything which will make this attempt to start business on a new basis a failure.

Cordially and faithfully yours,   [Woodrow Wilson]

CCL (WP, DLC).
¹ WCR to WW, March 27, 1919, and W. D. Hines to WW, March 28, 1919.

To Herbert Clark Hoover

My dear Hoover: Paris, 1 April, 1919.

Thank you for your letter and for the suggested telegrams.¹ I am sending them both today.

Cordially and faithfully yours,   [Woodrow Wilson]

CCL (WP, DLC).
¹ See HCH to WW, March 31, 1919 (second letter of that date).

From Edward Nash Hurley

Washington. April 1, 1919.

1406. For The President from Hurley.¹

"We will put forth every effort to comply with your request to allocate additional 500,000 tons of ships to Hoover for April in addition to the 800,000 tons which he has had at his disposal for months. We have granted every request Hoover has made on us but it has always been hard to learn just what he wants, and then when we do secure the information it is on such short notice that it is almost impossible for us to comply therewith. We appreciate the seriousness of the situation and have cabled him urging that he have the French waive delivery of freight cars for which they have contracted for the next couple of months so that we may allocate to him the 100,000 tons of ships which would otherwise be used for this purpose and in addition have assigned his commission 300,000 tons within the last few days for his April food program. Hurley."   Phillips,   Acting.

T telegram (WP, DLC).
¹ Hurley was responding to WW to ENH, March 28, 1919.

From the American Hungarian Press Association

Washington, April 1st, 1919.

1400. For the President from the American Hungarian Press Association.

"The members of the American Hungarian Press Association respectfully beg Your Excellency to use your exalted influence in order to stop the spreading of Bolshevism in their native land, Hungary. It is our earnest conviction that the present state of affairs existing in Hungary were brought about by the intolerable political and economic conditions prevailing now in that land. It is our firm belief that the Hungarian nation is not willingly accepting Bolshevistic rule, and is ready to destroy it if Your Excellency will see to it that the fate of Hungary is decided on your noble principles. It is our firm belief that if the nationalities of Hungary are allowed without interference to solve their own national problems on the basis of self-determination, and establish a true democratic government, then Bolshevism will cease to exist there.

We firmly believe that the sentiments expressed here are shared by all Americans of Hungarian extraction. Praying for Your Excellency's good health and may the Almighty give you strength that you may carry out the noble principles for the good of all humanity, we remain your most obedient servants. Executive Members, American Hungarian Press Association."   Phillips   Acting.

T telegram (WP, DLC).

Brand Whitlock to Gilbert Fairchild Close

Dear Mr. Close: Brussels 1st April, 1919.

During the President's absence in America a medal was presented at the Legation for him, and I decided to keep it until his return, or until his visit to Brussels, thinking that I could perhaps best give it to him then. But, as his visit is being delayed, I am sending it to you herewith, with the request that you give it to him. It was presented under most interesting circumstances. One afternoon a crowd of a thousand persons, each bearing an American flag, and headed by a band, marched to the Legation, and a committee entered, explaining that they were the men and women who had worked in the Comité National during the war, in the clothing department. Several speeches were made and an address was presented to the President, with a gold medal, which they asked him to accept. I replied to the addresses, saying that the President would be glad to receive this touching evidence of their admiration and reverence for him, and went out on the balcony of the Legation while the bands played the Belgian and American national hymns.

I think all that it is necessary to do has been done; but if you could authorize me to send a word to these working people, thanking them, on behalf of the President, it would doubtless be very gratifying to them.

I am, my dear Mr. Close,
                    Ever yours sincerely,   Brand Whitlock

TLS (WP, DLC).

From the Diary of Dr. Grayson

Wednesday, April 2, 1919.

The Council of Four resumed their sessions this morning, and we had another magnificent exhibition of the absolute impossibility of securing any action from the French. The question of the Rhine came up for consideration. This has been a very knotty problem from the start because the French have been insisting that there should be created here a separate Rhinish Republic, which would act as a buffer state between Alsace-Lorraine and Germany proper. When the President told Clemenceau about a week ago that under no circumstance could the United States consent to the creation of any such alien country inasmuch as the residents of the Rhine district are entirely German in their thoughts and sympathies, they temporarily abandoned the plan. When they met today they brought up a new line. They wanted all of the fortifications on both sides of the Rhine razed completely. They wanted nothing of a military character on the left bank of the Rhine between Alsace-Lorraine and the Rhine while they wanted a permanent prohibition on the erection of landing platforms at any point along the Rhine on the right bank. The excuse that they gave was that they wanted to be prepared to offset any sudden attempt by Germany to raid France. Clemenceau persisted in his arguments not only for this action but for a renewed policy of confiscation designed against the Saar Valley metallurgical wealth. The result was that the President found himself up against an opposition that was subtle, disingenuous, and entirely erroneous.

The question also of sending the Polish troops into Poland via Dantzig was raised and Marshal Foch was present. The French plan, which was endorsed by the British, was to load these troops on vessels despite the great scarcity of shipping for foodstuffs and the grave necessity of saving time and sending them through the Skagarack [Skagerrak] via the Baltic to Dantzig, thereby wasting very, very valuable time. The President wanted to know why they could not be sent through Germany by rail, calling attention to the fact that such an arrangement was entirely equitable under one of the provisions of the League of Nations Constitution. He let it be known that there would be no objection from Germany if these troops were to pass through in that way. As a matter of fact, the Germans would very gladly have them transferred there rather than to transport them into Dantzig and create a situation there which would be fraught with great danger. However, Marshal Foch could not see the reason, and the President afterwards suggested that while he might be a wonderful military leader it was necessary to deal with him exactly as one would with a child in explaining all the fundamentals of a proposition of this sort. For more than an hour there was wrangling on the subject, and it required absolute insistence by the President, coupled with a sharp threat that he would not stand for any more nonsense to secure approval of this plan. The morning conference again emphasized that it was impossible for the President to secure the slightest cooperation from the French officials, who at the present time were misrepresenting the French people.

After the Polish Army transport problem was disposed of the question came up of how the German economic delegates, who arrived in France yesterday,[1] were to communicate back and forth with their government. The original plan was that they would be quartered in a hotel in Versailles, and that the economic experts of the allied and associated governments would confer with them there, and that there would be freedom of communication back and forth. Today, however, Clemenceau said that he could not consent to this plan and that the delegates would be housed in a chateau at Pont Sainte Mexence. The chateau which was assigned to them belonged to M. Jacques Stern, a Paris banker, and it had been entirely surrounded by French troops, who were guarding the German delegates. This chateau is inaccessible, being more than an hour out by fast automobile, and the change from Versailles was one that there seemed no apparent excuse [for]. However, when the President broached the problem of how these men were to communicate freely with their own government in order to expedite business, he discovered to his amazement that the French and British wanted to place an absolute limitation. Their plan was that a French gendarme should be assigned to carry all the official reports from these delegates to German territory, and there turn them over to German couriers to proceed the rest of the way to Berlin. The President demanded an explanation of why such a plan should be arranged. He said that they should have their own couriers and their own rights, exactly the rights and only the rights which are guaranteed under international law in connection with diplomatic correspondence. No real explanation was forthcoming from Clemenceau, and Lloyd-George declared that the President was entirely right. However, Clemenceau wanted to know what objection there could be to the French gendarmes being employed and was very promptly told that the great objection was that there would be no way of guaranteeing the inviolability of the despatches. As a matter of fact, from the very attitude of M. Clemenceau it was evident that the plan of the French government was to inspect all communications that were sent out before they were delivered to the German courier. The President emphatically declared that he would be no party to any proposition that was in any way in violation of international law and he demanded that the Germans be permitted to have their own courier, said courier to be accompanied if necessary in his journeys to and fro by the French gendarme if they (the French) were apprehensive that the Germans might do something contrary to law while in France. The French excuse had been that there was a possibility that the Germans might take advantage of their trips to inaugurate a system of espionage, to which the President demanded, with well-deserved sarcasm, what there was to be spied upon in these perilous days. The President was greatly incensed over the French attitude and, addressing himself directly to M. Clemenceau and Marshal Foch said: "Why, you are wasting hours over a minor proposition while all Europe is going to pieces. This is a matter that must be settled and settled right." The French finally consented to the plan proposed by the President, and the morning session broke up with practically the entire time having been wasted, and the President in the most angry mood that he has been in since he has arrived in France.

In the afternoon the President again met with the Council of Four. The morning conference had completely disturbed the President to such an extent that he was not prepared to go further into the Saar Valley question or any of the matters that directly affected the French, and Clemenceau was not present at the afternoon session. Clemenceau had a council of his ministers during this afternoon, and the other Commissioners informally considered the Belgian propositions. The request of the Belgian representatives for priority was emphasized by the two Belgian High Commissioners, who appeared before the Council, preparatory to the arrival in Paris of King Albert, who had evinced a desire to be heard in person.

While the President was at the Council meeting Mrs. Wilson visited the American Red Cross Tent City on the Champ-de-Mars. She was taken throughout the entire kitchen, and the Red Cross women explained to her the methods of preparing food. She was also shown an auto truck loaded with fresh apple pies. A French war cripple, who had lost an arm, presented her with a bouquet of flowers, tied with the French national colors. Mrs. Wilson was received at the Camp by Major Francis Boyer, of the Red Cross, and, before she left, at her own request, a large number of American soldiers who were standing by were brought over and presented to her, she shaking hands with them.

That evening the President worked on his papers in his private study until after 11:00 o'clock. Before he retired I treated his nose and throat.

[1] These delegates had come to Paris to discuss the exchange of German securities for foodstuffs necessary for the implementation of the Brussels Agreement (about which see EMH to WW, March 7, 1919, n. 1, Vol. 55). The principal German negotiators were Max Moritz Warburg, head of the merchant banking firm of M. M. Warburg & Co. of Hamburg and an older brother of Paul Moritz Warburg, and Dr. Carl Melchior, a partner in M. M. Warburg & Co.

Mantoux's Notes of Two Meetings of the Council of Four

April 2, 1919, 11 a.m.

Reading of a memorandum from the embassy of Japan asking that no question concerning that country be discussed without the presence of the Japanese delegates.

Wilson. We can only accept this observation, which is presented in a most moderate form.

Lloyd George. We might respond that we are meeting among the four of us to study purely European questions, and that the delegates of Japan will be welcome when we touch on a question of such a nature as to interest them.

Clemenceau. I am in full agreement with you, and I think that our response should be written with the greatest courtesy.

Marshal Foch and General Weygand are introduced.

Foch. I wish to speak to you about the manner in which I should conduct the negotiations at Spa on the subject of the transport of Polish troops. I have received three instructions, on March 24, March 29, and April 1. There are some differences among these texts.

On the 24th, it was decided to demand of the Germans that they assure free passage for General Haller's troops through Danzig in conformity with Article 16 of the Armistice, and to warn them that a refusal would constitute a breach of the Armistice. This decision was communicated to them.

On the 29th, it was decided that the Germans would be invited to send a plenipotentiary to Spa; that I would demand of him, in the name of the powers, the passage of Polish troops through Danzig; but that I would be authorized, without renouncing Danzig, to accept the passage of a portion of these troops by way of Königsberg and Stettin.

Yesterday, April 1st, you gave me rather different instructions, as follows: "If the Germans recognize in writing their obligation to allow Polish troops to pass through Danzig, in conformity with the Armistice agreement, Marshal Foch will consider the transport of these troops across Germany by rail."

We seem to be abandoning Danzig, especially if we compare this text with those of March 24 and March 29.

Wilson. There is no contradiction among these successive decisions. We have constantly sought to maintain our right. Our instructions have only changed because of circumstances. The essential principle has not been modified.

Marshal Foch is authorized, not to propose but to take into consideration, if it is proposed by the Germans, the solution which consists of transporting Polish troops by German railways. We know that the Germans are inclined to make this proposal, which will have the great advantage of surmounting the difficult question of tonnage.

Foch. Then, the fundamental condition of my negotiation is our right to have these troops pass through Danzig.

Wilson. It is not a matter of actual passage but of our right to have them pass.

Foch. That right is recognized by the Armistice; we do not have to reclaim it but to impose it.

Clemenceau. If I understand the Marshal rightly, what he means is this: "I should open the negotiations by demanding passage through Danzig."

Foch. I am not going to Spa to win a right which I possess but to win an advantageous and practical execution.

Lloyd George. It is most important to get these troops to Poland as soon as possible. Our goal is not to seek a quarrel with the Germans, but to see that General Haller's troops arrive promptly in Warsaw.

Foch. Do we have any information about the proposal of the Germans? Have they made a proposal properly speaking?

Wilson. The information I have received comes from a source which I do not know directly, and which has permitted the officers who represent me in Germany to furnish this piece of information to me. There is nothing official about it. It is an indirect report which lets us know that the Germans are ready to make the proposal.

Lloyd George. The utilization of Stettin would permit us to double the opportunities for debarkation offered by Danzig; this new proposal would permit the entire transport to be made in one third the time. Each change in our first resolution has thus represented progress.

Reading by General Weygand of a dispatch from General d'Anselme[1] announcing that the military situation at Odessa is reestablished, but that, because of the lack of provisions which has forced us to share supplies of the army of occupation with the population, evacuation has been ordered. It will begin with the Allied civilian population and will continue with the troops, who will retire behind the Dniester.

Clemenceau. I would remark that this decision seems to precede the reception of the order which we ourselves had sent, which proves how necessary was the decision that we made.

Foch. I return to the question of the Polish troops. The transport of these troops by railway across Germany cannot be made without guarantees. For example, the trains must be accompanied by Allied officers; the Germans must provide the supplies and the personnel. If the proposal is made, it should not be accepted with eyes shut and without conditions. I think that I have the right, if these conditions are not admitted by the Germans, to refuse this solution?

Wilson. I would observe that the troops to be transported are Allied troops.

Foch. I mean that it would be advisable to place Allied officers in the trains, who would be there in case of an incident between the Poles and the Germans.

Lloyd George. I envisage senior officers.

Wilson. What is the point of your observation about the supplies?

Weygand. We must know whether supplies will be furnished by us or by the Germans. If the Germans are to furnish them, precise promises must be extracted from them. If it is we who send cars and locomotives across Germany, we must be assured that this

[1] Gen. Philippe Henri Joseph d'Anselme, commander of Allied forces operating near Odessa.

matériel will come back to us. There are similar stipulations to be made with regard to personnel.

Wilson. If they furnish the supplies, we will undoubtedly have to pay for them, because the Germans are not obliged to furnish us with cars for this type of transport.

Lloyd George. I believe that it would be better to furnish the supplies ourselves, as we would be doing if these troops were transported by sea.

Clemenceau. But the Germans will furnish the coal, for it could not be done otherwise.

Wilson. Since this proposal is a German proposal, they have every interest in presenting it with satisfactory conditions, in order to make it acceptable.

Foch. I would like your instructions on another point. When the convention of February 16 was concluded, we included a clause to stop hostilities between Poles and Germans. The execution was entrusted to an inter-Allied commission in Poland. Hostilities did stop, in fact; but the Noulens mission did not succeed in negotiating with the Germans. Must we take up this business at Spa and again ask the questions already asked by M. Noulens at Posen? Such as it is, this problem is not pressing, but it has remained without a definite solution.

Lloyd George. It is not worth the trouble, since we are approaching the date when the preliminaries of peace will give a real solution. From a practical point of view, there is no urgency, since hostilities have ceased.

Foch. I have also to inform you of a request made by the German financial commission which has just arrived in France.

Weygand. Herr Melchior, who is head of that delegation, asks that he be permitted to establish daily communications with the German government by means of a German courier who would be covered by diplomatic immunity. This courier would circulate either between the Château de Villette and Berlin, or between Villette and Spa. We have already provided for a courier service from Villette to Spa, protected by French gendarmes. But Herr Melchior asks to have his own courier, with diplomatic privilege.

Clemenceau. What does Marshal Foch think of this?

Foch. So long as the peace has not been signed, I do not wish to have a German courier free from all control on territory occupied by our armies.

Lloyd George. Is this request so unreasonable? Minor vexations without serious object must be avoided; and all that a courier could do would be to take to Germany scraps of information about our conference.

Clemenceau. I concur in Marshal Foch's objection, since there is already a functioning courier system.

Wilson. It is we who invited this commission to come to France; we can grant it certain facilities.

Clemenceau. If the Marshal consents, I also consent. But do they have a complaint about the gendarmes who carry their mail?

Lloyd George. I understand their feeling rather well, although I believe that your gendarmes do transport their dispatches most scrupulously. Herr Melchior is a capable man, and we must not desire his departure. We have nothing to gain by petty harassments. Herr Melchior knows that the French gendarme can always open the dispatch, even if he does not do so, and that restricts his correspondence. Could we not grant him the courier which he asks and add that this courier must be accompanied by a French gendarme?

Clemenceau. I would gladly accept that solution.

Foch. Then there would be a German courier accompanied by a gendarme. But would he have the right to send entire car loads like other diplomatic couriers? In any case he could carry whatever he wanted; we do not know what he could do, what people he could meet, or of what system of espionage he might be the agent. We have introduced a German into our midst; by this decision, we could give him the right to send and to receive whatever he wishes, and to correspond about any subjects that would please him.

Clemenceau. We give him this same right if the letters are carried by a French gendarme.

Foch. Yes, but then he would be on his guard.

Clemenceau. My opinion is that you should watch whatever is transported in this manner. If abuses occur, you should be able to warn us and even to arrest the courier.

Foch. He must be under my orders.

Wilson. If he does anything irregular, the gendarme accompanying him makes a report. That should suffice; he must have the right to pass freely.

Clemenceau. If he wants to stop en route without justification, or if he takes a route other than that which he himself has requested, the gendarme could arrest him immediately and warn you telegraphically.

April 2, 1919, 4 p.m.

Wilson. It seems that our disagreeable friends the Poles raise a new difficulty about the truce which they must conclude with the Ukrainians. They refuse to sign it, except under conditions which prejudge the tenor of the armistice. Our adviser, Dr. Lord, proposes to send a telegram reminding them about the decision taken previously and about our proposal to follow the existing truce with an armistice to be negotiated in Paris, under the mediation of the conference. But the first condition should be that the text of the agreement to suspend hostilities must contain nothing which prejudices the stipulations of the armistice.

The text of the telegram is adopted.[2]

Lloyd George. I would like to discuss with you the question of responsibilities. Our commission[3] declared itself against bringing to trial those who are in different degrees responsible for the declaration of war.[4] Personally, I regret this decision, but I accept it. In my opinion, if we could hold responsible for this greatest of all

[2] Addressed to the Polish Minister of Foreign Affairs, it reads as follows: "It will be recalled that in its note of March 19th, the conference suggested to both the Polish and Ukranian Governments that a suspension of arms should be arranged in Eastern Galicia pending the discussion at Paris of an armistice under the mediation of the Allied and Associated Governments. To further those objects the conference has decided to appoint an armistice commission to hear the representatives of the two belligerents and this Commission will begin its sittings in Paris as soon as it is informed that a truce has been concluded and that accredited Polish and Ukranian representatives are ready to present their views. To save time it is suggested that representatives be appointed from the Polish delegation now in Paris. If the plan of mediation proposed by the Allied and Associated Governments is to be carried out it is essential that the convention for the suspension of arms which is now being arranged in Eastern Galicia should contain nothing that would pre-judge the nature of the future armistice, and the Allied and Associated Governments cannot doubt that in the negotiation for a suspension of arms, the Polish Government will act upon this principle."

Someone signed Wilson's, Lloyd George's, Clemenceau's, and Orlando's names at the bottom of this document, which is a CC MS in WP, DLC.

[3] That is, the Commission on the Responsibility of the Authors of the War and on Enforcement of Penalties, created by the Plenary Session on January 25, 1919.

[4] The Commission on Responsibility had submitted its final report on March 29, 1919. It was printed as Commission on the Responsibility of the Authors of the War, REPORT PRESENTED TO THE PRELIMINARY PEACE CONFERENCE. It is reprinted in *The American Journal of International Law*, XIV (1920), 95-154. The "final proof" of the report was printed shortly after April 4, 1919. A copy of this version is in WP, DLC.

Lloyd George's statement, to say the least, was a curious one. The majority report not only recommended the *criminal* prosecution of persons guilty of crimes against the laws of war; it also called for the trial of *all* former enemies guilty of violations of "usages established among civilised peoples," "the laws of humanity," and "the dictates of public conscience." Finally, it stated (in the form of articles to be inserted in the treaty of peace) that the "*Enemy* Government" agreed to hand over to *any* of the Allied and Associate states *any* person for trial before a high tribunal or a "national court"; also, all records necessary for the prosecution of those trials.

Robert Lansing and James Brown Scott, the American representatives on the commission, had long and strongly fought against the inclusion of any provisions for the *criminal* prosecution of the former German Emperor for alleged violations of treaties, responsibility for war atrocities, etc. Lansing reviews this controversy briefly in the minutes of the meeting of the American commissioners of March 5, 1919, printed in *PPC*, XI, 93-94. See also James W. Garner, "Punishment of Offenders against the Laws and Customs of War," *The American Journal of International Law*, XIV (1920), 70-94; J. B. Scott, "The Trial of the Kaiser," in House and Seymour, eds., *What Really Happened at Paris*: pp. 231-58; Tillman, *Anglo-American Relations at the Paris Peace Conference*, pp. 312-13; and, most particularly, Klaus Schwabe, *Woodrow Wilson, Revolutionary Germany, and Peacemaking, 1918-1919* (Chapel Hill, N. C., 1985), *passim*.

Lansing's and Scott's "reservations" to the majority report are printed in the two versions of the report already cited. There is a T MS of these "reservations" in WP, DLC. We print the digest of their "Memorandum of Reservations," which Wilson read, at April 4, 1919.

crimes the high and mighty men who unleashed such scourges, the greatest of all, there would be less danger of war in the future.

On the other hand, responsibility has been admitted for violation of treaties which caused the death of millions of men. The same for acts against individuals, atrocities of all sorts committed under orders, the kidnaping of girls for forced prostitution, the destruction of ships on the high seas by submarines, leaving ships' crews in boats hundreds of miles from shore. In the text of the treaty, we will demand that the enemy recognize our right to judge these crimes and promise to deliver the guilty to us. We must also have the right to demand the production of all German documents which would be necessary to enlighten the tribunal.

Finally, the commission proposes the establishment of a court of justice in which all the belligerent nations, great and small, would be represented, and which would pronounce judgments.

Wilson. You know that the representatives of the United States signed a minority report. I believe that certain recent proposals, such as that renouncing prosecution of the authors of the war, bring them somewhat closer to your advisers than previously.

Lloyd George. I have to inform you of Japan's objection to the admission of the Kaiser's responsibility: the Mikado is a god who cannot be held responsible.

I am also told that the Americans do not wish to create a precedent which could be invoked against the President of the United States.

Wilson. That I do not believe. In fact, in the United States it is the Congress that declares war. However, I recognize that true responsibility, if not legal responsibility, belongs to the President, if it is he who advises war as I did. At the time of the Spanish-American conflict, on the other hand, President McKinley was opposed to war; it was against his advice that the Congress decided it.[5]

It is difficult for us today to determine what the Kaiser's responsibility is. Probably it is very great. However, certain stories show him signing the orders with regret and saying to those who had advised him: "You will regret what we are doing."

Lloyd George. All that we want is to punish those responsible, whoever they may be.

Wilson. I ask that we do not link the American objection with the Japanese objection, which, from our point of view, rests on a ridiculous principle.

---

[5] For a summary of the complex diplomatic and political maneuvering which led to the Spanish-American War of 1898, see Charles S. Campbell, *The Transformation of American Foreign Relations, 1865-1900* (New York, 1976), pp. 250-78, and David F. Trask, *The War with Spain in 1898* (New York and London, 1981).

Lloyd George. I do not know, after all: the Japanese principle is the English principle, that the King can commit no crime. In England, if the question of the origins of the war should arise, it is Mr. Asquith who would be responsible, and not King George. However, the case of the German Emperor is completely different, because he had direct executive power.

Wilson. I have doubts about our right to set up a tribunal composed only of the belligerents. The parties would be at the same time the judges.

Lloyd George. I do not consider England and the United States as injured parties. Both of us made war for justice.

Wilson. We have done justice by arms; but arms have not delivered to us the guilty ones whom we wish to punish.

Lloyd George. I argue that we are claiming them by virtue of the success of our arms. Their case is analogous to that of prisoners who, in conformity to the laws of war, may be judged by military tribunals if, after their capture, crimes they have committed are discovered.

Wilson. It would create a dangerous precedent to try our enemies by judges who represent us. Suppose that, in the future, a single nation be victorious over another which had attacked it in violation of international law. Would it alone judge those who were guilty of crimes against international law, of which it would have been the victim?

Lloyd George. Not at all; in that case, the League of Nations, conforming to the fundamental rules that we have given it, must intervene, and it is it which will judge. In the present case, it is not Belgium or France which judges its offenders; we judge with them, and we intervene in order to make justice triumph.

If we wish to give the League of Nations a chance of success, it must not appear to be a paper document. It is necessary that it can, from this time forward, punish crimes against international law. The violation of treaties is precisely the kind of crime directly involving the League of Nations.

Wilson. We must think about that. But I will observe that, up until now, the responsibility for international crimes has been solely a collective responsibility. It is not just to make an act of this type an individual crime after it was committed. That would be to give retroactive force to the principles we set down, contrary to all juridical tradition.

Undoubtedly certain crimes committed would be crimes punishable within each of the nations involved. But these are not the crimes for which an international tribunal existed at the time they were committed. If you declare that, in the future, crimes recognized as such within each nation, if they are committed during an international conflict, can be punished by an international tribunal, you will substitute individual responsibility for collective responsibility, alone recognized in the past. But you cannot act according to this principle before it has been recognized.

Lloyd George. In time of war, one has always recognized the right of belligerents to punish summarily violations of the laws of war. We did not contest it even among our enemies, except when they invoked it wrongly, as against Captain Fryatt.[6]

Wilson. Is it just to include in the peace treaty a usage customary during hostilities?

Lloyd George. We can say that the state of peace will not exist until the guilty ones have been delivered to us. That is what Austria said to Serbia in 1914, attributing to her a crime of which she was not guilty.

Wilson. Suppose that the Austrian version of the crime of Sarajevo had been true; the entire world would have accepted it if Austria had demanded from Serbia the condemnation of those guilty by Serbian courts. If we could obtain from Germany those whom she herself judges guilty, there would be no cause for the objections which I have made.

What I wish to avoid is leaving to historians any sympathy whatsoever for Germany. I wish to consign Germany to the execration of history and to do nothing to permit it to be said that we went beyond our rights in a just cause. We must prevent history from reproaching us for having judged before establishing the juridical principle for the sentence.

Lloyd George. My opinion is that history can also condemn us for our weakness. We would have the absolute right to obtain punishment for these crimes if the guilty ones were in our hands. These are crimes for which no equivalent can be found in the Napoleonic wars, nor in any war of the last two centuries. Napoleon was punished for having ravaged the world by his ambition, but not for having committed international crimes like those for which we blame the Germans.

Wilson. I recently reread the documents on the war of 1870, and it seems to me that the conduct of the Germans at that time resembles that for which we blame them today.

Clemenceau. There is no similarity. They were brutal in 1870; but we did not have to reproach them for having committed crimes

[6] About whom, see n. 9 to the Enclosure printed with RL to WW, Aug. 11, 1916 (second letter of that date), Vol. 38.

under orders, and there was not, during the war or immediately afterward, the same hatred of the German soldier that you would find today among the belligerents.

Lloyd George. We are in the presence of crimes committed under orders, of which one of the most striking examples is the submarine war. I would go so far as to say that it would not be worth the trouble to make peace if one could believe that all these crimes would go unpunished. I see no disadvantage, moreover, in having the League of Nations establish this tribunal.

Wilson. Unless we wait a long time to go through this process, the judgment will be rendered in an atmosphere of passion. For myself, every time that I have read the documents on the atrocities committed, I saw red, and I have been very careful not to make a decision in such moments, in order always to be able to judge and act according to reason.

Lloyd George. The truth is rather that our capacity for indignation is almost exhausted on account of hearing the frightful stories that we have been hearing for five years. In fifty years, one would judge more severely than today.

Wilson. You think me insensitive. But I struggle constantly against emotion, and I am obliged to put pressure on myself to safeguard the soundness of my judgment.

Clemenceau. Nothing is done without emotion. Was not Jesus Christ driven by passion on the day when he chased the merchants from the temple?

Lloyd George. If what we call the Concert of Europe had had common sanctions at its disposal, it could have kept the peace. If we terrible things we shall do the next time; but this time we will be content to set forth this principle." The world would not take us seriously.

Clemenceau. The first tribunal must have been summary and brutal; it was nevertheless the beginning of a great thing.

Lloyd George. If what we call the Concert of Europe had had common sanctions at its disposal, it could have kept the peace. If we wish the League of Nations to possess in the future the power which we wish it to possess, it must demonstrate from the beginning that it is capable of punishing crime.

Wilson. I agree with you about the crimes committed, but I want us to act, ourselves, in a manner which satisfies our consciences.

Mantoux, I, 115-24.

From the Diary of Vance Criswell McCormick

April 2 (Wednesday) [1919]

British, French, Italian and U. S. delegation on reparation negotiations went to Finance Ministry to discuss supposed first draft of reparation clauses for treaty with categories. Groups all met about 11.00 and discussed draft until lunch time. Looked as though we were getting closer together especially British and United States. After lunch Dulles and I went to meet Montague, Sumner and Keynes on categories to get them to expand their draft to suit ours. They stated Big Four had agreed to categories only on claims for destruction of property and destruction of life. I was worried considerably at this statement because I could see, if true, that the British, after they got pensions in categories, were now trying to reduce the categories which would give France and others their just claims which we held had been admitted in 14 points and armistice terms. Dulles and I so stated but without effect.

We then started for the full committee meeting, at Finance Ministry. On the way down in the car with Montague he acknowledged to me if he could make his deal with France on the side as to distribution, he did not care what was in the categories. I saw the game Lloyd George was trying to put over on the President and I made up my mind to get busy. Met all afternoon discussing draft; made small progress; adjourned until 9.30 P.M.

I dined alone and was very tired.

At 9.30 we went at it again and argued until after midnight agreeing with British in draft of reparations except on categories. I cut loose with the British representatives about their discussing categories as a means of trading with the other Allies rather than upon the points of justice and equity of claims. I could see they sympathized and were embarrassed by their Chief's orders. Made up my mind to inform the President who had not been properly posted by Davis of the Finance Section.

Returned 1.00 A.M. after one of the most strenuous days of conference. I knew there would be difficulties over the division of the spoils but I could not foresee the political reasons of these countries keeping from their people the truth about Germany's ability to pay and now they have to work out a treaty clause which postpones the evil day and conceals temporarily the true situation. I wish we could blow up the whole plan, but the governments would fall and only Germany would benefit.

Second Draft of an Accord on Reparations

[April 2, 1919]

Text tentatively agreed upon by the British
and American Delegates.

1. The Allied and Associated Governments affirm the responsibility of the Enemy States for causing all the loss and damage to which the Allied and Associated Governments and their nationals have been subjected as a consequence of the war imposed upon them by the aggression of the enemy states.

2. The Allied and Associated Governments recognize that the financial resources of the enemy states are not unlimited and, after taking into account permanent diminutions of such resources which will result from other treaty clauses, they judge that it will be impracticable for enemy states to make complete reparation for all such loss and damage. The Allied and Associated Governments, however, require that the enemy states, to the extent of their utmost capacity, make compensation for all damage done to the civilian population of the Allied and Associated Powers and to their property by the aggression of the enemy states by land, by sea, and from the air.

(See Annex for interpretation clause prepared by the British.)

3. The amount of such damage for which compensation is to be made shall be determined by an inter-allied commission, to be constituted in such form as the Allied and Associated Governments shall forthwith determine. This commission shall examine into the claims and give to the enemy states a just opportunity to be heard. The findings of the commission as to the amount of damage defined in Article 2 shall be concluded and communicated to the enemy states on or before May 1st, 1921. The commission at the same time shall also draw up a schedule of payments up to or within the total sum thus due, which in their judgment Germany should be able to liquidate within a period of thirty years, and this schedule of payments shall then be communicated to Germany as representing the extent of her obligations.

4. The inter-allied commission shall further have discretion to modify from time to time the date and mode of the schedule of payments fixed in clause 3 and, if necessary, to extend them in part beyond thirty years, by acceptance of long period bonds or otherwise, if subsequently such modification or extension appears necessary, after giving Germany a just opportunity to be heard. Payment may be required and, with the approval of the commission, accepted in the form of properties, chattels, businesses, rights, and concessions in ceded territory; of ships, of gold and silver, of prop-

erties, chattels, businesses, rights and concessions, of bonds, shares and securities of all kinds, of foreign currencies or the currency of the enemy state, or of German Government bonds.

5. In order to enable the Allied and Associated Powers to proceed at once to the restoration of their industrial and economic life, pending the full determination of their claim, the enemy states shall pay in such instalments and in such manner (whether in gold, commodities, ships, securities or otherwise) as the inter-allied commission may fix, in 1919 and 1920 the equivalent of $5,000,000,000 gold towards the liquidation of the above claims, out of which the expenses of the army of occupation subsequent to the Armistice, shall first be met, provided that such supplies of food and raw materials as may be judged by the Allied and Associated Governments to be essential to enable Germany to meet her obligations for reparation may, with the approval of the Allied and Associated Governments, be paid for out of the above sum.

6. The successive instalments paid over by the enemy states in satisfaction of the above claims shall be divided by the Allied and Associated Governments in proportions which have been determined upon by them in advance, on a basis of general equity, and of the rights of each.

7. The payments mentioned above do not include restitution in kind of cash taken away, seized or sequestered, nor the restitution in kind of animals, objects of every nature and securities taken away, seized or sequestered, in the cases in which it proves possible to identify them in enemy territory. If at least half the number of the animals taken by the enemy from the invaded territories cannot be identified and returned, the balance, up to a total of half the number taken, shall be delivered by Germany by way of restitution.

8. The attention of the four Chiefs of the respective Governments is to be called to the following:

(a) That necessary guarantees to insure the due collection of the sums fixed for reparation should be planned; and

(b) That there are other financial clauses which this conference has not been charged to deal with.

T MS (WP, DLC).

U. S. Annex to Clause 2.

Personal Injury
(1) Personal injury to or death of civilians resulting from military operations or mistreatment by the enemy.

Pensions
(2) Damage to the civilian population resulting from the absence, incapacitation or death, in military service, of persons upon whom they are de-

pendent and which damage is met by pensions or payments of like nature made by the State. (French scale to govern.)

Damage to Labor

(3) Damage to civilians resulting from their being forced by the enemy to labor without just remuneration, or to abstain from labor.

Damage to Property

(4) Damage to non-military property and property rights caused by military operations or illegal act of the enemy or war measures in the nature of requisitions or sequestrations, taken by the enemy.

Fines, etc.

(5) Damage in the form of levies, fines and other similar exactions imposed by the enemy upon the civilian population.

Violations of law and engagements

(6) Damage resulting from acts in violation of international law (as found by the Commission on Responsibilities) and in violation of formal engagements.

Note: Where the State or other public authority has already itself made compensation for the damage, it may present the claim in its own behalf.

T MS (WP, DLC).

April 2nd.

G. B. INTERPRETATION OF CLAUSE 2.

Compensation may be claimed under Clause 2 under the following categories of damage:

I.

a) Damage caused to civilian victims of acts of war (including bombardments or other attacks on land, on sea or from the air and all the direct consequences thereof and of all operations of war by the two groups of belligerents wherever arising) and to the surviving dependents of such victims.

b) Damage caused to civilian victims of acts, cruelties, violence or maltreatment (including injuries to life or health as a consequence of imprisonment, deportation, internment, or evacuation, of exposure at sea, or of being forced to labour by the enemy) committed or ordered by the enemy wherever arising and to the surviving dependents of such victims.

c) Damage caused to civilian victims of all acts of the enemy in occupied, invaded or enemy territory, injurious to health or capacity for work or to honour and to the surviving dependents of such victims.

II.

a) All pensions and compensations in the nature of pensions to naval and military victims of war, whether mutilated, wounded, sick or invalided, and to the dependents of such victims.

b) Cost of assistance by the State to prisoners of war and to their families and dependents.

c) Allowances by the State to the families and dependents of mobilized persons, or persons serving with the forces.

III.

Damage in respect of all property belonging to any of the Allied and Associated States or to any of their subjects, with the exception of military works or material, which has been carried off, seized, injured or destroyed by the acts of the enemy on land, on sea, or from the air, or damaged directly in consequence of hostilities or any operations of war.

CC MS (WP, DLC).

From the Diary of Colonel House

April 2, 1919.

Frazier, Gordon, Wiseman and practically all of my entourage have been worried for the last day or two because they did not think I was pushing the President as hard as I ought, and that I was letting matters drift. I have done this deliberately. I saw that things were coming to an impasse and the more I let them alone, the quicker this impasse would come. Frazier was urging me yesterday to see the President. I replied that when the President really needed me, he would not hesitate to call. This call came about eight o'clock tonight and we talked for three quarters of an hour over the telephone.

We went over the situation from start to finish. The Sarre Basin, the Rhenish Republic, the protection of France, Dantzig, Fiume, Reparations and what-not. He declared that the old man was stubborn and that he could not get him to come to a decision. What he really means is that he cannot get Clemenceau to come to his way of thinking.

He asked if I would see Tardieu and find what could be done in that direction. I have asked for Tardieu to be here at ten in the morning. The President asked if I thought Lloyd George was sincere with him. I had my doubts. The general impression is that George is playing him for a rupture with the French. I told the President I could see trouble ahead with George. When one talks of the sea, shipping, etc. an Englishman becomes as crazy as a Frenchman when a German is mentioned. He asked to what I referred. I replied "the merchant fleet and the navy building program." He talked as if he would stand firm on both propositions. If he does, he will find that the row he is having with Clemenceau is a frolic compared to that which he will have with Lloyd George.

He wishes me to outline to Orlando the boundary and other terms for Italy. I do not relish the job but I promised to do it. I shall see Orlando on Friday and tell him just where we wish the northern and eastern boundaries of Italy to be.

The President tried to get me to admit that the solution which our Experts have proposed and which Clemenceau might be willing to take as to the Sarre Valley, was inconsistent with the Fourteen Points. I replied that there were many who thought otherwise.

I told the President that I intended to tell Tardieu that unless a conclusion was reached within the next ten days that he, the President, would probably go back to America and that we would all go with him. I suggested that I use the necessity for calling in Special Session Congress and passing appropriation bills as the reason why it would be necessary for his early return.

I asked him if he had anyone at the Council of Four meetings who was taking notes. Professor Mantoux is there to do the interpreting for Signor Orlando. The President admitted that he thought Mantoux did not like him. He said, "indeed, I am not sure that anybody does." Mantoux is a Frenchman having a Chair at the London University. I consider the President imprudent and reckless to go into these acrimonious meetings with no member of his own staff there to actually report what goes on.

From the Diary of Edith Benham

April 2, 1919

I have never seen the President more irritated than he was today after luncheon. We came out and Mrs. Wilson suggested his going out for a walk. He said he would, but first he had to unburden himself about the morning's proceedings and the constant hindrances and petty objections coming up all the time. They had had Foch at the "Big 4" conferences. There is an army of Poles recruited from the Poles in the French Army of some 60,000 to 70,000. These, as you have read, are to be under command of General Haller. The terms of the Armistice provides the passage of allied troops through Dantzig to restore order in Poland. The Germans admitted this clause but say there is a large Polish and Jugo Slav population. Anyway, they were fearful of some trouble and asked if the troops could go via Konigsberg and Stettin. The French objected, why no one knows. In the meantime our Army secret service discovered that the Germans had been making arrangements to transport the troops from the Rhine across by train which would take a few weeks, whereas this other way would use up shipping and take a couple of months and the object of the whole thing was to prevent the spread of Bolshevism across the eastern frontier of Poland and get an Army in there. The French objected and it took time to beat that down. Finally Foch was directed to inquire how the Germans proposed to get the troops across, not mentioning the Rhine project as that was indirect Secret Service information, and he was also told to say to the Germans that they must acknowledge in writing the right to use the Dantzig as per the armistice terms, and Foch was told to say the Allies would consider the use of Konigsberg and Stettin. But as the President said, these French military commanders never seem to obey orders given them.

Another thing was the German Envoys who were supposed to come to Versailles for a conference about food, I think. It was some minor commission. The President said when the French Government invited the allied governments here for a conference they were supposed to talk to whom they wanted and now it refused permission for them to come to Paris and said they must go to Chateau Villette. They, the Germans, asked for the right to send mail back to Germany with their own courier under French guard, but be allowed diplomatic immunity. This the French refused saying the mail must be sent by French courier and the President says he is convinced that it might be opened and read and naturally the Germans were fearful of this and the President says they are quite within their rights in asking for diplomatic immunity. Foch says these Germans might communicate with spies and establish a spy system, but as the President said, what will they have to tell. Then the French are in a state of panic over what Germany will do. She is to be allowed no munition works and no forts within fifty miles of the Rhine and an army of only 100,000, and the President asked Foch how could they possibly make munitions over night, and he asked what the French were afraid of. What is it? and no one could explain. So the days go by and the President is blamed for the delay and the whole world waits and as he expresses it, "Europe is going to pieces." He said he had sent an ultimatum to Clemenceau not wishing to have a row directly with the old man that "the Allies had agreed to the 14 points as a basis for peace." These were accepted and a decision would have to be reached within a few days or he would go home. I have never seen him so irritated, so thoroughly in a rage. He characterized the attitude of the French and the delays as "damnable." He is usually so patient, so calm, and now he is just outdone with it all.

From the Diary of Ray Stannard Baker

Wednesday Apr 2 [1919].

I found the President to-night again much discouraged. The sitting of the Four adjourned about 6 o'clock & he & Mrs. Wilson had gone out for a little drive and some fresh air. He looks tired. He said that it began to seem to him that the French were intentionally delaying the proceedings by endless talk: for what purpose he could not see. Foch had been before them again to get his instructions for the meeting at Spa—mostly ground that had been covered before.

"Foch may be a great general," said the President, "but he is a dull man."

He said they had [undecipherable word: discussed?] the Verseilles meeting to receive the German peace delegates and that the French insisted upon going into this whole matter—the staging of their victory—(rubbing salt into the wounds of the Germans)—at length & spent precious time discussing whether or not the Germans should be permitted to use their own messengers between Verseilles & Berlin, or whether all their despatches should be transmitted by the hands of French couriers. This while the world is burning up!

I suggested that the time might come soon when he would have to speak out. The other day when I made a similar proposal he said: "That would break up the Peace Conference. I must do everything I can to keep things together." But tonight it was plain that he had been thinking of the possible necessity of making such a move. "If I speak out," he said, "I should have to tell the truth & place the blame exactly where it belongs—upon the French."

"The downfall of a government in France," I said, "is not as serious a matter as it would be in England."

I told him I had heard that Clemenceau had already been conferring with Poincaire about his possible resignation—& had even talked with Barthou,[1] who is said to be his choice as his successor.

"A new premier would probably be no better than Clemenceau," he said.

He referred also to the attacks in the French press & the evident effort to separate him & Lloyd-George. I said that Wickham Steed & the Northcliffe press were sharpening their campaign against Lloyd-George.

"Yes," he said, "the Northcliff[e] press is like the Hearst press—only a little better."

He said that it could not go on many days longer: that if some decision could not be reached by the middle of next week, he might have to make some positive break.

The question of a plenary conference to pass upon the completed L. of N. covenant came up: & the President spoke emphatically "No, we cannot have it. It would only give old Hughes of Australia an opportunity to talk & object. We must have it signed by everyone. If Hughes refuses to sign we shall simply have to let him go. No, we can't spend the time now on a plenary session."

I spoke of the feeling of unrest in the world: & of the blame that was everywhere being charged, unjustly, against him. "I know that," he said, "I know that." He paused. "But we've got to make peace on the principles laid down & accepted, or not make it at all."

In the meantime there are reports of new revolts in Germany[2] & spreading unrest in Hungary. Where are we going?

[1] Louis Jean Firmin Barthou, holder of various cabinet posts since 1894 and Premier of France, March-December 1913.

[2] He probably referred to the continuing revolutionary events in Bavaria, about which see EMH to WW, March 4, 1919, Vol. 55. Actually, there was much continuing unrest in many parts of Germany, including attempted general strikes in the Ruhr, Saxony, and Berlin. However, the central government, established under the Weimar Constitution in February, was gradually asserting its control over the country with the aid of the army and *Freikorps*. Even the Bavarian Soviet Republic, which was declared on April 7, was to be suppressed by the *Freikorps* by May 7. See A. J. Ryder, *The German Revolution of 1918: A Study of German Socialism in War and Revolt* (Cambridge, 1967), pp. 208-17, and Allan Mitchell, *Revolution in Bavaria, 1918-1919: The Eisner Regime and the Soviet Republic* (Princeton, N. J., 1965), pp. 304-31.

Two Letters to Herbert Clark Hoover

My dear Hoover: Paris, 2 April, 1919.

I gave Mr. Clemenceau a copy of the telegram you quote in your letter of the 31st of March about the holding of the food train at Zagrab [Zagreb]. He assured me that on the afternoon of the same day, that is yesterday, he had sent a telegram directing its release.

In haste,   Faithfully yours,   Woodrow Wilson

TLS (Hoover Archives, CSt-H).

My dear Hoover: Paris, 2 April, 1919.

I promised Mr. Clemenceau that I would ask you if it were feasible to send food directly to Bavaria through Switzerland without subtracting from the total supply for Germany or increasing the proportional supply due to Bavaria. Is this feasible?

Cordially and faithfully yours,   [Woodrow Wilson]

CCL (WP, DLC).

From William Allen White

Sir: [Paris] April 2, 1919.

From Colonel House, who gave me the only official notice I had of my selection as a delegate to Prinkipo, I have had no official notice of its abandonment; but I have presumed that the onrush of events has made that particular conference impossible. My contract for three months reporting the Peace Conference has expired, and naturally I feel like going home. But of course if there is the slightest possibility that I may be of service here in any other conference with the Russians, I should be happy to stay. For Russia is very much on my heart. During the last ten weeks—especially since I was asked to go to Prinkipo—I have made Russia a kind of major study. And I must not close this episode without giving you—quite briefly—the result of my inquiry.

Russian conditions are profoundly confused. There seems to be in Russia a reversion to some ancient type of feeling, somewhat racial, somewhat medieval, somewhat ethical; yet deeply removed from things of this modern world. One cannot say what it is, but certainly the Russian condition is a tinder box from which the world may strike fire at any time. The appeal to the mad court of war which has plunged all humanity into this world insanity after the late war, should convince us what vast folly must come from the crazy decisions of that court. And to go there with the Russian case—it is unthinkable. Half a dozen wars are raging there now, which we should hasten to stamp out with all the spiritual energy we have left. But to do that we must know how. That means study; not study a few days or a few weeks, but a long, serious, unbiased investigation by men of academic and political and military training—men not of one nation but men from at least England and America—who will go into Russia—all Russia (Moscow and Petrograd of course) but the exterior countries as well, and then formulate a policy for the civilized world to follow in Russia. If I could help on such a commission, I should be greatly pleased. But no one man is important. The commission itself is vital. So if there is no further need for me in Europe I shall leave for England next week—and then home. I feel that there also much must be done in making sentiment for the League of Peace. I am eager to get into the fight. So I hope in any event I shall have the honor of striving with you for the common ideal[s] which in the past few years have drawn forward walking men together from all castes and creeds.   Sincerely,   W. A. White

TLS (WP, DLC).

To William Allen White

My dear Mr. White: Paris, 2 April, 1919.

It was shabby to treat you as you were treated in the matter of the Prinkipo conference. You ought to have had official notice of each stage of the matter but I am sure you will forgive irregularities in the presence of so uncertain and unforeseen a situation as the Russian.

The suggestion you make about a small commission of observation in Russia impresses me as a very reasonable one and I would be inclined to urge that it be acted on at once if it were not evident that such an investigation, to bear its full fruit, would have to continue through several months and before it was concluded we would have signed the Peace. I would very much like to have your idea about that, that is to say as to whether investigation should go on irrespective of the Peace conclusions and in the meantime leaving Russia out of the settlement.

It is very hard to know what advice to give in the case of a man like yourself. As a matter of fact it is desirable, highly desirable, that you should be on both sides of the Atlantic. I am eager to have you get into the fight at home for the League of Nations and yet I am not sure that we can spare you over here.

Cordially and sincerely yours,   [Woodrow Wilson]

CCL (WP, DLC).

From David Lloyd George, with Enclosure

My dear Mr President   Paris. April 2nd 1919

I enclose reply I am sending to Clemenceau's paper.[1]

I thought on the whole it was better not to take it too seriously

Ever sincerely   D Lloyd George

ALS (WP, DLC).
[1] That is, the Enclosure printed with G. Clemenceau to WW, March 31, 1919.

E N C L O S U R E

1 April 1919

If the document put in by M. Clemenceau[1] in reply to my statement[2] really represents the attitude of France towards the various questions which come up for settlement, there ought to be no difficulty in making a peace with Germany which will satisfy everybody, especially the Germans.

Judging by the Memorandum, France seems to attach no importance to the rich German African colonies which she is in possession of. She attaches no importance to Syria, she attaches no importance to indemnity and compensation, not even although an overwhelming priority in the matter of compensation is given her as I proposed in my Memorandum. She attaches no importance to the fact that she has Alsace Lorraine with most of the iron mines and a large proportion of the potash of Germany. She attaches no importance to receiving a share of the German ships for the French ships sunk by submarines or to receiving any part of the German battle fleet. She attaches no importance to the Disarmament of Germany on land and sea. She attaches no importance to a British and American guarantee of the inviolability of her soil. All these are treated as matters which only concern "maritime people who have not know[n] invasion." What France really cares for is that the Dantzig Germans should be handed over to the Poles. Several months of insistent controversy on Syria and compensation and the disarmament of Germany and the guarantees of the inviolability of French soil, etc. etc. had led me to that conclusion that France attached an overwhelming importance to these vital matters. But M. Clemenceau knows France best and as he does not think all these things worth mentioning I am perforce driven to reverse my views on this subject. Especially would it be welcome to a large section of opinion in England who dislike entangling alliances to know that M. Clemenceau attaches no importance to the pledge I offer on behalf of Britain to come to the support of France if the invader threatens. M. Clemenceau suggests that the peace we propose is one which is entirely in the interests of Britain. I claim nothing for Britain which France would not equally get. In compensation although including the expenses of the war it has cost as much to Britain as to France, I propose that France should get twice as much of the indemnity and if my proposals seem to M. Clemenceau to favour Britain it is because I was, until I read his document, under the delusion that France also attached importance to colonies, to ships, to compensation, to disarmament, to Syria and to a British guarantee to stand by France with all her strength if she were attacked. I regret my error and shall be careful not to repeat it.

I may be permitted to correct one out of many misrepresentations of my document. It is true I suggested temporary ownership of the whole of the Saar coalfield with guarantees for permanent access to the coal, but this proposal was made as an alternative to another which I placed first—namely the restoration of the 1814 frontier.

Inasmuch, however, as M. Clemenceau treats this suggestion as a further proof of British selfishness I promptly withdraw it.

(Signed)   D Lloyd George.[3]

TS MS (WP, DLC).
[1] Again, the Enclosure printed with G. Clemenceau to WW, March 31, 1919.
[2] That is, the so-called Fontainebleau Memorandum, printed at March 25, 1919.
[3] Lloyd George obviously did not send this letter to Clemenceau.

From Herbert Clark Hoover

My dear Mr. President: Paris, 2 April 1919.

I have been for many days filled with the greatest anxiety over the feeding of Poland, due to the proposed transportation of troops through Dantzig, the absorption of the railway facilities, and the conviction on the part of all of our staff that bloodshed and disturbances will break out, probably requiring considerable military occupation. It is not alone the attitude of the German Government, but the local feeling is so high that I do not conceive that these troops can be taken through without trouble from the local people.

I have not hitherto said anything about it as I assumed that it was the only course to be pursued. I had of course made up my mind that there must be a longer or shorter break in the food supply and that the Allies were taking the account of the balance of starving populations versus more soldiers in their calculations. I learn however today from General Bliss that the Germans show a disposition to transport these troops overland direct from France. I cannot urge upon you too strongly the importance of taking this action and leaving the port of Dantzig alone to the food people until its fate has been settled be [by] peace negotiations. These proposed military plans for Dantzig, together with the military actions taken at Budapest and other instances through Europe, make the whole problem of trying to maintain stability by food completely discouraging.

Faithfully yours,   Herbert Hoover

TLS (WP, DLC).

From Robert Lansing

My Dear Mr. President: Paris, April 2, 1919.

With regard to my letter to you of March 29th, and to your reply of April 1st, concerning the bill from the Director of State Railroads of the French Republic, covering the cost of providing special trains for the Presidential Party in December and February, I beg to inform you that the Commission is now in receipt of the enclosed bill from the "Compagnie Internationale des Wagon-Lits," for dining car service amounting to francs 4,736.35. It is also our understanding that this latter expense was to be borne by the French Government; and we therefore would appreciate it if you would be good enough to favor us with an expression of your wishes in the matter.

I am, my dear Mr. President,

Faithfully yours,   Robert Lansing

TLS (WP, DLC).

From Robert Lansing, with Enclosures

My dear Mr. President: Paris. 2nd April, 1919.

I enclose herewith for your information copies of telegrams received from the Department relative to the political and economic conditions of the Soviet Republic in Russia and their request for recognition by the Government of the United States. Would you kindly give me your views on the matter?

Faithfully yours,   Robert Lansing.

TLS (WP, DLC).

E N C L O S U R E   I

Washington. March 25, 1919.

1270. For the Secretary of State.

Department has received following communication dated March 18, 1919:

"Honorable Robert Lansing, Secretary of State, Washington. Sir: I have the honor to hand you herewith original credentials of my appointment as representative of the Russian Socialist Federal Soviet Republic in the United States of North America, together with an English translation of the same. I also have the honor to submit a memorandum of the present political and economic conditions of the Soviet Russia based upon information supplied to me by my Government, and furthermore I enclose a translation of the constitution of the Russian Socialist Federal Soviet Republic, holding myself entirely at the disposal of the United States Government for any additional information or for any conference, official or unofficial. I am, Sir, Very respectfully yours, L. Martens,[1] Representative of the Russian Socialist Federal Soviet Republic in the United States of North America. S. Nuorteva,[2] Secretary of the Bureau."

You will recall that Nuorteva, Secretary of the Bureau, announced himself as official representative of the Red Guard early last year and has since claimed to represent the Bolsheviki. The memorandum referred to, which covers eleven pages of foolscap describing the success of the Bolshevik regime, concludes with the following passage:

"Fully realizing that economic prosperity of the world at large including Soviet Russia depends on uninterrupted interchange of products between various countries the Soviet Government of Russia desires to establish commercial relations with other countries, and especially with the United States. The Soviet Government is prepared at once to buy from the United States, vast amounts of finished products on the terms of payment fully satisfactory to parties concerned. My Government also desires to reach an agreement in respect to exports from Russia of the raw material needed by other countries and of which considerable surpluses exist in Russia. In order to reestablish the integrity of Russia and to insure uninterrupted commercial relations, the Russian workers and peasants are prepared to go to any length of concessions as far as the real interests of other countries are concerned, of course with the understanding that no agreements entered into should impair the sovereignty of the Russian people as expressed by the Russian Socialist Federal Soviet Republic.

On the part of the Russian Socialist Federal Soviet Republic there thus exist no obstacles to the establishment of the proper relations with other countries especially with the United States. The Soviet Government of Russia is willing to open its doors to citizens of other countries for peaceful pursuit of opportunity and it invites any scrutiny and investigation of its conditions which I feel sure will prove that peace and prosperity in Russia and elsewhere, in as far as the prosperity of Russia affects other countries, may be attained by the cessation of the present policy of non-intercourse with the Soviet Russia and by the establishment of material and intellectual intercourse. Russia is now prepared to purchase in the American market great quantities of the following commodities commensurate with the needs of 150,000,000 people: railroad supplies, agricultural implements and machinery, factory machinery, tools, mining machinery and supplies, electrical supplies, printing machinery, textile manufactures, shoes and clothing, fats and canned meat, rubber goods, typewriter and office supplies, automobiles and trucks, chemicals, medical supplies, etcetera. Russia is prepared to sell the following commodities: flax, hemp, hides, bristles, furs, lumber, grain, platinum, metals, for additional Russian purchases in the United States. I think that diplomatic negotiations with my Government will evolve propositions fully acceptable for this and that the Russian Government in the event of trade being opened with the United States is prepared to place at once in banks in Europe, quantities of American gold to the amount of $200,000,000 to cover the price of initial purchases.

To insure a basis for credits, I am empowered by my Government to negotiate for the speedy opening of commercial relations for the mutual benefit of Russia and America and I shall be glad to discuss details at the earliest possible opportunity. Respectfully, L. Martens, Representative of the Russian Socialist Federal Soviet Republic in the United States of North America. S. Nuorteva, Secretary of the Bureau."

I assume you have official text of Soviet constitution and would refer to division 1, chapter 2, section 3, and division 2, chapter 5, sections 9 and 10 as apparently summarizing the purpose of the Soviet Government. It is interesting to note that division 3, chapter 6, section 28 provides that the representatives to the City Soviets are elected on the basis of one deputy for 25,000 electors while the representatives of the Provincial Soviets where the population is agricultural, are elected on one deputy for every 125,000 inhabitants. If you have no official text of the constitution let me know if you wish me to transmit by cable. I am sending copies of all mentioned above by next mail. The fact that these credentials and proposals have been presented to the Department is being widely circulated in the press. The credentials themselves also seem to present more clearly than heretofore the question of the attitude which this Government should assume towards a regime whose constitution as officially communicated stipulates, that among its fundamental tasks, are the securing of the victory of Socialism in the countries, the abolition of private property, the repudiation of foreign obligations, and the complete elimination of whole classes from all share in Government.

In this connection you will note the ingeniousness of the proposal of the Bolshevik Representatives to deposit $200,000,000 in gold in the United States and Allied countries when the Government he represents has repudiated the foreign debts of Russia including $187,000,000 advanced by the United States to the Provisional Government.

Please instruct me what action you desire to take in regard to the communication quoted above.   Phillips,   Acting.

---

[1] Ludwig Christian Alexander Karlovich Martens (1875-1948). An old comrade in arms of Lenin, Trotsky, and other Bolsheviks, he had moved to New York in 1916 and had been associated with the Socialist daily newspaper, *Novy Mir*. Martens had been appointed as plenipotentiary to the United States on January 2, 1919. He had established the Russian Soviet Government Bureau in New York to encourage commercial relations

between Russia and the United States. Deported in 1921, he became a prominent engineer in Russia.

[2] Santeri Alexander Fedorovich Nuorteva (1881-1929). Born in Finland, he had fled to the United States in order to avoid imprisonment for writing articles critical of the Tsar. He had been active in the Socialist party in New York for a number of years. Under threat of deportation, he left the United States in 1920.

E N C L O S U R E   I I

Washington March 29, 1919.

1362. Referring to the Department's No. 1270, March 25th, 1:00 p.m.

Communication from American Russia Chamber of Commerce in New York states that Martens the Bolshevik representative and Professor Lomonosooff[1] are banking on the fact that Bullit[t] and his party will make a favorable report to the Mission and the President regarding conditions in Soviet Russia and that on the basis of this report the Government of the United States will favor dealing with the Soviet Government as proposed by Martens.

Phillips,   Acting

T telegrams (WP, DLC).
[1] Iurii Vladimirovich Lomonosov, or George Vladimir Lomonossoff, as he was known in the West, was a railroad expert and former professor at the Institute of Transport in Petrograd. He had headed a Russian Railway Mission to the United States sent by the Provisional Government. He had created a furor by appearing at a rally in support of recognition of the Soviet government by the United States held in Madison Square Garden on June 11, 1918. He had insisted that he was not himself a Bolshevik but declared that the regime of Lenin was the legitimate government of Russia and was far better than the former tsarist government. Boris Aleksandrovich Bakhmet'ev had immediately removed him from his post. Martens had announced on March 31, 1919, that Lomonosov would again be in charge of railroad affairs in his Soviet mission to the United States. Lomonosov returned to Russia early in 1920. See the *New York Times*, June 11-13 and 16, 1918, and April 1, 1919. Biographical sketches of Lomonosov appear in *ibid.*, Dec. 12, 1920, Sect. VII, and Nov. 21, 1952.

Two Telegrams from Joseph Patrick Tumulty

The White House, 2 April 1919.

#47 The proposed recognition of Lenine has caused consternation here.[1]   Tumulty.

[1] As early as March 24, 1919, the *New York Tribune* had carried a circumstantial, though sarcastic, account, datelined Paris, March 23, of the Bullitt mission to Russia. Under the heading, "Wilson sees Russia by Steffens' Eyes," the report began as follows: "William C. Bullitt, one time newspaper man and now preacher of radicalism and a new social order, is returning to Paris after several weeks on the trail of the Bolsheviki to tell President Wilson all about Lenine and Trotzky and darkest Russia. The trip, which was undertaken in secrecy by this State Department official, has finally been made the subject of an explanation at the Hotel Crillon as the result of adverse criticism regarding its nature. It was pointed out that Mr. Gullitt [Bullitt] was sent to Russia on the quiet, to pick up information on Russian conditions for the American peace delegation, whose members still profess ignorance on the Russian situation. Lincoln Steffens, who has

been acting as the eyes and ears for President Wilson in Europe, accompanied Mr. Bullitt to Russia. It is understood that the other Allied powers have been notified of Bullitt's and Steffens's mission." Extant records do not reveal who gave the "explanation" at the Crillon on March 23. It was undoubtedly Colonel House; Bullitt did not arrive in Paris until the evening of March 25.

The New York *Sun*, March 28, 1919, reported (dateline Paris, March 27) that a Russian policy was being framed "with the greatest secrecy" by the political leaders in Paris. It was known, the report continued, that Wilson had Bullitt's report before him. The writer noted that Bullitt and Steffens were likely to favor negotiations with the Bolsheviks and that it was probable that the Big Four would go along with this policy. The New York *Evening Post*, March 28, 1919 (dateline March 28), and the *New York Times*, March 29, 1919, both reported that a rumor was current in Paris that Lenin and Trotsky had sent a note to the United States requesting recognition of the Soviet government. In a related dispatch in the *New York Times* of the same date, Charles Albert Selden reported from Paris on March 28 as follows: "An American representative who recently returned from Russia, where he talked with Lenine, will soon make a statement on which some new plan of dealing with the Bolsheviki may be based." Finally, in a third report in the same issue, Richard V. Oulahan not only noted that Bullitt had given the Moscow government "rather a clean bill of health" in his report, but had also suggested that it was a widespread opinion, "among men not interested in Bolshevism or friendly to it," that Lenin would have to be called to Paris before the foundations for real peace could be laid.

However, the chief occasion of Tumulty's telegram, and certainly the source of the "consternation" mentioned by him was an article by George Rothwell Brown, under the headline "British Favor Lenine," in the *Washington Post*, April 1, 1919. "The Paris peace conference," wrote Brown, a political writer and foreign correspondent of the *Post*, "at the instance of Great Britain, is disposed to recognize the bolshevik government of Russia at an early date." He said that Lloyd George, while opposed to Bolshevism and to Lenin's methods, had decided that *de facto* recognition of Lenin and his regime was the only practical solution to the complex Russian problem. Brown believed that Clemenceau and Orlando were opposed to recognition and that Wilson occupied "a half-way position between Lloyd George and Clemenceau," being "not so fixed in his attitude." Brown warned that recognition of the Lenin government meant the establishment of Soviet embassies and legations in the nations of the world, including the United States, and that these diplomatic posts would become centers for the spread of Bolshevism. Brown noted at the end of his article that Bullitt had "recently returned to Paris from Moscow with a report favoring the recognition of Lenine."

The editorial writers of the *Washington Post* responded to Brown's article with two scathing editorials, "Proposed Recognition of Lenine" and "No Dealings With the Enemy," printed on April 1 and 2, 1919, respectively. Both painted grim pictures of what would happen to the world in general and the United States in particular if Lenin and Bolshevism were given the openings which *de facto* recognition implied. The second editorial expressed the hope that Wilson would "stand firm against the recognition of the Lenine government." It warned further against the alleged proposal in a typical paragraph:

"Twisted brains in American skulls are giving Lenine aid and comfort. Certain treacherous Americans are doing their best to forward this arch murderer's cause. They have not hesitated to prostitute their own reputations in serving Lenine. They advocate false doctrine with glib tongues and lying hearts. They gloss over the bestiality and fiendishness of the Lenine code of war on civilization, trying to make the ignorant believe that Lenine is the apostle of a new and improved method of securing justice and happiness among men. Many of the American followers of Lenine are merely defectives whose brains have proved inadequate to the strain of war. Others, however, are veritable birds of prey who scent carrion in the breakup of civilized governments."

[The White House] April 2 [1919]

No. 48. At McAdoo's request, cable you following:

"McAdoo being pressed for speeches on League of Nations. Feels he must soon speak if he can be helpful. He asks in strict confidence whether you contemplate any amendments with respect to 'the Monroe Doctrine; limitation permitting withdrawal from League upon notice; Article X, so as to provide for review of the territorial boundaries which may be established in the peace treaty; explicitly providing for a unanimous vote on all questions in Executive Council or Body of Delegates except as otherwise specifically provided for; reserving specifically as domestic questions immigration, tariffs, naturalization, etc.; changes with respect to any other matters.' "   Tumulty.

T telegrams (WP, DLC).

From Vance Criswell McCormick

My dear Mr. President: Paris. April 2, 1919.

I am enclosing a copy of a cable that we are sending to the War Trade Board in Washington for Mr. Woolley's attention.[1]

We have talked this matter over with Mr. Baruch, and he agrees with us that it would be a most helpful thing, in many ways, if a program of this character could be carried out.

If you approve, might I suggest that a cable from you to Secretary Redfield, expressing your approval as to the plan outlined in the enclosed cable, would be most helpful?

Very sincerely yours,   Vance C. McCormick

TLS (WP, DLC).
[1] G. McFadden to C. M. Woolley, April 1, 1919, TC telegram (WP, DLC). McFadden recommended that Woolley and Redfield set about establishing trade bureaus in Stockholm, Copenhagen, Rotterdam, Trieste, Prague, Vienna, Constantinople, Vladivostok, and "other important points of distribution in foreign countries" to collect accurate information on economic and commercial conditions and to assist American exporters in securing "responsible business connections in foreign countries." This proposal was intended to counter similar intensive efforts already under way by the British and French governments.

George McFadden was a member of the firm of George H. McFadden & Bro., cotton brokers of Philadelphia and New York, and had served as a representative in Paris of the United States Food Administration and the War Trade Board. At this time, he was a technical adviser on economic and commercial questions in the A.C.N.P.

To the Very Reverend Hardwicke Drummond Rawnsley

My dear Canon Rawnsley: Paris, 2 April, 1919.

Just a line to accompany the enclosed draft for two hundred pounds which it gives me great pleasure to contribute to the fund you are collecting to buy an annuity for Mrs. Yates. I know you will pardon the haste.

Cordially and faithfully yours,   Woodrow Wilson

TLS (WC, NjP).

From the Diary of Dr. Grayson

Thursday, April 3, 1919.

The morning session of the Council of Four was devoted to the consideration of the Hungarian situation and the plans which had been made for the investigations to be conducted by General Smuts, who has gone to the Hungary front for that purpose. Some progress was made at the morning session as a result of the President's warning to Clemenceau that unless matters were brought to a head within ten days there would be nothing left for the American delegates to do but to withdraw from France and to handle their negotiations separately. No official announcement, however, was made regarding the matter.

At 2:00 o'clock King Albert of Belgium visited the President. The King came in a rather democratic fashion, being accompanied only by a single Aide. The King was garbed in the uniform of a Field Marshal of the Belgian Army, wore tan shoes, with spurs, and wrapped leggings, and carried a light bamboo cane. He also wore tan leather gloves. I met him at the entrance and escorted him to the second floor. The King said to me as we were going up the stairs: "I am glad to meet you. You are the President's doctor." I asked him if he didn't think it was rather risky to come over in an airplane. He said: "No, it took me 2 hours and 20 minutes to make the trip from Brussels. There were no motors on the road and there was plenty of room up above! The air was perfectly smooth and the trip was speedy and very comfortable."

I ushered the King into the reception room, and a moment later the President came up stairs and entered the room. Addressing the King, the President said: "I am very glad indeed to have this pleasure of meeting you. It is a pleasure that I have been looking forward to." They shook hands and the President said: "Won't you be seated?" The King said: "It is a very great honor to me to meet you. I feel that we have had many things in common, and I am glad to have the privilege of telling you so. Every home in Belgium admires your great work for the world, and they have a deep affection for you." The President then complimented the King on what he had done in the trying situation through which he had passed during the war, and especially in the early days, telling him that the hearts of the American people had gone out to him and the Belgians themselves for their heroic work. He told the King that civilization owed much to what he and his people had personally contributed in the early stages of the world conflict. The conversation between the King and the President was extremely informal and democratic, rather more like the talk of two old friends than of two men who had met now for the first time.

The King had a slight cold and the President sympathized with him. The King said: "Thank you but it is now decreasing."

After this informal talk the subject matter of the King's visit was taken up, the King and the President discussing Belgian conditions generally and especially her attitude so far as the Peace Conference was concerned. The President asked the King whether he had come to any conclusion regarding the indemnity which he believed Belgium should exact from Germany. The King gave him the figures, and the President said: "I think your estimates are fair, but they differ considerably from those put forward by your Prime Minister, M. Hymans, who asks a very much larger sum." The President asked the King whether it would not be possible for him to appear before the Big Four and personally present to them the claims which he had just suggested to the President. The King in reply said: "I would not like to make a speech; I would be embarrassed to come to make a speech." The President said: "This meeting is very informal, and you do not have to make a speech; we all sit around; there will only be four besides yourself." Then the King said that he would be glad to come but that he would not like to come without bringing his Prime Minister with him. This rather pleased the President because of the divergence of views and figures between the King and the Prime Minister, and he told him he would be very glad to have both the King and the Prime Minister appear—and it was agreed that this should be done at 11:00 o'clock tomorrow morning.

With the business disposed of the President and the King resumed their informal talk, and the King, who knows a great deal about the United States, having visited there incognito while he was Crown Prince of Belgium before the death of King Leopold, told the President that he had heard an American call another American a lobster, and he was unable to understand what was meant. He asked the President why that name had been called, and the President said that the practice of calling a man a lobster as a term of derision originated back in the time of the Revolutionary War in Massachusetts, when the colonials affixed that name on the paid Hessian troops that Great Britain had imported to fight the colonials. Their very scarlet uniform coat, with the white face, resembled very much a freshly cooked lobster after it had been pulled out of the pot. The King seemed to get the application.

At this juncture the King said: "We are looking forward anxiously, and with much pleasure, to having you and Mrs. Wilson visit Belgium. We want you to invite whoever you would like to have there at the time. We would be glad to entertain as many guests as you would be pleased to bring." The King added: "The people of Belgium will give you a heartfelt welcome—every one of them will do this. They admire you, look up to you, and their hope for settling the peace of Europe is centered in you." The President thanked him for the invitation and told him that he was sorry that he had not been able to visit Belgium before this but he felt it was his duty first to sit on the job here and do what he could to help bring matters to a peaceful adjustment, but that he would certainly give himself this pleasure to visit Brussels at the very first available opportunity.

The President expressed the hope that the Queen[1] was in good health, and said that she was very much admired in America, especially for her noble work during the war.

The King then asked if he could have the pleasure of calling on Mrs. Wilson. He bade good-afternoon to the President and went down to Mrs. Wilson's sitting-room, where they enjoyed about a five minutes' conversation. He told Mrs. Wilson that: "We and Belgium are looking forward to a visit to Belgium from you and the President. We think that your husband is a very great man and we have respect and great admiration for him. We will always be grateful to him for the interest and help which he gave Belgium in the terribly trying days of the war." He said the President's help and counsel gave Belgium optimism when she was much depressed. Mrs. Wilson was very much pleased with the compliment and explained to the King that while she might be partial as the wife of the President, still she agreed in full with all that the King had said about him. She said: "It pleases me very much to hear the people say about him what I think."

The King said to me as he was leaving: "I hope that you are going to come to Brussels. We want you to know that we will give you a warm welcome. We know you as the President's doctor."

After the King left the Big Four meeting was resumed, with Orlando absent, he having to attend a council of the Italian peace delegation. However, he had made it plain that he would not consent to sit when the Jugo-Slav delegations were admitted to present their claims dealing with Fiume and the Dalmatian Coast. Therefore, his absence was more in the nature of an excuse than because of necessity. The Jugo-Slav delegation presented their statistics designed to show that Italy had no right to any part of the lower eastern Adriatic Coast.

Before they completed the presentation of their case the President was taken violently ill.[2] The conference had to adjourn summarily, and the President went to his room. He sent for me and said: "I am feeling terribly bad. My equatorial zone was considerably upset soon after lunch but I was anxious to proceed with the afternoon conference, which I was barely able to do owing to intense pains in my back and stomach and head. It has now turned into a very severe coughing spell and I can't control this cough, which is very distressing and harassing." I immediately got him to bed, and in the course of an hour I got him comfortably relieved. He said, "I don't think I have any fever"; but upon taking his temperature I found he had 103 degrees.

The President developed several violent coughing spells during the night, and it was necessary for me to use every possible remedy in order to relieve his condition and end the paroxysms, which were very seriously weakening him. The President passed a very restless night—and so did I.

---

[1] That is, Queen Elisabeth. She was Elisabeth Valerie, daughter of Karl Theodor, Duke in Bavaria (Tegernsee).

[2] Both Cary T. Grayson, *Woodrow Wilson: An Intimate Memoir* (New York, 1960), p. 85, and Edwin A. Weinstein, *Woodrow Wilson: A Medical and Psychological Biography* (Princeton, N. J., 1981), p. 328, have diagnosed this illness as influenza.

It seems to the Editors that, based upon the full evidence presented by Dr. Grayson in this and subsequent entries in his diary, this diagnosis has to be called into question. The reader will note that Grayson avoided using the word "influenza" until April 5, 1919, when he issued a press release on Wilson's illness. In this statement, Grayson said that Wilson had "come very near having a serious attack of influenza." This observation is, to say the least, puzzling. In a fairly detailed report to Tumulty on April 10, 1919, Grayson wrote that Wilson's illness was "the beginning of an attack of influenza." This statement, too, is puzzling. If Wilson did in fact have influenza, then what would "the beginning" of an attack of influenza" be?

We have submitted all the evidence relating to Wilson's illness to three specialists in infectious diseases and are pleased to give their conclusions:

A. Stanley Link, Jr., M.D., a specialist in infectious diseases and epidemiologist of the Forsyth Memorial Hospital, Winston-Salem, North Carolina, writes:

"President Wilson became violently ill with the symptoms of upset stomach and a severe coughing spell associated with a temperature of 103 degrees. Initially, his illness was characterized by severe paroxysmal cough, and his condition was described as 'distinctly serious.' Two days later his 'bronchial tubes were filled up with mucous,' and wheezing was described by the President while breathing. In his newspaper statement, Grayson said: 'The President has come very near having a serious attack of influenza.'

"Sunday, three days after he first became ill, Wilson's temperature was described as being only one degree above normal and showing signs of improvement. Thereafter, he evidently did improve quite rapidly and was able to carry out business from his bedside that day. Monday, four days after he first became ill, his temperature was described as being normal, and he said that he felt 'first rate.' However, for several days after this, the President was depicted as being somewhat weak and showing the effects of the infection, but he evidently did recover fairly rapidly and returned to a vigorous schedule.

"It is obvious that he suffered from an acute respiratory illness that was self-limited and resolved very rapidly. I would think that one of the respiratory viruses would be the most likely etiologic agent. Certainly the course of Wilson's illness is somewhat short for classic influenza. Likewise, the illness would seem unlikely to have been a bacterial pneumonia for it to have improved as rapidly as it did without antibiotic therapy. I think it would be impossible to say what virus we are talking about. However, the following viruses have all been implicated as causing acute respiratory illness: respiratory syncytial virus, para-influenza virus, rhino-virus, adeno-virus, and entero-virus.

"President Wilson's illness was most likely, in my opinion, a self-limited viral illness, which apparently resolved without residual damage."

Richard S. Marx, M.D., of Winston-Salem, also a practitioner in infectious diseases, writes: "I agree with Dr. Link that one cannot make a definitive statement about the diagnosis of the febrile illness which President Wilson contracted. Although the time period of his illness is atypical for influenza, there are individuals with some prior immunity to a related virus who might have a less severe course of the infection. The diarrhea mentioned is not common in influenza but can occur in some individuals and certainly the high fever would be compatible with this virus."

Samuel Pegram, M.D., Associate Professor of Medicine at the Bowman Gray School of Medicine, submitted the following report:

"The sign and symptom complex experienced by President Wilson in early April, 1919 was most certainly the manifestation of a viral infection. Because of the worldwide impact of the Great Swine (or Spanish) Flu pandemic of 1918, influenza has been blamed for most unexplained febrile, respiratory illnesses occurring around that time. In addition, Wilson's clinical course (acute onset, prominent respiratory complaints, self-limited disease, and post-illness fatigability) could all be explained by a case of un-complicated influenza.

"However, a number of other viral respiratory pathogens (all of which can mimic influenza clinically) may be more reasonable choices as the etiology of Wilson's problems. The height of the Spanish-influenza epidemic occurred in October and November of 1918, and shortly thereafter the plague that had swept the world began to pass as inexplicably as it had arrived. By late January, and certainly by March, no new cases were being identified. Any viral respiratory infection occurring in April with no mention of others similarly infected would strongly favor a *sporadic* pathogen and not influenza. Interestingly, gastro-intestinal symptomatology ('profuse diarrhea') is distinctly rare in influenza despite the label 'intestinal flu.'

"At least two other etiologic possibilities might be entertained: 1) Toxin exposure (unlikely that Wilson would be singularly affected); 2) Hypersensitivity pneumonitis (unlikely because of severity of Wilson's attack)."

As Dr. Pegram points out, it is extremely unlikely that Wilson had so-called Spanish influenza. It is true that the pandemic had passed by mid-November 1918, and no cases of Spanish influenza were reported in Paris in the spring of 1919. More important, headache and aching at the back of the eyes, or inside the head in front occurred in nearly all the cases of Spanish influenza for which we have reports. A. A. Hoehling, *The Great Epidemic* (Boston, 1961), p. 122. As Grayson's record reveals, Wilson did not suffer headaches.

If these assumptions are correct, then we must say that all previous diagnoses have greatly exaggerated the importance of this particular episode, and that we can see no evidence that this illness had any impact upon Wilson's decisions during the few days that he was confined to his bed. Moreover, after his quick recovery, Wilson worked with his normal drive and acuity. If Wilson made any mistake in judgment during the early period of his illness, it might have been to appoint Colonel House to represent him on the Council of Four. However, this is a subjective editorial comment. It should also be pointed out that Wilson made this appointment because Lloyd George, Clemenceau, and Orlando insisted upon it.

Weinstein, pp. 338-39, concludes that Wilson also suffered encephalitis as a sequela of influenza. In a letter to the Editor of March 1, 1986, Dr. Weinstein casts serious doubt upon the diagnosis of encephalitis. The Editors see no evidence to support that diagnosis. They will deal with this question when they come to the episode which Weinstein, in his book, says gives dramatic demonstration that Wilson was in a state of euphoria induced by encephalitis.

To look ahead, something very serious did happen to Wilson on about April 28, 1919, so serious that, at times, it rendered him incompetent. We are now working with a team of medical specialists on this illness, which has gone completely unnoticed by all previous biographers and historians, and we will present the findings of these specialists at the appropriate place.

From the Diary of Colonel House

April 3, 1919.

I did not feel like strenuous work this morning but it was nec-essary. Admiral Benson came in first to tell his usual story about our Naval Building Program which the British not only wish us to discont[in]ue, but wish us to promise that it shall never reach a point where it will compete with their Navy. Benson is a little obsessed with this idea. I do not think anyone wishes to make a promise to Great Britain that our Navy shall never equal hers, but

I told him if the League of Nations was to have a chance of life, it would not do to start its existence by increasing armaments instead of diminishing them. He agrees to this, but insists there is a great principle involved.

He wanted me to ask the President to keep Secretary Daniels away from Paris now that he has gone to Italy. The President flatly refused this when I put the matter to him.

Tardieu followed Benson. I gave the talk which the President and I agreed upon last night. It had some effect upon him and I hope when it is repeated it will have some effect on Clemenceau. I put our case as strongly as I could and took occasion to say that as far as I could see, France had not reciprocated in any way. I disliked to recount our services to them but I thought it necessary. I disliked even more to tell him of our unselfish purposes. We were demanding nothing, and were merely trying to hold to the principles upon which the Armistice had been made and to which all the belligerents had agreed.

The Sarre Valley was injected as an entirely new proposal—a proposal which the Prime Minister himself agreed not to put forth if I thought it unreasonable. When this proposal was suggested, the only consideration brought forward was the value and necessity for the coal which was to be given France in lieu of the destruction of the coal mines around Lens. The President had been in sympathy with this request and was willing to give France in fee simple the coal mines, but he was entirely unwilling to place under French sovereignty an absolutely German population. In our opinion, it was not only inconsistent with the Fourteen Points, but it meant trouble in the future for France, and if we consented, it meant an immediate demand by Italy for Dalmatia and other enemy territory to which she had no just claim.

In reply to this, Tardieu brought attention to the fact that Foch had threatened to resign unless France insisted upon the permanent occupation of the Rhine, although Clemenceau did not go that far. The upshot of our interview was that Tardieu is to see what practical arrangement can be worked out concerning the use of the mines by France. We will then take the next step, if indeed, there is to be any next.

We agreed that in the event the impasse continued we would get together on Sunday and try to work out something between ourselves. I let him know if these matters were not settled within the next ten days, it was the intention of the President to go home because of the urgent public business requiring his presence in Washington. . . .

The President and I had an interesting conversation over the telephone concerning my interview with Tardieu, King Albert and various other matters.

Mantoux's Notes of a Meeting of the Council of Four

April 3, 1919, 11 a.m.

Lloyd George. I wonder if it would not be advisable to hold a plenary session soon to approve the report of the commission on international labor legislation, which has finished its task. That would make a very good impression, and would enable us to give the debate all desired scope.

Clemenceau. In fact I think that that could be beneficial before May 1st.

Lloyd George. We can try to schedule this plenary session for the soonest possible date, but without interrupting our present discussions, which must be pushed with all possible continuity.

Wilson. Professor Haskins, Mr. Headlam Morley, and M. Tardieu, who met to study the plan that we had outlined about Danzig, have reached agreement.[1]

Lloyd George. We were already in accord among ourselves, except for the reservation made by M. Clemenceau.

Clemenceau. I have thought, and I am inclined to fall in with your opinion. The essential thing is to reach a solution acceptable to the Poles. I do not wish to break with them, and you know they are not always accommodating.

Wilson. In summary, the question is to create in Danzig and the territory immediately surrounding it inhabited by German peoples, a little state economically bound to Poland by a customs union. In the province of Marienwerder, the areas inhabited by Germans would be consulted by plebiscite and could, if they desired it, be united to East Prussia. In this case, the Vistula would be placed under the regime of international rivers, such as our special commission envisages. The Germans could obtain the right to create in peacetime direct rail service across the territory of Danzig toward East Prussia and Russia.

Lloyd George. An equivalent right must be provided for Polish communications between Danzig and Warsaw, for the Mlawa line will cross the area of Marienwerder.

Clemenceau. On the whole, I do not dislike this plan.

Lloyd George. Then we agree. What is Mr. Orlando's opinion?

Orlando. I also agree.

---

[1] That is, the plan embodied in the memorandum enclosed with S. E. Mezes to WW, April 1, 1919.

Clemenceau. Have we taken a decision on the subject of the rest of the German-Polish border?

Wilson. We have accepted the commission's report, reserving the right to examine it again when we take decisions together on the German frontiers.

Lloyd George. I had no comment to make concerning the commission's report, except on the question of Danzig.

I wish to say a few words to you about the interview I had last evening with the King of the Belgians. I found him full of good sense and moderation. He does not demand territories. Concerning Luxembourg, he only wants to strengthen relations between this country and Belgium, perhaps by a customs union.

Clemenceau. The German dynasty must also disappear.

Lloyd George. I believe that there would be a great advantage to hearing the King of the Belgians here if, according to the reservation he himself made, the Constitution permits him. We could invite him by letter.

Wilson. I believe that it would be more respectful to visit him about the matter.

Clemenceau. I am prepared, if you wish, to go to Versailles, where it seems he is residing.

Wilson. I must see him today at two o'clock.

Clemenceau. In that case, the simplest thing is for the President to speak to him in our name.

Wilson. Which commissions have not yet completed their reports? I know that the financial commission is still debating some difficult points, notably concerning the responsibility of the new states formed out of the dissolution of Austria-Hungary.

Lloyd George. Truly I find it rather unjust that, if Poland includes the better part of Silesia, she does not bear its part of what the enemy owes us. She has little intention of doing so; moreover, no more than the Czechs and the Yugoslavs who are all vying with one another to reject responsibilities, in order to begin their existence without a burden of debt. It is a little hard also to think that Danzig, which is a very flourishing city, will pay nothing because we will make her a free city.

Wilson. I propose to ask the commissions to complete their reports still unfinished by next Monday at noon.

Clemenceau. That would be very desirable.

Lloyd George. I also believe that it would be in our interest, before finishing with the German questions, to know immediately the point of view of the Italian government on the question of the Adriatic.

Orlando. The question in general is well known; as for our point of view, we regard the Treaty of London as a compromise to which the mixture of nationalities in the Adriatic region obliged us. The question of Fiume arose later, for reasons which I can explain to you.

Clemenceau. Would it not be best to hear M. Orlando on this subject?

Lloyd George. Yes, we are listening.

Orlando. Italy had renounced Fiume in order to reach the compromise of which I have just spoken. We believed then that Austria-Hungary would survive the war; no one considered a total dissolution possible, and it was thought impossible to leave this great continental state without an outlet to the sea; the necessary outlet was Fiume.

This question is not unrelated to that of Danzig. The countries which form the true hinterland of Fiume are all of Hungary, a part of Bohemia and of Austria, as well as Croatia. Italy had understood the necessity of giving up this Italian city: but the situation has changed and, with it, the status of the problem.

Several reasons intervene. The most important is the national reason. Austria-Hungary was a country in which several nationalities lived side by side. This mixture itself created a sort of equilibrium in which Italians could find certain guarantees. In Fiume, Italian interests were relatively well respected, because of the equilibrium created by the rivalry between the Hungarians and the Croats.

Lloyd George. Are there many Hungarians in Fiume?

Orlando. A certain number, and the rivalry between the two interests was such that the city had been constituted as an autonomous organization between Croatia and Hungary. The rupture of that equilibrium is today complete, and the consequence is that the Italian element in Fiume risks being submerged. It is no longer only a question of renouncing political union with an Italian city, but of condemning the *italianità* to death.

As for the economic argument which we took account of in 1916— knowing that Fiume is the outlet of a vast hinterland—that argument now speaks in our favor. Of the merchandise which passes through the port of Fiume, no more than 7 per cent is of Croatian origin. All the rest is Hungarian, Bohemian, or Austrian. Thus, Fiume is not the natural outlet of Yugoslavia, but of other more distant countries. It is impossible to give Fiume to all these countries at the same time. That being the case, it is natural enough to allow the national claim of Italy to prevail. The administration of the city by Italy will give more guarantees to the different peoples who form the clientele of Fiume than a Yugoslav administration would do. Italy can have no other interest than the prosperity of the city.

Thus the economic argument, in the new situation created by the dismemberment of Austria-Hungary, reinforces the national argument. Moreover, Italy is ready to accept all stipulations which would establish and guarantee the freedom of international trade in the port of Fiume.

Another aspect of the question is that the Yugoslav countries do not lack outlets to the sea. Poland deprived of Danzig has no other port. In spite of that, we have been prevented from giving Danzig to Poland by concern about handing over this purely German city to the Poles. The Yugoslav state, on the contrary, will have several hundred kilometers of coast with magnificent ports such as Cattaro, Ragusa, Spalato, Mitrovic, which is the best port of Montenegro, and, in the Quarnero, Porto Re, Buccari, and Segno, which has for a long time been a port used by the Croats. Thus one cannot say that the Yugoslavs need to possess Fiume in order to have access to the sea. Finally, Fiume is at the extremity of their territory. That is why Fiume is much more a Hungarian port than a Croatian port.

If it were only a matter of the port, I would prefer to destroy the port of Fiume and to construct another port for the Yugoslavs at the expense of Italy, rather than to renounce having this Italian city enter into Italian unity.

Lloyd George. What would happen if Fiume were a free city under the control of the League of Nations?

Orlando. I would accept that solution for the port, but not for the city.

If we look at it simply from the economic point of view, what reason could one invoke, if not distrust of Italy? To make Fiume a free city is to prepare for the absorption of the Italian element by the Croatian populations which surround the city.

Wilson. I am so especially interested in this problem that there is not a solution which I have not studied. I sent the most competent and disinterested man[2] I could find to Fiume, to inform me about the sentiments of the population. I have his report in my hands. He assures me that there is in Fiume a true unanimity in favor of autonomy.[3] The opinions differ as to the degree of this autonomy, up to and including complete independence.

[2] Lt. Col. Sherman Miles, a member of the Coolidge mission who had been stationed as an observer in various parts of present day Yugoslavia, including Fiume and, most recently, Spalato (now called Split).

[3] Wilson had read either S. Miles to A. C. Coolidge, Report No. 16, March 15, 1919, printed in PPC, XII, 479-83, or a summary of that report, printed in Miller, My Diary at the Conference of Paris, VII, 172. Miles' conclusion, as set forth in the summary, was that the people of Fiume desired autonomy "of a greater or less degree." Only "propagandists" desired absolute incorporation of Fiume into either Italy or Yugoslavia.

I was very much struck by the conversation which I had, shortly before my recent departure for America, with several leading people of Fiume, members of the municipal administration. They told me that they wished to be placed neither under the jurisdiction of Italy nor under that of the Yugoslavs, and they showed me a zone to establish around the city in order to form an autonomous territory.

Undoubtedly this local opinion must be subordinated to our international view, should there be a contradiction between the two; but this contradiction does not exist. The dismemberment of Austria-Hungary makes it more desirable than ever that no particular nationality be in exclusive possession of an outlet common to the peoples of the former monarchy. Free competition between Trieste and Fiume will be much more fruitful if these two cities are not placed under the same jurisdiction. It will be in the interest of all the peoples for which Fiume is the outlet to work toward its development. Trieste has clientele which will not abandon it.

What M. Orlando has just said about the other ports which the Yugoslavs can use did not convince me, because although these ports are very fine, they have only difficult communications with the interior.

I earnestly beg M. Orlando to take into serious consideration the plan to make Fiume a free city without customs ties with any of its neighboring states. In that way, Fiume would not be the port of the Yugoslavs, but the one of all the interior. This solution seems to me the best one by far. I would not like to ask guarantees of a great nation like Italy. We have complete confidence in her; we would not wish to seem to be imposing conditions upon her.

Orlando. I take occasion to express my gratitude to President Wilson for what he has said, and for the careful study which he has made of the question. But I beg him to consider the political situation of the representative of Italy. One can show deference and personal respect toward a man one esteems, by allowing him the right to decide about his own interests. But when one speaks, not for oneself, but for a nation, one does not have that possibility

---

The "Independent Party" preferred Yugoslav rule to Italian if autonomy could not be had. The Spalato area was the only location where a port to replace Fiume could be built. However, Fiume was a prepared port with loading facilities, railroad connections, and so forth, while Spalato could not have them for years. Moreover, it would be very difficult to build a railroad from Spalato over the mountains into the interior. Miles found that the families of Fiume were divided among themselves in their national sympathies. He believed that the best solution for Fiume short of internationalization was to make the city a free port under a Yugoslav mandate. He also submitted a map with a proposed boundary line between Italy and Yugoslavia (reproduced in *ibid.*, facing p. 172).

Wilson had probably also read S. Miles to A. C. Coolidge, March 20 and 29, 1919, printed in *PPC*, XII, 491-96, as well as a memorandum on Dalmatia and Fiume of March 18, 1919, by Charles Seymour, Clive Day, William E. Lunt, and Douglas W. Johnson, printed in Baker, *Woodrow Wilson and World Settlement*, III, 263-65. The latter document concluded that both Fiume and Dalmatia should go to Yugoslavia.

and is constrained to remain within the limits of the national mandate. I must say this to justify the opposition which I am obliged to express, against the opinion of a man whom I respect.

The economic difficulty is not insurmountable. If access to other ports is costly, that will not stop us, for modern engineers have solved greater problems. If, on the other hand, Croatian trade is not profitable enough to justify or to pay for the necessary works, the argument is in our favor.

For us, the question is above all a matter of sentiment. If, nevertheless, we consider it from the economic point of view, I would say to you that the question of Fiume is very closely related to that of Trieste. I would accept their competition, if I did not fear that it would be manipulated in some way. We have reason to believe, without being able to furnish proof, that the Czechs and the Yugoslavs have a secret agreement to use Fiume in preference to Trieste. If this agreement is carried out, it would divert part of the commerce of Trieste to the port of Fiume. But that is secondary. For the Italians, the question of Fiume is a question of sentiment. We do not wish to abandon our brothers, whose liberation was the great goal of our national war.

You tell me that it is the people who want autonomy. It is difficult to believe that without absolute proof. I can tell you that the deputy of Fiume[4] and the mayor of that city,[5] who are both in Paris, tell me that they do not wish to hear any talk of its constitution as a free city. That is a hypothesis which they reject absolutely. If I could be sure that Fiume prefers this solution, that would not fail to have much influence upon my decision. But all that I know leads me to think that it is not so.

Wilson. You say that you have fought to liberate your compatriots of Fiume. However, you declared war after having signed a treaty according to which Fiume would remain outside of Italy.

Mr. Lloyd George reads a letter from Mr. Balfour: the King of the Belgians will attend the meeting of the heads of government tomorrow, accompanied by M. Hymans who, "like well bred children, will be seen but not heard."

Mantoux, I, 125-31.

[4] Andrea Ossoinack, formerly the deputy from Fiume in the Hungarian Parliament, at this time a member of the delegation from Fiume to the peace conference.

[5] Antonio Vio.

From Vittorio Emanuele Orlando

Mr. President,   Paris, April 3rd, 1919.

The quite unexpected way in which the Italian questions came up for discussion to-day, made it impossible to examine more thoroughly the many difficult points, including even questions of procedure, which present themselves.

I had not been able to come to an understanding with my colleagues on the Delegation, nor had my colleague, the Minister of Foreign Affairs, Baron Sonnino, come to the meeting, as it had been agreed that he would do, and as was done in the case of Mr. Tardieu when the problem of the French frontiers was under consideration.

As for the very delicate matter of giving a further hearing to the representatives of the Slovenes and Croats,—against whom Italy has been at war for four years,—I would not insist against it, just as I would not exclude the advisability of giving a hearing to the representatives of any other enemy people on whom it is a question of imposing conditions. But, on the other hand, as no such debate has yet been granted, I insist in thinking it advisable to abstain from taking part in a meeting which, as things stand, must necessarily give rise to debate.

I realize, with keen regret, that my absence may give rise to an impression, which I should be the first to wish to avoid, that a misunderstanding has arisen between the Italian Government and the Allied and Associated Governments. I think however that such an impression will not be given, as the meeting this afternoon is not the meeting of the representatives of the four Powers, but a conversation between the President of the United States and the Prime Ministers of Great Britain and France with those Gentlemen.

I earnestly hope, Mr. President, that in this way the reason for my absence will be seen in its true light, i.e. not as an evidence of disagreement, but as an act of consideration towards colleagues, whose wish it is to obtain all the data available in order to form their own opinion on the grave matters under consideration.

Believe me, Mr. President,

Sincerely yours   V. E. Orlando

TLS (WP, DLC).

Mantoux's Notes of a Meeting of the Council of Four

April 3, 1919, 4 p.m.

Clemenceau. We have heard a statement from M. Orlando on the question of Fiume; we wished to hear a representative of the Yugoslavs on the same subject.

Trumbić. I am ready to respond to your questions, although I was only designated for this mission barely an hour ago.

The city of Fiume is a Slavic city. Today a majority of the population is Italian speaking; but that is above all the result of the favor accorded that element by the Magyar domination since 1868. It is also the consequence of the growth of the port of Fiume.

If we go back to 1848, we see that, at that time, the city had only 12,600 inhabitants, of whom 11,600 were Slavs and only 1,000 Italians. In 1868, Fiume passed under the political power of Hungary through the well-known forgery of the Hungarian-Croatian Convention. I recall that incident. After Sadowa, the imperial government was obliged to accept dualism, Hungary becoming an autonomous State. In 1868, an agreement between Croatia and Hungary gave the Croats a species of autonomy, which they enjoyed until the present war. In fixing the territorial limit between the two countries, the Croat commission and the Hungarian commission could not agree on the question of Fiume, and an article of the convention, Article 66, stated the disagreement purely and simply. The text was approved in this form by the Parliament of Pest and by the Parliament of Zagreb, and signed by the Emperor. But the Austro-Hungarian Foreign Minister had stuck in the place of Article 66, which stated that an accord could not be reached about Fiume, another text which gave that city to Hungary. I have brought you the photograph of the forged document, and we have the original text, without alteration, conserved in the archives of Croatia.

After that, the Magyars seized the city of Fiume, removing all Croatian authorities, even eliminating Croatian-speaking schools after ten years. The Slavic population had access to only one secondary school which, being located in the suburb of Susak, on the other side of the Resina river, was in Croatian territory. At that time, there were no Magyars in Fiume, but only Croats and Italians. The latter were used by the Magyars as an instrument of their policy, because they were anti-Croat.

The government of Pest tried to make Fiume a great port, constructed a railroad, wharves, docks, which created a certain sympathy for the Magyars among elements of the population associated with those works. Until the present war, the Italian element had no political aspirations; irredentism did not exist in Fiume. The

Italians were only one of the elements in the local game played by the Magyars. The latter handed over the schools to the Italians and gave them the most important role in the city, for the sole aim of excluding the Croats. It is thus that the Italian element grew and prospered, animated by a Hungarian political spirit, or as an instrument of Hungarian policy.

Lloyd George. When was the railroad constructed?

Trumbić. Between 1870 and 1880.

Lloyd George. Fiume was not a great port before this time?

Trumbić. No, the port grew only afterward.

Lloyd George. It is the Hungarian government which had these works done?

Trumbić. It is the government of Budapest, acting as the common government of Hungary and Croatia, with funds voted by both Parliaments.

Official statistics show that in 1880 there were in Fiume 11,175 Slavs and 9,920 Italians; in 1890, 13,478 Slavs and 13,012 Italians; in 1910, 24,212 Italians, forming the majority, 15,696 Slavs, 6,493 Hungarians and 2,315 Germans. I would remark on the appearance of these two new elements, which explains better what I said about the growth of the Italian population, itself attracted by the development of the port.

These figures only apply to the city of Fiume proper, excluding the suburb of Susak which, although an integral part of the same conglomeration, is administratively separate, and is part of Croatia.

The *italianità* of Fiume is an artificial creation. The Italians are not an indigenous population; that is essentially Slavic. The Italians are immigrants, come to work on the port and the railroad. Under Magyar rule, the Slavic element was subjected to a complete political boycott. The municipal statute of the city was drawn up in such a way as to exclude the Croats from the administration; the regulations for elections deprive them of any chance of having a seat on the municipal council, which was until now formed entirely of Italians and Hungarians acting in concert.

It was to weaken the Slavic element that the suburb of Susak was separated from Fiume. Susak counts 11,705 Slavs and 658 Italians, a few families. Fiume, with Susak, according to the statistics furnished by the Italo-Magyar municipality itself, had before the war a population of 27,392 Slavs, 24,870 Italians, 6,492 Magyars, and 2,315 Germans. Thus we can conclude that the city of Fiume must not be considered an Italian city; the Italian element is interesting from a demographic point of view, not from a political point of view. Rijeka—that is the original name of the city, translated into Italian as "Fiume"—belongs to Croatia, of which it is geographic part. Moreover, it is surrounded on all sides by exclusively Slavic peoples, as the ethnographic map shows.

The Slavic element has always maintained a primary economic position in Fiume, and its preponderance is well demonstrated by the following facts. The city of Fiume, in the strict sense of the word, numbers 2,756 property owners: 1,193 are Yugoslavs. The most noteworthy buildings in the center of the city and on the wharves belong to Yugoslavs. The navigation companies of Fiume are the following: (1) the Hungarian-Croatian Company for Coastwise Trade—forty-two vessels, 15,506 gross tons; (2) the Hungarian-Croatian Company for Free Navigation—six vessels, 22,606 tons; these enterprises are completely Croatian in capital, officers and crews; the name given them can be explained by the fact that the Hungarian government granted them a subsidy for the postal service and for the export of Hungarian flour; (3) the Oriental Company—six vessels, 26,405 tons; (4) the Levant Company—eleven vessels, 39,436 tons; (5) the Atlantica Company—ten vessels, 41,550 tons; (6) the Adria Company—thirty-two vessels, 74,555 tons. Several small businesses should be added, which have together eight vessels.

I said that the first two are almost exclusively Yugoslav; the last three have capital principally Hungarian, but with Yugoslav participation; in the Oriental Company, this participation is important. If we take all these companies together, the capital is divided in the following proportions: Hungarian capital 68 per cent; Yugoslav capital 28 per cent; Italian capital 6 per cent.

The merchant fleet of Fiume employs 283 captains and 269 engineers; 199 captains and 169 engineers are Yugoslavs. As for the personnel, it is recruited from the coastal region, and it is 98 per cent Yugoslav. In Fiume's banks, the ratio of Yugoslav to Italian capital is ten to one.

Wilson. What is the nature of the commerce of Fiume? What is the origin of the merchandise? What is the proportion which comes from Yugoslav lands? What are the relations with the different countries of the hinterland, such as Hungary and Bohemia?

Trumbić. In 1913, the commerce of Fiume reached a level of approximately 2,100,000 [metric] tons—927,500 entering and 1,180,000 departing. It is impossible to say exactly what belongs properly to Yugoslav lands and that because of the dualist regime which permitted distinctions only between Austrian and Hungarian regions. But I can say that the coastal traffic, purely Yugoslav, because all the coastal region is inhabited by our peoples, reached a level of approximately 330,000 tons.

The principal export—27 per cent of the total—is wood. Now this product comes almost exclusively from Croatia, with a small portion coming from Carniola; this is a Yugoslav export. The division between Hungary and Austria of official statistical documents does not permit us to distinguish specifically what comes from Bohemia.

On the other hand, I can give some figures on imports. English coal—160,000 tons—was destined almost exclusively for the commercial fleet and railroad of Fiume. Rice from the Indies—120,000 tons—went to the rice husking factory in Fiume. Australian ore—5,500 tons—was destined for the lead foundry of Martin Sitza. Oil seeds—27,000 tons—went to the oil and chemical factories in Fiume. Phosphates from the Indies and North Africa were destined for the agriculture of our countries.

Serbian trade did not pass through Fiume, because Serbia, boycotted economically by Austria, sought its outlet on the coast of Saloniki. In our unified State, Fiume would drain the trade of Croatia, of Slavonia, of Serbia, of the Banat, of the Backa; it is the only outlet to the sea for these countries.

Lloyd George. What are the outlets for Hungary and Bohemia?

Trumbić. Of necessity the port of the Hungarians is Fiume; the port for Bohemia, an industrial country and particularly rich, is Trieste. The eastern part of the Czechoslovakian Republic will gravitate toward Fiume through Pressburg. The principal items in Fiume's export trade are wood and wine; both are in the hands of the Yugoslavs. Of twenty-seven commercial establishments which conduct commerce in wood, sixteen are Yugoslav, the others belonging mostly to the Hungarians. The wine trade is in the hands of the Dalmatians and the Slavs of Istria. The most important establishment of the entire coastal area is the Maison Boubokovitch of Lesina.

Fiume's trade is only at the beginning of its development. Our new state, by the construction of a new network linking the Banat, the Backa, Serbia and Bosnia, and by the suppression of artificial obstacles which have impeded the port's trade, will allow it to take flight. It is a well known fact that the Germans, by constructing their railroad, established there a system of tariffs designed especially to favor Hungary, particularly the city of Budapest, while sacrificing Croatian interests. For example, to send a sack of flour from Sisak, which is located about two hours east of Zagreb, to Fiume, it was necessary to pay more than to send it to Budapest, which is much further away. In fact, it was arranged so that the first journey was divided into two zones, while the second crossed only one.

Wilson. What are the possibilities of the development of a port such as Spalato?

Trumbić. Very little: there is no railroad to Spalato; moreover, a series of mountain ranges parallel to the coast would make construction very difficult and very costly.

I would like to say a word about the banks. I have already indicated that the ratio between Slavic interests and Italian interests is as ten to one. Four great banks of Fiume are in the hands of Yugoslavs; together they have a capital of twenty-nine million crowns, with reserves of eight million. Their annual turnover in 1917 was 2.5 billion crowns. The major Italian bank, the Cooperative Bank, had a turnover in the same year of only 246 million, with a capital of only two million crowns.

Lloyd George. Do these Yugoslav banks have branches in different parts of Croatia?

Trumbić. I do not believe so; but in Fiume there are branches of the Zagreb banks.

Wilson. I understand that the companies are Croatian, but are the capital and deposits principally Yugoslav, or do they contain an Italian element?

Trumbić. These are businesses almost exclusively Yugoslav. The Italians do business with or deposit their capital in Italian or Hungarian banks. That is the natural consequence of the political situation. I did not mention the Banca Commerciale di Fiume and the Hungarian Realty Bank. The first was created by the Commercial Bank of Budapest, and the second is the creation of the Hungarian Discount Bank.

The Croatian banking agencies in Zagreb do much to encourage business in Fiume. For example, the agency of the first Savings Bank of Zagreb had in 1917 an annual turnover of two billion crowns. The entire economic life of Fiume proves that it is the Croatian people who furnish this city with the greatest part of its capital. Hungary did everything it could to suppress Croatian activity through licit or illicit means; but it did not succeed.

Lloyd George. What do the Italians do?

Trumbić. They are shopkeepers, employees; they form part of the personnel of the port and railroads.

Lloyd George. This does not correspond to the figure of 24,000 Italians for the city of Fiume.

Trumbić. It must not be forgotten that this figure is the statistic established by the Italo-Hungarian municipality, figures based, not upon nationality, but upon habitual language. It is a well known procedure to enter a house and to say "Good morning" in Italian. One answers you in Italian, which everyone knows how to speak in our country; I myself speak it like an Italian, having been born in Spalato. So it is written on the list that the family is Italian. The same thing happens in Austria with regard to the German language. It is the system used everywhere to the advantage of the language of the nation which holds power.

Cordial relations between Italians and Magyars were reinforced by memories of 1848; the two peoples fought as one against the Habsburgs. The great Hungarian patriot Kossuth died in Italy. The Magyars had no reason to fear the Italian population of Fiume, which formed only a small island, while they feared the Croats. On the other hand, under the rule of the Triple Alliance, the Hungarian government made concessions to the Italians in order to avoid giving offense to Italy. It was the Croats who paid the price and were constantly accused of being the instruments of Pan-Slavism and of the Russian drive toward the Mediterranean.

Wilson. Those who speak for Italy contest these statistics. What is the source of yours?

Trumbić. I drew them from official Hungarian sources and, for those concerning banks, from information gathered right on the spot.

Mantoux, I, 132-38.

From Nicholas I

Dear and Great Friend,   Paris, April 3rd, 1919.

Six months will soon have passed since the collapse of brute force, personified in Prussian militarism, thanks to the bravery of the Allied peoples, but thanks especially to the admirable energy of the United States. The latter, from the first day of their intervention, by the enormous moral and material forces they brought with them, became the decisive factor in the realization of the supreme ideal of humanity—the consecration of the right to live, for the small as well as for the great.

The history, six centuries old, of my country, and liberty, which has been its corollary, are nothing but an uninterrupted chain of bloody struggles for the realisation of this ideal.

I am proud of my country, for Montenegro, like your glorious nation, has been the country which threw itself into the strife without imposing utilitarian conditions nor with selfish, hidden calculation, but solely in order to collaborate, in so far as it was able, in the triumph of right and justice over brute force and all that was arbitrary.

A conscious victim of its generous and spontaneous action, Montenegro had the undoubted right to complete restoration on the same grounds as Belgium and Serbia, a right which was solemnly recognized as due to it by yourself, Mr. President, in the name of the United States, and by all the Governments of the other great Allied Powers. Furthermore, the hard combats and suffering which, alone, Montenegro has undergone in the past; the struggles and sacrifices endured in common in these days; ought to have sufficed, perhaps, to procure for it, on the part of the Allies, certain rewards of a moral and political order. Alas! it was in no way so. Worse still, certain Allies did not hesitate even to put its very existence as a sovereign and independent State in question.

Montenegro is today the victim of the worst of oppressions. The Serbian army of occupation, constituted, organized and equipped by the Allies, acting under the orders of a French general, Commander-in-Chief of the Armies of the Near East,[1] has invaded my country, and this at a time when not one enemy soldier remained on Montenegrin soil. Immediately on their arrival, these invaders proclaimed the annexation of Montenegro to Serbia—an Allied State.

During this time, my Government and myself, have not only been prevented from forming a combattant unit of Montenegrin refugees and emigrants from America, but, further, at the moment of the evacuation of Montenegro by enemy troops, we were forbidden to leave the land of exile under a threat of: *the immediate breaking off of diplomatic relations on the part of the French Government if we tried to return to Montenegro.*

In this manner official Montenegro has been virtually held in captivity, whereas the Command of the Allied Armies in the Near East, favored Serbian invasion and the return to the country of a small number of Montenegrin renegades in the pay of the Serbian Government, so that, taking advantage of the confusion in which the country found itself, the Serbians might proceed more easily with the destruction of our national institutions and the suppression of the independence of Montenegro.

Mr. President, I believe that the most elementary justice as well as the solemn undertakings of the Allies and the universal conscience of which you are the noble mouthpiece imperatively demand that Montenegro be restored at the earliest possible moment to the full rights it enjoyed before the war. That is what the majority of the Montenegrin people demand. That is why it has risen in insurrection and why it is still struggling and suffering today.

Mr. President, as soon as the Montenegrin State shall have been restored and I am back in my country, I shall call a parliament in conformity with the constitutional dispositions and laws of the Montenegrin State. This constitution, which is in spirit more liberal than the constitution of the Kingdom of Serbia, is a guarantee that this parliament will be the true interpreter of the wish of the people of Montenegro.

I declare to you, Mr. President, solemnly, that I will accept, without reserve, any and every decision of the parliament thus legally convened, even though such decision be unfavorable to me as a sovereign.

Moved solely by the interests of the Montenegrin people, whose rights are at present ignored, I take this step of appealing to you, Mr. President, which I pray you to consider as a solemn engagement on my part towards the President of the Republic of the United States. And if among the great Allies there is to be found one who should try to cast a doubt upon the sincerity of my undertaking, I declare that I submit in advance to any decision which you, Mr. President, may think fit to take to ensure the legality and sincerity of the consultation of the Montenegrin people as well as the carrying out of the decisions of parliament legally convoked.

I pray Your Excellency, dear and great friend, to believe me,

Your very sincere friend   Nicolas.

TLS (WP, DLC).
    [1] That is, Gen. Franchet d'Espérey.

From Herbert Clark Hoover

Dear Mr. President: Paris, France. April 3, 1919.

With respect to feeding Bavaria through Switzerland, this is totally infeasible in any volume worth considering, both from a transportation, food and financial point of view.

For your confidential information, the whole of this question has been repeatedly agitated up by the French Minister at Berne,[1] who is constantly endeavoring to create a Separatist spirit in Bavaria and who wishes to send a few carloads of food into Bavaria under the French flag. The pressure from this quarter became so great in this particular about ten days ago that it was raised before the Council of Four Ministers of Foreign Affairs,[2] and I gathered Mr. Lansing and Mr. Balfour were against this encouragement towards Separatist movement from the rest of Germany, and its moral violation of the Brussels agreement.[3]

Foodstuffs are moving into the ports of Germany as rapidly as we can secure transportation and the large industrial centers in the North are in far more acute distress than Bavaria. While we are insistent that some portion of shipments should be made to Bavaria, I myself consider it fundamental that we should get some American food at the earliest possible moment into the larger centers of the North and East.

As quickly as the first German passenger ship left the German harbors, and before any of the financial arrangements were completed, I diverted several cargoes intended for other quarters into German harbors, anticipating by about two weeks the settlement of financial questions. I was able to do this by virtue of the reserve of some two or three millions of dollars which I had from the fund you supplied me with, and you would I believe, be extremely pleased with the reaction created in Germany by this act, which is evidenced by the German press. The question of food to Germany from the United States has become a byword in Germany due to the three months delay arising from our difficulties in negotiations with the Allies, and its realization without quibbling over detailed arrangements has created a certain amount of confidence by the people that we are good for our undertakings. I may add, however, that the situation in Germany is extremely dangerous and that I am not at all sure that our food supplies have not arrived sixty days too late. In any event, it is a neck and neck race as to whether food will maintain stability as against the other forces that have grown out of hunger in the meantime.

Faithfully yours,   Herbert Hoover

TLS (WP, DLC).
  [1] That is, Paul Eugène Dutasta, who was also at this time the Secretary General of the Paris Peace Conference.
  [2] For the minutes of this meeting of the Council of Foreign Ministers, held on March 27, 1919, see *PPC*, IV, 515-21.
  [3] Again, about which see EMH to WW, March 7, 1919, n. 1, Vol. 55. The reader will recall that the first American food ship, S.S. *West Carnifex*, landed at Hamburg on March 25, 1919.

From Fridtjof Nansen[1]

My dear Mr. President: Paris, April 3, 1919.

The present food situation in Russia, where hundreds of thousands of people are dying monthly from sheer starvation and disease, is one of the problems now uppermost in all men's minds. As it appears that no solution of this food and disease question has so far been reached in any direction, I would like to make a suggestion from a neutral point of view for the alleviation of this gigantic misery, on purely humanitarian grounds.

It would appear to me possible to organize a purely humanitarian Commission for the provisioning of Russia, the foodstuffs and medical supplies to be paid for perhaps to some considerable extent by Russia itself, the justice of distribution to be guaranteed by such a Commission, the membership of the Commission to be comprised of Norwegian, Swedish, and possibly Dutch, Danish and Swiss nationalities. It does not appear that the existing authorities in Russia would refuse the intervention of such a Commission of wholly non-political order, devoted solely to the humanitarian purpose of saving life. If thus organized upon the lines of the Belgian Relief Commission, it would raise no question of political recognition or negotiations between the Allies with the existing authorities in Russia.

I recognize keenly the large political issues involved, and I would be glad to know under what conditions you would approve such an enterprise and whether such Commission could look for actual support in finance, shipping and food and medical supplies from the United States Government.

I am addressing a similar note to Messrs. Orlando, Clemenceau and Lloyd George.

Believe me, my dear Mr. President,

Yours most respectfully,   Fridtjof Nansen

TCL (WP, DLC).
    [1] The Norwegian Arctic explorer and oceanographer. He had recently come to Paris because of his concern over the Russian situation and the plight of prisoners of war of all nations. For the immediate background of this letter, reportedly drafted by House and Hoover, see Thompson, *Russia, Bolshevism, and the Versailles Peace*, pp. 250-51, and Herbert Hoover, *The Ordeal of Woodrow Wilson* (New York, Toronto, and London, 1958), pp. 120-21.

From Newton Diehl Baker

Washington. April 4 [3], 1919.[1]

1431. For the President.

"Reference Mission telegram 1421, April 1st.[2] Proposed instructions to General Graves. The situation now is that General Graves has been instructed to use his troops as requested by Stevens to guard the railway. The definite assumption by inter-Allied agreement of [the responsibility for a strip six miles wide, practically to Omsk, would require for effective military control] a very large force, perhaps 500,000 men, and any such definite control would inevitably mean either very large additions to the Japanese forces or additions to our own. In any case it would sanction a very large section under Japanese control penetrating practically through Siberia. Conflicts between the soldiers and officers of the inter-Allied forces and with various elements of the native population and forces are of daily occurrence. Would not the establishment of this long zone increase the frequency of such conflicts and so make possible local disturbances which would appear to justify assumption of civil

control and perhaps military repression which in effect would mean
occupation and administration of Siberia by Japan? Would it not
be better to have State Department take up with Allied nations
represented in Siberia the formulation of a policy limiting the ob-
jectives of our military forces to the preservation of order about the
railroad, its stations and trains, as those in charge of the railroad
may request, and also stating definitely as one of late [its] objects
the common desire to bring about the cessation of local violence
by conflicting Russian forces merely as such actions affect the
dispatch of trains or operation of the railroad? In seeking such an
agreement I think our State Department should be clear in its
expression of disinclination on the part of The United States to add
to its troops now in Siberia or to see additions [made] by other
nations. This would limit military activity to the railroad and to
existing forces and give no implied sanction to great increases by
any nation or extension of its political or military activities. Baker."

Phillips,   Acting.[3]

T telegram (WP, DLC).
   [1] Corrections in square brackets from the copy, dated April 3, 1919, in the N. D. Baker
Papers, DLC.
   [2] RL to FLP, April 1, 1919.
   [3] This was sent as NDB to WW, April 4, 1919, T telegram (SDR, RG 59, 861.00/4197,
DNA).

From the Diary of Ray Stannard Baker

Thursday the 3rd April [1919]

To cap the climax the President fell ill to-day just after the Council
of Four meeting & Admiral Grayson put him to bed. He has a severe
cold with fever. They had up the Adriatic problems this afternoon
& Signor Orlando, refusing to be present when the Jugo-Slavs
(represented by Mr. Trumbic) set forth their case. The Four jumps
about from question to question & decides nothing. There is unlimited greedy bargaining, especially by the French & Italians, only
the President, growing grayer & grimmer all the time, standing
upon principles of justice & right. He will probably be beaten. I
only hope he goes down fighting for his own principles & does not
yield. It will be better for him & for the principles—for the world—
in the long run. The King of the Belgians flew down from Brussels
& came in this morning to see Col. House & this afternoon saw
the President. He is a tall, blond, youthful looking man—handsome
& engaging. I saw him this morning. All agree that he is frank &
honest—& much more moderate in his demands than some of the
Belgian delegates. . . .

I had a long talk this evening with Col. House who was sitting in his long lounge with a figured blanket over his chilly legs—quite serenely dictating his diary to Miss Denton. More & more he impresses me as the dilletante—the lover of the game—the eager secretary without profound responsibility. He stands in the midst of great events, to lose nothing. He gains experiences to put in his diary, makes great acquaintances, plays at getting important men together for the sheer joy in making them agree. He is a matchless conciliator but with the faults of his victim for he conciliates over the border of minor disagreements into the solid flesh of principle. I found him to-night quite cheerful: quite optimistic. Told me that if he had it to do he could make peace in an hour! Were the Italians going home: well & good, let them go! Was Lloyd-George going to issue a defense (as I intimated to him) which might compromise the President—all right, let him issue it! I told him of the President's illness (of which I had just been talking with Grayson) & said that Grayson told me that the President had probably contracted his cold from contact with Clemenceau who coughs fearfully. "I hope," said the Colonel genially, "that Clemenceau will pass on the germ to Lloyd-George." The Colonel had conferences to-day with Tardieu & Orlando & told them (as he assured me) just what the American position was.

Thus, a bright, lively little man, optimistic in the presence of tragic events! While the great serious man of the conference—gray, grim, lonely there on the hill—fights a losing battle against heavy odds. He can escape no responsibility & must go to his punishment not only for his own mistakes and weaknesses of temperament but for the greed & selfishness of the world. I do not love him—but beyond any other man I admire & respect him. *He is real.* He is the only great man here. Clemenceau is serious & honest but serious for smaller causes, immediate gains, selfish ends. Lloyd-George is a poor third & yet he too is a serious man. But he lives for the moment, is pleased with every new thing, seizes any compromise, promises any future benefit for each present gain. Orlando is an amiable sentimental [?] Italian without depth of vision, playing little games of local politics while the world is afire.

In the meantime Germany drifts always nearer bolshevism.

The Second American Draft of Categories of Damages

April 3, 1919.

ANNEX TO CLAUSE 2.

Personal Injury	(1) Personal injury to or death of civilians resulting from acts of war on land and sea and from the air or mistreatment by the enemy.
Pensions	(2) Damage to the civilian population resulting from the absence, incapacitation or death of persons serving with the forces and which damage is met by pensions or allowances of like nature made by the State. (French scale to govern.)
Damage to Labor	(3) Damage to civilians resulting from their being forced by the enemy to labor without just remuneration or abstain from labor.
Damage to Property	(4) Damage to or interference with non-military property, as from date of damage or interference, directly caused by acts of war on land and sea and from the air, or illegal acts of the enemy or war measures in the nature of requisitions or sequestrations, taken by the enemy.
Fines, etc.	(5) Damage in the form of levies, fines and other similar exactions imposed by the enemy upon the civilian population.
Violations of law and of Engagements	(6) Damage resulting from acts in violation of international law (as found by the Commission on Responsibilities) and in violation of formal engagements.

NOTE: Where the State or other public authority has already itself made compensation for the damage, it may present the claim in its own behalf.

T MS (WP, DLC).

From the Diary of Vance Criswell McCormick

April 3 (Thursday) [1919]

Got started early this A.M. as Davis, Lamont, Baruch and I were to call on President, to explain situation in regard to categories as stated to us by the British. He acknowledged Lloyd George had nearly put it over on him and Davis, who with him had been present at all of the meetings and did not know enough about the categories to keep the President straight.[1] President this morning, however,

saw the point and approved the categories Dulles and I had worked
out during the night and early morning,[2] much to my relief, as we
had what I believe was a just claim against Germany in accordance
with the President's 14 points and for a proper distribution among
the Allies. I went with Dulles to see Montague and Keynes to show
our plan approved by the President. They agreed to submit to Lloyd
George before afternoon meeting. . . .

Davis and I went to President to report. Found him in bed with
a bad cold at 6.00 P.M., very tired and I know discouraged. Allies
acting like the devil. We are proposing most liberal terms and French
particularly unreasonable. President told us he was willing French
should take over Saar coal mines as reparations for destroyed coal
mines of France, with freedom of operation, but could not take over
territory as he only agreed to Alsace Lorraine; also agreed to most
liberal military curtailment on Rhine; no fortifications within fifty
kilometers of Rhine, no troops or maneuvers east of Rhine and no
railroad sidings or facilities for mobilization, active and military
occupation by Allies for reasonable period. All refused—he is at a
loss to know what to do if impasse continues. Disgusted, threatening to go home as he must call Congress in May. I really pitied
him as they are trying to make him the goat and he is powerless
to fight publicly in the open because it would only help Germany
by showing serious discord among the Allies.

[1] See the extract from the McCormick Diary printed at April 2, 1919.
[2] That is, the preceding document.

From the Peace Conference Diary of Thomas William Lamont

[Paris] April 3 [1919]

At 9.30, NHD[,] BMB[,] McC & I called on Pres't & explained
text of Reparation as tenatively agreed to by Am. & British Del.
including the 30 yr period with permission to demand at end of
that period a bond from Germany covering all unpaid instalments.
Pres't appd. of all. I pted out to him that on whole matter we had
been proceeding on theory that Germany was not to be hampered
with trade restrictions, for if she were she could not pay the reparation. There might be a few minor exceptions for the transitory
period, like the Alsace Lorraine-Germany tariff, but nothing formidable. The Pres't absolutely agreed. He then said very solemnly
that he wanted to consult us on his most difficult situation. The
whole peace settlement was being held up by Clemenceau who
would not agree to stand on the 14 pts. He wd not realize that a

bargain, good or bad, had been made w. Germany & must be lived up to. He explained again about Saar Basin—how Clemenceau insisted on taking over sovereignty because under the unjust treaty of 1815 (after the 100 days war) it had been wrenched away by Prussia. He retorted to C. that unfortunately while he (W.W.) had said that the wrong of 1871 must be righted he had said nothing about the wrong of 1815, as he had not been posted to that end. He went on to explain that he tho't he had gone a great distance in saying that while Germany must retain sovereignty over Saar, France could insist upon ownership in fact forever of Saar coal fields, crediting to Germany a fair price for them. He went on to explain how France seemed to think that from the ground, or sky or somewhere, an enemy was going to arise & crush her. To meet that they had laid down the most drastic disarmament & military terms & L-G had agreed to come to France's aid if she were ever attacked by Germany. W.W. also gave his own view of what he proposed for America under that formula. I asked him how about the League of Nations. He was so upset & puzzled by how he could bring this impasse to an end that he wondered whether the course was to pick up & go home or to tell the American people the whole story & let them decide.

Tasker Howard Bliss to Newton Diehl Baker

No. 51

My dear Mr. Secretary: Paris, April 3, 1919.

. . . A few days ago,[1] just after the revolution in Hungary occurred, Mr. Wilson sent for me at his house and told me that in the session of the Council of Four that afternoon they had considered various telegrams from the French general in Roumania[2] in regard to the critical situation of the Allied forces in Odessa. They finally sent for Marshal Foch and he again reverted to his plan. He said that he did not believe that Odessa was worth holding and that it would be better to transfer the forces there to Roumania and have the Allies strengthen the Roumanians and the Polish Army. It seems that the British, French and Italians agreed to this and then asked Mr. Wilson what supplies he could furnish to the Roumanian Army. He told them that he did not know what he could do under the law but he would consult his advisors about it. He asked me to make him a report on the subject. I consulted Mr. Norman Davis and learned from him that he had been informed by the Roumanian Prime Minister[3] that some time before the Hungarian revolution occurred the British and French had agreed to finance and supply the Roumanian Army themselves. They had not informed the President of this and it looked to Mr. Davis and myself as though they were deliberately attempting to unload a part of the expense upon the United States. I made my report to the President, closing it with the following paragraphs:

["]After my conversation with Mr. Norman Davis last night, I came to the conclusion that, if my advice were asked, I would suggest that you say to the Prime Ministers that the United States is doing, apparently, some eight times more for the checking of Bolshevism by general relief work in Europe than the other Powers combined; that, inasmuch as we can continue this relief work without the embarrassment that would probably result from having to ask Congress for authority to engage directly or indirectly in operations of war in Eastern Europe, it would be better if they were to agree that we should continue to furnish assistance in this way and let them charge themselves with the equipment and maintenance of armies. To my mind, any nation which takes upon itself expenditures for military operations intended to check the universal revolutionary tendency in Europe, will be assuming a burden that will last for indefinite years. If we are once committed to it, in any degree, it will be difficult to withdraw. We may easily find ourselves tied up in a military situation which will subsequently demand the sending of our troops. Notwithstanding all of the talk of the withdrawal of the Archangel expedition, I think that it is not improbable that the Allies will make a demand upon us for further considerable reinforcements to that expedition. When we once engage ourselves in that sort of adventure, a thousand unforeseen reasons crop up for our continuing in it and for engaging ourselves in it more deeply than before. The Allies want to engage in extensive military operations, but they are afraid to do so on account of expense and the unwillingness of their own peoples. Nevertheless, they appear to be unwilling to face the alternative, which is a complete cessation of such operations. The assistance which we are asked to give in Roumania and in Poland brings us face to face with the final and positive determination of our future policy in European affairs. You must remember that the request made of us to furnish supplies to the Roumanian Army is a continuing request of indefinite continuance. If we take the first step which commits us to this policy, we shall have to continue in that course. And that will commit us to what may be perhaps a long series of wars for the purpose of throttling the revolutionary movement in Europe. The long-continued Napoleonic Wars resulted in the unchaining of those forces of revolution which the Holy Alliance attempted to combat. In the same way, this horrible war, which concentrated in itself all of and more than the energies of destruction of twenty-five years of Napoleonic Wars, has again broken up all of the foundations of the great political deep. I cannot convince myself that it is wise, from any point of view, for the United States to engage in the work of combating these new forces of revolution."

I do not know what action the President has finally taken but the French insist that he has agreed to furnish supplies. If he has, I am afraid that it will prove a serious matter. They will expect the furnishing of supplies to be continuous. If we do that, it will be an expensive matter, and if we do not do it, they will say we have gone back on our word. I still hope that he has not agreed to it.

At the session of the Council of Four on the afternoon of March 27th I received word at the last moment to be present at the discussion of a new plan to be presented by Marshal Foch to meet the Hungarian situation. This plan proved to be a modification of his original plan for fighting Russia and was evidently directed at the former object. It involved, among other things, the immediate occupation of Vienna by an American army, with Allied contingents, under an American general! As it was entirely a question of *policy*, I supposed that the four heads of governments would dismiss the military men (there were present General Diaz, Marshal Foch, General Sir Henry Wilson and myself) and discuss it as a matter of policy among themselves. Instead of that, after Marshal Foch had made his speech, Mr. Clemenceau called on General Diaz who entered into a long discussion of Bolshevism. Then he called on General Sir Henry Wilson who, like myself, was of the opinion that so momentous a military plan heard then for the first time, could not be sanely discussed on the spur of the moment. When he called on me, I took the view that, if I had to speak at all, it would be on the line of general policy and not on the line of the military merits of the plan. I accordingly "unloaded" myself of the remarks which I attach hereto.[4]

Now the courier is waiting and I must get this letter off. I have said enough to prove to you that we are talking more of war than of peace, as I said at the beginning.

We are all hoping that the President will announce to his colleagues that if they do not promptly come to an agreement he will go home and let Congress decide for itself what it will do. If anything will bring them to time, such an announcement will do it.

With kindest regards, believe me,

Sincerely yours,   [Tasker H. Bliss]

CCL (T. H. Bliss Papers, DLC).
[1] That is, on March 25.
[2] That is, Gen. Berthelot.
[3] That is, Ionel (or Ion I. C.) Brătianu.
[4] They are missing, but see Bliss' remarks as recorded in the minutes of the Council of Four, March 27, 1919, 3:30 p.m.

From the Diary of Dr. Grayson

Friday, April 4, 1919.

This morning the President's condition was distinctly serious. The question, therefore, of what should be said to the public was one which I had to decide. The President had no objection to my announcing that he was sick in bed; in fact, he advised that I do so because, as he pointed out, he did not want any one to attribute to him any indication of quitting, as only the fact that he could not sit up prevented him from continuing the work of the Peace Conference. I got in touch with the newspaper correspondents immediately and told them that the President was suffering from a severe cold and that I had put him to bed and was insisting that he remain there so that he could have the proper care and attention, which was absolutely imperative at the present time.

The President then asked me to go across the street to the British Headquarters and see Premier Lloyd-George, and explain to him why he (the President) could not be present at the morning session of the Big Four, but that he hoped that they would go on with the business, especially as the King of Belgium had promised to be present. Lloyd-George suggested that Colonel House be the substitute for the President, instead of Secretary Lansing. He said: "If you have Secretary Lansing there, every other Secretary of State of all the other countries will deem it their duty to be present and it will be equal to a council of ten.["] Lloyd-George said to me: "You have Scotch in your blood, haven't you?" And I said: "Yes, a generation removed." He said: "That's all right. I feel satisfied that you can handle him then. I don't have to give you any advice."

The Council of Four, with Colonel House substituting, held its meeting in the temporary White House as originally scheduled, and the King of the Belgians and his Prime Minister presented their views on behalf of Belgium. Nothing that was transacted, however, was brought to the attention of the President, he being allowed to remain quiet.

When the King arrived here for the morning session he said: "I am very sorry to hear that the President is ill. Please take good care of him, because the world is counting on him, and give him a greeting with best wishes for me."

As the day wore on the President showed some manifestations of improvement, and I was able to give him some nourishment in the form of oyster soup and hot coffee. Afterward he fell into a sleep and his temperature was reduced to 101.

When the meeting of the Big Four adjourned, I made it a point to see Lloyd-George and asked him if he had any information to convey to the President. He told me that the King of Belgium had practically gone over everything that had been discussed at previous meetings, and that they really had made no progress. Lloyd-George further said: "Tell the President that we are going to have a meeting at four o'clock this afternoon. I think it is the wise thing to do, notwithstanding the fact that I do not believe we will accomplish anything without the President's presence."

Colonel and Mrs. Birch,[1] and Mrs. Willard and Miss Willard[2] were the guests at luncheon today. Colonel Birch is our Minister to Portugal, and Mrs. Willard and Miss Willard are the wife and daughter of our Ambassador to Spain. They were, of course, much disappointed because the President could not be present on account of his illness. The President was represented by Mrs. Wilson. Colonel Birch was bubbling with good spirits and humor. I asked him how he liked the wine in Portugal and he said that when he first went there it went to his head, but later on it went to his big toe— so he had to vote "dry." The Colonel told many amusing and interesting stories.

The President had a very bad night and I was called to see him a number of times in order to give him whatever relief was possible.

[1] Wilson's old friends, Thomas Howard and Helen Louise Barr Birch.
[2] Belle Layton Wyatt (Mrs. Joseph Edward) Willard and Mary Elizabeth Willard.

From the Diary of Colonel House

April 4, 1919.

I received word from the President this morning asking me to take his place in the Council of Four which was to meet at his residence.

Before going, I had several people to see, among them Thomas Lamont, who had just returned from the French Chateau where the German fifnancial [financial] experts are stopping. Max Warburg, one of the experts, told Lamont a sad story of conditions in Germany and asked him to give a message to the President and to me. We were the only two, he thought, among the many delegates in Paris, who would care. He said they were on the verge of Bolshevism, and the present Government would not last longer than a few weeks. Conditions in Germany were worse now than at any time during the war, and largely because the French had executed the terms of the Armistice in a spirit entirely different from that which was meant.

At the Place des Etats-Unis, Orlando, Clemenceau, George and myself received King Albert of Belgium. For two hours he told us the story of Belgium's desires. I received a better impression of him than I have had before. He is a level headed, slow talking and slow thinking gentleman. He asked nothing unreasonable and said nothing foolish—something to be commended in these days of misty minds. I tried to get Lloyd George down to the matter of priority, but it was impossible. That was too near accomplishment. I can easily see how the time has been wasted in the Council of Four. They did not come to grips with the King about anything. It was all talk and a promise to look into matters later.

We did not break up until one o'clock. I saw Mrs. Wilson for a moment and she asked me to remain to lunch, but I had an engagement with Frazier.

Lord Robert Cecil and I had a long conference about the situation as it exists today. We both see the world crumbling about our feet, and we both see the need not only for peace but the lifting of all trade restrictions and the bringing the world back to the normal. Even after peace is made, our troubles will not end, for it will be many weary months before it will be possible to start industries and get the currents of commerce properly flowing.

I told Cecil of my desire to have the first meeting of the League of Nations at Washington. I suggested that it be held in the East Room of the White House on the first day of October. In the meanwhile, after this Conference had finished its work, he and I could work out an organization in England for the League and prepare, or have prepared, the different subjects for settlement which might properly be brought to the League's attention. This would take all summer and would make October about the right time for the first meeting. I was glad to have Cecil respond so quickly to the thought of holding the first meeting at Washington under the Chairmanship of the President. We agreed that it would give it an impetus and a setting to the League that could not be obtained elsewhere.

At four o'clock I went to the Ministry of War where a meeting of the Council of Four was to be held. We had decided this morning to take up the question of the Czecho-Slovak boundaries. Our Experts had drawn a line which ran in and out of the old territory, throwing some of the old Austria into Germany and placing many Germans in Austria.[1] The French and English agreed upon the entire line.

I reached the Ministry of War five or six minutes in advance of George and Orlando and by the time they arrived, Clemenceau and I had agreed to adopt the old historic boundary line and not attempt the new one. It was so much simpler and less full of possibilities for trouble. We had but little difficulty in persuading both George and Orlando to accept our conclusions, George seeming to know but little about it. The question of Teschen came up and I suggested that no decision be arrived at there, but that it be placed under a commission for a report at some very much later time.

George wanted to postpone our next meeting until Sunday, alleging that the President would then be well enough to attend. Clemenceau and I insisted upon having it tomorrow and he finally acquiesced. We also agreed to take up the question of Reparations. I found in talking with Clemenceau that George or someone had misinformed him as to the American position and that he thought the entire cause of the trouble and disagreement lay with our experts. Lamont and Davis have done everything possible to save George because of his election promises, and in return he uses us to mislead Clemenceau into believing that what we have tried to do to help him, was our own idea and not for him.

I told them that in my opinion it was more important to bring about peace quickly than it was to haggle over details. That I would rather see an immediate peace and the world brought to order than I would to see a better peace and delay. I jestingly remarked that by tomorrow night we ought to be able to settle all subjects necessary for a peace with Germany and all the differences between us. I told Clemenceau I disliked evading problems which had to be solved. He replied that he was no "dodger." Then, I said, we will come to grips tomorrow.

When George saw that it was likely we would get together on some of the questions affecting France, he brought up the subject of Syria. He is determined to have this settled before he lets the French get what they want. He has told me many times of this, and his bringing it up today is an evidence of his determination in this direction. When we went out of the room he said he was sorry the subject of Reparations was coming up tomorrow when the President was away, for he believed that he and the President were nearer together than he an[d] I. This, I answered, might be, nevertheless, I thought there should be no delay in getting at it.

When I reached the Crillon, I told Lamont, Davis and Mc-Cormick, who will be present at the meeting tomorrow, that we must expose the situation and let the French know the story as it was. Clemenceau, I said, believed that we were the hindrance and we must make it clear in a pleasant, impersonal and cordial way, where the real trouble was. I am looking forward with interest to our meeting.

Tardieu was another visitor. We discussed the left bank of the Rhine and the Sarre Valley. It was a continuation of our discussion of the last few days and the memorandum which he brought on the subject is a part of the record.[2] We have come closer together.

I was glad to hear, in talking with Mrs. Wilson over the telephone, that the President was better. I explained what I had done at the two meetings. After she had told the President, he was evidently alarmed at the rapidity of the decisions and had her telephone me back that he hoped I would not commit myself on the question of the Sarre Valler [Valley] and the left bank of the Rhine. I replied that these question[s] had been up with Tardieu only and I was not committed any further than that Tardieu knew my views and knowing them, had prepared the memorandum.

[1] Actually, Charles Seymour and Allen W. Dulles, the American representatives on the Commission on Czechoslovak Affairs, had sought to draw boundaries which would minimize the number of Germans included within Czechoslovakia. For a detailed discussion of their efforts, see Perman, *The Shaping of the Czechoslovak State*, pp. 138-45, 153-54, 169-72.
[2] It is printed as Enclosure I with WW to EMH, April 12, 1919.

From the Diary of Vance Criswell McCormick

April 4 (Friday) [1919]

Met with Lamont, Davis and Dulles to discuss reparations and later went to Colonel House's office to discuss program for meeting with Prime Ministers in the morning, to try to force final settlement between British and French. They are playing a sordid game and playing for advantage in the division of the spoils and trying to lay the blame of the delay in making of the Peace Treaty on the President. The Chief is getting mad and I think we will have an explosion soon, which will be justified. President still indisposed to-day. . . .

Baruch and McFadden came in before bed. Baruch very sore at our Allies on account of unfair tactics at Economic meeting, also sore at Colonel's crowd, which he thought too free in criticising President to outsiders.

These are strange days and everyone tired and irritable and we will have to keep our heads and keep cool for we are just passing over the peak and still have some rough going before we land.

From the Diary of Ray Stannard Baker

Friday April 4 [1919]

The Four met to-day with Col. House taking the President's place. The Colonel prefers to work with Clemenceau rather than Lloyd-George. He told me to-day that L.G. said to him: "You & I do not agree as well as the President and I agree." The Colonel is still optimistic! . . .

The Colonel sides with the group which desires a swift peace on any terms: the President struggles almost alone to secure some constructive & idealistic result out of the general ruin. If these old leaders only knew it Wilson is the only strong bulwark against Leninism left of the old order: he would save the present democratic system by making it just, decent, honest. What they are doing, with their greedy demands & selfish interests, is to give new arguments, new force to Lenin & his extreme policy of decentralization & horizontal internationalism. They can't see this—& plunge on to their doom.

Wilson is really the supreme champion of the old order, the old nationalism & would save it. He does not even *see* the new social revolution as a wily[?] Colonel House sees it & would, as usual, conciliate it. So does Lloyd-George see it! & would temporize with it. So does Clemenceau see it—& would fight it.

Mantoux's Notes of Two Meetings of the Council of Four

[Paris] April 4, 1919, 11 a.m.

Clemenceau. We ask your Majesty[1] to inform us about what he has to say.

The King. We believe that Belgium, if the promises which have been made to her are carried out, has the right to a priority in the reparations. The invasion caused her to lose nearly all her means of production. Raw materials and most of the industrial machinery were carried off. The Belgian state was forced to pay to the enemy war levies rising to 2.6 billion, and this figure rises to 3 billion if forced contributions by cities are added. Belgium lost not only nearly all the machinery of its great industrial establishments, but also half its livestock.

Lloyd George. What is the state of your coal mines?

The King. In peacetime, Belgium already imported more coal than it exported. It is a country which lives by its exports, since eight-tenths of its population is involved in industry.

Lloyd George. What is the nature of the war levies which the cities had to pay? Did a part represent works done for their benefit?

The King. Not at all: they are penalties. For example, the people of Brussels, because they gave an ovation to Cardinal Mercier, had to pay two million. The city of Brussels paid on different occasions fifty millions francs. Tournai, which has only 30,000 to 40,000

---

[1] Albert.

inhabitants, paid around thirty million francs during the war. Many small cities paid one or two million. That is what raises the figure of our war levies from approximately 2.5 billion to 3 billion.

House. One has envisaged the possibility of actual reconstruction by the Germans of all buildings destroyed. But sums paid as war levies should obviously be repaid by pure and simple restitution.

The King. At present we have in Belgium 800,000 unemployed, and more than 1,600,000 people on state assistance. It is as if there were in the United States twelve million unemployed, and twenty-five million persons to support by allocations. If we cannot be immediately assisted, Belgium will find itself in a very grave situation. The state debt is increasing enormously, without any compensation in sight.

France, which has suffered much, it is true, has at least a great part of her territory intact and in a state of production. Eighty-five per cent of Belgian production is paralyzed. In France there is not enough labor for the necessary works of repair; but in our country, there is more labor than work.

Clemenceau. Your mines did not stop working?

The King. No.

Clemenceau. Has the work in them been completely restored?

The King. Yes, but I remind you again that our coal needs have always surpassed our production, particularly of long burning coal, which our steel mills import from England.

House. Is it not possible to employ this labor in the reconstruction of the devastated regions?

The King. It is difficult to employ in building trades men trained for example in the textile industry.

Lloyd George. Would it not be possible to recover your stolen machines? The Germans are very orderly and write everything down.

Clemenceau. Truly they are thieves who are orderly. We were able to recover many objects stolen from France, thanks to the way in which they had been registered.

The King. In fact there are commissions of recuperation in Mainz and Wiesbaden; but their work can only yield rather slow results.

We are completely lacking in raw materials, in metals for our metallurgy, in wool and cotton for our textile industry. During his occupation and withdrawal, the enemy emptied Belgium. He took foodstuffs in considerable quantity. That is why, moreover, there are so many marks in Belgium; for he paid for a part of what he took. These marks represent in some way the liquidation of Belgium, and we are obliged to reimburse our citizens at a rate of 1.25 francs, which is far from an advantageous operation for the state.

Lloyd George. The *Frankfurter Zeitung* had the audacity to speak of this German money left in Belgium as a great benefaction from Germany. Can greater impudence be imagined?

What is most important at this time is to know what can be put in the stipulations in the peace treaty between us and Germany; the question of distribution is one to be settled among ourselves and does not concern the Germans.

The King. You have received a memorandum from the Belgian government indicating what we claim.

Lloyd George. I should inform Your Majesty that we arrived here at a provisional arrangement about the nature of damages for which we will ask reparations. We divide these damages into damages to property and damages to persons, putting into this second category, the losses by death or mutilation which necessitate pensions.

The King. This classification would be very unfavorable to us; damages to persons have very little place in the sum of our claims, because Belgium, having been invaded very rapidly, was not able to raise any army. Otherwise, instead of 150,000 men under arms, she would have had 800,000.

Lloyd George. We would prefer to have living men than to receive pensions for the dead.

The King. What I say is meant only to indicate that there is a factual reason, independent of our will. I will observe moreover that an indemnity to persons always takes the form of annuities, while it is impossible to put destroyed businesses on their feet without capital.

Lloyd George. They tell me that France lost up to 58 per cent of her young men between the ages of twenty and thirty. It is a terrible figure. No material reparation could ever suffice to compensate for such losses.

The King. It is indeed frightful. I believe that Serbia lost even more.

Clemenceau. Probably.

Lloyd George. On the first point, that is concerning damages to property, the Germans seem inclined to repair them directly.

Clemenceau. I recall one of President Wilson's Fourteen Points, which promises complete reparation to France and to Belgium.

Lloyd George. Does Your Majesty see another category of losses to be repaired? We mentioned the restitution of sums extorted in the form of war levies, machinery, raw materials, foodstuffs, livestock; all that is included in our categories.

The King. There are also damages to railroads and to public works.

Lloyd George. We have provided for these. However, military

works, such as your forts at Liège destroyed by German cannon, are not included.

The King. Does your classification include public works [tunnels, bridges, etc.], forests?

Lloyd George. Yes, as well as orchards and all agricultural resources.

If Belgium has other suggestions to make to us, we will be happy to know them. This classification exhausts what the Germans will have to know. The distribution of payments remains a matter among ourselves.

Clemenceau. Another question which should be settled by the peace preliminaries with Germany is the question of Malmédy.

Hymans. This small territory is composed of the circle of Malmédy and the canton of Eupen. Eupen is a small German city, but the great forest adjoining it sits astride the German-Belgian frontier. The Belgian portion of this forest was destroyed by the enemy during the war, so that possession of the other portion would be compensation for Belgium; and this cession is only conceivable if it includes the small city where exploitation of the forest is concentrated.

As for Malmédy, it is a Walloon city of 4,600 inhabitants who speak French; before the war they had French schools and French newspapers. It is the same for the villages surrounding Malmédy. The frontier must be traced in such a way as to give us the railway from Malmédy to Eupen, which otherwise would cross a portion of German territory. Altogether this is not much and does not represent more than 10,000 souls.

Clemenceau. Does Your Majesty wish to speak to us about the question of the Scheldt?

The King. It is the events of 1914 which called into question the validity of the Treaty of 1839.[2] The essential clause of this treaty was the neutrality of Belgium, which was violated by German aggression.

Two questions are bound to that of the Treaty of 1839; the security of Belgium and the interests of Antwerp. I was surprised to see that the British Admiralty seems to prefer the status quo, that is the possession by Holland of the banks of the Scheldt. The Admiralty seems to consider it as inevitable that Belgium would be invaded in case of war and prefers, in that eventuality, that Holland close the Scheldt.

Lloyd George. The Admiralty is reasoning as it did in 1793. But I see nothing in Tardieu's report about the Scheldt.

---

[2] About which see the minutes of the meeting of the Council of Four printed at March 31, 1919, 3 p.m., n. 8.

Hymans. Tardieu's report concludes simply at the revision of the Treaty of 1839 and at the invitation to Holland to examine this revision with the Allies.

The King. The Conference approved this report and consequently agreed to bring up the matter again.

Lloyd George. It is certain that the régime of the Scheldt such as it was in 1914 is absurd. We were obliged to blow up some English ships in the Scheldt which we had time to withdraw, simply so as not to violate Holland's neutrality. It is true that Grey, who was then Foreign Secretary, was particularly scrupulous. I do not know if I would have been as much. It is an absurd situation. Belgium must have free access to the sea by way of the Scheldt without having to ask Holland's consent.

Clemenceau. There is no difficulty in that.

Lloyd George. No; the territorial question is another matter.

The King. The worst effects of the Treaty of 1839 were not felt until nearly seventy-five years after its signature. But it contained a series of stipulations favorable to Holland and unfavorable to Belgium. For example, it was impossible to create a navigable canal between Antwerp and the Meuse, because Holland told us that the construction of a railway had exhausted our right.

Concerning Limburg, the important thing is to know if Holland can defend it.

Lloyd George. It is certain that she has not done so, and that she allowed the Germans to pass in retreat with all their supplies under conditions which are questionable.

Could not the question of the Scheldt be settled by our commission on navigable waterways?

Hymans. There would be some disadvantage in cutting into two the Belgian claims, the same question being treated here in some respects, and, in other respects, by the commission on navigable waterways.

Lloyd George. That commission is concerned with assuring free passage on international rivers.

Hymans. The Scheldt is not properly speaking an international river, since from an economic point of view it is exclusively Belgian. We are asking for sovereignty over this river.

Lloyd George. I would approve of everything which would give Belgium free use of the Scheldt.

Undoubtedly Your Majesty wishes to speak to us about the problem of the occupation of the left bank of the Rhine?

The King. What I would have to say depends upon the regime foreseen for that region.

Lloyd George. What we foresee is a complete disarmament of the left bank of the Rhine and of a zone extending up to fifty kilometers on the right bank.

The King. That seems to me a sound plan.

Clemenceau. I must observe that our frontier, which touches the Rhine in Alsace, diverges from it by up to 100 kilometers, and there could be danger that a German army could be only fifty kilometers from the river, while we would be twice as far from it.

I have thought of different solutions, notably to increase this distance of fifty kilometers; but I rejected that. We say to President Wilson: in case of invasion, the French and Belgians will be obliged to rise to battle before you will have had time to arrive. President Wilson responds: "It is absurd to reason as if the Germans could build up an army from 100,000 men to a million men without anyone noticing it." This response is acceptable, but on condition that Germany be watched. If she increases her army from 100,000 to 120,000 men, or even her artillery from 1,000 to 1,500 cannon, we would perhaps not declare war for that; but it would be necessary, if this movement should grow, that we be able immediately to warn England and America of a violation by Germany of the treaty she had signed. We must be able to ask the English and Americans to come to ascertain the fact and to join us in taking the necessary remedies; without that, I would only have a scrap of paper in my hands.

I favor making practical stipulations, in such a way as not ourselves to provoke the danger that we fear. Our military leaders are against a surveillance of this kind; I have to fight against them. President Wilson does not like the idea of permanent commissions watching the military state of Germany. I do not favor permanent commissions, but we must have a means of immediate inquiry in case of need.

House. I must say that I do not share President Wilson's feelings about the commissions. In my opinion, if a power is only doing what it has the right to do, it has no reason to resent any kind of inspection.

Lloyd George. Yes, on the condition that the inspection be universal. But we must agree that an inspection made by a foreign power in a single country, during perhaps fifty years, could cause some difficulties.

The King. One objection against the occupation is the following: Germany will not be very dangerous before twenty or twenty-five years; it is precisely then that Germany will have so recovered that the occupation will end.

Lloyd George. Then I understand that Your Majesty does not favor a prolonged occupation of German cities?

The King. All the military leaders that I see, including your generals, tell me that the German army no longer exists. The danger is not during the coming years, but much later, and Belgian opinion would not favor a prolonged occupation.

Lloyd George. About this, English opinion is the same.

Clemenceau. I am no longer asking for that prolonged occupation.

The King. In addition, we have no interest in making the Rhenish provinces suffer, which might lead them to envy Saxony or Bavaria, and where purely German sentiment might be reinforced by that.

Clemenceau. On the contrary, we have an interest in treating the Rhineland relatively well.

Orlando. The only policy to follow in Germany is to try to profit from the divisions between Catholics and Protestants, and the Rhineland is Catholic.

The King. I myself will raise the question of Luxembourg. Negotiation is going on between us and the government of Luxembourg; we would be happy to see France approve of this negotiation, and to declare that its success would conform to the interests of the two countries in question and of all of Europe.

Clemenceau. May I ask what are the intentions of Belgium? I have understood that she wanted the annexation of Luxembourg.

Hymans. We have simply asked that France favor the free rapprochement of the two countries.

Clemenceau. You cannot ask me to tell the people of Luxembourg: "I want you to become Belgians." They must be left their freedom of choice. You know very well that I am not claiming Luxembourg for France.

I consider the present government of Luxembourg to be German, and I do not wish to enter into relations with it. That is why I did not send a plenipotentiary there. You have done so; that is very good. I ask only one thing: the disappearance of the German dynasty.

Concerning the fate of Luxembourg, the conference should be approached by Luxembourg herself. I ask nothing for France. I ask that Luxembourg say what she wants. I will not send anyone there; I am ready to withdraw the last French soldier. You have acted differently; you have acted in Luxembourg, and you have provoked protests.

The King. There have also been protests against French propaganda.

Clemenceau. A French general intervened in Luxembourg's affairs; I punished him. This defines my attitude. I will be happy if Luxembourg becomes Belgian; but this change must be made by the Luxemburgers.

The King. We did not seek out the people of Luxembourg; it is the government of Luxembourg which entered into negotiations with us.

Clemenceau. The only thing which I do not accept is that M. Hymans ask me to invite Luxembourg to talk with Belgium. That is a pressure that I cannot agree to do. What I myself want is to withdraw my troops from Luxembourg, and to play no role whatever in that country. I complain about your government's procedures, which wants to force our hand. If Luxembourg was Belgian, I repeat that I would be very happy.

The King. The acquisition of Luxembourg would give France a bad frontier. On the other hand, if Luxembourg is reunited to Belgium, the violation of the least part of Luxembourg's frontier would immediately set into action the participation of the Belgian army.

Clemenceau. All that I wish is that no one force my hand.

The King. I should remind you that at several times during the course of the war, we received assurances concerning Luxembourg from President Poincaré, M. Ribot, and other French statesmen. In the past Luxembourg was united to Belgium. Some Luxemburgian deputies sat among Belgian deputies after the revolution of 1830.

Clemenceau. Do not ask me to throw the people of Luxembourg into the arms of the Belgians; I do not know their feelings. All that I know is that we had 1,500 Luxemburgian volunteers in the French army, and that there were only 170 in the Belgian army. However, I am not saying that in order to claim Luxembourg.

The King. The Luxemburgian colony in Paris consists of 30,000 persons, and it is undoubtedly that which furnished volunteers for the French army. The invasion of Belgium was so rapid that Belgian Luxembourg itself could not furnish us with soldiers.

Clemenceau. The advice which I gave to M. Hymans, when he came to Paris, was to leave things to work themselves out. He did not listen to me, he caused agitation there. The only thing I do not want is that the reunion of Luxembourg to Belgium take place in such a way that it would seem to be a setback for France.

The King. There has been French agitation in Luxembourg.

Clemenceau. I already told you how I punished the general who interfered in Luxembourg's affairs. I said to M. Hymans: "I shall inflict punishment if you inform me of other acts." He did not inform me of any.

Believe me, it is easy for us to agree.

Lloyd George. This affair must be settled, but by what means?

Clemenceau. At the conference, President Wilson and Mr. Lansing proposed a plebiscite. M. Hymans said that the time was not favorable and that it would be better to wait. If you have a decent way to resolve the problem, indicate it. I do not want to do anything about Luxembourg. Belgium's friendship for France is worth ten Luxembourgs. But I ask you to do the thing as it should be done.

Lloyd George. What is the means?

Clemenceau. I have not suggested it. But I refuse to negotiate with the present government of Luxembourg, which is a German government.

The King. There has been a change of personnel. Herr Eyschen[3] is no longer in power.

Clemenceau. I only ask you to assist me in overcoming all obstacles to what you wish. Undoubtedly the best means is to consult the population, which can be done under American occupation, General Pershing being responsible for the maintenance of order.

The King. The misfortune is that there is no clear orientation; the people of Luxembourg await an indication from the great powers.

Clemenceau. At this moment you make them speak. It is probable that, if one put to them, purely and simply, the question of knowing what they wish to become, they would reply: "We wish to remain what we are." But if one asked them: "Would you like to be attached to France or to Belgium?" we do not know what they will say.

Lloyd George. What is the language of Luxembourg?

The King. The official language is French, but the popular language is a low-German dialect.

Lloyd George. What is the political regime?

Hymans. Since 1867, Luxembourg is independent and neutralized. Hence the danger that it constitutes for its neighbors.

Clemenceau. I hope that Your Majesty will pardon me for the frankness of my language. From the first day, I have said to Belgium that I ask nothing for France, and I have added: "If you remain tranquil, no difficulty will arise between us." I want to reach agreement with you, but I also want to avoid 150 deputies coming to tell me: "Luxembourg wishes to be French; you have not allowed that, you have given her to Belgium." I am with you; but it is necessary only that what takes place should not appear a defeat for France.

[Paris] April 4, 1919, 4 p.m.

Clemenceau. I have just studied the report of the expert commission on the frontier between Bohemia and Germany. The solution is very complicated and makes all sorts of changes, some of which include cessions of territory to the Germans; that seems very

---

[3] Paul Eyschen had been Prime Minister of Luxembourg from 1889 until his death on October 12, 1915. There had been several prime ministers since that date. The current incumbent was Émile Reuter.

useless to me. The simplest is to maintain the frontier such as it was before the war, and to leave to Bohemia and Germany the task of making territorial exchanges between themselves as they judge appropriate.

As for the question of the Germans of Bohemia, that has nothing to do with the preliminaries of peace between us and Germany.

Lloyd George. It is indeed a question related to the division of the former Austrian Empire. I agree with you that the old frontier between Bohemia and Germany should be respected. As for the question of Teschen, that is also part of the Austrian questions.

House. That solution seems the best to me. On the subject of Teschen, we could establish a commission which will make a report to the League of Nations.

Clemenceau. The question of Ratibor and of Upper Silesia, which concerns both Poland and Bohemia, could be treated at the same time as the Polish questions.

Thus we conclude—reserving the opinion of President Wilson— to maintain purely and simply the old frontier between Bohemia and Germany.

An exchange of comments takes place on the agenda. Colonel House proposes that the financial experts be heard tomorrow at eleven o'clock, in order to reach a decision in the afternoon. The meeting will be held at the Place des États-Unis, so that Colonel House can immediately ascertain the opinion of President Wilson.

M. Orlando makes known that, in a conversation between the English, American, and Italian delegates and the German financial commission at the Chateau de Villette, the Germans insisted particularly upon the necessity of stipulations informing Germany clearly about the obligations which will be imposed upon her. "Germany," they say, "will work and do what she can to pay; but she cannot bear remaining in uncertainty about her obligations."

Colonel House believes that the moment has come to make a decision and that it is possible to do it quickly.

Mantoux, I, 139-50.

From Norman Hezekiah Davis and Vance Criswell McCormick, with Enclosure

My dear Mr. President: [Paris] April 4, 1919.

Supplementing our conversation with you of last night, we hand you herewith a schedule showing the basic text of the reparation clauses and categories of damage, together with the comment and reserves in regard thereto made by the representatives of the Four Powers who have been participating in the discussions.

These comments and reserves are taken from the record and may appear to you to be somewhat formidable. As a matter of fact we believe that serious question exists only with reference to Article 3, to which the French appear to make serious objection. There is also the hesitation of the British relative to the acceptance of the categories. We have reason to believe that the Italians are prepared to accept our text in toto.

Sincerely yours,   Norman H. Davis
Vance C. McCormick

TLS (WP, DLC).

E N C L O S U R E

REPARATION CLAIMS

TEXT

1. The Allied and Associated Governments affirm the responsibility of the enemy States for causing all the loss and damage to which the Allied and Associated Governments and their nationals have been subjected as a consequence of the war imposed upon them by the aggression of the enemy States.

2. The Allied and Associated Governments recognize that the financial resources of the enemy States are not unlimited, and, after taking into account permanent diminutions of such resources which will result from other treaty clauses, they judge that it will be impracticable for enemy States to make com-

BRITISH, FRENCH, ITALIAN AND U. S. COMMENT AND RESERVES.

Article 1 is agreed to subject to:

(a) Italian reserve with respect to substituting for "enemy States" where it first occurs, the word "Germany," thus proclaiming the liability of Germany for all consequences of the war of herself and her Allies;

(b) French reserve as to political policy of incorporating article 1 and the first half of Article 2, as this is in the nature of a preamble and might be omitted or placed in the general preambles of the Treaty.

Article 2 is agreed to, subject to the observation of the French that the phrase "to the extent of their utmost capacity" is inconsistent with the 30-year limitation in Article 3.

With regard to the parenthetical reference to categories, it is left undetermined as to whether these shall or shall not

plete reparation for all such loss and damage. The Allied and Associated Governments, however, require that the enemy States, to the extent of their utmost capacity, make compensation for all damage done to the civilian population of the Allied or Associated Powers and to their property by the aggression of the enemy States by land, by sea, and from the air.

(Reference to Categories may be inserted here.)

3. The amount of such damage for which compensation is to be made should be determined by an inter-allied commission, to be constituted in such form as the Allied and Associated Governments shall forthwith determine. This commission shall examine into the claims and give to the enemy States a just opportunity to be heard. The findings of the commission as to the amount of damage defined in Article 2 shall be concluded and communicated to the enemy States on or before May 1, 1921. The commission shall also, concurrently, draw up a schedule of payments up to or within the total sum thus due, which in their judgment Germany should be able to liquidate within a period of thirty years, and this schedule of payments shall then be communicated to Germany as representing the extent of her obligations.

4. The inter-allied commission shall further have discretion to modify from time to time

be incorporated in the first instance in the treaty as to be proposed to Germany. The British, French and Italians regard this as indispensable; the United States reserved their view as being a question of strategy to be subsequently decided.

Article 3 is agreed to, except as to France, which rejects the paragraph particularly in that it does not insure the complete payment of the debt to be established in accordance with Article 2. The French contend that the Commission should be required to secure complete payment but have discretion so as to permit such proportion of this as may be necessary to be paid in marks and German internal bonds.

Article 4 is accepted, subject to any modifications which might be required if Article 3 the date and mode of the schedule of payments fixed in clause 3, and, if necesary, to extend them in part beyond thirty years, by acceptance of long period bonds or otherwise, if subsequently such modification or extension appear necessary, after giving Germany a just opportunity to be heard.

5. In order to enable the Allied and Associated Powers to proceed at once to the restoration of their industrial and economic life, pending the full determination of their claim, Germany shall pay in such installments and in such manner (whether in gold, commodities, ships, securities or otherwise) as the inter-allied commission may fix, in 1919 and 1920, the equivalent of $5,000,000,000 gold towards the liquidation of the above claims, out of which the expenses of the Army of Occupation subsequent to the Armistice shall first be met, provided that such supplies of food and raw materials as may be judged by the Allied and Associated Governments to be essential to enable Germany to meet her obligations for reparation may, with the approval of the Allied and Associated Governments, be paid for out of the above sum.

6. The successive installments paid over by the enemy States in satisfaction of the above claims shall be divided by the Allied and Associated Governments in proportions which have been determined

is changed in accordance with the French view.

Article 5 is accepted by the British and Americans. The French and Italians propose the following alternative text:

"Germany shall pay, in such installments and in such manner (either in gold, commodities, ships, securities or otherwise) as the inter-allied commission may fix, in 1919 and 1920, the equivalent of $5,000,000,000 gold, of which $4,500,000,000 shall be applied to meet the expenses of the Armies of Occupation and the reparation of damage above contemplated, and $500,000,000 shall be applied to the payment of supplies of food and raw materials, approved and controlled by the Allied and Associated [Governments] for the purpose of supplying Germany up to May 1, 1921."

Article 6 is agreed to, subject to the Italian reservation that in the event of the inability of the Allied and Associated Governments to agree upon a division of the reparation payments, the question shall be upon by them in advance, on a basis of general equity, and of the rights of each.

7. The payments mentioned above do not include restitution in kind of cash taken away, seized or sequestrated, nor the restitution in kind of animals, objects of every nature and securities taken away, seized, or sequestrated in the cases in which it proves possible to identify them in enemy territory. If at least half the number of the animals taken by the enemy from the invaded territories cannot be identified and returned, the balance, up to a total of half the number taken, shall be delivered by Germany by way of restitution.

N.B. The attention of the four chiefs of the respective Governments is to be called to the following:

(a) That necessary guarantees to insure the due collection of the sums fixed for reparation should be planned; and

(b) That there are other financial clauses which this conference has not been charged to deal with.

arbitrated by or under the direction of the President of the United States.

Article 7 is agreed to, subject to the British reservation of the word "cash" in the first sentence. The British have proposed that the propriety of including cash be decided by the American delegation. The French reserve the question of their willingness to accept such decision.

ANNEX

Compensation may be claimed under Article 2 for the following categories of damage:

(1) Personal injury to or death of civilians resulting from acts of war on land and sea and from the air or mistreatment by the enemy.

(2) Damage to the civilian population resulting from the absence, incapacitation or death of persons serving with the forces and which damage is met by pensions or allowances of like nature made by the State. (French scale to govern.)

(3) Damage to civilians resulting from their being forced by the enemy to labor without just remuneration or abstain from labor.

(4) Damage to or interference with non-military property, as from date of damage or interference, directly caused by acts of war on land and sea and from the air, or illegal acts of the enemy or war measures in the nature of requisitions or sequestrations, taken by the enemy.

(5) Damage in the form of levies, fines and other similar exactions imposed by the enemy upon the civilian population.

(6) Damage resulting from acts in violation of international law (as found by the Commission on Responsibilities) and in violation of formal engagements.

NOTE: Where the State or other public authority has already itself made compensation for the damage, it may present the claim in its own behalf.

(These categories are accepted, subject to the following:

   (a) British do not oppose, but state present instructions from Mr. Lloyd George do not permit them to accept all of the categories;[1]

   (b) French propose additional categories: (1) expense of relief to prisoners of war, (2) Expense involved in repurchase of Marks;

   (c) Italians state they construe Category 6 to permit of claim for expense in providing defense against air raids and gas attack. Other delegations do not accept this construction.)

T MS (WP, DLC).

[1] See the British interpretation of Clause 2, printed as an Annex to the Second Anglo-American Draft of an Accord on Reparations, April 2, 1919.

From Robert Lansing, with Enclosure

My dear Mr. President: Paris, April 4, 1919.

I am enclosing to you a memorandum which was handed to me today by Mr. H. M. Robinson, who was a member of the Labor Commission with Mr. Gompers. I think that his views should receive careful consideration. They impressed me very much when he stated them to me orally at the time of a meeting of the Ministers of Foreign Affairs at which Mr. Barnes was present[1] and I followed closely his suggestions in regard to the course which I there took.

Mr. Robinson feels that a very serious injustice will be done to the American representatives of Labor if this matter should now be reopened after their departure for America.

           Faithfully yours,   Robert Lansing

TLS (WP, DLC).

[1] On April 1. See PPC, IV, 536-43.

ENCLOSURE

Paris, 4 April 1919

MEMORANDUM FROM Mr. H. M. Robinson
            TO   Hon. Robert Lansing
                    Secretary of State
SUBJECT: *Proposed Reopening of Work of Labor Commission*

The Commission on International Legislation for Labor held thirty-five meetings between February 1st and March 24th. Labor leaders of various countries were present at the meetings. The head of the Federation of Labor of the United States was President of the Commission, and M. Jouhaux,[1] head of the French Federation of Labor, sat in most of the meetings as a delegate.

As a result of unusually full discussion covering practically every word in the proposed draft convention for the setting up of a labor conference, and practically every word in every principle offered by the various delegates, the Commission finally adopted the Draft Convention and principles now under discussion by a unanimous vote,[2] the Japanese delegation alone held a reservation on Article 19 of the Draft Convention.

The members of the Commission and the Commission as a whole regarded their work as completed, and asked to be permitted to present through their president, Mr. Samuel Gompers, to a plenary session of the Peace Conference, the Draft Convention and principles so unanimously adopted.

My understanding is that this was objected to at the time by Mr. Lloyd George.

There have been in Paris during all of these sessions, five of the Presidents of various labor organizations in the United States and Mr. Andrew Foruseth, President of the International Seamen's Union, and many other labor leaders. All of the American labor leaders have left for home, having left England a few days since, and I am confident they left without the slightest idea that the work so thoroughly done would be undone.

I submit that the work of the Commission as such is complete: that the report should go to the Peace Conference, accompanied by memoranda of any amendments offered by Japan for which reservations were made: that the Peace Conference then adopt the report with such changes and amendments as it deems proper: that to reopen the work of the Commission, particularly under the conditions, would be irregular and unfair, and would be fraught with very great danger for all: that the American labor leaders would certainly feel that they had been tricked if the work of the Commission were reopened: that the Draft Convention itself provides ample means for the making of amendments, if any are desired after the Peace Conference has acted upon the report they could be made at the first conference, which it is proposed shall be held in October, where it is fair to assume all parties would be properly represented.

I attach an excerpt from one of the Paris papers[3] which may give you a hint as to what is going on.

T MS (WP, DLC).
  [1] That is, Léon Jouhaux.
  [2] About which, see H. M. Robinson to WW, March 24, 1919.
  [3] It is missing.

From Henry Mauris Robinson

Dear Mr. President: Hotel Crillon, 4 April 1919

At a meeting of the Conference of Five[1] on Tuesday, April 1st, Mr. Barnes of the British Labor Ministry, Vice-President of the Commission on International Legislation for Labor, made a request for the holding of a plenary session of the Peace Conference to submit informally the report of the Commission.

His request was based on:

1. Need for best publicity for the work of the Commission.

2. In order that the Commission might be set up again to pass upon suggested amendments, to the proposed Draft Convention for a permanent conference, that might be offered as a result of the publicity.

The Commission held thirty-five meetings between February 1st and March 24th. Labor leaders of various countries were present at the meetings. Mr. Samuel Gompers of the United States was President of the Commission. M. Jouhaux, head of the French Federation of Labor, attended most of the meetings as delegate. In addition five of the heads of various labor organizations of the United States, and Andrew Furuseth, President of the International Seamen's Union, were present at some or all of the meetings.

The discussion covered practically every word in the proposed Draft Convention for the setting up of labor conferences, and practically every word in every principle offered by various delegates.

The Commission adopted the Draft Convention and principles by unanimous vote, except that the Japanese delegation alone held a reservation on Article 19.

A copy of the Draft Convention and of the substitute amendment for Article 19 were sent you under date of March 24th.

Everyone regarded the work as completed. No indication that it was proposed to open up for a new discussion the various articles had been made until this request of Vice-President Barnes. This request was made after all the American labor leaders had left for home and, I am certain, without the slightest idea that the work so thoroughly done could again be gone into by the Commission.

I am fearful both of the purpose and the result of a reopening in the Commission of the authority to amend the Draft Convention as reported. I am clearly of the opinion that the Draft Convention, accompanied by any amendments which may be offered by Japan, for which reservations were made, should be submitted to the Peace Conference, and that it lies within the competence of that conference to adopt the report with such changes and amendments as it deems proper: that the Draft Convention provides ample means for the making of amendments by its own members: that a conference is planned for October when amendments could be made: that to reopen the work of the Commission, particularly under these conditions, would be irregular, unfair, and fraught with very great danger for all: that the American labor leaders would certainly feel that they had been tricked if the Commission were again to act upon the Draft Convention: that, if the matter is again opened for the Commission's action, it would be entirely possible to force the United States delegation into a position where it would have to make a separate report, and where because of constitutional limitations, the United States could not become a party to the Draft Convention.

To my mind this is a very great danger. I have spoken to Mr. Secretary Lansing with regard to the matter, and he shares my fears.   Very respectfully yours,   Henry M. Robinson

TLS (WP, DLC).
   [1] That is, the Council of Foreign Ministers.

William Phillips to the American Commissioners

Washington April 4, 1919

1432. Your 1421, April 1st. Please see Secretary of War's message to the President forwarded today,[1] which was drafted with concurrence of General March. I share Secretary Baker's view and believe that the establishment of a zone six miles in width and of such great length would tend to convey the impression to the people of Siberia that foreign governments had undertaken to control not only for police purposes but also politically and commercially a considerable part of Siberian territory and that the use of the term "zone" would afford the enemies of inter-allied control a good opportunity for criticising the altruistic purposes of the United States and its associates. Is not a zone of occupation unnecessary in view of the great distances between stations? It would seem that the same purpose might be accomplished by limiting military activity to preservation of order along the railroad rather than to inject a political character which might readily follow the establishment of a zone of any definite width.   Phillips,   Acting.

T telegram (WP, DLC).
   [1] That is, NDB to WW, April 3, 1919.

From William Edward Lunt and Others, with Enclosure[1]

[Paris] April 4, 1919

From: Chiefs of the Italian Division, the Balkan Division, the Austro-Hungarian Division, the Division of Boundary Geography, and the Division of Economics.
To: President Wilson.
Subject: Disposition of Fiume.

The following statement of facts and opinions is respectfully submitted for the President's consideration:

1) The port of Fiume is vitally necessary to the economic life of Jugo-Slavia.

2) It has no economic significance for Italy, except as its development would prevent Italy from controlling trade which might otherwise be artificially deflected to Trieste.

3) The large business interests of Fiume, the banking houses, and the shipping are mainly in Hungarian and Jugo-Slav hands. Italian capital did not develop the port. The Italians constitute the small traders and shop keepers and to some extent the professional classes.

4) According to the last official census the Italians constituted only a plurality of the population of Fiume, even when its artificial separation from the Slavic Susak is maintained.

   [1] This memorandum was not transmitted to Wilson until April 6. In the afternoon of April 5, Johnson and Miller had discussed an earlier draft of the memorandum, and Miller had promised to submit a written comment on the subject. Miller received a copy of the final draft of the memorandum in the late evening of April 5. The next morning, he dictated a letter to Johnson and handed it to him at the Crillon. Johnson, in turn, attached Miller's letter to this memorandum and forwarded both to Wilson on the same day. See Miller, *My Diary at the Conference of Paris*, I, 225-26.
   The "Experts" who signed the memorandum of April 4, 1919, had been arguing consistently and strongly for the award of Fiume (and Dalmatia, as well) to Yugoslavia. For a narrative of their recommendations to this date, see René Albrecht-Carrié, *Italy at the Paris Peace Conference* (New York, 1938), pp. 117-23. Albrecht-Carrié, pp. 417-18 and 424-28, prints all their memoranda on Fiume and the Adriatic question to April 4, 1919, including the memorandum cited in n. 1 to T. N. Page to the American Mission, March 28, 1919.
   The "Experts' " memorandum of April 4, 1919, was also a rebuke to Mezes, who, in a letter to House on March 16, 1919, had recommended the award of Fiume and the Dalmatian islands to Italy. As Albrecht-Carrié, p. 123, says, the "Experts' " memorandum reflected their "indignation" evoked by Mezes' recommendation. It should also be pointed out that the memorandum of April 4 was the "Experts' " first direct appeal to Wilson, over Mezes' head, on the Italian question.

5) The Italian plurality in the restricted Fiume:
   a) Is of recent development (since 1880 or 1890).
   b) Includes an unknown but considerable number who have not given up Italian citizenship.
   c) Has probably resulted from artificial encouragement by the Hungarian government, which had a comprehensible interest in developing an alien rather than a Slav majority in the city.
6) The Italian agitation in favor of annexing Fiume is only a few months old. Last summer it was generally admitted in high Italian circles that Fiume would and should go to Jugo-Slavia.

In view of the foregoing considerations the American specialists are unanimously of the opinion:

1) That Fiume should be given to the Jugo-Slav State without restriction.

This solution is the only one which in our opinion will prove attractive at the same time to Jugo-Slav capital and to outside capital (Hungarian, Czecho-Slovak, etc.); it will best serve the vital economic interests of both city and state; and in view of the facts regarding the nature and origin of the Italian population, it seems to us the most just morally.

2) That the interests of the Italian minority of greater Fiume should be assured by the establishment of adequate guarantees of protection.

Similar guarantees should be extended, in a spirit of equality and justice, to the other Italian minorities in Jugo-Slavia, and to the much larger Slavic minorities in Trieste and other areas transferred to Italy by the recommended new frontier.

3) That it is unwise to make of Fiume a free city.

Our unanimity of opinion on this point is due to the approximate equality of the two antagonistic elements of the population, the testimony of observers as to the inability of the Italians of Fiume properly to administer the port, the justified sensitiveness of the Slavs toward any infringement of sovereignty over their only good port and chief commercial city, and the serious economic and political disadvantages which such infringement would entail under the peculiar physical conditions which obtain at Fiume. (See attached letter by Mr. Miller.)

4) That if for reasons not connected with the best interests of the city and its hinterland it is deemed necessary that Fiume be made a free city, its right of local self-government should be accompanied by the following safe-guards of the interests of the Jugo-Slav State:
   a) The moles, docks, basins, and other instrumentalities of the port must be under Jugo-Slav sovereignty as well as Jugo-

Slav ownership, and it must be possible for the Jugo-Slavs to acquire the land and other property needed for their extension.

b) The railways and other means of communication with the interior (e.g., telephones, telegraphs, and postal service) must likewise be under Jugo-Slav control.

c) There must be no discrimination with respect to political and economic rights of any kind, nor with respect to schools and churches.

d) The city (except for a possible free port) must be included within the Slav customs frontier.

e) The organization of the city must be such as to abolish the present artificial division of the port into two parts.

These safe-guards are necessary: *1*) To ensure conditions of sufficient stability to justify expenditures by the government and by Jugo-Slav and foreign private capitalists for the improvement and development of the port; *2*) To prevent Italian interference with the development of the port and with its full use; *3*) To give the Slavs a fair opportunity to achieve a position in the industrial and political life of the community strong enough to safe-guard their vital interests.   W E Lunt   Chief of the Italian Division.

Clive Day   Chief of the Balkan Division.

Charles Seymour   Chief of the Austro-
Hungarian Division.

Douglas Johnson   Chief of the Division
of Boundary Geography.

Allyn A. Young   Chief of the Division
of Economics.

TS MS (WP, DLC).

E N C L O S U R E

David Hunter Miller to Douglas Wilson Johnson

Dear Major Johnson: [Paris] 6 April, 1919.

In our conversation yesterday you asked my views as to the creation of an independent territory comprising, with certain exceptions, the districts of Fiume and Susak under the hypothesis that the territory surrounding these districts was entirely within the limits of Jugo-Slavia, and under the further hypothesis that the entire port facilities of Fiume as well as any land necessary for their extension would likewise be under the sovereignty of Jugo-Slavia, and that the railroads running into Fiume and the other means of communication with the interior, such as telephones, telegraphs, and postal service, should be under the control of Jugo-Slavia.

I do not doubt that such an arrangement is a legal possibility, but there are certain legal questions to which attention should be directed as they involve matters of practical importance.

Under the hypothesis the territory in question would be independent but the character of the locus is such as to make it doubtful whether that independence could be more than theoretical.

From the maps which you showed me it appears that what I will call the proposed "free area" while of very irregular shape, would run along the coast for ten or twelve miles, extending into the interior for a very short distance except in the center of the strip where it would be perhaps five or six miles wide, and even from this area would have to be deducted all of the docks, etc., which extend over most although not all of the waterfront. Furthermore, the control of the railroads by Jugo-Slavia would result in dividing the territory to be administered in the free area into three parts; the first what may be called the interior on the land side of the railroad, and the other two small strips of the coast between the railroad and the sea, lying on either side of the docks.

It should be added that under your statement of the hypothesis the area would for customs purposes be part of Jugo-Slavia, and that the population of the area is perhaps 60,000 persons, of whom no doubt a certain number reside in the portion devoted to the docks.

Under any form of agreement it seems to me that the difficulties of the administration of such a very small area as an independent unit would be enormous, and to be successful would require almost complete co-operation and harmony between the government of the free area and the government of Jugo-Slavia. Take for example the question of police. The jurisdiction of police over the docks, etc. would necessarily be Jugo-Slav, and also similar jurisdiction over the railroads and their appurtenances, and even if the latter were not technically under the sovereignty but only under the control of Jugo-Slavia. Thus the police of the free area would be over three distinct pieces of territory with the consequent necessity of free passage and repassage over the railroad.

It may be assumed, although you did not so state, that there is one water supply for the territory which would be within the free area, and for the docks, etc. Such a water supply would be under two distinct sovereignties and yet would of necessity be under a single management; indeed, it would be quite important to determine in making such an agreement where the source of the water supply of Fiume was located, for if this source is in the interior outside of the free area a still very difficult complication would be presented.

Without attempting to go into further detail I may mention that somewhat similar questions of administration would be presented in regard to the protection of health, the sewage system, the prevention of fire, and the means of communication between the two areas.

These matters are not mentioned for the purpose of expressing any opinion upon the questions of policy involved, but chiefly, as you suggest, in order, if such an arrangement is to be made, that very detailed knowledge of the local conditions may be obtained so that so far as possible future difficulties may be foreseen and perhaps avoided.

Very sincerely yours,　David Hunter Miller

P.S. The two maps[1] and the memorandum which you handed me are returned herewith.　D.H.M.

TLS (WP, DLC).
[1] The two maps cannot be found. However, Wilson, in WW to EMH, April 7, 1919, refers to them and says that he has to stand by them.

A Memorandum[1]

MEMORANDUM OF RESERVATIONS
*presented by the American Representatives
to the report of the*
COMMISSION ON RESPONSIBILITIES
April 4th, 1919

The American members of the Commission on Responsibilities, in presenting their reservations to the report of the Commission, declare that they are as earnestly desirous as the other members of the Commission that those persons responsible for causing the Great War and those responsible for violations of the laws and customs of war should be punished for their crimes, moral and legal. The differences which have arisen between them and their colleagues lie in the means of accomplishing this common desire. The American members therefore submit to the Conference on the Preliminaries of Peace a memorandum of the reasons for their dissent from the report of the Commission and suggestions as to the course of action which they consider should be adopted in dealing with the subjects upon which the Commission on Responsibilities was directed to report.

Preliminary to a consideration of the points at issue and the irreconcilable differences which have developed and which make this dissenting report necessary, we desire to express our high appreciation of the conciliatory and considerate spirit manifested

[1] About the provenance of this memorandum, see n. 4 to the minutes of the Council of Four printed at April 2, 1919, 4 p.m.

by our colleagues throughout the many and protracted sessions of the Commission. From the first of these held on February 3, 1919, there was an earnest purpose shown to compose the differences which existed, to find a formula acceptable to all, and to render, if possible, a unanimous report. That this purpose failed was not because of want of effort on the part of any member of the Commission. It failed because after all the proposed means of adjustment had been tested with frank and open minds, no practicable way could be found to harmonize the differences without an abandonment of principles which were fundamental. This the representatives of the United States could not do and they could not expect it of others.

In the early meetings of the Commission and the three Sub-Commissions appointed to consider various phases of the subject submitted to the Commission the American members declared that there were two classes of responsibilities, those of a legal nature and those of a moral nature, that legal offenses were justiciable and liable to trial and punishment by appropriate tribunals, but that moral offenses, however iniquitous and infamous and however terrible in their results, were beyond the reach of judicial procedure and subject only to moral sanctions.

While this principle seems to have been adopted by the Commission in the report so far as the responsibility for the authorship of the war is concerned, the Commission appeared unwilling to apply it in the case of indirect responsibility for violations of the laws and customs of war. It is respectfully submitted that this inconsistency was due in large measure to a determination to punish certain persons, high in authority, particularly the heads of enemy States, even though heads of States were not hitherto legally responsible for the atrocious acts committed by subordinate authorities. To such an inconsistency the American members of the Commission were unwilling to assent, and from the time it developed that this was the unchangeable determination of certain members of the Commission they doubted the possibility of a unanimous report. Nevertheless they continued their efforts in behalf of the adoption of a consistent basis of principle, appreciating the desirability of unanimity if it could be attained. That their efforts were futile they deeply regret.

With the manifest purpose of trying and punishing those persons to whom reference has been made, it was proposed to create a high tribunal with an international character and to bring before it those who had been marked as responsible not only for directly ordering illegal acts of war but for having abstained from preventing such illegal acts.

Appreciating the importance of a judicial proceeding of this nature, as well as its novelty, the American Representatives laid before the Commission a memorandum upon the constitution and procedure of a tribunal of an international character which, in their opinion, should be formed by the union of existing national military tribunals or commissions of admitted competence in the premises. And in view of the fact that "customs" as well as "laws" were to be considered, they filed another memorandum, attached hereto, as to the principles which should guide the Commission in considering and reporting on this subject.

The practice proposed in the memorandum as to the military commissions was in part accepted, but the purpose of constituting a high tribunal for the trial of persons exercising sovereign rights was persisted in and the abstention from preventing violations of the laws and customs of war and of humanity was insisted upon. It was frankly stated that the purpose was to bring before this tribunal the ex-Kaiser of Germany, and that the jurisdiction of the tribunal must be broad enough to include him even if he had not directly ordered the violations.

To the unprecedented proposal of creating an international criminal tribunal and to the doctrine of negative criminality the American members refused to give their assent.

On January 25, 1919, the Conference on the Preliminaries of Peace in plenary session recommended the appointment of a commission to examine and to report to the Conference upon the following five points:

1. The responsibility of the authors of the war.
2. The facts as to the violations of the Laws and Customs of War committed by the forces of the German Empire and its Allies, on land, on sea, and in the air in the course of the present war.
3. The degree of responsibility for these crimes attaching to particular members of the enemy forces, including members of the General Staffs, and other individuals, however highly placed.
4. The constitution and procedure of a Tribunal appropriate for the trial of these crimes.
5. Any other matters cognate or ancillary to the above points which may arise in the course of the enquiry, and which the Commission finds it useful and proper to take into consideration.

The conclusions reached by the Commission as to the responsibility of the authors of the War with which the Representatives of the United States agree are thus stated:

The war was premeditated by the Central Powers together with their Allies, Turkey and Bulgaria, and was the result of acts deliberately committed in order to make it unavoidable.

Germany, in agreement with Austria-Hungary, deliberately worked to defeat all the many conciliatory proposals made by the Entente Powers and their repeated efforts to avoid war.

The American representatives are happy to declare that they not only concur in these conclusions, but also in the process of reasoning by which they are reached and justified. However, in addition to the evidence adduced by the Commission, based for the most part upon official memoranda issued by the various governments in justification of their attitude toward the Serbian question and the War which resulted because of the deliberate determination of Austria-Hungary and Germany to crush that gallant little country which blocked the way to the Dardanelles and to the realization of their larger ambitions, the American Representatives call attention to four documents, three of which have been made known by his Excellency Milenko R. Vesnitch, Serbian Minister at Paris. Of the three, the first is reproduced for the first time, and two of the others were only published during the sessions of the Commission.

The first of these documents is a report of Von Wiesner,[2] the Austro-Hungarian agent sent to Sarajevo to investigate the assassination at that place on June 28, 1914, of the Archduke Francis Ferdinand, heir to the Austro-Hungarian throne, and the Duchess of Hohenberg, his morganatic wife.

The material portion of this report in the form of a telegram is as follows:

"Herr von Wiesner, to the Foreign Ministry, Vienna

Sarajevo, 15 July 1914, 1:10 P.M.

Cognizance on the part of the Serbian Government, participation in the murderous assault or in its preparation and supplying the weapons is proved by nothing, nor is it even to be suspected. On the contrary there are indications which cause this to be rejected." (1)

The second is likewise a telegram, dated Berlin, July 25, 1914, from Count Szoegany,[3] Austro-Hungarian Ambassador at Berlin, to the Minister of Foreign Affairs at Vienna,[4] and reads as follows:

"Here it is generally taken for granted that in case of a possible refusal on the part of Serbia, our immediate declaration of war will be coincident with military operations. Delay in beginning military operations is here considered as a great danger because of the intervention of other Powers. We are urgently advised to proceed at once and to confront the world with a fait accompli."

---

[2] Friedrich von Wiesner, legal counselor of the Austro-Hungarian Foreign Ministry in 1914.

[3] Ladislaus, Count von Szögyény-Marich.

[4] Leopold Anton Johann Sigismund Joseph Korsinus Ferdinand, Count von Berchtold von und zu Ungarschitz, Fratting, und Pullitz, Austro-Hungarian Foreign Minister, 1912-1915.

(2)

The third, likewise a telegram in cipher, marked "strictly confidential" and dated Berlin, July 27, 1914, two days after the Serbian reply to the Austro-Hungarian ultimatum and the day before the Austro-Hungarian declaration of war upon that devoted kingdom, was from the Austro-Hungarian Ambassador at Berlin to the Minister of Foreign Affairs at Vienna. The material portion of this document is as follows:

"The Secretary of State informed me very definitely and in the strictest confidence that in the near future possible proposals for mediation on the part of England would be brought to Your Excellency's knowledge by the German Government.

"The German Government gives its most binding assurance that *it does not in any way associate itself with the proposals*, on the contrary it is absolutely opposed to their consideration and only transmits them in compliance with the English request."

(3)

Of the English proposition, to which reference is made in the above telegram, the following may be quoted, which, under date of July 30, 1914, Sir Edward Grey, Secretary of State for Foreign Affairs, telegraphed to Sir Edward Goschen, British Ambassador at Berlin:

"If the peace of Europe can be preserved, and the present crisis safely passed, my own endeavor will be to promote some arrangement to which Germany could be a party, by which she could be assured that no aggressive or hostile policy would be pursued against her or her allies by France, Russia, and ourselves, jointly or separately." (4)

While comment on these telegrams would tend to weaken their force and effect, it may nevertheless be observed that the last of them was dated two days before the declaration of war by Germany against Russia, which might have been prevented, had not Germany, flushed with the hope of certain victory and of the fruits of conquest, determined to force the war.

The report of the Commission treats separately the violation of the neutrality of Belgium and of Luxemburg and reaches the conclusion, in which the American Representatives concur, that the neutrality of both of these countries was deliberately violated. The American Representatives believe, however, that it is not enough to state or to hold with the Commission that "the war was premeditated by the Central Powers," that "Germany, in agreement with Austria-Hungary deliberately worked to defeat all the many conciliatory proposals made by the Entente Powers and their repeated efforts to avoid war," and to declare that the neutrality of Belgium, guaranteed by the Treaty of the 19th April, 1839, and that of Luxembourg, guaranteed by the Treaty of the 11th May, 1867, were deliberately violated by Germany and Austria-Hungary. They are of the opinion that these acts should be condemned in no uncertain terms and that their perpetrators should be held up to the execration of mankind. They therefore propose that the Conference, accepting this portion of the report of the Commission, should nevertheless intervene and of its own initiative and on behalf of an outraged world adopt, proclaim, and give the widest publicity to the following recommendation and declaration:

It is recommended that the Conference of the Allied and Associated Governments issue at the time of the signature of a treaty of peace with an enemy power and annex the same to such treaty the following declaration:

DECLARATION BY THE REPRESENTATIVES OF
(NAMES OF COUNTRIES) IN CONFERENCE ASSEMBLED.

The moral right to wage war only exists when there is an imperative necessity to employ force in the protection of national life, in the maintenance of national right or in the defence of liberty and humanity.

War inspired by any other motive is wanton, needless and violative of international morality and justice. It cannot be justified.

Judged by this standard, the war which was begun in 1914 was unrighteous and indefensible. It was a war of aggression. The masters of the Central Powers, inflamed by the passion to possess the territory and sovereignty of others, entered upon a war of conquest, a war, which in magnitude, in waste of life and property, in merciless cruelties and in intolerable woes surpasses all wars of modern times. The evidence of this moral crime against mankind is convincing and conclusive.

Restrained by reverence for law which is inseparable from that high sense of justice which is essential to social order, the nations, which have suffered so grievously, may be unable to mete out through judicial channels retribution to the guilty. But the authors of this atrocious war ought not to pass unscathed into history. They should be summoned before the bar of universal public opinion to listen to the verdict which mankind passes upon the perpetrators of this greatest crime against the world.

Therefore in the name of those who sacrificed their lives that liberty might live, in the name of [the] helpless who endured unspeakable atrocities, the name of those who[se] ruined and plundered lands bear witness to the wickedness of the accused, in the name of humanity, of righteousness and of civilization, an outraged world denounces as infamous and demands the judgment of the ages against

Wilhelm of Hohenzollern, once German Emperor and King of
Prussia

etc.   Etc.   etc.

Note 1.
Herr v. Wiesner an Ministerium des Aeussern in Wien[5]

Sarajevo, 13 Juli 1914.
1 h. 10 p.m.

Mitwissenschaft serbischer Regierung, Leitung an Attentat oder
dessen Vorbereitung und Beistellung der Waffen durch nichts er-
wiesen oder auch nur zu vermuthen. Es bestehen vielmehr An-
haltspunkte, dies als ausgeschlossen anzusehen.

Note 2.
Graf Szoegyény an Minister des Aeussern in Wien

Berlin, 25 Juli 1914.

285.
Hier wird allgemein vorausgesetzt, dass auf eventuelle abweisende
Antwort Serbiens sofort unsere Kriegserklaerung verbunden mit
kriegerischen Operationen erfolgen werde. Man sieht hier in jeder
Verzoegerung des Beginnes der kriegerischen Operationen grosse
Gefahr betreffs Einmischung anderer Maechte. Man raet uns drin-
gendst sofort vorzugehen und Welt vor ein fait accompli zu stellen.

Note 3.
Graf Szoegyény an Ministerium des Aeussern in Wien.

Berlin, 27 Juli, 1914.

307. Streng vertraulich.
Staatssekretaer erklaerte mir in streng vertraulicher Form sehr
entschieden, dass in der naechsten Zeit eventuell Vermittlungs-
vorschlaege Englands durch die deutsche Regierung zur Kenntnis
Euer Exc. gebracht wuerden.

  Die deutsche Regierung versichere auf das Buendigste, *dass sie
sich in keiner Weise mit den Vorschlaegen identificire*, sogar entschieden gegen deren Beruecksichtigung sei und dieselben nur,
um der englischen Bitte Rechnung zu tragen, weitergebe.

Note 4. British Parliamentary Papers, Miscellaneous No. 10 (1915),
          Collected Documents relating to the Outbreak of the Eu-
          ropean War, p. 78.

CC MS (WP, DLC).

[5] We have corrected numerous misspellings and typographical errors in the following
German texts.

From Carter Glass

Washington. April 4th, 1919.

1441. From Glass to the President.

Pursuing the subject of former communication the Industrial Board appointed by Secretary Redfield has proceeded along lines distinctly not approved by other Members of Cabinet with whom I have conferred. Its actions involve a plain violation of Sherman Anti-Trust Law. My opinion on this point concurred in by Palmer, Baker and Burleson. Aside from this consideration, it is sought in effect to compel Railway Administration and other Government purchasing agencies to buy at figures established by Industrial Board in conference with certain Industrial interests against protest of Railway Administration. In my judgement the entire proceeding is contrary to the original proposal and is fundamentally wrong. We are trying to extricate the Industrial Board from its predicament, if it will consent to be rescued. Meanwhile it is my judgement, concurred in by Baker, Burleson and Palmer and Lane, that you should not be drawn into approval of the action taken by the Industrial Board.   Polk,   Acting.

T telegram (WP, DLC).

From Joseph Patrick Tumulty

The White House, 4 April 1919.

Number Fifty. Following is sent at request of Attorney General:

"I am opposed to granting any respite or clemency in the case of Eugene Debs. He was convicted on a charge of inciting wage-earners to refrain from aiding their Government in the war. In his speech to the jury he said:

'I have been accused of obstructing the war. I admit it. Gentlemen, I abhor war. I would oppose the war if I stood alone.'

He was given an eminently fair trial; the decision of the Supreme Court in affirming his conviction was unanimous. Since the decision of the Supreme Court he has publicly said that he despised the law and defied the Government. He has violently criticized the Supreme Court and announced that if an effort is made to imprison him a general strike will be called on May-Day headed by the Indiana miners. His attitude of challenging and defying the administration of law makes it imperative that no respite or clemency be shown at the present time. UNQUOTE.

I agree with the Attorney General in this conclusion.

Tumulty.

T telegram (WP, DLC).

From Alexander Mitchell Palmer

My dear Mr. President: [Washington] April 4, 1919.

You will remember that Mr. Gregory informed you that my Department was making a detailed study of all convictions under the Espionage Act,[1] with a view to recommending pardons or commutations of sentence in those cases in which such action was warranted in order to bring about a just result.

As a result of that investigation, I am forwarding to you herewith for your signature warrants for one pardon and fifty-one commutations of sentence, all of which I hereby recommend.

These represent cases in which my Department either doubts whether the facts justified the verdict or in which the sentence was excessive and probably intended for reduction after the war.

In some of these cases the trial judges have recommended immediate release. The investigation of so large a group of cases has necessarily involved considerable delay. I beg, therefore, to recommend that you give this matter as early attention as your more important engagements will permit.

Faithfully yours, A. Mitchell Palmer

TCL (WP, DLC).
[1] See Enclosure II printed with JPT to WW, March 1, 1919, Vol. 55 (first letter of that date).

From William Cox Redfield

My dear Mr. President: Washington April 4, 1919.

I am taking advantage of Secretary Baker's visit to Europe to transmit a letter, through him, to you. He is familiar with the subject matter and will doubtless give his own views concerning the problem I have in mind.

I understand that the Food Administration Grain Corporation will continue to act until the guaranty for the 1919 wheat is effectuated. There are two theories on which the Corporation may proceed. It may try to handle the matter so that the Treasury may stand no loss. It has handled the guaranty up to date on that basis, and, I understand, has a surplus to the credit of the government. Apparently Mr. Barnes indicated, in a statement to the House Committee, that the 1919 guaranty could be so managed as to prevent loss to the Treasury, and, from the record, it seems that it may be his policy to attempt this. I believe that there ought not to be a *desire* on the part of the Grain Corporation to handle the wheat primarily with a view to prevent loss to the Treasury. If the market price of wheat should be below the guaranteed price, I believe it would be in the national interest to let the price drop to the market price and let the Treasury stand the loss. If this is not done and the price of wheat is artificially kept up, then there will be great difficulty in the way of a resumption of industry throughout the Nation and much resulting hardship, especially to the less fortunate classes in the Nation.

I realize that it may be difficult to determine what the market price is or should be. I imagine that during the next year or two the forces of supply and demand will not normally operate. I assume that foreign nations will have central purchasing agencies and, in respect to wheat, this country will have a central control. In a measure, these centralized agencies will interfere with the operation of normal laws and the price of wheat and other foodstuffs will, to a certain extent, be the result of the negotiations of these national bodies. The point that I present involves mainly a matter of attitude and policy. There can be either the policy of trying to save the Treasury from loss, or the policy of assisting in a gradual return to the normal in the matter of prices. If Mr. Barnes could take the latter view, I think it would greatly assist us in the process of readjustment about which we are greatly concerned. Unless there is rapid readjustment and a resumption of business operations, we are in danger of having a considerable number of idle laborers, with consequent unrest. Manufacturers are showing a disposition to reduce their prices and some agreements have been reached, but they are naturally solicitous as to the course of food products. Obviously, if the price of wheat is artificially kept up, other food supplies will sympathetically remain high.

If you concur in this view, I trust you may see fit to intimate to Mr. Hoover and Mr. Barnes that you are sympathetic with the policy of facilitating readjustment by a return of all prices towards normal rather than with a policy, in respect to wheat, of preventing loss to the Treasury. Secretary Houston authorizes me to say that he shares the view that, if possible, prices should not, by government action, be prevented from returning towards the normal.

Yours very truly,   William C Redfield

TLS (WP, DLC).

From Walker Downer Hines

Dear Mr. President: Washington April 4, 1919.

I attach memorandum[1] which I have prepared for your considtion and which recommends that the railroads should be relinquished on December 31, 1919, and that if such relinquishment is to be made an announcement to that effect be made as soon as the extra session is called. I read this memorandum on the 2nd inst. to Secretaries Glass, Baker and Lane. They all authorized me to say that they concur in it. I strongly believe that the course therein outlined will be highly desirable. I would like to emphasize the following additional points:

I do not think it would be advisable to propose a relinquishment prior to December 31st. An earlier relinquishment would not afford the reasonable opportunity for permanent legislation, and it has already been announced that it is the intention to afford this opportunity. Besides, it is almost certain that any relinquishment earlier than December would come before there had been time for a reasonable adjustment of business conditions and would cause serious financial alarm whereas the proposal to relinquish on December 31st would give a much greater promise of business conditions improving to the point where the railroads would be reasonably able to pay their way.

If there should be made, say, in April or May, an announcement in accordance with the attached memorandum, the public would then have before it the railroad operations up to and including only February or March, as the case may be. Such operations will be exceedingly unfavorable because the business has fallen off substantially and it has been impossible to make any corresponding reduction in the expense. The disposition of financial interests will be to assume that these unfavorable conditions will continue throughout the year and therefore that when the relinquishment shall take place on December 31 the railroads will still be unable (in the absence of a further increase in rates) to sustain themselves. I believe, however, that this sentiment will not prove seriously disturbing because everyone will feel that there will be an ample opportunity for business conditions to improve and also for remedial action to be taken. As the months go by, there will either develop a showing of increased business which will make the railroad results less unfavorable, or a showing of a settled condition of unfavorable business which will serve as a proper basis for the Railroad Administration to consider (preferably with the cooperation of the Interstate Commerce Commission, although this is not necessary under the law) the question of increasing the rates so as to make the situation reasonably self-sustaining at the time the relinquishment shall take place. Even if an increase in rates should be necessary, my firm conviction is that it would be far better for the Administration to make this increase and turn the railroads back to private control on December 31st than to retain the railroads after that date without any clarification of the situation and either incur a heavy deficit or increase the rates to meet it.

These considerations emphasize to my mind the importance, if the plan recommended meets your approval, of announcing it at the earliest possible date after announcement of the extra session shall be made. I assume that the announcement should not be made prior to calling the extra session because if so made there will be immediately a great clamor for the calling of the extra session so as to have an opportunity to consider the subject.

Some classes of the public, and particularly labor, may look with disfavor upon the proposed relinquishment, but if influential portions of the public object to the relinquishment, the obvious step for them to take is to insist upon Congress making an appropriate clarification of the situation. Unless the necessity for definite action is forced on Congress, and if without definite legislation the railroads shall be retained in Federal Control, I believe the Administration will get no credit whatever from the classes which wish continuance of such control and yet will be held as exclusively responsible for the continuance of such control by all classes who are anxious for Federal Control to end, even though they do not wish it to end until there is legislation.

If you approve the principle of this recommendation, the question may arise as to what is the preferable procedure. It may be a convenience to you for me to put in concrete form the alternatives which occur to me, the first being the one which is definitely recommended by the memorandum.

1. Immediately after the calling of the extra session, and before that session assembles, my thought would be that it would be in order for you to state that since the extra session just called would afford an adequate opportunity to consider a constructive permanent program of railroad legislation, and since the present status of Federal Control with its early termination is not satisfactorily adapted to peace conditions, it would be your purpose to relinquish the railroads from that control on December 31, 1919, and that it seems appropriate to give timely notice of that intention to the end that all persons interested may prepare to expedite the disposition of the problem. I think the advantage of making the announcement immediately after the calling of the extra session would be that it would probably stimulate the activities of Congress and of those having plans to discuss, so that the time intervening between the call of the session and its assembling would be profitably employed in making progress.

2. The other plan that occurs to me would be for you in your address to the Congress upon its reassembling to announce your

intention as to relinquishment December 31, 1919, substantially in the same sense as is stated above. I assume that whether you announce such intention prior to the actual assembling of Congress or in your address, you will wish to state in your address such views as you may entertain as to the lines which the permanent solution ought to follow. I am hoping to communicate with you in a few days on this important question.

Sincerely yours,   Walker D Hines

TLS (WP, DLC).
¹ W. D. Hines, "MEMORANDUM FOR THE PRESIDENT," April 1, 1919, TS MS (WP, DLC).

From Norman Hezekiah Davis

Dear Mr. President: [Paris] April 4, 1919.

Secretary Glass has requested me by cable to obtain your approval for the establishment of further credits in favor of the British Government, up to $150,000,000, beyond the credits previously authorized by you. British Government credits authorized by you, but not yet established, approximate $200,000,000, but the British Government estimates that their cash requirements during April will almost absorb this amount, and Secretary Glass now thinks it advisable to have your approval for the establishment of credits in favor of the British Government up to $150,000,000.

May I therefore request that, if this meets with your approval, you sign the enclosed letter for transmittal to Secretary Glass.

Cordially yours,   Norman H. Davis

TLS (WP, DLC).

To Carter Glass

Dear Mr. Secretary: [Paris] April 4, 1919

Mr. Norman H. Davis has transmitted to me your request for my approval of the establishment of further credits in favor of the British Government, up to $150,000,000, beyond amounts previously authorized by me, and I have pleasure in advising you of my approval of the establishment of such credits.

Very sincerely yours,   Woodrow Wilson

TLS (WP, DLC).

INDEX

NOTE ON THE INDEX

THE alphabetically arranged analytical table of contents at the front of the volume eliminates duplication, in both contents and index, of references to certain documents, such as letters. Letters are listed in the contents alphabetically by name, and chronologically within each name by page. The subject matter of all letters is, of course, indexed. The Editorial Notes and Wilson's writings are listed in the contents chronologically by page. In addition, the subject matter of both categories is indexed. The index covers all references to books and articles mentioned in text or notes. Footnotes are indexed. Page references to footnotes which place a comma between the page number and "n" cite both text and footnote, thus: "418,n1." On the other hand, absence of the comma indicates reference to the footnote only, thus: "59n1"—the page number denoting where the footnote appears.

The index supplies the fullest known form of names and, for the Wilson and Axson families, relationships as far down as cousins. Persons referred to by nicknames or shortened forms of names can be identified by reference to entries for these forms of the names.

All entries consisting of page numbers only and which refer to concepts, issues and opinions (such as democracy, the tariff, the money trust, leadership, and labor problems), are references to Wilson's speeches and writings. Page references that follow the symbol Δ in such entries refer to the opinions and comments of others who are identified.

Three cumulative contents-index volumes are now in print: Volume 13, which covers Volumes 1-12, Volume 26, which covers Volumes 14-25, and Volume 39, which covers Volumes 27-38. Volume 52, covering volumes 40-49 and 51, is in production.

INDEX

WOODROW WILSON

and issue of Senate ratification of peace treaty, 58,n4, 67-69, 97-98; on not permitting T. Roosevelt to lead volunteer division in France, 87; unable to visit Dublin for freedom of the city, 96; on transport of Haller's Army, 133, 134, 135-36, 138-40, 141, 144; French society of workmen name their association after, 183,n2,3; visits French battlefront, 194-200, 244; and White House sheep, 204; concern over civilian staff wives being in Paris, 235; House on "nimbleness of mind of," 335; gives Daniels tour of Paris White House, 338; as decision maker, 338; confrontation with Clemenceau, 349-50, 351, 353, 353-54, 365-68, 434; talk of going home, 354, 540, 580, 581, 583; receives medal from French Academy of Moral and Political Sciences, 428,n2, 440; a day's schedule, 441; and French bill for traveling expenses, 444, 513,n1, 547-48; anger over Steed's formula for Saar Basin, 517n1; House on stubbornness and anger of, 517-18; Whitlock forwards Belgian medal to, 521-22; *see also* Council of Four: Paris Peace Conference

APPEARANCE

518; tired, 179-80, 337, 542; during confrontation with Clemenceau, 351; "growing grayer and grimmer," 577, 578

APPOINTMENT SUGGESTIONS, APPOINTMENTS AND RESIGNATIONS

Hapgood appointed minister to Denmark, 101, 191,n1; and U.S. Minister to Czechoslovakia, 122,n1; and U.S. Minister to Poland, 123-24,n2; suggestions for mideastern commission, 155-56, 179, 200, 310; and